THE INTELLIGENT INVESTOR

THE DEFINITIVE BOOK ON VALUE INVESTING

THIRD EDITION

BENJAMIN GRAHAM
With Jason Zweig

HARPER
BUSINESS
An Imprint of HarperCollins*Publishers*

Without limiting the exclusive rights of any author, contributor or the publisher of this publication, any unauthorized use of this publication to train generative artificial intelligence (AI) technologies is expressly prohibited. HarperCollins also exercise their rights under Article 4(3) of the Digital Single Market Directive 2019/790 and expressly reserve this publication from the text and data mining exception.

While the method of investment described in this book is believed to be effective there is no guarantee that the method will be profitable in specific applications, owing to the risk that is involved in investing of almost any kind. Thus, neither the publisher nor the author assume liability for any losses that may be sustained by the use of the method described in this book, and any such liability is hereby expressly disclaimed.

Grateful acknowledgment is made for permission to reprint:

"The Superinvestors of Graham-and-Doddsville," by Warren E. Buffett, from the Fall 1984 issue of *Hermes*, Magazine of Columbia Business School. Reprinted by permission of *Hermes*, Magazine of Columbia Business School, copyright © 1984 The Trustees of Columbia University and Warren E. Buffett.

"Benjamin Graham," by Warren E. Buffett, from the November/December 1976 issue of *Financial Analyst Journal*. Reprinted by permission of Financial Analysts Federation.

THE INTELLIGENT INVESTOR, THIRD EDITION. Copyright © 1973 by Benjamin Graham. Updated text copyright © 2024 by Jason Zweig. All rights reserved. No part of this book may be used or reproduced in any manner whatsoever without written permission except in the case of brief quotations embodied in critical articles and reviews. For information, address HarperCollins Publishers, 195 Broadway, New York, NY 10007. In Europe, HarperCollins Publishers, Macken House, 39/40 Mayor Street Upper, Dublin 1, D01 C9W8, Ireland.

HarperCollins books may be purchased for educational, business, or sales promotional use. For information, please email the Special Markets Department at SPsales@harpercollins.com.

hc.com

FIRST EDITION

The Library of Congress has catalogued the hardcover edition as follows:

Names: Graham, Benjamin, 1894–1976, author. | Zweig, Jason, author.
Title: The intelligent investor : the definitive book on value investing / Benjamin Graham ; with Jason Zweig.
Description: Third edition. | New York : Harper Business, an Imprint of HarperCollinsPublishers, 2024. | Includes bibliographical references and index. |
Identifiers: LCCN 2024019180 (print) | LCCN 2024019181 (ebook) | ISBN 9780063356726 (hardcover) | ISBN 9780063356733 (ebook)
Subjects: LCSH: Securities. | Investments.
Classification: LCC HG4521 .G665 2024 (print) | LCC HG4521 (ebook) | DDC 332.67/8—dc23/eng/20240716
LC record available at https://lccn.loc.gov/2024019180
LC ebook record available at https://lccn.loc.gov/2024019181

Printed in the United States of America.

ISBN 978-0-06-349747-4

$PrintCode

"Enduring wisdom from the man who trained Warren Buffett, with commentary by preeminent financial columnist Jason Zweig showing how relevant Graham's principles are today. This treatise deserves a central place on the bookshelf of every intelligent investor."

—Burton G. Malkiel, author of
A Random Walk Down Wall Street

"Jason Zweig has done an important favor for all serious investors by representing Benjamin Graham's great book, enhanced by footnotes and chapter-by-chapter commentary full of insights and contemporary examples. Expert investors and beginning investors—and all investors between—will enjoy and profit from making the time to enjoy and learn from this wonderful book!"

—Charles D. Ellis, founder of Greenwich Associates
and author of *Winning the Loser's Game*

"Ben Graham was the most learned of professional investors and *The Intelligent Investor* is the bible of value investing. Jason Zweig, the wisest of financial journalists, has done something remarkable: created a new edition that is even better than the original. A must read for any serious investor."

—Bill Miller, founder of Miller Value Partners

Praise for *The Intelligent Investor, Third Edition*

"The most important investing book ever written. Jason Zweig's masterful commentary provides a modern lens to this timeless wisdom."

—Morgan Housel, author of *The Psychology of Money*

"*The Intelligent Investor* teaches that value investing occurs at the intersection of fundamental investment analysis and psychology. It's the marriage of a calculator and a contrarian streak. If you find the right balance between the two, you inhabit a fruitful space that most investors won't have the tenacity, patience, or stamina to occupy. Zweig's latest update weaves recent market developments, fads, and follies into this classic guide, making it more relevant than ever before. The principles, though, need no updating."

—Seth A. Klarman, CEO of the Baupost Group

"Benjamin Graham is no longer here to advise investors when markets act up, but no one channels him better than Jason Zweig, who brings the great master's counsel into the twenty-first century with cutting-edge academic research, dead-on commentary, and trademark wit. It's easy to imagine Graham nodding to himself, and occasionally chuckling, as he turns the pages of this new edition of *The Intelligent Investor*."

—William J. Bernstein, author of *The Four Pillars of Investing*

To E.M.G.

Through chances various, through all
vicissitudes, we make our way. . . .

—Aeneid

Contents

	Preface to the Revised Edition, by Warren E. Buffett	xiii
	Foreword: A Note About Benjamin Graham, by Jason Zweig	xvii
	Introduction: What This Book Expects to Accomplish	1
	Commentary on the Introduction	12
1.	Investment versus Speculation: Results to Be Expected by the Intelligent Investor	17
	Commentary on Chapter 1	34
2.	The Investor and Inflation	47
	Commentary on Chapter 2	57
3.	A Century of Stock-Market History: The Level of Stock Prices in Early 1972	65
	Commentary on Chapter 3	80
4.	General Portfolio Policy: The Defensive Investor	89
	Commentary on Chapter 4	102
5.	The Defensive Investor and Common Stocks	113
	Commentary on Chapter 5	124
6.	Portfolio Policy for the Enterprising Investor: Negative Approach	134
	Commentary on Chapter 6	146
7.	Portfolio Policy for the Enterprising Investor: The Positive Side	157
	Commentary on Chapter 7	180

8.	The Investor and Market Fluctuations	185
	Commentary on Chapter 8	209
9.	Investing in Investment Funds	220
	Commentary on Chapter 9	236
10.	The Investor and His Advisers	246
	Commentary on Chapter 10	260
11.	Security Analysis for the Lay Investor: General Approach	269
	Commentary on Chapter 11	290
12.	Things to Consider About Per-Share Earnings	295
	Commentary on Chapter 12	307
13.	A Comparison of Four Listed Companies	316
	Commentary on Chapter 13	325
14.	Stock Selection for the Defensive Investor	333
	Commentary on Chapter 14	352
15.	Stock Selection for the Enterprising Investor	362
	Commentary on Chapter 15	382
16.	Convertible Issues and Warrants	398
	Commentary on Chapter 16	413
17.	Four Extremely Instructive Case Histories	420
	Commentary on Chapter 17	436
18.	A Comparison of Eight Pairs of Companies	444
	Commentary on Chapter 18	471
19.	Shareholders and Managements: Dividend Policy	486
	Commentary on Chapter 19	495
20.	"Margin of Safety" as the Central Concept of Investment	505
	Commentary on Chapter 20	518
	Postscript	530
	Commentary on the Postscript	533

Appendixes
    1. The Superinvestors of Graham-and-Doddsville   535
    2. The New Speculation in Common Stocks   559
    3. Technological Companies as Investments   571
Notes   573
Acknowledgments from Jason Zweig   583
Index   585

The text reproduced here is the Fourth Revised Edition, updated by Graham in 1971–1972 and initially published in 1973. Please be advised that the text of Graham's original footnotes (designated in his chapters with superscript numerals) can be found in the Notes section beginning on p. 573. The new footnotes that Jason Zweig has introduced appear at the bottom of Graham's pages (and, in the typeface used here, as occasional additions to Graham's endnotes).

Preface to the Revised Edition, by Warren E. Buffett

I read the first edition of this book early in 1950, when I was nineteen. I thought then that it was by far the best book about investing ever written. I still think it is.

To invest successfully over a lifetime does not require a stratospheric IQ, unusual business insights, or inside information. What's needed is a sound intellectual framework for making decisions and the ability to keep emotions from corroding that framework. This book precisely and clearly prescribes the proper framework. You must supply the emotional discipline.

If you follow the behavioral and business principles that Graham advocates—and if you pay special attention to the invaluable advice in Chapters 8 and 20—you will not get a poor result from your investments. (That represents more of an accomplishment than you might think.) Whether you achieve outstanding results will depend on the effort and intellect you apply to your investments, as well as on the amplitudes of stock-market folly that prevail during your investing career. The sillier the market's behavior, the greater the opportunity for the business-like investor. Follow Graham and you will profit from folly rather than participate in it.

To me, Ben Graham was far more than an author or a teacher. More than any other man except my father, he influenced my life. Shortly after Ben's death in 1976, I wrote the following short remembrance about him in the *Financial Analysts Journal*. As you read the book, I believe you'll perceive some of the qualities I mentioned in this tribute.

BENJAMIN GRAHAM
1894–1976

Several years ago Ben Graham, then almost eighty, expressed to a friend the thought that he hoped every day to do "something foolish, something creative and something generous."

The inclusion of that first whimsical goal reflected his knack for packaging ideas in a form that avoided any overtones of sermonizing or self-importance. Although his ideas were powerful, their delivery was unfailingly gentle.

Readers of this magazine need no elaboration of his achievements as measured by the standard of creativity. It is rare that the founder of a discipline does not find his work eclipsed in rather short order by successors. But over forty years after publication of the book that brought structure and logic to a disorderly and confused activity, it is difficult to think of possible candidates for even the runner-up position in the field of security analysis. In an area where much looks foolish within weeks or months after publication, Ben's principles have remained sound—their value often enhanced and better understood in the wake of financial storms that demolished flimsier intellectual structures. His counsel of soundness brought unfailing rewards to his followers—even to those with natural abilities inferior to more gifted practitioners who stumbled while following counsels of brilliance or fashion.

A remarkable aspect of Ben's dominance of his professional field was that he achieved it without that narrowness of mental activity that concentrates all effort on a single end. It was, rather, the incidental by-product of an intellect whose breadth almost exceeded definition. Certainly I have never met anyone with a mind of similar scope. Virtually total recall, unending fascination with new knowledge, and an ability to recast it in a form applicable to seemingly unrelated problems made exposure to his thinking in any field a delight.

But his third imperative—generosity—was where he succeeded beyond all others. I knew Ben as my teacher, my employer, and my friend. In each relationship—just as with all his students, employees, and friends—there was an absolutely open-ended, no-scores-kept generosity of ideas, time, and spirit. If clarity of thinking was required, there was no better place to go. And if encouragement or counsel was needed, Ben was there.

Walter Lippmann spoke of men who plant trees that other men will sit under. Ben Graham was such a man.

Reprinted from the *Financial Analysts Journal*, November/December 1976.

Benjamin Graham in Sevilla, Spain, October 1964. Photo courtesy Benjamin Graham, Jr.

A Note About Benjamin Graham, by Jason Zweig

> The test of integrity is its blunt refusal to be compromised.
>
> —*Chinua Achebe*[1]

Who was Benjamin Graham, and why should you listen to him?

Graham was one of the greatest investors who ever lived. He also was one of the smartest, and he may well have been the wisest.[2]

How great an investor was Graham?

He didn't merely earn superior returns; he did so during some of the most difficult times investors have ever seen, including the end of the Great Depression. His Graham-Newman Corp. beat the market by an average of roughly five percentage points annually between 1936 and 1956.[3] Few other investors have ever rivaled so great a margin of outperformance over so long a career—foremost among them Warren Buffett, who learned how to invest from Graham himself.

---

[1] *The Trouble with Nigeria* (Heinemann, 1984), p. 42.

[2] For more on this remarkable man, see Jason Zweig, "A Note on Benjamin Graham," bit.ly/40XkE7h; the *Beyond Ben Graham* blog, bit.ly/442IEX8; and Benjamin Graham, *Benjamin Graham: The Memoirs of the Dean of Wall Street* (McGraw-Hill, 1996).

[3] According to Warren Buffett, Graham's full returns aren't precisely knowable over his entire career from 1923 through 1956, but were "far more terrific" than usual estimates indicate (personal communication, April 14, 2023). In addition to their gains on Graham's fund, his investors earned high returns on shares in Government Employees Insurance Co. or GEICO, which Graham-Newman Corp. paid out in July 1948 as a special dividend.

How smart was Graham?

He entered Columbia University at age 17; he should have been admitted a year earlier, but the college bungled his paperwork. He finished in two and a half years, ranked second in his class. Before Graham even graduated, Columbia offered him faculty positions in three different departments: philosophy, mathematics, and English. Needing to support his widowed mother, he took a better-paying job on Wall Street instead.

Graham's book *Security Analysis*, written with David Dodd and published in 1934, became the foundational text for financial analysts worldwide. But his brilliance knew no bounds. When Graham was 23, the *American Mathematical Monthly* published his article on how to improve the teaching of calculus. He went on to patent two innovative handheld calculators. He wrote two books on how to stabilize global currencies and numerous articles on law, taxation, and unemployment. In his spare time, Graham wrote a Broadway play, taught himself Spanish and translated a Uruguayan novel, and read voraciously in French, ancient Greek, and Latin.

Above all, Graham was wise. In his decades on Wall Street, he encountered every kind of scam and fraud: insider trading, promoters touting worthless stocks, dirty accounting tricks, companies shafting their own shareholders. He witnessed markets in which millions of people lost their minds, fooling themselves into thinking they were investing geniuses just because they had bought a few stocks that had gone up—temporarily. He had also seen investors stripped of their wealth by listening to "experts" who told them they could get rich quick.

Graham learned not only from the mistakes of others but from his own:

- He had chased hot stocks—and gotten burned.
- He had traded too much—and learned to be patient.
- He had taken too much risk—and learned to be cautious.
- He had invested with borrowed money—and never used leverage again.
- He had tried and tested countless investing methods—and understood the pitfalls of attempting to predict the future with inadequate data from the past.

Graham understood that investing is a lonely activity in which isolated individuals, yearning for connection and the approval of their peers, easily fall prey to manipulators and crooks. In recent years, the profoundly human desire to join the crowd has been hijacked by social media and smartphone brokerage apps until millions of people ended up trading the same stocks all at once, motivated by FOMO: the fear of missing out. Once you join such a financial flash mob, making a sensible plan and sticking to it become all but impossible. This book will help you think for yourself instead of letting millions of strangers tell you what to think.

Graham also knew that even the most honest people aren't always honest with themselves. We all hate admitting our own shortcomings. Graham's advice focuses not only on what investors *ought* to do, but on what they *can* do. He never misleads his readers with bogus promises about the markets or themselves. This book will help you understand your own strengths and weaknesses, giving you the intellectual and emotional framework for making good investing decisions—and, more importantly, for sticking with them.

To stand out from the crowd, you must stand apart from the crowd. To be an intelligent investor, you must be disciplined and you must think differently.

Four Cornerstones

Graham teaches four great principles:

- **You can't be an investor without trading, but you can trade without ever investing.** If you know nothing about a stock except that its price has gone up or "everybody" is buying it, you're not investing; you're speculating. The intelligent investor does thorough research and makes deliberate, consistent, measurable decisions.
- **A stock isn't a ticker symbol or a pulsating series of prices on your smartphone; it's an ownership interest in a business with a fundamental value independent of its share price.** The intelligent investor studies the business, not the stock. (See Table 0.1.)
- **Most of the time, market prices are approximately right, but when they are wrong they can be abysmally wrong.** Graham invented a character called Mr. Market, a mythical figure who goes wild with greed and euphoria when stocks go up but wallows in fear

and misery when stocks go down.[4] The intelligent investor is a realist who sells to optimists and buys from pessimists. You must never let your emotions be taken hostage by Mr. Market's mood swings.
- **Most investors commit their biggest mistakes when they focus on how much money they could make if they turn out to be right—and forget to consider how much they could lose if they turn out to be wrong.** The intelligent investor always maintains what Graham called a "margin of safety," a cushion of humility that will allow you to survive your losses if your analysis is incorrect.

TABLE 0-1: Stocks vs. Businesses

	Stocks	Businesses
Appraised by	Price	Value
Numerical format	Precise to the penny	Approximate range
Basis for appraisal	What someone will pay today for the ability to own or trade it, subject to market moods	The present worth of the total future cash generated by the business
How often they change	Up to thousands of times a day	At most a few times a year
Why they change	Quarterly earnings growth; strength of stock market; geopolitical events; noise	Long-term earnings growth; strength of business; competition
Typical holding period	One year or less	A generation or more
Risk	Continuous, momentary volatility of market price	Permanent decline in business value

[4] See Chapter 8.

A Note About Benjamin Graham

The Intelligent Investor was first published in 1949. The goal of this commemorative 75th anniversary edition is to integrate Graham's classic insights with today's market realities.

This edition, like the previous version published in 2003, follows Graham's own plan. *The Intelligent Investor* isn't—and Graham never intended it to be—a step-by-step guide to stock picking or an instructional handbook on how to analyze and evaluate businesses. Instead, it lays down the guidelines and principles that are the indispensable foundation for investing success. As Graham put it:

Comparatively little will be said here about the technique of analyzing securities; attention will be paid chiefly to investment principles and investors' attitudes.

All of Graham's original chapters remain intact.[5] I've also highlighted many of Graham's passages in **boldface type** to signal their importance.

In the commentaries that accompany each of Graham's chapters, I've included recent examples that show how powerful his principles still are. The commentaries are printed in sans serif type, like this. Graham's original chapters are printed in serif type, like this.

This book will help you build the habits and cultivate the discipline that are essential for succeeding as an investor. Warren Buffett calls *The Intelligent Investor* "by far the best book about investing ever written" because no one else has ever understood and conveyed these principles better than Graham.

With this book in your hands, you are well on your way to becoming an intelligent investor. In the next chapter, we'll talk about what that means and what it takes.

---

[5] However, three of Graham's appendixes, discussing long-ago companies and obsolete tax rules, aren't included in this edition. To see those, please reference the 2003 revised edition of *The Intelligent Investor*.

INTRODUCTION:
What This Book Expects to Accomplish
by Benjamin Graham

*T*he purpose of this book is to supply, in a form suitable for laymen, guidance in the adoption and execution of an investment policy. Comparatively little will be said here about the technique of analyzing securities; attention will be paid chiefly to investment principles and investors' attitudes. We shall, however, provide a number of condensed comparisons of specific securities—chiefly in pairs appearing side by side in the New York Stock Exchange list—in order to bring home in concrete fashion the important elements involved in specific choices of common stocks.

But much of our space will be devoted to the historical patterns of financial markets, in some cases running back over many decades. To invest intelligently in securities one should be forearmed with an adequate knowledge of how the various types of bonds and stocks have actually behaved under varying conditions—some of which, at least, one is likely to meet again in one's own experience. **No statement is more true and better applicable to Wall Street than the famous warning of Santayana: "Those who do not remember the past are condemned to repeat it."**

Our text is directed to investors as distinguished from speculators, and our first task will be to clarify and emphasize this now all but forgotten distinction. We may say at the outset that this is not a "how to make a million" book. **There are no sure and easy paths to riches on Wall Street or anywhere else.** It may be well to point up what we have just said by a bit of financial history—especially since there is more than one moral to be drawn from it. In the climactic year 1929 John J. Raskob, a most important figure nationally as well as on Wall Street, extolled the blessings of capitalism in an article in the *Ladies' Home Journal*, entitled "Everybody Ought to Be Rich."* His thesis was that savings of only $15 per month invested in good common stocks—with dividends reinvested—would produce an estate of $80,000 in twenty years against total contributions of only $3,600. If the General Motors tycoon was right, this was indeed a simple road to riches. How nearly right was he? Our rough calculation—based on assumed investment in the 30 stocks making up the Dow Jones Industrial Average (DJIA)—indicates that if Raskob's prescription had been followed during 1929–1948, the investor's holdings at the beginning of 1949 would have been worth about $8,500. This is a far cry from the great man's promise of $80,000, and it shows how little reliance can be placed on such optimistic forecasts and assurances. But, as an aside, we should remark that the return actually realized by the 20-year operation would have been better than 8% compounded annually—and this despite the fact that the investor would have begun his purchases with the DJIA at 300 and ended with a valuation based on the 1948 closing level of 177. This record may be regarded as a persuasive argument for the principle of regular monthly purchases of strong common stocks through thick and thin—a program known as "dollar-cost averaging."

Since our book is not addressed to speculators, it is not meant for those who trade in the market. Most of these people are guided by charts or other largely mechanical means of determining the right moments to buy and sell. **The one principle that applies to nearly all these so-called "technical approaches" is that one should buy *because* a stock or the market has gone up and one should sell *because* it has declined. This is the exact opposite of sound business sense everywhere else, and it is most unlikely that it can lead to lasting success on Wall Street.** In our own stock-

---

* Raskob (1879–1950) was a director of Du Pont, the giant chemical company, and chairman of the finance committee at General Motors. Calculations by finance professor Jeremy Siegel confirm that Raskob's plan would have grown to just under $9,000 after 20 years, although inflation would have eaten away much of that gain. For a look at Raskob's views on long-term stock investing, see the essay by investment adviser William Bernstein at bit.ly/3QuKk8H.

market experience and observation, extending over 50 years, we have not known a single person who has consistently or lastingly made money by thus "following the market." We do not hesitate to declare that this approach is as fallacious as it is popular. We shall illustrate what we have just said—though, of course this should not be taken as proof—by a later brief discussion of the famous Dow theory for trading in the stock market.*

Since its first publication in 1949, revisions of *The Intelligent Investor* have appeared at intervals of approximately five years. In updating the current version we shall have to deal with quite a number of new developments since the 1965 edition was written. These include:

1. An unprecedented advance in the interest rate on high-grade bonds.
2. A fall of about 35% in the price level of leading common stocks, ending in May 1970. This was the highest percentage decline in some 30 years. (Countless issues of lower quality had a much larger shrinkage.)
3. A persistent inflation of wholesale and consumer's prices, which gained momentum even in the face of a decline of general business in 1970.
4. The rapid development of "conglomerate" companies, franchise operations, and other relative novelties in business and finance. (These include a number of tricky devices such as "letter stock,"[1] proliferation of stock-option warrants, misleading names, use of foreign banks, and others.)†
5. Bankruptcy of our largest railroad, excessive short- and long-term debt of many formerly strongly entrenched companies,

---

* Graham's "brief discussion" is in two parts, on p. 32 and pp. 188–189. For more detail on the Dow theory, see bit.ly/4b3xhT8.
† Mutual funds bought "letter stock" in private transactions, then immediately revalued these shares at a higher public price (see Graham's definition on p. 230). That enabled these "go-go" funds to report unsustainably high returns in the mid-1960s. The U.S. Securities and Exchange Commission cracked down on this abuse in 1969, and it is no longer a concern for fund investors. Graham explains stock-option warrants in Chapter 16.

and even a disturbing problem of solvency among Wall Street houses.*
6. The advent of the "performance" vogue in the management of investment funds, including some bank-operated trust funds, with disquieting results.

These phenomena will have our careful consideration, and some will require changes in conclusions and emphasis from our previous edition. The underlying principles of sound investment should not alter from decade to decade, but the application of these principles must be adapted to significant changes in the financial mechanisms and climate.

The last statement was put to the test during the writing of the present edition, the first draft of which was finished in January 1971. At that time the DJIA was in a strong recovery from its 1970 low of 632 and was advancing toward a 1971 high of 951, with attendant general optimism. As the last draft was finished, in November 1971, the market was in the throes of a new decline, carrying it down to 797 with a renewed general uneasiness about its future. We have not allowed these fluctuations to affect our general attitude toward sound investment policy, which remains substantially unchanged since the first edition of this book in 1949.

The extent of the market's shrinkage in 1969–70 should have served to dispel an illusion that had been gaining ground during the past two decades. This was that leading common stocks could be bought at any time and at any price, with the assurance not only of ultimate profit but also that any intervening loss would soon be recouped by a renewed advance of the market to new high levels. That was too good to be true. At long last the stock market has "returned to normal," in the sense that both speculators and

---

* The Penn Central Transportation Co., then the biggest railroad in the United States, sought bankruptcy protection on June 21, 1970—shocking investors, who had never expected such a giant company to go under (see p. 347). Among the companies with "excessive" debt Graham had in mind were Ling-Temco-Vought and National General Corp. (see pp. 423 and 409). The "problem of solvency" emerged between 1968 and 1971, when several prestigious brokerages went bust.

stock investors must again be prepared to experience significant and perhaps protracted falls as well as rises in the value of their holdings.

In the area of many secondary and third-line common stocks, especially recently floated enterprises, the havoc wrought by the last market break was catastrophic. This was nothing new in itself—it had happened to a similar degree in 1961–62—but there was now a novel element in the fact that some of the investment funds had large commitments in highly speculative and obviously overvalued issues of this type. Evidently it is not only the tyro who needs to be warned that **while enthusiasm may be necessary for great accomplishments elsewhere, on Wall Street it almost invariably leads to disaster.**

The major question we shall have to deal with grows out of the huge rise in the rate of interest on first-quality bonds. Since late 1967 the investor has been able to obtain more than twice as much income from such bonds as he could from dividends on representative common stocks. At the beginning of 1972 the return was 7.19% on highest-grade bonds versus only 2.76% on industrial stocks. (This compares with 4.40% and 2.92% respectively at the end of 1964.) It is hard to realize that when we first wrote this book in 1949 the figures were almost the exact opposite: the bonds returned only 2.66% and the stocks yielded 6.82%.[2] In previous editions we have consistently urged that at least 25% of the conservative investor's portfolio be held in common stocks, and we have favored in general a 50–50 division between the two media. We must now consider whether the current great advantage of bond yields over stock yields would justify an all-bond policy until a more sensible relationship returns, as we expect it will. Naturally the question of continued inflation will be of great importance in reaching our decision here. A chapter will be devoted to this discussion.*

In the past we have made a basic distinction between two kinds of investors to whom this book was addressed—the "defensive"

---

* See Chapter 2. As of the beginning of 2024, U.S. Treasury bonds maturing in 10 years yielded 3.9%, while stocks (as measured by the Dow Jones Industrial Average) yielded 1.95%. (Note that this relationship is not all that different from the 1964 figures that Graham cites.) The income generated by top-quality bonds fell steadily between 1981 and 2020.

and the "enterprising." **The defensive (or passive) investor will place his chief emphasis on the avoidance of serious mistakes or losses.** His second aim will be freedom from effort, annoyance, and the need for making frequent decisions. **The determining trait of the enterprising (or active, or aggressive) investor is his willingness to devote time and care to the selection of securities that are both sound and more attractive than the average.** Over many decades an enterprising investor of this sort could expect a worthwhile reward for his extra skill and effort, in the form of a better average return than that realized by the passive investor. We have some doubt whether a really substantial extra recompense is promised to the active investor under today's conditions. But next year or the years after may well be different. We shall accordingly continue to devote attention to the possibilities for enterprising investment, as they existed in former periods and may return.

It has long been the prevalent view that the art of successful investment lies first in the choice of those industries that are most likely to grow in the future and then in identifying the most promising companies in these industries. For example, smart investors—or their smart advisers—would long ago have recognized the great growth possibilities of the computer industry as a whole and of International Business Machines in particular. And similarly for a number of other growth industries and growth companies. But this is not as easy as it always looks in retrospect. To bring this point home at the outset let us add here a paragraph that we included first in the 1949 edition of this book.

> Such an investor may for example be a buyer of air-transport stocks because he believes their future is even more brilliant than the trend the market already reflects. For this class of investor the value of our book will lie more in its warnings against the pitfalls lurking in this favorite investment approach than in any positive technique that will help him along his path.*

---

* "Air-transport stocks" generated as much excitement in the late 1940s and early 1950s as internet stocks did a half century later. Among the hottest mutual funds of that era were Aeronautical Securities and the Missiles-Rockets-Jets & Automation Fund. They, like the stocks they owned, turned

The pitfalls have proved particularly dangerous in the industry we mentioned. It was, of course, easy to forecast that the volume of air traffic would grow spectacularly over the years. Because of this factor their shares became a favorite choice of the investment funds. But despite the expansion of revenues—at a pace even greater than in the computer industry—a combination of technological problems and overexpansion of capacity made for fluctuating and even disastrous profit figures. In the year 1970, despite a new high in traffic figures, the airlines sustained a loss of some $200 million for their shareholders. (They had shown losses also in 1945 and 1961.) The stocks of these companies once again showed a greater decline in 1969–70 than did the general market. The record shows that even the highly paid full-time experts of the mutual funds were completely wrong about the fairly short-term future of a major and nonesoteric industry.

On the other hand, while the investment funds had substantial investments and substantial gains in IBM, the combination of its apparently high price and the impossibility of being *certain* about its rate of growth prevented them from having more than, say, 3% of their funds in this wonderful performer. Hence the effect of this excellent choice on their overall results was by no means decisive. Furthermore, many—if not most—of their investments in computer-industry companies other than IBM appear to have been unprofitable. From these two broad examples we draw two morals for our readers:

1. **Obvious prospects for physical growth in a business do not translate into obvious profits for investors.**
2. **The experts do not have dependable ways of selecting and concentrating on the most promising companies in the most promising industries.**

---

out to be an investing disaster. It is commonly accepted today that the cumulative earnings of the airline industry over its entire history have been negative. The lesson Graham is driving at is not that you should avoid buying airline stocks, but that you should never succumb to the "certainty" that *any* industry will outperform all others in the future.

The author did not follow this approach in his financial career as fund manager, and he cannot offer either specific counsel or much encouragement to those who may wish to try it.

What then will we aim to accomplish in this book? Our main objective will be to guide the reader against the areas of possible substantial error and to develop policies with which he will be comfortable. We shall say quite a bit about the psychology of investors. For indeed, **the investor's chief problem—and even his worst enemy—is likely to be himself.** ("The fault, dear investor, is not in our stars—and not in our stocks—but in ourselves....") This has proved the more true over recent decades as it has become more necessary for conservative investors to acquire common stocks and thus to expose themselves, willy-nilly, to the excitement and the temptations of the stock market. By arguments, examples, and exhortation, we hope to aid our readers to establish the proper mental and emotional attitudes toward their investment decisions. **We have seen much more money made and *kept* by "ordinary people" who were temperamentally well suited for the investment process than by those who lacked this quality, even though they had an extensive knowledge of finance, accounting, and stock-market lore.**

Additionally, we hope to implant in the reader a tendency to measure or quantify. **For 99 issues out of 100 we could say that at some price they are cheap enough to buy and at some other price they would be so dear that they should be sold. The habit of relating what is paid to what is being offered is an invaluable trait in investment.** In an article in a women's magazine many years ago we advised the readers to buy their stocks as they bought their groceries, not as they bought their perfume. **The really dreadful losses of the past few years (and on many similar occasions before) were realized in those common-stock issues where the buyer forgot to ask "How much?"**

In June 1970 the question "How much?" could be answered by the magic figure 9.40%—the yield obtainable on new offerings of high-grade public-utility bonds. This has now dropped to about 7.3%, but even that return tempts us to ask, "Why give any other answer?" But there are other possible answers, and these must be carefully considered. Besides which, we repeat that both we and our readers must be prepared in advance for the possibly quite different conditions of, say, 1973–1977.

We shall therefore present in some detail a positive program for common-stock investment, part of which is within the purview of both classes of investors and part is intended mainly for the enterprising group. Strangely enough, we shall suggest as one of our chief requirements here that our readers limit themselves to issues selling not far above their tangible-asset value.* The reason for this seemingly outmoded counsel is both practical and psychological. Experience has taught us that, while there are many good growth companies worth several times net assets, the buyer of such shares will be too dependent on the vagaries and fluctuations of the stock market. By contrast, the investor in shares, say, of public-utility companies at about their net-asset value can always consider himself the owner of an interest in sound and expanding businesses, acquired at a rational price—regardless of what the stock market might say to the contrary. The ultimate result of such a conservative policy is likely to work out better than exciting adventures into the glamorous and dangerous fields of anticipated growth.

The art of investment has one characteristic that is not generally appreciated. A creditable, if unspectacular, result can be achieved by the lay investor with a minimum of effort and capability; but to improve this easily attainable standard requires much application and more than a trace of wisdom. If you merely try to bring *just a little* extra knowledge and cleverness to bear upon your investment program, instead of realizing a little better than normal results, you may well find that you have done worse.

Since anyone—by just buying and holding a representative list—can equal the performance of the market averages, **it would seem a comparatively simple matter to "beat the averages"; but as a matter of fact the proportion of smart people who try this and fail is surprisingly large.** Even the majority of the investment funds, with all their experienced personnel, have not performed so well

---

* Tangible assets include a company's physical property (like real estate, factories, equipment, and inventories) as well as its financial balances (such as cash, short-term investments, and accounts receivable). Among the elements not included in tangible assets are brands, copyrights, patents, franchises, goodwill, and trademarks. To see how to calculate tangible-asset value, see footnote † on p. 194.

over the years as has the general market. Allied to the foregoing is the record of the published stock-market predictions of the brokerage houses, for there is strong evidence that their calculated forecasts have been somewhat less reliable than the simple tossing of a coin.

In writing this book we have tried to keep this basic pitfall of investment in mind. The virtues of a simple portfolio policy have been emphasized—the purchase of high-grade bonds plus a diversified list of leading common stocks—which any investor can carry out with a little expert assistance. The adventure beyond this safe and sound territory has been presented as fraught with challenging difficulties, especially in the area of temperament. **Before attempting such a venture the investor should feel sure of himself and of his advisers—particularly as to whether they have a clear concept of the differences between investment and speculation and between market price and underlying value.**

A strong-minded approach to investment, firmly based on the margin-of-safety principle, can yield handsome rewards. But a decision to try for these emoluments rather than for the assured fruits of defensive investment should not be made without much self-examination.

A final retrospective thought. When the young author entered Wall Street in June 1914 no one had any inkling of what the next half-century had in store. (The stock market did not even suspect that a World War was to break out in two months, and close down the New York Stock Exchange.) Now, in 1972, we find ourselves the richest and most powerful country on earth, but beset by all sorts of major problems and more apprehensive than confident of the future. Yet if we confine our attention to American investment experience, there is some comfort to be gleaned from the last 57 years. Through all their vicissitudes and casualties, as earth-shaking as they were unforeseen, it remained true that **sound investment principles produced generally sound results. We must act on the assumption that they will continue to do so**.

Note to the Reader: This book does not address itself to the *overall* financial policy of savers and investors; it deals only with that portion of their funds which they are prepared to place in marketable (or redeemable) securities, that is, in bonds and stocks. Consequently we do not discuss such important media as savings and time desposits, savings-and-loan-association accounts, life insurance, annuities, and real-estate mortgages or equity ownership. The reader should bear in mind that when he finds the word "now," or the equivalent, in the text, it refers to late 1971 or early 1972.*

---

* That applies to Graham's chapters. The chapter commentaries by Jason Zweig are current through early 2024.

Commentary on the Introduction
by Jason Zweig

> I can't tell you how to get rich quickly. I can only tell you how to get poor quickly: by trying to get rich quickly.
> —André Kostolany[1]

"The investor's chief problem—and even his worst enemy—is likely to be himself."

With these simple words, Graham signals what investing is all about.

Our message in this book is that investing is the exact opposite of what you've been led to believe.

Financial television, blogs, brokerage ads, and social media portray investing as a struggle for survival in a hostile wilderness. They want you to think you're locked in a lifelong battle against the stock market, hedge funds, central banks, or other dark and mysterious forces.

Such propaganda stokes fear. It makes you feel you're in a competition that you can win only if everyone else loses. Conveniently for the people who spout this message, once you start believing it, you become willing to pay them high fees in a desperate quest to survive.

You will also feel compelled to learn the "secrets" of successful investors, check the value of your investments every few minutes, get swept up in conspiracy theories about how the market is rigged, or trade obsessively at blazing speed.

That way, it seems, you can beat the professionals at their own game.

Yet they can't win it themselves. Roughly three-quarters of professional investors fail to beat the market—even though they have decades of training and experience, command computers that can

---

[1] UndervaluedJapan blog, November 11, 2020, bit.ly/43sXdnG.

trade thousands of times per second, and get instantaneous access to all the market-moving news on earth.

If *they* can't win their game, why would you even want to play?

The good news is that you don't have to.

With Graham as your guide, you can forget all that nonsense about being in a fight to the death against the markets—and forgo all the stress, fees, and failure that go with it.

However, you will have to wage another, even more challenging struggle.

To be an intelligent investor, there is a dark and mysterious force you must conquer. But it isn't the market.

It's yourself.

You—not the market—are your own worst investing enemy.

That's because the human mind is a brilliant mechanism for solving difficult problems—but it is even more adept at the simple task of self-deception.

Millions of investors spend their entire lives fooling themselves: taking risks they don't understand, chasing the phantoms of past performance, selling their winning assets too soon, holding their losers too long, paying outlandish fees in pursuit of the unobtainable, bragging about beating the market without even measuring their returns.

They are willfully blind to the fact that they are their own worst enemy. They preserve their self-esteem with self-delusion. They look in the mirror and see Warren Buffett.

As an investor, if you know what you're doing, you can make more money than you ever dreamed possible. If you only *think* you know what you're doing, you will lose more money than you ever envisioned in your worst nightmares. Fooling yourself can be even more costly than being fooled by someone else.

What Is an Intelligent Investor?

Conventional measures of intelligence have little to do with whether you can be what Graham calls an intelligent investor. In 1720, Sir Isaac Newton, one of the smartest people who ever lived, lost a fortune trading shares in the South Sea Co.[2] In 1998, Long-Term Capital

---

[2] Andrew Odlyzko, "Newton's Financial Misadventures in the South Sea Bubble," bit.ly/3psYyvF.

Management L.P., a hedge fund run by mathematicians, computer scientists, and two Nobel Laureates in economics, lost roughly 80% of its capital in a few weeks and had to be rescued in a $3.6 billion bailout.[3]

No matter how brilliant you are, you can't be—or become—an intelligent investor unless you learn to be honest with yourself. In the first edition of this book, Graham wrote:

> The word "intelligent" in our title will be used . . . in its common and dictionary sense as meaning "endowed with the capacity for knowledge and understanding." It will not be taken to mean "smart" or "shrewd," or gifted with unusual foresight or insight. [It] is a trait more of the character than of the brain.[4]

"You don't need to be a rocket scientist," Warren Buffett has said. "Investing is not a game where the guy with the 160 IQ beats the guy with a 130 IQ. Rationality is essential." Buffett and his partner, Charlie Munger, have repeatedly emphasized the vital importance of what they call "temperament."

The Seven Virtues of Great Investors

Graham doesn't list all the character traits that constitute the temperament of an intelligent investor, but the great money managers I've met share a few indispensable qualities. I call them the seven virtues:[5]

> **Curiosity.** Ordinary investors are afraid of what they don't know. Intelligent investors are also afraid of what they think they *do* know, because they realize it might be biased, incomplete, or wrong.
> So they never deviate from their relentless lifelong quest to learn

---

[3] A hedge fund is a pool of money, largely unregulated, that invests for wealthy clients; see the Commentary on Chapter 6. For the collapse of LTCM, see Roger Lowenstein, *When Genius Failed* (Random House, 2000).
[4] Benjamin Graham, *The Intelligent Investor* (Harper & Row, 1949), p. 4.
[5] Jason Zweig, "The Seven Virtues of Great Investors," bit.ly/42MxqWA.

more. They read constantly and never stop asking questions. They are learning machines.

Skepticism. Wall Street purports to sell investments, but its real business is selling hopes and dreams to people who want to believe in magic. *Save for retirement by getting in on the ground floor of the artificial-intelligence revolution! Earn high income at low risk! Get exclusive access to the lucrative returns on alternative assets!*

In this book, you'll learn to sharpen your skepticism and recognize when an ostensible opportunity is too good to be true.

Independence. The single most valuable investment asset you will ever have is your own mind. If you let other people do your thinking for you, you've traded away your greatest asset—and made your emotions and your results captive to the whims of millions of strangers. Great investors like Graham, Buffett, and Munger don't try to step in with the crowd; they step away. The approval of others means nothing to them. Nor should it to you.

As Graham writes in Chapter 20: "You are neither right nor wrong because the crowd disagrees with you. You are right because your data and reasoning are right."

Humility. The most dangerous thing about buying any asset that goes up is that *profit feels like proof.* Making money makes you think you know what you're doing and what the future holds—even when you're wrong. That's why hanging on to humility is so important. The more you learn, the more you should realize how little you know; the longer you invest, the more you should realize that your luck is bigger than you are.

Many people think humility is about managing what others think of you, which would be easy. Instead, it's about being honest with yourself, which is hard.

Discipline. To be an intelligent investor, you can't make things up as you go along, following your gut wherever it goes, trying a little of this and a little of that to see what happens. Instead, you need to impose discipline on yourself with policies, procedures, and rules you follow before making any decision. That way, you treat investing as a continuous process you can practice improving at every step, rather than a series of haphazard events.

Discipline doesn't just mean consistently doing what you should do, when and how you should do it; it also means consistently not doing what you shouldn't do.

Patience. Why bother trying to be patient in a world of instant gratification, an endless deluge of information, and stocks and cryptocurrencies that go to the moon? Why not just try to get rich quick?

Because almost nobody who gets rich quick stays rich for long.

The money you make in a few months or weeks or days or hours will almost certainly disappear at least as fast as it came. Hot streaks go cold, good luck turns bad, surprises blow your profits to bits.

To earn—and keep—long-term gains, you can't be a short-term thinker. You must build your wealth slowly and steadily.

Courage. It's easy to say you'll buy more if the stock market falls, but being brave is a lot harder than saying you are. Courage is losing more than 55% of your money between late 2007 and early 2009—and then buying more stocks, not despite the global financial crisis, but *because of it*. Courage is losing 34% in only five weeks during the pandemic panic in February and March 2020—and then hanging on, not despite the fear and dread that surrounded you, but *because of them*.

To be an investor you must believe in a better tomorrow. History shows that financial faith pays off the best after the times when it is hardest to hold.

With Graham as your guide, you can acquire and cultivate these virtues. They will serve you well not only in investing but in life. With this book in hand, you can become a more intelligent investor and a wiser person. Read on, and learn!

CHAPTER 1

Investment versus Speculation: Results to Be Expected by the Intelligent Investor
by Benjamin Graham

This chapter will outline the viewpoints that will be set forth in the remainder of the book. In particular we wish to develop at the outset our concept of appropriate portfolio policy for the individual, nonprofessional investor.

Investment versus Speculation

What do we mean by "investor"? Throughout this book the term will be used in contradistinction to "speculator." As far back as 1934, in our textbook *Security Analysis*,[1] we attempted a precise formulation of the difference between the two, as follows: **"An investment operation is one which, upon thorough analysis, promises safety of principal and an adequate return. Operations not meeting these requirements are speculative."**

While we have clung tenaciously to this definition over the ensuing 38 years, it is worthwhile noting the radical changes that have occurred in the use of the term "investor" during this period. After the great market decline of 1929–1932 *all* common stocks were widely regarded as speculative by nature. (A leading authority stated flatly that only bonds could be bought for investment.[2]) Thus we had then to defend our definition against the charge that it gave too wide scope to the concept of investment.

Now our concern is of the opposite sort. We must prevent our readers from accepting the common jargon which applies the term "investor" to anybody and everybody in the stock market. In our last edition we cited the following headline of a front-page article of our leading financial journal in June 1962:

SMALL INVESTORS BEARISH, THEY ARE SELLING ODD-LOTS SHORT

In October 1970 the same journal had an editorial critical of what it called "reckless investors," who this time were rushing in on the buying side.

These quotations well illustrate the confusion that has been dominant for many years in the use of the words investment and speculation. Think of our suggested definition of investment given above, and compare it with the sale of a few shares of stock by an inexperienced member of the public, who does not even own what he is selling, and has some largely emotional conviction that he will be able to buy them back at a much lower price. (It is not irrelevant to point out that when the 1962 article appeared the market had already experienced a decline of major size, and was now getting ready for an even greater upswing. It was about as poor a time as possible for selling short.) In a more general sense, the later-used phrase "reckless investors" could be regarded as a laughable contradiction in terms—something like "spendthrift misers"—were this misuse of language not so mischievous.

The newspaper employed the word "investor" in these instances because, in the easy language of Wall Street, everyone who buys or sells a security has become an investor, regardless of what he buys, or for what purpose, or at what price, or whether for cash or on margin. Compare this with the attitude of the public toward common stocks in 1948, when over 90% of those queried expressed themselves as opposed to the purchase of common stocks.[3] About half gave as their reason "not safe, a gamble," and about half, the reason "not familiar with."* It is indeed ironical

---

* The survey Graham cites was published in the *Federal Reserve Bulletin*, July 1948. Only 4% thought common stock would offer a "satisfactory" return; 26% considered it "not safe" or a "gamble." From 1949 through 1958, the U.S. stock market earned one of its highest 10-year returns in history, averaging 18.7% annually.

(though not surprising) that common-stock purchases of all kinds were quite generally regarded as highly speculative or risky at a time when they were selling on a most attractive basis, and due soon to begin their greatest advance in history; conversely the very fact they had advanced to what were undoubtedly dangerous levels as judged by *past experience* later transformed them into "investments," and the entire stock-buying public into "investors."

The distinction between investment and speculation in common stocks has always been a useful one and its disappearance is a cause for concern. We have often said that Wall Street as an institution would be well advised to reinstate this distinction and to emphasize it in all its dealings with the public. Otherwise the stock exchanges may some day be blamed for heavy speculative losses, which those who suffered them had not been properly warned against. Ironically, once more, much of the recent financial embarrassment of some stock-exchange firms seems to have come from the inclusion of speculative common stocks in their own capital funds. We trust that the reader of this book will gain a reasonably clear idea of the risks that are inherent in common-stock commitments—risks which are inseparable from the opportunities of profit that they offer, and both of which must be allowed for in the investor's calculations.

What we have just said indicates that there may no longer be such a thing as a simon-pure investment policy comprising representative common stocks—in the sense that one can always wait to buy them at a price that involves no risk of a market or "quotational" loss large enough to be disquieting. **In most periods the investor must recognize the existence of a *speculative factor* in his common-stock holdings. It is his task to keep this component within minor limits, and to be prepared financially and psychologically for adverse results that may be of short or long duration.**

Two paragraphs should be added about stock speculation per se, as distinguished from the speculative component now inherent in most representative common stocks. Outright speculation is neither illegal, immoral, nor (for most people) fattening to the pocketbook. More than that, some speculation is necessary and unavoidable, for in many common-stock situations there are substantial possibilities of both profit and loss, and the risks therein must be assumed by someone.* There is intelligent speculation as there is intelligent investing. But **there are many ways in which speculation may be unintelligent. Of these the foremost are: (1) speculating when you think you are investing; (2) speculating seriously instead of as a pastime, when you lack proper knowledge and skill for it; and (3) risking more money in speculation than you can afford to lose.**

In our conservative view every nonprofessional who operates *on margin*† should recognize that he is *ipso facto* speculating, and it is his broker's duty so to advise him. And everyone who buys a so-called "hot" common-stock issue, or makes a purchase in any way similar thereto, is either speculating or gambling. Speculation is always fascinating, and it can be a lot of fun while you are ahead of the game. **If you want to try your luck at it, put aside a portion—the smaller the better—of your capital in a separate fund for this purpose. Never add more money to this account just because the market has gone up and profits are rolling in.** (That's the time to think of taking money *out* of your speculative fund.) Never mingle your speculative and investment operations in the same account, nor in any part of your thinking.

Results to Be Expected by the Defensive Investor

We have already defined the defensive investor as one interested chiefly in safety plus freedom from bother. In general what course should he follow and what return can he expect under "average normal conditions"—if such conditions really exist? To answer these questions we shall consider first what we wrote on the subject

---

* Speculation is beneficial on two levels: First, without it, innovative young companies (like Tesla or, in earlier times, the Edison Electric Light Co.) wouldn't be able to raise the necessary capital for growth. The alluring hope of a huge gain is the grease that lubricates the machinery of innovation. Speculation is also the "self-adjustment of society to the probable," as Justice Oliver Wendell Holmes wrote in 1905—the continuous capture of information that enables markets to update prices.

† A margin account enables you to buy stocks using money you borrow from the brokerage firm. By investing with borrowed money, you make more when your stocks go up—but you can be wiped out when they go down. The

seven years ago, next what significant changes have occurred since then in the underlying factors governing the investor's expectable return, and finally what he should do and what he should expect under present-day (early 1972) conditions.

1. What We Said Six Years Ago

We recommended that the investor divide his holdings between high-grade bonds and leading common stocks; that the proportion held in bonds be never less than 25% or more than 75%, with the converse being necessarily true for the common-stock component; that his simplest choice would be to maintain a 50–50 proportion between the two, with adjustments to restore the equality when market developments had disturbed it by as much as, say, 5%. As an alternative policy he might choose to reduce his common-stock component to 25% "if he felt the market was dangerously high," and conversely to advance it toward the maximum of 75% "if he felt that a decline in stock prices was making them increasingly attractive."

In 1965 the investor could obtain about 4½% on high-grade taxable bonds and 3¼% on good tax-free bonds. The dividend return on leading common stocks (with the DJIA at 892) was only about 3.2%. This fact, and others, suggested caution. We implied that "at normal levels of the market" the investor should be able to obtain an initial dividend return of between 3½% and 4½% on his stock purchases, to which should be added a steady increase in underlying value (and in the "normal market price") of a representative stock list of about the same amount, giving a return from dividends and appreciation combined of about 7½% per year. The half and half division between bonds and stocks would yield about 6% before income tax. We added that the stock component should carry a fair degree of protection against a loss of purchasing power caused by large-scale inflation.

It should be pointed out that the above arithmetic indicated expectation of a much lower rate of advance in the stock market than had been realized between 1949 and 1964. That rate had

---

collateral for the loan is the value of the investments in your account—so you must put up more money if that value falls below a required amount. For more on margin, see the Commentary on Chapter 6.

averaged a good deal better than 10% for listed stocks as a whole, and it was quite generally regarded as a sort of guarantee that similarly satisfactory results could be counted on in the future. Few people were willing to consider seriously the possibility that the high rate of advance in the past means that stock prices are "now too high," and hence that "the wonderful results since 1949 would imply not very good but *bad* results for the future."[4]

2. What Has Happened Since 1964

The major change since 1964 has been the rise in interest rates on first-grade bonds to record high levels, although there has since been a considerable recovery from the lowest prices of 1970. The obtainable return on good corporate issues is now about 7½% and even more against 4½% in 1964. In the meantime the dividend return on DJIA-type stocks had a fair advance also during the market decline of 1969–70, but as we write (with "the Dow" at 900) it is less than 3.5% against 3.2% at the end of 1964. The change in going interest rates produced a maximum decline of about 38% in the market price of medium-term (say 20-year) bonds during this period.

There is a paradoxical aspect to these developments. In 1964 we discussed at length the possibility that the price of stocks might be too high and subject ultimately to a serious decline; but we did not consider specifically the possibility that the same might happen to the price of high-grade bonds. (Neither did anyone else that we know of.) We did warn (on p. 90 of the 1965 edition) that "a long-term bond may vary widely in price in response to changes in interest rates." In the light of what has since happened we think that this warning—with attendant examples—was insufficiently stressed. For the fact is that if the investor had a given sum in the DJIA at its closing price of 874 in 1964 he would have had a small profit thereon in late 1971; even at the lowest level (631) in 1970 his indicated loss would have been less than that shown on good long-term bonds. On the other hand, if he had confined his bond-type investments to U.S. savings bonds, short-term corporate issues, or savings accounts, he would have had no loss in market value of his principal during this period and he would have enjoyed a higher income return than was offered by good stocks. It turned out, therefore, that true "cash equivalents" proved to be better investments in 1964 than common stocks—in spite of the inflation experience that in theory should have favored stocks over cash. The decline in quoted principal value of good longer-term bonds was due to developments in the money market, an abstruse area which ordinarily does not have an important bearing on the investment policy of individuals.

This is just another of an endless series of experiences over time that have demonstrated that the future of security prices is never predictable.* Almost always bonds have fluctuated much less than stock prices, and investors generally could buy good bonds of any maturity without having to worry about changes in their market value. There were a few exceptions to this rule, and the period after 1964 proved to be one of them. We shall have more to say about change in bond prices in a later chapter.

3. Expectations and Policy in Late 1971 and Early 1972

Toward the end of 1971 it was possible to obtain 8% taxable interest on good medium-term corporate bonds, and 5.7% tax-free on good state or municipal securities. In the shorter-term field the investor could realize about 6% on U.S. government issues due in five years. In the latter case the buyer need not be concerned about a possible loss in market value, since he is sure of full repayment, including the 6% interest return, at the end of a comparatively short holding period. The DJIA at its recurrent price level of 900 in 1971 yields only 3.5%.

Let us assume that now, as in the past, the basic policy decision to be made is how to divide the fund between high-grade bonds (or other so-called "cash equivalents") and leading DJIA-type stocks. What course should the investor follow under present conditions, if we have no strong reason to predict either a significant upward or a significant downward movement for some time in the future?

---

* Read Graham's sentence again, and note what this greatest of investing experts is saying: The future of security prices is never predictable. And as you read ahead in the book, notice how everything else Graham tells you is designed to help you grapple with that truth. Since you cannot predict the behavior of the markets, you must learn how to predict and control your own behavior.

First let us point out that if there is no serious adverse change, the defensive investor should be able to count on the current 3.5% dividend return on his stocks and also on an *average* annual appreciation of about 4%. As we shall explain later, this appreciation is based essentially on the reinvestment by the various companies of a corresponding amount annually out of undistributed profits. On a before-tax basis the combined return of his stocks would then average, say, 7.5%, somewhat less than his interest on high-grade bonds.* On an after-tax basis the average return on stocks would work out at some 5.3%.[5] This would be about the same as is now obtainable on good tax-free medium-term bonds.

These expectations are much less favorable for stocks against bonds than they were in our 1964 analysis. (That conclusion follows inevitably from the basic fact that bond yields have gone up much more than stock yields since 1964.) We must never lose sight of the fact that the interest and principal payments on good bonds are much better protected and therefore more certain than the dividends and price appreciation on stocks. Consequently we are forced to the conclusion that now, toward the end of 1971, bond investment appears clearly preferable to stock investment. If we could be sure that this conclusion is right we would have to advise the defensive investor to put *all* his money in bonds and *none* in common stocks until the current yield relationship changes significantly in favor of stocks.

But of course we cannot be certain that bonds will work out better than stocks from today's levels. The reader will immediately

---

* How well did Graham's forecast pan out? At first blush, it seems, very well: From the beginning of 1972 through the end of 1981, stocks earned an annual average return of 6.5%. (Graham did not specify the time period for his forecast, but he probably intended a 10-year time horizon.) However, inflation raged at 8.6% annually over this period, eating up the entire gain that stocks produced. In this section of his chapter, Graham is summarizing what is known as the "Gordon equation," which holds that the stock market's future rate of return is the sum of the current dividend yield and expected dividend growth. With a yield under 2% in early 2024, and long-term dividend growth of just over 2%, a future average annual return of roughly 4% (after inflation) is plausible. (See the Commentary on Chapter 3.)

think of the inflation factor as a potent reason on the other side. In the next chapter we shall argue that our considerable experience with inflation in the United States during this century would not support the choice of stocks against bonds at present differentials in yield. But there is always the possibility—though we consider it remote—of an accelerating inflation, which in one way or another would have to make stock equities preferable to bonds payable in a fixed amount of dollars.* There is the alternative possibility—which we also consider highly unlikely—that American business will become so profitable, without stepped-up inflation, as to justify a large increase in common-stock values in the next few years. Finally, there is the more familiar possibility that we shall witness another great speculative rise in the stock market without a real justification in the underlying values. Any of these reasons, and perhaps others we haven't thought of, *might* cause the investor to regret a 100% concentration on bonds even at their more favorable yield levels.

Hence, after this foreshortened discussion of the major considerations, we once again enunciate the same basic compromise policy for defensive investors—namely that at all times they have a significant part of their funds in bond-type holdings and a significant part also in equities. It is still true that they may choose between maintaining a simple 50–50 division between the two components or a ratio, dependent on their judgment, varying between a minimum of 25% and a maximum of 75% of either. We shall give our more detailed view of these alternative policies in a later chapter.

Since at present the overall return envisaged from common stocks is nearly the same as that from bonds, the presently expectable return (including growth of stock values) for the

---

* Since 1997, when Treasury Inflation-Protected Securities (TIPS) were introduced, stocks have no longer been automatically superior to bonds when inflation increases. TIPS, unlike other bonds, tend to rise in value when the Consumer Price Index goes up, generally immunizing the investor against losing money after inflation. Stocks carry no such guarantee and are an imperfect hedge against high rates of inflation. (For more details, see the Commentary on Chapter 2.)

investor would change little regardless of how he divides his fund between the two components. As calculated above, the aggregate return from both parts should be about 7.8% before taxes or 5.5% on a tax-free (or estimated tax-paid) basis. A return of this order is appreciably higher than that realized by the typical conservative investor over most of the long-term past. It may not seem attractive in relation to the 14%, or so, return shown by common stocks during the 20 years of the predominantly bull market after 1949. But it should be remembered that between 1949 and 1969 the price of the DJIA had advanced more than fivefold while its earnings and dividends had about doubled. Hence the greater part of the impressive market record for that period was based on a change in investors' and speculators' attitudes rather than in underlying corporate values. To that extent it might well be called a "bootstrap operation."

In discussing the common-stock portfolio of the defensive investor, we have spoken only of leading issues of the type included in the 30 components of the Dow Jones Industrial Average. We have done this for convenience, and not to imply that these 30 issues alone are suitable for purchase by him. Actually, there are many other companies of quality equal to or excelling the average of the Dow Jones list; these would include a host of public utilities (which have a separate Dow Jones average to represent them).* But the major point here is that the defensive investor's overall results are not likely to be decisively different from one diversified or representative list than from another, or—more accurately—that neither he nor his advisers could predict with certainty whatever differences would ultimately develop. It is true that the art of skillful or shrewd investment is supposed to lie particularly in the selection of issues that will give better results than the general market. For reasons to be developed elsewhere we are skeptical of the ability of defensive investors generally to get better than average results—

---

* Today, the most widely available alternatives to the Dow Jones Industrial Average are the Standard & Poor's 500-stock index (the "S&P 500") and the FT Wilshire 5000 index. The S & P focuses on about 500 large, well-known companies that make up about 80% of the total capitalization of the U.S. equity market. The FT Wilshire 5000 follows the returns of nearly every which in fact would mean to beat their own overall performance.* (Our skepticism extends to the management of large funds by experts.)

Let us illustrate our point by an example that at first may seem to prove the opposite. Between December 1960 and December 1970 the DJIA advanced from 616 to 839, or 36%. But in the same period the much larger Standard & Poor's weighted index of 500 stocks rose from 58.11 to 92.15, or 58%. Obviously the second group had proved a better "buy" than the first. But who would have been so rash as to predict in 1960 that what seemed like a miscellaneous assortment of all sorts of common stocks would definitely outperform the aristocratic "thirty tyrants" of the Dow? All this proves, we insist, that only rarely can one make dependable predictions about price changes, absolute or relative.

We shall repeat here without apology—for the warning cannot be given too often—that **the investor cannot hope for better than average results by buying new offerings, or "hot" issues of any sort, meaning thereby those recommended for a quick profit.**† The contrary is almost certain to be true in the long run. The defensive investor must confine himself to the shares of important companies with a long record of profitable operations and in strong financial condition. (Any security analyst worth his salt could make up such a list.) Aggressive investors may buy other types of common stocks, but they should be on a definitely attractive basis as established by intelligent analysis.

To conclude this section, let us mention briefly three supplementary concepts or practices for the defensive investor. The first is the purchase of the shares of well-established investment

---

significant, publicly traded stock in America, approximately 3,500 in all; but, since the largest companies account for most of the market value of the index, the return of the FT Wilshire 5000 is usually quite similar to that of the S&P 500. Low-cost index funds enable investors to hold the stocks in these indexes as a single, convenient portfolio. Index funds are available worldwide, to the benefit of investors almost everywhere. (See Chapter 9 and its Commentary.)

* See pp. 348–351 and pp. 362–366.
† For greater detail, see Chapter 6 and its Commentary.

funds as an alternative to creating his own common-stock portfolio. He might also utilize one of the "common trust funds," or "commingled funds," operated by trust companies and banks in many states; or, if his funds are substantial, use the services of a recognized investment-counsel firm. This will give him professional administration of his investment program along standard lines. The third is the device of "dollar-cost averaging," which means simply that the practitioner invests in common stocks the same number of dollars each month or each quarter. In this way he buys more shares when the market is low than when it is high, and he is likely to end up with a satisfactory overall price for all his holdings. Strictly speaking, this method is an application of a broader approach known as "formula investing." The latter was already alluded to in our suggestion that the investor may vary his holdings of common stocks between the 25% minimum and the 75% maximum, in inverse relationship to the action of the market. These ideas have merit for the defensive investor, and they will be discussed more amply in later chapters.*

Results to Be Expected by the Aggressive Investor

Our enterprising security buyer, of course, will desire and expect to attain better overall results than his defensive or passive companion. But first he must make sure that his results will not be worse. **It is no difficult trick to bring a great deal of energy, study, and native ability into Wall Street and to end up with losses instead of profits.** These virtues, if channeled in the wrong directions, become indistinguishable from handicaps. Thus it is most essential that the enterprising investor start with a clear conception as to which courses of action offer reasonable chances of success and which do not.

First let us consider several ways in which investors and speculators generally have endeavored to obtain better than average results. These include:

---

* For more advice on "well-established investment funds," see Chapter 9. "Professional administration" by "a recognized investment-counsel firm" is discussed in Chapter 10. "Dollar-cost averaging" is explained in Chapter 5.

1. Trading in the market. This usually means buying stocks when the market has been advancing and selling them after it has turned downward. The stocks selected are likely to be among those which have been "behaving" better than the market average. A small number of professionals frequently engage in short selling. Here they will sell issues they do not own but borrow through the established mechanism of the stock exchanges. Their object is to benefit from a subsequent decline in the price of these issues, by buying them back at a price lower than they sold them for. (As our quotation from the *Wall Street Journal* on p. 18 indicates, even "small investors"—perish the term!—sometimes try their unskilled hand at short selling.)

2. Short-term selectivity. This means buying stocks of companies which are reporting or expected to report increased earnings, or for which some other favorable development is anticipated.

3. Long-term selectivity. Here the usual emphasis is on an excellent record of past growth, which is considered likely to continue in the future. In some cases also the "investor" may choose companies which have not yet shown impressive results, but are expected to establish a high earning power later. (Such companies belong frequently in some technological area—e.g., computers, drugs, electronics—and they often are developing new processes or products that are deemed to be especially promising.)

We have already expressed a negative view about the investor's overall chances of success in these areas of activity. The first we have ruled out, on both theoretical and realistic grounds, from the domain of investment. **Stock trading is not an operation "which, on thorough analysis, offers safety of principal and a satisfactory return."** More will be said on stock trading in a later chapter.*

In his endeavor to select the most promising stocks either for the near term or the longer future, the investor faces obstacles of two kinds—the first stemming from human fallibility and the second from the nature of his competition.

---

* See Chapter 8 and the Commentaries on Chapters 5, 8, and 14.

He may be wrong in his estimate of the future; or even if he is right, the current market price may already fully reflect what he is anticipating. In the area of near-term selectivity, the current year's results of the company are generally common property on Wall Street; next year's results, to the extent they are predictable, are already being carefully considered. **Hence the investor who selects issues chiefly on the basis of this year's superior results, or on what he is told he may expect for next year, is likely to find that others have done the same thing for the same reason.**

In choosing stocks for their *long-term* prospects, the investor's handicaps are basically the same. The possibility of outright error in the prediction—which we illustrated by our airlines example on p. 7—is no doubt greater than when dealing with near-term earnings. Because the experts frequently go astray in such forecasts, it is theoretically possible for an investor to benefit greatly by making correct predictions when Wall Street as a whole is making incorrect ones. But that is only theoretical. **How many enterprising investors could count on having the acumen or prophetic gift to beat the professional analysts at their favorite game of estimating long-term future earnings?**

We are thus led to the following logical if disconcerting conclusion: **To enjoy a reasonable chance for continued better than average results, the investor must follow policies which are (1) inherently sound and promising, and (2) not popular on Wall Street.**

Are there any such policies available for the enterprising investor? In theory once again, the answer should be yes; and there are broad reasons to think that the answer should be affirmative in practice as well. Everyone knows that speculative stock movements are carried too far in both directions, frequently in the general market and at all times in at least some of the individual issues. Furthermore, a common stock may be undervalued because of lack of interest or unjustified popular prejudice. We can go further and assert that **in an astonishingly large proportion of the trading in common stocks, those engaged therein don't appear to know—in polite terms—one part of their anatomy from another**. In this book we shall point out numerous examples of (past) discrepancies between price and value. Thus it seems that any intelligent person, with a good head for figures, should have a veritable picnic on Wall Street, battening off other people's foolishness. So it seems, but somehow it doesn't work out that simply. Buying a neglected and therefore undervalued issue for profit generally proves a protracted and patience-trying experience. And selling short a too popular and therefore overvalued issue is apt to be a test not only of one's courage and stamina but also of the depth of one's pocketbook.* The principle is sound, its successful application is not impossible, but it is distinctly not an easy art to master.†

There is also a fairly wide group of "special situations," which over many years could be counted on to bring a nice annual return of 20% or better, with a minimum of overall risk to those who knew their way around in this field. They include intersecurity arbitrages, payouts or workouts in liquidations, protected hedges of certain kinds. The most typical case is a projected merger or acquisition which offers a substantially higher value for certain shares than their price on the date of the announcement. The number of such deals increased greatly in recent years, and it should have been a highly profitable period for the cognoscenti. But with the multiplication of merger announcements came a multiplication of obstacles to mergers and of deals that didn't go through; quite a few individual losses were thus realized in these once-reliable

---

* In "selling short" (or "shorting") a stock, you make a bet that its share price will go down, not up. Shorting is a three-step process: First, you borrow shares from someone who owns them; then you immediately sell the borrowed shares; finally, you replace them with shares you buy later. If the stock drops, you will be able to buy your replacement shares at a lower price. The difference between the price at which you sold your borrowed shares and the price you paid for the replacement shares is your gross profit (reduced by dividend or interest charges, along with brokerage costs). However, if the stock goes up in price instead of down, your potential loss is unlimited—making short sales unacceptably speculative for most individual investors.
† Another way enterprising investors can earn "better than average results": by stepping forward to buy when professional investors are panic-selling, as occurred in 2000–02, 2008–09, and early 2020. Courage is often more common on Main Street than on Wall Street.

operations. Perhaps, too, the overall rate of profit was diminished by too much competition.*

The lessened profitability of these special situations appears one manifestation of a kind of self-destructive process—akin to the law of diminishing returns—which has developed during the lifetime of this book. In 1949 we could present a study of stock-market fluctuations over the preceding 75 years, which supported a formula—based on earnings and current interest rates—for determining a level to buy the DJIA below its "central" or "intrinsic" value, and to sell out above such value. It was an application of the governing maxim of the Rothschilds: "Buy cheap and sell dear."† And it had the advantage of running directly counter to the ingrained and pernicious maxim of Wall Street that stocks should be bought because they have gone up and sold because they have gone down. Alas, after 1949 this formula no longer worked. A second illustration is provided by the famous "Dow Theory" of stock-market movements, in a comparison of its indicated splendid results for 1897–1933 and its much more questionable performance since 1934.

A third and final example of the golden opportunities not recently available: A good part of our own operations on Wall Street had been concentrated on the purchase of *bargain issues* easily identified as such by the fact that they were selling at less than their share in the net current assets (working capital) alone, not counting

---

* In the late 1980s, as hostile corporate takeovers and leveraged buyouts multiplied, Wall Street set up institutional arbitrage desks to profit from any errors in pricing these complex deals. They became so good at it that the easy profits disappeared and many of these desks have been closed down. Although Graham discusses it again (see pp. 174–176), this sort of trading is no longer feasible or appropriate for most people, since only multimillion-dollar trades are large enough to justify earning a slim profit per share. Wealthy individuals and institutions can utilize this strategy through hedge funds that specialize in merger or "event" arbitrage.

† The Rothschild family, led by Nathan Mayer Rothschild, was a dominant power in European investment banking and brokerage in the nineteenth century. See Niall Ferguson, *The House of Rothschild: Money's Prophets, 1798–1848* (Viking, 1998).

the plant account and other assets, and after deducting all liabilities ahead of the stock. It is clear that these issues were selling at a price well below the value of the enterprise as a private business. No proprietor or majority holder would think of selling what he owned at so ridiculously low a figure. Strangely enough, such anomalies were not hard to find. In 1957 a list was published showing nearly 200 issues of this type available in the market. In various ways practically all these bargain issues turned out to be profitable, and the average annual result proved much more remunerative than most other investments. But they too virtually disappeared from the stock market in the next decade, and with them a dependable area for shrewd and successful operation by the enterprising investor. However, at the low prices of 1970 there again appeared a considerable number of such "sub-working-capital" issues, and despite the strong recovery of the market, enough of them remained at the end of the year to make up a full-sized portfolio.

The enterprising investor under today's conditions still has various possibilities of achieving better than average results. The huge list of marketable securities must include a fair number that can be identified as undervalued by logical and reasonably dependable standards. These should yield more satisfactory results on the average than will the DJIA or any similarly representative list. In our view the search for these would not be worth the investor's effort unless he could hope to add, say, 5% before taxes to the average annual return from the stock portion of his portfolio. We shall try to develop one or more such approaches to stock selection for use by the active investor.

Commentary on Chapter 1
by Jason Zweig

> If you don't know who you are, [the stock market] is an expensive place to find out.
> —"Adam Smith" (George J. W. Goodman)[1]

Before you buy any stock or other financial asset, the first thing to understand isn't what you are buying, but rather who you are.

Are You an Investor?

The word "invest" comes from the Latin *vestire*, to clothe, surround, or envelop. To invest means to wrap yourself in a financial asset and hold it close. To do that, you should have a reasonable basis for confidence that you understand what you're doing—based not on what other people say or do, but on your own careful research.

As Graham writes:

> An investment operation is one which, upon thorough analysis, promises safety of principal and an adequate return. Operations not meeting these requirements are speculative.[2]

Graham calls it "an investment *operation*" because investing is a process, not an event. It unfolds over years and decades. It depends on structured decision-making, in which every action you take conforms to criteria you have set in advance. It requires the discipline

---

[1] "Adam Smith," *The Money Game* (Random House, 1968), p. 30.
[2] P. 17. Graham sometimes used the phrase "satisfactory return" instead of "adequate return."

of thorough and consistent analysis, not just an impulsive swipe on your smartphone.

The sources of return for an investment are *intrinsic*: the interest income of bonds, the earnings and dividends of stocks. An investor understands that a stock isn't a plaything; it's an ownership stake in an underlying business. And a stock can't go up persistently unless that business consistently generates more cash than it consumes.

An investor never buys a stock merely because its price has been going up or sells it just because its price has been falling. An investor looks beyond the short-term behavior of the stock to evaluate the long-term health of the *business*.

The investor asks: *What is this worth to me? How long can I hold it?*

Are You a Speculator?

In the past few years, many investors lost their way. They became speculators, often without realizing it.

To "speculate" comes from the Latin words *speculum* (mirror) and *specula* (watchtower).

A speculator should look *inward*, in an act of self-reflection, as in a mirror—as well as *forward* into the future, like a sentry in a watchtower.[3]

In practice, however, many speculators never look inward and barely look forward. Often, they buy just because other people are.

Speculation unfolds over short horizons: months, weeks, sometimes hours or even minutes. The sources of return for a speculation are *extrinsic*: who else owns an asset, how popular it is, whether its price has been rising or falling. The speculator asks: *What is this worth to somebody else? How soon can I sell it?*

For many people, speculation is an endless cycle of emotional swings, beginning in doubt, progressing through hope and confidence to complacency and greed, falling into fear and despair, fading back into doubt, then starting all over again. It's a hamster wheel of trading on hunches, throwing money into stocks, options, and other assets and flipping them as soon as possible, just for the fun of it—until it isn't fun anymore.

---

[3] Gayle Rogers, *Speculation: A Cultural History from Aristotle to AI* (Columbia, 2021).

FIGURE 1-1: The Behavioral Life Cycle of the Speculator

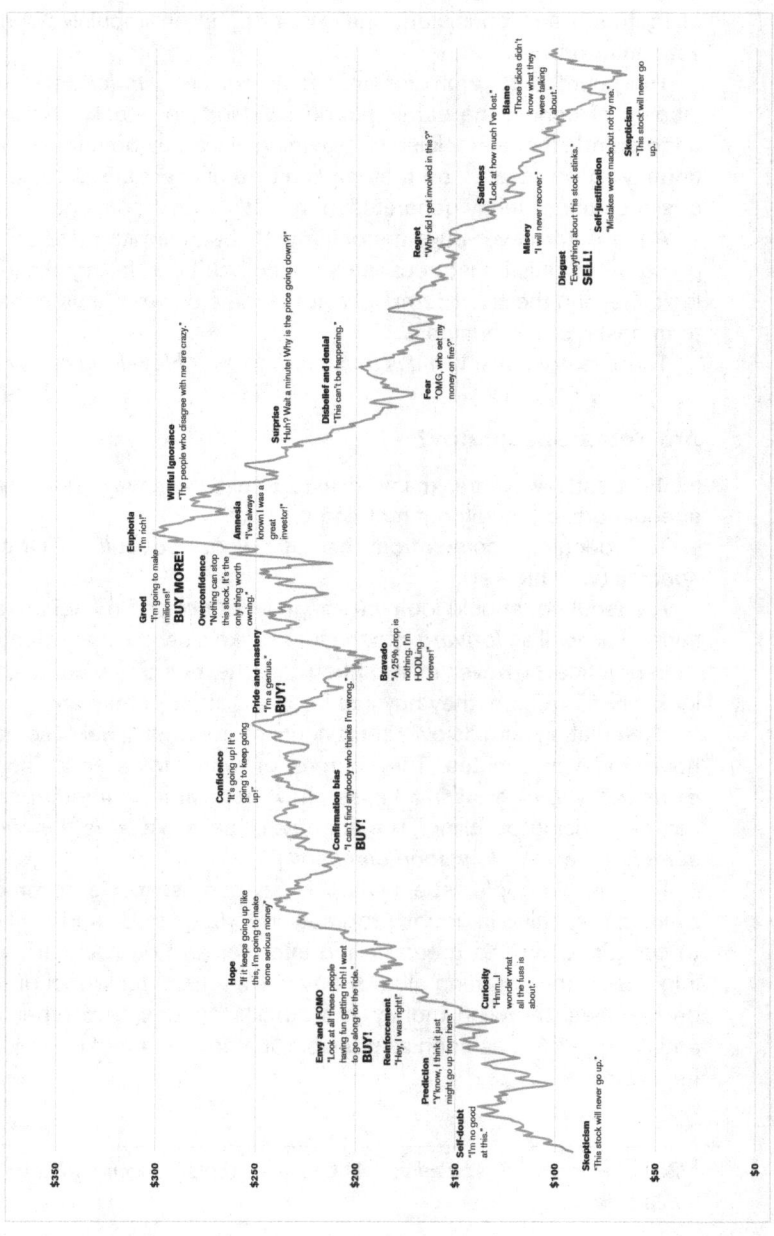

All that is understandable. The urge to gamble is part of human nature; our ancestors appear to have been gambling with dice at least 10,000 years ago. And speculation is exciting: Even a ridiculously remote chance of a big jackpot opens the gates of hope and possibility. Betting $1 on a one-in-a-million long shot leaves you $1 poorer if you lose—as you almost certainly will. But if, against all odds, you happen to win, you will suddenly be $1 million richer—and, you feel, your life will never be the same. What's more, the odds of making money speculating in the stock market are less adverse than the odds in a casino or the lottery.

> ### Investing as Endeavor
>
> To endeavor is to work conscientiously toward a specified goal or purpose; it is rooted in the French word *devoir*, or duty. Such a goal might be to buy a house, pay for your children's tuition, fund care for an aging parent, finance your retirement, or simply achieve the serenity of not needing to worry about money. You can't fulfill those purposes in a moment, with a single trade or one shrewd decision. Getting there takes years, even decades, of discipline and patience. That's why you should treat investing as an endeavor.

> ### Investing as Entertainment
>
> To be entertained is *to have fun*! And if you treat investing as entertainment, you probably will have fun—for a while, anyway. But that joyride is likely to end in losses, leaving you farther away from your goals. Investing for entertainment can bring the thrill of a near miss—*I came this close to being rich!*—or even the elation of hitting the jackpot. Part of what makes hitting the jackpot so exciting, though, is that losses occur much more often. The remote odds of nailing a giant winner can't provide the reliability you need to meet your long-term financial goals.

The Silence of the Losers

Like eating and drinking and drugs and sex, speculation can be pleasurable in moderation. Overeat, though, and you can endanger your health. Drink too much, and you can become an alcoholic. Abuse drugs or sex, and you can become an addict or end up in prison. And if you speculate with more than a tiny portion of your money, you are likely to end up losing all of it.

The odds in financial markets usually aren't fixed or predetermined. They depend partly on how many people are speculating and on how much money they are betting. The higher speculators drive the price of an asset in the present, the lower its returns are likely to be in the future. The more people speculate in the short run, the lower the odds that any one of them can profit in the long run.

The more people start speculating, though, the more tempted you might be to give it a try. Everybody seems to be doing it, and some of them are getting rich. Most of the losers are too embarrassed to talk about their losses, while the winners all seem to be yelling through megaphones. Even if they don't know what they're talking about, people with extreme views seem more credible and trustworthy as they "double down" to escalate their commitment. After all, they've put their money where their mouth is.

So stories triumph over statistics: You can't avoid the boasting of the winners, while the evidence that most people have gotten wiped out never even comes to your attention. The hope of striking it rich feels especially appealing when big institutions that took reckless risks keep getting bailed out by the government. If they got away with taking shortcuts, why shouldn't you? If you're working hard but can't seem to get ahead, why not try gambling on stocks?

And speculation is often habit-forming. The thrill of making money can quickly trap you in the cycle of addiction: Like someone with a substance-abuse problem, you need a bigger fix each time to match the previous high, and losses simply make you crave gains even more. Every addict says, "I can quit anytime I want," but quitting can become all but impossible. Chasing the next short-term hit, you can lose sight of your long-term goals. You may end up flinging good money after bad until nothing is left.

Free Money

In 2020 and 2021, as the Covid pandemic raged, the stock market quickly turned into the biggest online video game ever played.

More than 110 million people lost their jobs worldwide and were

> **Trade-a-holics**
>
> From the end of 2019 through early 2021, the online brokerage Robinhood grew from just over 5 million accounts to 18 million. That means roughly 13 million people—one out of every 25 Americans—opened a new account in 15 months.
>
> In the first quarter of 2021, those 18 million customers traded stocks, options, and cryptocurrencies an average of 7.6 million times per day.
>
> A Singapore-based online brokerage, Moomoo, reported in 2021 that its younger customers were trading an average of more than 140 times a year.
>
> According to Massachusetts regulators, Robinhood allowed one customer with no investment experience to make 12,748 trades in just over six months—an average of approximately 92 trades per day.[1]
>
> Even people who didn't trade as if their underpants were on fire had become obsessed: In 2020, Robinhood reported that customers who opened its app used it seven times a day on average.
>
> Are you trading almost 150 times a year or checking on your accounts seven times a day?
>
> Then you aren't an investor.
>
> You're an addict.
>
> You aren't just impairing your financial health, but your mental health as well.
>
> ---
>
> [1] bit.ly/46BxTga.

quarantined from their family and friends. Most businesses shut down—but stock markets were open. Governments squashed interest rates to zero and flooded the global economy with trillions of dollars in cash payments to individuals and companies.

With nowhere to go and nothing to do with all that free money, people flung it into the financial markets.

Everything went up.

By late March 2021, the U.S. stock market had gained 85% in 12 months, with the smallest stocks rising more than 120% on average. In fact, 96% of all U.S. stocks had a positive total return over the prior 12 months. It was as if the stock market had become a slot machine that spewed out a jackpot on every play.

Markets were roaring around the world. Over the year ending March 31, 2021, stocks in China gained 47%, Brazil 52%, Germany 67%, and India 84%.

You could make good money on good stocks. You could make good money on bad stocks. Dogecoin, a cryptocurrency that was set up as a joke and served no practical purpose, gained more than 15,000% in the first five months of 2021.

Why bother trying to distinguish good assets from bad? When knowing nothing pays off, why learn anything?

"I Don't Know What the F— I'm Doing"

Such willful ignorance was typical.

- On the Reddit online forum WallStreetBets, many members felt that carefully analyzing an investment made "no sense," the group's founder, Jaime Rogozinski, said in 2020. "They just regard the volatility as an opportunity for fun . . . they don't know what they're doing, and they don't care that they don't know what they're doing."
- In mid-2020, a sports blogger and self-described "degenerate gambler" named Dave Portnoy began live-tweeting videos in which he bought any stock whose ticker symbol matched the letters he pulled randomly from a bag of Scrabble tiles. He often sold the stocks the same day he bought them, openly mocking the idea that learning anything about a company was worthwhile.[4]
- In early 2021, a bright-eyed young couple named Chad and Jenny became instant celebrities with a TikTok video on how to make money without working a 9-to-5 job. "I see a stock going up and I buy it," said Chad with a cheerfully clueless shrug. "And I just

---

[4] "The Dave Portnoy Origin Story," bit.ly/48SWkqF; Akane Otani, "The New Stock Influencers Have Huge—and Devoted—Followings," bit.ly/41ZDqfv.

watch it until it stops going up, and then I sell it. And I do that over and over, and it pays for our whole lifestyle."
- "I don't know what the f— I'm doing," 22-year-old Danny Tran said in a TikTok video in January 2021. "I just know I'm making money." He quickly racked up roughly 500,000 followers. Asked if he did any research before trading, Mr. Tran laughed, "When I tell you I don't know what the f— I'm doing, I really mean it. It's all just a game to me." He added, "Knowing what you're doing would always be good, but in this market anything is possible."

"Something That Is Imitated"

In 2020 and 2021, millions of novice traders stampeded into such "meme stocks" as AMC Entertainment Holdings, Bed Bath & Beyond, GameStop, and Virgin Galactic Holdings, regardless of the health of the underlying businesses.

The term "meme," coined by the biologist Richard Dawkins in 1976, is from the Greek *mimema*, "something that is imitated." Everybody else was buying, and that was all that mattered.[5]

For a few glorious months in 2020 and 2021, it worked. Then, one after another, these overpriced stocks shattered like overheated flashbulbs.

While a few early buyers captured enormous profits, most people bought too late, paid too much, and bailed out near the bottom. One trader made $1.5 million treating the market "like a casino"—only to lose it all, ending up working at a deli in Las Vegas for $14 an hour.[6]

One of investing's few universal rules is this: *Whenever making money becomes effortlessly easy, keeping it is about to become extraordinarily hard.*

---

[5] The best account of this madness is Spencer Jakab, *The Revolution That Wasn't* (Portfolio, 2022).
[6] Gunjan Banerji, "The Retreat of the Amateur Investors," bit.ly/3F3VKcE.

TABLE 1-1: Memes of Dreams

Stock	High price	Date of high	Low price	Date of low	% change
AMC Entertainment Holdings Inc.	38.43	06/02/21	3.84	12/28/22	-90.0
Bed Bath & Beyond Inc.	46.08	01/27/21	2.39	12/28/22	-94.8
BlackBerry Ltd.	24.65	01/27/21	3.19	12/28/22	-87.1
Clover Health Investments Corp.	22.15	06/08/21	0.87	12/28/22	-96.1
Coinbase Global Inc.	357.39	11/09/21	32.53	12/28/22	-90.9
DraftKings Inc.	71.98	03/19/21	10.27	05/11/22	-85.7
FuelCell Energy Inc.	27.96	02/09/21	2.55	12/28/22	-90.9
GameStop Corp.	86.88	01/27/21	17.92	12/28/22	-79.4
Lordstown Motors Corp.	461.25	02/11/21	15.75	12/27/22	-96.6

Stock	High price	Date of high	Low price	Date of low	% change
MicroStrategy Inc.	1272.94	02/09/21	136.63	12/29/22	-89.3
Nikola Corp.	28.58	01/27/21	2.11	12/14/22	-92.6
NIO Inc.	62.84	02/09/21	9.25	11/09/22	-85.3
Palantir Technologies Inc.	39.00	01/27/21	6.00	12/27/22	-84.6
Peloton Interactive Inc.	167.42	01/13/21	6.93	09/30/22	-95.9
PlugPower Inc.	73.18	01/26/21	11.71	12/28/22	-84.0
Riot Blockchain Inc.	77.90	02/17/21	3.29	12/28/22	-95.8
Rivian Automotive Inc.	172.01	11/16/21	17.74	12/28/22	-89.7
Sundial Growers Inc.	29.50	02/10/21	1.99	12/28/22	-93.3
Virgin Galactic Holdings Inc.	59.41	02/11/21	3.29	12/27/22	-94.5

Stock	High price	Date of high	Low price	Date of low	% change
Zoom Video Communications Inc.	444.51	02/16/21	65.36	12/28/22	-85.3
S&P 500 index	4796.56	01/03/22	3577.03	10/12/22	-25.4

Daily closing prices, $ per share; dividends not included in % change. Riot Blockchain later renamed Riot Platforms Inc.; Sundial Growers later renamed SNDL Inc.

Source: FactSet.

Protecting Yourself from Your Worst Enemy

I must warn you that a tension runs throughout this book. Any attempt to beat the market is probably futile, especially when you can match the market with no effort and nearly no cost by buying and holding an index fund. On the other hand, it's human nature to hate settling for "average," and trying to outwit the billion-brained market is an exciting challenge many people can't completely renounce.

Our goal is to bridge that tension. You should feel no shame in settling for average; that makes you what Graham calls a defensive investor.[7] If, however, you are an enterprising investor who wants to try to outperform, you've set an improbable—although not quite impossible—goal. To stand a chance of achieving it, you will need to follow rules, policies, and procedures with rigorous discipline.

If you still want to speculate, then the key is to contain it (see the sidebar on p. 46). Even the most cautious people can get a kick out of gambling every once in a while; that's fine, so long as you risk no more than you can afford to lose, and you are honest enough with yourself to know you probably *will* lose.

But the heat of the moment can melt your resolve. That's why you must control your impulses and structure your decisions with the techniques we'll discuss in Chapters 4, 5, 7, 11, and the accompanying Commentaries.

And what if you speculated and got burned so badly that you can finally admit you've hit bottom?

Good for you. The rest of this book will map out how you can get on track as an investor and how to stay there.

---

[7] And earning the "average" return of the stock market by holding an index fund is likely to give you a result far *above* average; see the Commentary on Chapter 9.

Mad Money

If you have the urge to speculate, segregate it in a "mad money" account. Limit it to a maximum of 5% of your assets; that way, you can make a decent amount if any of your speculations pay off, but you won't lose a dangerous amount if they go to zero. Quarantine the mad money from the rest of your assets, in an isolated account at a different financial institution. No matter what happens, *never* add more money to it.

CHAPTER 2

The Investor and Inflation
by Benjamin Graham

*I*nflation, and the fight against it, has been very much in the public's mind in recent years. The shrinkage in the purchasing power of the dollar in the past, and particularly the fear (or hope by speculators) of a serious further decline in the future, has greatly influenced the thinking of Wall Street. It is clear that those with a fixed dollar income will suffer when the cost of living advances, and the same applies to a fixed amount of dollar principal. Holders of stocks, on the other hand, have the possibility that a loss of the dollar's purchasing power may be offset by advances in their dividends and the prices of their shares.

On the basis of these undeniable facts many financial authorities have concluded that (1) bonds are an inherently undesirable form of investment, and (2) consequently, common stocks are by their very nature more desirable investments than bonds. We have heard of charitable institutions being advised that their portfolios should consist 100% of stocks and zero percent of bonds.* This is quite a reversal from the earlier days when trust investments were restricted by law to high-grade bonds (and a few choice preferred stocks).

---

* By the late 1990s, this advice—which can be appropriate for a foundation or endowment with a perpetual investment horizon—had spread to individual investors, whose life spans are finite. In the 1994 edition of his influential book *Stocks for the Long Run*, finance professor Jeremy Siegel recommended that "risk-taking" investors should buy on margin, borrowing more than a third of their net worth to sink 135% of their assets into stocks.

47

Our readers must have enough intelligence to recognize that even high-quality stocks cannot be a better purchase than bonds under all conditions—i.e., regardless of how high the stock market may be and how low the current dividend return compared with the rates available on bonds. A statement of this kind would be as absurd as was the contrary one—too often heard years ago—that any bond is safer than any stock. In this chapter we shall try to apply various measurements to the inflation factor, in order to reach some conclusions as to the extent to which the investor may wisely be influenced by expectations regarding future rises in the price level.

In this matter, as in so many others in finance, we must base our views of future policy on a knowledge of past experience. Is inflation something new for this country, at least in the serious form it has taken since 1965? If we have seen comparable (or worse) inflations in living experience, what lessons can be learned from them in confronting the inflation of today? Let us start with Table 2-1, a condensed historical tabulation that contains much information about changes in the general price level and concomitant changes in the earnings and market value of common stocks. Our figures will begin with 1915, and thus cover 55 years, presented at five-year intervals. (We use 1946 instead of 1945 to avoid the last year of wartime price controls.)

The first thing we notice is that we have had inflation in the past—lots of it. The largest five-year dose was between 1915 and 1920, when the cost of living nearly doubled. This compares with the advance of 15% between 1965 and 1970. In between, we have had three periods of declining prices and then six of advances at varying rates, some rather small. On this showing, the investor should clearly allow for the probability of continuing or recurrent inflation to come.

Can we tell what the rate of inflation is likely to be? No clear answer is suggested by our table; it shows variations of all sorts. It would seem sensible, however, to take our cue from the rather consistent record of the past 20 years. The average annual rise in the consumer price level for this period has been 2.5%; that for 1965–1970 was 4.5%; that for 1970 alone was 5.4%. Official government policy has been strongly against large-scale inflation, and there are some reasons to believe that Federal policies will be more effective in the future than in recent

TABLE 2-1 The General Price Level, Stock Earnings, and Stock Prices at Five-Year Intervals, 1915–1970

	Price Level[a]		S & P 500-Stock Index[b]		Percent Change from Previous Level			
Year	Wholesale	Consumer	Earnings	Price	Wholesale Prices	Consumer Prices	Stock Earnings	Stock Prices
1915	38.0	35.4		8.31				
1920	84.5	69.8		7.98	+96.0%	+96.8%		− 4.0%
1925	56.6	61.1	1.24	11.15	−33.4	−12.4		+41.5
1930	47.3	58.2	.97	21.63	−16.5	−4.7	−21.9%	+88.0
1935	43.8	47.8	.76	15.47	−7.4	−18.0	−21.6	−26.0
1940	43.0	48.8	1.05	11.02	−0.2	+2.1	+33.1	−28.8
1946[c]	66.1	68.0	1.06	17.08	+53.7	+40.0	+1.0	+55.0
1950	86.8	83.8	2.84	18.40	+31.5	+23.1	+168.0	+21.4
1955	97.2	93.3	3.62	40.49	+6.2	+11.4	+27.4	+121.0
1960	100.7	103.1	3.27	55.85	+9.2	+10.5	−9.7	+38.0
1965	102.5	109.9	5.19	88.17	+1.8	+6.6	+58.8	+57.0
1970	117.5	134.0	5.36	92.15	+14.6	+21.9	+3.3	+4.4

[a] Annual averages. For price level 1957 = 100 in table; but using new base, 1967 = 100, the average for 1970 is 116.3 for consumers' prices and 110.4 for wholesale prices for the stock index.
[b] 1941–1943 average = 10.
[c] 1946 used, to avoid price controls.

years.* We think it would be reasonable for an investor at this point to base his thinking and decisions on a *probable* (far from certain) rate of future inflation of, say, 3% per annum. (This would compare with an annual rate of about 2½% for the entire period 1915–1970.)[1]

What would be the implications of such an advance? It would eat up, in higher living costs, about one-half the income now obtainable on good medium-term tax-free bonds (or our assumed after-tax equivalent from high-grade corporate bonds). This would be a serious shrinkage, but it should not be exaggerated. It would not mean that the true value, or the purchasing power, of the investor's fortune need be reduced over the years. If he spent half his interest income after taxes he would maintain this buying power intact, even against a 3% annual inflation.

But the next question, naturally, is, "Can the investor be reasonably sure of doing better by buying and holding other things than high-grade bonds, even at the unprecedented rate of return offered in 1970–1971?" Would not, for example, an all-stock program be preferable to a part-bond, part-stock program? Do not common stocks have a built-in protection against inflation, and are they not almost certain to give a better return over the years than will bonds? Have not in fact stocks treated the investor far better than have bonds over the 55-year period of our study?

The answer to these questions is somewhat complicated. Common stocks have indeed done better than bonds over a long period of time in the past. The rise of the DJIA from an average of 77 in 1915 to an average of 753 in 1970 works out at an annual compounded rate of just about 4%, to which we may add another 4% for average dividend return. (The corresponding figures for the S & P composite are about the same.) These combined figures of 8% per year are of course much better than the return enjoyed from bonds over the same 55-year period. But they do not exceed that *now* offered by high-grade bonds. This brings us to the next logical

---

* This is one of Graham's rare misjudgments. In 1973, just two years after President Richard Nixon imposed wage and price controls, inflation hit 8.7%, its highest level since the end of World War II. The decade from 1973 through 1982 was the most inflationary in modern U.S. history, as the cost of living more than doubled.

question: Is there a persuasive reason to believe that common stocks are likely to do much better in future years than they have in the last five and one-half decades?

Our answer to this crucial question must be a flat *no*. Common stocks *may* do better in the future than in the past, but they are far from certain to do so. We must deal here with two different time elements in investment results. The first covers what is likely to occur over the long-term future—say, the next 25 years. The second applies to what is likely to happen to the investor—both financially and psychologically—over short or intermediate periods, say five years or less. His frame of mind, his hopes and apprehensions, his satisfaction or discontent with what he has done, above all his decisions what to do next, are all determined not in the retrospect of a lifetime of investment but rather by his experience from year to year.

On this point we can be categorical. There is no close time connection between inflationary (or deflationary) conditions and the movement of common-stock earnings and prices. The obvious example is the recent period, 1966–1970. The rise in the cost of living was 22%, the largest in a five-year period since 1946–1950. But both stock earnings and stock prices as a whole have declined since 1965. There are similar contradictions in both directions in the record of previous five-year periods.

Inflation and Corporate Earnings

Another and highly important approach to the subject is by a study of the earnings rate on capital shown by American business. This has fluctuated, of course, with the general rate of economic activity, but it has shown no general tendency to advance with wholesale prices or the cost of living. Actually this rate has fallen rather markedly in the past twenty years in spite of the inflation of the period. (To some degree the decline was due to the charging of more liberal depreciation rates. See Table 2-2.) Our extended studies have led to the conclusion that the investor cannot count on much above the recent five-year rate earned on the DJIA group—about 10% on net tangible assets (book value) behind the shares.[2] Since the market value of these issues is well above their book value—say, 900 market vs. 560 book in mid-1971—the earnings on current market price work out only at some 6¼%. (This relationship is generally expressed in the reverse, or "times earnings," manner—e.g., that the DJIA price of 900 equals 18 times the actual earnings for the 12 months ended June 1971.)

Our figures gear in directly with the suggestion in the previous chapter* that the investor may assume an average dividend return of about 3.5% on the market value of his stocks, plus an appreciation of, say, 4% annually resulting from reinvested profits. (Note that each dollar added to book value is here assumed to increase the market price by about $1.60.)

The reader will object that in the end our calculations make no allowance for an increase in common-stock earnings and values to result from our projected 3% annual inflation. Our justification is the absence of any sign that the inflation of a comparable amount in the past has had any *direct* effect on reported per-share earnings. The cold figures demonstrate that *all* the large gain in the earnings of the DJIA unit in the past 20 years was due to a proportionately large growth of invested capital coming from reinvested profits. If inflation had operated as a separate favorable factor, its effect would have been to increase the "value" of previously existing capital; this in turn should increase the rate of earnings on such old capital and therefore on the old and new capital combined. But nothing of the kind actually happened in the past 20 years, during which the wholesale price level has advanced nearly 40%. (Business earnings should be influenced more by wholesale prices than by "consumer prices.") The only way that inflation can add to common stock values is by raising the rate of earnings on capital investment. On the basis of the past record this has not been the case.

In the economic cycles of the past, good business was accompanied by a rising price level and poor business by falling prices. It was generally felt that "a little inflation" was helpful to business profits. This view is not contradicted by the history of 1950–1970, which reveals a combination of generally continued prosperity and generally rising prices. But the figures indicate that the effect of all this on the *earning power* of common-stock capital ("equity capital") has been quite limited; in fact it has not even served to maintain the

---

* See p. 24.

rate of earnings on the investment. Clearly there have been important offsetting influences which have prevented any increase in the real profitability of American corporations as a whole. Perhaps the most important of these have been (1) a rise in wage rates exceeding the gains in productivity, and (2) the need for huge amounts of new capital, thus holding down the ratio of sales to capital employed.

Our figures in Table 2-2 indicate that so far from inflation having benefited our corporations and their shareholders, its effect has been quite the opposite. The most striking figures in our table are those for the growth of corporate debt between 1950 and 1969. It is surprising how little attention has been paid by economists and by Wall Street to this development. The debt of corporations has expanded nearly fivefold while their profits before taxes a little more than doubled. With the great rise in interest rates during this period, it is evident that the aggregate corporate debt is now an adverse economic factor of some magnitude and a real problem for many individual enterprises. (Note that in 1950 net earnings after interest but before income tax were about 30% of corporate debt, while in 1969 they were only 13.2% of debt. The 1970 ratio must

TABLE 2-2 Corporate Debt, Profits, and Earnings on Capital, 1950–1969

		Corporate Profits		Percent Earned on Capital	
	Net Corporate	Before	After		
	Debt	Income Tax	Tax	S & P	Other
Year	(billions)	(millions)	(millions)	Data[a]	Data[b]
1950	$140.2	$42.6	$17.8	18.3%	15.0%
1955	212.1	48.6	27.0	18.3	12.9
1960	302.8	49.7	26.7	10.4	9.1
1965	453.3	77.8	46.5	10.8	11.8
1969	692.9	91.2	48.5	11.8	11.3

[a] Earnings of Standard & Poor's industrial index divided by average book value for year.

[b] Figures for 1950 and 1955 from Cottle and Whitman; those for 1960–1969 from *Fortune*.

have been even less satisfactory.) In sum it appears that a significant part of the 11% being earned on corporate equities as a whole is accomplished by the use of a large amount of new debt costing 4% or less after tax credit. If our corporations had maintained the debt ratio of 1950, their earnings rate on stock capital would have fallen still lower, in spite of the inflation.

The stock market has considered that the public-utility enterprises have been a chief victim of inflation, being caught between a great advance in the cost of borrowed money and the difficulty of raising the rates charged under the regulatory process. But this may be the place to remark that the very fact that the unit costs of electricity, gas, and telephone services have advanced so much less than the general price index puts these companies in a strong strategic position for the future.³ They are entitled by law to charge rates sufficient for an adequate return on their invested capital, and this will probably protect their shareholders in the future as it has in the inflations of the past.

All of the above brings us back to our conclusion that the investor has no sound basis for expecting more than an average overall return of, say, 8% on a portfolio of DJIA-type common stocks purchased at the late 1971 price level. But even if these expectations should prove to be understated by a substantial amount, the case would not be made for an all-stock investment program. If there is one thing guaranteed for the future, it is that the earnings and average annual market value of a stock portfolio will *not* grow at the uniform rate of 4%, or any other figure. In the memorable words of the elder J. P. Morgan, *"They will fluctuate."** This means, first, that the common-stock buyer at today's prices—or tomorrow's—will be running a real risk of having unsatisfactory results therefrom over a period of years. It took 25 years for General Electric (and the DJIA itself) to recover the ground lost in the 1929–1932 debacle. Besides that, if the investor concentrates his portfolio on common stocks

---

* John Pierpont Morgan Sr. was the most powerful financier of the late nineteenth and early twentieth centuries. Often asked what the stock market would do next, Morgan developed a mercifully short and unfailingly accurate answer: "It will fluctuate." See Jean Strouse, *Morgan: American Financier* (Random House, 1999), p. 11.

he is very likely to be led astray either by exhilarating advances or by distressing declines. This is particularly true if his reasoning is geared closely to expectations of further inflation. For then, if another bull market comes along, he will take the big rise not as a danger signal of an inevitable fall, not as a chance to cash in on his handsome profits, but rather as a vindication of the inflation hypothesis and as a reason to keep on buying common stocks no matter how high the market level nor how low the dividend return. That way lies sorrow.

Alternatives to Common Stocks as Inflation Hedges

The standard policy of people all over the world who mistrust their currency has been to buy and hold gold. This has been against the law for American citizens since 1935—luckily for them. In the past 35 years the price of gold in the open market has advanced from $35 per ounce to $48 in early 1972—a rise of only 35%. But during all this time the holder of gold has received no income return on his capital, and instead has incurred some annual expense for storage. Obviously, he would have done much better with his money at interest in a savings bank, in spite of the rise in the general price level.

The near-complete failure of gold to protect against a loss in the purchasing power of the dollar must cast grave doubt on the ability of the ordinary investor to protect himself against inflation by putting his money in "things."* Quite a few categories of valuable objects have had striking advances in market value over the years—such as diamonds, paintings by masters, first editions of books, rare stamps and coins, etc. But in many, perhaps most, of these cases there seems to be an element of the artificial or the precarious or even the unreal about the quoted prices. Somehow it is hard to think of paying $67,500 for a U.S. silver dollar dated 1804 (but not even minted that year) as an "investment operation."[4] We acknowledge we are out of our depth in this area. Very few of our readers will find the swimming safe and easy there.

The outright ownership of real estate has long been considered

---

* For more on gold, see pp. 60–61.

as a sound long-term investment, carrying with it a goodly amount of protection against inflation. Unfortunately, real-estate values are also subject to wide fluctuations; serious errors can be made in location, price paid, etc.; there are pitfalls in salesmen's wiles. Finally, diversification is not practical for the investor of moderate means, except by various types of participations with others and with the special hazards that attach to new flotations—not too different from common-stock ownership. This too is not our field. All we should say to the investor is, "Be sure it's yours before you go into it."

Conclusion

Naturally, we return to the policy recommended in our previous chapter. Just because of the uncertainties of the future the investor cannot afford to put all his funds into one basket—neither in the bond basket, despite the unprecedentedly high returns that bonds have recently offered; nor in the stock basket, despite the prospect of continuing inflation.

The more the investor depends on his portfolio and the income therefrom, the more necessary it is for him to guard against the unexpected and the disconcerting in this part of his life. It is axiomatic that the conservative investor should seek to minimize his risks. We think strongly that the risks involved in buying, say, a telephone-company bond at yields of nearly 7½% are much less than those involved in buying the DJIA at 900 (or any stock list equivalent thereto). But the possibility of *large-scale* inflation remains, and the investor must carry some insurance against it. There is no certainty that a stock component will insure adequately against such inflation, but it should carry more protection than the bond component.

This is what we said on the subject in our 1965 edition (p. 97), and we would write the same today:

> It must be evident to the reader that we have no enthusiasm for common stocks at these levels (892 for the DJIA). For reasons already given we feel that the defensive investor cannot afford to be without an appreciable proportion of common stocks in his portfolio, even if we regard them as the lesser of two evils—the greater being the risks in an all-bond holding.

Commentary on Chapter 2
by Jason Zweig

> A nickel ain't worth a dime anymore.
>
> —Yogi Berra[1]

For investors, inflation isn't an event. It's the environment.

That was easy to forget over the long period, from 2009 to 2020, when the cost of living—at least as many governments measure it—barely budged.

The Money Illusion

Investors tend to overreact to high inflation in the short run, while underreacting to low inflation in the long run. Most of us suffer from a fundamental misperception that psychologists call "money illusion."

Imagine three people: Amelia, Bella, and Charlotte. At different times, each inherited $500,000 and spent it all to buy a house, then sold the house one year later.

During the year Amelia owned her house, severe deflation reduced the cost of living by 25%. At the end of that year, she sold the house for $385,000, or 23% less than she paid for it.

During the year Bella owned her house, the cost of living didn't change; there was no inflation or deflation. At the end of that year, she sold the house for $495,000, or 1% less than she paid for it.

During the year Charlotte owned her house, inflation ran at

---

[1] Yogi Berra, *The Yogi Book* (Workman, 1998), p. 19.

25%. At the end of that year, she sold the house for $615,000, or 23% more than she paid for it.

Who made the best deal? Who made the worst deal?

Surveys suggest that most people will say Charlotte made out the best, followed by Bella, with Amelia coming out the worst.

Yet Amelia did the best of all three. She's the only one who came out ahead after changes in the cost of living. Goods and services became 25% cheaper, but she sold her house for only 23% less than it cost her—leaving her 2% better off.

That adjustment for the changing cost of living takes extra mental effort, whereas the nominal price—unadjusted for inflation—is obvious, simple, and salient. It's hard to ignore how much bigger $615,000 is than $500,000. Only if you stop to think about it (or grab a calculator) will you realize that Charlotte would have had to sell her house for $625,000 to break even after inflation.[2]

Likewise, investors tend to forget that commonly cited investment returns don't adjust for inflation. Assuming that the cost of living will tend to rise by at least 3% per year in the long term, you should get in the habit of subtracting 3% annually from any expected return. Someone who projects that stocks will rise an average of 10% annually is really saying you should expect no more than 7% annually, net of inflation.

To be an intelligent investor, you must counteract the money illusion. Keep your expectations realistic by always subtracting a plausible inflation rate from projected returns.

But inflation never dies. The trick, for intelligent investors, is to defend against it without overreacting to it.

Edges or Hedges?

Which financial assets provide the best protection against inflation?

When inflation flares up, scary rhetoric can blind you to faulty logic, so be sure to base your decisions on statistics rather than stories.

---

[2] Adapted from Eldar Shafir et al., "Money Illusion," bit.ly/45jx0YE.

Commentary on Chapter 2

> ### You Are an Egg
>
> As you consider defending against inflation, sort your assets into three mental buckets.
>
> **Financial capital** consists of cash, bonds, stocks, publicly traded real estate, commodities, and other marketable assets. Some shield better than others against the rising costs of living. To protect you from inflation, financial capital should be liquid, or quickly and easily convertible into cash.
>
> **Human capital** is the present value of all the income that your job, career, and education will produce. By going back to school for another degree, studying for a professional certification, acquiring proficiency in a vital new skill, moonlighting in a part-time job, or starting your own business, you can augment your human capital and push the growth in your total income well past the rate of inflation. Don't invest too much of your financial capital in the same industry where your human capital is concentrated. (When you're taking care not to put all your eggs in one basket, remember to count yourself among the eggs.)
>
> **Physical capital** is your material possessions: your home, cars, farmland or timberland, and fine collectibles like art, antiques, wine, jewelry, coins, or stamps. Over decades and even centuries, some physical or "real" assets have tended to hold their value during inflationary periods, particularly if they are high quality. They don't generate income, though.
>
> Don't forget to consider your human and physical capital when you're hedging against inflation. Otherwise, the investment industry's propaganda machine will fixate all your attention on your financial capital. That way, you'll be scared into buying funds tailored to look good—and generate high fees—when inflation heats up. Many such funds aren't liquid or don't generate income, limiting their usefulness as inflation fighters.

Financial advisers and other investment marketers rarely remind clients of the basic fact Graham emphasizes: An inflation-hedging asset should earn consistently higher returns as the cost of living rises.

By definition, then, it must earn consistently lower returns as the rate of inflation falls.

An asset that does well when inflation is hot *and* when it is not would be an investment paradise. It's also an impossibility. Wall Street is not Shangri-la.

Insurance Isn't Free

To insure against inflation, you must pay a price, just as you do to cover your car, home, and life. Here are the main ways to insure against inflation; each comes at a cost.

- **Gold** has served as a store of value for a remarkably long time. The same quantity of gold that a Roman centurion earned annually under Emperor Augustus (27 B.C. to A.D. 14) would still have covered one year's pay for a U.S. Army captain more than 2,000 years later.[3]

    However, from 1900 through 2022, gold earned an average return of less than 0.8% annually after inflation—only slightly better than cash.[4] Had you invested $1,000 in gold on January 1, 1900, you'd have finished 2022 with about $2,500—compared with roughly $7,800 in U.S. bonds and more than $2 million in stocks if you'd put the same $1,000 in each.

    Along the way, the price of gold swung up and down almost as erratically as stocks did, so it often lagged inflation instead of beating it. In 2021, as the cost of living surged, gold fell 3.5%; in 2022, with inflation breaking all modern records, the precious metal lost 0.4%. In 2023, as inflation fell, gold rose 13%.

---

[3] Claude B. Erb and Campbell R. Harvey, "The Golden Dilemma," bit.ly/3Ja7TPF. Gold equivalent of U.S. Army pay is for a captain with four years' experience, using a gold price of about $2,000 per ounce, as of 2023.
[4] Throughout these Commentaries, I will use "average annual return" or "average return of X% annually" as nontechnical wording to describe geometric mean, or compound annualized, returns. For most assets, cumulative changes in value occur in highly variable increments over time; restating that growth as a geometric mean treats the return as if it had occurred at a constant rate throughout the entire period.

In the very long run, gold has been a good way to sustain purchasing power. In the shorter run, it's an unreliable way to hedge against inflation.

- **I bonds** are savings bonds issued by the U.S. government whose interest rate adjusts twice a year to track the official rise in consumer prices. They are essentially risk-free: The U.S. Treasury guarantees to pay you your original money back, plus any inflation that has accrued along the way. That means your I bonds will preserve their purchasing power for up to 30 years, no matter how much damage inflation does. (They will not grow above the rate of inflation, though.)

  I bonds also have tax advantages. However, you can't easily invest more than $10,000 per year, they're available exclusively at TreasuryDirect.gov, and you aren't likely to be able to buy them unless you're a U.S. citizen or resident. You can't sell I bonds at all for the first year, and you'll forfeit three months' interest if you sell within the first five years. While they offer excellent protection against inflation, I bonds are imperfectly liquid and are hard to buy in bulk.[5]

- **Inflation-linked bonds** can also help cushion the rising cost of living. Called Treasury Inflation-Protected Securities or TIPS in the U.S., "linkers" are issued by many other governments in Europe, Asia, Latin America, and elsewhere. Such bonds automatically adjust their principal—the amount that the issuer will repay you by the maturity date—as inflation rises and falls.

  Unfortunately, inflation-linked bonds can become overpriced and are hypersensitive to changes in interest rates. In 2022, U.S. TIPS lost 11%, and the longest-term TIPS, maturing in 30 years, fell more than 40%.

  In early 2024, though, long-term U.S. TIPS offered investors the opportunity to lock in a guaranteed return of at least 2% annually, after inflation, for the next 30 years. While that's a modest rate of growth above the rising cost of living, it was priced like an ultrasafe, long-term insurance policy.

  If you're approaching retirement, when your wage income will

---

[5] For more: TreasuryDirect, "I Bonds," bit.ly/48EDPqJ; TIPSWatch, "Q&A on I Bonds," bit.ly/47IYf0H; and Jason Zweig, "Fight Runaway Inflation with I Bonds," bit.ly/43UbCsY.

cease and the value of your human capital will dwindle, inflation-protected bonds are an ideal way to guarantee that your financial capital will survive increases in the cost of living as you age.[6]
- **Real estate** is shelter—although it might not shelter you from inflation as well as you think. Between 1890 and 2014, the average growth rate of U.S. home prices was 0.3% annually after inflation, according to Yale University economist Robert Shiller.[7]

    Your house is a home, not a hedge. And commercial real estate is so sensitive to rising interest rates that it only partially protects against inflation.
- **Stocks** do fine when the cost of living rises moderately, up to about 4% annually. However, once inflation hits double digits, as it did in the U.S. around the end of World Wars I and II and in the late 1970s, stocks perform abysmally, with real losses averaging more than 7% annually. The same has been true worldwide for more than a century, with stocks earning an average real return of less than 1% annually when inflation exceeds 7.5% and average real losses of nearly 10% annually when the cost of living rises in the high double digits.

That certainly doesn't mean you should avoid stocks. An asset doesn't have to perform well *all* the time to perform well over time. When the rate of inflation moves up quickly and significantly, stocks will incur severe losses that can take years to recover from. Over very long periods, however, stocks have historically far outpaced the rise in consumer prices.[8]

The all-but-certain short-term decline in the market value

---

[6] That assumes you buy when TIPS offer positive "real," or after-inflation, yields and that you hold to maturity. For more on TIPS: Bogleheads.org, "Treasury Inflation Protected Security," bit.ly/3JizCxP; E-piphany, "How TIPS Work," bit.ly/3RGxSDE; The Finance Buff, "TIPS: Inflation Linked Bonds," bit.ly/3Q4hYSh; and Allan Roth, "The 4% Rule Just Became a Whole Lot Easier," bit.ly/3JN3lyF.

[7] Robert J. Shiller, *Irrational Exuberance* (Princeton, 2015), pp. 19–28; Brent W. Ambrose et al., "House Prices and Fundamentals," bit.ly/46EDkLg.

[8] See the Commentary on Chapter 3 and Jim O'Shaughnessy, "Inflation and the US Bond and Stock Markets," bit.ly/3Nscnns.

of stocks during an inflation spike is one price you must pay to capture their higher longer-term returns.

Changes in the cost of living vary across time and nations, so it makes sense to keep a substantial portion of your stock portfolio in companies whose shares are listed in markets outside your home country. That can provide a source of return from assets whose values aren't being eroded as fast by inflation.

- **Bitcoin** has often been touted in recent years as a sort of digital Terminator that can pulverize inflation. That's partly because the supply of this cryptocurrency is limited to 21 million units; after the last of those is created, no more will ever exist—which should mean that bitcoin's value can't be diluted by too much issuance.

By contrast, the supply of conventional, government-issued currencies is potentially unlimited, degrading their value over time. Fueled largely by such rhetoric, bitcoin gained 94% in 2019, 308% in 2020, and 57% in 2021, according to Bitwise Asset Management.

However, bitcoin didn't even begin trading publicly until July 2010. You can't draw sweeping conclusions from returns over such a short history, especially because inflation was so low over most of that period.

And in 2022, as inflation raged, bitcoin fell far worse than most other assets, crashing by almost two-thirds. At exactly the time when investors most urgently needed protection from inflation, bitcoin deflated. In 2023, as inflation fell, bitcoin soared more than 156%—again, not what an inflation hedge should do.

Will bitcoin continue to provide high returns?

That's anybody's guess. A superior cryptocurrency might arise later, making bitcoin obsolete, although that seems unlikely. Software updates might introduce critical flaws, undermining confidence. Central banks could introduce their own digital currencies, marginalizing bitcoin. Or its price might go into a protracted decline that feeds on itself, making bitcoin's network less attractive.

Rather than thinking of bitcoin purely as money, consider it a scarce collectible that can also function as a currency, like gold. Possessing such a rare object gives collectors pride and pleasure—even if the object no longer remains fashionable. That suggests that bitcoin may retain some value even if it never becomes fully accepted as a currency.

How much might it end up being worth? Bitcoin might turn out to be as stable a store of value, measured over centuries, as gold. Or it might resemble rare artwork, whose value tends to rise over time, but with extreme fluctuations along the way. Or bitcoin might turn out to be almost as ephemeral as Beanie Babies, Cabbage Patch Kids, or Pet Rocks—whose prices peaked in wild fads decades ago and have never recovered.

Warren Buffett has joked that if he were teaching a class on valuing stocks, he would ask on the final exam how much a speculative internet company was worth. "And anybody that gave me an answer," he quipped, "I would flunk."

By the same token, bitcoin could someday end up being worth $1,000,000 or more—or next to nothing. That gamble just might pay off, but given bitcoin's short history and wild volatility, its effectiveness as an inflation hedge remains unproven.

- **Commodities** are a popular but imperfect hedge. Leading commodity funds gained 20% to 30% or more in 2022, handily beating the rise in consumer prices.

  However, the returns on individual commodities vary wildly over time. Coal gained 161% in 2021, then lost 48% in 2022 and another 10% in 2023. Lithium lost 55% in 2019, fell another 38% in 2020, then gained an astonishing 443% in 2021 and another 72% in 2022; in 2023, it fell a ghastly 81%.

  Their popularity in recent years may have distorted the market in commodities, undermining their ability to combat future inflation. Over the longer run, a $1 investment in U.S. stocks in 1871 would have grown to $1,896 by the end of 2022. In commodities, it would have grown to only $744.[9]

In short, no single asset can fully protect against the rising cost of living. By supplementing a stock portfolio with a big slug of inflation-protected bonds, you can build your financial capital into a stronger bulwark. And your human capital and physical capital should bolster you, too.

---

[9] These returns are the excess performance over what cash earned. Elroy Dimson et al., "Global Investment Returns Yearbook 2023," bit.ly/3CBJr6l; Henry Neville et al., "The Best Strategies for Inflationary Times," bit.ly/3Q4bORZ.

CHAPTER 3

A Century of Stock-Market History: The Level of Stock Prices in Early 1972
by Benjamin Graham

*T*he investor's portfolio of common stocks will represent a small cross-section of that immense and formidable institution known as the stock market. Prudence suggests that he have an adequate idea of stock-market history, in terms particularly of the major fluctuations in its price level and of the varying relationships between stock prices as a whole and their earnings and dividends. With this background he may be in a position to form some worthwhile judgment of the attractiveness or dangers of the level of the market as it presents itself at different times. By a coincidence, useful statistical data on prices, earnings, and dividends go back just 100 years, to 1871. (The material is not nearly as full or dependable in the first half-period as in the second, but it will serve.) In this chapter we shall present the figures, in highly condensed form, with two objects in view. The first is to show the general manner in which stocks have made their underlying advance through the many cycles of the past century. The second is to view the picture in terms of successive ten-year averages, not only of stock prices but of earnings and dividends as well, to bring out the varying relationship between the three important factors. With this wealth of material as a background we shall pass to a consideration of the level of stock prices at the beginning of 1972.

The long-term history of the stock market is summarized in two tables and a chart. Table 3-1 sets forth the low and high points of nineteen bear- and bull-market cycles in the past 100 years. We have used two indexes here. The first represents a combination of an early study by the Cowles Commission going back to 1870, which

TABLE 3-1 Major Stock-Market Swings Between 1871 and 1971

Average Year	Cowles-Standard 500 Composite			Dow-Jones		Industrial
	High	Low	Decline	High	Low	Decline
1871		4.64				
1881	6.58					
1885		4.24	28%			
1887	5.90					
1893		4.08	31			
1897					38.85	
1899				77.6		
1900					53.5	31%
1901	8.50			78.3		
1903		6.26	26		43.2	45
1906	10.03			103		
1907		6.25	38		53	48
1909	10.30			100.5		
1914		7.35	29		53.2	47
1916–18	10.21			110.2		
1917		6.80	33		73.4	33
1919	9.51			119.6		
1921		6.45	32		63.9	47
1929	31.92			381		
1932		4.40	86		41.2	89
1937	18.68			197.4		
1938		8.50	55		99	50
1939	13.23			158		
1942		7.47	44		92.9	41
1946	19.25			212.5		
1949		13.55	30		161.2	24
1952	26.6			292		
1952–53		22.7	15		256	13
1956	49.7			521		
1957		39.0	24		420	20
1961	76.7			735		
1962		54.8	29		536	27
1966–68	108.4			995		
1970		69.3	36		631	37
early 1972	100		—	900		—

has been spliced on to and continued to date in the well-known Standard & Poor's composite index of 500 stocks. The second is the even more celebrated Dow Jones Industrial Average (the DJIA, or "the Dow"), which dates back to 1897; it contains 30 companies, of which one is American Telephone & Telegraph and the other 29 are large industrial enterprises.[1]

Chart I, presented by courtesy of Standard & Poor's, depicts the market fluctuations of its 425-industrial-stock index from 1900 through 1970. (A corresponding chart available for the DJIA will look very much the same.) The reader will note three quite distinct patterns, each covering about a third of the 70 years. The first runs from 1900 to 1924, and shows for the most part a series of rather similar market cycles lasting from three to five years. The annual advance in this period averaged just about 3%. We move on to the "New Era" bull market, culminating in 1929, with its terrible aftermath of collapse, followed by quite irregular fluctuations until 1949. Comparing the average level of 1949 with that of 1924, we find the annual rate of advance to be a mere 1½%; hence **the close of our second period found the public with no enthusiasm at all for common stocks. By the rule of opposites the time was ripe for the beginning of the greatest bull market in our history,** presented in the last third of our chart. This phenomenon may have reached its culmination in December 1968 at 118 for Standard & Poor's 425 industrials (and 108 for its 500-stock composite). As Table 3-1 shows, there were fairly important setbacks between 1949 and 1968 (especially in 1956–57 and 1961–62), but the recoveries therefrom were so rapid that they had to be denominated (in the long-accepted semantics) as recessions in a single bull market, rather than as separate market cycles. Between the low level of 162 for "the Dow" in mid-1949 and the high of 995 in early 1966, the advance had been more than sixfold in 17 years—which is at the average compounded rate of 11% per year, not counting dividends of, say, 3½% per annum. (The advance for the Standard & Poor's composite index was somewhat greater than that of the DJIA—actually from 14 to 96.)

These 14% and better returns were documented in 1963, and later, in a much publicized study.*[2] It created a natural satisfaction

---

* The study was Lawrence Fisher and James H. Lorie, "Rates of Return on Investments in Common Stock," bit.ly/3vwu52P.

CHART 1

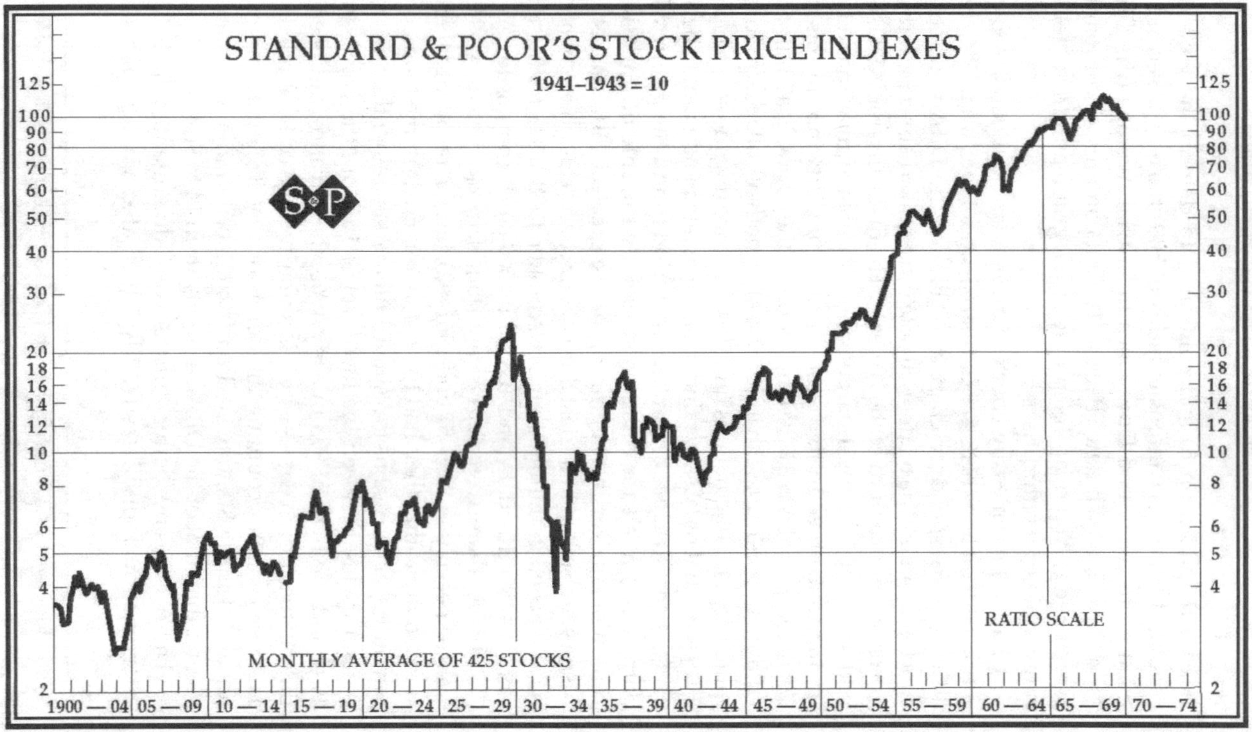

STANDARD & POOR'S STOCK PRICE INDEXES
1941–1943 = 10
S&P
MONTHLY AVERAGE OF 425 STOCKS
RATIO SCALE
125
100
90
80
70
60
50
40
30
20
18
16
14
12
10
8
6
5
4
2
1900 — 04
05 — 09
10 — 14
15 — 19
20 — 24
25 — 29
30 — 34
35 — 39
40 — 44
45 — 49
50 — 54
55 — 59
60 — 64
65 — 69
70 — 74

on Wall Street with such fine achievements, and a quite illogical and dangerous conviction that equally marvelous results could be expected for common stocks in the future. Few people seem to have been bothered by the thought that the very extent of the rise might indicate that it had been overdone. The subsequent decline from the 1968 high to the 1970 low was 36% for the Standard & Poor's composite (and 37% for the DJIA), the largest since the 44% suffered in 1939–1942, which had reflected the perils and uncertainties after Pearl Harbor. In the dramatic manner so characteristic of Wall Street, the low level of May 1970 was followed by a massive and speedy recovery of both averages, and the establishment of a new all-time high for the Standard & Poor's industrials in early 1972. The annual rate of price advance between 1949 and 1970 works out at about 9% for the S & P composite (or the industrial index), using the average figures for both years. That rate of climb was, of course, much greater than for any similar period before 1950. (But in the last decade the rate of advance was much lower—5¼% for the S & P composite index and only the once familiar 3% for the DJIA.)

The record of price movements should be supplemented by corresponding figures for earnings and dividends, in order to provide an overall view of what has happened to our share economy over the ten decades. We present a conspectus of this kind in our Table 3-2 (p. 71). It is a good deal to expect from the reader that he study all these figures with care, but for some we hope they will be interesting and instructive.

Let us comment on them as follows: The full decade figures smooth out the year-to-year fluctuations and leave a general picture of persistent growth. Only two of the nine decades after the first show a decrease in earnings and average prices (in 1891–1900 and 1931–1940), and no decade after 1900 shows a decrease in average dividends. But the rates of growth in all three categories are quite variable. In general the performance since World War II has been superior to that of earlier decades, but the advance in the 1960s was less pronounced than that of the 1950s. Today's investor cannot tell from this record what percentage gain in earnings dividends and prices he may expect in the next ten years, but it does supply all the encouragement he needs for a consistent policy of common-stock investment.

However, a point should be made here that is not disclosed in our table. The year 1970 was marked by a definite deterioration in the overall earnings posture of our corporations. The rate of profit on invested capital fell to the lowest percentage since the World War years. Equally striking is the fact that a considerable number of companies reported net losses for the year; many became "financially troubled," and for the first time in three decades there were quite a few important bankruptcy proceedings. These facts as much as any others have prompted the statement made above* that the great boom era may have come to an end in 1969–1970.

A striking feature of Table 3-2 is the change in the price/earnings ratios since World War II.† In June 1949 the S & P composite index sold at only 6.3 times the applicable earnings of the past 12 months; in March 1961 the ratio was 22.9 times. Similarly, the dividend yield on the S & P index had fallen from over 7% in 1949 to only 3.0% in 1961, a contrast heightened by the fact that interest rates on high-grade bonds had meanwhile risen from 2.60% to 4.50%. This is certainly the most remarkable turnabout in the public's attitude in all stock-market history.

To people of long experience and innate caution the passage from one extreme to another carried a strong warning of trouble ahead. They could not help thinking apprehensively of the 1926–1929 bull market and its tragic aftermath. But these fears have not been confirmed by the event. True, the closing price of the DJIA in 1970 was the same as it was 6½ years earlier, and the much heralded "Soaring Sixties" proved to be mainly a march up a series of high hills and then down again. But nothing has happened either to

---

* See pp. 50–51.

† The "price/earnings ratio" (P/E) of a stock, or of a market average like the S&P 500-stock index, is a simple tool for taking the market's temperature. If a company earned $1 per share of net income over the past year, and its stock is selling at $8.93 per share, its price/earnings ratio would be 8.93; if, however, the stock is at $69.70, then the P/E would be 69.7. In general, a P/E below 10 is considered very low, between 10 and 20 is considered low to moderate, and greater than 20 is considered expensive. (For more on P/Es, see Chapters 7 and 11.)

TABLE 3-2 A Picture of Stock-Market Performance, 1871–1970[a]

Period	Average Price	Average Earnings	Average P/E Ratio	Dividend Average	Average Yield	Average Payout	Annual Growth Rate[b] Earnings	Dividends
1871–1880	3.58	0.32	11.3	0.21	6.0%	67%	—	—
1881–1890	5.00	0.32	15.6	0.24	4.7	75	−0.64%	−0.66%
1891–1900	4.65	0.30	15.5	0.19	4.0	64	−1.04	−2.23
1901–1910	8.32	0.63	13.1	0.35	4.2	58	+6.91	+5.33
1911–1920	8.62	0.86	10.0	0.50	5.8	58	+3.85	+3.94
1921–1930	13.89	1.05	13.3	0.71	5.1	68	+2.84	+2.29
1931–1940	11.55	0.68	17.0	0.78	5.1	85	−2.15	−0.23
1941–1950	13.90	1.46	9.5	0.87	6.3	60	+10.60	+3.25
1951–1960	39.20	3.00	13.1	1.63	4.2	54	+6.74	+5.90
1961–1970	82.50	4.83	17.1	2.68	3.2	55	+5.80[c]	+5.40[c]
1954–1956	38.19	2.56	15.1	1.64	4.3	65	+2.40[d]	+7.80[d]
1961–1963	66.10	3.66	18.1	2.14	3.2	58	+5.15[d]	+4.42[d]
1968–1970	93.25	5.60	16.7	3.13	3.3	56	+6.30[d]	+5.60[d]

[a] The following data based largely on figures appearing in N. Molodovsky's article, "Stock Values and Stock Prices," *Financial Analysts Journal*, May 1960. These, in turn, are taken from the Cowles Commission book *Common Stock Indexes* for years before 1926 and from the spliced-on Standard & Poor's 500-stock composite index for 1926 to date.
[b] The annual growth-rate figures are Molodovsky compilations covering successive 21-year periods ending in 1890, 1900, etc.
[c] Growth rate for 1968–1970 vs. 1958–1960.
[d] These growth-rate figures are for 1954–1956 vs. 1947–1949, 1961–1963 vs. 1954–1956, and for 1968–1970 vs. 1958–1960.

business or to stock prices that can compare with the bear market and depression of 1929–1932.

The Stock-Market Level in Early 1972

With a century-long conspectus of stock, prices, earnings, and dividends before our eyes, let us try to draw some conclusions about the level of 900 for the DJIA and 100 for the S & P composite index in January 1972.

In each of our former editions we have discussed the level of the stock market at the time of writing, and endeavored to answer the question whether it was too high for conservative purchase. The reader may find it informing to review the conclusions we reached on these earlier occasions. This is not entirely an exercise in self-punishment. It will supply a sort of connecting tissue that links the various stages of the stock market in the past twenty years and also a taken-from-life picture of the difficulties facing anyone who tries to reach an informed and critical judgment of current market levels. Let us, first, reproduce the summary of the 1948, 1953, and 1959 analyses that we gave in the 1965 edition:

> In 1948 we applied conservative standards to the Dow Jones level of 180, and found no difficulty in reaching the conclusion that "it was not too high in relation to underlying values." When we approached this problem in 1953 the average market level for that year had reached 275, a gain of over 50% in five years. We asked ourselves the same question—namely, "whether in our opinion the level of 275 for the Dow Jones Industrials was or was not too high for sound investment." In the light of the subsequent spectacular advance, it may seem strange to have to report that it was by no means easy for us to reach a definitive conclusion as to the attractiveness of the 1953 level. We did say, positively enough, that "from the standpoint of value indications—our chief investment guide—the conclusion about 1953 stock prices must be favorable." But we were concerned about the fact that in 1953, the averages had advanced for a longer period than in most bull markets of the past, and that its absolute level was historically high. Setting these factors against our favorable value judgment, we advised a cautious or compromise policy. As it turned out, this was not a

particularly brilliant counsel. A good prophet would have foreseen that the market level was due to advance an additional 100% in the next five years. Perhaps we should add in self-defense that few if any of those whose business was stock-market forecasting—as ours was not—had any better inkling than we did of what lay ahead.

At the beginning of 1959 we found the DJIA at an all-time high of 584. Our lengthy analysis made from all points of view may be summarized in the following (from page 59 of the 1959 edition): "In sum, we feel compelled to express the conclusion that the present level of stock prices is a dangerous one. It may well be perilous because prices are already far too high. But even if this is not the case the market's momentum is such as inevitably to carry it to unjustifiable heights. Frankly, **we cannot imagine a market of the future in which there will never be any serious losses**, and in which every tyro will be guaranteed a large profit on his stock purchases."

The caution we expressed in 1959 was somewhat better justified by the sequel than was our corresponding attitude in 1954. Yet it was far from fully vindicated. The DJIA advanced to 685 in 1961; then fell a little below our 584 level (to 566) later in the year; advanced again to 735 in late 1961; and then declined in near panic to 536 in May 1962, showing a loss of 27% within the brief period of six months. At the same time there was a far more serious shrinkage in the most popular "growth stocks"—as evidenced by the striking fall of the indisputable leader, International Business Machines, from a high of 607 in December 1961 to a low of 300 in June 1962.

This period saw a complete debacle in a host of newly launched common stocks of small enterprises—the so-called hot issues—which had been offered to the public at ridiculously high prices and then had been further pushed up by needless speculation to levels little short of insane. Many of these lost 90% and more of the quotations* in just a few months.

The collapse in the first half of 1962 was disconcerting, if not disastrous, to many self-acknowledged speculators and perhaps to many more imprudent people who called themselves "in-

---

* Graham's term "quotations" is a synonym for "share price" or "market value."

vestors." But the turnabout that came later that year was equally unsuspected by the financial community. The stock-market averages resumed their upward course, producing the following sequence:

	DJIA	Standard & Poor's 500-Stock Composite
December 1961	735	72.64
June 1962	536	52.32
November 1964	892	86.28

The recovery and new ascent of common-stock prices was indeed remarkable and created a corresponding revision of Wall Street sentiment. At the low level of June 1962 predictions had appeared predominantly bearish, and after the partial recovery to the end of that year they were mixed, leaning to the skeptical side. But at the outset of 1964 the natural optimism of brokerage firms was again manifest; nearly all the forecasts were on the bullish side, and they so continued through the 1964 advance.

We then approached the task of appraising the November 1964 levels of the stock market (892 for the DJIA). After discussing it learnedly from numerous angles we reached three main conclusions. The first was that "**old standards (of valuation) appear inapplicable; new standards have not yet been tested by time.**" The second was that the investor "must base his policy on the existence of major uncertainties. The possibilities compass the extremes, on the one hand, of a protracted and further advance in the market's level—say by 50%, or to 1350 for the DJIA; or, on the other hand, of a largely unheralded collapse of the same magnitude, bringing the average in the neighborhood of, say, 450" (p. 63 of the 1965 edition). The third was expressed in much more definite terms. We said: "Speaking bluntly, if the 1964 price level is not too high how could we say that *any* price level is too high?" And the chapter closed as follows:

WHAT COURSE TO FOLLOW

Investors should not conclude that the 1964 market level is dangerous merely because they read it in this book. They must weigh our reasoning against the contrary reasoning they will hear from most competent and experienced people on Wall Street. In the end each one must make his own decision and accept responsibility therefor. We suggest, however, that if the investor is in doubt as to which course to pursue he should choose the path of caution. The principles of investment, as set forth herein, would call for the following policy under 1964 conditions, in order of urgency:

1. No borrowing to buy or hold securities.
2. No increase in the proportion of funds held in common stocks.
3. A reduction in common-stock holdings where needed to bring it down to a maximum of 50 per cent of the total portfolio. The capital-gains tax must be paid with as good grace as possible, and the proceeds invested in first-quality bonds or held as a savings deposit.

Investors who for some time have been following a bona fide dollar-cost averaging plan can in logic elect either to continue their periodic purchases unchanged or to suspend them until they feel the market level is no longer dangerous. We should advise rather strongly against the initiation of a new dollar-averaging plan at the late 1964 levels, since many investors would not have the stamina to pursue such a scheme if the results soon after initiation should appear highly unfavorable.

This time we can say that our caution was vindicated. The DJIA advanced about 11% further, to 995, but then fell irregularly to a low of 632 in 1970, and finished that year at 839. The same kind of debacle took place in the price of "hot issues"—i.e., with declines running as much as 90%—as had happened in the 1961–62 setback. And, as pointed out in the Introduction, the whole financial picture appeared to have changed in the direction of less enthusiasm and greater doubts. A single fact may summarize the story: The DJIA closed 1970 at a level lower than six years before—the first time such a thing had happened since 1944.

Such were our efforts to evaluate former stock-market levels. Is there anything we and our readers can learn from them? We considered the market level favorable for investment in 1948 and 1953 (but too cautiously in the latter year), "dangerous" in 1959 (at 584 for DJIA), and "too high" (at 892) in 1964. All of these judgments could be defended even today by adroit arguments. But it is doubtful if they have been as useful as our more pedestrian counsels—in favor of a consistent and controlled common-stock policy on the one hand, and discouraging endeavors to "beat the market" or to "pick the winners" on the other.

Nonetheless we think our readers may derive some benefit from a renewed consideration of the level of the stock market—this time as of late 1971—even if what we have to say will prove more interesting than practically useful, or more indicative than conclusive. **There is a fine passage near the beginning of Aristotle's *Ethics* that goes: "It is the mark of an educated mind to expect that amount of exactness which the nature of the particular subject admits. It is equally unreasonable to accept merely probable conclusions from a mathematician and to demand strict demonstration from an orator." The work of a financial analyst falls somewhere in the middle between that of a mathematician and of an orator.**

At various times in 1971 the Dow Jones Industrial Average stood at the 892 level of November 1964 that we considered in our previous edition. But in the present statistical study we have decided to use the price level and the related data for the Standard & Poor's composite index (or S & P 500), because it is more comprehensive and representative of the general market than the 30-stock DJIA. We shall concentrate on a comparison of this material near the four dates of our former editions—namely the year-ends of 1948, 1953, 1958 and 1963—plus 1968; for the current price level we shall take the convenient figure of 100, which was registered at various times in 1971 and in early 1972. The salient data are set forth in Table 3-3. For our earnings figures we present both the last year's showing and the average of three calendar years; for 1971 dividends we use the last twelve months' figures; and for 1971 bond interest and wholesale prices those of August 1971.

The 3-year price/earnings ratio for the market was lower in October 1971 than at year-end 1963 and 1968. It was about the same as in 1958, but much higher than in the early years of the

TABLE 3-3 Data Relating to Standard & Poor's Composite Index in Various Years

Year[a]	1948	1953	1958	1963	1968	1971
Closing price	15.20	24.81	55.21	75.02	103.9	100[d]
Earned in current year	2.24	2.51	2.89	4.02	5.76	5.23
Average earnings of last 3 years	1.65	2.44	2.22	3.63	5.37	5.53
Dividend in current year	.93	1.48	1.75	2.28	2.99	3.10
High-grade bond interest[a]	2.77%	3.08%	4.12%	4.36%	6.51%	7.57%
Wholesale-price index	87.9	92.7	100.4	105.0	108.7	114.3
Ratios:						
Price/last year's earnings	6.3 ×	9.9 ×	18.4 ×	18.6 ×	18.0 ×	19.2 ×
Price/3-years' earnings	9.2 ×	10.2 ×	17.6 ×	20.7 ×	19.5 ×	18.1 ×
3-Years' "earnings yield"[c]	10.9 %	9.8 %	5.8 %	4.8 %	5.15%	5.53%
Dividend yield	5.6 %	5.5 %	3.3 %	3.04%	2.87%	3.11%
Stock-earnings yield/bond yield	3.96×	3.20×	1.41×	1.10×	.80×	.72×
Dividend yield/bond yield	2.1 ×	1.8 ×	.80×	.70×	.44×	.41×
Earnings/book value[e]	11.2 %	11.8 %	12.8 %	10.5 %	11.5 %	11.5 %

[a] Yield on S & P AAA bonds.
[b] Calendar years in 1948–1968, plus year ended June 1971.
[c] "Earnings yield" means the earnings divided by the price, in %.
[d] Price in Oct. 1971, equivalent to 900 for the DJIA.
[e] Three-year average figures.

long bull market. This important indicator, taken by itself, could not be construed to indicate that the market was especially high in January 1972. But when the interest yield on high-grade bonds is brought into the picture, the implications become much less favorable. The reader will note from our table that the ratio of stock returns (earnings/price) to bond returns has grown worse during the entire period, so that the January 1972 figure was less favorable to stocks, by this criterion, than in any of the previous years examined. When dividend yields are compared with bond yields we find that the relationship was completely reversed between 1948 and 1972. In the early year stocks yielded twice as much as bonds; now bonds yield twice as much, and more, than stocks.

Our final judgment is that the adverse change in the bond-yield/stock-yield ratio fully offsets the better price/earnings ratio for late 1971, based on the 3-year earnings figures. Hence our view of the early 1972 market level would tend to be the same as it was some 7 years ago—i.e., that it is an unattractive one from the standpoint of conservative investment. (This would apply to most of the 1971 price range of the DJIA: between, say, 800 and 950.)

In terms of historical market swings the 1971 picture would still appear to be one of irregular recovery from the bad setback suffered in 1969–1970. In the past such recoveries have ushered in a new stage of the recurrent and persistent bull market that began in 1949. (This was the expectation of Wall Street generally during 1971.) After the terrible experience suffered by the public buyers of low-grade common-stock offerings in the 1968–1970 cycle, it is too early (in 1971) for another twirl of the new-issue merry-go-round. Hence that dependable sign of imminent danger in the market is lacking now, as it was at the 892 level of the DJIA in November 1964, considered in our previous edition. Technically, then, the outlook would appear to favor another substantial rise far beyond the 900 DJIA level before the next serious setback or collapse. But we cannot quite leave the matter there, as perhaps we should. To us, the early-1971-market's disregard of the harrowing experiences of less than a year before is a disquieting sign. Can such heedlessness go unpunished? We think the investor must be prepared for difficult times ahead—perhaps in the form of a fairly quick replay of the 1969–1970 decline, or perhaps in the form of another bull-market fling, to be followed by a more catastrophic collapse.[3]

What Course to Follow

Turn back to what we said in the last edition, reproduced on p. 75. This is our view at the same price level—say 900—for the DJIA in early 1972 as it was in late 1964.

Commentary on Chapter 3
by Jason Zweig

> In my nearly fifty years of experience in Wall Street I've found that I know less and less about what the stock market is going to do, but I know more and more about what investors ought to do.
> —Benjamin Graham[1]

What can the stock market's past tell us about the future?

As Graham points out in Chapter 3, stocks generally go up over multidecade periods, but the course is seldom smooth and never predictable. Reconciling yourself to that uncertainty can be troubling at first, but I promise to bring you hope in the end.

Where You Stand Depends on Where You Sit

If you are in your working and saving years, you need to be *accumulating* wealth. Falling stock markets make it easier for you to buy more shares at lower prices for longer.

Assuming stocks do ultimately recover, an early stretch of falling prices can function like rocket fuel to propel your wealth as you grow older.

If you are retired and no longer earning a salary, however, you are *decumulating*, and a market decline can be a disaster. Unless you're able to rely on income from bonds, real estate, pensions, or Social Security or the equivalent, you will have to pay your expenses by selling some of your stocks. If you happen to sell into the teeth of a bear market, you will lock in permanent losses—and the more the

---

[1] Benjamin Graham, "Securities in an Insecure World," bit.ly/449pBuT.

market goes down, the more stocks you will have to sell to generate a constant stream of income.

Socks vs. Stocks

The problem with *stocks* is that the word contains the letter T. Take that away, and you have *socks*. If stocks were socks, people would view a 20% drop in price not as a selloff but as a sale. Instead of panicking, people would be purchasing.

When socks are 20% off, you don't feel a sudden urge to get rid of the ones you already own; you check your sock drawer to see if you need any. Young investors should learn to think of stocks like socks:

Socks	Stocks
You buy them when you need them.	You buy them when other people want them.
You want to buy more when the price goes down.	You want to buy more when the price goes up.
You keep them even if they have some holes.	You sell them as soon as the price goes down.
Then you mend them or save them to use as rags.	You don't want them again until the price goes back *up*.

CAPE Fear

If you could determine when a crash will strike, you could sell at the top, step aside into the safety of cash, then buy back into stocks at the bottom.

One measure has become a popular way to try making such predictions. This indicator, the cyclically adjusted price/earnings or CAPE ratio, divides the current price of the S&P 500 index by its average earnings over the past 10 years, adjusting both the price and the earnings for inflation. It was devised by Yale University finance professor Robert Shiller, partly inspired by Benjamin Graham himself.

Many market commentators argue that when CAPE is higher than average, future returns will be below average. That makes intuitive sense: The more it costs you to buy stocks now, the less return you are likely to earn later.

And a higher-than-average CAPE has tended to be followed by lower-than-average returns, as this scatterplot shows:

FIGURE 3-1: CAPE of Little Hope

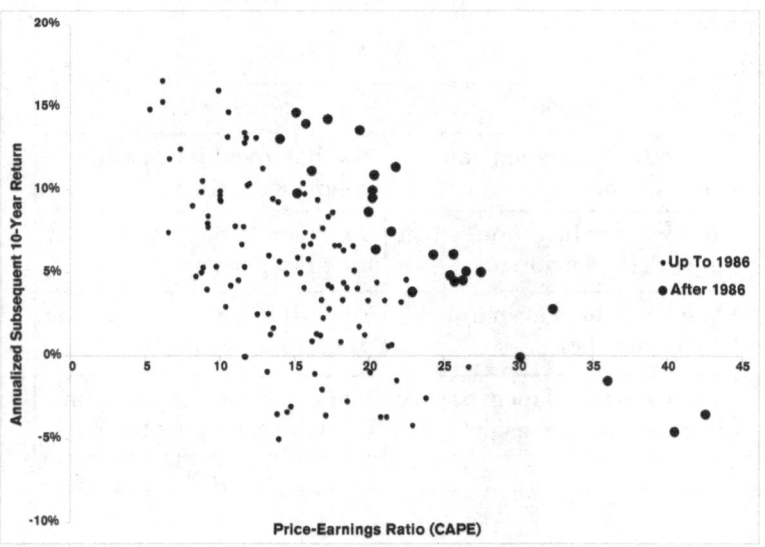

Source: Robert Shiller, Yale University.

That's a tendency, however. It isn't a law.

As you can see in Figure 3.1, after CAPE hit 40.4 in 1999 (the lowest point at the far right), stocks went on to lose an average of 4.6% annually over the ensuing 10 years. And CAPE's 42.5 level in 2000 (the second-lowest point at the far right) preceded average annual losses of 3.5% over the following decade.

Sometimes, though, high CAPEs foretell high—not low—returns. After the ratio hit 21.8 in 2011, stocks nevertheless gained an annual average of 11.4% in the next 10 years. This is one of several points clustered in the upper center of the figure, where both CAPE *and* subsequent long-term returns are above average. (All these returns are after inflation.)

In late 2021, CAPE nearly reached 39, one of the highest levels on record and far above its average of 17.4 over its more than 140-year history. But that average has changed over time. Over the 30 years ending in 1910, CAPE averaged 17; over the next three decades, 12.7; over the 30 years after that, 15.7. Over the most recent three decades, it's averaged almost 27.

History isn't static. It's unstable, changing continuously as the present gets absorbed into the past.

So, when you compare CAPE to its past "average," which past should you use? The last 140 years? The last 50? The last 30? The longer the period, the more you rely on data that might no longer be relevant. The shorter the period, the more the results will be skewed by the recent past, which could be an anomaly.

"The market is supposed to estimate the value of earnings, but the value of the earnings depends on people's perception of what they can sell it for," Professor Shiller says. Today's level "might be high relative to history," he points out, "but how do we know that history hasn't changed?"

Except for a brief period in late 2008 and early 2009, U.S. stocks have traded above their long-term average CAPE every month since late 1988. If you wanted stocks to become cheap again by the longest historical standards before you bought them, you would still be waiting—more than one-third of a century later.

In short, stocks that already seem overvalued can get even more expensive—and stay that way for a bewilderingly long time. As Graham says, "anyone who tries to reach an informed and critical judgment of current market levels" faces extreme "difficulties."[2]

---

[2] Many proponents of CAPE as a market-timing tool are cheating: They look at CAPE's average over its full history to the present day, find past periods when it was above that level, and declare that stocks were obviously overvalued then. But those past periods didn't include CAPE's subsequent history!

> ### The Simplest Rule of Thumb
>
> To estimate the future long-term return on stocks, you can use the Gordon equation. Devised in the late 1950s by economist Myron Gordon, the formula assumes that market prices depend on the income and growth that stocks can produce.
>
> The stock market's future performance should approximate its current dividend yield plus the average rate at which dividends grow. In early 2024, the dividend yield on the S&P 500 index was 1.4%. Over the previous half-century, dividends grew 2.2% annually on average, adjusted for inflation. Add those two numbers and you get 3.6%. That's an imprecise but plausible estimate of the average annual return of stocks, after inflation, over the coming decades. While it's lower than the long-term historical average, it is likely to enable patient investors to reach their goals.[1]
>
> ---
>
> [1] For further discussion, see William J. Bernstein, *The Four Pillars of Investing* (McGraw-Hill, 2023).

Stocks for the Wrong Run

Beginning in the 1990s, investors' minds were infected with a new belief: Stocks aren't risky.

By 2010, a survey of more than 2,200 investors found that 31% believed that "stocks *always* do better than safe investments" like cash and bonds over periods of five years or more.

That notion is nonsense. It distorts history and misinterprets what risk means.

Let's take the history first.

In his book *Stocks for the Long Run*, first published in 1994, finance professor Jeremy Siegel argued that "the risks in stocks are *less than* those found in bonds or even [U.S. Treasury] bills." He based his argument on data going back to 1802 suggesting that U.S. stocks had outperformed both bonds and cash over nearly every period of

20 years or more—and had never lost money, after inflation, over such long periods.[3]

That argument has at least three critical flaws:

Inaccuracy. Correcting for survivorship bias (see sidebar on p. 86), business professor Edward McQuarrie has adjusted the historical record and found that stocks *underperformed* bonds in the U.S. for most of the nineteenth century.[4] Bonds beat stocks in one-third of all 20-year periods since 1793—not in less than one-tenth of those periods, as Siegel claimed. In several other major markets around the world, bonds have outperformed stocks for decades on end.

Incomparability. In the past, brokerage commissions and management fees were at least 10 times higher, and market-tracking index funds didn't exist. Diversification was costly and cumbersome, making stocks riskier than they are now. Investors had to be compensated for that risk in the form of higher returns. Now that diversification is easy and cheap, stocks are less risky, so their future returns are likely to be lower.

Impracticality. Historical rates of return assume that investors took the income from dividends and plowed it back into more shares, generating growth on top of growth. Until the late 1970s, though, investors rarely used their dividends to buy more shares. Instead, many took dividends as cash, which they saved or spent; it couldn't grow from being reinvested in the stock market.[5]

---

[3] Jeremy J. Siegel, *Stocks for the Long Run* (Irwin, 1994), pp. 31–33; italics in original.

[4] Edward F. McQuarrie, "Stocks for the Long Run? Sometimes Yes. Sometimes No," bit.ly/48guZhU. See also Rob Arnott, "Bonds: Why Bother?," bit.ly/44vclfS.

[5] Until then, brokerage commissions on small trades could exceed 5% and full diversification wasn't feasible, putting the stock market's average return out of reach for most investors.

Survivor

Imagine visiting a nursing home for retired lumberjacks and being struck by how old they are. You might conclude that the average worker in the logging industry lives to a ripe old age. What you should realize instead is that logging is one of the world's most dangerous occupations and that you saw only the extreme outliers—the old and rare survivors, not a broad and typical sample. Your first impression was misleading, because you encountered no trace of the many loggers who tragically died young.[1]

I'm describing *survivorship bias*, which overweights history's winners by overlooking the losers. It warps our perceptions of statistical evidence by painting an unrepresentative picture. It's like a rearview mirror made of rose-colored glass.

In the nineteenth-century U.S., entire industries, such as wooden turnpikes and whale oil, steamboats and stagecoaches, sprang up, shut down, and wiped investors out. Stock exchanges boomed and withered in Bisbee, Arizona; Charleston, South Carolina; Honolulu, Hawaii; Wheeling, West Virginia; and many other forgotten venues.[2]

Investors lost real money, but the magic wand of survivorship waves those losses away. Correcting for this data bias would significantly reduce the early returns of stocks.[3]

---

[1] According to the Bureau of Labor Statistics (bit.ly/43UD3TG), logging has the highest incidence of fatal job-related injuries of any occupation in the U.S.

[2] Almost a century ago, scholars who tried tracking the earliest U.S. stocks warned that their cherry-picked indexes "might fail to measure" returns "with the maximum accuracy desirable"; Walter Buckingham Smith and Arthur Harrison Cole, *Fluctuations in American Business, 1790–1860* (bit.ly/3NoRY1A), pp. 23 and 44.

[3] From the start of the twentieth century onward, stock-market data and indexes like the S&P 500 are generally *not* contaminated with survivorship bias, although performance databases for mutual funds, as well as hedge funds and other "alternative" assets, often are.

Risky Business

History shows that the longer you hang on to stocks, the less their rate of return has varied. Over the long term, U.S. stocks have gone up by an average of roughly 10% annually (or about 7% after inflation). Even in the devastating bear market of 2007–09, when U.S. stocks fell more than 55%, their long-term average annual rate of return shrank only slightly, from 10.4% to 9.3%.

If "risk" is the chance of deviating from the average historical rate of return, that *has* declined if you held stocks for decades.

However, after a 55% crash, you need a 122% return just to get back to where you were. You are *not* going to be thinking, "Hey, stocks aren't risky! Their average rate of return since 1926 has only declined from 10.4% to 9.3%." Instead, you'll be thinking, "If getting more than half my wealth eviscerated in 17 months isn't risk, what is?"

As we've seen from looking at CAPE, it's impossible to be certain when stocks are dangerously high. And if you buy at what turns out to be a peak, the long run might feel like eons.

As Warren Buffett has noted about investing for the long run: "People say that stocks have to be better than bonds, but I've pointed out just the opposite: That all depends on the starting price."[6]

People who bought the technology-heavy NASDAQ stock index in early 2000 didn't break even for more than 15 years. Japanese investors waited more than three decades to get back to that country's record-high stock prices of 1989. Worldwide, in such markets as France, Germany, Switzerland, Taiwan, and Thailand, stocks have sometimes earned negative returns after inflation for 20 years or more.[7]

The belief that simply extending your holding period can eliminate the risk of stocks is bogus. Time might be your ally, but it also might turn out to be your enemy. A longer horizon gives you more opportunities to recover from crashes, but it also gives you more opportunities to experience them. You can't erase that risk, even if you hold stocks for a century.

---

[6] Jason Zweig, "Sometimes the Stock Market Needs 'Knights of Faith,'" bit.ly/42YKEiC; "Don't Let a Market Crash Hit You at the Finish Line," bit.ly/3CKOJfW.

[7] Elroy Dimson et al., "Irrational Optimism," bit.ly/3RWhK0O.

"Investors Hate Uncertainty"

Paradoxically, all this brings us to a place of hope.

One of Wall Street's favorite sayings is "investors hate uncertainty." But if you could ever be certain that stocks would have high returns, they wouldn't seem risky. And that perceived absence of risk would create more risk than ever.

If stocks seemed certain to outperform, everyone would buy them, driving prices so high that there would be no room left for future growth, making a crash inevitable. That's exactly what happened in 1720 and 1929 and 2000, among many other occasions.

Stocks *are* risky. Without any warning, after years of gains, you can lose an ungodly amount of money for an agonizingly long time. But the most subtle risk of owning stocks is that you can never be sure when they are overpriced or underpriced—or how long it will take for them to return to "normal."

The only certainty you can derive from past financial data is that the future is always surprising. And it will most brutally surprise those who are the most certain they know what is about to happen.

To be an intelligent investor, you must accept that stocks are likely—but *not* certain—to outperform over long periods. Instead of trying to build a portfolio that would thrive if what you think will happen does happen, strive to build a portfolio that should thrive no matter what happens. Stop fruitlessly trying to predict the unknowable. You will exert much more control by accepting how little you can control. That will free you up to establish policies and procedures to structure all the decisions over which you *do* have control.

CHAPTER 4

General Portfolio Policy: The Defensive Investor
by Benjamin Graham

The basic characteristics of an investment portfolio are usually determined by the position and characteristics of the owner or owners. At one extreme we have had savings banks, life-insurance companies, and so-called legal trust funds. A generation ago their investments were limited by law in many states to high-grade bonds and, in some cases, high-grade preferred stocks. At the other extreme we have the well-to-do and experienced businessman, who will include any kind of bond or stock in his security list provided he considers it an attractive purchase.

It has been an old and sound principle that those who cannot afford to take risks should be content with a relatively low return on their invested funds. From this there has developed the general notion that the rate of return which the investor should aim for is more or less proportionate to the degree of risk he is ready to run. Our view is different. The rate of return sought should be dependent, rather, on the amount of intelligent effort the investor is willing and able to bring to bear on his task. The minimum return goes to our passive investor, who wants both safety and freedom from concern. The maximum return would be realized by the alert and enterprising investor who exercises maximum intelligence and skill. In 1965 we added: "In many cases there may be less real risk associated with buying a 'bargain issue' offering the chance of a large profit than with a conventional bond purchase yielding about 4½%." This statement had more truth in it than we ourselves suspected, since in subsequent years even the best long-term bonds lost a substantial part of their market value because of the rise in interest rates.

The Basic Problem of Bond-Stock Allocation

We have already outlined in briefest form the portfolio policy of the defensive investor.* He should divide his funds between high-grade bonds and high-grade common stocks.

We have suggested as a fundamental guiding rule that the investor should never have less than 25% or more than 75% of his funds in common stocks, with a consequent inverse range of between 75% and 25% in bonds. There is an implication here that the standard division should be an equal one, or 50–50, between the two major investment mediums. According to tradition the sound reason for increasing the percentage in common stocks would be the appearance of the "bargain price" levels created in a protracted bear market. Conversely, sound procedure would call for reducing the common-stock component below 50% when in the judgment of the investor the market level has become dangerously high.

These copybook maxims have always been easy to enunciate and always difficult to follow—because they go against that very human nature which produces that excesses of bull and bear markets. **It is almost a contradiction in terms to suggest as a feasible policy for the average stockowner that he lighten his holdings when the market advances beyond a certain point and add to them after a corresponding decline. It is because the average man operates, and apparently must operate, in opposite fashion that we have had the great advances and collapses of the past; and—this writer believes—we are likely to have them in the future.**

If the division between investment and speculative operations were as clear now as once it was, we might be able to envisage investors as a shrewd, experienced group who sell out to the heedless, hapless speculators at high prices and buy back from them at depressed levels. This picture may have had some verisimilitude in bygone days, but it is hard to identify it with financial developments since 1949. There is no indication that

---

* See Graham's "Conclusion" to Chapter 2, p. 56.

such professional operations as those of the mutual funds have been conducted in this fashion. The percentage of the portfolio held in equities by the two major types of funds—"balanced" and "common-stock"—has changed very little from year to year. Their selling activities have been largely related to endeavors to switch from less to more promising holdings.

If, as we have long believed, the stock market has lost contact with its old bounds, and if new ones have not yet been established, then we can give the investor no reliable rules by which to reduce his common-stock holdings toward the 25% minimum and rebuild them later to the 75% maximum. We can urge that in general the investor should not have more than one-half in equities unless he has strong confidence in the soundness of his stock position and is sure that he could view a market decline of the 1969–70 type with equanimity. It is hard for us to see how such strong confidence can be justified at the levels existing in early 1972. Thus we would counsel against a greater than 50% apportionment to common stocks at this time. But, for complementary reasons, it is almost equally difficult to advise a reduction of the figure well below 50%, unless the investor is disquieted *in his own mind* about the current market level, and will be satisfied also to limit his participation in any further rise to, say, 25% of his total funds.

We are thus led to put forward for most of our readers what may appear to be an oversimplified 50–50 formula. Under this plan the guiding rule is to maintain as nearly as practicable an equal division between bond and stock holdings. When changes in the market level have raised the common-stock component to, say, 55%, the balance would be restored by a sale of one-eleventh of the stock portfolio and the transfer of the proceeds to bonds. Conversely, a fall in the common-stock proportion to 45% would call for the use of one-eleventh of the bond fund to buy additional equities.

Yale University followed a somewhat similar plan for a number of years after 1937, but it was geared around a 35% "normal holding" in common stocks. In the early 1950s, however, Yale seems to have given up its once famous formula, and in 1969 held 61% of its portfolio in equities (including some convertibles). (At that time the endowment funds of 71 such institutions, totaling $7.6 billion, held 60.3% in common stocks.) The Yale example illustrates the almost lethal effect of the great market advance upon the once popular *formula approach* to investment. Nonetheless we are convinced that our 50–50 version of this approach makes good sense for the defensive investor. **It is extremely simple; it aims unquestionably in the right direction; it gives the follower the feeling that he is at least making some moves in response to market developments; most important of all, it will restrain him from being drawn more and more heavily into common stocks as the market rises to more and more dangerous heights.**

Furthermore, a truly conservative investor will be satisfied with the gains shown on half his portfolio in a rising market, while in a severe decline he may derive much solace from reflecting how much better off he is than many of his more venturesome friends.

While our proposed 50–50 division is undoubtedly the simplest "all-purpose program" devisable, it may not turn out to be the best in terms of results achieved. (Of course, no approach, mechanical or otherwise, can be advanced with any assurance that it will work out better than another.) The much larger income return now offered by good bonds than by representative stocks is a potent argument for favoring the bond component. The investor's choice between 50% or a lower figure in stocks may well rest mainly on his own temperament and attitude. If he can act as a cold-blooded weigher of the odds, he would be likely to favor the low 25% stock component at this time, with the idea of waiting until the DJIA dividend yield was, say, two-thirds of the bond yield before he would establish his median 50–50 division between bonds and stocks. Starting from 900 for the DJIA and dividends of $36 on the unit, this would require either a fall in taxable bond yields from 7½% to about 5.5% without any change in the present return on leading stocks, or a fall in the DJIA to as low as 660 if there is no reduction in bond yields and no increase in dividends. A combination of intermediate changes could produce the same "buying point." A program of that kind is not especially complicated; the hard part is to adopt it and to stick to it, not to mention the possibility that it may turn out to have been much too conservative.

The Bond Component

The choice of issues in the bond component of the investor's portfolio will turn about two main questions: Should he buy taxable or tax-free bonds, and should he buy shorter- or longer-term maturities? The tax decision should be mainly a matter of arithmetic, turning on the difference in yields as compared with the investor's tax bracket. In January 1972 the choice in 20-year maturities was between obtaining, say, 7½% on "grade Aa" corporate bonds and 5.3% on prime tax-free issues. (The term "municipals" is generally applied to all species of tax-exempt bonds, including state obligations.) There was thus for this maturity a loss in income of some 30% in passing from the corporate to the municipal field. Hence if the investor was in a maximum tax bracket higher than 30% he would have a net saving after taxes by choosing the municipal bonds; the opposite, if his maximum tax was less than 30%. A single person starts paying a 30% rate when his income after deductions passes $10,000; for a married couple the rate applies when combined taxable income passes $20,000. It is evident that a large proportion of individual investors would obtain a higher return after taxes from good municipals than from good corporate bonds.

The choice of longer versus shorter maturities involves quite a different question, viz.: Does the investor want to assure himself against a decline in the price of his bonds, but at the cost of (1) a lower annual yield and (2) loss of the possibility of an appreciable *gain* in principal value? We think it best to discuss this question in Chapter 8, "The Investor and Market Fluctuations."

For a period of many years in the past the only sensible bond purchases for individuals were the U.S. savings issues. Their safety was—and is—unquestioned; they gave a higher return than other bond investments of first quality; they had a money-back option and other privileges which added greatly to their attractiveness. In our earlier editions we had an entire chapter entitled "U.S. Savings Bonds: A Boon to Investors."

As we shall point out, U.S. savings bonds still possess certain unique merits that make them a suitable purchase by any individual investor. For the man of modest capital—with, say, not more than $10,000 to put into bonds—we think they are still the easiest and the best choice. But those with larger funds may find other mediums more desirable.

Let us list a few major types of bonds that deserve investor consideration, and discuss them briefly with respect to general description, safety, yield, market price, risk, income-tax status, and other features.

1. U.S. savings bonds, Series E and Series H. We shall first summarize their important provisions, and then discuss briefly the numerous advantages of these unique, attractive, and exceedingly convenient investments. The Series H bonds pay interest semi-annually, as do other bonds. The rate is 4.29% for the first year, and then a flat 5.10% for the next nine years to maturity. Interest on the Series E bonds is not paid out, but accrues to the holder through increase in redemption value. The bonds are sold at 75% of their face value, and mature at 100% in 5 years 10 months after purchase. If held to maturity the yield works out at 5%, compounded semi-annually. If redeemed earlier, the yield moves up from a minimum of 4.01% in the first year to an average of 5.20% in the next 4⅚ years.

Interest on the bonds is subject to Federal income tax, but is exempt from state income tax. However, Federal income tax on the Series E bonds may be paid at the holder's option either annually as the interest accrues (through higher redemption value), or not until the bond is actually disposed of.

Owners of Series E bonds may cash them in at any time (shortly after purchase) at their current redemption value. Holders of Series H bonds have similar rights to cash them in at par value (cost). Series E bonds are exchangeable for Series H bonds, with certain tax advantages. Bonds lost, destroyed, or stolen may be replaced without cost. There are limitations on annual purchases, but liberal provisions for co-ownership by family members make it possible for most investors to buy as many as they can afford. *Comment:* There is no other investment that combines (1) absolute assurance of principal and interest payments, (2) the right to demand full "money back" at any time, and (3) guarantee of at least a 5% interest rate for at least ten years. Holders of the earlier issues of Series E bonds have had the right to extend their bonds at maturity, and thus to continue to accumulate annual values at successively higher rates. The deferral of income-tax payments over these long periods has been of great dollar advantage; we calculate it has increased the effective net-after-tax rate received by as much as a third in typical cases. Conversely, the right to cash in the bonds at cost price or better has given the purchasers in former years of low interest rates complete protection against the shrinkage in principal value that befell many bond investors; otherwise stated, it gave them the possibility of *benefiting* from the rise in interest rates by switching their low-interest holdings into very-high-coupon issues on an even-money basis.

In our view the special advantages enjoyed by owners of savings bonds now will more than compensate for their lower current return as compared with other direct government obligations.

2. Other United States bonds. A profusion of these issues exists, covering a wide variety of coupon rates and maturity dates. All of them are completely safe with respect to payment of interest and principal. They are subject to Federal income taxes but free from state income tax. In late 1971 the long-term issues—over ten years—showed an average yield of 6.09%, intermediate issues (three to five years) returned 6.35%, and short issues returned 6.03%.

In 1970 it was possible to buy a number of old issues at large discounts. Some of these are accepted at par in settlement of estate taxes. Example: The U.S. Treasury 3½s due 1990 are in this category; they sold at 60 in 1970, but closed 1970 above 77.

It is interesting to note also that in many cases the indirect obligations of the U.S. government yield appreciably more than its direct obligations of the same maturity. As we write, an offering appears of 7.05% of "Certificates Fully Guaranteed by the Secretary of Transportation of the Department of Transportation of the United States." The yield was fully 1% more than that on direct obligations of the U.S., maturing the same year (1986). The certificates were actually issued in the name of the Trustees of the Penn Central Transportation Co., but they were sold on the basis of a statement by the U.S. Attorney General that the guarantee "brings into being a general obligation of the United States, backed by its full faith and credit." Quite a number of indirect obligations of this sort have been assumed by the U.S. government in the past, and all of them have been scrupulously honored.

The reader may wonder why all this hocus-pocus, involving an apparently "personal guarantee" by our Secretary of Transportation, and a higher cost to the taxpayer in the end. The chief reason for the indirection has been the debt limit imposed on government borrowing by the Congress. Apparently guarantees by the government are not regarded as debts—a semantic windfall for shrewder investors. Perhaps the chief impact of this situation has been the creation of tax-free Housing Authority bonds, enjoying the equivalent of a U.S. guarantee, and virtually the only tax-exempt issues that are equivalent to government bonds. Another type of government-backed issues is the recently created New Community Debentures, offered to yield 7.60% in September 1971.

3. *State and municipal bonds.* These enjoy exemption from Federal income tax. They are also ordinarily free of income tax in the state of issue but not elsewhere. They are either direct obligations of a state or subdivision, or "revenue bonds" dependent for interest payments on receipts from a toll road, bridge, building lease, etc. Not all tax-free bonds are strongly enough protected to justify their purchase by a defensive investor. He may be guided in his selection by the rating given to each issue by Moody's or Standard & Poor's. One of the three highest ratings by both services—Aaa (AAA), Aa (AA), or A—should constitute a sufficient indication of adequate safety. The yield on these bonds will vary both with the quality and the maturity, with the shorter maturities giving the lower return. In late 1971 the issues represented in Standard & Poor's municipal bond index averaged AA in quality rating, 20 years in maturity, and 5.78% in yield. A typical offering of Vineland, N.J., bonds, rated AA for A and gave a yield of only 3% on the one-year maturity, rising to 5.8% to the 1995 and 1996 maturities.[1]

4. *Corporation bonds.* These bonds are subject to both Federal and state tax. In early 1972 those of highest quality yielded 7.19% for a 25-year maturity, as reflected in the published yield of Moody's Aaa corporate bond index. The so-called lower-medium-grade issues—rated Baa—returned 8.23% for long maturities. In each class shorter-term issues would yield somewhat less than longer-term obligations.

Comment. The above summaries indicate that the average investor has several choices among high-grade bonds. Those in high income-tax brackets can undoubtedly obtain a better net yield from good tax-free issues than from taxable ones. For others the early 1972 range of taxable yield would seem to be from 5.00% on U.S. savings bonds, with their special options, to about 7½% on high-grade corporate issues.

Higher-Yielding Bond Investments

By sacrificing quality an investor can obtain a higher income return from his bonds. Long experience has demonstrated that the ordinary investor is wiser to keep away from such high-yield bonds. While, taken as a whole, they may work out somewhat better in terms of overall return than the first-quality issues, they expose the owner to too many individual risks of untoward developments, ranging from disquieting price declines to actual default. (It is true that bargain opportunities occur fairly often in lower-grade bonds, but these require special study and skill to exploit successfully.)*

Perhaps we should add here that the limits imposed by Congress on direct bond issues of the United States have produced at least two sorts of "bargain opportunities" for investors in the purchase of government-backed obligations. One is provided by the tax-exempt "New Housing" issues, and the other by the recently created (taxable) "New Community debentures." An offering of New Housing issues in July 1971 yielded as high as 5.8%, free from both Federal and state taxes, while an issue of (taxable) New Community debentures sold in September 1971 yielded 7.60%. Both obligations have the "full faith and credit" of the United States government behind them and hence are safe without question. And—on a net basis—they yield considerably more than ordinary United States bonds.†

Savings Deposits in Lieu of Bonds

An investor may now obtain as high an interest rate from a savings deposit in a commercial or savings bank (or from a bank certificate of deposit) as he can from a first-grade bond of short maturity. The interest rate on bank savings accounts may be lowered

---

* Graham's objection to high-yield bonds is largely mitigated today by the widespread availability of mutual funds and exchange-traded funds that spread the "individual risk."

† The "New Housing" bonds and "New Community debentures," backed by the U.S. Department of Housing and Urban Development (HUD), have not been issued since 1974 and 1983, respectively.

in the future, but under present conditions they are a suitable substitute for short-term bond investment by the individual.*

Convertible Issues

These are discussed in Chapter 16. The price variability of bonds in general is treated in Chapter 8, "The Investor and Market Fluctuations."

Call Provisions

In previous editions we had a fairly long discussion of this aspect of bond financing, because it involved a serious but little noticed injustice to the investor. In the typical case bonds were callable fairly soon after issuance, and at modest premiums—say 5%—above the issue price.† This meant that during a period of wide fluctuations in the underlying interest rates the investor had to bear the full brunt of unfavorable changes and was deprived of all but a meager participation in favorable ones.

Example: Our standard example has been the issue of American Gas & Electric 100-year 5% debentures, sold to the public at 101 in 1928. Four years later, under near-panic conditions, the price of these good bonds fell to 62½, yielding 8%. By 1946, in a great reversal, bonds of this type could be sold to yield only 3%, and the 5% issue *should* have been quoted at close to 160. But at that point the company took advantage of the call provision and redeemed the issue at a mere 106.

The call feature in these bond contracts was a thinly disguised instance of "heads I win, tails you lose." At long last, the bond-buying institutions refused to accept this unfair arrangement; in recent years most long-term high-coupon issues have been protected against redemption for ten years or more after issuance. This still limits their possible price rise, but not inequitably.

In practical terms, we advise the investor in long-term issues

---

* Unfortunately, this hasn't been true in recent decades.
† A "callable" bond may be forcibly bought back by the issuer, usually at the worst time for the investor.

to sacrifice a small amount of yield to obtain the assurance of noncallability—say for 20 or 25 years. Similarly, there is an advantage in buying a low-coupon bond* at a discount rather than a high-coupon bond selling at about par and callable in a few years. For the discount—e.g., of a 3½% bond at 63½%, yielding 7.85%— carries full protection against adverse call action.

Straight—i.e., Nonconvertible—Preferred Stocks

Certain general observations should be made here on the subject of preferred stocks. Really good preferred stocks can and do exist, but they are good in spite of their investment form, which is an inherently bad one. The typical preferred shareholder is dependent for his safety on the ability and desire of the company to pay dividends on its *common stock*. Once the common dividends are omitted, or even in danger, his own position becomes precarious, for the directors are under no obligation to continue paying him unless they also pay on the common. On the other hand, the typical preferred stock carries no share in the company's profits beyond the fixed dividend rate. Thus the preferred holder lacks both the legal claim of the bondholder (or creditor) and the profit possibilities of a common shareholder (or partner).

These weaknesses in the legal position of preferred stocks tend to come to the fore recurrently in periods of depression. Only a small percentage of all preferred issues are so strongly entrenched as to maintain an unquestioned investment status through all vicissitudes. Experience teaches that the time to buy preferred stocks is when their price is unduly depressed by temporary adversity. (At such times they may be well suited to the aggressive investor but too unconventional for the defensive investor.)

In other words, they should be bought on a bargain basis or not at all. We shall refer later to convertible and similarly privileged issues, which carry some special possibilities of profits. These are not ordinarily selected for a conservative portfolio.

Another peculiarity in the general position of preferred

---

* A bond's "coupon" is its interest rate; a "low-coupon" bond pays a rate of interest income below the market average.

stocks deserves mention. They have a much better tax status for corporation buyers than for individual investors. Corporations pay income tax on only 15% of the income they receive in dividends, but on the full amount of their ordinary interest income. Since the 1972 corporate rate is 48%, this means that $100 received as preferred-stock dividends is taxed only $7.20, whereas $100 received as bond interest is taxed $48. On the other hand, individual investors pay exactly the same tax on preferred-stock investments as on bond interest, except for a recent minor exemption. Thus, in strict logic, all investment-grade preferred stocks should be bought by corporations, just as all tax-exempt bonds should be bought by investors who pay income tax.*

Security Forms

The bond form and the preferred-stock form, as hitherto discussed, are well-understood and relatively simple matters. A bondholder is entitled to receive fixed interest and payment of principal on a definite date. The owner of a preferred stock is entitled to a fixed dividend, and no more, which must be paid before any common dividend. His principal value does not come due on any specified date. (The dividend may be cumulative or noncumulative. He may or may not have a vote.)

The above describes the standard provisions and, no doubt, the majority of bond and preferred issues, but there are innumerable departures from these forms. The best-known types are convertible and similar issues, and income bonds. In the latter type, interest does not have to be paid unless it is earned by the company. (Unpaid interest may accumulate as a charge against future earnings, but the period is often limited to three years.)

Income bonds should be used by corporations much more extensively than they are. Their avoidance apparently arises from a mere accident of economic history—namely, that they were first employed in quantity in connection with railroad reorganizations,

---

* Preferred stock, overwhelmingly issued by banks, dealt devastating losses to investors during the financial crisis of 2008–09. An issuer may suspend the dividend on preferred stock at any time.

and hence they have been associated from the start with financial weakness and poor investment status. But the form itself has several practical advantages, especially in comparison with and in substitution for the numerous (convertible) preferred-stock issues of recent years. Chief of these is the deductibility of the interest paid from the company's taxable income, which in effect cuts the cost of that form of capital in half. From the investor's standpoint it is probably best for him in most cases that he should have (1) an unconditional right to receive interest payments *when they are earned* by the company, and (2) a right to *other* forms of protection than bankruptcy proceedings if interest is not earned and paid. The terms of income bonds can be tailored to the advantage of both the borrower and the lender in the manner best suited to both. (Conversion privileges can, of course, be included.) The acceptance by everybody of the inherently weak preferred-stock form and the rejection of the stronger income-bond form is a fascinating illustration of the way in which traditional institutions and habits often tend to persist on Wall Street despite new conditions calling for a fresh point of view. With every new wave of optimism or pessimism, we are ready to abandon history and time-tested principles, but we cling tenaciously and unquestioningly to our prejudices.

Commentary on Chapter 4
by Jason Zweig

> Not being able to rule events, I rule myself, and adapt myself to them if they do not adapt themselves to me.
> —Michel de Montaigne[1]

The hardest part of being a defensive investor is defending yourself from yourself. Most conventional investing wisdom focuses on what to do. Intelligent investors focus most of their energy on what *not* to do.

This Is Not a Test

How much risk should you take?

The conventional answer depends on what financial advisers call your "risk tolerance," a nebulous concept they often measure by asking you as few as a half dozen questions, including this nonsensical favorite: *If the stock market dropped 20%, would you sell, hold, or buy more?*

When markets are calm, it's easy to say you'd buy more in a market crash, the same way you might say *of course* you'd rush into a burning building to rescue the people inside.

However, saying you'll run into a burning building is a lot easier than running into a burning building. And saying you'll buy stocks in a market crash is a lot easier than doing it.

A market crash is not a quiz.

When every stock price is blazing bloodred on your phone, the headlines are apocalyptic, market pundits are shrieking on television that you should sell everything before it's too late, and your family is

---

[1] "Of Presumption," *The Complete Essays of Montaigne* (Stanford, 1965), p. 488.

begging you to stop throwing money into the flames, buying more isn't an act of bravado; it's terrifying.

Your tolerance for risk doesn't stay constant most of your life. It might not even stay constant from hour to hour. That's why Graham warns against picking your portfolio based on how much risk you (or your financial adviser) think you can stomach.

> ### Your "Risk Tolerance" Is Out of Control
>
> Economists and psychologists have shown that how much financial risk you're willing to take at any moment depends on:
>
> - how well the stock market has done lately;
> - how well your own investments have done lately;
> - whether you're investing alone or as part of a group;
> - whether you're feeling happy, angry, sad, anxious, fearful, or disgusted;
> - how much money you had between the ages of 18 and 25;
> - which country or culture you come from;
> - whether stock prices end in the digits 4, 8, or 9;
> - where you got the money you're investing;
> - what time of year it is;
> - what time of day it is;
> - how well you slept;
> - how long ago you last ate;
> - whether the sun is shining;
> - how recently you read about an airplane crash;
> - whether your favorite sports team won or lost the big game.
>
> These are just a few of the factors that have been identified. They're all a reminder that, without policies and procedures to guide you, you will be at the mercy of the market's ever-changing moods—and your own.[1]
>
> ---
> [1] Elke U. Weber and Joachim Klement, "Risk Tolerance and Circumstances," bit.ly/45dJzp1.

Defensive versus Enterprising

Based on the faulty assumption that people's risk tolerance is stable, financial advisers often offer "conservative," "moderate," or "aggressive" portfolios whose riskiness is defined by their exposure to stocks. A conservative portfolio might have no more than 40% in stocks; a moderate allocation, 60%; an aggressive basket, 80% or more.

Graham thinks this is ludicrous. When the stock market soars, "conservative" investors forget they ever wanted protection against loss. They become consumed with envy over the gains they would have earned if only they'd had more than that measly 40% in stocks. Desperate to make up for lost time, sick of listening to other people brag about getting rich, they buy stocks urgently—right before a crash.

After the market crashes, "aggressive" investors forget their original goal of making as much money as possible. Reeling from the wreckage of their wealth, they flee stocks and rush into the safety of cash. Brave as lions when stocks were expensive, they morph into mice when stocks become cheap.

Instead of using phony notions about risk tolerance, Graham draws a different distinction: How much risk you should take depends on how much time and "the amount of intelligent effort" you're willing and able to put into investing.

If you're too busy or don't feel qualified to put in much more time and effort than it takes to read this book, then Graham wants you to consider yourself a *defensive* investor. That means you don't have to bother working hard at it.

That doesn't mean being a defensive investor is easy. You will need to muster the discipline to follow an investment policy statement (see p. 107). You also must accept that bull markets will leave you behind, that someone you know will always be making more money than you, and above all that you don't know—and don't care—what the financial markets are going to do.

But *you should feel no shame whatsoever* in deciding you're a defensive investor. It isn't a confession of weakness, an abdication of responsibility, or an admission that you aren't smart or skillful. It's simply a recognition that incurring higher fees and costs in pursuit of superior returns is a waste of money unless you can also commit the time and effort it takes to be an enterprising investor.

On the other hand, if you enjoy studying businesses and analyzing financial statements, then you probably *are* an enterprising investor.

You, too, will need a formal investment policy.

And you will have to invest not only your money but also a lot of your time and energy.

First, you will have to probe deeply into any investment before you make it and so long as you continue to own it. You will have to analyze yourself even more deeply, creating a continuous learning environment that will enable you to identify your mistakes, benefit from feedback, and develop and follow consistent rules.[2]

The beauty of Graham's distinction between defensive and enterprising investors is that—unlike your purported risk tolerance—it isn't prone to change just because the markets make a big move up or down. A defensive investor is much less likely than a "conservative" investor to suffer the fear of missing out when stocks soar, and an enterprising investor is much more likely than an "aggressive" one to remain disciplined when stocks crumble.

Better Questions

Here are some questions that can help you start getting honest answers about how much money you should have in stocks.

What are my circumstances, preferences, and objectives?

- Age
- Marital status
- Income or earnings potential of spouse or partner
- Expected job security
- Do I own, rent, or plan to buy a home?
- Do I or will I have children and tuition to pay?
- Will I inherit money or will I need to provide for my parents?
- How ample is my employer-sponsored retirement plan?
- How reliant am I on my investments to produce regular income?
- How much physical capital do I have? How much can I make my human capital grow? (see p. 59)

---

[2] See Chapters 5, 7, 11, and their accompanying Commentaries.

What did I do during past down markets?

The best guide to how you'll behave in the next crash is how you behaved in the last one. We all tend to rewrite our own history, making ourselves braver in memory than we were in reality. If you can recall the financial crisis of 2008–09, you may well believe you bought more stock when, in fact, you sold or froze. You might also feel you bought more during the Covid crash of 2020 when you were, in real time, too scared to do anything.

Dig up your old account statements. If you sold or sat on your hands in past crashes, you probably will in the next one. Don't raise your stock exposure now above where it was then.

How flexible are my goals?

Your ability to withstand risk depends partly on how much money you have and can earn—but also on how much control you have over the timing of your future spending. If you can't defer buying that expensive house or your children must attend private schools, your capacity for taking risk is more limited than your cash balance might imply. Always having enough cash to cover at least six to 12 months of your spending needs will improve your flexibility.

How well do I understand the risks in the rest of my portfolio?

Many financial advisers have talked their clients into assets like emerging-market debt, bank-loan funds, and non-traded real estate. In a crisis, these income-producing but risky investments may go down at least as much as U.S. stocks. Long-term bonds, even U.S. Treasuries, will suffer steep losses if interest rates rise. Trendy holdings such as private equity, venture capital, hedge funds, and other "alternative assets" can be difficult to sell if you need cash in a hurry. If such investments have supplanted cash and short-to-medium-term government bonds in your portfolio, you're less able to withstand a stock crash than you think.

Have I turned rules into habits?

It's human nature to believe, when times are calm, that you will do the right thing in the heat of the moment. In a market crash, however, willpower is worthless. You can stay calm only if you have practiced beneficial rules until they've become good habits. If you check the value of your portfolio multiple times a day during a bull market, you've formed a toxic habit—and you're kidding yourself if you think you won't freak out and sell during a bear market.

The ABCs of an IPS

An investment policy statement, or IPS, is a formal document that spells out your investing circumstances, preferences, and goals. It explains how you plan to achieve your objectives, make significant decisions, and measure your progress. It also serves as a constant reminder of what you're committing *not* to do.

Every IPS, like every investor, is unique. You should customize the following generic template to your own needs and circumstances, changing it as much as necessary.[3]

Start with a mission statement:

The primary objective of this portfolio is long-term growth, with an ultimate horizon of ____ years, to help fund the coming decades' expenses for ourselves, for our children, and for our grandchildren. We will pursue this goal with patience and prudence, taking no unnecessary risks and never seeking to maximize short-term returns. The secondary objective will be to provide regular income. The primary decision-makers will be _____ and _____.

Then spell out structure:

The portfolio will be broadly diversified. Based on a careful review of our objectives, constraints, and reasonable expectations for returns on the following assets, it will allocate __% to cash, __% to bonds, __% to U.S. stocks, __% to international stocks, __% to public real estate, and __% to _____. Each allocation will be broadly diversified, with a minimum of ___ underlying holdings. We will never use margin or other borrowed money.[4] We will maintain enough cash to cover at least six months of expenses.

---

[3] For more on drafting an IPS, see CFA Institute, "Elements of an Investment Policy Statement for Individual Investors," bit.ly/3rDrKBn, and Bogleheads .org, "Investment Policy Statement," bit.ly/3NEVjtb.

[4] See the Commentary on Chapter 6.

Then describe implementation:

> We will bolster our patience by rebalancing _____ times per year and by dollar-cost averaging. We will select mutual funds, ETFs, and other investments by the lowest cost, not by the highest return. Total annual expenses, including all fees and trading costs, must not exceed 1%. We will never buy any asset only because its price has gone up or sell only because its price has gone down. All purchases and sales must fully conform to the criteria in our checklist, which must be filled out before any trade. If we have a "mad money" account, it will be funded with no more than 5% of our financial capital and will be segregated at a separate financial institution from the rest of our assets; under no circumstances of either gain or loss can we add more money to it.[5]

Finally, discuss monitoring:

> We will update the value of all our holdings no more than four times a year. We will measure performance relative to the _____ benchmarks, evaluating multiyear returns first and recent returns last.
>
> Once a year we will review this IPS to consider whether our circumstances, preferences, or objectives have changed.
>
> Any departure from this IPS must be justified in writing and agreed to by everyone who is a party to it.

I've often suggested, only half-jokingly, that investors should keep the printed original of their IPS in one of those red emergency boxes labeled IN CASE OF FIRE, BREAK GLASS. If you can't rewrite any detail of the document unless you first smash open its glass case with a hammer, you'll hesitate before impulsively changing it the next time the market goes down.

---

[5] For rebalancing, see p. 109; dollar-cost averaging, Chapter 5 and its Commentary; annual expenses, the Commentary on Chapter 9; checklists, the Commentary on Chapter 11; "mad-money" accounts, Chapter 1 and its accompanying Commentary.

Passive or Active?

If you're a defensive investor, you shouldn't bother picking specific stocks or attempting to beat the market. If you can't commit the time and effort, there's no point trying to do something you won't succeed at.

Fortunately, by choosing to admit that you're a defensive investor, you don't preclude the possibility of good results.

Once you renounce attempting to pick specific stocks and trying to beat the market, you can own all the stocks and match the market. *Index funds* own practically everything in a benchmark like the S&P 500 or the MSCI All-Country World Index. Through them, you own all the stocks all the time. The winners grow and the losers fade, and you never need to trade.

Because index funds cost almost nothing to run, their low expenses mean nearly all the market's return flows through to you. That, in turn, means they outperform most investors who incur high trading and research expenses. Over time, index funds tend to earn higher returns than at least two-thirds of professional investors. Graham himself was one of the earliest advocates of indexing.[6]

As a defensive investor, you could buy an index fund, hold it for the rest of your life, and almost never need to make another significant investing decision. Even better, you could rest assured that in the long run you'd do better than most professionals—at a fraction of the cost and aggravation.

Regaining Your Balance

As a defensive investor, you need yet another weapon in your arsenal.

Buy low, sell high: That's one of the most basic principles of investing. But even if you own only index funds, you still might end up doing the opposite: buying high and selling low.

The way the human brain works, buying high and selling low feel natural and necessary, while buying low and selling high feel frightening and wrong.

---

[6] See Chapter 9, its Commentary, and Jason Zweig, "Would Benjamin Graham Have Hated Index Funds?," bit.ly/3qb7iXS.

Buying high can be thrilling, especially when you're on a hot streak. If the market flips on you, then selling low often feels like the only way to stop your wealth from being sucked into a black hole of loss. When we invest, our neural circuitry automatically makes some harmful actions easier than beneficial behavior.[7]

To guard against that cycle of performance chasing, Graham suggests a simple rule: "Never have less than 25% or more than 75%" of your assets in stocks. That also means you should never have more than 75% or less than 25% in bonds. You would hold more in stocks when they appear cheap by historical standards and less when they seem expensive; most of the time, you would favor a 50–50 "standard division" between stocks and bonds.[8]

Because, as I explained in the Commentary on Chapter 3, you can never be *certain* that the stock market is overvalued or undervalued, Graham's rule prevents you from ever taking an all-or-nothing approach. When stocks have doubled or tripled and you might be tempted to put all your money in them because you're sure they're going up even more, his rule still requires you to stop at 75%—just in case you're wrong. And even when the market is crashing and seems to be heading to oblivion, Graham's rule still won't permit you to go below 25% in stocks—just in case you're wrong again.

Today's equivalent of Graham's policy is *rebalancing*, a procedure that sets a target proportion of your total assets to keep in stocks. Once a year, or after any big rise or fall in the stock market, reset your holdings back to your targets by selling some of whichever asset has gone up the most and buying some of whichever has gone down the most. Adjust enough to restore your target percentages. The best place to rebalance is in your retirement account, where sales won't trigger immediate tax consequences.[9]

For simplicity's sake, let's assume your assets consist of two broadly diversified exchange-traded index funds, one holding stocks and the other holding bonds. In your investment policy, you've set your target

---

[7] Jason Zweig, *Your Money and Your Brain* (Simon and Schuster, 2007).

[8] Graham also discusses his version of rebalancing in Chapter 8.

[9] For a more advanced discussion, see William J. Bernstein, "The Rebalancing Bonus," bit.ly/3rbDElh.

allocation at half in stocks, half in bonds.[10] If stocks fall 20% and bonds gain 20%, here's what rebalancing would look like:

Rather than emotionally buying high and selling low, you're automatically buying low and selling high. And you're making the market your servant instead of your master.

After all, the ultimate goal of being a defensive investor isn't freedom from effort; it's freedom from worry.

---

[10] The same method applies regardless of whether your target allocation is 50/50, 60/40, 70/30, 80/20, 90/10, 76/24, or any other combination. In each case, you would sell enough of the winning asset and buy enough of the loser to get back to your target.

TABLE 4-1: Rebalancing Act

	Original balance	Change in market value	New balance	Action needed to rebalance	Resulting balance
Stocks	$5,000	-20%	$4,000	Buy $1000	$5,000
Bonds	$5,000	+20%	$6,000	Sell $1000	$5,000
Total	$10,000	—	$10,000		$10,000

CHAPTER 5

The Defensive Investor and Common Stocks
by Benjamin Graham

Investment Merits of Common Stocks

In our first edition (1949) we found it necessary at this point to insert a long exposition of the case for including a substantial common-stock component in all investment portfolios.* Common stocks were generally viewed as highly speculative and therefore unsafe; they had declined fairly substantially from the high levels of 1946, but instead of attracting investors to them because of their reasonable prices, this fall had had the opposite effect of undermining confidence in equity securities. We have commented on the converse situation that has developed in the ensuing 20 years, whereby the big advance in stock prices made them appear safe and profitable investments at record high levels which might actually carry with them a considerable degree of risk.†

The argument we made for common stocks in 1949 turned on two main points. The first was that they had offered a considerable

---

* At the beginning of 1949, the average annual return produced by stocks over the previous 20 years was 3.1%, versus 3.9% for long-term Treasury bonds. Naturally enough, 1949 turned out to be a fabulous time to buy stocks: Over the next decade, the S&P 500 gained an average of 20.1% annually, one of the best long-term returns in history.
† Graham's earlier comments on this subject appear on pp. 18–19. Just imagine what he would have thought about the markets of the late 1990s or 2021, in which each new record high was considered further "proof" that stocks were the riskless way to wealth!

degree of protection against the erosion of the investor's dollar caused by inflation, whereas bonds offered no protection at all. The second advantage of common stocks lay in their higher average return to investors over the years. This was produced both by an average dividend income exceeding the yield on good bonds and by an underlying tendency for market value to increase over the years in consequence of the reinvestment of undistributed profits.

While these two advantages have been of major importance—and have given common stocks a far better record than bonds over the long-term past—we have consistently warned that these benefits could be lost by the stock buyer if he pays too high a price for his shares. This was clearly the case in 1929, and it took 25 years for the market level to climb back to the ledge from which it had abysmally fallen in 1929–1932.* Since 1957 common stocks have once again, through their high prices, lost their traditional advantage in dividend yield over bond interest rates.† It remains to be seen whether the inflation factor and the economic-growth factor will make up in the future for this significantly adverse development.

It should be evident to the reader that we have no enthusiasm for common stocks in general at the 900 DJIA level of late 1971. For reasons already given‡ we feel that the defensive investor cannot afford to be without an appreciable proportion of common

---

* See the Commentary on Chapter 3.
† Why do the "high prices" of stocks affect their dividend yields? A stock's yield is the ratio of its cash dividend to the price of one share of common stock. If a company pays a $2 annual dividend when its stock price is $100 per share, its yield is 2%. But if the stock price doubles while the dividend stays constant, the dividend yield will drop to 1%. In 1959, when the trend Graham spotted in 1957 became noticeable to everyone, most Wall Street pundits declared that it could not possibly last. After all, since stocks are riskier than bonds, why would anyone buy them at all without being able to earn extra dividend income to compensate for the greater risk? The experts argued that bonds would outyield stocks for a few months at most, and then things would revert to "normal." Except for brief periods between 2008 and 2021, bonds have outyielded stocks ever since.
‡ See pp. 56 and 90.

stocks in his portfolio, even if he must regard them as the lesser of two evils—the greater being the risks attached to an all-bond holding.

Rules for the Common-Stock Component

The selection of common stocks for the portfolio of the defensive investor should be a relatively simple matter. Here we would suggest four rules to be followed:

1. There should be adequate though not excessive diversification. This might mean a minimum of ten different issues and a maximum of about thirty.*

2. Each company selected should be large, prominent, and conservatively financed. Indefinite as these adjectives must be, their general sense is clear. Observations on this point are added at the end of the chapter.

3. Each company should have a long record of continuous dividend payments. (All the issues in the Dow Jones Industrial Average met this dividend requirement in 1971.) To be specific on this point we would suggest the requirement of continuous dividend payments beginning at least in 1950.†

4. The investor should impose some limit on the price he will pay for an issue in relation to its average earnings over, say, the past seven years. We suggest that this limit be set at 25 times such average earnings, and not more than 20 times those of the last twelve-month period. But such a restriction would eliminate nearly all the strongest and most popular companies from the portfolio. In particular, it would ban virtually the entire category of "growth stocks," which have for some years past been the favorites of both speculators and institutional investors. We must give our reasons for proposing so drastic an exclusion.

---

* For more on diversification, see the Commentaries on Chapters 7 and 14.
† Today's defensive investor who wishes to pursue such a strategy can choose among numerous dividend-oriented exchange-traded funds.

Growth Stocks and the Defensive Investor

The term "growth stock" is applied to one which has increased its per-share earnings in the past at well above the rate for common stocks generally and is expected to continue to do so in the future. (Some authorities would say that a true growth stock should be expected at least to double its per-share earnings in ten years—i.e., to increase them at a compounded annual rate of over 7.1%.)* Obviously stocks of this kind are attractive to buy and to own, provided the price paid is not excessive. The problem lies there, of course, since growth stocks have long sold at high prices in relation to current earnings and at much higher multiples of their average profits over a past period. This has introduced a speculative element of considerable weight in the growth-stock picture and has made successful operations in this field a far from simple matter.

The leading growth issue has long been International Business Machines, and it has brought phenomenal rewards to those who bought it years ago and held on to it tenaciously. But we have already pointed out[†] that this "best of common stocks" actually lost 50% of its market price in a six-months' decline during 1961–62 and nearly the same percentage in 1969–70. Other growth stocks have been even more vulnerable to adverse developments; in some cases not only has the price fallen back but the earnings as well, thus causing a double discomfiture to those who owned them. A good second example for our purpose is Texas Instruments, which in six years rose from 5 to 256, without paying a dividend, while its earnings increased from 40 cents to $3.91 per share. (Note that the price advanced five times as fast as the profits; this is characteristic of popular common stocks.) But two

---

* The "Rule of 72" is a handy mental tool. To estimate the length of time an amount of money takes to double, simply divide its assumed growth rate into 72. At 6%, for instance, money will double in roughly 12 years (72 divided by 6 = 12). At the 7.1% rate cited by Graham, a growth stock will double its earnings in just over 10 years (72/7.1 = about 10.1 years).

[†] Graham makes this point on p. 73.

years later the earnings had dropped off by nearly 50% and the price by *four-fifths*, to 49.*

The reader will understand from these instances why we regard growth stocks as a whole as too uncertain and risky a vehicle for the defensive investor. Of course, wonders can be accomplished with the right individual selections, bought at the right levels, and later sold after a huge rise and before the probable decline. But the average investor can no more expect to accomplish this than to find money growing on trees. In contrast we think that the group of large companies that are relatively unpopular, and therefore obtainable at reasonable earnings multipliers,† offers a sound if unspectacular area of choice by the general public. We shall illustrate this idea in our chapter on portfolio selection.

Portfolio Changes

It is now standard practice to submit all security lists for periodic inspection in order to see whether their quality can be improved. This, of course, is a major part of the service provided for clients by investment counselors. Nearly all brokerage houses are ready to make corresponding suggestions, without special fee, in return for the commission business involved. Some brokerage houses maintain investment services on a fee basis.

Presumably our defensive investor should obtain—at least once a year—the same kind of advice regarding changes in his portfolio as he sought when his funds were first committed. Since he will have little expertness of his own on which to rely, it is essential that he entrust himself only to firms of the highest reputation; otherwise he may easily fall into incompetent or unscrupulous hands. It is important, in any case, that at every

---

* To show that Graham's observations are perennially true, consider the recent example of Zoom Video Communications. From early 2019 through late 2020, the stock soared from $62 to $568 as earnings rose roughly 30-fold during the Covid pandemic. Then, as the economy reopened, Zoom's profits collapsed, and the stock fell nearly 90% in the next two years. As always, the hotter they are, the harder they fall.

† "Earnings multiplier" is a synonym for P/E ratios. (See footnote † on p. 70.)

such consultation he make clear to his adviser that he wishes to adhere closely to the four rules of common-stock selection given earlier in this chapter. Incidentally, if his list has been competently selected in the first instance, there should be no need for frequent or numerous changes.

Dollar-Cost Averaging

The New York Stock Exchange has put considerable effort into popularizing its "monthly purchase plan," under which an investor devotes the same dollar amount each month to buying one or more common stocks. This is an application of a special type of "formula investment" known as dollar-cost averaging. During the predominantly rising-market experience since 1949 the results from such a procedure were certain to be highly satisfactory, especially since they prevented the practitioner from concentrating his buying at the wrong times.

In Lucile Tomlinson's comprehensive study of formula investment plans,[1] the author presented a calculation of the results of dollar-cost averaging in the group of stocks making up the Dow Jones industrial index. Tests were made covering 23 ten-year purchase periods, the first ending in 1929, the last in 1952. Every test showed a profit either at the close of the purchase period or within five years thereafter. The average indicated profit at the end of the 23 buying periods was 21.5%, exclusive of dividends received. Needless to say, in some instances there was a substantial temporary depreciation at market value. Miss Tomlinson ends her discussion of this ultrasimple investment formula with the striking sentence: "No one has yet discovered any other formula for investing which can be used with so much confidence of ultimate success, regardless of what may happen to security prices, as Dollar Cost Averaging."

It may be objected that dollar-cost averaging, while sound in principle, is rather unrealistic in practice, because few people are so situated that they can have available for common-stock investment the same amount of money each year for, say, 20 years. It seems to me that this apparent objection has lost much of its force in recent years. Common stocks are becoming generally accepted as a necessary component of a sound savings-investment program.

Thus, systematic and uniform purchases of common stocks may present no more psychological and financial difficulties than similar continuous payments for United States savings bonds and for life insurance—to which they should be complementary. The monthly amount may be small, but the results after 20 or more years can be impressive and important to the saver.*

The Investor's Personal Situation

At the beginning of this chapter we referred briefly to the position of the individual portfolio owner. Let us return to this matter, in the light of our subsequent discussion of general policy. To what extent should the type of securities selected by the investor vary with his circumstances? As concrete examples representing widely different conditions, we shall take: (1) a widow left $200,000 with which to support herself and her children; (2) a successful doctor in mid-career, with savings of $100,000 and yearly accretions of $10,000; and (3) a young man earning $200 per week and saving $1,000 a year.†

For the widow, the problem of living on her income is a very difficult one. On the other hand the need for conservatism in her investments is paramount. A division of her fund about equally between United States bonds and first-grade common stocks is a compromise between these objectives and corresponds to our general prescription for the defensive investor. (The stock component may be placed as high as 75% if the investor is psychologically prepared for this decision, and if she can be almost certain she is not buying at too high a level. Assuredly this is *not* the case in early 1972.)

We do not preclude the possibility that the widow may qualify as an enterprising investor, in which case her objectives and methods will be quite different. The one thing the widow must *not* do is to take speculative chances in order to "make some extra income." By this we mean trying for profits or high income without the

---

* For more on dollar-cost averaging, see the Commentary on this chapter and Nick Maggiulli, *Just Keep Buying* (Harriman House, 2022).
† To update Graham's figures for inflation, take each dollar amount in this section and multiply it by 8.

necessary equipment to warrant full confidence in overall success. It would be far better for her to draw $2,000 per year out of her principal, in order to make both ends meet, than to risk half of it in poorly grounded, and therefore speculative, ventures.

The prosperous doctor has none of the widow's pressures and compulsions, yet we believe that his choices are pretty much the same. Is he willing to take a serious interest in the business of investment? If he lacks the impulse or the flair, he will do best to accept the easy role of the defensive investor. The division of his portfolio should then be no different from that of the "typical" widow, and there would be the same area of personal choice in fixing the size of the stock component. The annual savings should be invested in about the same proportions as the total fund.

The average doctor may be more likely than the average widow to elect to become an enterprising investor, and he is perhaps more likely to succeed in the undertaking. He has one important handicap, however—the fact that he has less time available to give to his investment education and to the administration of his funds. In fact, medical men have been notoriously unsuccessful in their security dealings. The reason for this is that they usually have an ample confidence in their own intelligence and a strong desire to make a good return on their money, without the realization that to do so successfully requires both considerable attention to the matter and something of a professional approach to security values.

Finally, the young man who saves $1,000 a year—and expects to do better gradually—finds himself with the same choices, though for still different reasons. Some of his savings should go automatically into Series E bonds. The balance is so modest that it seems hardly worthwhile for him to undergo a tough educational and temperamental discipline in order to qualify as an aggressive investor. Thus a simple resort to our standard program for the defensive investor would be at once the easiest and the most logical policy.

Let us not ignore human nature at this point. Finance has a fascination for many bright young people with limited means. They would like to be both intelligent and enterprising in the placement of their savings, even though investment income is much less important to them than their salaries. This attitude is all to the good. **There is a great advantage for the young capitalist to begin his** financial education and experience early. If he is going to operate as an aggressive investor he is certain to make some mistakes and to take some losses. Youth can stand these disappointments and profit by them. We urge the beginner in security buying not to waste his efforts and his money in trying to beat the market. Let him study security values and initially test out his judgment on price versus value with the smallest possible sums.

Thus we return to the statement, made at the outset, that **the kind of securities to be purchased and the rate of return to be sought depend not on the investor's financial resources but on his financial equipment in terms of knowledge, experience, and temperament.**

Note on the Concept of "Risk"

It is conventional to speak of good bonds as less risky than good preferred stocks and of the latter as less risky than good common stocks. From this was derived the popular prejudice against common stocks because they are not "safe," which was demonstrated in the Federal Reserve Board's survey of 1948. We should like to point out that the words "risk" and "safety" are applied to securities in two different senses, with a resultant confusion in thought.

A bond is clearly proved unsafe when it defaults its interest or principal payments. Similarly, if a preferred stock or even a common stock is bought with the expectation that a given rate of dividend will be continued, then a reduction or passing of the dividend means that it has proved unsafe. It is also true that an investment contains a risk if there is a fair possibility that the holder may have to sell at a time when the price is well below cost.

Nevertheless, the idea of risk is often extended to apply to a possible decline in the price of a security, even though the decline may be of a cyclical and temporary nature and even though the holder is unlikely to be forced to sell at such times. These chances are present in all securities, other than United States savings bonds, and to a greater extent in the general run of common stocks than in senior issues as a class. But we believe that what is here involved is not a true risk in the useful sense of the term. The man who holds a mortgage on a building might have to take a substantial loss if he were forced to sell it at an unfavorable time. That element is not taken into account in judging the safety or risk of ordinary real-estate mortgages, the only criterion being the certainty of punctual payments. In the same way **the risk attached to an ordinary commercial business is measured by the chance of its losing money, not by what would happen if the owner were forced to sell.**

In Chapter 8 we shall set forth our conviction that **the bona fide investor does not lose money merely because the market price of his holdings declines; hence the fact that a decline may occur does not mean that he is running a true risk of loss. If a group of well-selected common-stock investments shows a satisfactory overall return, as measured through a fair number of years, then this group investment has proved to be "safe." During that period its market value is bound to fluctuate, and as likely as not it will sell for a while under the buyer's cost. If that fact makes the investment "risky," it would then have to be called both risky and safe at the same time.** This confusion may be avoided if we apply the concept of risk solely to a loss of value which either is realized through actual sale, or is caused by a significant deterioration in the company's position—or, more frequently perhaps, is the result of the payment of an excessive price in relation to the intrinsic worth of the security.[2]

Many common stocks do involve risks of such deterioration. But it is our thesis that a properly executed group investment in common stocks does not carry any substantial risk of this sort and that therefore it should not be termed "risky" merely because of the element of price fluctuation. But such risk is present if there is danger that the price may prove to have been clearly too high by intrinsic-value standards—even if any subsequent severe market decline may be recouped many years later.

Note on the Category of "Large, Prominent, and Conservatively Financed Corporations"

The quoted phrase in our caption was used earlier in the chapter to describe the kind of common stocks to which defensive investors should limit their purchases—provided also that they had paid continuous dividends for a considerable number of years. A criterion based on adjectives is always ambiguous. Where is the dividing line for size, for prominence, and for conservatism of financial structure? On the last point we can suggest a specific standard that, though arbitrary, is in line with accepted thinking. An industrial company's finances are not conservative unless the common stock (at book value) represents at least half of the total capitalization, including all bank debt.[3] For a railroad or public utility the figure should be at least 30%.

The words "large" and "prominent" carry the notion of substantial size combined with a leading position in the industry. Such companies are often referred to as "primary"; all other common stocks are then called "secondary," except that growth stocks are ordinarily placed in a separate class by those who buy them as such. To supply an element of concreteness here, let us suggest that to be "large" in present-day terms a company should have $50 million of assets or do $50 million of business.* Again to be "prominent" a company should rank among the first quarter or first third in size within its industry group.

It would be foolish, however, to insist upon such arbitrary criteria. They are offered merely as guides to those who may ask for guidance. But any rule which the investor may set for himself and which does no violence to the common-sense meanings of "large" and "prominent" should be acceptable. By the very nature of the case there must be a large group of companies that some will and others will not include among those suitable for defensive investment. There is no harm in such diversity of opinion and action. In fact, it has a salutary effect upon stock-market conditions, because it permits a gradual differentiation or transition between the categories of primary and secondary stock issues.

---

* In today's U.S. markets, to be considered large, a company should have a total stock value (or "market capitalization") of at least $15 billion, or book value and annual revenue approximating at least $5 billion and $10 billion, respectively.

Commentary on Chapter 5
by Jason Zweig

> The line I draw in the sand is that if an asset has cash flow or the likelihood of cash flow in the near term and is not purely dependent on what a future buyer might pay, then it's an investment. If an asset's value is totally dependent on the amount a future buyer might pay, then its purchase is speculation.
> —Seth Klarman[1]

The defensive investor, as Graham wrote in Chapter 4, wants to minimize the time and effort that investing takes and wants "freedom from concern."

The stock market isn't your only concern, though. You face two great external dangers as a defensive investor.

First, you need to fend off the brokerage industry.

Because defensive investors almost never trade, they generate no revenue for brokerage firms. What's called "the democratization of investing"—low-cost trading for anyone who has a smartphone with a brokerage app—is a compelling delusion. It sounds empowering, but it can transform defensive investors into hyperactive traders who make brokers rich.

You also need to defend against social contagion.

Once you let other people do your thinking for you, your single most valuable asset—your intellectual independence—is impaired. And once you lose part of your sense of self, losing financial wealth won't be far behind. By the time you recognize you've lost the ability to think for yourself, it will be too late.

---

[1] Jason Zweig, "Why One Legendary Investor Is More Worried Than Ever," May 18, 2010, bit.ly/3tS6V6i.

Gamification or Gamblification?

The companies behind such trading apps as eToro, Robinhood, tastytrade, and Webull often describe them as "gamification," but "gamblification" would be more accurate. We shouldn't liken trading apps to the games that can make education, fitness, dieting, and other activities more engaging and achievable. We should classify them with the poker, casino, and sports-betting apps and gambling machines that exploit vulnerable users and addict many of them.

A gamblified investing tool is fun to use, but it has three insidious features. It's designed to encourage short-term trading. It's potentially addictive. And it relies on manipulative techniques perfected by the gambling industry.[2]

Among those are:

- **bright, energetic audiovisual displays** that make stock prices resemble the spinning reels on a slot machine—highlighting the changes in your wealth, not the amount of your wealth;
- **scratch-off rewards** resembling lottery tickets, giving you a share of a random stock when you first sign up—and the excitement of playing with what feels like free money;
- **frequent alerts** notifying you of big moves and goading you to trade;
- **badges, trophies, or levels** ("Silver," "Gold," "Platinum"), getting your competitive juices flowing;
- **lists** of the hottest or most-popular stocks;
- **copying and liking**, in which you can mimic or praise other people's trades (as they can yours);
- **leaderboards** showing who's making the most money.

Gamblified apps also goad users into trading options contracts, which are much riskier and generate far higher brokerage fees.[3]

Casinos are designed to maximize what operators call TOD, or

---

[2] Philip W. S. Newall and Leonardo Weiss-Cohen, "The Gamblification of Investing," bit.ly/44nZ0Kl; Maèva Flayelle et al., "A Taxonomy of Technology Design Features That Promote Potentially Addictive Online Behaviours," bit.ly/3wm9IWC.

[3] See the Commentary on Chapter 16.

"time on device." The longer you spend in front of a slot machine, the more certain you are to lose. You should immediately walk away if you hit the jackpot, but casinos have learned to glue you to your seat with hypnotic audiovisuals and "nanomonetization," the ability to place many small bets simultaneously. Gamblified brokerage apps follow the same principle of maximizing TOD. In 2020, while testing Robinhood, I temporarily became a trading addict myself.[4]

A study by the Ontario Securities Commission found that earning rewards prompted people to trade 39% more often; seeing a weekly list of top-traded stocks led participants to increase their trading of those same stocks by 14%. Gamblifying a brokerage app by adding badges, levels, and leaderboards can also change how investors think. Instead of seeking to fulfill their own financial goals, they will instead strive to beat everybody else—becoming up to twice as likely to buy a highly risky stock.[5]

The Faster You Run, the Behinder You Get

The fast trading encouraged by brokerage apps provides short-term fun—and long-term loss.

- Among more than 66,000 U.S. households using a major discount brokerage, those who traded the most underperformed those who traded the least by more than 7 percentage points annually.
- A study of roughly 20,000 retail brokerage customers in Brazil found that among those who kept making short-term trades for at least 300 days, 97% lost money.
- Fewer than 3% of active day traders in Taiwan earn a profit, although most can't stop trading. People with a history of losing money generate 75% of total trading.
- Contracts for difference, or CFDs, are a popular way to place

---

[4] Natasha Dow Schüll, *Addiction by Design: Machine Gambling in Las Vegas* (Princeton, 2014); Jason Zweig, "I Started Trading Hot Stocks on Robinhood. Then I Couldn't Stop," bit.ly/3NVuYHw.

[5] Ontario Securities Commission, "Digital Engagement Practices in Retail Investing," bit.ly/3rg29hb; Christoph Hüller et al., "When Financial Platforms Become Gamified, Consumers' Risk Preferences Change," bit.ly/3QcDCCT.

short-term bets on whether an asset's price will move up or down. On average, 74% to 89% of customers who trade CFDs lose money.⁶

The stock market should be what economists call a positive-sum game: As companies grow, their increasing earnings generate dividends and rising stock prices, enabling investors to build wealth.

If you gamble instead of investing, however, you turn the stock market into a negative-sum game: You miss out on reaping the rewards of long-term ownership, create unnecessary trading costs, and generate punitive tax bills. Instead of going along for the ride, you get taken for a ride.⁷

Is Gamblification an Education?

Proponents of gamblified brokerage apps defend them with such arguments as "Making investing fun is a great way to get young people to try it, even if they lose money at first," or "You have to take risks to learn how to manage them."

Why should inexperienced investors have to behave dangerously to learn how to behave safely? We don't get teenagers to drink responsibly by challenging them to chug down 50 shots of whiskey; we don't instruct young people how to drive by urging them to crash cars into brick walls at 100 mph; nor do we teach firearm safety by having novices take target practice by blasting shotguns at their own feet.

Gamblified brokerage apps that encourage impressionable people to practice dangerous investing behaviors are terrible—if not tragic—training for life.

---

⁶ Brad M. Barber and Terrance Odean, "Trading Is Hazardous to Your Wealth," bit.ly/3LZdE49; Fernando Chague et al., "Day Trading for a Living?," bit.ly/45D0qkU; Brad M. Barber et al., "Learning, Fast or Slow," bit.ly/3tvNn7n; European Securities and Markets Authority, bit.ly/45z1kyy.

⁷ The so-called "free" trading at apps like Robinhood isn't free. Although you may not pay a commission, costs *are* embedded in the price. Brokerage

The Wisdom of Crowds

It can seem rational to join the herd.

Our everyday experience and our evolutionary history teach us that crowds are often correct.

You probably wouldn't eat at a completely empty restaurant, purchase a product that has no positive online reviews, or buy a house that nobody else wants to bid on.

Learning from other people facilitates cooperation and collective problem-solving; groups often know more than one person does.

Also, it feels safer inside the herd. We all want to be popular, to belong to the "in" crowd. The bigger the group we belong to, the more compelling and irresistible its message will feel—and the size of an online crowd has no physical constraints. Millions can join. Own a soaring stock that you can chat about online with thousands of other people who all love it, and you will feel you belong to a pride of lions. Own a falling stock that nobody wants to touch, and you will feel like a skunk at a garden party.

What's more, if you're acting alone and make a mistake, you have no one to blame but yourself. If you go along with the crowd and it turns out to be wrong, you can shrug and say, "Everybody else was wrong, too."

Finally, a crowd can make things happen. Starting in 2020, swarms of investors coalescing on Reddit, Twitter, and Discord began to pool their buying power and drive up the prices of their favorite stocks: AMC Entertainment Holdings, GameStop, Bed Bath & Beyond, and many more. The leaders and early birds made profits hundreds of times larger than what they put in. By channeling the buying power of millions of small investors into a tiny number of stocks, they created a giant force that could send a company's shares soaring just by mentioning it online. Anyone could go along for the ride. Why not join the fun?

---

firms may pocket a portion of the bid/ask spread, the difference between the highest bid (the top price at which anyone offers to buy) and the lowest ask (the least anyone will accept to sell). They also earn "payment for order flow," a legal but almost invisible kickback.

The Madness of Crowds

Yet crowds aren't always right, and their errors are contagious.

That can be catastrophic, as when millions of people fall under the spell of murderous rabble-rousers like Hitler or Mussolini. Or it can be insidious, as when conspiracy theories become mental epidemics—and when baseless beliefs about investing go viral.

What separates the wisdom from the madness of the crowd?

In 1907, the statistician Francis Galton described the results of a contest at an agricultural fair in which nearly 800 visitors tried to guess the weight of an ox. Although many knew little or nothing about oxen and their guesses varied widely, the visitors' average estimate turned out to be the exact weight of the ox.[8]

Francis Galton's guessers had a variety of viewpoints, sought to win a prize for the most accurate guess, didn't know other people's estimates, and had to pay an entry fee. The sponsors of the contest collected all the guesses and tallied them fairly.

The judgments of that crowd were independent, confidential, diverse, incentivized, and aggregated—and, therefore, remarkably accurate at estimating simple values.[9]

In today's financial markets, online and social-media mobs seethe with emotion, but valuable information is scarce. Predictions are made in public, with countless strangers trying to influence other people's opinions. Popular "influencers" can set off stampedes, crushing cognitive diversity as millions of people rush to embrace the same beliefs. There are no barriers to entry, no easy way to authenticate claims of expertise, and no registry of how accurate or how extreme the opinions are.

All too often, the judgments of this sort of crowd are the opposite of Galton's: interdependent, public, homogenized, non-incentivized, and disaggregated. That can turn the wisdom of the crowd into madness.

The weight of an ox doesn't change with people's estimates of it.

---

[8] Francis Galton, "Vox Populi," bit.ly/44kPaZY, and "The Ballot-Box," bit.ly/3PzB9U3; Kenneth Wallis, "Revisiting Francis Galton's Forecasting Competition," bit.ly/443G5Fh.

[9] James Surowiecki, *The Wisdom of Crowds* (Doubleday, 2004); Michael J. Mauboussin, "Explaining the Wisdom of Crowds," bit.ly/3D0j4Hu; William J. Bernstein, *The Delusions of Crowds* (Grove Atlantic, 2021).

However, if millions of speculators suddenly decide that a stock is worth $100,000, it will skyrocket—at least temporarily—even if it's worthless.

Herd on the Street

Learning what other people think changes how you think. When you find out that a group of your peers disagrees with you, your choices become up to three times more likely to match theirs, although you will have no conscious awareness of being influenced. A single exposure to an opinion from someone described as an expert enhances your memory of the information and how favorably you view it. And agreeing with your peers or with purported experts will activate the same regions of the brain that process the anticipation of reward.

As information becomes more complex or ambiguous, you become more prone to interpret it the same way the crowd does. And social media, by design, amplifies views that resemble your own. One recent study found that investors on social media are five times more likely to follow users who agree with them and will see nearly three times as many messages they agree with than disagree with. Falling into this kind of echo chamber, the study showed, leads people to trade more—and earn lower returns.[10]

The more people "like" a post on social media, the higher the odds that you will like it as well. "Liking" a post already liked by lots of other people activates a key reward center in the human brain more intensely than liking a less-popular post. On public brokerage platforms, having other people "like" your trades can lead you to trade three times more often than those who don't receive such feedback.

Meanwhile, bucking the consensus engages circuits in the brain that generate pain, fear, anxiety, and disgust. If you've ever rooted against the home team in a crowded stadium or spoken up for your candidate in a room full of members of an opposing political party, you know how hard it feels not to fit in. The larger the group, the more painful standing alone becomes.[11]

---

[10] J. Anthony Cookson et al., "Echo Chambers," bit.ly/44KpkiC.
[11] Professional fund managers face the same pressures as individual investors—and seem to have little more success resisting them: Harrison

Worse, the algorithms embedded in social-media platforms like Facebook, Twitter, and TikTok appear to be designed to maximize the time you spend on your device. They do that by fixating your attention on celebrities, on people who agree with you, and on information and imagery that inflame your emotions. That makes certain content seem more prevalent than it is and thus more persuasive than it should be. These algorithms are an invisible but pervasive force field that pulls you away from thinking for yourself.[12]

Vaccinating Yourself Against Contagion

Because you may never realize how much a group is influencing your behavior and decisions, it's vital to protect yourself *before* you join the crowd.

First, don't join a group that has different values. You should marry your investments, not speed-date them—and associating with people who trade promiscuously is bound to infect your behavior. Seek out patient, like-minded investors at such online communities as bogleheads.org, HumbleDollar.com, MutualFundObserver.com, or ValueInvestorsClub.com.

Look for posts that:

- steer clear of "hot takes" on the latest headlines;
- avoid anger, boasting, and mockery;
- and reveal their sources by linking to long-term data and peer-reviewed research, rather than just making assertions without evidence.

Hong et al., "Thy Neighbor's Portfolio," bit.ly/44KJyZq; Richard W. Sias, "Institutional Herding," bit.ly/3pOeB7G; David S. Scharfstein and Jeremy C. Stein, "Herd Behavior and Investment," bit.ly/3JZJ8WS; Hao Jiang and Michela Verardo, "Does Herding Behavior Reveal Skill?," bit.ly/44p0aWN.

[12] Lauren E. Sherman et al., "The Power of the *Like* in Adolescence," bit.ly/4a596CG; Matthias Pelster and Bastian Breitmayer, "Attracting Attention from Peers," bit.ly/44M8osi; William J. Brady et al., "Algorithm-Mediated Social Learning in Online Social Networks," bit.ly/44GszY4.

> If you have views about which asset or investing strategy is right for you, write down your reasons for those beliefs before you explore what some online group is saying. Take no action without reviewing your original rationale and determining that there's a reasonable basis for changing it—grounded in data and evidence, not just the opinions of random people online.
>
> Remember that the internet and social media are reality-distortion fields: "Likes" and "upvotes" go to the loudest and brashest advice, not the best. Conflicts of interest abound but are often undisclosed. Automated bots skew which posts get the most attention.
>
> Paradoxically, the more expertise people have, the more often they will say "I don't know" or "It depends"—leading them to sound as if they know less than those who are often wrong but never in doubt. The ones who admit the limits of their knowledge are the ones to listen to.

Be an Investing Inchworm

To succeed as a defensive investor, you must be able to turn your back on the crowd; otherwise, you'll run the risk of almost constantly overreacting to news, opinion, and rumor.

Don't speculate; automate.

With *dollar-cost averaging*, you can invest a fixed amount of money at predetermined intervals: every week, every month, every quarter, every year, whenever you can, whatever you can afford. Your brokerage or fund company will automatically move the money from your bank in an electronic transfer, so you don't have to lift a finger.

Many corporate retirement plans and government pension systems do this for you, but using additional money of your own is another way to impose discipline on yourself.

Rather than jumping in and out of the market in giant leaps, become an inchworm, steadily adding more no matter what the market does. Such an automatic investment plan can't guarantee you won't lose money. But it compels you to keep investing even when the stock market is crashing, and it prevents you from heaving money impulsively into the market when stocks are soaring. These automated purchases are out of sight, out of mind, so you aren't making frequent ad-hoc decisions that you will second-guess or regret later.

By dollar-cost averaging with a simple basket of index funds and trading only to rebalance, you can put your entire portfolio on multiple levels of autopilot.

As Graham wrote about dollar-cost averaging in 1962:

> Such a policy will pay off ultimately, regardless of when it is begun, **provided** that it is adhered to conscientiously and courageously under all intervening conditions. This . . . presupposes that the dollar-cost-averager . . . will not be subject to the alternations of exhilaration and deep gloom that have accompanied the gyrations of the stock market for generations past.

In a speech the next year, he added:

> That way you buy more shares of stocks when the market level is low and fewer shares when it's high. That method has worked out extremely well for those who have had (a) the money, (b) the time, and (c) the character necessary to pursue a consistent policy over the years regardless of whether the market has been going up or down. If you can do that you are guaranteed satisfactory success in your investments. . . .[13]

Rather than following the herd, follow Graham's policies. In the short run, you'll miss out on a little fun; in the long run, you'll build a lot more wealth.

---

[13] Benjamin Graham, "Some Investment Aspects of Accumulation Through Equities," bit.ly/3RLiNjV, and "Securities in an Insecure World," bit.ly/449pBuT.

CHAPTER 6

Portfolio Policy for the Enterprising Investor: Negative Approach
by Benjamin Graham

The "aggressive" investor should start from the same base as the defensive investor, namely, a division of his funds between high-grade bonds and high-grade common stocks bought at reasonable prices.* He will be prepared to branch out into other kinds of security commitments, but in each case he will want a well-reasoned justification for the departure. There is a difficulty in discussing this topic in orderly fashion, because there is no single or ideal pattern for aggressive operations. The field of choice is wide; the selection should depend not only on the individual's competence and equipment but perhaps equally well upon his interests and preferences.

The most useful generalizations for the enterprising investor are of a negative sort. Let him leave high-grade preferred stocks to corporate buyers. Let him also avoid inferior types of bonds and preferred stocks unless they can be bought at bargain levels—which means ordinarily at prices at least 30% under par for high-coupon

---

* Here Graham has made a slip of the tongue. After insisting in Chapter 1 that the definition of an "enterprising" investor depends not on the amount of risk you seek, but the amount of work you are willing to put in, Graham falls back on the conventional notion that enterprising investors are more "aggressive." The rest of the chapter, however, makes clear that Graham stands by his original definition. (The great British economist John Maynard Keynes appears to have been the first to use the term "enterprise" as a synonym for analytical investment.)

issues, and much less for the lower coupons.* He will let someone else buy foreign-government bond issues, even though the yield may be attractive. He will also be wary of all kinds of new issues, including convertible bonds and preferreds that seem quite tempting and common stocks with excellent earnings confined to the recent past.

For standard bond investments the aggressive investor would do well to follow the pattern suggested to his defensive confrere, and make his choice between high-grade taxable issues, which can now be selected to yield about 7¼%, and good-quality tax-free bonds, which yield up to 5.30% on longer maturities.†

Second-Grade Bonds and Preferred Stocks

Since in late 1971 it is possible to find first-rate corporate bonds to yield 7¼%, and even more, it would not make much sense to buy second-grade issues merely for the higher return they offer. In fact corporations with relatively poor credit standing have found it virtually impossible to sell "straight bonds"—i.e., nonconvertibles—to the public in the past two years. Hence their debt financing has been done by the sale of convertible bonds (or bonds with warrants attached), which place them in a separate category. It follows that virtually all the nonconvertible bonds of inferior rating represent older issues which are selling at a large discount. Thus they offer the possibility of a substantial gain in principal value under favorable future conditions—which would mean here a combination of an improved credit rating for the company and lower general interest rates.

But even in the matter of price discounts and resultant chance of principal gain, the second-grade bonds are in competition with better issues. Some of the well-entrenched obligations with "old-

---

* "High-coupon issues" are corporate bonds paying above-average interest rates (in today's markets, at least 8%) or preferred stocks paying large dividend yields (6% or more). If a company must pay such high rates to borrow money, that is a fundamental signal that it is risky. "Second-grade bonds" are now called "high-yield" or "junk bonds."
† As of early 2024, the equivalent yields are roughly 5.5% on high-grade corporate bonds and 3.5% on 20-year tax-free municipal bonds.

style" coupon rates (2½% to 4%) sold at about 50 cents on the dollar in 1970. Examples: American Telephone & Telegraph 2⅝s, due 1986 sold at 51; Atchison Topeka & Santa Fe RR 4s, due 1995, sold at 51; McGraw-Hill 3⅞s, due 1992, sold at 50½.

Hence under conditions of late 1971 the enterprising investor can probably get from good-grade bonds selling at a large discount all that he should reasonably desire in the form of both income and chance of appreciation.

Throughout this book we refer to the possibility that **any well-defined and protracted market situation of the past may return in the future.** Hence we should consider what policy the aggressive investor might have to choose in the bond field if prices and yields of high-grade issues should return to former normals. For this reason we shall reprint here our observations on that point made in the 1965 edition, when high-grade bonds yielded only 4½%.

Something should be said now about investing in second-grade issues, which can readily be found to yield any specified return up to 8% or more. The main difference between first- and second-grade bonds is usually found in the number of times the interest charges have been covered by earnings. Example: In early 1964 Chicago, Milwaukee, St. Paul and Pacific 5% income debenture bonds, at 68, yielded 7.35%. But the total interest charges of the road, before income taxes, were earned only 1.5 times in 1963, against our requirement of 5 times for a well-protected railroad issue.[1]

Many investors buy securities of this kind because they "need income" and cannot get along with the meager return offered by top-grade issues. **Experience clearly shows that it is unwise to buy a bond or a preferred which lacks adequate safety merely because the yield is attractive.** (Here the word "merely" implies that the issue is not selling at a large discount and thus does not offer an opportunity for a substantial gain in principal value.) Where such securities are bought at full prices—that is, not many points under 100*—the chances are very great that at some future

---

* Bond prices are quoted in percentages of "par value," or 100. A bond priced at "85" is selling at 85% of its principal value; a bond originally offered for $10,000, but now selling at 85, will cost $8,500. When bonds sell below 100, they are called "discount" bonds; above 100, they become "premium" bonds.

time the holder will see much lower quotations. For when bad business comes, or just a bad market, issues of this kind prove highly susceptible to severe sinking spells; often interest or dividends are suspended or at least endangered, and frequently there is a pronounced price weakness even though the operating results are not at all bad.

As a specific illustration of this characteristic of second-quality senior issues, let us summarize the price behavior of a group of ten railroad *income bonds* in 1946–47. These comprise all of those which sold at 96 or more in 1946, their high prices averaging 102½. By the following year the group had registered low prices averaging only 68, a loss of one-third of the market value in a very short time. Peculiarly enough, the railroads of the country were showing much better earnings in 1947 than in 1946; hence the drastic price decline ran counter to the business picture and was a reflection of the selloff in the general market. But it should be pointed out that the shrinkage in these income bonds was proportionately larger than that in the *common stocks* in the Dow Jones industrial list (about 23%). Obviously the purchaser of these bonds at a cost above 100 could not have expected to participate to any extent in a further rise in the securities market. The only attractive feature was the income yield, averaging about 4.25% (against 2.50% for first-grade bonds, an advantage of 1.75% in annual income). Yet the sequel showed all too soon and too plainly that for the minor advantage in annual income the buyer of these second-grade bonds was risking the loss of a substantial part of his principal.

The above example permits us to pay our respects to the popular fallacy that goes under the sobriquet of a "businessman's investment." That involves the purchase of a security showing a larger yield than is obtainable on a high-grade issue and carrying a correspondingly greater risk. **It is bad business to accept an acknowledged possibility of a loss of principal in exchange for a mere 1 or 2% of additional yearly income.** If you are willing to assume some risk you should be certain that you can realize a really substantial gain in principal value if things go well. Hence a second-grade 5.5 or 6% bond *selling at par* is almost always a bad purchase. The same issue at 70 might make more sense—and if you are patient you will probably be able to buy it at that level.

Second-grade bonds and preferred stocks possess two

contradictory attributes which the intelligent investor must bear clearly in mind. Nearly all suffer severe sinking spells in bad markets. On the other hand, a large proportion recover their position when favorable conditions return, and these ultimately "work out all right." This is true even of (cumulative) preferred stocks that fail to pay dividends for many years. There were a number of such issues in the early 1940s, as a consequence of the long depression of the 1930s. During the postwar boom period of 1945–1947 many of these large accumulations were paid off either in cash or in new securities, and the principal was often discharged as well. As a result, large profits were made by people who, a few years previously, had bought these issues when they were friendless and sold at low prices.[2]

It may well be true that, in an overall accounting, the higher yields obtainable on second-grade senior issues will prove to have offset those principal losses that were irrecoverable. In other words, an investor who bought all such issues at their offering prices might conceivably fare as well, *in the long run,* as one who limited himself to first-quality securities, or even somewhat better.[3]

But for practical purposes the question is largely irrelevant. Regardless of the outcome, the buyer of second-grade issues at full prices will be worried and discommoded when their prices decline precipitately. Furthermore, he cannot buy enough issues to assure an "average" result, nor is he in a position to set aside a portion of his larger income to offset or "amortize" those principal losses which prove to be permanent. Finally, it is mere common sense to abstain from buying securities at around 100 if long experience indicates that they can probably be bought at 70 or less in the next weak market.

Foreign Government Bonds

All investors with even small experience know that foreign bonds, as a whole, have had a bad investment history since 1914. This was inevitable in the light of two world wars and an intervening world depression of unexampled depth. Yet every few years market conditions are sufficiently favorable to permit the sale of some new foreign issues at a price of about par. This phenomenon tells us a good deal about the working of the average investor's mind—and not only in the field of bonds.

We have no *concrete reason* to be concerned about the future history of well-regarded foreign bonds such as those of Australia or Norway. But we do know that, if and when trouble should come, the owner of foreign obligations has no legal or other means of enforcing his claim. Those who bought Republic of Cuba 4½s as high as 117 in 1953 saw them default their interest and then sell as low as 20 cents on the dollar in 1963. The New York Stock Exchange bond list in that year also included Belgian Congo 5¼s at 36, Greek 7s at 30, and various issues of Poland as low as 7. How many readers have any idea of the repeated vicissitudes of the 8% bonds of Czechoslovakia, since they were first offered in this country in 1922 at 96½? They advanced to 112 in 1928, declined to 67¾ in 1932, recovered to 106 in 1936, collapsed to 6 in 1939, recovered (unbelievably) to 117 in 1946, fell promptly to 35 in 1948, and sold as low as 8 in 1970!

Years ago an argument of sorts was made for the purchase of foreign bonds here on the grounds that a rich creditor nation such as ours was under moral obligation to lend abroad. Time, which brings so many revenges, now finds us dealing with an intractable balance-of-payments problem of our own, part of which is ascribable to the large-scale purchase of foreign bonds by American investors seeking a small advantage in yield. For many years past we have questioned the inherent attractiveness of such investments from the standpoint of the buyer; perhaps we should add now that the latter would benefit both his country and himself if he declined these opportunities.

New Issues Generally

It might seem ill-advised to attempt any broad statements about new issues as a class, since they cover the widest possible range of quality and attractiveness. Certainly there will be exceptions to any suggested rule. Our one recommendation is that **all investors should be wary of new issues—which means, simply, that these should be subjected to careful examination and unusually severe tests before they are purchased**.

There are two reasons for this double caveat. The first is that new issues have special salesmanship behind them, which calls therefore for a special degree of sales resistance.* The second is that most new issues are sold under "favorable market conditions"—which means favorable for the seller and consequently less favorable for the buyer.†

The effect of these considerations becomes steadily more important as we go down the scale from the highest-quality bonds through second-grade senior issues to common-stock flotations at the bottom. A tremendous amount of financing, consisting of the repayment of existing bonds at call price and their replacement by new issues with lower coupons, was done in the past. Most of this was in the category of high-grade bonds and preferred stocks. The buyers were largely financial institutions, amply qualified to protect their interests. Hence these offerings were carefully priced to meet the going rate for comparable issues, and high-powered salesmanship had little effect on the outcome. As interest rates fell lower and lower the buyers finally came to pay too high a price for these issues, and many of them later declined appreciably in the market. This is one aspect of the general tendency to sell new securities of all types when conditions are most favorable to the issuer; but in the case of first-quality issues the ill effects to the purchaser are likely to be unpleasant rather than serious.

The situation proves somewhat different when we study the lower-grade bonds and preferred stocks sold during the 1945–46 and 1960–61 periods. Here the effect of the selling effort is more apparent, because most of these issues were probably placed with

---

* New issues of common stock—initial public offerings or IPOs—normally are sold with an "underwriting discount" (a built-in commission) of 4% or more. By contrast, the buyer's commission on older shares of common stock can be close to zero. Whenever Wall Street makes much more for selling something new than for selling something old, the new will get the harder sell.

† Companies tend to offer new shares to the public when the stock market is near a peak. See Lubos Pastor and Pietro Veronesi, "Rational IPO Waves," bit.ly/450Y1Rd, and Owen Lamont and Jeremy Stein, "Investor Sentiment and Corporate Finance," bit.ly/3Kzmzc2.

individual and inexpert investors. It was characteristic of these offerings that they did not make an adequate showing when judged by the performance of the companies over a sufficient number of years. They did look safe enough, for the most part, if it could be assumed that the recent earnings would continue without a serious setback. The investment bankers who brought out these issues presumably accepted this assumption, and their salesmen had little difficulty in persuading themselves and their customers to a like effect. Nevertheless it was an unsound approach to investment, and one likely to prove costly.

Bull-market periods are usually characterized by the transformation of a large number of privately owned businesses into companies with quoted shares. This was the case in 1945–46 and again beginning in 1960. The process then reached extraordinary proportions until brought to a catastrophic close in May 1962. After the usual "swearing-off" period of several years the whole tragicomedy was repeated, step by step, in 1967–1969.*

New Common-Stock Offerings

The following paragraphs are reproduced unchanged from the 1959 edition, with comment added:

> Common-stock financing takes two different forms. In the case of companies already listed, additional shares are offered pro rata to the existing stockholders. The subscription price is set below the current market, and the "rights" to subscribe have an initial

---

* In the two years from June 1960 through May 1962, more than 850 companies sold their stock to the public for the first time—an average of more than one per day. In late 1967 the IPO market heated up again; in 1969 an astonishing 781 new stocks were born. That oversupply helped create the bear markets of 1969 and 1973–1974. In 1974 the IPO market was so dead that only nine new stocks were created all year. That undersupply fed the bull market of the 1980s, when roughly 4,000 new stocks sprang up, ultimately triggering the overenthusiasm that led to the 1987 crash. In the late 1990s, Wall Street got back into the business of creating new stocks, cranking out nearly 5,000

money value.* The sale of the new shares is almost always underwritten by one or more investment banking houses, but it is the general hope and expectation that all the new shares will be taken by the exercise of the subscription rights. Thus the sale of additional common stock of listed companies does not ordinarily call for active selling effort on the part of distributing firms.

The second type is the placement with the public of common stock of what were formerly privately owned enterprises. **Most of this stock is sold for the account of the controlling interests to enable them to cash in on a favorable market and to diversify their own finances.** (When new money is raised for the business it comes often via the sale of preferred stock, as previously noted.) This activity follows a well-defined pattern, which by the nature of the security markets must bring many losses and disappointments to the public. The dangers arise both from the character of the businesses that are thus financed and from the market conditions that make the financing possible.

In the early part of the century a large proportion of our leading companies were introduced to public trading. As time went on, the number of enterprises of first rank that remained closely held steadily diminished; hence original common-stock flotations have tended to be concentrated more and more on relatively small concerns. By an unfortunate correlation, during

---

IPOs. Then, after the bubble burst in 2000, only 88 IPOs were issued in 2001—the lowest annual total since 1979. In every case, the public has gotten burned on IPOs, stayed away for at least two years, then returned for another scalding. For as long as stock markets have existed, investors have gone through this manic-depressive cycle. In America's first great IPO boom, back in 1825, a man was said to have been squeezed to death in the stampede of speculators trying to buy shares in the new Bank of Southwark; the wealthiest buyers hired thugs to punch their way to the front of the line. Sure enough, by 1829, stocks had lost roughly 25% of their value.

* Here Graham is describing rights offerings, in which investors who already own a stock are asked to pony up even more money to maintain the same proportional interest in the company. This form of financing, still widespread in Europe, has become rare in the U.S., except among closed-end funds.

the same period the stock-buying public has been developing an ingrained preference for the major companies and a similar prejudice against the minor ones. This prejudice, like many others, tends to become weaker as bull markets are built up; **the large and quick profits shown by common stocks as a whole are sufficient to dull the public's critical faculty, just as they sharpen its acquisitive instinct.** During these periods, also, quite a number of privately owned concerns can be found that are enjoying excellent results—although most of these would not present too impressive a record if the figures were carried back, say, ten years or more.

When these factors are put together the following consequences emerge: Somewhere in the middle of the bull market the first common-stock flotations make their appearance. These are priced not unattractively, and some large profits are made by the buyers of the early issues. As the market rise continues, this brand of financing grows more frequent; the quality of the companies becomes steadily poorer; the prices asked and obtained verge on the exorbitant. One fairly dependable sign of the approaching end of a bull swing is the fact that new common stocks of small and nondescript companies are offered at prices somewhat higher than the current level for many medium-sized companies with a long market history. (It should be added that very little of this common-stock financing is ordinarily done by banking houses of prime size and reputation.)*

The heedlessness of the public and the willingness of selling organizations to sell whatever may be profitably sold can have only one result—price collapse. In many cases the new issues lose 75% and more of their offering price. The situation is worsened by the aforementioned fact that, at bottom, the public

---

* In Graham's day, the most prestigious investment banks generally steered clear of the IPO business, which was regarded as an undignified exploitation of naïve investors. By the peak of the IPO boom in late 1999 and early 2000, however, Wall Street's biggest investment banks had jumped in with both feet. And the frenzy among major brokerage firms to foist SPACs on the eager speculative public in 2020 and 2021 should live in financial infamy for decades to come. (See the Commentary on this chapter.)

has a real aversion to the very kind of small issue that it bought so readily in its careless moments. Many of these issues fall, proportionately, as much below their true value as they formerly sold above it.

An elementary requirement for the intelligent investor is an ability to resist the blandishments of salesmen offering new common-stock issues during bull markets. Even if one or two can be found that can pass severe tests of quality and value, it is probably bad policy to get mixed up in this sort of business. Of course the salesman will point to many such issues which have had good-sized market advances—including some that go up spectacularly the very day they are sold. But all this is part of the speculative atmosphere. It is easy money. **For every dollar you make in this way you will be lucky if you end up by losing only two.**

Some of these issues may prove excellent buys—a few years later, when nobody wants them and they can be had at a small fraction of their true worth.

In the 1965 edition we continued our discussion of this subject as follows:

> While the broader aspects of the stock market's behavior since 1949 have not lent themselves well to analysis based on long experience, the development of new common-stock flotations proceeded exactly in accordance with ancient prescription. It is doubtful whether we ever before had so many new issues offered, of such low quality, and with such extreme price collapses, as we experienced in 1960–1962.[4] The ability of the stock market as a whole to disengage itself rapidly from that disaster is indeed an extraordinary phenomenon, bringing back long-buried memories of the similar invulnerability it showed to the great Florida real-estate collapse in 1925.
>
> Must there be a return of the new-stock-offering madness before the present bull market can come to its definitive close? Who knows? But we do know that an intelligent investor will not forget what happened in 1962 and will let others make the next batch of quick profits in this area and experience the consequent harrowing losses.

Portfolio Policy for the Enterprising Investor: Negative Approach

We followed these paragraphs in the 1965 edition by citing "A Horrible Example," namely, the sale of stock of Aetna Maintenance Co. at $9 in November 1961. In typical fashion the shares promptly advanced to $15; the next year they fell to 2⅜, and in 1964 to ⅞. The later history of this company was on the extraordinary side, and illustrates some of the strange metamorphoses that have taken place in American business, great and small, in recent years. The curious reader will find the older and newer history of this enterprise in Appendix 5 (see pp. 575–576 of the 2003 edition).

It is by no means difficult to provide even more harrowing examples taken from the more recent version of "the same old story," which covered the years 1967–1970. Nothing could be more pat to our purpose than the case of AAA Enterprises, which happens to be the first company then listed in Standard & Poor's *Stock Guide*. The shares were sold to the public at $14 in 1968, promptly advanced to 28, but in early 1971 were quoted at a dismal 25¢. (Even this price represented a gross overvaluation of the enterprise, since it had just entered the bankruptcy court in a hopeless condition.) There is so much to be learned, and such important warnings to be gleaned, from the story of this flotation that we have reserved it for detailed treatment below, in Chapter 17.

Commentary on Chapter 6

by Jason Zweig

> If you can admit a mistake when it is the size of an acorn, it will be easier to repair than if you wait until it becomes the size of a tree, with deep, wide-ranging roots.
> —Carol Tavris and Elliot Aronson[1]

Even if you're an enterprising investor, you still need to be on the defensive—both against those who want you to lock up your money and those who want you to keep it in constant motion.

Focusing on what to do is fun, but focusing on what not to do is vital. Otherwise, as Graham warns, "for every dollar you make" as an enterprising investor, "you will be lucky if you end up by losing only two."

The Alternative Universe

One potential mistake of enterprising investors is locking money up for years at high fees in pursuit of big gains.

What investors *see* often depends on its *fee*. The more bankers, brokers, and financial advisers can earn from an asset, the harder they'll push to sell it.

In the 1980s and 1990s, that meant constant pressure on investors to buy high-cost mutual funds and annuities, as well as initial public offerings (IPOs).[2] Lately, the arm-twisting has shifted to "alternative"

---

[1] Carol Tavris and Elliot Aronson, *Mistakes Were Made (but Not by Me)* (Mariner, 2020), p. 296.

[2] Chapter 9 and its Commentary discuss mutual funds. Annuities are insurance contracts that provide income, usually over a multiyear period, in exchange for an upfront fee and other charges. In an IPO, a private company sells some of its shares to the public, generating 4% or more in fees for investment banks and brokerage firms.

assets such as hedge funds, private-equity funds that buy out entire companies, venture capital that finances start-ups, private-credit funds specializing in non-traded debt, and portfolios of private real estate.

These assets are tantalizing for enterprising investors, promising potentially superior returns and the warm glow of owning funds that historically were available only to the elite.

Prestige comes at a price.

Between 2013 and 2022, private-equity, venture-capital, real-estate, and other private funds raised a total of $11.7 trillion worldwide, according to PitchBook Data. Investors paid managers and marketers hundreds of billions of dollars in cumulative fees and expenses.

The costs investors pay at one popular "fund of funds"—a non-traded portfolio that invests in a bundle of other non-traded funds—are extreme but hardly unique:

TABLE 6-1: Fee Hive

Fees and expenses at a leading "alternative" fund:

Upfront fees	
Maximum sales charge	3.00%
Annual expenses	
Advisory fee	1.20%
Interest payments on borrowed funds	0.02%
Other expenses	1.60%
Acquired funds' fees and expenses	4.67%
Total annual expenses	7.49%

Notes: Sales charge is percentage of offering price. Expenses are percentages of net assets.

Source: Prospectus, SkyBridge Multi-Adviser Hedge Fund Portfolios LLC Multi-Strategy Series G, July 23, 2023, bit.ly/3GuDGcp.

Here, two things are possible, and one is certain.
  You *might* get a good return.
  You *might* be able to get your money out when you need to.
  You *will* pay high fees.

Alternative funds often don't trade publicly or even disclose exactly what they own. Many update their prices (and permit withdrawals) only monthly or quarterly—sometimes even less often. Promoters say these funds operate in private markets dominated by sophisticated investors immune to the short-term pressures of public markets. Therefore, the story goes, alternatives offer longer investment horizons, lower risks, and higher returns—making their fees worth paying.

Let's think about that.

Does the absence of public trading mean prices can't go down? Of course not. Venture-capital funds slumped 65% as technology stocks collapsed in the early 2000s; private real-estate funds lost 63% during the global financial crisis in the late 2000s.

Markets work best when they are both deep (with many participants) and wide (with strong differences of opinion). That's a good description of public trading in the stock market much of the time.[3]

Private markets have far fewer participants, who tend to move in the same circles, share similar beliefs, and hold similar portfolios. Instead of being deep and wide, private markets are shallow and narrow; rather than being independent, they're codependent. In such a clubby atmosphere, private-market valuations can end up relying more on faith, guesswork, and groupthink than on original analysis.

A survey of nearly 900 venture capitalists reported that when deciding which companies to invest in, 44% "often make a gut decision," and 9% said they use no financial metrics at all. A survey of dozens of private-equity executives found that whether a company is cheap isn't a major determinant of whether to invest, and "very few" evaluate companies by estimating future earnings or cash flows.[4]

Look at the fiascos of blood-testing start-up Theranos Inc., office-sharing firm WeWork, and cryptocurrency exchange FTX.

---

[3] Not *all* the time. See Chapter 8 and its Commentary.
[4] Paul A. Gompers et al., "How Do Venture Capitalists Make Decisions?," bit.ly/3XOsTBL; and "What Do Private Equity Firms Say They Do?," bit.ly/3rnxoHr.

The private venture-capital market valued Theranos at $9 billion in 2014, FTX at $32 billion in 2022, and WeWork at $47 billion in 2018.[5]

Theranos shut down in 2018; its founder was sentenced to 11 years in prison for fraud. FTX and WeWork filed for bankruptcy protection in late 2022 and in 2023, respectively. FTX's founder Sam Bankman-Fried was sentenced in March 2024 to serve 25 years in prison for stealing billions of dollars from the exchange's customers.

These flame-outs were funded by some of the world's most renowned hedge funds and private-equity and venture-capital firms—which charged gigantic fees for due diligence they apparently didn't do.

The public stock market makes absurd mistakes, too, but it doesn't pretend to be omniscient and doesn't charge an arm and a leg.

To Invest Like Yale, *Be* Like Yale

The longtime head of Yale University's endowment, David Swensen, who died in 2021, pioneered investing in such alternatives as hedge funds, private equity, and non-traded real estate. Over his 35-year tenure, Yale's portfolio gained an average of 13.1% annually, far surpassing its peers and U.S. and global stock markets.

Swensen explained that private assets were more risky and less liquid than stocks and bonds—and, therefore, could earn higher returns. At the same time, he warned, the gap between winners and losers in private assets is much wider than in public markets. Therefore, the potentially superior returns in alternative funds can be captured *only* by specialized investors who can withstand higher risk and lower liquidity.[1]

To invest like Yale, you must be like Yale. It has extraordinary advantages:

---

[1] David F. Swensen, *Pioneering Portfolio Management* (Free Press, 2000).

---

[5] For brilliant accounts of the rise and fall of WeWork and Theranos, respectively, see Eliot Brown and Maureen Farrell, *The Cult of We* (Crown, 2021), and John Carreyrou, *Bad Blood* (Knopf, 2018).

- **Expertise.** A large, experienced staff at Yale specializes in analyzing these funds. Do you or your advisers have long, deep experience studying alternative funds' fees, managers, and methods of valuing assets?
- **Time.** Founded in 1701 and likely to survive for centuries more, Yale has the luxury of investing for decades at a time. Do you?
- **Size.** Yale's endowment exceeds $40 billion, granting it special access to the world's best alternative funds and enabling it to diversify across many at once. Can you?
- **Resilience.** As a perpetual institution, Yale can outlast severe interim—even permanent—losses on its private funds. Can you survive deep losses and the inability to sell?
- **Cash.** Yale derives additional income from tuition, gifts, and grants, so it can cut spending if its portfolio underperforms. And it can deploy surplus capital when falling markets create bargains. Do you have multiple sources of ample income?

If—*but only if*—you can answer yes to all five of those questions, alternative investments may be right for you.[2]

---

[2] Laurence B. Siegel, "Alternatives for the Masses?," bit.ly/3O7T2YZ.

Push Back Against What's Being Pushed

Pensions and endowments—the ultimate "sophisticated" investors—have sunk 30% to 60% of their assets into alternative funds. As a result, investment consultant Richard Ennis estimates, these institutions have underperformed a simple portfolio of roughly 70% stocks and 30% bonds by as much as two percentage points annually since 2008.[6]

---

[6] Richard M. Ennis, "Excellence Gone Missing," bit.ly/3NQ4xmH. For other evidence of below-average returns, see Arthur Korteweg, "Risk Adjustment in Private Equity Returns," bit.ly/3Of4NNf; Simon Lack, *The Hedge Fund Mirage* (Wiley, 2012); and Daniel Rasmussen, "Private Equity: Overvalued and Overrated?," bit.ly/3XPsn6F.

Yet promoters say *you* can use alternative funds to earn superior returns.

Can you? In addition to the guidelines in "To Invest Like Yale, Be Like Yale," you should rely on some of the virtues I described in the Commentary on the Introduction. *Independence* will tell you not to invest in alternatives just because "everybody else" is. *Humility* will counsel you that, as an individual investor, you're unlikely to be offered the opportunity to invest in the few superlative funds that welcome giants like Yale. *Skepticism* will remind you that private funds are hyped by salespeople earning fat fees, that survivorship bias skews the reported numbers, and that even most institutional investors don't come out ahead on alternative assets.

Margin for Error

While the financial industry pressured many enterprising investors to lock up money in alternative funds that will charge high fees in perpetuity, it was goading others into putting money into perpetual motion.

During the boom of 2020–21, many inexperienced investors bought risky assets with *margin debt*, money they borrowed from their broker.

Like all forms of leverage, margin increases your potential gains—and magnifies your potential losses. Many trading apps encouraged newly minted investors to take on margin by describing it as a way of doubling your "buying power."

Margin also doubles your losing power.

Imagine you buy 100 shares of stock at $50 using 50% margin, the regulatory limit in the U.S. Of the $5,000 you paid, $2,500 is your money; $2,500 came from your broker. If the stock goes up to $75, the shares are worth a total of $7,500, a gain of $2,500—or a 100% profit on the money you put in. If you'd put up the entire $5,000 yourself without borrowing, you'd have "only" a 50% gain.

What happens if the stock goes down, not up, $25? If you'd used only your own money to buy it, your holding would be worth $2,500, a 50% loss. If you used margin, that $2,500 loss would incinerate your entire investment.[7]

---

[7] SEC.gov, "Understanding Margin Accounts," bit.ly/3O6Zb7U. You also owe the broker interest on the margin loan.

Ben Graham himself was nearly wiped out by margin debt in the Great Depression—a mistake he never repeated. "I haven't the slightest doubt," he said in 1963, "that nine people out of ten who have margin accounts with brokers are *ipso facto* speculators."[8]

I believe what Graham meant is that using margin can transform you, unwittingly and unwillingly, from an investor into a speculator.

Let's say, to use Graham's words from Chapter 1, that "upon thorough analysis," you've decided a stock "promises safety of principal and an adequate return" and you intend to hold it for years, even decades.

If you bought that stock on margin and it goes down, it has become even cheaper than when you first bought it. But you might no longer be able to buy more; you'll have to add cash to your account just to keep your broker from seizing the stock from you in a "margin call." Constant updates from the brokerage app on your phone may crank up your anxiety (see the sidebar on p. 153). Fear could make you freak out and sell a stock you intended to hold.

In 2022, margin loans plunged from $519 billion to $371 billion, according to the Federal Reserve, probably because brokerage customers paid them off with panic-selling of stock to prevent even worse losses.

One final point: Hedge funds, private-equity and private-credit funds, as well as other alternative portfolios, commonly use leverage. Even though *you* might not have borrowed to invest in them, if *they* borrowed to buy their assets, then you have effectively taken on margin through them.

That makes your overall portfolio riskier—a handicap the promoters of alternatives almost never mention.

---

[8] Benjamin Graham, "The Future of Financial Analysis," in Jason Zweig and Rodney N. Sullivan, *Benjamin Graham: Building a Profession* (McGraw-Hill, 2010), p. 240.

> **App-sorbed**
>
> Half the world's population is expected to suffer from myopia by 2050. Although the problem is too new to have been comprehensively studied, some vision scientists believe that excessive use of smartphones may be contributing to this worldwide epidemic of nearsightedness.
>
> Just as staring at that little screen for a few hours every day might retrain your eye away from easily focusing on distant objects, so it might retrain your mind away from setting and achieving long-term investing goals.
>
> Studies in Brazil, China, South Korea, and elsewhere have found that young people who can't put their smartphones down tend to make impulsive decisions. Smartphone addicts prefer smaller rewards sooner over larger rewards later; they also are relatively indifferent to losses and struggle to distinguish profitable from unprofitable gambles. Overusing your smartphone may also impair your ability to solve math problems and think creatively.
>
> The people who run your online brokerage know all this. That's why they want you to trade using smartphone apps. The more time you spend on that device, the more often you're likely to trade, making money for the brokerage regardless of whether you make any for yourself.
>
> In the old days, you had to talk with your stockbroker over the phone or face-to-face before a purchase or sale. That—and your broker's punitively high commissions—introduced a layer of friction between your impulses and your actions. Your stockbroker was out to pick your pocket, and you knew it.
>
> Nowadays, your stockbroker is *in* your pocket, on your phone. That could lead not just to visual myopia, but investing myopia as well.

SPACulative Fever

Another temptation for enterprising investors is to be a player: to join forces with celebrities and glide along in their slipstream toward greater wealth.

In recent years, such wealthy "influencers" as professional athletes Stephen Curry and Serena Williams, musicians Justin Bieber and Eminem, and actors Gwyneth Paltrow and Kevin Hart touted their NFTs, or non-fungible tokens—helping set off a buying frenzy in these digital assets. Among the hottest of NFTs were the Bored Ape Yacht Club, colorful electronic caricatures of weary-eyed, stubbly-faced primates in sailor suits, sometimes selling for more than $1 million. By late 2022, trading volume had collapsed, and many NFTs had fallen in price by more than 90%.

Perhaps no recent investment benefited more from famous backers than special-purpose acquisition companies. SPACs have no assets or earnings. They're a bet on something that doesn't exist yet, as they raise money through an IPO, or initial public offering of stock, to buy other firms by a predetermined deadline, often 24 months.

In 2020–21, such celebrity entrepreneurs as airline and music magnate Richard Branson and former Facebook executive Chamath Palihapitiya attracted countless investors to buy shares in their SPACs.

For a brief and shining moment, fame seemed to ensure fortune.

In 2020, 248 SPACs raised a total of $83 billion in the U.S.; in 2021, 613 raised more than $160 billion, mostly in the beginning of the year. Gains of more than 50% in a single day attracted swarms of new buyers.

Unfortunately, as Graham warns in Chapter 6, "large and quick profits . . . are sufficient to dull the public's critical faculty, just as they sharpen its acquisitive instinct." You can't build long-term wealth with blind-faith bets that billionaires will act in your best interest, or that assets and earnings will materialize out of thin air.

And if the only research you did was to notice the presence of a famous name, you forgot Graham's injunction that enterprising investors must commit significant time and energy before buying any asset.

SPACs bristle with conflicts of interest. Even a glance at the IPO prospectus, or disclosure document, of the typical offering should unfurl blazing red flags, including:

- insiders pay as little as a tenth of a penny per share to control 20% of the company;

- insiders reserve the right to compete directly against the SPAC with their own companies;
- managers potentially get paid by acquisition targets, giving them incentives to recommend deals they personally benefit from;
- "independent" directors, meant to serve as watchdogs, receive tens of thousands of shares at a fraction of market value;
- no assurance that insiders will remain invested in the SPAC;
- no assurance that the SPAC will ever find a business to buy.

SPACs are often called blank-check companies because outside investors give the insiders carte blanche to spend the proceeds on

FIGURE 6-1: SPACtacular

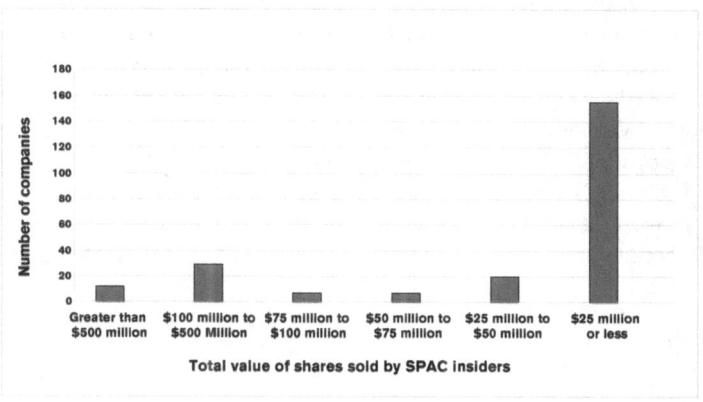

Source: *The Wall Street Journal.*

just about anything. Investment banks earn fees of 2% to 5% or more.

When insiders can make hundreds of millions of dollars for pushing an asset onto the investing public, they have an incentive to push very hard—and to get out while the getting's good.

As deal after deal fizzled, SPACs imploded. Between February and August 2021, SPACs lost $100 billion in combined market value.[9] Seldom has any investment turned so fast from a success to a slaughterhouse.

No Shortcuts

The problem isn't that investors never learn a lesson. It's that they learn the wrong lessons.

If you speculated on NFTs or SPACs and got wiped out, the lesson you learned was probably *Never speculate on NFTs or SPACs again!* The lesson you should have learned, however, is *Never speculate again!*

That's because the next bout of market madness won't tempt you with NFTs or SPACs. It will be some new disruption or transformation that sounds completely different and utterly seductive.

Every investing craze turns out to be another iteration of the same old story: the quest for the Holy Grail of high returns at low risk with no work. In the 1980s and early 1990s, it was mutual funds run by active managers. In the mid-1990s, it was emerging markets. In the late 1990s, it was internet stocks. In the early 2000s, it was real estate. Then it was "inverse" funds that benefit from falling markets. Next it was private alternatives, then cryptocurrency, NFTs, and SPACs.

The quest for the investing Holy Grail is always futile. To earn higher-than-average returns, you must take extra risk and you must commit additional time and effort. You're kidding yourself if you think there's a shortcut.

---

[9] Tom McGinty et al., "Company Insiders Made Billions Before SPAC Bust," bit.ly/3rXfSdy; Amrith Ramkumar, "SPAC Rout Erases $75 Billion in Startup Value," bit.ly/46wXd7F; Michael Klausner et al., "A Sober Look at SPACs," bit.ly/3M0G4eh.

CHAPTER 7

Portfolio Policy for the Enterprising Investor: The Positive Side

by Benjamin Graham

The enterprising investor, by definition, will devote a fair amount of his attention and efforts toward obtaining a better than run-of-the-mill investment result. In our discussion of general investment policy we have made some suggestions regarding *bond investments* that are addressed chiefly to the enterprising investor. He might be interested in special opportunities of the following kinds:

(1) Tax-free New Housing Authority bonds effectively guaranteed by the United States government.
(2) Taxable but high-yielding New Community bonds, also guaranteed by the United States government.
(3) Tax-free industrial bonds issued by municipalities, but serviced by lease payments made by strong corporations.

References have been made to these unusual types of bond issues in Chapter 4.*

At the other end of the spectrum there may be lower-quality bonds obtainable at such low prices as to constitute true bargain opportunities. But these would belong in the "special situation"

---

* As already noted (see p. 97, footnote †), the New Housing Authority and New Community bonds are no longer issued.

area, where no true distinction exists between bonds and common stocks.*

Operations in Common Stocks

The activities specially characteristic of the enterprising investor in the common-stock field may be classified under four heads:

1. Buying in low markets and selling in high markets
2. Buying carefully chosen "growth stocks"
3. Buying bargain issues of various types
4. Buying into "special situations"

General Market Policy—Formula Timing

We reserve for the next chapter our discussion of the possibilities and limitations of a policy of entering the market when it is depressed and selling out in the advanced stages of a boom. For many years in the past this bright idea appeared both simple and feasible, at least from first inspection of a market chart covering its periodic fluctuations. We have already admitted ruefully that the market's action in the past 20 years has not lent itself to operations of this sort on any mathematical basis. The fluctuations that have taken place, while not inconsiderable in extent, would have required a special talent or "feel" for trading to take advantage of them. This is something quite different from the intelligence which we are assuming in our readers, and we must exclude operations based on such skill from our terms of reference.

---

* Today these "lower-quality bonds" in the "special situation" area are known as distressed or defaulted bonds. When a company is in (or approaching) bankruptcy, its common stock becomes essentially worthless, since U.S. bankruptcy law entitles bondholders to a much stronger legal claim than shareholders. But if the company reorganizes successfully and comes out of bankruptcy, the bondholders often receive stock in the new firm, and the value of the bonds usually recovers once the company is able to pay interest again. In these special situations, as Graham puts it, "no true distinction exists between bonds and common stocks."

Portfolio Policy for the Enterprising Investor: The Positive Side

The 50–50 plan, which we proposed to the defensive investor and described on p. 91, is about the best specific or automatic formula we can recommend to all investors under the conditions of 1972. But we have retained a broad leeway between the 25% minimum and the 75% maximum in common stocks, which we allow to those investors who have strong convictions about either the danger or the attractiveness of the general market level. Some 20 years ago it was possible to discuss in great detail a number of clear-cut formulas for varying the percentage held in common stocks, with confidence that these plans had practical utility.[1] The times seem to have passed such approaches by, and there would be little point in trying to determine new levels for buying and selling out of the market patterns since 1949. That is too short a period to furnish any reliable guide to the future.*

Growth-Stock Approach

Every investor would like to select the stocks of companies that will do better than the average over a period of years. A growth stock may be defined as one that has done this in the past and is expected to do so in the future.[2] Thus it seems only logical that the intelligent investor should concentrate upon the selection of growth stocks. Actually the matter is more complicated, as we shall try to show.

It is a mere statistical chore to identify companies that have "outperformed the averages" in the past. The investor can obtain a list of 50 or 100 such enterprises from his broker.[†] Why, then, should he not merely pick out the 15 or 20 most likely looking issues of this group and lo! he has a guaranteed-successful stock portfolio?

---

* Note carefully what Graham is saying here. Writing in 1972, he contends that the period since 1949—a stretch of more than 22 years—is too short a period from which to draw reliable conclusions! With his mastery of mathematics, Graham never forgets that objective conclusions require very long samples of large amounts of data. The charlatans who peddle "back-tested" stock-picking gimmicks almost always base their hypothetical results on smaller samples than Graham would ever accept. (Graham often used 50-year periods to analyze past data.)

† Today, you can assemble such a list by googling a phrase such as "best performing stocks last 10 years" (or any other period you choose).

There are two catches to this simple idea. The first is that common stocks with good records and apparently good prospects sell at correspondingly high prices. The investor may be right in his judgment of their prospects and still not fare particularly well, merely because he has paid in full (and perhaps overpaid) for the expected prosperity. The second is that his judgment as to the future may prove wrong. Unusually rapid growth cannot keep up forever; when a company has already registered a brilliant expansion, its very increase in size makes a repetition of its achievement more difficult. At some point the growth curve flattens out, and in many cases it turns downward.

It is obvious that if one confines himself to a few chosen instances, based on hindsight, he could demonstrate that fortunes can readily be either made or lost in the growth-stock field. How can one judge fairly of the overall results obtainable here? We think that reasonably sound conclusions can be drawn from a study of the results achieved by the investment funds specializing in the growth-stock approach. The authoritative manual entitled *Investment Companies*, published annually by Arthur Wiesenberger & Company, members of the New York Stock Exchange, computes the annual performance of some 120 such "growth funds" over a period of years. Of these, 45 have records covering ten years or more. The average overall gain for these companies—unweighted for size of fund—works out at 108% for the decade 1961–1970, compared with 105% for the S & P composite and 83% for the DJIA.[3] In the two years 1969 and 1970 the majority of the 126 "growth funds" did worse than either index. Similar results were found in our earlier studies. The implication here is that no outstanding rewards came from diversified investment in growth companies as compared with that in common stocks generally.*

There is no reason at all for thinking that the average intelligent

---

* Over the 20 years ending December 31, 2002, 95.6% of funds investing in large growth companies—today's equivalent of what Graham calls "growth funds"—underperformed their benchmark. However, 90.9% of "large value" funds investing in more reasonably priced big companies also underperformed their respective benchmark over the same period. See bit.ly/47yjBwQ.

investor, even with much devoted effort, can derive better results over the years from the purchase of growth stocks than the investment companies specializing in this area. Surely these organizations have more brains and better research facilities at their disposal than you do. Consequently we should advise against the usual type of growth-stock commitment for the enterprising investor.* This is one in which the excellent prospects are fully recognized in the market and already reflected in a current price-earnings ratio of, say, higher than 20. (For the defensive investor we suggested an upper limit of purchase price at 25 times average earnings of the past seven years. The two criteria would be about equivalent in most cases.)†

The striking thing about growth stocks as a class is their tendency toward wide swings in market price. This is true of the largest and longest-established companies—such as General Electric and International Business Machines—and even more so of newer and smaller successful companies. They illustrate our thesis that the main characteristic of the stock market since 1949 has been the injection of a highly speculative element into the shares

---

* For another approach, see "What Makes Superstocks Super" in the Commentary on Chapter 15.

† Notice that Graham insists on calculating the price/earnings ratio based on a multiyear average of past earnings. That way, you lower the odds that you will overestimate a company's value based on a temporarily high burst of profitability. Imagine that a company earned $3 per share over the past 12 months, but an average of only 50 cents per share over the previous six years. Which number—the sudden $3 or the steady 50 cents—is more likely to represent a sustainable trend? At 25 times the $3 it earned in the most recent year, the stock would be priced at $75. But at 25 times the average earnings of the past seven years ($6 in total earnings, divided by seven, equals 85.7 cents per share in average annual earnings), the stock would be priced at only $21.43. Which number you pick makes a big difference. The prevailing method on Wall Street today—basing price/earnings ratios primarily on "next year's earnings"—would be anathema to Graham. How can you value a company based on earnings it hasn't even generated yet? That's like setting house prices based on a rumor that Cinderella will be building her new castle right around the corner.

of companies which have scored the most brilliant successes, and which themselves would be entitled to a high investment rating. (Their credit standing is of the best, and they pay the lowest interest rates on their borrowings.) **The investment caliber of such a** *company* **may not change over a long span of years, but the risk characteristics of its** *stock* **will depend on what happens to it in the stock market. The more enthusiastic the public grows about it, and the faster its advance as compared with the actual growth in its earnings, the riskier a proposition it becomes.***

But is it not true, the reader may ask, that the really big fortunes from common stocks have been garnered by those who made a substantial commitment in the early years of a company in whose future they had great confidence, and who held their original shares unwaveringly while they increased 100-fold or more in value? The answer is "Yes." But the big fortunes from single-company investments are almost always realized by persons who have a close relationship with the particular company—through employment, family connection, etc.—which justifies them in placing a large part of their resources in one medium and holding on to this commitment through all vicissitudes, despite numerous temptations to sell out at apparently high prices along the way. An investor without such close personal contact will constantly be faced with the question of whether too large a portion of his funds are in this one medium.† Each decline—however temporary it proves in the sequel—will accentuate his problem; and internal and external pressures are likely to force him to take what seems to be a goodly profit, but one far less than the ultimate bonanza.[4]

---

* That's why the stocks of fast-growing companies can drop 20% or more if they fall even one penny short of meeting Wall Street's high expectations for growth in earnings per share.

† Today's equivalent of investors "who have a close relationship with the particular company" are control persons—senior managers or directors who run the company and own huge blocks of stock. Executives like Elon Musk of Tesla or Mark Zuckerberg of Meta Platforms, Facebook's parent, have direct control over a company's destiny—and outside investors want them to maintain large shareholdings as a vote of confidence. But less-senior

TABLE 7-1 Average Results of "Growth Funds," 1961–1970[a]

	1 year 1970	5 years 1966–1970	10 years 1961–1970	1970 Dividend Return
17 large growth funds	−7.5%	+23.2%	+121.1%	2.3%
106 smaller growth funds—group A	−17.7	+20.3	+102.1	1.6
38 smaller growth funds—group B	−4.7	+23.2	+106.7	1.4
15 funds with "growth" in their name	−14.2	+13.8	+97.4	1.7
Standard & Poor's composite	+3.5%	+16.1	+104.7	3.4
Dow Jones Industrial Average	+8.7	+2.9	+83.0	3.7

[a] These figures are supplied by Wiesenberger Financial Services.

Three Recommended Fields for "Enterprising Investment"

To obtain better than average investment results over a long pull requires a policy of selection or operation possessing a twofold merit: (1) It must meet objective or rational tests of underlying soundness; and (2) it must be different from the policy followed by most investors or speculators. Our experience and study leads us to recommend three investment approaches that meet these criteria. They differ rather widely from one another, and each may require a different type of knowledge and temperament on the part of those who assay it.

The Relatively Unpopular Large Company

If we assume that it is the habit of the market to overvalue common stocks which have been showing excellent growth or are glamorous for some other reason, it is logical to expect that it will undervalue—relatively, at least—companies that are out of favor because of unsatisfactory developments of a temporary nature. This may be set down as a fundamental law of the stock market, and it suggests an investment approach that should prove both conservative and promising.

The key requirement here is that the enterprising investor concentrate on the larger companies that are going through a period of unpopularity. While small companies may also be undervalued for similar reasons, and in many cases may later increase their earnings and share price, they entail the risk of a definitive loss of profitability and also of protracted neglect by the market in spite of better earnings. The large companies thus have a double advantage over the others. First, they have the resources in capital and brain power to carry them through adversity and back to a satisfactory earnings base. Second, the market is likely to respond with reasonable speed to any improvement shown.

---

managers and rank-and-file workers can't influence the company's share price with their individual decisions; thus they should not put more than a small percentage of their assets in their own employer's stock. As for outside investors, no matter how well they think they know the company, the same objection applies.

Portfolio Policy for the Enterprising Investor: The Positive Side

A remarkable demonstration of the soundness of this thesis is found in studies of the price behavior of the unpopular issues in the Dow Jones Industrial Average. In these it was assumed that an investment was made each year in either the six or the ten issues in the DJIA which were selling at the lowest multipliers of their current or previous year's earnings. These could be called the "cheapest" stocks in the list, and their cheapness was evidently the reflection of relative unpopularity with investors or traders. It was assumed further that these purchases were sold out at the end of holding periods ranging from one to five years. The results of these investments were then compared with the results shown in either the DJIA as a whole or in the highest multiplier (i.e., the most popular) group.

The detailed material we have available covers the results of annual purchases assumed in each of the past 53 years.[5] In the early period, 1917–1933, this approach proved unprofitable. But since 1933 the method has shown highly successful results. In 34 tests made by Drexel & Company (now Drexel Firestone)* of one-year holding—from 1937 through 1969—the cheap stocks did definitely worse than the DJIA in only three instances; the results were about the same in six cases; and the cheap stocks clearly outperformed the average in 25 years. The consistently better performance of the low-multiplier stocks is shown (Table 7-2) by the average results for successive five-year periods, when compared with those of the DJIA and of the ten high-multipliers.

The Drexel computation shows further that an original investment of $10,000 made in the low-multiplier issues in 1936, and switched each year in accordance with the principle, would have grown to $66,900 by 1962. The same operations in high-multiplier stocks would have ended with a value of only $25,300; while an operation in all thirty stocks would have increased the original fund to $44,000.[†]

---

* Drexel Firestone, a Philadelphia investment bank, merged in 1973 with Burnham & Co. and later became Drexel Burnham Lambert, famous for its junk-bond financing of the 1980s takeover boom.
† This strategy of buying the cheapest stocks in the Dow Jones Industrial Average is nicknamed the "Dogs of the Dow." It became popular in the 1990s but has only worked sporadically in recent years.

TABLE 7-2 Average Annual Percentage Gain or Loss on Test Issues, 1937–1969

Period	10 Low-Multiplier Issues	10 High-Multiplier Issues	30 DJIA Stocks
1937–1942	−2.2	−10.0	−6.3
1943–1947	17.3	8.3	14.9
1948–1952	16.4	4.6	9.9
1953–1957	20.9	10.0	13.7
1958–1962	10.2	−3.3	3.6
1963–1969 (8 years)	8.0	4.6	4.0

The concept of buying "unpopular large companies" and its execution on a group basis, as described above, are both quite simple. But in considering individual companies a special factor of opposite import must sometimes be taken into account. Companies that are inherently speculative because of widely varying earnings tend to sell both at a relatively high price and at a relatively low multiplier in their good years, and conversely at low prices and high multipliers in their bad years. These relationships are illustrated in Table 7-3, covering fluctuations of Chrysler Corp. common. In these cases the market has sufficient skepticism as to the continuation of the unusually high profits to value them conservatively, and conversely when earnings are low or nonexistent. (Note that, by the arithmetic, if a company earns "next to nothing" its shares must sell at a high multiplier of these minuscule profits.)

As it happens Chrysler has been quite exceptional in the DJIA list of leading companies, and hence it did not greatly affect the low-multiplier calculations. It would be quite easy to avoid inclusion of such anomalous issues in a low-multiplier list by requiring also that the price be low in relation to past *average* earnings or by some similar test.

While writing this revision we tested the results of the DJIA-low-multiplier method applied to a group assumed to be bought at the end of 1968 and revalued on June 30, 1971. This time the

TABLE 7-3 Chrysler Common Prices and Earnings, 1952–1970

Year	Earnings Per Share	High or Low Price	P/E Ratio
1952	$ 9.04	H 98	10.8
1954	2.13	L 56	26.2
1955	11.49	H 101½	8.8
1956	2.29	L 52 (in 1957)	22.9
1957	13.75	H 82	6.7
1958	(def.) 3.88	L 44[a]	—
1968	24.92[b]	H 294[b]	11.8
1970	def.	L 65[b]	—

[a] 1962 low was 37½.
[b] Adjusted for stock splits. def.: Net loss.

figures proved quite disappointing, showing a sharp loss for the low-multiplier six or ten and a good profit for the high-multiplier selections. This one bad instance should not vitiate conclusions based on 30-odd experiments, but its recent happening gives it a special adverse weight. Perhaps the aggressive investor should start with the "low-multiplier" idea, but add other quantitative and qualitative requirements thereto in making up his portfolio.

Purchase of Bargain Issues

We define a bargain issue as one which, on the basis of facts established by analysis, appears to be worth considerably more than it is selling for. The genus includes bonds and preferred stocks selling well under par, as well as common stocks. To be as concrete as possible, let us suggest that an issue is not a true "bargain" unless the indicated value is at least 50% more than the price. What kind of facts would warrant the conclusion that so great a discrepancy exists? How do bargains come into existence, and how does the investor profit from them?

There are two tests by which a bargain common stock is detected. The first is by the method of appraisal. This relies largely on estimating future earnings and then multiplying these by a

factor appropriate to the particular issue. If the resultant value is sufficiently above the market price—and if the investor has confidence in the technique employed—he can tag the stock as a bargain. The second test is the value of the business to a private owner. This value also is often determined chiefly by expected future earnings—in which case the result may be identical with the first. But in the second test more attention is likely to be paid to the realizable value of the *assets*, with particular emphasis on the net current assets or working capital.

At low points in the general market a large proportion of common stocks are bargain issues, as measured by these standards. (A typical example was General Motors when it sold at less than 30 in 1941, equivalent to only 5 for the 1971 shares. It had been earning in excess of $4 and paying $3.50, or more, in dividends.) It is true that current earnings and the immediate prospects may both be poor, but a levelheaded appraisal of average future conditions would indicate values far above ruling prices. Thus the wisdom of having courage in depressed markets is vindicated not only by the voice of experience but also by application of plausible techniques of value analysis.

The same vagaries of the market place that recurrently establish a bargain condition in the general list account for the existence of many individual bargains at almost all market levels. **The market is fond of making mountains out of molehills and exaggerating ordinary vicissitudes into major setbacks. Even a mere lack of interest or enthusiasm may impel a price decline to absurdly low levels. Thus we have what appear to be two major sources of undervaluation: (1) currently disappointing results and (2) protracted neglect or unpopularity.**

However, neither of these causes, if considered by itself alone, can be relied on as a guide to successful common-stock investment. How can we be sure that the currently disappointing results are indeed going to be only temporary? True, we can supply excellent examples of that happening. The steel stocks used to be famous for their cyclical quality, and the shrewd buyer could acquire them at low prices when earnings were low and sell them out in boom years at a fine profit. A spectacular example is supplied by Chrysler Corporation, as shown by the data in Table 7-3.

If this were the *standard* behavior of stocks with fluctuating earnings, then making profits in the stock market would be an easy matter. Unfortunately, we could cite many examples of declines in earnings and price which were not followed automatically by a handsome recovery of both. One such was Anaconda Wire and Cable, which had large earnings up to 1956, with a high price of 85 in that year. The earnings then declined irregularly for six years; the price fell to 23½ in 1962, and the following year it was taken over by its parent enterprise (Anaconda Corporation) at the equivalent of only 33.

The many experiences of this type suggest that the investor would need more than a mere falling off in both earnings and price to give him a sound basis for purchase. He should require an indication of at least reasonable stability of earnings over the past decade or more—i.e., no year of earnings deficit—plus sufficient size and financial strength to meet possible setbacks in the future. The ideal combination here is thus that of a large and prominent company selling both well below its past average price and its past average price/earnings multiplier. This would no doubt have ruled out most of the profitable opportunities in companies such as Chrysler, since their low-price years are generally accompanied by high price/earnings ratios. But let us assure the reader now—and no doubt we shall do it again—that **there is a world of difference between "hindsight profits" and "real-money profits."** We doubt seriously whether the Chrysler type of roller coaster is a suitable medium for operations by our enterprising investor.

We have mentioned protracted neglect or unpopularity as a second cause of price declines to unduly low levels. A current case of this kind would appear to be National Presto Industries. In the bull market of 1968 it sold at a high of 45, which was only 8 times the $5.61 earnings for that year. The per-share profits increased in both 1969 and 1970, but the price declined to only 21 in 1970. This was less than 4 times the (record) earnings in that year and less than its net-current-asset value. In March 1972 it was selling at 34, still only 5½ times the last reported earnings, and at about its enlarged net-current-asset value.

Another example of this type is provided currently by Standard Oil of California, a concern of major importance. In early 1972 it was selling at about the same price as 13 years before, say 56. Its earnings had been remarkably steady, with relatively small growth but with only one small decline over the entire period. Its book value was about equal to the market price. With this conservatively favorable 1958–71 record the company has never shown an average annual price as high as 15 times its current earnings. In early 1972 the price/earnings ratio was only about 10.

A third cause for an unduly low price for a common stock may be the market's failure to recognize its true earnings picture. Our classic example here is Northern Pacific Railway, which in 1946–47 declined from 36 to 13½. The true earnings of the road in 1947 were close to $10 per share. The price of the stock was held down in great part by its $1 dividend. It was neglected also because much of its earnings power was concealed by accounting methods peculiar to railroads.

The type of bargain issue that can be most readily identified is a common stock that sells for less than the company's net working capital alone, after deducting all prior obligations.* This would mean that the buyer would pay nothing at all for the fixed assets—buildings, machinery, etc., or any good-will items that might exist. Very few companies turn out to have an ultimate value less than the working capital alone, although scattered instances may be found. The surprising thing, rather, is that there have been so many enterprises obtainable which have been valued in the market on this bargain basis. A compilation made in 1957, when the market's level was by no means low, disclosed about 150 of such common stocks. In Table 7-4 we summarize the result of buying, on December 31, 1957, one share of each of the 85 companies in that list for which data appeared in Standard & Poor's *Monthly Stock Guide*, and holding them for two years.

By something of a coincidence, each of the groups advanced in the two years to somewhere in the neighborhood of the aggregate net-current-asset value. The gain for the entire "portfolio" in that period was 75%, against 50% for Standard & Poor's 425 industrials. What is more remarkable is that none of the issues showed significant losses, seven held about even, and 78 showed appreciable gains.

Our experience with this type of investment selection—on

---

* By "net working capital," Graham means a company's current assets (such as cash, marketable securities, and inventories) minus its total liabilities (including preferred stock and long-term debt).

TABLE 7-4 Profit Experience of Undervalued Stocks, 1957–1959

Location of Market	Number of Companies	Aggregate Net Current Assets Per Share	Aggregate Price Dec. 1957	Aggregate Price Dec. 1959
New York S.E.	35	$ 748	$ 419	$ 838
American S.E.	25	495	289	492
Midwest S.E.	5	163	87	141
Over the counter	20	425	288	433
Total	85	$1,831	$1,083	$1,904

a diversified basis—was uniformly good for many years prior to 1957. It can probably be affirmed without hesitation that it constitutes a safe and profitable method of determining and taking advantage of undervalued situations. However, during the general market advance after 1957 the number of such opportunities became extremely limited, and many of those available were showing small operating profits or even losses. The market decline of 1969–70 produced a new crop of these "sub-working-capital" stocks. We discuss this group in Chapter 15, on stock selection for the enterprising investor.

Bargain-Issue Pattern in Secondary Companies

We have defined a secondary company as one that is not a leader in a fairly important industry. Thus it is usually one of the smaller concerns in its field, but it may equally well be the chief unit in an unimportant line. By way of exception, any company that has established itself as a growth stock is not ordinarily considered "secondary."

In the great bull market of the 1920s relatively little distinction was drawn between industry leaders and other listed issues, provided the latter were of respectable size. The public felt that a middle-sized company was strong enough to weather storms and that it had a better chance for really spectacular expansion than one that was already of major dimensions. The depression years 1931–32, however, had a particularly devastating impact on the companies below the first rank either in size or in inherent stability. As a result of that experience investors have since developed a pronounced preference for industry leaders and a corresponding lack of interest most of the time in the ordinary company of secondary importance. This has meant that the latter group have usually sold at much lower prices in relation to earnings and assets than have the former. It has meant further that in many instances the price has fallen so low as to establish the issue in the bargain class.*

When investors rejected the stocks of secondary companies, even though these sold at relatively low prices, they were expressing a belief or fear that such companies faced a dismal future. In fact, at least subconsciously, they calculated that *any* price was too high for them because they were heading for extinction—just as in 1929 the companion theory for the "blue chips" was that no price was too high for them because their future possibilities were limitless. Both of these views were exaggerations and were productive of serious investment errors. Actually, the typical middle-sized listed company is a large one when compared with the average privately owned business. There is no sound reason why such companies should not continue indefinitely in operation, undergoing the vicissitudes characteristic of our economy but earning on the whole a fair return on their invested capital.

This brief review indicates that the stock market's attitude toward secondary companies tends to be unrealistic and consequently to create in normal times innumerable instances of major undervaluation. As it happens, the World War II period and the postwar boom were more beneficial to the smaller concerns than to the larger ones, because then the normal competition for sales was suspended and the former could expand sales and profit margins more spectacularly. Thus by 1946 the market's pattern had completely reversed itself from that before the war. Whereas the leading stocks in the Dow Jones Industrial Average had advanced only 40% from the end of 1938 to the 1946 high, Standard & Poor's index of low-priced stocks had shot up no less than 280% in the

---

* This is no longer true. Private-equity firms, with trillions of dollars to spend, have bid up the share prices of "secondary" companies past bargain levels.

same period. Speculators and many self-styled investors—with the proverbial short memories of people in the stock market—were eager to buy both old and new issues of unimportant companies at inflated levels. Thus the pendulum had swung clear to the opposite extreme. The very class of secondary issues that had formerly supplied by far the largest proportion of bargain opportunities was now presenting the greatest number of examples of overenthusiasm and overvaluation. In a different way this phenomenon was repeated in 1961 and 1968—the emphasis now being placed on new offerings of the shares of small companies of less than secondary character, and on nearly all companies in certain favored fields such as "electronics," "computers," "franchise" concerns, and others.*

As was to be expected the ensuing market declines fell most heavily on these overvaluations. In some cases the pendulum swing may have gone as far as definite *under*valuation.

If most secondary issues tend normally to be undervalued, what reason has the investor to believe that he can profit from such a situation? For if it persists indefinitely, will he not always be in the same market position as when he bought the issue? The answer here is somewhat complicated. Substantial profits from the purchase of secondary companies at bargain prices arise in a variety of ways. First, the dividend return is relatively high. Second, the reinvested earnings are substantial in relation to the price paid and will ultimately affect the price. In a five- to seven-year period these advantages can bulk quite large in a well-selected list. Third, a bull market is ordinarily most generous to low-priced

---

* From 1975 through 1983, small ("secondary") stocks outperformed large stocks by an amazing average of 17.6 percentage points per year. The investing public eagerly embraced small stocks, mutual fund companies rolled out hundreds of new funds specializing in them, and small stocks obliged by *underperforming* large stocks by five percentage points per year over the next decade. The cycle recurred in 1999, when small stocks beat big stocks by nearly nine percentage points, inspiring investment bankers to sell hundreds of hot little high-tech stocks to the public for the first time. Instead of "electronics," "computers," or "franchise" in their names, the new buzzwords were ".com," "optical," "wireless," and even prefixes like "e-" and "I-." Investing buzzwords always turn into buzz saws, tearing apart anyone who believes in them.

issues; thus it tends to raise the typical bargain issue to at least a reasonable level. Fourth, even during relatively featureless market periods a continuous process of price adjustment goes on, under which secondary issues that were undervalued may rise at least to the normal level for their type of security. Fifth, the specific factors that in many cases made for a disappointing record of earnings may be corrected by the advent of new conditions, or the adoption of new policies, or by a change in management.

An important new factor in recent years has been the acquisition of smaller companies by larger ones, usually as part of a diversification program. In these cases the consideration paid has almost always been relatively generous, and much in excess of the bargain levels existing not long before.

When interest rates were much lower than in 1970, the field of bargain issues extended to bonds and preferred stocks that sold at large discounts from the amount of their claim. Currently we have a different situation in which even well-secured issues sell at large discounts if carrying coupon rates of, say, 4½% or less. Example: American Telephone & Telegraph 2⅝s, due 1986, sold as low as 51 in 1970; Deere & Co. 4½s, due 1983, sold as low as 62. These may well turn out to have been bargain opportunities before very long—if ruling interest rates should decline substantially. For a bargain bond issue in the more traditional sense perhaps we shall have to turn once more to the first-mortgage bonds of railroads now in financial difficulties, which sell in the 20s or 30s. Such situations are not for the inexpert investor; lacking a real sense of values in this area, he may burn his fingers. But there is an underlying tendency for market decline in this field to be overdone; consequently the group as a whole offers an especially rewarding invitation to careful and courageous analysis. In the decade ending in 1948 the billion-dollar group of defaulted railroad bonds presented numerous and spectacular opportunities in this area. Such opportunities have been quite scarce since then; but they seem likely to return in the 1970s.

Special Situations, or "Workouts"

Not so long ago this was a field which could almost guarantee an attractive rate of return to those who knew their way around in it; and this was true under almost any sort of general market situation. It was not actually forbidden territory to members of the general public. Some who had a flair for this sort of thing could learn the ropes and become pretty capable practitioners without the necessity of long academic study or apprenticeship. Others have been keen enough to recognize the underlying soundness of this approach and to attach themselves to bright young men who handled funds devoted chiefly to these "special situations." But in recent years, for reasons we shall develop later, the field of "arbitrages and workouts" became riskier and less profitable. It may be that in years to come conditions in this field will become more propitious. In any case it is worthwhile outlining the general nature and origin of these operations, with one or two illustrative examples.

The typical "special situation" has grown out of the increasing number of acquisitions of smaller firms by large ones, as the gospel of diversification of products has been adopted by more and more managements. It often appears good business for such an enterprise to acquire an existing company in the field it wishes to enter rather than to start a new venture from scratch. In order to make such acquisition possible, and to obtain acceptance of the deal by the required large majority of shareholders of the smaller company, it is almost always necessary to offer a price considerably above the current level. Such corporate moves have been producing interesting profit-making opportunities for those who have made a study of this field, and have good judgment fortified by ample experience.

A great deal of money was made by shrewd investors not so many years ago through the purchase of bonds of railroads in bankruptcy—bonds which they knew would be worth much more than their cost when the railroads were finally reorganized. After promulgation of the plans of reorganization a "when issued" market for the new securities appeared. These could almost always be sold for considerably more than the cost of the old issues which were to be exchanged therefor. There were risks of nonconsummation of the plans or of unexpected delays, but on the whole such "arbitrage operations" proved highly profitable.

There were similar opportunities growing out of the breakup of public-utility holding companies pursuant to 1935 legislation. Nearly all these enterprises proved to be worth considerably more when changed from holding companies to a group of separate operating companies.

The underlying factor here is the tendency of the security markets to undervalue issues that are involved in any sort of complicated legal proceedings. An old Wall Street motto has been: "Never buy into a lawsuit." This may be sound advice to the speculator seeking quick action on his holdings. But the adoption of this attitude by the general public is bound to create bargain opportunities in the securities affected by it, since the prejudice against them holds their prices down to unduly low levels.*

The exploitation of special situations is a technical branch of investment which requires a somewhat unusual mentality and equipment. Probably only a small percentage of our enterprising investors are likely to engage in it, and this book is not the appropriate medium for expounding its complications.[6]

Broader Implications of Our Rules for Investment

Investment policy, as it has been developed here, depends in the first place on a choice by the investor of either the defensive (passive) or aggressive (enterprising) role. The aggressive investor must have a considerable knowledge of security values—enough, in fact, to warrant viewing his security operations as equivalent to a business enterprise. There is no room in this philosophy for a middle ground, or a series of gradations, between the passive and aggressive status. Many, perhaps most, investors seek to place themselves in such an intermediate category; in our opinion that is a compromise that is more likely to produce disappointment than achievement.

As an investor you cannot soundly become "half a businessman," expecting thereby to achieve half the normal rate of business profits on your funds.

It follows from this reasoning that the majority of security owners should elect the defensive classification. They do not have the time,

---

* The outcomes of more-recent lawsuits and regulatory actions have often been large, sudden, and unpredictable. Thus, "never buy into a lawsuit" remains a valid rule for all but the most intrepid investors to live by.

or the determination, or the mental equipment to embark upon investing as a quasi-business. They should therefore be satisfied with the excellent return now obtainable from a defensive portfolio (and with even less), and they should stoutly resist the recurrent temptation to increase this return by deviating into other paths.

The enterprising investor may properly embark upon any security operation for which his training and judgment are adequate and which appears sufficiently promising *when measured by established business standards.*

In our recommendations and caveats for this group of investors we have attempted to apply such business standards. In those for the defensive investor we have been guided largely by the three requirements of underlying safety, simplicity of choice, and promise of satisfactory results, in terms of psychology as well as arithmetic. The use of these criteria has led us to exclude from the field of recommended investment a number of security classes that are normally regarded as suitable for various kinds of investors. These prohibitions were listed in our first chapter on p. 29.

Let us consider a little more fully than before what is implied in these exclusions. We have advised against the purchase at "full prices" of three important categories of securities: (1) foreign bonds, (2) ordinary preferred stocks, and (3) secondary common stocks, including, of course, original offerings of such issues. By "full prices" we mean prices close to par for bonds or preferred stocks, and prices that represent about the fair business value of the enterprise in the case of common stocks. The greater number of defensive investors are to avoid these categories regardless of price; the enterprising investor is to buy them only when obtainable at bargain prices—which we define as prices not more than two-thirds of the appraisal value of the securities.

What would happen if all investors were guided by our advice in these matters? That question was considered in regard to foreign bonds, on p. 138, and we have nothing to add at this point. Investment-grade preferred stocks would be bought solely by corporations, such as insurance companies, which would benefit from the special income-tax status of stock issues owned by them.

The most troublesome consequence of our policy of exclusion is in the field of secondary common stocks. If the majority of investors, being in the defensive class, are not to buy them at all, the field of possible buyers becomes seriously restricted. Furthermore, if aggressive investors are to buy them only at bargain levels, then these issues would be doomed to sell for less than their fair value, except to the extent that they were purchased unintelligently.

This may sound severe and even vaguely unethical. Yet in truth we are merely recognizing what has actually happened in this area for the greater part of the past 40 years. Secondary issues, for the most part, *do* fluctuate about a central level which is well below their fair value. They reach and even surpass that value at times; but this occurs in the upper reaches of bull markets, when the lessons of practical experience would argue against the soundness of paying the prevailing prices for common stocks.

Thus we are suggesting only that aggressive investors recognize the facts of life as it is lived by secondary issues and that they accept the central market levels that are normal for that class as their guide in fixing their own levels for purchase.

There is a paradox here, nevertheless. The average well-selected secondary company may be fully as promising as the average industrial leader. What the smaller concern lacks in inherent stability it may readily make up in superior possibilities of growth. Consequently it may appear illogical to many readers to term "unintelligent" the purchase of such secondary issues at their full "enterprise value." We think that the strongest logic is that of experience. **Financial history says clearly that the investor may expect satisfactory results, on the average, from secondary common stocks only if he buys them for less than their value to a private owner, that is, on a bargain basis.**

The last sentence indicates that this principle relates to the ordinary *outside* investor. Anyone who can *control* a secondary company, or who is part of a cohesive group with such control, is fully justified in buying the shares on the same basis as if he were investing in a "close corporation" or other private business. The distinction between the position, and consequent investment policy, of insiders and of outsiders becomes more important as the enterprise itself becomes *less* important. It is a basic characteristic of a primary or leading company that a single detached share is ordinarily worth as much as a share in a controlling block. In secondary companies the *average* market value of a detached share is substantially less than its worth to a controlling owner. Because of this fact, the matter of shareholder-management relations and of those between inside and outside shareholders tends to be much more important and controversial in the case of secondary than in that of primary companies.

At the end of Chapter 5 we commented on the difficulty of making any hard and fast distinction between primary and secondary companies. The many common stocks in the boundary area may properly exhibit an intermediate price behavior. It would not be illogical for an investor to buy such an issue at a *small* discount from its indicated or appraisal value, on the theory that it is only a small distance away from a primary classification and that it may acquire such a rating unqualifiedly in the not too distant future.

Thus the distinction between primary and secondary issues need not be made too precise; for, if it were, then a small difference in quality must produce a large differential in justified purchase price. In saying this we are admitting a middle ground in the classification of common stocks, although we counseled against such a middle ground in the classification of investors. Our reason for this apparent inconsistency is as follows: No great harm comes from some uncertainty of viewpoint regarding a single security, because such cases are exceptional and not a great deal is at stake in the matter. But the investor's choice as between the defensive or the aggressive status is of major consequence to him, and he should not allow himself to be confused or compromised in this basic decision.

Commentary on Chapter 7
by Jason Zweig

> There's a person in my life I just do not trust. . . . And that person is me. You should not trust yourself! Decisions? It's like handing over bubble wrap to a five-year-old. You know what's going to happen!
>
> —Sendhil Mullainathan[1]

Graham has already told us that even enterprising investors should never put 100% of their assets in stocks.[2] Risk is a function not only of the probabilities of being right, but of the consequences if you turn out to be wrong. No matter how bullish you feel, your judgments could still be mistaken. And by never putting all—or none—of your money in stocks, you protect yourself against the most extreme consequences of being wrong.

You must also protect against less severe consequences, too—those that arise from repeated and avoidable mistakes. The costs of unforced errors can turn what would have been superior returns into underperformance.

Pretend Portfolios

The first step for an enterprising investor is to test your ideas and train yourself. To do that, Graham urges, you should spend a full year studying and picking a few stocks—but don't buy any.[3]

Just about every brokerage or investing website and app enables

---

[1] *The Knowledge Project* podcast with Shane Parrish, bit.ly/3JXBnRu.
[2] See Chapters 1 and 4.
[3] Patricia A. Dreyfus, "Investment Analysis in Two Easy Lessons," bit.ly/3rlxejF.

you to track stocks in a model portfolio without putting up any money. Creating a pretend portfolio in an online portfolio tracker is the equivalent of being an actor or musician rehearsing behind closed doors before a public performance.

Use your pretend portfolio to see what works. The point isn't to make the most money in the shortest time—you aren't using real money!—but to see whether you can develop a system to identify good businesses whose stocks are undervalued. To assemble your portfolio, follow a checklist (see "Gut Check" in the Commentary on Chapter 11, p. 291).

Hang on to all your picks for the full year; don't trade in and out. Judge your success less by how much your stock picks go up than by how many of them go up—and why. Did they rise in price because the original rationale in your checklist was right—or for reasons you didn't anticipate or understand?

Over the course of the year, continue to read the companies' financial statements, sample their products or services, and learn about their competitors. When the 12 months are up, take a hard look at your pretend portfolio. Compare its performance against that of a broad market index like the S&P 500. It should be obvious

---

Graham's Final Fund

Late in life, Graham advocated what he called a "group approach," buying baskets of stocks that all met simple criteria of cheapness—"regardless of the industry and with very little attention to the individual company."

Graham should be regarded as a pioneer of what today is often called "factor" or "smart-beta" investing: holding bundles of stocks that all clear a set of statistical hurdles.

After studying 50 years of data to determine the past performance of hypothetical portfolios of stocks with various characteristics, Graham recommended looking for companies with:

1. debt no greater than equity (50% or less of total capital);
2. an annual dividend at least two-thirds as high as the yield on high-quality corporate bonds (then, a dividend of at least 5%;

today, with investment-grade bonds yielding 5.5%, a dividend of at least 3.7%);
3. an earnings yield—net income per share divided by price per share—that was at least twice the yield on high-quality corporate bonds (in Graham's day, an earnings yield of 14; today, approximately 11).[1]

Graham's junior research partner, James Rea, formed a fund in 1976 to pursue this approach. Its design was a bit odd: The fund would keep one-third of its portfolio in U.S. government bonds, a third in companies whose shares were trading at less than net current asset value, and a third in stocks that passed Graham's dividend and earnings tests. It would sell any holding after a 50% gain or after two years, whichever came first.

Graham died a few months later. The Rea-Graham fund earned robust gains for several years, then faded into obscurity. It seems to have faltered because it sold its winners too soon, held bonds in a time of rising inflation, and rejiggered its rules after Graham's death. To turn a pretend portfolio into a real one, consistency is key.

---

[1] Earnings yield and the more commonly used price/earnings ratio are reciprocal. When a stock has an earnings yield of 11, its P/E ratio is [1 / 11] * 100 = 9.1. When the P/E is 50, the earnings yield is 2.

whether you are good at this, getting better, or have no aptitude. If your pretend portfolio's results are significantly worse than those of the benchmark, you have a lot more to learn about investing—and might not be prepared to put in the time and effort that will take. Maybe you should concede that you're a defensive investor—and you should feel no shame in doing so.

Wait-Watching

Another way to structure your decisions so you don't rely on gut feelings alone: Keep a watchlist of companies you're already familiar with and would like to own if their stock prices fall to bargain levels.

Many brokerage websites permit you to set up notifications that will alert you whenever a stock falls below a target price, which you might set (for example) 25% below where it is now. If you've already analyzed the business thoroughly enough to be confident of the price range within which its stock would be attractive, mark your watchlist to flag the stock for you if it falls to that range.

While you wait, continue to read the company's financial reports to make sure it remains healthy. That way, if the stock takes a dive but the business is unimpaired, you will be ready to buy.

A watchlist helps override the instinctive, destructive tendency to buy high and sell low. It automatically compels you to consider buying low and to embrace a falling market rather than flee from it.

Memorialize Your Mistakes

In the offices of Davis Advisors in New York, at least a dozen and a half framed stock certificates hang on what's called the "mistake wall." Among them: American International Group, which fell 96% in 2008, and Lucent Technologies, which dropped 94% between 1999 and 2001.

The mistake wall includes both "sins of commission," or misinterpretations of available data, and "sins of omission," or failures to take all relevant information into account. The stock certificates are unavoidable daily reminders that something went wrong, while brief descriptions of each explain what went wrong. Davis keeps even more records of its mistakes in extensive files on each of the companies.

The idea, says chairman Christopher Davis, is to shift the focus from *outcome* (how bad the decision was) to *process* (what led to the bad decision and how to avoid repeating it). That helps the firm recognize when it may be about to echo a mistake it's made before. "It gives us a toolkit that makes it easier for people to change their minds," says Davis. "It's a way to evaluate our work that helps keep us more focused on the North Star of valuing businesses versus just trading stocks."

You should memorialize your mistakes, too. You don't need to use a stock certificate. Put a sample of a company's products in your home office; post an image of its logo on your wall, your computer monitor, or your desktop.

Remember, too, that your mistakes aren't just the stocks you bought that you shouldn't have.

If you're serious about being an enterprising investor, you'll use a portfolio tracker to monitor not only the stocks you *hold* but the stocks you *sold*. Are the companies you no longer own doing better than the ones you kept? Then you're probably making the common mistake of selling too soon.

You'll also track the stocks you considered buying but didn't. Are the ones you almost bought doing better than those you did buy? Then you need to refine the criteria in your checklist and watchlist.

You can't be an investor without taking risks, and you can't take risks without making mistakes. But you can't learn from your mistakes if you never admit you make any. Only by studying your mistakes can you keep improving your policies and procedures. Making fewer mistakes will help you incur fewer and smaller losses. And that will give you more capital to work with, enabling you to make the most of your skills as they improve.

CHAPTER 8

The Investor and Market Fluctuations
by Benjamin Graham

To the extent that the investor's funds are placed in high-grade bonds of relatively short maturity—say, of seven years or less—he will not be affected significantly by changes in market prices and need not take them into account. (This applies also to his holdings of U.S. savings bonds, which he can always turn in at his cost price or more.) His longer-term bonds may have relatively wide price swings during their lifetimes, and his common-stock portfolio is almost certain to fluctuate in value over any period of several years.

The investor should know about these possibilities and should be prepared for them both financially and psychologically. He will want to benefit from changes in market levels—certainly through an advance in the value of his stock holdings as time goes on, and perhaps also by making purchases and sales at advantageous prices. This interest on his part is inevitable, and legitimate enough. But it involves the very real danger that it will lead him into speculative attitudes and activities. **It is easy for us to tell you not to speculate; the hard thing will be for you to follow this advice. Let us repeat what we said at the outset: If you want to speculate do so with your eyes open, knowing that you will probably lose money in the end; be sure to limit the amount at risk and to separate it completely from your investment program.**

We shall deal first with the more important subject of price changes in common stocks, and pass later to the area of bonds. In Chapter 3 we supplied a historical survey of the stock market's action over the past hundred years. In this section we shall return to that material from time to time, in order to see what the past record promises the investor—in either the form of long-term appreciation of a portfolio held relatively unchanged through successive rises and declines, or in the possibilities of buying near bear-market lows and selling not too far below bull-market highs.

Market Fluctuations as a Guide to Investment Decisions

Since common stocks, even of investment grade, are subject to recurrent and wide fluctuations in their prices, the intelligent investor should be interested in the possibilities of profiting from these pendulum swings. There are two possible ways by which he may try to do this: the way of *timing* and the way of *pricing*. By timing we mean the endeavor to anticipate the action of the stock market—to buy or hold when the future course is deemed to be upward, to sell or refrain from buying when the course is downward. By pricing we mean the endeavor to buy stocks when they are quoted below their fair value and to sell them when they rise above such value. A less ambitious form of pricing is the simple effort to make sure that when you buy you do not pay too much for your stocks. This may suffice for the defensive investor, whose emphasis is on long-pull holding; but as such it represents an essential minimum of attention to market levels.[1]

We are convinced that the intelligent investor can derive satisfactory results from pricing of either type. We are equally sure that **if he places his emphasis on timing, in the sense of forecasting, he will end up as a speculator and with a speculator's financial results**. This distinction may seem rather tenuous to the layman, and it is not commonly accepted on Wall Street. As a matter of business practice, or perhaps of thoroughgoing conviction, the stock brokers and the investment services seem wedded to the principle that both investors and speculators in common stocks should devote careful attention to market forecasts.

The farther one gets from Wall Street, the more skepticism one will find, we believe, as to the pretensions of stock-market forecasting or timing. **The investor can scarcely take seriously the innumerable predictions which appear almost daily and are his for the asking. Yet in many cases he pays attention to them and even acts upon them. Why? Because he has been** persuaded that it is important for him to form *some* opinion of the future course of the stock market, and because he feels that the brokerage or service forecast is at least more dependable than his own.*

We lack space here to discuss in detail the pros and cons of market forecasting. A great deal of brain power goes into this field, and undoubtedly *some people* can make money by being good stock-market analysts. But it is absurd to think that the *general public* can ever make money out of market forecasts. For who will buy when the general public, at a given signal, rushes to sell out at a profit? If you, the reader, expect to get rich over the years by following some system or leadership in market forecasting, you must be expecting to try to do what countless others are aiming at, and to be able to do it better than your numerous competitors in the market. There is no basis either in logic or in experience for assuming that any typical or average investor can anticipate market movements more successfully than the general public, of which he is himself a part.

There is one aspect of the "timing" philosophy which seems to have escaped everyone's notice. Timing is of great psychological importance to the speculator because he wants to make his profit in a hurry. The idea of waiting a year before his stock moves up is repugnant to him. But a waiting period, as such, is of no consequence to the investor. What advantage is there to him in having his money uninvested until he receives some (presumably) trustworthy signal that the time has come to buy? He enjoys an advantage only if by waiting he succeeds in buying later at a sufficiently *lower price* to offset his loss of dividend income. What this means is that **timing is of no real value to the investor unless it coincides with pricing—that is, unless it enables him to repurchase his shares at substantially under his previous selling price.**

---

* Wall Street's highly paid "market strategists," economists, and other forecasters not only fail, year after year, to predict the rate of stock returns accurately; they often don't even get the direction correct. They frequently forecast that the market will fall when, in fact, it ends up rising—and vice versa.

In this respect the famous Dow theory for timing purchases and sales has had an unusual history.* Briefly, this technique takes its signal to buy from a special kind of "breakthrough" of the stock averages on the up side, and its selling signal from a similar breakthrough on the down side. The calculated—not necessarily actual—results of using this method showed an almost unbroken series of profits in operations from 1897 to the early 1960s. On the basis of this presentation the practical value of the Dow theory would have appeared firmly established; the doubt, if any, would apply to the dependability of this published "record" as a picture of what a Dow theorist would actually have done in the market.

A closer study of the figures indicates that the quality of the results shown by the Dow theory changed radically after 1938—a few years after the theory had begun to be taken seriously on Wall Street. Its spectacular achievement had been in giving a sell signal, at 306, about a month before the 1929 crash and in keeping its followers out of the long bear market until things had pretty well righted themselves, at 84, in 1933. But from 1938 on the Dow theory operated mainly by taking its practitioners out at a pretty good price but then putting them back in again at a higher price. For nearly 30 years thereafter, one would have done appreciably better by just buying and holding the DJIA.[2]

In our view, based on much study of this problem, the change in the Dow-theory results is not accidental. It demonstrates an inherent characteristic of forecasting and trading formulas in the fields of business and finance. **Those formulas that gain adherents and importance do so because they have worked well over a period, or sometimes merely because they have been plausibly adapted to the statistical record of the past. But as their acceptance increases, their reliability tends to diminish. This happens for two reasons: First, the passage of time brings new conditions which the old formula no longer fits. Second, in stock-market affairs the popularity of a trading theory has itself an influence on the market's behavior which detracts in the long run from its profit-making possibilities.** (The popularity of something like

---

* See p. 32.

the Dow theory may seem to create its own vindication, since it would make the market advance or decline by the very action of its followers when a buying or selling signal is given. A "stampede" of this kind is, of course, much more of a danger than an advantage to the public trader.)

Buy-Low–Sell-High Approach

We are convinced that the average investor cannot deal successfully with price movements by endeavoring to forecast them. Can he benefit from them *after* they have taken place—i.e., by buying after each major decline and selling out after each major advance? The fluctuations of the market over a period of many years prior to 1950 lent considerable encouragement to that idea. In fact, a classic definition of a "shrewd investor" was "one who bought in a bear market when everyone else was selling, and sold out in a bull market when everyone else was buying." If we examine our Chart I, covering the fluctuations of the Standard & Poor's composite index between 1900 and 1970, and the supporting figures in Table 3-1 (p. 66), we can readily see why this viewpoint appeared valid until fairly recent years.

Between 1897 and 1949 there were ten complete market cycles, running from bear-market low to bull-market high and back to bear-market low. Six of these took no longer than four years, four ran for six or seven years, and one—the famous "new-era" cycle of 1921–1932—lasted eleven years. The percentage of advance from the lows to highs ranged from 44% to 500%, with most between about 50% and 100%. The percentage of subsequent declines ranged from 24% to 89%, with most found between 40% and 50%. (It should be remembered that a decline of 50% fully offsets a preceding advance of 100%.)

Nearly all the bull markets had a number of well-defined characteristics in common, such as (1) a historically high price level, (2) high price/earnings ratios, (3) low dividend yields as against bond yields, (4) much speculation on margin, and (5) many offerings of new common-stock issues of poor quality. Thus to the student of stock-market history it appeared that the intelligent investor should have been able to identify the recurrent bear and bull markets, to buy in the former and sell in the latter, and to do so for the most part at reasonably short intervals of time. Various methods were developed for determining buying and selling levels of the general market, based on either value factors or percentage movements of prices or both.

But we must point out that even prior to the unprecedented bull market that began in 1949, there were sufficient variations in the successive market cycles to complicate and sometimes frustrate the desirable process of buying low and selling high. The most notable of these departures, of course, was the great bull market of the late 1920s, which threw all calculations badly out of gear.* Even in 1949, therefore, it was by no means a certainty that the investor could base his financial policies and procedures mainly on the endeavor to buy at low levels in bear markets and to sell out at high levels in bull markets.

It turned out, in the sequel, that the opposite was true. The market's behavior in the past 20 years has not followed the former pattern, nor obeyed what once were well-established danger signals, nor permitted its successful exploitation by applying old rules for buying low and selling high. Whether the old, fairly regular bull-and-bear-market pattern will eventually return we do not know. But it seems unrealistic to us for the investor to endeavor to base his present policy on the classic formula—i.e., to wait for demonstrable bear-market levels before buying *any* common stocks. Our recommended policy has, however, made provision for changes in the *proportion* of common stocks to bonds in the portfolio, if the investor chooses to do so, according as the level of stock prices appears less or more attractive by value standards.†

---

* Without bear markets to take stock prices back down, anyone waiting to "buy low" will feel completely left behind—and, all too often, will end up abandoning any former caution and jumping in with both feet. That's why Graham's message about the importance of *emotional discipline* is so important. The longer a bull market lasts, the more severely investors will be afflicted with amnesia; after five years or so, many people no longer believe that bear markets are even possible. All those who forget are doomed to be reminded; and, in the stock market, recovered memories are always unpleasant.

† Graham discusses this "recommended policy" in Chapter 4 (p. 90).

Formula Plans

In the early years of the stock-market rise that began in 1949–50 considerable interest was attracted to various methods of taking advantage of the stock market's cycles. These have been known as "formula investment plans." The essence of all such plans—except the simple case of dollar averaging—is that the investor automatically does *some* selling of common stocks when the market advances substantially. In many of them a very large rise in the market level would result in the sale of all common-stock holdings; others provided for retention of a minor proportion of equities under all circumstances.

This approach had the double appeal of sounding logical (and conservative) and of showing excellent results when applied retrospectively to the stock market over many years in the past. Unfortunately, its vogue grew greatest at the very time when it was destined to work least well. Many of the "formula planners" found themselves entirely or nearly out of the stock market at some level in the middle 1950s. True, they had realized excellent profits, but in a broad sense the market "ran away" from them thereafter, and their formulas gave them little opportunity to buy back a common-stock position.*

There is a similarity between the experience of those adopting the formula-investing approach in the early 1950s and those who embraced the purely mechanical version of the Dow theory some 20 years earlier. In both cases the advent of popularity marked almost the exact moment when the system ceased to work well. We have had a like discomfiting experience with our own "central value method" of determining indicated buying and selling levels of the Dow Jones Industrial Average. The moral seems to be that **any approach to moneymaking in the stock market which can be easily described and followed by a lot of people is by its terms too simple and too easy to last.** Spinoza's concluding remark applies

---

* Many of these "formula planners" would have sold all their stocks at the end of 1954, after the U.S. stock market rose 52.6%, the second-highest yearly return then on record. Over the next five years, these market-timers would likely have stood on the sidelines as stocks doubled.

to Wall Street as well as to philosophy: "All things excellent are as difficult as they are rare."

Market Fluctuations of the Investor's Portfolio

Every investor who owns common stocks must expect to see them fluctuate in value over the years. The behavior of the DJIA since our last edition was written in 1964 probably reflects pretty well what has happened to the stock portfolio of a conservative investor who limited his stock holdings to those of large, prominent, and conservatively financed corporations. The overall value advanced from an average level of about 890 to a high of 995 in 1966 (and 985 again in 1968), fell to 631 in 1970, and made an almost full recovery to 940 in early 1971. (Since the individual issues set their high and low marks at different times, the fluctuations in the Dow Jones group as a whole are less severe than those in the separate components.) We have traced through the price fluctuations of other types of diversified and conservative common-stock portfolios and we find that the overall results are not likely to be markedly different from the above. In general, the shares of second-line companies* fluctuate more widely than the major ones, but this does not necessarily mean that a group of well-established but smaller companies will make a poorer showing over a fairly long period. In any case **the investor may as well resign himself in advance to the probability rather than the mere possibility that most of his holdings will advance, say, 50% or more from their low point and decline the equivalent one-third or more from their high point at various periods in the next five years.**[†]

---

* Today's equivalent of what Graham calls "second-line companies" would be any of the thousands of stocks not included in the S&P 500.
† Note carefully what Graham is saying here. It is not just possible, but probable, that most of the stocks you own will gain at least 50% from their lowest price and lose at least 33% from their highest price—regardless of which stocks you own or whether the market as a whole goes up or down. If you can't live with that—or you think your portfolio is somehow magically exempt from it—then you are not yet entitled to call yourself an

A serious investor is not likely to believe that the day-to-day or even month-to-month fluctuations of the stock market make him richer or poorer. But what about the longer-term and wider changes? Here practical questions present themselves, and the psychological problems are likely to grow complicated. **A substantial rise in the market is at once a legitimate reason for satisfaction and a cause for prudent concern, but it may also bring a strong temptation toward imprudent action.** Your shares have advanced, good! You are richer than you were, good! But has the price risen *too* high, and should you think of selling? Or should you kick yourself for not having bought more shares when the level was lower? Or—worst thought of all—should you now give way to the bull-market atmosphere, become infected with the enthusiasm, the overconfidence and the greed of the great public (of which, after all, you are a part), and make larger and dangerous commitments? Presented thus in print, the answer to the last question is a self-evident no, but even the intelligent investor is likely to need considerable willpower to keep from following the crowd.

It is for these reasons of human nature, even more than by calculation of financial gain or loss, that **we favor some kind of mechanical method for varying the proportion of bonds to stocks in the investor's portfolio.** The chief advantage, perhaps, is that such a formula will give him *something to do*. As the market advances he will from time to time make sales out of his stockholdings, putting the proceeds into bonds; as it declines he will reverse the procedure. These activities will provide some outlet for his otherwise too-pent-up energies. If he is the right kind of investor he will take added satisfaction from the thought that his operations are exactly opposite from those of the crowd.*

---

investor. (Graham refers to a 33% decline as the "equivalent one-third" because a 50% gain takes a $10 stock to $15. From $15, a 33% loss [or $5 drop] takes it right back to $10, where it started.)

* For today's investor, the ideal strategy for pursuing this "formula" is rebalancing; see pp. 109–112.

Business Valuations versus Stock-Market Valuations

The impact of market fluctuations upon the investor's true situation may be considered also from the standpoint of the shareholder as the part owner of various businesses. The holder of marketable shares actually has a double status, and with it the privilege of taking advantage of either at his choice. On the one hand his position is analogous to that of a minority shareholder or silent partner in a private business. Here his results are entirely dependent on the profits of the enterprise or on a change in the underlying value of its assets. He would usually determine the value of such a private-business interest by calculating his share of the net worth as shown in the most recent balance sheet. On the other hand, the common-stock investor holds a piece of paper, an engraved stock certificate, which can be sold in a matter of minutes at a price which varies from moment to moment—when the market is open, that is—and often is far removed from the balance-sheet value.*

The development of the stock market in recent decades has made the typical investor more dependent on the course of price quotations and less free than formerly to consider himself merely a business owner. The reason is that the successful enterprises in which he is likely to concentrate his holdings sell almost constantly at prices well above their net asset value (or book value, or "balance-sheet value"). In paying these market premiums the investor gives precious hostages to fortune, for he must depend on the stock market itself to validate his commitments.†

---

* Most companies today provide "an engraved stock certificate" only upon special request. Stocks exist, for the most part, in purely electronic form (much as your bank account contains computerized credits and debits, not actual currency) and thus have become even easier to trade than they were in Graham's day.

† Net asset value, book value, balance-sheet value, and tangible-asset value are all synonyms for net worth, or the total value of a company's physical and financial assets minus all its liabilities. It can be calculated using the balance sheets in a company's annual and quarterly reports; from total shareholders' equity, subtract all "soft" assets such as goodwill, trademarks, and other

This is a factor of prime importance in present-day investing, and it has received less attention than it deserves. The whole structure of stock-market quotations contains a built-in contradiction. The better a company's record and prospects, the less relationship the price of its shares will have to their book value. But the greater the premium above book value, the less certain the basis of determining its intrinsic value—i.e., the more this "value" will depend on the changing moods and measurements of the stock market. Thus we reach the final paradox, that **the more successful the company, the greater are likely to be the fluctuations in the price of its shares.** This really means that, in a very real sense, **the better the quality of a common stock, the more *speculative* it is likely to be**—at least as compared with the unspectacular middle-grade issues.* (What we have said applies to a comparison of the leading growth companies with the bulk of well-established concerns; we exclude from our purview here those issues which are highly speculative because the businesses themselves are speculative.)

The argument made above should explain the often erratic price behavior of our most successful and impressive enterprises. Our favorite example is the monarch of them all—International Business Machines. The price of its shares fell from 607 to 300 in seven months in 1962–63; after two splits its price fell from 387 to 219 in 1970. Similarly, Xerox—an even more impressive earnings

---

intangibles. Divide by the fully diluted number of shares outstanding to arrive at book value per share.

* Graham's use of the word "paradox" is probably an allusion to a classic article by David Durand, "Growth Stocks and the Petersburg Paradox," bit .ly/3Qt2xn9, which compares investing in high-priced growth stocks to betting on a series of coin flips in which the payoff escalates with each flip of the coin. Durand points out that if a growth stock could continue to grow at a high rate for an indefinite period of time, an investor should (in theory) be willing to pay an infinite price for its shares. Why, then, has no stock ever sold for a price of infinity dollars per share? Because the higher the assumed future growth rate, and the longer the time period over which it is expected, the wider the margin for error grows, and the higher the cost of even a tiny miscalculation becomes. Graham discusses this problem further in Appendix 2 (p. 566).

gainer in recent decades—fell from 171 to 87 in 1962–63, and from 116 to 65 in 1970. These striking losses did not indicate any doubt about the future long-term growth of IBM or Xerox; they reflected instead a lack of confidence in the premium valuation that the stock market itself had placed on these excellent prospects.

The previous discussion leads us to a conclusion of practical importance to the conservative investor in common stocks. If he is to pay some special attention to the selection of his portfolio, it might be best for him to concentrate on issues selling at a reasonably close approximation to their tangible-asset value—say, at not more than one-third above that figure. Purchases made at such levels, or lower, may with logic be regarded as related to the company's balance sheet, and as having a justification or support independent of the fluctuating market prices. The premium over book value that may be involved can be considered as a kind of extra fee paid for the advantage of stock-exchange listing and the marketability that goes with it.

A caution is needed here. A stock does not become a sound investment merely because it can be bought at close to its asset value. The investor should demand, in addition, a satisfactory ratio of earnings to price, a sufficiently strong financial position, and the prospect that its earnings will at least be maintained over the years. This may appear like demanding a lot from a modestly priced stock, but the prescription is not hard to fill under all but dangerously high market conditions. Once the investor is willing to forgo brilliant prospects—i.e., better than average expected growth—he will have no difficulty in finding a wide selection of issues meeting these criteria.

In our chapters on the selection of common stocks (Chapters 14 and 15) we shall give data showing that more than half of the DJIA issues met our asset-value criterion at the end of 1970. The most widely held investment of all—American Tel. & Tel.—actually sells below its tangible-asset value as we write. Most of the light-and-power shares, in addition to their other advantages, are now (early 1972) available at prices reasonably close to their asset values.

The investor with a stock portfolio having such book values behind it can take a much more independent and detached view of stock-market fluctuations than those who have paid high multipliers of both earnings and tangible assets. As long as the earning power of his holdings remains satisfactory, he can give as little attention as he pleases to the vagaries of the stock market. More than that, at times he can use these vagaries to play the master game of buying low and selling high.

The A. & P. Example

At this point we shall introduce one of our original examples, which dates back many years but which has a certain fascination for us because it combines so many aspects of corporate and investment experience. It involves the Great Atlantic & Pacific Tea Co. Here is the story:

A. & P. shares were introduced to trading on the "Curb" market, now the American Stock Exchange, in 1929 and sold as high as 494. By 1932 they had declined to 104, although the company's earnings were nearly as large in that generally catastrophic year as previously. In 1936 the range was between 111 and 131. Then in the business recession and bear market of 1938 the shares fell to a new low of 36.

That price was extraordinary. It meant that the preferred and common were together selling for $126 million, although the company had just reported that it held $85 million in cash alone and a working capital (or net current assets) of $134 million. A. & P. was the largest retail enterprise in America, if not in the world, with a continuous and impressive record of large earnings for many years. Yet in 1938 this outstanding business was considered on Wall Street to be worth less than its current assets alone—which means less as a going concern than if it were liquidated. Why? First, because there were threats of special taxes on chain stores; second, because net profits had fallen off in the previous year; and, third, because the general market was depressed. The first of these reasons was an exaggerated and eventually groundless fear; the other two were typical of temporary influences.

Let us assume that the investor had bought A. & P. common in 1937 at, say, 12 times its five-year average earnings, or about 80. We are far from asserting that the ensuing decline to 36 was of no importance to him. He would have been well advised to scrutinize the picture with some care, to see whether he had made any miscalculations. But if the results of his study were reassuring—

as they should have been—he was entitled then to disregard the market decline as a temporary vagary of finance, unless he had the funds and the courage to take advantage of it by buying more on the bargain basis offered.

Sequel and Reflections

The following year, 1939, A. & P. shares advanced to 117½, or three times the low price of 1938 and well above the average of 1937. Such a turnabout in the behavior of common stocks is by no means uncommon, but in the case of A. & P. it was more striking than most. In the years after 1949 the grocery chain's shares rose with the general market until in 1961 the split-up stock (10 for 1) reached a high of 70½ which was equivalent to 705 for the 1938 shares.

This price of 70½ was remarkable for the fact it was 30 times the earnings of 1961. Such a price/earnings ratio—which compares with 23 times for the DJIA in that year—must have implied expectations of a brilliant growth in earnings. This optimism had no justification in the company's earnings record in the preceding years, and it proved completely wrong. Instead of advancing rapidly, the course of earnings in the ensuing period was generally downward. The year after the 70½ high the price fell by more than half to 34. But this time the shares did not have the bargain quality that they showed at the low quotation in 1938. After varying sorts of fluctuations the price fell to another low of 21½ in 1970 and 18 in 1972—having reported the first quarterly *deficit* in its history.

We see in this history how wide can be the vicissitudes of a major American enterprise in little more than a single generation, and also with what miscalculations and excesses of optimism and pessimism the public has valued its shares. In 1938 the business was really being given away, with no takers; in 1961 the public was clamoring for the shares at a ridiculously high price. After that came a quick loss of half the market value, and some years later a substantial further decline. In the meantime the company was to turn from an outstanding to a mediocre earnings performer; its profit in the boom-year 1968 was to be less than in 1958; it had paid a series of confusing small stock dividends not warranted by the current additions to surplus; and so forth. A. & P. was a larger company in

1961 and 1972 than in 1938, but not as well-run, not as profitable, and not as attractive.*

There are two chief morals to this story. The first is that the stock market often goes far wrong, and sometimes an alert and courageous investor can take advantage of its patent errors. The other is that most businesses change in character and quality over the years, sometimes for the better, perhaps more often for the worse. The investor need not watch his companies' performance like a hawk; but he should give it a good, hard look from time to time.

Let us return to our comparison between the holder of marketable shares and the man with an interest in a private business. We have said that the former has the *option* of considering himself merely as the part owner of the various businesses he has invested in, or as the holder of shares which are salable at any time he wishes at their quoted market price.

But note this important fact: The true investor scarcely ever *is forced to sell* his shares, and at all other times he is free to disregard the current price quotation. He need pay attention to it and act upon it only to the extent that it suits his book, and no more.†Thus the investor who permits himself to be stampeded or unduly worried by unjustified market declines in his holdings is perversely transforming his basic advantage into a basic disadvantage. That man would be better off if his stocks had no market quotation at all, for he would then be spared the mental anguish caused him by *other persons'* mistakes of judgment.‡

Incidentally, a widespread situation of this kind actually existed during the dark depression days of 1931–1933. There was then a

---

* More recently, A&P's share price fluctuated wildly before it sought bankruptcy protection in 2015.

† "Only to the extent that it suits his book" means "only to the extent that the price is favorable enough to justify selling the stock." In traditional brokerage lingo, the "book" is an investor's ledger of holdings and trades.

‡ In these 113 words Graham sums up his lifetime of experience. You cannot read these words too often; they are like Kryptonite for bear markets. If you keep them close at hand and let them guide you throughout your investing life, you can survive whatever the markets throw at you.

psychological advantage in owning business interests that had no quoted market. For example, people who owned first mortgages on real estate that continued to pay interest were able to tell themselves that their investments had kept their full value, there being no market quotations to indicate otherwise. On the other hand, many listed corporation bonds of even better quality and greater underlying strength suffered severe shrinkages in their market quotations, thus making their owners believe they were growing distinctly poorer. In reality the owners were better off with the listed securities, despite the low prices of these. For if they had wanted to, or were compelled to, they could at least have sold the issues—possibly to exchange them for even better bargains. Or they could just as logically have ignored the market's action as temporary and basically meaningless. But it is self-deception to tell yourself that you have suffered no shrinkage in value *merely because* your securities have no quoted market at all.

Returning to our A. & P. shareholder in 1938, we assert that as long as he held on to his shares he suffered no loss in their price decline, beyond what his own judgment may have told him was occasioned by a shrinkage in their underlying or intrinsic value. If no such shrinkage had occurred, he had a right to expect that in due course the market quotation would return to the 1937 level or better—as in fact it did the following year. In this respect his position was at least as good as if he had owned an interest in a private business with no quoted market for its shares. For in that case, too, he might or might not have been justified in mentally lopping off part of the cost of his holdings because of the impact of the 1938 recession—depending on what had happened to his company.

Critics of the value approach to stock investment argue that listed common stocks cannot properly be regarded or appraised in the same way as an interest in a similar private enterprise, because the presence of an organized security market "injects into equity ownership the new and extremely important attribute of liquidity." **But what this liquidity really means is, first, that the investor has the benefit of the stock market's daily and changing appraisal of his holdings,** *for whatever that appraisal may be worth,* **and, second, that the investor is able to increase or decrease his investment at the market's daily figure**—*if he chooses.* **Thus the** existence of a quoted market gives the investor *certain options* that he does not have if his security is unquoted. But it does not impose the current quotation on an investor who prefers to take his idea of value from some other source.

Let us close this section with something in the nature of a parable. Imagine that in some private business you own a small share that cost you $1,000. One of your partners, named Mr. Market, is very obliging indeed. Every day he tells you what he thinks your interest is worth and furthermore offers either to buy you out or to sell you an additional interest on that basis. Sometimes his idea of value appears plausible and justified by business developments and prospects as you know them. Often, on the other hand, Mr. Market lets his enthusiasm or his fears run away with him, and the value he proposes seems to you a little short of silly.

If you are a prudent investor or a sensible businessman, will you let Mr. Market's daily communication determine your view of the value of a $1,000 interest in the enterprise? Only in case you agree with him, or in case you want to trade with him. You may be happy to sell out to him when he quotes you a ridiculously high price, and equally happy to buy from him when his price is low. But the rest of the time you will be wiser to form your own ideas of the value of your holdings, based on full reports from the company about its operations and financial position.

The true investor is in that very position when he owns a listed common stock. He can take advantage of the daily market price or leave it alone, as dictated by his own judgment and inclination. He must take cognizance of important price movements, for otherwise his judgment will have nothing to work on. Conceivably they may give him a warning signal which he will do well to heed—this in plain English means that he is to sell his shares *because* the price has gone down, foreboding worse things to come. In our view such signals are misleading at least as often as they are helpful. Basically, price fluctuations have only one significant meaning for the true investor. They provide him with an opportunity to buy wisely when prices fall sharply and to sell wisely when they advance a great deal. At other times he will do better if he forgets about the stock market and pays attention to his dividend returns and to the operating results of his companies.

Summary

The most realistic distinction between the investor and the speculator is found in their attitude toward stock-market movements. **The speculator's primary interest lies in anticipating and profiting from market fluctuations. The investor's primary interest lies in acquiring and holding suitable securities at suitable prices.** Market movements are important to him in a practical sense, because they alternately create low price levels at which he would be wise to buy and high price levels at which he certainly should refrain from buying and probably would be wise to sell.

It is far from certain that the typical investor should regularly hold off buying until low market levels appear, because this may involve a long wait, very likely the loss of income, and the possible missing of investment opportunities. On the whole it may be better for the investor to do his stock buying whenever he has money to put in stocks, *except* when the general market level is much higher than can be justified by well-established standards of value. If he wants to be shrewd he can look for the ever-present bargain opportunities in individual securities.

Aside from forecasting the movements of the general market, much effort and ability are directed on Wall Street toward selecting stocks or industrial groups that in matter of price will "do better" than the rest over a fairly short period in the future. Logical as this endeavor may seem, we do not believe it is suited to the needs or temperament of the true investor—particularly since he would be competing with a large number of stock-market traders and first-class financial analysts who are trying to do the same thing. As in all other activities that emphasize price movements first and underlying values second, the work of many intelligent minds constantly engaged in this field tends to be self-neutralizing and self-defeating over the years.

The investor with a portfolio of sound stocks should expect their prices to fluctuate and should neither be concerned by sizable declines nor become excited by sizable advances. He should always remember that market quotations are there for his convenience, either to be taken advantage of or to be ignored. He should never buy a stock *because* it has gone up or sell one *because* it has gone down. He would not be far wrong if this motto read more simply: "Never buy a stock immediately after a substantial rise or sell one immediately after a substantial drop."

An Added Consideration

Something should be said about the significance of average market prices as a measure of managerial competence. The shareholder judges whether his own investment has been successful in terms both of dividends received and of the long-range trend of the average market value. The same criteria should logically be applied in testing the effectiveness of a company's management and the soundness of its attitude toward the owners of the business.

This statement may sound like a truism, but it needs to be emphasized. For as yet there is no accepted technique or approach by which management is brought to the bar of market opinion. On the contrary, managements have always insisted that they have no responsibility *of any kind* for what happens to the market value of their shares. It is true, of course, that they are not accountable for those *fluctuations* in price which, as we have been insisting, bear no relationship to underlying conditions and values. But it is only the lack of alertness and intelligence among the rank and file of shareholders that permits this immunity to extend to the entire realm of market quotations, including the permanent establishment of a depreciated and unsatisfactory price level. **Good managements produce a good average market price, and bad managements produce bad market prices.***

Fluctuations in Bond Prices

The investor should be aware that even though safety of its principal and interest may be unquestioned, a long-term bond could vary widely in market price in response to changes in interest rates. In Table 8-1 we give data for various years back to 1902 covering yields for high-grade corporate and tax-free issues.

---

* Graham has much more to say on what is now known as "corporate governance." See Chapter 19 and its Commentary.

As individual illustrations we add the price fluctuations of two representative railroad issues for a similar period. (These are the Atchison, Topeka & Santa Fe general mortgage 4s, due 1995, for generations one of our premier noncallable bond issues, and the Northern Pacific Ry. 3s, due 2047—originally a 150-year maturity!—long a typical Baa-rated bond.)

Because of their inverse relationship the low yields correspond to the high prices and vice versa. The decline in the Northern Pacific 3s in 1940 represented mainly doubts as to the safety of the issue. It is extraordinary that the price recovered to an all-time high in the next few years, and then lost two-thirds of its price chiefly because of the rise in general interest rates. There have been startling variations, as well, in the price of even the highest-grade bonds in the past forty years.

Note that bond prices do not fluctuate in the same (inverse) proportion as the calculated yields, because their fixed maturity value of 100% exerts a moderating influence. However, for very long maturities, as in our Northern Pacific example, prices and yields change at close to the same rate.

Since 1964 record movements *in both directions* have taken place in the high-grade bond market. Taking "prime municipals" (tax-free) as an example, their yield more than doubled, from 3.2% in January 1965 to 7% in June 1970. Their price index declined, correspondingly, from 110.8 to 67.5. In mid-1970 the yields on high-grade long-term bonds were higher than *at any time in the nearly 200 years of this country's economic history.** Twenty-five years earlier, just before our protracted bull market began, bond yields were at their *lowest* point in history; long-term municipals returned as little as 1%, and industrials gave 2.40% compared with the 4½ to 5% formerly considered "normal." Those of us with a long experience on Wall Street had seen Newton's law of "action and reaction, equal and

---

* By what Graham calls "the rule of opposites," in 2020 the yields on long-term U.S. Treasury bonds hit their *lowest* levels since 1963. Since bond yields move inversely to prices, those low yields meant that prices had risen—making investors most eager to buy just as bonds were at their most expensive. In 2022, long-term U.S. Treasury bonds lost as much as 39%, delivering brutal losses to recent buyers.

TABLE 8-1 Fluctuations in Bond Yields, and in Prices of Two Representative Bond Issues, 1902–1970

	Bond Yields			Bond Prices	
	S & P AAA Composite	S & P Municipals		A. T. & S. F. 4s, 1995	Nor. Pac. 3s, 2047
1902 low	4.31%	3.11%	1905 high	105½	79
1920 high	6.40	5.28	1920 low	69	49½
1928 low	4.53	3.90	1930 high	105	73
1932 high	5.52	5.27	1932 low	75	46¾
1946 low	2.44	1.45	1936 high	117¼	85¼
1970 high	8.44	7.06	1939–40 low	99½	31½
1971 close	7.14	5.35	1946 high	141	94¾
			1970 low	51	32¾
			1971 close	64	37¼

opposite" work itself out repeatedly in the stock market—the most noteworthy example being the rise in the DJIA from 64 in 1921 to 381 in 1929, followed by a record collapse to 41 in 1932. But this time the widest pendulum swings took place in the usually staid and slow-moving array of high-grade bond prices and yields. Moral: **Nothing important on Wall Street can be counted on to occur exactly in the same way as it happened before. This represents the first half of our favorite dictum:** *"The more it changes, the more it's the same thing."*

If it is virtually impossible to make worthwhile predictions about the price movements of stocks, it is completely impossible to do so for bonds. In the old days, at least, one could often find a useful clue to the coming end of a bull or bear market by studying the prior action of bonds, but no similar clues were given to a coming change in interest rates and bond prices. Hence the investor must choose between long-term and short-term bond investments on the basis chiefly of his personal preferences. If he wants to be certain that the market values will not decrease, his best choices are probably U.S. savings bonds, Series E or H, which were described above, p. 94. Either issue will give him a 5% yield (after the first year), the Series E for up to 5⅚ years, the Series H for up to ten years, with a guaranteed resale value of cost or better.

If the investor wants the 7.5% now available on good long-term corporate bonds, or the 5.3% on tax-free municipals, he must be prepared to see them fluctuate in price. Banks and insurance companies have the privilege of valuing high-rated bonds of this type on the mathematical basis of "amortized cost," which disregards market prices; it would not be a bad idea for the individual investor to do something similar.

The price fluctuations of *convertible* bonds and preferred stocks are the resultant of three different factors: (1) variations in the price of the related common stock, (2) variations in the credit standing of the company, and (3) variations in general interest rates. A good many of the convertible issues have been sold by companies that have credit ratings well below the best.[3] Some of these were badly affected by the financial squeeze in 1970. As a result, convertible issues as a whole have been subjected to triply unsettling influences in recent years, and price variations have been unusually wide. In the typical case, therefore, the investor would delude himself if he expected to find in convertible issues that ideal combination of the safety of a high-grade bond and price protection plus a chance to benefit from an advance in the price of the common.

This may be a good place to make a suggestion about the "long-term bond of the future." Why should not the effects of changing interest rates be divided on some practical and equitable basis between the borrower and the lender? One possibility would be to sell long-term bonds with interest payments that vary with an appropriate index of the going rate. The main results of such an arrangement would be: (1) the investor's bond would always have a principal value of about 100, if the company maintains its credit rating, but the interest received will vary, say, with the rate offered on conventional new issues; (2) the corporation would have the advantages of long-term debt—being spared problems and costs of frequent renewals of refinancing—but its interest costs would change from year to year.[4]

Over the past decade the bond investor has been confronted by an increasingly serious dilemma: Shall he choose complete stability of principal value, but with varying and usually low (short-term) interest rates? Or shall he choose a fixed-interest income, with considerable variations (usually downward, it seems) in his principal value? It would be good for most investors if they could compromise between these extremes, and be assured that neither their interest return nor their principal value will fall below a stated minimum over, say, a 20-year period. This could be arranged, without great difficulty, in an appropriate bond contract of a new form. Important note: In effect the U.S. government has done a similar thing in its combination of the original savings-bonds contracts with their extensions at higher interest rates. The suggestion we make here would cover a longer fixed investment period than the savings bonds, and would introduce more flexibility in the interest-rate provisions.*

---

* As mentioned in the Commentary on Chapter 2, Treasury Inflation-Protected Securities, or TIPS, are a new and improved version of what Graham is suggesting here.

It is hardly worthwhile to talk about nonconvertible preferred stocks, since their special tax status makes the safe ones much more desirable holdings by corporations—e.g., insurance companies—than by individuals. The poorer-quality ones almost always fluctuate over a wide range, percentagewise, not too differently from common stocks. We can offer no other useful remark about them. Table 16-2 below, p. 401, gives some information on the price changes of lower-grade nonconvertible preferreds between December 1968 and December 1970. The average decline was 17%, against 11.3% for the S & P composite index of common stocks.

Commentary on Chapter 8
by Jason Zweig

> When everyone is moving toward depravity, no one seems to be moving, but if someone stops he shows up the others who are rushing on, by acting as a fixed point.
>
> —Blaise Pascal[1]

The true investor scarcely ever **is forced to sell** his shares, and at all other times he is free to disregard the current price quotation. He need pay attention to it and act upon it only to the extent that it suits his book, and no more. Thus the investor who permits himself to be stampeded or unduly worried by unjustified market declines in his holdings is perversely transforming his basic advantage into a basic disadvantage. That man would be better off if his stocks had no market quotation at all, for he would then be spared the mental anguish caused him **by other persons'** mistakes of judgment.

In the previous edition, I wrote that those words in Chapter 8 "may well be the single most important paragraph in Graham's entire book."

I was wrong: Those words may well be the single most important paragraph about investing ever written.

Meet Mr. Market

In this chapter, Graham introduces the brilliant metaphor of Mr. Market. Let's say you own a private business, perhaps a restaurant, a bike shop,

---

[1] Blaise Pascal, *Pensées* (Penguin, 1995), p. 220.

a yoga studio, a clothing store, or a computer-software consulting firm. Mr. Market is an imaginary partner in your business. Every day he knocks on your door and tells you what he thinks the business is worth.

Mr. Market's moods are unstable, and his estimates of value are determined as much by how he is feeling as by how your business is doing. He normally names a number that sounds about right. But some days Mr. Market is euphoric and puts a value on the business that's ridiculously high. Other days, Mr. Market is miserable and names a number that's absurdly low.

Before he knocks on your door, you never know how Mr. Market will be feeling. The more extreme his mood swings, the more intensely he will pressure you to trade with him at the wacky prices he comes up with.

Should you let either your own mood, or your appraisal of what the business is worth, be determined by this guy? Should you buy from him when he wants to sell? Should you sell to him when he wants to buy?

Mr. Market, of course, is more than a metaphor. He *is* the stock market: a collective beast made up of millions of minds, usually sensible, but sometimes giddy and sometimes grim. You cannot be an intelligent investor—either defensive or enterprising—if you let yourself become his emotional hostage.

Individuals versus Institutions

In this sentence . . .

> Thus the investor who permits himself to be stampeded or unduly worried by unjustified market declines in his holdings is perversely transforming his basic advantage into a basic disadvantage.

. . . what does Graham mean by the investor's "basic advantage"?

He means that listening to Mr. Market is an *option*, not an *obligation*. You don't have to trade with him because he wants you to, and you don't have to let his outlook become yours.

Why is that your basic advantage?

Professional investors aren't in the business of maximizing the returns on the portfolios they manage. They are in the business of maximizing the *fees* on the portfolios they manage.

You are a *principal*; an investment manager is only your *agent*. An agent has different incentives and preferences than you do.

TABLE 8-1: Institutions vs. Individuals

Institutions must...	You can...
...answer to clients, regulators, the media	...answer to no one but yourself
...measure performance against the market annually, quarterly, monthly, weekly, daily	...measure performance against long-term personal goals and ignore short-term market fluctuations
...shun strategies that diverge widely from the market, create "reputational risk," or jeopardize management fees	...be as unconventional as you wish
...buy and sell in vast quantities	...buy and sell in small amounts
...pay high trading costs	...incur close to zero trading cost
...dodge criticism by selling stocks on which they incur big losses	...hold on after big losses in expectation of eventual recovery
...typically sell a small stock that gets big	...hold a formerly small stock no matter how big it becomes
...keep as little cash as possible	...keep as much cash you wish
...charge management fees, reducing net return	...avoid management fees entirely
...generally trade with no regard for tax consequences	...trade opportunistically to minimize tax liability
...buy more at market highs and sell more at market lows	...buy or sell only when you wish

Decades ago, institutions had the edge over individuals. They could trade at lower cost and diversify more easily. They could obtain privileged access to companies' managers and unearth original research beyond the reach of individual investors.

Those days are gone.

Because institutions run giant portfolios, they often need to buy millions of dollars' worth of the typical stock to build a position big enough to make a meaningful contribution to performance. Their purchases drive up the price of the stock they want to own before they can finish buying it. Conversely, when they sell, they drive down the price before they can get out.

Individuals can buy and sell nearly any stock without affecting the price at all. They can diversify completely, at extremely low cost, with a total stock-market index fund. Regulatory reforms long ago eliminated the selective disclosures that gave institutions an informational edge.[2]

Because clients give more money to portfolio managers when markets are hot and withdraw it when returns are poor, the professionals are compelled to buy stocks as they get more expensive and sell as they get cheaper. You are free to do the opposite.

Small companies generate their best returns as they grow into big companies. Many portfolio managers are forced to sell too soon, because small-stock funds aren't supposed to own large stocks.[3] You can hang on indefinitely.

Big funds regularly dump stocks on which they incurred big losses, lest their clients blame them for blundering. You can hang on to losers you expect will recover. Institutions also tend not to buy stocks that have suffered severe recent losses; you can.

In the short term, an investment firm that ignores Mr. Market is all but certain to generate returns that deviate widely from average—

---

[2] Institutions still have access to more and better data, which they can process and analyze faster than individuals can, although only a few institutions have consistently outperformed as a result. See Gregory Zuckerman, *The Man Who Solved the Market: How Jim Simons Launched the Quant Revolution* (Portfolio, 2019).

[3] Eugene F. Fama and Kenneth R. French, "Migration," bit.ly/44W1O26.

which will spook clients into withdrawing money, reducing the firm's management fees.

In the long term, to have any chance of outperforming, a portfolio manager "should be eccentric, unconventional and rash in the eyes of average opinion," the economist John Maynard Keynes wrote in 1936. However, Keynes added:

> If he is successful, that will only confirm the general belief in his rashness; and if in the short run he is unsuccessful, which is very likely, he will not receive much mercy. Worldly wisdom teaches [fund managers] that it is better for reputation to fail conventionally than to succeed unconventionally.[4]

This simple matrix in Figure 8-1 shows how clients compare a portfolio manager's decisions to the rest of the market.

A manager who follows the herd in picking either a good or bad stock (see the right column) isn't likely to be criticized or fired. But

FIGURE 8-1: Wrong and Alone

		Portfolio manager's decision	
		Alone	Along with the crowd
Outcome of decision	Right	idiosyncratic	comforting
	Wrong	reckless	understandable

Source: Adapted from Mark Kritzman, Windham Capital Management.

---

[4] John Maynard Keynes, *The General Theory of Employment, Interest, and Money* (Macmillan, 1936), chapter 12, bit.ly/3rF2SsN.

clients will view a manager who stands alone in picking a good stock (upper left) as either lucky or eccentric, while if an unorthodox stock pick loses money (lower left) they will regard the manager as dangerous.

Professional investors never want to be in the bottom left corner, "wrong and alone," where clients might desert them. So they go along with the crowd—thereby minimizing the chance that their clients can ever outperform, but maximizing the odds that their own fees won't be impaired. You, however, don't have to cave to that kind of pressure.[5]

As markets move faster and trading becomes more volatile, the basic advantage of individuals looms even larger. No one can fire you for buying an unpopular stock. You are free to seek value in the most obscure companies and to find hope in the darkest hour. Your ability to invest for the long term in a short-term world is a superpower.[6]

You *can* outperform the professionals, because you don't have their handicaps of size, myopia, rigidity, conformity, and high cost. To beat the professionals, however, you can't play their game. You must play your own game. You must put Mr. Market in his place by trading only when it is in your interest, not his.

How Mr. Market Messes with Your Mind

Listening to Mr. Market will obliterate your individuality. Once you begin to conform with the crowd, your mind is no longer entirely your own.

If you were investing on a desert island, you would care only about the probabilities and consequences of your decisions. But you aren't on a desert island, so you probably also care about other people's

---

[5] Mark Kritzman, "Wrong and Alone," Peter L. Bernstein, Inc., *Economics & Portfolio Strategy* (1998); Dimitri Vayanos and Paul Woolley, "An Institutional Theory of Momentum and Reversal," bit.ly/3Kcbg9t; Jason Zweig, "The Velocity of Learning and the Future of Active Management," bit.ly/3Yhl4VH.
[6] In a speech in 1974, Graham said: "I am convinced that an individual *investor* with sound principles, and soundly advised, can do distinctly better over the long pull than a large institution." A half-century later, the handicaps on institutions have become as heavy as chains, while those formerly faced by individuals have fallen away.

How to Turn Your Basic Advantage into a Disadvantage

The great investor Charlie Munger, vice chairman of Berkshire Hathaway until his death in 2023, liked to solve problems by "inverting" them. To figure out how you can succeed, think about what it would take to fail.

- If the *option* of cheap trading makes you feel you have an *obligation* to trade as often as professionals do, you'll end up sandpapering your money away and jacking up your tax bill.
- If the *option* of diversifying cheaply creates the sense of *obligation* to diversify indiscriminately, you'll end up owning a triple-leveraged fund that uses artificial intelligence to pick socially responsible lithium start-ups based in southeastern Western Sahara.[1]
- If you let the *option* of being able to ignore Mr. Market turn into an *obligation* to act on every whim, you'll end up feeding your own ego and forgetting the importance of making structured decisions.

The Nobel Prize–winning economist James Tobin once wrote that the trustees of an endowment, such as a university or charitable foundation, are "the guardians of the future against the claims of the present." Their task is "to preserve equity among generations."[2]

Likewise, you are the guardian of your future against the claims of the present. You, too, must preserve equity among generations.

To meet those responsibilities, you must distinguish between options and obligations. Otherwise, you turn your basic advantages into crippling disadvantages.

---

[1] For leveraged funds, see the Commentary on Chapter 9.
[2] James Tobin, "What Is Permanent Endowment Income?," bit.ly/3OnubR3.

decisions, what they think about your decisions, and what they think about you.

Being part of the crowd feels safer, especially if you're a novice, facing unfamiliar challenges, or taking on high risks. You may tend to defer to the consensus even more when decisions are harder, because being able to deflect blame over big mistakes feels even better.

When you pay attention to the same thing at the same time as other people, you will remember it better, feel intensified emotions, make more extreme judgments, and be more motivated to act. Think of the difference between watching a sporting event by yourself on a delayed video feed at home and attending it live in a stadium—or even just watching it live on your phone.[7]

The internet and social media create borderless communities in which thousands, even millions, can focus together on the same topic or event. When everyone has simultaneous mutual access to information, each can immediately see and hear that all are paying attention to the same thing at the same time. In this state of shared attention, you can feel other people's minds converging with your own. Your experience is collective. Your confidence surges from knowing you're not alone in what you believe. *You* become *we*.

Humans evolved to cooperate in clans or small groups; the ability for countless people, no matter how widely dispersed, to coalesce into one collective mind is unprecedented in human history. Our individual brains haven't learned how to cope with it yet.

Technology has turned Mr. Market into a monster.

The individuals who flocked to buy such meme stocks as AMC Entertainment and GameStop in 2020 and 2021 exemplify the pitfalls of this phenomenon.

WallStreetBets, the online forum, ended December 2020 with 1.8 million subscribers. A month later it had 8.4 million. On January 26, 2021—the day Elon Musk tweeted "Gamestonk!!"—WallStreetBets subscribers posted an astounding 352,597 comments, mostly about GameStop. On January 28, WallStreetBets generated more than 271 million page views, making it the third-most-visited website in the world that day, behind only

---

[7] Marwa El Zein and Bahador Bahrami, "Joining a Group Diverts Regret and Responsibility Away from the Individual," bit.ly/452X2zx; Garriy Shteynberg, "A Collective Perspective: Shared Attention and the Mind," bit.ly/3OvXWzt.

Google and YouTube. From its closing price on January 21 to its high on January 28, GameStop stock rose more than 1,020%.[8]

A few people, who sold at the top, made money.

Most hung on, hoping for more. They incurred massive losses as the stock went into a kamikaze dive in February, losing 69%.

With shared attention intensifying their memory, emotions, and motivation, many still remember every twitch in the prices of their stocks, remain outraged over their losses, believe discredited conspiracy theories, and refuse to sell even though their holdings have shriveled before their eyes.

How Mr. Market Messes with Your Heart

The emotional mood swings of the stock market can wreak havoc on your feelings. Psychologists have shown that emotions shape both our perceptions and our actions—creating *unconscious biases* that can govern our behavior even if we're never aware of it. Even a faint whiff of emotion can skew your decisions:

> **Anger** fires up urgency, confidence, and the sensation of being in control. Angry people rely more on snap judgments. They also think good things are more likely—and bad things less likely—to happen to them than to others. Angry people, especially men, take greater risks.[9]
>
> **Anxiety** makes you more sensitive to the magnitude of a possible reward than to the probability of receiving it. Long-shot bets look better when you're anxious—especially if you've been losing money.[10]

---

[8] Elon Musk tweet, bit.ly/3Ur5OUC; Daniel Bradley et al., "Place Your Bets?," bit.ly/453LdcE. "Stonk," as in "Gamestonk," is an intentional misspelling of "stock" that online commenters use to flaunt their indifference to conventional investing analysis.

[9] Jennifer S. Lerner et al., "Emotion and Decision Making," bit.ly/3q37okj; Rebecca A. Ferrer et al., "Revisiting the Effects of Anger on Risk-Taking," bit.ly/3Kccp0O.

[10] Catherine A. Hartley and Elizabeth A. Phelps, "Anxiety and Decision-Making," bit.ly/3uaGYPg; George F. Loewenstein et al., "Risk as Feelings," bit.ly/3Y76rnr; Jason Zweig, "Fear," bit.ly/3Do3CF8.

Loneliness can make you less likely to seek out information that could contradict what you already believe. It also can increase your anxiety, impair your reasoning, and shred your attention span. "Cabin fever" can undermine your self-control and make you more impulsive.[11]

Sadness makes people prefer smaller rewards sooner over larger rewards later. It also can raise the price you're willing to pay to buy something you don't own. Feeling sad makes riskier bets more attractive and deferring gratification more difficult. Sadness is emotional poison for patience.[12]

Stress impairs working memory and makes focusing on long-term goals difficult; it can lead to perseveration, in which people follow the same failing behaviors regardless of feedback. Under stress, you might jump to conclusions and neglect novel solutions to problems. Stress can also trigger increased risk-taking.[13]

Is it any wonder that, during the Covid pandemic, when hundreds of millions of people felt angry, anxious, lonely, sad, and stressed, tens of millions started impetuously trading stocks?

Talking Back to Mr. Market

Today the stock market crashed more than 30%.

Your phone is flaring with news alerts, electronic stock tickers are an endless crawl of crimson, the president is urging the public to remain calm, television pundits are shrieking that everyone should sell everything, friends and family are texting you to dump your stocks while you still can. Whether you realize it or not, your heart is racing, your muscles are tense, your palms are sweating.

---

[11] John T. Cacioppo and Louise C. Hawkley, "Perceived Social Isolation and Cognition," bit.ly/3O8ctQe.

[12] Jennifer S. Lerner et al., "The Financial Costs of Sadness," bit.ly/3Kw0MSH; Rajagopal Raghunathan and Michel Tuan Pham, "All Negative Moods Are Not Equal," bit.ly/43vHjrK.

[13] Anthony J. Porcelli and Mauricio R. Delgado, "Stress and Decision Making," bit.ly/3rxcEgj; Katrin Starcke and Matthias Brand, "Decision Making Under Stress," bit.ly/44C4Ngk; Elizabeth A. Phelps et al., "Emotion and Decision Making," bit.ly/3q1R0R3.

Mr. Market is red in the face as he bangs on your door, yelling that every dollar you had in stocks yesterday is worth less than 70 cents today.

How do you answer him?

You have the *option* to sell, but the *obligation* to think before you act.

Go to a quiet room and imagine that somebody else had just suffered these losses and is asking you for advice. That should prompt you to reflect on questions like these:

- Other than stock prices, which specific aspects of the businesses you own have changed?
- How large a tax bill would you incur if you sell?
- If this stock or fund were a gift rather than a purchase, would you return it to the person who gave it to you now that it's fallen in price?
- Has this stock or fund ever gone down this much before? If so, would you have done better if you had sold out—or if you had bought more?
- If you liked this asset well enough to buy it at a higher price, shouldn't you like it more now that the price has fallen?

Such questions will take some research to answer—which is as it should be. This way, you stop Mr. Market's overreaction to a change in *price* from contaminating your view of underlying *value*. He might be right; he might be wrong. Only by comparing price against value will you be able to tell.

You can use the same approach whether a single stock, an industry, or the entire market collapses. You can also invert the questions whenever prices go up farther and faster than you expected.

Sooner or later, Mr. Market will go off the rails.

Be prepared, so you can stay on track.

CHAPTER 9

Investing in Investment Funds
by Benjamin Graham

One course open to the defensive investor is to put his money into investment-company shares. Those that are redeemable on demand by the holder, at net asset value, are commonly known as "mutual funds" (or "open-end funds"). Most of these are actively selling additional shares through a corps of salesmen. Those with nonredeemable shares are called "closed-end" companies or funds; the number of their shares remains relatively constant. All of the funds of any importance are registered with the Securities & Exchange Commission (SEC), and are subject to its regulations and controls.

The industry is a very large one. At the end of 1970 there were 383 funds registered with the SEC, having assets totaling $54.6 billions. Of these 356 companies, with $50.6 billions, were mutual funds, and 27 companies with $4.0 billions, were closed-end.*

There are different ways of classifying the funds. One is by the broad division of their portfolio; they are "balanced funds" if they have a significant (generally about one-third) component of bonds, or "stock-funds" if their holdings are nearly all common stocks. (There are some other varieties here, such as "bond funds," "hedge funds," "letter-stock funds," etc.)† Another is by their objectives, as

---

* As of late 2023, in the U.S. 6,973 mutual funds held a total of $18.82 trillion in net assets; 426 closed-end funds held $243 billion; and 3,076 exchange-traded funds held $7.63 trillion. Worldwide, mutual funds' assets totaled $63.39 trillion.

† Letter-stock funds no longer exist, while hedge funds are generally not available in a mutual-fund format.

their primary aim is for income, price stability, or capital appreciation ("growth"). Another distinction is by their method of sale. "Load funds" add a selling charge (generally about 9% of asset value on minimum purchases) to the value before charge.[1] Others, known as "no-load" funds, make no such charge; the managements are content with the usual investment-counsel fees for handling the capital. Since they cannot pay salesmen's commissions, the size of the no-load funds tends to be on the low side.* The buying and selling prices of the *closed-end* funds are not fixed by the companies, but fluctuate in the open market as does the ordinary corporate stock.

Most of the companies operate under special provisions of the income-tax law, designed to relieve the shareholders from double taxation on their earnings. In effect, the funds must pay out virtually all their ordinary income—i.e., dividends and interest received, less expenses. In addition they can pay out their realized long-term profits on sales of investments—in the form of "capital-gains dividends"—which are treated by the shareholder as if they were his own security profits. (There is another option here, which we omit to avoid clutter.)† Nearly all the funds have but one class of security outstanding. A new wrinkle, introduced in 1967, divides the capitalization into a preferred issue, which will receive all the ordinary income, and a capital issue, or common stock, which will receive all the profits on security sales. (These are called "dual-purpose funds.")‡

Many of the companies that state their primary aim is for capital gains concentrate on the purchase of the so-called "growth stocks," and they often have the word "growth" in their name. Some

---

* Today, the maximum sales load on a stock fund tends to be around 5.75%, although most financial advisers will waive the upfront charge; instead, you will pay "distribution fees" that can reach 1% per year.

† Nearly every mutual fund today is taxed as a "regulated investment company," which is exempt from corporate income tax so long as it pays out essentially all of its income to its shareholders. In the "option" that Graham omits "to avoid clutter," a fund can ask the SEC for special permission to distribute some of its holdings directly to its shareholders—as his Graham-Newman Corp. did in 1948, parceling out shares in GEICO to the fund's own investors. This sort of distribution is extraordinarily rare.

‡ Dual-purpose funds, popular in the late 1980s, have disappeared.

specialize in a designated area such as chemicals, aviation, overseas investments; this is usually indicated in their titles.

The investor who wants to make an intelligent commitment in fund shares has thus a large and somewhat bewildering variety of choices before him—not too different from those offered in direct investment. In this chapter we shall deal with some major questions, viz:

1. Is there any way by which the investor can assure himself of better than average results by choosing the right funds? (Subquestion: What about the "performance funds"?)*

2. If not, how can he avoid choosing funds that will give him worse than average results?

3. Can he make intelligent choices between different types of funds—e.g., balanced versus all-stock, open-end versus closed-end, load versus no-load?

Investment-Fund Performance as a Whole

Before trying to answer these questions we should say something about the performance of the fund industry as a whole. Has it done a good job for its shareholders? In the most general way, how have fund investors fared as against those who made their investments directly? We are quite certain that the funds in the aggregate have served a useful purpose. They have promoted good habits of savings and investment; they have protected countless individuals against costly mistakes in the stock market; they have brought their participants income and profits commensurate with the overall returns from common stocks. On a comparative basis we would hazard the guess that the average individual who put his money exclusively in investment-fund shares in the past ten years has fared better than the average person who made his common-stock purchases directly.

The last point is probably true even though the actual

---

* "Performance funds" were all the rage in the late 1960s. After one or two hot years, they scorched their investors and then went cold.

performance of the funds seems to have been no better than that of common stocks as a whole, and even though the cost of investing in mutual funds may have been greater than that of direct purchases. The real choice of the average individual has not been between constructing and acquiring a well-balanced common-stock portfolio or doing the same thing, a bit more expensively, by buying into the funds. More likely his choice has been between succumbing to the wiles of the doorbell-ringing mutual-fund salesman on the one hand, as against succumbing to the even wilier and much more dangerous peddlers of second- and third-rate new offerings. We cannot help thinking, too, that **the average individual who opens a brokerage account with the idea of making conservative common-stock investments is likely to find himself beset by untoward influences in the direction of speculation and speculative losses; these temptations should be much less for the mutual-fund buyer.**

But how have the investment funds performed as against the general market? This is a somewhat controversial subject, but we shall try to deal with it in simple but adequate fashion. Table 9-1 gives some calculated results for 1961–1970 of our ten largest stock funds at the end of 1970, but choosing only the largest one from each management group. It summarizes the overall return of each of these funds for 1961–1965, 1966–1970, and for the single years 1969 and 1970. We also give average results based on the sum of one share of each of the ten funds. These companies had combined assets of over $15 billion at the end of 1969, or about one-third of all the common-stock funds. Thus they should be fairly representative of the industry as a whole. (In theory, there should be a bias in this list on the side of better than industry performance, since these better companies should have been entitled to more rapid expansion than the others; but this may not be the case in practice.)

Some interesting facts can be gathered from this table. First, we find that the overall results of these ten funds for 1961–1970 were not appreciably different from those of the Standard & Poor's 500-stock composite average (or the S & P 425-industrial stock average). But they were definitely better than those of the DJIA. (This raises the intriguing question as to why the 30 giants in the DJIA did worse than the much more numerous and apparently

TABLE 9-1 Management Results of Ten Large Mutual Funds[a]

	(Indicated) 5 years, 1961–1965 (all +)	5 years, 1966–1970	10 years, 1961–1970 (all +)	1969	1970	Net Assets, December 1970 (millions)
Affiliated Fund	71%	+19.7%	105.3%	−14.3%	+2.2%	$1,600
Dreyfus	97	+18.7	135.4	−11.9	−6.4	2,232
Fidelity Fund	79	+31.8	137.1	−7.4	+2.2	819
Fundamental Inv.	79	+1.0	81.3	−12.7	−5.8	1,054
Invest. Co. of Am.	82	+37.9	152.2	−10.6	+2.3	1,168
Investors Stock Fund	54	+5.6	63.5	−80.0	−7.2	2,227
Mass. Inv. Trust	18	+16.2	44.2	−4.0	+0.6	1,956
National Investors	61	+31.7	112.2	+4.0	−9.1	747
Putnam Growth	62	+22.3	104.0	−13.3	−3.8	684
United Accum.	74	−2.0	72.7	−10.3	−2.9	1,141
Average	72	18.3	105.8	−8.9	−2.2	$13,628 (total)
Standard & Poor's composite index	77	+16.1	104.7	−8.3	+3.5	
DJIA	78	+2.9	83.0	−11.6	+8.7	

[a] These are the stock funds with the largest net assets at the end of 1970, but using only one fund from each management group. Data supplied by Wiesenberger Financial Services.

rather miscellaneous list used by Standard & Poor's.)* A second point is that the funds' aggregate performance as against the S & P index has improved somewhat in the last five years, compared with the preceding five. The funds' gain ran a little lower than S & P's in 1961–1965 and a little higher than S & P's in 1966–1970. The third point is that a wide difference exists between the results of the individual funds.

We do not think the mutual-fund industry can be criticized for doing no better than the market as a whole. Their managers and their professional competitors administer so large a portion of all marketable common stocks that what happens to the market as a whole must necessarily happen (approximately) to the sum of their funds. (Note that the trust assets of insured commercial banks included $181 billion of common stocks at the end of 1969; if we add to this the common stocks in accounts handled by investment advisers, plus the $56 billion of mutual and similar funds, we must conclude that the combined decisions of these professionals pretty well determine the movements of the stock averages, and that the movement of the stock averages pretty well determines the funds' aggregate results.)

Are there better than average funds and can the investor select these so as to obtain superior results for himself? Obviously all investors could not do this, since in that case we would soon be back where we started, with no one doing better than anyone else. Let us consider the question first in a simplified fashion. Why shouldn't the investor find out what fund has made the best showing of the lot over a period of sufficient years in the past, assume from this that its management is the most capable and will therefore do better than average in the future, and put his money in that fund? This idea appears the more practicable because, in the case of the mutual funds, he could obtain this "most capable management" without paying any special premium for it as against the other funds. (By contrast, among noninvestment corporations

---

* For periods as long as 10 years, the returns of the Dow and the S&P 500 can diverge by fairly wide margins. Over the course of the typical investing lifetime, however—say 25 to 50 years—their returns have tended to converge quite closely.

the best-managed companies sell at correspondingly high prices in relation to their current earnings and assets.)

The evidence on this point has been conflicting over the years. But our Table 9-1 covering the ten largest funds indicates that the results shown by the top five performers of 1961–1965 carried over *on the whole* through 1966–1970, even though two of this set did not do as well as two of the other five. Our studies indicate that the investor in mutual-fund shares may properly consider comparative performance over a period of years in the past, say at least five, *provided* the data do not represent a large net upward movement of the market as a whole. In the latter case spectacularly favorable results may be achieved in unorthodox ways—as will be demonstrated in our following section on "performance" funds. Such results in themselves may indicate only that the fund managers are taking undue speculative risks, and getting away with same *for the time being*.

"Performance" Funds

One of the new phenomena of recent years was the appearance of the cult of "performance" in the management of investment funds (and even of many trust funds). We must start this section with the important disclaimer that it does not apply to the large majority of well-established funds, but only to a relatively small section of the industry which has attracted a disproportionate amount of attention. The story is simple enough. **Some of those in charge set out to get much better than average (or DJIA) results. They succeeded in doing this for a while, garnering considerable publicity and additional funds to manage. The aim was legitimate enough; unfortunately, it appears that, in the context of investing really sizable funds, the aim cannot be accomplished without incurring sizable risks. And in a comparatively short time the risks came home to roost.**

Several of the circumstances surrounding the "performance" phenomenon caused ominous headshaking by those of us whose experience went far back—even to the 1920s—and whose views, for that very reason, were considered old-fashioned and irrelevant to this (second) "New Era." In the first place, and on this very point, nearly all these brilliant performers were young men—in their thirties and forties—whose direct financial experience was limited to the all but continuous bull market of 1948–1968. Secondly, they often acted as if the definition of a "sound investment" was a stock that was likely to have a good rise in the market in the next few months. This led to large commitments in newer ventures at prices completely disproportionate to their assets or recorded earnings. They could be "justified" only by a combination of naïve hope in the future accomplishments of these enterprises with an apparent shrewdness in exploiting the speculative enthusiasms of the uninformed and greedy public.

This section will not mention people's names. But we have every reason to give concrete examples of companies. The "performance fund" most in the public's eye was undoubtedly Manhattan Fund, Inc., organized at the end of 1965. Its first offering was of 27 million shares at $9.25 to $10 per share. The company started out with $247 million of capital. Its emphasis was, of course, on capital gains. Most of its funds were invested in issues selling at high multipliers of current earnings, paying no dividends (or very small ones), with a large speculative following and spectacular price movements. The fund showed an overall gain of 38.6% in 1967, against 11% for the S & P composite index. But thereafter its performance left much to be desired, as is shown in Table 9-2.

The portfolio of Manhattan Fund at the end of 1969 was unorthodox to say the least. It is an extraordinary fact that two of its largest investments were in companies that filed for bankruptcy within six months thereafter, and a third faced creditors' actions in 1971. It is another extraordinary fact that shares of at least one of these doomed companies were bought not only by investment funds but by university endowment funds, the trust departments of large banking institutions, and the like.* A third extraordinary

---

* One of the "doomed companies" Graham refers to was National Student Marketing Corp., a con game masquerading as a stock, whose saga was told brilliantly in Andrew Tobias's *The Funny Money Game* (Playboy Press, 1971). Among the supposedly sophisticated investors who were snookered by NSM's charismatic founder, Cort Randell, were the endowment funds of Cornell and Harvard and the trust departments at such prestigious banks as Morgan Guaranty and Bankers Trust.

TABLE 9-2 A Performance-Fund Portfolio and Performance
(Larger Holdings of Manhattan Fund, December 31, 1969)

Shares Held (thousands)	Issue	Price	Earned 1969	Dividend 1969	Market Value (millions)
60	Teleprompter	99	$ .99	none	$ 6.0
190	Deltona	60½	2.32	none	11.5
280	Fedders	34	1.28	$ .35	9.5
105	Horizon Corp.	53½	2.68	none	5.6
150	Rouse Co.	34	.07	none	5.1
130	Mattel Inc.	64¼	1.11	.20	8.4
120	Polaroid	125	1.90	.32	15.0
244[a]	Nat'l Student Mkt'g	28½	.32	none	6.1
56	Telex Corp.	90½	.68	none	5.0
100	Bausch & Lomb	77¾	1.92	.80	7.8
190	Four Seasons Nursing	66	.80	none	12.3[b]
20	Int. Bus. Machines	365	8.21	3.60	7.3
41.5	Nat'l Cash Register	160	1.95	1.20	6.7
100	Saxon Ind.	109	3.81	none	10.9
105	Career Academy	50	.43	none	5.3
285	King Resources	28	.69	none	8.1
					$130.6
				Other common stocks	93.8
				Other holdings	19.6
				Total investments[c]	$244.0

[a] After 2-for-1 split.
[b] Also $1.1 million of affiliated stocks.
[c] Excluding cash equivalents.

Annual Performance Compared with S & P Composite Index

	1966	1967	1968	1969	1970	1971
Manhattan Fund	– 6 %	+38.6%	– 7.3%	–13.3%	–36.9%	+ 9.6%
S & P Composite	–10.1%	+23.0%	+10.4%	– 8.3%	+ 3.5%	+13.5%

fact was that the founder-manager of Manhattan Fund sold his stock in a separately organized management company to another large concern for over $20 million in its stock; at that time the management company sold had less than $1 million in assets. This is undoubtedly one of the greatest disparities of all times between the results for the "manager" and the "managees."

A book published at the end of 1969[2] provided profiles of nineteen men "who are tops at the demanding game of managing billions of dollars of other people's money." The summary told us further that "they are young ... some earn more than a million dollars a year ... they are a new financial breed ... they all have a total fascination with the market ... and a spectacular knack for coming up with winners." A fairly good idea of the accomplishments of this top group can be obtained by examining the published results of the funds they manage. Such results are available for funds directed by twelve of the nineteen persons described in *The Money Managers*. Typically enough, they showed up well in 1966, and brilliantly in 1967. In 1968 their performance was still good in the aggregate, but mixed as to individual funds. In 1969 they all showed losses, with only one managing to do a bit better than the S & P composite index. In 1970 their comparative performance was even worse than in 1969.

We have presented this picture in order to point a moral, which perhaps can best be expressed by the old French proverb: *Plus ça change, plus c'est la même chose*. **Bright, energetic people—usually quite young—have promised to perform miracles with "other people's money" since time immemorial. They have usually been able to do it for a while—or at least to appear to have done it—and they have inevitably brought losses to their public in the end.***
About a half century ago the "miracles" were often accompanied by flagrant manipulation, misleading corporate reporting, outrageous

---

* As later proof that "the more things change, the more they stay the same," consider that 29-year-old Ryan Jacob launched the Jacob Internet Fund at year-end 1999, after producing a 216% return at his previous dot-com fund. Investors poured nearly $300 million into Jacob's fund in the first few weeks of 2000. It then proceeded to lose 79.1% in 2000, 56.4% in 2001, and 13% in 2002—a cumulative collapse of 92%.

capitalization structures, and other semifraudulent financial practices. All this brought on an elaborate system of financial controls by the SEC, as well as a cautious attitude toward common stocks on the part of the general public. The operations of the new "money managers" in 1965–1969 came a little more than one full generation after the shenanigans of 1926–1929.* The specific malpractices banned after the 1929 crash were no longer resorted to—they involved the risk of jail sentences. But in many corners of Wall Street they were replaced by newer gadgets and gimmicks that produced very similar results in the end. Outright manipulation of prices disappeared, but there were many other methods of drawing the gullible public's attention to the profit possibilities in "hot" issues. Blocks of "letter stock"[3] could be bought well below the quoted market price, subject to undisclosed restrictions on their sale; they could immediately be carried in the reports at their full market value, showing a lovely and illusory profit. And so on. It is amazing how, in a completely different atmosphere of regulation and prohibitions, Wall Street was able to duplicate so much of the excesses and errors of the 1920s.

No doubt there will be new regulations and new prohibitions. The specific abuses of the late 1960s will be fairly adequately banned from Wall Street. But **it is probably too much to expect that the urge to speculate will ever disappear, or that the exploitation of that urge can ever be abolished. It is part of the armament of the intelligent investor to know about these "Extraordinary Popular Delusions,"[4] and to keep as far away from them as possible.**

The picture of most of the performance funds is a poor one if we start *after* their spectacular record in 1967. With the 1967 figures included, their overall showing is not at all disastrous. On that basis one of "The Money Managers" operators did quite a bit better than the S & P composite index, three did distinctly worse, and six did about the same. Let us take as a check another group of performance funds—the ten that made the best showing in 1967,

---

* The disastrous boom and bust of 1999–2002 also came roughly 35 years after the previous cycle of insanity. The binges and crashes of 2007-09 and 2020-22 came at shorter intervals, however. Intelligent investors should brace themselves for booms and busts at any moment.

with gains ranging from 84% up to 301% in that single year. Of these, four gave a better overall four-year performance than the S & P index, if the 1967 gains are included; and two excelled the index in 1968–1970. None of these funds was large, and the average size was about $60 million. Thus, there is a strong indication that smaller size is a necessary factor for obtaining continued outstanding results.

The foregoing account contains the implicit conclusion that there may be special risks involved in looking for superior performance by investment-fund managers. All financial experience up to now indicates that large funds, soundly managed, can produce at best only slightly better than average results over the years. If they are unsoundly managed they can produce spectacular, but largely illusory, profits for a while, followed inevitably by calamitous losses. There have been instances of funds that have consistently outperformed the market averages for, say, ten years or more. But these have been scarce exceptions, having most of their operations in specialized fields, with self-imposed limits on the capital employed—and not actively sold to the public.*

Closed-End versus Open-End Funds

Almost all the mutual funds or open-end funds, which offer their holders the right to cash in their shares at each day's valuation of the portfolio, have a corresponding machinery for selling new shares. By this means most of them have grown in size over the years. The closed-end companies, nearly all of which were organized a long time ago, have a fixed capital structure, and thus have diminished in relative dollar importance. Open-end companies are being sold by many thousands of energetic and persuasive salesmen; the closed-end shares have no one especially interested in distributing them. Consequently it has been possible to sell most "mutual funds" to

---

* Today's equivalent of Graham's "scarce exceptions" tend to be open-end funds that are closed to new investors—meaning that the managers have stopped taking in any more cash. While that reduces the management fees they can earn, it maximizes the returns their existing shareholders can earn. Because most fund managers would rather look out for No. 1 than be No. 1, closing a fund to new investors is a rare and courageous step.

the public at a fixed premium of about 9% above net asset value (to cover salesmen's commissions, etc.), while the majority of close-end shares have been consistently obtainable at *less* than their asset value. This price discount has varied among individual companies, and the average discount for the group as a whole has also varied from one date to another. Figures on this point for 1961–1970 are given in Table 9-3.

TABLE 9-3 Certain Data on Closed-End Funds, Mutual Funds, and S & P Composite Index

Year	Average Discount of Closed-End Funds	Average Results of Closed-End Funds[a]	Average Results of Mutual Stock Funds[b]	Results of S & P Index[c]
1970	− 6%	even	− 5.3%	+ 3.5%
1969		− 7.9%	−12.5	− 8.3
1968	(+ 7)[d]	+13.3	+15.4	+10.4
1967	− 5	+28.2	+37.2	+23.0
1966	−12	− 5.9	− 4.1	−10.1
1965	−14	+14.0	+24.8	+12.2
1964	−10	+16.9	+13.6	+14.8
1963	− 8	+20.8	+19.3	+24.0
1962	− 4	−11.6	−14.6	− 8.7
1961	− 3	+23.6	+25.7	+27.0
Average of 10 yearly figures:		+ 9.14%	+ 9.95%	+ 9.79%

[a] Wiesenberger average of ten diversified companies.
[b] Average of five Wiesenberger averages of common-stock funds each year.
[c] In all cases distributions are added back.
[d] Premium.

It does not take much shrewdness to suspect that the lower relative price for closed-end as against open-end shares has very little to do with the difference in the overall investment results between the two groups. That this is true is indicated by the comparison of the annual results for 1961–1970 of the two groups included in Table 9-3.

Thus we arrive at one of the few clearly evident rules for investors' choices. If you want to put money in investment funds, buy a group of closed-end shares at a discount of, say, 10% to 15% from asset value, instead of paying a premium of about 9% above asset value for shares of an open-end company. Assuming that the future dividends and changes in asset values continue to be about the same for the two groups, you will thus obtain about one-fifth more for your money from the closed-end shares.*

The mutual-fund salesman will be quick to counter with the argument: "Ah, but if you own closed-end shares you can never be sure what price you can sell them for. The discount can be greater than it is today, and you will suffer from the wider spread. With our shares you are guaranteed the right to turn in your shares at 100% of asset value, never less." Let us examine this argument a bit; it will be a good exercise in logic and plain common sense. Question: Assuming that the discount on closed-end shares does widen, how likely is it that you will be worse off with those shares than with an otherwise equivalent purchase of open-end shares?

This calls for a little arithmetic. Assume that Investor A buys some open-end shares at 109% of asset value, and Investor B buys closed-end shares at 85% thereof, plus 1½% commission. Both sets of shares earn and pay 30% of this asset value in, say, four years, and end up with the same value as at the beginning. Investor A redeems his shares at 100% of value, losing the 9% premium he paid. His overall return for the period is 30% less 9%, or 21% on asset value. This, in turn, is 19% on his investment. How much must Investor B realize on his closed-end shares to obtain the same return on his investment as Investor A? The answer is 73%, or a discount of 27% from asset value. In other words, the closed-end man could suffer a

---

* In the 2020s, closed-end funds generally have several handicaps: They are thinly traded, often leveraged with borrowed money, and have high annual expenses. That makes them riskier and costlier than ETFs or conventional mutual funds. So, with rare exceptions (particularly during a market crash), closed-end funds are not worth exploring unless they can be bought at discounts of at least 15% below net asset value.

TABLE 9-4 Average Results of Diversified Closed-End Funds, 1961–1970[a]

	1970	5 years, 1966–1970	1961–1970	Premium or Discount, December 1970
Three funds selling at premiums	−5.2%	+25.4%	+115.0%	11.4% premium
Ten funds selling at discounts	+1.3	+22.6	+102.9	9.2% discount

[a] Data from Wiesenberger Financial Services.

widening of 12 points in the market discount (about double) before his return would get down to that of the open-end investor. An adverse change of this magnitude has happened rarely, if ever, in the history of closed-end shares. Hence it is very unlikely that you will obtain a lower overall return from a (representative) closed-end company, bought at a discount, if its investment performance is about equal to that of a representative mutual fund. If a small-load (or no-load) fund is substituted for one with the usual "8½%" load, the advantage of the closed-end investment is of course reduced, but it remains an advantage.

The fact that a few closed-end funds are selling at *premiums* greater than the true 9% charge on most mutual funds introduces a separate question for the investor. Do these premium companies enjoy superior management of sufficient proven worth to warrant their elevated prices? If the answer is sought in the comparative results for the past five or ten years, the answer would appear to be no. Three of the six premium companies have mainly foreign investments. A striking feature of these is the large variation in prices in a few years' time; at the end of 1970 one sold at only one-quarter of its high, another at a third, another at less than half. If we consider the three domestic companies selling above asset value, we find that the average of their ten-year overall returns was somewhat better than that of ten discount funds, but the opposite was true in the last five years. A comparison of the 1961–1970 record

TABLE 9-5 Comparison of Two Leading Closed-End Companies[a]

	1970	5 years, 1966–1970	10 years, 1961–1970	Premium or Discount, December 1970
General Am. Investors Co.	–0.3%	+34.0%	+165.6%	7.6% discount
Lehman Corp.	–7.2	+20.6	+108.0	13.9% premium

[a] Data from Wiesenberger Financial Services.

of Lehman Corp. and of General American Investors, two of our oldest and largest closed-end companies, is given in Table 9-5. One of these sold 14% above and the other 7.6% below its net-asset value at the end of 1970. The difference in price to net-asset relationships did not appear warranted by these figures.

Investment in Balanced Funds

The 23 balanced funds covered in the Wiesenberger Report had between 25% and 59% of their assets in preferred stocks and bonds, the average being just 40%. The balance was held in common stocks. It would appear more logical for the typical investor to make his bond-type investments directly, rather than to have them form part of a mutual-fund commitment. The average income return shown by these balanced funds in 1970 was only 3.9% per annum on asset value, or say 3.6% on the offering price. The better choice for the bond component would be the purchase of United States savings bonds, or corporate bonds rated A or better, or tax-free bonds, for the investor's bond portfolio.

Commentary on Chapter 9

by Jason Zweig

> [Fund managers] allocate the funds between themselves and their clients in the ancient classic manner, i.e., at the close of the day's business they take all the money and throw it up in the air. Everything that sticks to the ceiling belongs to the clients.
> —Fred Schwed, Jr.[1]

For decades, the fund industry had the investing public fooled.

Beginning in the 1920s, fund managers masqueraded as miracle workers who could minimize risk, find winners and shun losers, and beat the market to a bloody pulp—making big commissions and fat annual fees seem worth paying.

Only after the global financial crisis of 2008–09 did the public finally wake up.

The Futility of the Funds

Year after year, well-educated, highly trained professionals, armed with vast quantities of data and computing power, attempt to pick investments that will earn higher returns than a market average like the S&P 500 index. Year after year, most of these actively managed funds fail.

In 2022, 43% of actively managed U.S. mutual funds and ETFs outperformed their respective market average, according to Morningstar, down from 47% the year before. Only 10.5% of funds investing in large U.S. stocks survived for the full 10 years ending June 30, 2023, *and* beat their benchmark.

---

[1] Fred Schwed, Jr., *Where Are the Customers' Yachts?* (Wiley, 2006), p. 140.

Among those mutual funds that do beat the market one year, almost none go on to repeat:

TABLE 9-1: It's Lonely at the Top

Top half of U.S. stock funds in December 2020 (number)	Remaining in top half by December 2021 (percentage)	Remaining in top half by December 2022 (percentage)
975	32.1%	7.2%

Top quarter of U.S. stock funds in December 2020 (number)	Remaining in top quarter by December 2021 (percentage)	Remaining in top quarter by December 2022 (percentage)
488	4.1%	0.0%

Source: S&P Dow Jones Indices, bit.ly/3rPkBO8.

Three main handicaps cripple fund managers—and their investors.

Asset elephantiasis. As funds grow bigger, buying smaller stocks becomes harder. A fund with $100 million can put 1% in any stock; that's only $1 million. A fund with $10 billion putting 1% in a stock has to buy $100 million of it—a prohibitively huge hunk of most small companies. Trading costs may also go up as a fund becomes a giant. And the more money investors add, the greater the pressure to buy something, anything, that can put all that new cash to work.

Fees. In the U.S., the average stock fund charged 1.15% in annual expenses as of 2022, according to the Investment Company Institute.

Trading costs. Imagine a fund has a portfolio turnover rate of 100%, meaning the managers hold its typical stock for one year. Let's say it incurs 0.25% in brokerage costs to buy and to sell a stock. Trading would cost this fund's investors 0.5% annually.

If a fund charges 1.15% in expenses and racks up 0.5% in brokerage costs, that's a 1.65% annual drag. If the market goes up 10% in a year, the fund must gain 11.65% before expenses just to match the market's return after expenses. That means the fund must perform 16.5% better, before fees, to avoid underperforming after fees![2]

It isn't just beating the market that's hard for fund managers. Even *matching* the market is hard.

When "Average" Is Better than Average

Graham understood all this—decades before most other people. As early as 1951 he suggested that investors would be better off if they could invest in a market average. Graham emphasized the idea repeatedly until he died in 1976. That same year, John C. Bogle of Vanguard Group introduced the index mutual fund.[3]

Index funds hold practically every investment in a market benchmark like the S&P 500, MSCI All-Country World Index, or Bloomberg U.S. Aggregate Bond Index. They seek to match the market's return (before fees), not to beat it. They don't need to spend lavish sums on research or pay high trading costs, because they aren't trying to pick the best investments and avoid the worst—but only to buy and hold them all.

Automatically, the winners will grow and the losers shrink, with no need for the manager to analyze or trade them. Total costs at an index fund can be below 0.05% per year—well under one-tenth the cost of traditional funds seeking to beat the market. And, because they trade so seldom, index funds rarely generate high tax bills.

By settling for average, you end up doing much better than average. If one investor gains on a trade, another must have lost by the same amount; across the entire market, all that activity nets out to zero. And that's before costs. After the expenses of research and trading, most investors trying to beat the market get beaten by it.

Own an index fund instead, and you will match the market before

---

[2] Funds' trading costs are often higher than 0.25%; see Phil Mackintosh, "How Much Does Trading Cost the Buy Side?," bit.ly/3Dychoy. Trading costs aren't reported in a mutual fund or ETF's annual expenses; instead, they are deducted from its gross return. If the market went up only 5%, then the fund in our example would need to rise 6.65% to match it after expenses; that's 33% greater than the market's return.

[3] Jason Zweig, "Would Benjamin Graham Have Hated Index Funds?," bit.ly/3qb7iXS.

costs—thereby surpassing almost all the amateurs and professionals trying to beat it, after they pay their much higher expenses. Thus, by "settling for average" you can secure above-average results.[4]

Extremely Tempting Funds

You can index your portfolio with mutual funds or *exchange-traded funds*. Unlike mutual funds, which in the U.S. you can buy or sell only at one price at the end of the trading day, you can trade ETFs anytime.

ETFs are remarkably cheap, with expenses as low as 0.03%, or only $3 per year on a $10,000 investment.

Index mutual funds can be almost as cheap. But a traditional mutual fund seeking to beat the market that charges an average of 1.15% annually is *nearly 40 times more* expensive. Decades of research show that the single most important determinant of a fund's success is whether its fees are low.

The peril of ETFs is that you can trade them all day long, and many people do.

If you used ETFs this way, you would turn your basic advantage into a disadvantage. Why would you want to take an asset that you can hold at near-zero cost for decades and turn it into a short-term trading toy?

Another potential problem: You can find an ETF for every conceivable purpose, and some inconceivable ones too.

In 2023, various ETFs:

- offered exposure to Korean media companies;
- owned nickel-mining stocks;
- bought only stocks traded by Democratic members of the U.S. Congress;
- lost 2% for every 1% daily gain in Brazilian stocks;
- offered between 25% and 200% exposure to nothing but Tesla Inc. stock, depending on market conditions;
- used artificial intelligence to pick agriculture companies;

---

[4] William F. Sharpe, "The Arithmetic of Active Management," bit.ly/4572gud. See also Lasse Heje Pedersen, "Sharpening the Arithmetic of Active Management," bit.ly/3OgJucZ.

TABLE 9-2: Exuberantly Traded Funds

ETF	Ticker symbol	Average daily net assets	Average daily trading volume	Daily turnover rate	Annualized turnover rate
SPDR S&P 500	SPY	$394,849,683,157	$34,405,432,438	8.7%	2196%
iShares Core S&P 500	IVV	$327,548,869,939	$1,780,984,598	0.5%	137%
Vanguard S&P 500	VOO	$308,258,084,527	$1,551,640,052	0.5%	127%
Vanguard Total Stock Market	VTI	$297,061,149,892	$641,958,257	0.2%	54%
Invesco QQQ Trust Series 1	QQQ	$186,230,121,010	$17,957,771,186	9.6%	2430%
Vanguard FTSE Developed Markets	VEA	$110,636,676,983	$460,759,200	0.4%	105%
Vanguard Value	VTV	$100,219,303,401	$325,980,613	0.3%	82%
Vanguard Total Bond Market	BND	$92,587,446,741	$410,510,468	0.4%	112%
iShares Core MSCI EAFE	IEFA	$96,881,684,514	$582,906,057	0.6%	152%
Vanguard Growth	VUG	$86,279,720,336	$244,972,436	0.3%	72%

Notes: Data from 2023. A 100% annual turnover rate implies a holding period of 12 months; 200% annual turnover translates to a six-month holding period; 2,400% annual turnover equates to a two-week holding period. Annualized rate assumes 252 trading days.

Source: Strategas Securities.

- sought to generate returns that are the opposite of those earned by financial-television pundit Jim Cramer;
- captured the performance of stocks during the night but not during the day; or
- used borrowed money to trade marijuana stocks.

As December 31, 2023, the U.S. had 3,383 ETFs (and related products) with assets of $8.12 trillion, according to ETFGI, a research firm in London; the rest of the world had 8,486 ETFs with assets of $3.51 trillion.

Many ETFs fill narrow niches, owning few holdings rather than the broadest possible swath of securities. They often are based on indexes with short track records, making past performance an even poorer guide than usual. Because they tend to be small, they charge much higher fees and are far more likely to go out of business.[5]

Many such ETFs are *inverse* or *leveraged*. Inverse funds generate the opposite of a benchmark's return—for example, gaining 1% on a day when the underlying index loses 1%. Leveraged funds use borrowed money or other techniques to amplify their gains—and losses. A leveraged fund might double or even triple the daily gain of a market average. It will, by design, also double or triple any daily *loss*. If you don't know what you're doing, experimenting with these funds is like playing with matches in a warehouse full of dynamite.

Instead of diversifying your portfolio, these specialized ETFs do what Peter Lynch, the former manager of Fidelity Magellan Fund, calls di-worse-ifying: They clutter your portfolio with risky clusters of weird assets.

You have the *option* to buy eccentric ETFs. You do not have an *obligation*.

How to Pick an ETF

With thousands of ETFs, how should you pick one that's right for you?

Elisabeth Kashner, head of global fund analytics at FactSet Research Systems, suggests a simple mnemonic:

---

[5] Morningstar, "Mining for Alpha with Index Funds," bit.ly/3YhHZjw.

Efficiency,
Tradability, and
Fit.

Efficiency means low annual expenses, preferably 0.10% or less. "The longer you plan to hold the ETF, the more this cost matters," says Kashner, because expenses are a perennial drag on performance.

Tradability measures how much it costs to buy or sell an ETF. In the U.S., at least $250,000 of a fund's shares should trade daily. The bid/ask spread, or the gap between what buyers are willing to pay and what sellers will accept, should be 0.05% or less—ideally, 0.01%. "The longer you plan to hold the ETF, the less this cost matters," says Kashner, because it's a one-time cost you won't have to pay again until you ultimately sell the fund. Trade only with a *limit order* that specifies the highest price you're willing to pay if you're buying and the lowest you'll accept if you're selling.

Fit is another word for diversification: You want your fund to wrap itself snugly around the broadest possible bundle of assets. Total market ETFs are ideal. "One covering your home country and another covering the rest of the world" will serve you well, says Kashner.

The narrower the index the ETF tracks, the less money you should invest in it. (If a smidgen of a narrow ETF belongs anywhere, it belongs in your "mad money" account.[6])

Traditional index mutual funds work as well as ETFs, assuming their fees are as low.

An actively managed mutual fund or ETF might make sense if—but *only* if—its fees are also low, it holds stocks for years on end, and its portfolio is drastically different from the market.

Extremely Sanctimonious Gimmicks?

The latest craze on Wall Street is ESG funds, which purport to make businesses and the world [E]nvironmentally cleaner, [S]ocially fairer, and [G]overned better. They enable you to do good and do well at the same time, marketers say. Owning an ESG fund will give you that righteous glow from feeling you're on the side of the angels, and

---

[6] See p. 46. You can research how broadly an ETF is diversified on its website and on ETF.com, Finominal.com, PortfolioVisualizer.com, or VettaFi.com.

some studies suggest ESG funds have performed about as well as conventional portfolios.

Unfortunately, you might or might not do good, but you will pay more to feel good.

As James Mackintosh showed in a brilliant series of columns in *The Wall Street Journal*, ESG funds overpromise and underdeliver. Polluters and other bad corporate citizens have already sold their shares to the public, so refusing to buy their stock has no direct effect on them. If every "good" company divests its "bad" assets, then mines, oil wells, and factories will end up in the hands of operators that don't care about public opinion, producing more harm than ever. And the intense popularity of ESG helped drive the stock prices of many of the movement's darlings, like electric-vehicle manufacturer Tesla, to such unearthly heights that future returns are bound to be lower.

What's more, many ESG funds don't even pretend to own "good" companies; they own the least bad. With the demand from investors far exceeding the supply of ESG companies, the firms that screen companies end up promoting "the greenest within a dirty industry."

In 2021, a big holding in MSCI's Global Pollution Prevention Index and many ESG funds was a company that had been sued by the state of New Jersey for allegedly releasing such putrid odors that nearby residents suffered migraines. Other ESG funds raced to invest in a company mining the ocean floor for rare metals, even though environmentalists consider that an abomination.[7]

Finally, many ESG funds barely differ from the rest of the market. A team of economists found in 2022 that 68% of the holdings of ESG funds overlap perfectly with those of conventional funds. That means you pay high fees on 100% of your investment, even though only a third of it is customized. That's like paying a triple fee—estimated by the economists at 0.63% annually.

Overall, ESG funds probably don't do much to make the world a better place. Maybe, however, you don't expect a fund to make the world better; you just don't want any of your money in companies you feel are making the world worse.

---

[7] James Mackintosh, "Sustainable Investing," bit.ly/3rJxMA2; Justin Scheck et al., "Environmental Investing Frenzy Stretches Meaning of 'Green,'" bit.ly/3QkkvIE.

In that case, you're buying the fund not because it's a good value but because it enables you to feel you're acting on *your* good values. Fair enough—so long as you avoid high fees, confirm that the fund doesn't own any companies you disapprove of, and can live with returns that might be lower. You should also realize that if you want to make the world a better place, you'll have to take action yourself. Mutual funds and ETFs are baskets of investments; they aren't magical healers that can cure what ails the planet.

When Investments Make Money and Investors Don't

Imagine a fund that starts the year at $10 a share. It also finishes the year at $10. It fluctuated during the year, but didn't pay a dividend. That's an annual return of 0%.

Did all its investors have a 0% return?

Of course not. Some bought the fund when it was trading below $10, whereas others paid more than $10. Still others sold before year end—some at a profit and some at a loss.

How well the fund's investors fared depends not only on the fund's returns, but on their actions. If most of them bought at a market high or sold at a market low, they will collectively earn lower returns than the fund's portfolio itself.

In extreme cases, investors can lose billions of dollars in a fund that made money. Few examples have ever been more extreme than the ARK funds run by stock-picking celebrity Cathie Wood.

ARK Innovation, the flagship ETF in this fleet, gained 87% in 2017. It then was tiny, with only $12 million in assets at the beginning of the year, so that enormous gain was earned by only a few investors. ARK Innovation returned an astounding 153% in 2020. But even by the beginning of that year it had just $1.9 billion in total assets.

Finally, in 2020, the public poured money in. The fund's assets tripled to $6 billion between March and July 2020. From September 2020 through March 2021, investors inundated ARK Innovation with $13 billion in new money.

Right on cue, performance peaked. ARK Innovation lost 23% in 2021 and a bloodcurdling 67% in 2022.

The few early-bird investors who captured the fund's biggest gains were dwarfed by the flocks of latecomers who suffered its worst losses. Collectively, ARK Innovation's shareholders lost as much as

FIGURE 9-1: A Leaky ARKK

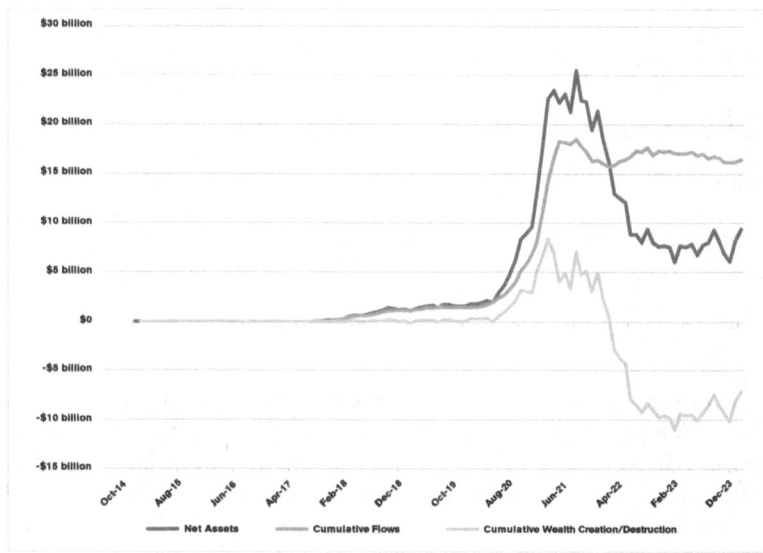

Source: Morningstar.

$10 billion even though the fund had racked up some of the biggest gains in history—and even after the fund went on to go up 68% in 2022.[8]

The lessons? It's investors, not investments, that make or lose money. How your fund behaves is much less important than how you behave. And if you chase hot performance, you will get burned.

---

[8] Jason Zweig, "How a Flood of Money Swamped Cathie Wood's ARK," bit.ly/3OeNDyo; Amy Arnott, "Why ARKK Shareholders Are Still Underwater," bit.ly/3qdh7Vb.

CHAPTER 10

The Investor and His Advisers
by Benjamin Graham

The investment of money in securities is unique among business operations in that it is almost always based in some degree on advice received from others. The great bulk of investors are amateurs. Naturally they feel that in choosing their securities they can profit by professional guidance. Yet there are peculiarities inherent in the very concept of investment advice.

If the reason people invest is to make money, then in seeking advice they are asking others to tell them how to make money. That idea has some element of naïveté. Businessmen seek professional advice on various elements of their business, but they do not expect to be told how to make a profit. That is their own bailiwick. When they, or nonbusiness people, rely on others to make *investment profits* for them, they are expecting a kind of result for which there is no true counterpart in ordinary business affairs.

If we assume that there are normal or standard *income* results to be obtained from investing money in securities, then the role of the adviser can be more readily established. **He will use his superior training and experience to protect his clients against mistakes and to make sure that they obtain the results to which their money is entitled. It is when the investor demands more than an average return on his money, or when his adviser undertakes to do better for him, that the question arises whether more is being asked or promised than is likely to be delivered.**

Advice on investments may be obtained from a variety of sources. These include: (1) a relative or friend, presumably knowledgeable in securities; (2) a local (commercial) banker; (3) a brokerage firm or investment banking house; (4) a financial service or periodical; and (5) an investment counselor. The miscellaneous character of this list suggests that no logical or systematic approach in this matter has crystallized, as yet, in the minds of investors.

Certain common-sense considerations relate to the criterion of normal or standard results mentioned above. **Our basic thesis is this: If the investor is to rely chiefly on the advice of others in handling his funds, then either he must limit himself and his advisers strictly to standard, conservative, and even unimaginative forms of investment, or he must have an unusually intimate and favorable knowledge of the person who is going to direct his funds into other channels. But if the ordinary business or professional relationship exists between the investor and his advisers, he can be receptive to *less conventional* suggestions only to the extent that he himself has grown in knowledge and experience and has therefore become competent to pass independent judgment on the recommendations of others. He has then passed from the category of defensive or unenterprising investor into that of aggressive or enterprising investor.**

Investment Counsel and Trust Services of Banks

The truly professional investment advisers—that is, the well-established investment counsel firms, who charge substantial annual fees—are quite modest in their promises and pretentions. For the most part they place their clients' funds in standard interest- and dividend-paying securities, and they rely mainly on normal investment experience for their overall results. In the typical case it is doubtful whether more than 10% of the total fund is ever invested in securities other than those of leading companies, plus government bonds (including state and municipal issues); nor do they make a serious effort to take advantage of swings in the general market.

The leading investment-counsel firms make no claim to being brilliant; they do pride themselves on being careful, conservative, and competent. Their primary aim is to conserve the principal value over the years and produce a conservatively acceptable rate of income. Any accomplishment beyond that—and they do strive to better the goal—they regard in the nature of extra service rendered. Perhaps their chief value to their clients lies in shielding them from costly mistakes. They offer as much as the defensive investor has the right to expect from any counselor serving the general public.

What we have said about the well-established investment-counsel firms applies generally to the trust and advisory services of the larger banks.

Financial Services

The so-called financial services are organizations that send out uniform bulletins (sometimes in the form of telegrams) to their subscribers. The subjects covered may include the state and prospects of business, the behavior and prospect of the securities markets, and information and advice regarding individual issues. There is often an "inquiry department" which will answer questons affecting an individual subscriber. The cost of the service averages much less than the fee that investment counselors charge their individual clients. Some organizations—notably Babson's and Standard & Poor's—operate on separate levels as a financial service and as investment counsel. (Incidentally, other organizations—such as Scudder, Stevens & Clark—operate separately as investment counsel and as one or more investment funds.)

The financial services direct themselves, on the whole, to a quite different segment of the public than do the investment-counsel firms. The latters' clients generally wish to be relieved of bother and the need for making decisions. The financial services offer information and guidance to those who are directing their own financial affairs or are themselves advising others. Many of these services confine themselves exclusively, or nearly so, to forecasting market movements by various "technical" methods. We shall dismiss these with the observation that their work does not concern "investors" as the term is used in this book.

On the other hand, some of the best known—such as Moody's Investment Service and Standard & Poor's—are identified with statistical organizations that compile the voluminous statistical data that form the basis for all serious security analysis. These services have a varied clientele, ranging from the most conservative-minded investor to the rankest speculator. As a result they must find it difficult to adhere to any clear-cut or fundamental philosophy in arriving at their opinions and recommendations.

An old-established service of the type of Moody's and the others must obviously provide something worthwhile to a broad class of investors. What is it? Basically they address themselves to the matters in which the average active investor-speculator is interested, and their views on these either command some measure of authority or at least appear more reliable than those of the unaided client.

For years the financial services have been making stock-market forecasts without anyone taking this activity very seriously. Like everyone else in the field they are sometimes right and sometimes wrong. Wherever possible they hedge their opinions so as to avoid the risk of being proved completely wrong. (There is a well-developed art of Delphic phrasing that adjusts itself successfully to whatever the future brings.) In our view—perhaps a prejudiced one—this segment of their work has no real significance except for the light it throws on human nature in the securities markets. **Nearly everyone interested in common stocks wants to be told by someone else what he thinks the market is going to do. The demand being there, it must be supplied.**

Their interpretations and forecasts of business conditions, of course, are much more authoritative and informing. These are an important part of the great body of economic intelligence which is spread continuously among buyers and sellers of securities and tends to create fairly rational prices for stocks and bonds under most circumstances. Undoubtedly the material published by the financial services adds to the store of information available and fortifies the investment judgment of their clients.

It is difficult to evaluate their recommendations of individual securities. Each service is entitled to be judged separately, and the verdict could properly be based only on an elaborate and inclusive study covering many years. In our own experience we have noted among them a pervasive attitude which we think tends to impair what could otherwise be more useful advisory work. This is their general view that a stock should be bought if the near-term prospects of the business are favorable and should be sold if these are unfavorable—*regardless of the current price.* Such a superficial principle often prevents the services from doing the sound analytical job of which their staffs are capable—namely, to ascertain whether a given stock appears over- or undervalued at the current price in the light of its indicated long-term future earning power.

The intelligent investor will not do his buying and selling solely on the basis of recommendations received from a financial service. Once this point is established, the role of the financial service then becomes the useful one of supplying information and offering suggestions.

Advice from Brokerage Houses

Probably the largest volume of information and advice to the security-owning public comes from stockbrokers. These are members of the New York Stock Exchange, and of other exchanges, who execute buying and selling orders for a standard commission. Practically all the houses that deal with the public maintain a "statistical" or analytical department, which answers inquiries and makes recommendations. A great deal of analytical literature, some of it elaborate and expensive, is distributed gratis to the firms' customers—more impressively referred to as clients.

A great deal is at stake in the innocent-appearing question whether "customers" or "clients" is the more appropriate name. A business has customers; a professional person or organization has clients. The Wall Street brokerage fraternity has probably the highest ethical standards of any *business*, but it is still feeling its way toward the standards and standing of a true profession.*

In the past Wall Street has thrived mainly on speculation, and stock-market speculators as a class were almost certain to lose money. Hence it has been logically impossible for brokerage houses to operate on a thoroughly professional basis. To do that would have required them to direct their efforts toward reducing rather than increasing their business.

The farthest that certain brokerage houses have gone in that direction—and could have been expected to go—is to refrain from

---

* More than half a century after Graham wrote this, the financial-advisory industry is "still feeling its way toward the standards and standing of a true profession," with no single set of educational requirements, qualifications of competency, or ethical criteria.

inducing or encouraging anyone to speculate. Such houses have confined themselves to executing orders given them, to supplying financial information and analyses, and to rendering opinions on the investment merits of securities. Thus, in theory at least, they are devoid of all responsibility for either the profits or the losses of their speculative customers.*

Most stock-exchange houses, however, still adhere to the old-time slogans that they are in business to make commissions and that the way to succeed in business is to give the customers what they want. Since the most profitable customers want speculative advice and suggestions, the thinking and activities of the typical firm are pretty closely geared to day-to-day trading in the market. Thus it tries hard to help its customers make money in a field where they are condemned almost by mathematical law to lose in the end.† By this we mean that the speculative part of their operations cannot be profitable over the long run for most brokerage-house customers. But to the extent that their operations resemble true investing they may produce investment gains that more than offset the speculative losses.

The investor obtains advice and information from stock-exchange houses through two types of employees, now known officially as "customers' brokers" (or "account executives") and financial analysts.

The customer's broker, also called a "registered representative," formerly bore the less dignified title of "customer's man." Today he is for the most part an individual of good character and considerable knowledge of securities, who operates under a rigid code of right conduct. Nevertheless, since his business is to earn commissions, he can hardly avoid being speculation-minded. Thus the security buyer

---

* In the late 1990s, and again in 2020–21, Wall Street foisted shoddy stocks onto the public without a whiff of remorse.

† Interestingly, this stinging criticism, which in his day Graham was directing at full-service brokers, ended up applying to discount internet brokers in the late 1990s and trading apps in the early 2020s. These firms spent millions of dollars on flashy marketing that goaded their customers into trading more and trading faster. Most of those customers ended up picking their own pockets, instead of paying someone else to do it for them.

who wants to avoid being influenced by speculative considerations will ordinarily have to be careful and explicit in his dealing with his customer's broker; he will have to show clearly, by word and deed, that he is not interested in anything faintly resembling a stock-market "tip." Once the customer's broker understands clearly that he has a real investor on his hands, he will respect this point of view and cooperate with it.

The financial analyst, formerly known chiefly as security analyst, is a person of particular concern to the author, who has been one himself for more than five decades and has helped educate countless others. At this stage we refer only to the financial analysts employed by brokerage houses. The function of the security analyst is clear enough from his title. It is he who works up the detailed studies of individual securities, develops careful comparisons of various issues in the same field, and forms an expert opinion of the safety or attractiveness or intrinsic value of all the different kinds of stocks and bonds.

By what must seem a quirk to the outsider there are no formal requirements for being a security analyst. Contrast with this the facts that a customer's broker must pass an examination, meet the required character tests, and be duly accepted and registered by the New York Stock Exchange. As a practical matter, nearly all the younger analysts have had extensive business-school training, and the oldsters have acquired at least the equivalent in the school of long experience. In the great majority of cases, the employing brokerage house can be counted on to assure itself of the qualifications and competence of its analysts.*

The customer of the brokerage firm may deal with the security analysts directly, or his contact may be an indirect one via the customer's broker. In either case the analyst is available to the client for a considerable amount of information and advice. Let us make an emphatic statement here. The value of the security analyst

---

* This remains true, although in an even stranger quirk, there are almost no formal licensing, educational, or competency requirements for managing other people's investments. In many U.S. states it is harder to become a cosmetologist than a financial adviser.

to the investor depends largely on the investor's own attitude. If the investor asks the analyst the right questions, he is likely to get the right—or at least valuable—answers. The analysts hired by brokerage houses, we are convinced, are greatly handicapped by the general feeling that they are supposed to be market analysts as well. When they are asked whether a given common stock is "sound," the question often means, "Is this stock likely to advance during the next few months?" As a result many of them are compelled to analyze with one eye on the stock ticker—a pose not conducive to sound thinking or worthwhile conclusions.

In the next section of this book we shall deal with some of the concepts and possible achievements of security analysis. A great many analysts working for stock exchange firms could be of prime assistance to the bona fide investor who wants to be sure that he gets full value for his money, and possibly a little more. As in the case of the customers' brokers, what is needed at the beginning is a clear understanding by the analyst of the investor's attitude and objectives. Once the analyst is convinced that he is dealing with a man who is value-minded rather than quotation-minded, there is an excellent chance that his recommendations will prove of real overall benefit.

The CFA Certificate for Financial Analysts

An important step was taken in 1963 toward giving professional standing and responsibility to financial analysts. The official title of chartered financial analyst (CFA) is now awarded to those senior practitioners who pass required examinations and meet other tests of fitness.[1] The subjects covered include security analysis and portfolio management. The analogy with the long-established professional title of certified public accountant (CPA) is evident and intentional. This relatively new apparatus of recognition and control should serve to elevate the standards of financial analysts and eventually to place their work on a truly professional basis.*

---

* Benjamin Graham was the prime force behind the establishment of the CFA program, which he advocated for nearly two decades before it became a reality.

Dealings with Brokerage Houses

One of the most disquieting developments of the period in which we write this revision has been the financial embarrassment—in plain words, bankruptcy or near-bankruptcy—of quite a few New York Stock Exchange firms, including at least two of considerable size.* This is the first time in half a century or more that such a thing has happened, and it is startling for more than one reason. For many decades the New York Stock Exchange has been moving in the direction of closer and stricter controls over the operations and financial condition of its members—including minimum capital requirements, surprise audits, and the like. Besides this, we have had 37 years of control over the exchanges and their members by the Securities and Exchange Commission. Finally, the stock-brokerage industry itself has operated under favorable conditions—namely, a huge increase in volume, fixed minimum commission rates (largely eliminating competitive fees), and a limited number of member firms.

The first financial troubles of the brokerage houses (in 1969) were attributed to the increase in volume itself. This, it was claimed, overtaxed their facilities, increased their overhead, and produced many troubles in making financial settlements. It should be pointed out **this was probably the first time in history that important enterprises have gone broke because they had more business than they could handle.** In 1970, as brokerage failures increased, they were blamed chiefly on "the falling off in volume." A strange complaint when one reflects that the turnover of the NYSE in 1970 totaled 2,937 million shares, the *largest* volume in its history and well

---

* The two firms Graham had in mind were probably Du Pont, Glore, Forgan & Co. and Goodbody & Co. Du Pont (founded by the heirs to the chemical fortune) was saved from insolvency in 1970 only after Texas entrepreneur H. Ross Perot lent more than $50 million to the firm; Goodbody, the fifth-largest brokerage in the United States, would have failed in late 1970 had Merrill Lynch not acquired it. Hayden, Stone & Co. would also have gone under if it had not been acquired. The farcical story of Wall Street's frenzied over-expansion in the late 1960s is beautifully told in John Brooks's *The Go-Go Years* (Wiley, 1999).

over twice as large as in any year before 1965. During the 15 years of the bull market ending in 1964 the annual volume had averaged "only" 712 million shares—one quarter of the 1970 figure—but the brokerage business had enjoyed the greatest prosperity in its history. If, as it appears, the member firms as a whole had allowed their overhead and other expenses to increase at a rate that could not sustain even a mild reduction in volume during part of a year, this does not speak well for either their business acumen or their financial conservatism.

A third explanation of the financial trouble finally emerged out of a mist of concealment, and we suspect that it is the most plausible and significant of the three. It seems that a good part of the capital of certain brokerage houses was held in the form of common stocks owned by the individual partners. Some of these seem to have been highly speculative and carried at inflated values. When the market declined in 1969 the quotations of such securities fell drastically and a substantial part of the capital of the firms vanished with them.[2] In effect the partners were speculating with the capital that was supposed to protect the customers against the ordinary financial hazards of the brokerage business, in order to make a double profit thereon. This was inexcusable; we refrain from saying more.

The investor should use his intelligence not only in formulating his financial policies but also in the associated details. These include the choice of a reputable broker to execute his orders. Up to now it was sufficient to counsel our readers to deal only with a member of the New York Stock Exchange, unless he had compelling reasons to use a nonmember firm. Reluctantly, we must add some further advice in this area. We think that people who do not carry margin accounts—and in our vocabulary this means *all* nonprofessional *investors*—should have the delivery and receipt of their securities handled by their bank. When giving a buying order to your brokers you can instruct them to deliver the securities bought to your bank against payment therefor by the bank; conversely, when selling you can instruct your bank to deliver the securities to the broker against payment of the proceeds. These services will cost a little extra but they should be well worth the expense in terms of safety and peace of mind. This advice may be disregarded, as no longer called for, after the investor is sure that all the problems of stock-exchange firms have been disposed of, but not before.*

Investment Bankers

The term "investment banker" is applied to a firm that engages to an important extent in originating, underwriting, and selling new issues of stocks and bonds. (To underwrite means to guarantee to the issuing corporation, or other issuer, that the security will be fully sold.) A number of the brokerage houses carry on a certain amount of underwriting activity. Generally this is confined to participating in underwriting groups formed by leading investment bankers. There is an additional tendency for brokerage firms to originate and sponsor a minor amount of new-issue financing, particularly in the form of smaller issues of common stocks when a bull market is in full swing.

Investment banking is perhaps the most respectable department of the Wall Street community, because it is here that finance plays its constructive role of supplying new capital for the expansion of industry. In fact, much of the theoretical justification for maintaining active stock markets, notwithstanding their frequent speculative excesses, lies in the fact that organized security exchanges facilitate the sale of new issues of bonds and stocks. If investors or speculators could not expect to see a ready market for a new security offered them, they might well refuse to buy it.

The relationship between the investment banker and the investor is basically that of the salesman to the prospective

---

* Nearly all brokerage transactions are now conducted electronically, and securities are no longer physically "delivered." Thanks to the establishment of the Securities Investor Protection Corporation, or SIPC, in 1970, investors are generally assured of recovering their full account values if their brokerage firm becomes insolvent. SIPC is a government-mandated consortium of brokers; all the members agree to pool their assets to cover losses incurred by the customers of any firm that becomes insolvent. SIPC's protection eliminates the need for investors to make payment and take delivery through a bank intermediary, as Graham urges.

buyer. For many years past the great bulk of the new offerings in dollar value has consisted of bond issues that were purchased in the main by financial institutions such as banks and insurance companies. In this business the security salesmen have been dealing with shrewd and experienced buyers. Hence any recommendations made by the investment bankers to these customers have had to pass careful and skeptical scrutiny. Thus these transactions are almost always effected on a businesslike footing.

But a different situation obtains in a relationship between the *individual* security buyer and the investment banking firms, including the stockbrokers acting as underwriters. Here the purchaser is frequently inexperienced and seldom shrewd. He is easily influenced by what the salesman tells him, especially in the case of common-stock issues, since often his unconfessed desire in buying is chiefly to make a quick profit. The effect of all this is that the public investor's protection lies less in his own critical faculty than in the scruples and ethics of the offering houses.[3]

It is a tribute to the honesty and competence of the underwriting firms that they are able to combine fairly well the discordant roles of adviser and salesman. But **it is imprudent for the buyer to trust himself to the judgment of the seller**. In 1959 we stated at this point: "The bad results of this unsound attitude show themselves recurrently in the underwriting field and with notable effects in the sale of new common stock issues during periods of active speculation." Shortly thereafter this warning proved urgently needed. As already pointed out, the years 1960–61 and, again, 1968–69 were marked by an unprecedented outpouring of issues of lowest quality, sold to the public at absurdly high offering prices and in many cases pushed much higher by heedless speculation and some semimanipulation. A number of the more important Wall Street houses have participated to some degree in these less than creditable activities, which demonstrates that **the familiar combination of greed, folly, and irresponsibility has not been exorcized from the financial scene**.

The intelligent investor will pay attention to the advice and recommendations received from investment banking houses, especially those known by him to have an excellent reputation; but he will be sure to bring sound and independent judgment to bear upon these suggestions—either his own, if he is competent, or that of some other type of adviser.*

Other Advisers

It is a good old custom, especially in the smaller towns, to consult one's local banker about investments. A commercial banker may not be a thoroughgoing expert on security values, but he is experienced and conservative. He is especially useful to the unskilled investor, who is often tempted to stray from the straight and unexciting path of a defensive policy and needs the steadying influence of a prudent mind. The more alert and aggressive investor, seeking counsel in the selection of security bargains, will not ordinarily find the commercial banker's viewpoint to be especially suited to his own objectives.†

We take a more critical attitude toward the widespread custom of asking investment advice from relatives or friends. The inquirer always thinks he has good reason for assuming that the person consulted has superior knowledge or experience. Our own observation indicates that **it is almost as difficult to select satisfactory lay advisers as it is to select the proper securities unaided. Much bad advice is given free.**

Summary

Investors who are prepared to pay a fee for the management of their funds may wisely select some well-established and well-recommended investment-counsel firm. Alternatively, they may use the investment department of a large trust company or the supervisory service supplied on a fee basis by a few of the leading New York Stock Exchange houses. The results to be expected are in no wise exceptional, but they are commensurate with those of the average well-informed and cautious investor.

---

* Those who heeded Graham's advice would not have been suckered into buying internet IPOs in 1999 and 2000, or SPACS in 2020 and 2021.
† This traditional role of bankers has for the most part been supplanted by financial planners.

Most security buyers obtain advice without paying for it specifically. It stands to reason, therefore, that in the majority of cases they are not entitled to and should not expect better than average results. They should be wary of all persons, whether customers' brokers or security salesmen, who promise spectacular income or profits. This applies both to the selection of securities and to guidance in the elusive (and perhaps illusive) art of trading in the market.

Defensive investors, as we have defined them, will not ordinarily be equipped to pass independent judgment on the security recommendations made by their advisers. But they can be explicit—and even repetitiously so—in stating the kind of securities they want to buy. If they follow our prescription they will confine themselves to high-grade bonds and the common stocks of leading corporations, preferably those that can be purchased at individual price levels that are not high in the light of experience and analysis. The security analyst of any reputable stock-exchange house can make up a suitable list of such common stocks and can certify to the investor whether or not the existing price level therefor is a reasonably conservative one as judged by past experience.

The aggressive investor will ordinarily work in active cooperation with his advisers. He will want their recommendations explained in detail, and he will insist on passing his own judgment upon them. This means that the investor will gear his expectations and the character of his security operations to the development of his own knowledge and experience in the field. **Only in the exceptional case, where the integrity and competence of the advisers have been thoroughly demonstrated, should the investor act upon the advice of others without understanding and approving the decision made.**

There have always been unprincipled stock salesmen and fly-by-night stock brokers, and—as a matter of course—we have advised our readers to confine their dealings, if possible, to members of the New York Stock Exchange. But we are reluctantly compelled to add the extra-cautious counsel that security deliveries and payments be made through the intermediary of the investor's bank. The distressing Wall Street brokerage-house picture may have cleared up completely in a few years, but in late 1971 we still suggest, "Better safe than sorry."

Commentary on Chapter 10

by Jason Zweig

> The prudent are crowned with knowledge.
> —Proverbs 14:18.

A good financial adviser can make or save you a fortune by preventing you from being your own worst enemy.

Good advisers can deter you from buying high and selling low. They can help you figure out how to afford to buy a house, pay for college, provide for your aging parents, and navigate the Kafkaesque complexities of tax, estate, and retirement planning. They can help you avoid scams and frauds.

Many defensive—and enterprising—investors could benefit from the counsel of a good adviser. If you carry too much debt, struggle to get your spending under control, lost a ton of money trading stocks, are juggling a jumble of assets that don't seem to work together, or just can't face difficult financial decisions, a good adviser can be a godsend. Finding the right one is nowhere near as easy as it should be, however.

Can't See the Forest for the Fees

As Graham warns:

> Most security buyers obtain advice without paying for it specifically. It stands to reason, therefore, that in the majority of cases they are not entitled to and should not expect better than average results.

Imagine two people going to the same dentist. Afterward, they discover that one patient's bill is five times higher, even though they received the same treatment. When the patient with the higher bill

> ### Should You Go Robo?
>
> Digital advisory firms, which use software to assemble investment portfolios online at low cost, have become popular. These "robo-advisers" arose over the past decade and manage roughly $750 billion in the U.S. Fees generally are about 0.25% annually; clients get a portfolio of ETFs, periodic rebalancing, and selective sales of losing positions to maximize tax efficiency. Such bare-bones service may make sense for defensive investors who have zero spare time or energy to monitor their own portfolios.[1]
>
> Some robo-advisers also offer financial-planning advice, typically from a human staffer. However, such firms specialize in automated portfolio management, so personalized financial planning is a lower priority.
>
> Eventually, artificial intelligence may bridge that gap. In professional chess, "centaurs" (the combination of a human and a computer) have tended to be able to beat either the best of human chess players or a well-trained computer. Financial planning might ultimately employ its own centaurs: an experienced financial planner coupled with an artificial-intelligence tool that can generate accurate and helpful advice. For now, however, most clients prefer to have a human do their financial planning.
>
> ---
>
> [1] If you're reading this book, you probably aren't *that* defensive.

demands an explanation, the office assistant says, "Your investment portfolio is five times bigger."

Would anyone—including the patient who paid less—think that's fair?

Yet that's how the financial-advice business works. Most advisers don't charge fees based on the services they provide—for example, to calculate your projected income during retirement or to review your estate plans. Instead, they charge an annual fee based on *assets under management* or AUM: how much money they oversee for you.

AUM fees give an adviser an interest in how well your investment portfolio performs. The more it goes up, the more your adviser earns. That might be better than paying brokers a commission for every transaction, which can create an incentive to trade as often as possible. But AUM fees also create perverse incentives by:

- rewarding advisers not for how good their advice is, but for how much money you have;
- creating pressure to take risks and actions, necessary or not, to justify "earning" those fees;
- encouraging advisers to push in-house investments that are often inferior;
- compensating advisers for providing investment management, which is a commodity available through index funds at virtually no cost—while paying them nothing for personalized financial planning, which can be extraordinarily valuable.

Expressed as a percentage, 1% sounds like a teeny number. But, on a $1 million account, it's $10,000 annually. If investors clearly understood how much they are paying, they surely would shop around for lower fees.[1]

Separate surveys of more than 1,000 financial advisers in the U.S. by industry analysts Bob Veres and Michael Kitces, in 2020 and 2022 respectively, found that advisers were charging a median of 0.9% to 1.0% annually to advise accounts of up to $1,000,000. Even accounts with $5 million paid 0.6% to 0.7%. These fees have barely budged in decades—even though, over the past few decades, the cost of investing through mutual funds and ETFs has fallen 90% or more.

That puts investors in the absurd position of having to pay far more to someone who *picks* funds than to the people who *manage* them. You can buy index mutual funds or ETFs for well under 0.1% annually—and then leave them undisturbed for decades. Why should you pay an adviser 1% every year for that? And why should complex financial advice be free but simple fund-picking so expensive?

None of that makes any sense. Look for an adviser who charges

---

[1] In what behavioral economist Richard Zeckhauser calls "denominator blindness," people tend to overlook the total values on which judgments of frequency or magnitude should be based. Clever marketers focus people's attention on a small number, like a percentage, that distracts them from the high costs they're paying. See Kimihiko Yamagishi, "When a 12.86% Mortality Is More Dangerous than 24.14%," bit.ly/3QnX5St.

Meet Max, the Top Financial Planner Who Didn't Even Have a Desk

Chances are, your doctor, lawyer, or accountant has only one or two framed documents hanging on the office wall: a medical or law degree, a CPA or other accountancy certificate. Financial advisers, though, often display an entire wall full of framed, diploma-like certificates and awards.

Because there are no national public standards of knowledge, competence, and professional ethics for financial advisers, private organizations claiming to confer official recognition have proliferated.

Some, like Chartered Financial Analyst or Certified Public Accountant, require years of rigorous study and training. Others, such as Certified Financial Planner, take less onerous but still diligent preparation.

Many, though, are meaningless. Some organizations will award a financial designation, suitable for framing, to anyone with a pulse willing to fork over a few hundred dollars.

If you have a relevant license or degree and three years of "related work experience," then the certificate for a Master Financial Planner or MFP is yours for $349, plus $29 shipping. No studying or exam is required.[1]

Job descriptions are also elastic. "Wealth manager" sounds impressive but is merely a self-appointed, self-important title with no legal definition.

Finally, awards are remarkably easy to get. Honored as one of "America's Top Financial Planners" in 2009, Maxwell Tailwagger won the accolade after financial planner Allan Roth of Colorado Springs, Colorado, "nominated" him by sending in a check for $183. In exchange, Max received an impressive plaque that he could display prominently on his desk—if, that is, he'd *had* a desk.

Consumers' Research Council of America, which purported to "help educate and assist consumers in obtaining the finest professional services," bestowed the award on Max even though he wasn't a financial planner at all.

Max was Mr. Roth's six-month-old dachshund puppy.

---

[1] See FINRA, "Professional Designations," bit.ly/47oJosS; Jason Zweig and Mary Pilon, "Is Your Adviser Pumping Up His Credentials?," bit.ly/3KvRkOO.

fees for service: pricing each task by how much time and expertise it takes, not by how much money you have. Some advisers charge by the hour, accept retainers, or even charge monthly subscription fees. Many will negotiate their fees—if you ask.

Searching for an Adviser

The first step in getting good financial advice is knowing what you need. Do you want an adviser who will mainly manage your investments? (Probably not, unless you are an extremely defensive investor.) Or do you want an adviser who can help primarily with the intricacies of financial planning?

Second, insist on an adviser who will act as a *fiduciary*, with obligations to provide advice in your best interest, to disclose all material facts about costs and conflicts of interest, and to ensure that conflicts don't corrupt the quality of the advice. Hiring a fiduciary doesn't guarantee that you'll get good guidance, but it's the basic prerequisite for a relationship built on trust.

In the U.S., start by visiting NAPFA.org and LetsMakeAPlan.org, which enable you to search for a financial planner in your geographic area.

Once you find a handful of advisers who seem like possible matches, do a quick background check: Go to brokercheck.finra.org and adviserinfo.sec.gov to see whether they have a disciplinary history. Look up the advisers *and* their firms. Watch for customer complaints, lawsuits and arbitrations, punishments from regulators, criminal cases, and personal bankruptcies.

Then download the Form ADV Part 2 brochure, available by searching for the name of the person or firm at adviserinfo.sec.gov. If fees are 1% or more, the disciplinary information doesn't match what you saw on brokercheck.finra.org, the adviser runs a commission-based insurance agency, or the adviser takes extra payments for referring clients into certain investments, find someone else.

Search the document for frequent use of the terms "annuities," "charting," "technical analysis," "tactical," and "private funds."

Annuities—insurance contracts that produce income, usually over time after an upfront purchase—are seldom appropriate. They're one of the last bastions of fat fees, sometimes carrying commissions up to 10% and annual expenses that can exceed 2%. A few advisers use annuities judiciously. Others cram them down clients' throats like foie-gras farmers stuffing feed pellets down the gullets of geese.

Charting, like technical analysis, attempts to predict future prices by studying the pattern of past prices. These are abstruse arts that are barely credible when practiced by trained specialists; in the amateur hands of many financial advisers, they create higher fees, unnecessary tax bills, and lousy performance.

Tactical advisers trade in and out. If they could reliably predict when markets are going to rise or fall, would they be sitting in some piddly office trying to get their mitts on your money? Or would they be on a yacht, counting their own?

Private funds, as we saw in the Commentary on Chapter 6, are extortionately expensive and riddled with conflicts; financial advisers who offer "proprietary" private funds have a powerful disincentive to recommend other investments, even if just about anything else would be better for you. With rare exceptions, private funds are another strike against a potential adviser.

Asking the Right Questions

Once you've winnowed down your list of possible advisory candidates to three to five, make appointments to interview them in person.

Ask each the same set of questions.

Here are a few that are critical, followed by the preferable answer:

Will you always act as a fiduciary, and will you state that in writing? (Yes.)

Do you focus mainly on investment management, or do you also advise on taxes, estates and retirement, budgeting, debt management, or insurance? (Here, your own needs will determine which answer is correct.)

Do you earn more (in cash or other incentives) for recommending certain products or services? (No.)

Do you earn fees to advise a private fund or other investments you may recommend to clients? (No.)

Are your fees negotiable, and will you charge by the hour or by the service, rather than on assets under management? (Yes.)

Have clients filed written complaints or arbitration claims against you or your firm? Have you or your firm been sued by clients? (No.[2])

Do you believe you can beat the market? (No.)

What's a reasonable expectation for future average annual returns on my portfolio, after expenses, your fees, inflation, and taxes? (4% at most. Anyone who gives a much higher number is either a fool or trying to fool you.[3])

Who manages your money? (I do, and I invest in the same assets I recommend to my clients.)

If asking so many questions in person feels awkward, submit them by email in advance. Ask each adviser to reply by email; they can always provide extra detail when you meet in person.

In advance, prepare a notepad or a spreadsheet to keep track of your questions and the advisers' responses. Rate each answer on a numerical scale from 1 (lowest) to 5 (best). By scoring all the answers on the same scale, you prevent yourself from arbitrarily overweighting a particular response.

Score each as soon as the adviser answers. If possible, you and your spouse or partner (or your closest friend or relative if you're unattached) should rate the answers independently.[4]

---

[2] An isolated complaint isn't necessarily cause for concern; a persistent pattern of complaints is cause for alarm. U.S. regulations permit advisers themselves to determine whether such events as civil lawsuits, customer complaints, and arbitration claims are "material" enough to disclose on their Form ADV, so you must also ask about them in person. See Jason Zweig, "You Don't Know What You Don't Know About Your Financial Adviser," bit.ly/44VryMo.

[3] Imagine your portfolio is 100% in stocks. After inflation, the long-term return on stocks has averaged about 7% annually. Unless it's entirely in broad index funds, expenses could reduce that return to 6%. A 1% advisory fee takes it down to 5%, and taxes could easily shave it to 4%. If future returns are lower than in the past (as they might well be), and your portfolio consists partly of cash and bonds (as it probably does), even 4% is high.

[4] For more on such interviews, see Jason Zweig, "The 19 Questions to Ask Your Financial Adviser," bit.ly/45kjlRJ, and "The Special Trick to Find the Right Financial Adviser," bit.ly/440yq9T.

Words of Warning

When you interview a potential adviser, be on the alert for words and phrases intended to stoke fear or greed, to invoke the illusion of certainty, and to prod you into taking urgent action. Does the adviser keep changing the subject away from your goals and circumstances to catchphrases like these?

- our proprietary algorithms
- our timing model
- our model portfolios
- options strategy
- guaranteed
- it's a sure thing
- monthly returns
- our exclusive private funds
- in this market, you have to have alternative investments
- we can get you access
- institutional quality
- we understand the markets
- we know how to identify . . .
- our stock recommendations are up ___%
- less volatility, lower risk, higher return
- we've done all the work for you
- everyone else is investing in this
- don't miss out on this opportunity
- you need to hurry
- this will be the best decision you can make
- the upside is potentially unlimited
- give us the chance to show what we can do for you
- we have no conflicts of interest[5]

---

[5] Ohio Securities Commissioner Andrea Seidt and Maryland Securities Commissioner Melanie Senter Lubin helped compile this list. For more on toxic investment pitches, see Joshua M. Brown, *Backstage Wall Street* (McGraw-Hill, 2012).

After you've met with the adviser, assign two more grades on the same five-point scale: one for communication, one for your overall impression.

Did the adviser bombard you with clichés? Or did you get clear, specific explanations of fees, strategies, and conflicts? Rate that on the same 1–5 scale.

Now rate your gut feelings about how competent, caring, and trustworthy the adviser is. Don't overthink it; close your eyes and quickly score your intuitive impression from 1 to 5.

After you've interviewed the advisers and recorded all your ratings, forget about your gut feelings: You've just accounted for them in your tally. Add up each adviser's scores and hire the one with the highest total.

You shouldn't view all this as more work than it's worth: You're about to consign your current wealth and financial future into this person's hands. Instead of picking that person by a hunch or by relying on a random referral, shouldn't you use a careful and deliberate process?

CHAPTER 11

Security Analysis for the Lay Investor: General Approach
by Benjamin Graham

*F*inancial analysis is now a well-established and flourishing profession, or semiprofession. The various societies of analysts that make up the National Federation of Financial Analysts have over 13,000 members, most of whom make their living out of this branch of mental activity. Financial analysts have textbooks, a code of ethics, and a quarterly journal.* They also have their share of unresolved problems. In recent years there has been a tendency to replace the general concept of "security analysis" by that of "financial analysis." The latter phrase has a broader implication and is better suited to describe the work of most senior analysts on Wall Street. It would be useful to think of security analysis as limiting itself pretty much to the examination and evaluation of stocks and bonds, whereas financial analysis would comprise that work, plus the determination of investment policy (portfolio selection), plus a substantial amount of general economic analysis.[1] In this chapter we shall use whatever designation is most applicable, with chief emphasis on the work of the security analyst proper.

The security analyst deals with the past, the present, and the future of any given security issue. He describes the business; he summarizes its operating results and financial position; he sets forth its strong and weak points, its possibilities and risks; he estimates its future earning

---

* The National Federation of Financial Analysts is now the CFA Institute, with more than 190,000 members worldwide.

power under various assumptions, or as a "best guess." He makes elaborate comparisons of various companies, or of the same company at various times. Finally, he expresses an opinion as to the safety of the issue, if it is a bond or investment-grade preferred stock, or as to its attractiveness as a purchase, if it is a common stock.

In doing all these things the security analyst avails himself of a number of techniques, ranging from the elementary to the most abstruse. He may modify substantially the figures in the company's annual statements, even though they bear the sacred *imprimatur* of the certified public accountant. He is on the lookout particularly for items in these reports that may mean a good deal more or less than they say.

The security analyst develops and applies standards of safety by which we can conclude whether a given bond or preferred stock may be termed sound enough to justify purchase for investment. These standards relate primarily to past average earnings, but they are concerned also with capital structure, working capital, asset values, and other matters.

In dealing with common stocks the security analyst until recently has only rarely applied standards of value as well defined as were his standards of safety for bonds and preferred stocks. Most of the time he contented himself with a summary of past performances, a more or less general forecast of the future—with particular emphasis on the next 12 months—and a rather arbitrary conclusion. The latter was, and still is, often drawn with one eye on the stock ticker or the market charts. In the past few years, however, much attention has been given by practicing analysts to the problem of valuing growth stocks. Many of these have sold at such high prices in relation to past and current earnings that those recommending them have felt a special obligation to justify their purchase by fairly definite projections of expected earnings running fairly far into the future. Certain mathematical techniques of a rather sophisticated sort have perforce been invoked to support the valuations arrived at.

We shall deal with these techniques, in foreshortened form, a little later. However, we must point out a troublesome paradox here, which is that **the mathematical valuations have become most prevalent precisely in those areas where one might consider them least reliable. For the more dependent the valuation becomes on anticipations of the future—and the less it is tied to a figure** demonstrated by past performance—the more vulnerable it becomes to possible miscalculation and serious error. A large part of the value found for a high-multiplier growth stock is derived from future projections which differ markedly from past performance—except perhaps in the growth rate itself. Thus it may be said that security analysts today find themselves compelled to become most mathematical and "scientific" in the very situations which lend themselves least auspiciously to exact treatment.*

Let us proceed, nonetheless, with our discussion of the more important elements and techniques of security analysis. The present highly condensed treatment is directed to the needs of the nonprofessional investor. At the minimum he should understand what the security analyst is talking about and driving at; beyond that, he should be equipped, if possible, to distinguish between superficial and sound analysis.

Security analysis for the lay investor is thought of as beginning with the interpretation of a company's annual financial report. This is a subject which we have covered for laymen in a separate book, entitled *The Interpretation of Financial Statements*.[2] We do not consider it necessary or appropriate to traverse the same ground in this chapter, especially since the emphasis in the present book is on principles and attitudes rather than on information and description. Let us pass on to two basic questions underlying the selection of investments. What are the primary tests of safety of a corporate bond or preferred stock? What are the chief factors entering into the valuation of a common stock?

---

* The higher the growth rate you project, and the longer the future period over which you project it, the more sensitive your forecast becomes to the slightest error. If, for instance, you estimate that a company earning $1 per share can raise that profit by 15% a year for the next 15 years, its earnings would end up at $8.14. If the market values the company at 35 times earnings, the stock would finish the period at roughly $285. But if earnings grow at 14% instead of 15%, the company would earn $7.14 at the end of the period—and, in the shock of that shortfall, investors would no longer be willing to pay 35 times earnings. At, say, 20 times earnings, the stock would end up around $140 per share, or 50% less.

Bond Analysis

The most dependable and hence the most respectable branch of security analysis concerns itself with the safety, or quality, of bond issues and investment-grade preferred stocks. The chief criterion used for corporate bonds is the number of times that total interest charges have been covered by available earnings for some years in the past. In the case of preferred stocks, it is the number of times that bond interest and preferred dividends combined have been covered.

The exact standards applied will vary with different authorities. Since the tests are at bottom arbitrary, there is no way to determine precisely the most suitable criteria. In the 1961 revision of our textbook, *Security Analysis,* we recommend certain "coverage" standards, which appear in Table 11-1.*

Our basic test is applied only to the *average* results for a period of years. Other authorities require also that a *minimum* coverage be shown for every year considered. We approve a "poorest-year" test as an *alternative* to the seven-year-average test; it would be sufficient if the bond or preferred stock met either of these criteria.

It may be objected that the large increase in bond interest rates since 1961 would justify some offsetting reduction in the coverage of charges required. Obviously it would be much harder for an industrial company to show a seven-times coverage of interest charges at 8% than at 4½%. To meet this changed situation we now suggest an alternative requirement related to the percent earned on the *principal* amount of the debt. These figures might be 33% before taxes for an industrial company, 20% for a public utility, and 25% for a railroad. It should be borne in mind here that the rate actually paid by most companies on their total debt is considerably less than the current 8% figure, since they have the benefit of older issues

---

* In 1972, investors in corporate bonds had little choice but to assemble their own portfolios. Today, hundreds of mutual funds and ETFs invest in corporate bonds, creating convenient, well-diversified bundles of securities. Since it often is not feasible to build a diversified bond portfolio on your own unless you have at least $100,000, the typical intelligent investor will be best off simply buying a low-cost bond fund and leaving the painstaking labor of credit research to its managers.

bearing lower coupons. The "poorest year" requirement could be set at about two-thirds of the seven-year requirement.

TABLE 11-1 Recommended Minimum "Coverage" for Bonds and Preferred Stocks

A. *For Investment-grade Bonds*

Minimum Ratio of Earnings to Total Fixed Charges:

Type of enterprise	Before Income Taxes		After Income Taxes	
	Average of Past 7 Years	Alternative: Measured by "Poorest Year"	Average of Past 7 Years	Alternative: Measured by "Poorest Year"
Public-utility operating company	4 times	3 times	2.65 times	2.10 times
Railroad	5	4	3.20	2.65
Industrial	7	5	4.30	3.20
Retail concern	5	4	3.20	2.65

B. *For Investment-grade Preferred Stocks*

The same minimum figures as above are required to be shown by the ratio of earnings *before* income taxes to the sum of fixed charges plus twice preferred dividends.

NOTE: The inclusion of twice the preferred dividends allows for the fact that preferred dividends are not income-tax deductible, whereas interest charges are so deductible.

C. *Other Categories of Bonds and Preferreds*

The standards given above are not applicable to (1) public-utility holding companies, (2) financial companies, (3) real-estate companies. Requirements for these special groups are omitted here.

In addition to the earnings-coverage test, a number of others are generally applied. These include the following:

1. *Size of Enterprise.* There is a minimum standard in terms of volume of business for a corporation—varying as between

industrials, utilities, and railroads—and of population for a municipality.

2. *Stock/Equity Ratio.* This is the ratio of the market price of the junior stock issues* to the total face amount of the debt, or the debt plus preferred stock. It is a rough measure of the protection, or "cushion," afforded by the presence of a junior investment that must first bear the brunt of unfavorable developments. This factor includes the market's appraisal of the future prospects of the enterprise.

3. *Property Value.* The asset values, as shown on the balance sheet or as appraised, were formerly considered the chief security and protection for a bond issue. Experience has shown that in most cases safety resides in the earning power, and if this is deficient the assets lose most of their reputed value. Asset values, however, retain importance as a separate test of ample security for bonds and preferred stocks in three enterprise groups: public utilities (because rates may depend largely on the property investment), real-estate concerns, and investment companies.

At this point the alert investor should ask, "How dependable are tests of safety that are measured by past and present performance, in view of the fact that payment of interest and principal depends upon what the future will bring forth?" The answer can be founded only on experience. Investment history shows that bonds and preferred stocks that have met stringent tests of safety, based on the past, have in the great majority of cases been able to face the vicissitudes of the future successfully. This has been strikingly demonstrated in the major field of railroad bonds—a field that has been marked by a calamitous frequency of bankruptcies and serious losses. In nearly every case the roads that got into trouble had long been overbonded, had shown an inadequate coverage of fixed charges in periods of average prosperity, and would thus have been

---

* By "junior stock issues" Graham means shares of common stock. Preferred stock is considered "senior" to common stock because the company must pay all dividends on the preferred before paying any dividends on the common. (See Chapter 4.)

ruled out by investors who applied strict tests of safety. Conversely, practically every road that has met such tests has escaped financial embarrassment. Our premise was strikingly vindicated by the financial history of the numerous railroads reorganized in the 1940s and in 1950. All of these, with one exception, started their careers with fixed charges reduced to a point where the current coverage of fixed-interest requirements was ample, or at least respectable. The exception was the New Haven Railroad, which in its reorganization year, 1947, earned its new charges only about 1.1 times. In consequence, while all the other roads were able to come through rather difficult times with solvency unimpaired, the New Haven relapsed into trusteeship (for the third time) in 1961.

In Chapter 17 below we shall consider some aspects of the bankruptcy of the Penn Central Railroad, which shook the financial community in 1970. An elementary fact in this case was that the coverage of fixed charges did not meet conservative standards as early as 1965; hence a prudent bond investor would have avoided or disposed of the bond issues of the system long before its financial collapse.

Our observations on the adequacy of the past record to judge future safety apply, and to an even greater degree, to the public utilities, which constitute a major area for bond investment. Receivership of a soundly capitalized (electric) utility company or system is almost impossible. Since Securities and Exchange Commission control was instituted,* along with the breakup of most of the holding-company systems, public-utility financing has been sound and bankruptcies unknown. The financial troubles of electric and gas utilities in the 1930s were traceable almost 100% to financial excesses and mismanagement, which left their imprint clearly on the companies' capitalization structures. Simple but stringent tests of safety, therefore, would have warned the investor away from the issues that were later to default.

Among industrial bond issues the long-term record has been

---

* After investors lost billions of dollars on the shares of recklessly assembled utility companies in 1929–1932, Congress authorized the SEC to regulate the issuance of utility stocks under the Public Utility Holding Company Act of 1935.

different. Although the industrial group as a whole has shown a better growth of earning power than either the railroads or the utilities, it has revealed a lesser degree of inherent stability for individual companies and lines of business. Thus in the past, at least, there have been persuasive reasons for confining the purchase of industrial bonds and preferred stocks to companies that not only are of major size but also have shown an ability in the past to withstand a serious depression.

Few defaults of industrial bonds have occurred since 1950, but this fact is attributable in part to the absence of a major depression during this long period. Since 1966 there have been adverse developments in the financial position of many industrial companies. Considerable difficulties have developed as the result of unwise expansion. On the one hand this has involved large additions to both bank loans and long-term debt; on the other it has frequently produced operating losses instead of the expected profits. At the beginning of 1971 it was calculated that in the past seven years the interest payments of all nonfinancial firms had grown from $9.8 billion in 1963 to $26.1 billion in 1970, and that interest payments had taken 29% of the aggregate profits before interest and taxes in 1971, against only 16% in 1963.[3] Obviously, the burden on many individual firms had increased much more than this. Overbonded companies have become all too familiar. There is every reason to repeat the caution expressed in our 1965 edition:

> We are not quite ready to suggest that the investor may count on an indefinite continuance of this favorable situation, and hence relax his standards of bond selection in the industrial or any other group.

Common-Stock Analysis

The ideal form of common-stock analysis leads to a valuation of the issue which can be compared with the current price to determine whether or not the security is an attractive purchase. This valuation, in turn, would ordinarily be found by estimating the average earnings over a period of years in the *future* and then multiplying that estimate by an appropriate "capitalization factor."

The now-standard procedure for estimating future earning power starts with average *past* data for physical volume, prices received, and operating margin. Future sales in dollars are then projected on the basis of assumptions as to the amount of change in volume and price level over the previous base. These estimates, in turn, are grounded first on general economic forecasts of gross national product, and then on special calculations applicable to the industry and company in question.

An illustration of this method of valuation may be taken from our 1965 edition and brought up to date by adding the sequel. The Value Line, a leading investment service, makes forecasts of future earnings and dividends by the procedure outlined above, and then derives a figure of "price potentiality" (or projected market value) by applying a valuation formula to each issue based largely on certain past relationships. In Table 11-2 we reproduce the projections for 1967–1969 made in June 1964, and compare them with the earnings, and average market price actually realized in 1968 (which approximates the 1967–1969 period).

The combined forecasts proved to be somewhat on the low side, but not seriously so. The corresponding predictions made six years before had turned out to be overoptimistic on earnings and dividends; but this had been offset by use of a low multiplier, with the result that the "price potentiality" figure proved to be about the same as the actual average price for 1963.

The reader will note that quite a number of the individual forecasts were wide of the mark. This is an instance in support of our general view that **composite or group estimates are likely to be a good deal more dependable than those for individual companies.** Ideally, perhaps, the security analyst should pick out the three or four companies whose future he thinks he knows the best, and concentrate his own and his clients' interest on what he forecasts for them. Unfortunately, it appears to be almost impossible to distinguish in advance between those individual forecasts which can be relied upon and those which are subject to a large chance of error. At bottom, this is the reason for the wide diversification practiced by the investment funds. **For it is undoubtedly better to concentrate on one stock that you *know* is going to prove highly profitable, rather than dilute your results to a mediocre figure, merely for diversification's sake. But this is not done, because it**

TABLE 11-2 The Dow Jones Industrial Average

The Value Line's Forecast for 1967–1969 (Made in Mid-1964) Compared With Actual Results in 1968

	Earnings		Price June 30 1964	Price Forecast 1967–1969	Average Price 1968[a]
	Forecast 1967–1969	Actual 1968[a]			
Allied Chemical	$3.70	$1.46	54½	67	36½
Aluminum Corp. of Am.	3.85	4.75	71½	85	79
American Can	3.50	4.25	47	57	48
American Tel. & Tel.	4.00	3.75	73½	68	53
American Tobacco	3.00	4.38	51½	33	37
Anaconda	6.00	8.12	44½	70	106
Bethlehem Steel	3.25	3.55	36½	45	31
Chrysler	4.75	6.23	48½	45	60
Du Pont	8.50	7.82	253	240	163
Eastman Kodak	5.00	9.32	133	100	320
General Electric	4.50	3.95	80	90	90½
General Foods	4.70	4.16	88	71	84½
General Motors	6.25	6.02	88	78	81½
Goodyear Tire	3.25	4.12	43	43	54
Internat. Harvester	5.75	5.38	82	63	69
Internat. Nickel	5.20	3.86	79	83	76
Internat. Paper	2.25	2.04	32	36	33
Johns Manville	4.00	4.78	57½	54	71½
Owens-Ill. Glass	5.25	6.20	99	100	125½
Procter & Gamble	4.20	4.30	83	70	91
Sears Roebuck	4.70	5.46	118	78	122½
Standard Oil of Cal.	5.25	5.59	64½	60	67
Standard Oil of N.J.	6.00	5.94	87	73	76
Swift & Co.	3.85	3.41[b]	54	50	57
Texaco	5.50	6.04	79½	70	81
Union Carbide	7.35	5.20	126½	165	90
United Aircraft	4.00	7.65	49½	50	106
U.S. Steel	4.50	4.69	57½	60	42
Westinghouse Elec.	3.25	3.49	30½	50	69
Woolworth	2.25	2.29	29½	32	29½
Total	138.25	149.20	2222	2186	2450
DJIA (Total % 2.67)	52.00	56.00	832	820	918[c]
DJIA Actual 1968	57.89				906[c]
DJIA Actual 1967–1969	56.26				

[a] Adjusted for stock-splits since 1964.
[b] Average 1967–1969.
[c] Difference due to changed divisor.

cannot be done *dependably*.[4] The prevalence of wide diversification is in itself a pragmatic repudiation of the fetish of "selectivity," to which Wall Street constantly pays lip service.*

Factors Affecting the Capitalization Rate

Though average future earnings are supposed to be the chief determinant of value, the security analyst takes into account a number of other factors of a more or less definite nature. Most of these will enter into his capitalization rate, which can vary over a wide range, depending upon the "quality" of the stock issue. Thus, although two companies may have the same figure of expected earnings per share in 1973–1975—say $4—the analyst may value one as low as 40 and the other as high as 100. Let us deal briefly with some of the considerations that enter into these divergent multipliers.

1. *General Long-Term Prospects.* **No one really knows anything about what will happen in the distant future, but analysts and investors have strong views on the subject just the same.** These views are reflected in the substantial differentials between the price/earnings ratios of individual companies and of industry groups. At this point we added in our 1965 edition:

> For example, at the end of 1963 the chemical companies in the DJIA were selling at considerably higher multipliers than the oil companies, indicating stronger confidence in the prospects of the former than of the latter. Such distinctions made by the

---

* For indisputably skilled investors like Warren Buffett, wide diversification would be foolish, because it would water down the concentrated force of a few great ideas. But for the typical fund manager or individual investor, *not* diversifying is foolish, since it is so difficult to select a limited number of stocks that will include most winners and exclude most losers. As you own more stocks, the damage any single loser can cause will decline, and the odds of owning at least some big winners will rise. The ideal choice for most investors is a total stock market index fund, a low-cost way to hold every stock worth owning.

market are often soundly based, but when dictated mainly by past performance they are as likely to be wrong as right.

We shall supply here, in Table 11-3, the 1963 year-end material on the chemical and oil company issues in the DJIA, and carry their earnings to the end of 1970. It will be seen that the chemical companies, despite their high multipliers, made practically no gain in earnings in the period after 1963. The oil companies did much better than the chemicals and about in line with the growth implied in their 1963 multipliers.[5] Thus our chemical-stock example proved to be one of the cases in which the market multipliers were proven wrong.*

2. *Management.* On Wall Street a great deal is constantly said on this subject, but little that is really helpful. Until objective, quantitative, and reasonably reliable tests of managerial competence are devised and applied, this factor will continue to be looked at through a fog. **It is fair to assume that an outstandingly successful company has unusually good management. This will have shown itself already in the past record; it will show up again in the estimates for the next five years, and once more in the previously discussed factor of long-term prospects. The tendency to count it still another time as a separate bullish consideration can easily lead to expensive overvaluations. The management factor is most useful, we think, in those cases in which a recent change has taken place that has not yet had the time to show its significance in the actual figures.**

---

* Graham's point about chemical and oil companies in the 1960s applies to nearly every industry in nearly every time period. Wall Street's consensus view of the future for any given sector is usually either too optimistic or too pessimistic. Worse, the consensus is at its most cheery just when the stocks are most overpriced—and gloomiest just when they are cheapest. History proves that Wall Street's "expert" forecasters are equally inept at predicting the performance of 1) the market as a whole, 2) industry sectors, and 3) specific stocks. As Graham points out, the odds that individual investors can do any better are not good. Intelligent investors excel by making decisions that are not dependent on the accuracy of anybody's forecasts, including their own. (See Chapter 8.)

TABLE 11-3 Performance of Chemical and Oil Stocks in the DJIA, 1970 versus 1964

	Closing Price	1963 Earned Per Share	P/E Ratio	Closing Price	1970 Earned Per Share	P/E Ratio
Chemical companies:						
Allied Chemical	55	2.77	19.8 ×	24⅛	1.56	15.5 ×
Du Pont[a]	77	6.55	23.5	133½	6.76	19.8
Union Carbide[b]	60¼	2.66	22.7	40	2.60	15.4
			25.3 ave.			
Oil companies:						
Standard Oil of Cal.	59½	4.50	13.2 ×	54½	5.36	10.2 ×
Standard Oil of N.J.	76	4.74	16.0	73½	5.90	12.4
Texaco[b]	35	2.15	16.3	35	3.02	11.6
			15.3 ave.			

[a] 1963 figures adjusted for distribution of General Motors shares.
[b] 1963 figures adjusted for subsequent stock splits.

Two spectacular occurrences of this kind were associated with the Chrysler Motor Corporation. The first took place as far back as 1921, when Walter Chrysler took command of the almost moribund Maxwell Motors, and in a few years made it a large and highly profitable enterprise, while numerous other automobile companies were forced out of business. The second happened as recently as 1962, when Chrysler had fallen far from its once high estate and the stock was selling at its lowest price in many years. Then new interests, associated with Consolidation Coal, took over the reins. The earnings advanced from the 1961 figure of $1.24 per share to the equivalent of $17 in 1963, and the price rose from a low of 38½ in 1962 to the equivalent of nearly 200 the very next year.[6]

3. *Financial Strength and Capital Structure.* Stock of a company with a lot of surplus cash and nothing ahead of the common is clearly a better purchase (at the same price) than another one with the same per share earnings but large bank loans and senior securities. Such factors are properly and carefully taken into account by security analysts. A modest amount of bonds or preferred stock, however, is not necessarily a disadvantage to the common, nor is the moderate use of seasonal bank credit. (Incidentally, a top-heavy structure—too little common stock in relation to bonds and preferred—may under favorable conditions make for a huge *speculative* profit in the common. This is the factor known as "leverage.")

4. *Dividend Record.* One of the most persuasive tests of high quality is an uninterrupted record of dividend payments going back over many years. We think that a record of continuous dividend payments for the last 20 years or more is an important plus factor in the company's quality rating. Indeed the defensive investor might be justified in limiting his purchases to those meeting this test.

5. *Current Dividend Rate.* This, our last additional factor, is the most difficult one to deal with in satisfactory fashion. Fortunately, the majority of companies have come to follow what may be called a standard dividend policy. This has meant the distribution of about two-thirds of their average earnings, except that in the recent period of high profits and inflationary demands for more capital the figure has tended to be lower. (In 1969 it was 59.5% for the stocks

in the Dow Jones average, and 55% for all American corporations.)*
Where the dividend bears a normal relationship to the earnings, the valuation may be made on either basis without substantially affecting the result. For example, a typical secondary company with expected average earnings of $3 and an expected dividend of $2 may be valued at either 12 times its earnings or 18 times its dividend, to yield a value of 36 in both cases.

However, an increasing number of growth companies are departing from the once standard policy of paying out 60% or more of earnings in dividends, on the grounds that the shareholders' interests will be better served by retaining nearly all the profits to finance expansion. The issue presents problems and requires careful distinctions. We have decided to defer our discussion of the vital question of proper dividend policy to a later section—Chapter 19—where we shall deal with it as a part of the general problem of management-shareholder relations.

Capitalization Rates for Growth Stocks

Most of the writing of security analysts on formal appraisals relates to the valuation of growth stocks. Our study of the various methods has led us to suggest a foreshortened and quite simple formula for the valuation of growth stocks, which is intended to produce figures fairly close to those resulting from the more refined mathematical calculations. Our formula is:

Value = Current (Normal) Earnings × (8.5 plus twice the expected annual growth rate)

The growth figure should be that expected over the next seven to ten years.[7]

---

* This figure, now known as the "dividend payout ratio," has dropped since Graham's day as American tax law discouraged investors from seeking, and corporations from paying, dividends. As of year-end 2023, the payout ratio was approximately 38% for the S&P 500. Include the effects of share buybacks and that number is considerably higher; see the Commentary on Chapter 19.

In Table 11-4 we show how our formula works out for various rates of assumed growth. **It is easy to make the converse calculation and to determine what rate of growth is anticipated by the current market price, assuming our formula is valid.** In our last edition we made that calculation for the DJIA and for six important stock issues. These figures are reproduced in Table 11-5. We commented at the time:

> The difference between the implicit 32.4% annual growth rate for Xerox and the extremely modest 2.8% for General Motors is indeed striking. It is explainable in part by the stock market's feeling that General Motors' 1963 earnings—the largest for any corporation in history—can be maintained with difficulty and exceeded only modestly at best. The price earnings ratio of Xerox, on the other hand, is quite representative of speculative enthusiasm fastened upon a company of great achievement and perhaps still greater promise.
>
> The implicit or expected growth rate of 5.1% for the DJIA compares with an actual annual increase of 3.4% (compounded) between 1951–1953 and 1961–1963.

We should have added a caution somewhat as follows: The valuations of expected high-growth stocks are necessarily on the low side, if we were to assume these growth rates will actually be realized. **In fact, according to the arithmetic, if a company could be assumed to grow at a rate of 8% or more *indefinitely* in the future its value would be infinite, and no price would be too high to pay for the shares.** What the valuer actually does in these cases is to introduce a *margin of safety* into his calculations—somewhat as an engineer does in his specifications for a structure.* On this basis the purchases would realize his assigned objective (in 1963, a future overall return of 7½% per annum) even if the growth rate actually realized proved substantially less than that projected in the formula. Of course, then, if that rate were actually realized the investor would be sure to enjoy a handsome additional return. There is really no way of valuing a high-growth company (with

---

* See Chapter 20 and its Commentary.

TABLE 11-4 Annual Earnings Multipliers Based on Expected Growth Rates, Based on a Simplified Formula

Expected growth rate	0.0%	2.5%	5.0%	7.2%	10.0%	14.3%	20.0%
Growth in 10 years	0.0	28.0%	63.0%	100.0%	159.0%	280.0%	319.0%
Multiplier of current earnings	8.5	13.5	18.5	22.9	28.5	37.1	48.5

TABLE 11-5 Implicit or Expected Growth Rates, December 1963 and December 1969

Issue	P/E Ratio, 1963	Projected[a] Growth Rate, 1963	Earned Per Share 1963	Earned Per Share 1969	Actual Annual Growth, 1963–1969	P/E Ratio, 1969	Projected[a] Growth Rate, 1969
American Tel. & Tel.	23.0 ×	7.3%	3.03	4.00	4.75%	12.2 ×	1.8%
General Electric	29.0	10.3	3.00	3.79[b]	4.0	20.4	6.0
General Motors	14.1	2.8	5.55	5.95	1.17	11.6	1.6
IBM	38.5	15.0	3.48[c]	8.21	16.0	44.4	17.9
International Harvester	13.2	2.4	2.29[c]	2.30	0.1	10.8	1.1
Xerox	25.0	32.4	.38[c]	2.08	29.2	50.8	21.2
DJIA	18.6	5.1	41.11	57.02	5.5	14.0	2.8

[a] Based on formula on p. 283.
[b] Average of 1968 and 1970, since 1969 earnings were reduced by strike.
[c] Adjusted for stock splits.

an expected rate above, say, 8% annually), in which the analyst can make realistic assumptions of *both* the proper multiplier for the current earnings and the expectable multiplier for the future earnings.

As it happened the actual growth for Xerox and IBM proved very close to the high rates implied from our formula. As just explained, this fine showing inevitably produced a large advance in the price of both issues. The growth of the DJIA itself was also about as projected by the 1963 closing market price. But the moderate rate of 5% did not involve the mathematical dilemma of Xerox and IBM. It turned out that the 23% price rise to the end of 1970, plus the 28% in aggregate dividend return received, gave not far from the 7½% annual overall gain posited in our formula. In the case of the other four companies it may suffice to say that their growth did not equal the expectations implied in the 1963 price and that their quotations failed to rise as much as the DJIA. *Warning:* This material is supplied for illustrative purposes only, and because of the inescapable necessity in security analysis to project the future growth rate for most companies studied. **Let the reader not be misled into thinking that such projections have any high degree of reliability or, conversely, that future prices can be counted on to behave accordingly as the prophecies are realized, surpassed, or disappointed.**

We should point out that **any "scientific," or at least reasonably dependable, stock evaluation based on anticipated future results must take future interest rates into account**. A given schedule of expected earnings, or dividends, would have a smaller present value if we assume a higher than if we assume a lower interest structure.* Such assumptions have always been difficult to make with any degree of confidence, and the recent violent swings in long-term

---

* Why is this? By "the rule of 72," at 10% interest a given amount of money doubles in just over seven years, while at 7% it doubles in just over 10 years. When interest rates are high, the amount of money you need to set aside today to reach a given value in the future is *lower*—since those high interest rates will enable it to grow at a more rapid rate. Thus a rise in interest rates today makes a future stream of earnings or dividends less valuable—since the alternative of investing in bonds has become relatively more attractive.

interest rates render forecasts of this sort almost presumptuous. Hence we have retained our old formula above, simply because no new one would appear more plausible.

Industry Analysis

Because the general prospects of the enterprise carry major weight in the establishment of market prices, it is natural for the security analyst to devote a great deal of attention to the economic position of the industry and of the individual company in its industry. Studies of this kind can go into unlimited detail. They are sometimes productive of valuable insights into important factors that will be operative in the future and are insufficiently appreciated by the current market. Where a conclusion of that kind can be drawn with a fair degree of confidence, it affords a sound basis for investment decisions.

Our own observation, however, leads us to minimize somewhat the practical value of most of the industry studies that are made available to investors. The material developed is ordinarily of a kind with which the public is already fairly familiar and that has already exerted considerable influence on market quotations. Rarely does one find a brokerage-house study that points out, with a convincing array of facts, that a popular industry is heading for a fall or that an unpopular one is due to prosper. Wall Street's view of the longer future is notoriously fallible, and this necessarily applies to that important part of its investigations which is directed toward the forecasting of the course of profits in various industries.

We must recognize, however, that the rapid and pervasive growth of technology in recent years is not without major effect on the attitude and the labors of the security analyst. More so than in the past, the progress or retrogression of the typical company in the coming decade may depend on its relation to new products and new processes, which the analyst may have a chance to study and evaluate *in advance*. Thus there is doubtless a promising area for effective work by the analyst, based on field trips, interviews with research men, and on intensive technological investigation on his own. **There are hazards connected with investment conclusions derived chiefly from such glimpses into the future, and not supported by presently demonstrable value. Yet there are**

perhaps equal hazards in sticking closely to the limits of value set by sober calculations resting on actual results. The investor cannot have it both ways. He can be imaginative and play for the big profits that are the reward for vision proved sound by the event; but then he must run a substantial risk of major or minor miscalculation. Or he can be conservative, and refuse to pay more than a minor premium for possibilities as yet unproved; but in that case he must be prepared for the later contemplation of golden opportunities foregone.

A Two-Part Appraisal Process

Let us return for a moment to the idea of valuation or appraisal of a common stock, which we began to discuss above on p. 276. A great deal of reflection on the subject has led us to conclude that this had better be done quite differently than is now the established practice. We suggest that analysts work out first what we call the "past-performance value," which is based solely on the past record. This would indicate what the stock would be worth—absolutely, or as a percentage of the DJIA or of the S & P composite—if it is assumed that its relative past performance will continue unchanged in the future. (This includes the assumption that its relative growth rate, as shown in the last seven years, will also continue unchanged over the next seven years.) This process could be carried out mechanically by applying a formula that gives individual weights to past figures for profitability, stability, and growth, and also for current financial condition. The second part of the analysis should consider to what extent the value based solely on past performance should be modified because of new conditions expected in the future.

Such a procedure would divide the work between senior and junior analysts as follows: (1) The senior analyst would set up the formula to apply to all companies generally for determining past-performance value. (2) The junior analysts would work up such factors for the designated companies—pretty much in mechanical fashion. (3) The senior analyst would then determine to what extent a company's performance—absolute or relative—is likely to differ from its past record, and what change should be made in the value to reflect such anticipated changes. It would be best if the senior analyst's report showed both the original valuation and the modified one, with his reasons for the change.

Is a job of this kind worth doing? Our answer is in the affirmative, but our reasons may appear somewhat cynical to the reader. We doubt whether the valuations so reached will prove sufficiently dependable in the case of the typical industrial company, great or small. We shall illustrate the difficulties of this job in our discussion of Aluminum Company of America (ALCOA) in the next chapter. Nonetheless it should be done for such common stocks. Why? First, many security analysts are bound to make current or projected valuations, as part of their daily work. The method we propose should be an improvement on those generally followed today. Secondly, because it should give useful experience and insight to the analysts who practice this method. Thirdly, because work of this kind could produce an invaluable body of recorded experience—as has long been the case in medicine—that may lead to better methods of procedure and a useful knowledge of its possibilities and limitations. The public-utility stocks might well prove an important area in which this approach will show real pragmatic value. Eventually the intelligent analyst will confine himself to those groups in which the future appears reasonably predictable,* or where the margin of safety of past-performance value over current price is so large that he can take his chances on future variations—as he does in selecting well-secured senior securities.

In subsequent chapters we shall supply concrete examples of the application of analytical techniques. But they will only be illustrations. If the reader finds the subject interesting he should pursue it systematically and thoroughly before he considers himself qualified to pass a final buy-or-sell judgment of his own on a security issue.

---

* Such industry groups would tend not to be overly vulnerable to shocks from interest rates or the prices of raw materials. They might include some consumer products, food and beverages, gaming, and waste management.

Commentary on Chapter 11
by Jason Zweig

> If you want to buy the same thing that is popular with your friends or popular with the investment analysts, you can't get a bargain. If you buy the same thing they buy you will get the same performance they get. If you are going to have a superior performance, you've got to buy what the other people are not buying or even what those are selling.
> —*Sir John Templeton*[1]

As an intelligent investor, if you hope to succeed at analyzing stocks in an always competitive and usually efficient market, you must follow Graham's essential principles: Be different from the crowd, and be disciplined.

You can't achieve either of those goals by acting on whims. If, however, you can become disciplined and stay that way, then you will be different from the crowd—by definition.[2]

"Kind" versus "Wicked"

Start by understanding that how much any of us can learn from our experience depends on the quality of the feedback we get. Robin Hogarth, a psychologist at Universitat Pompeu Fabra in Barcelona,

---

[1] "Investments, Insights and Inspiration: Words of Wisdom from Sir John Templeton," Franklin Templeton Investments.

[2] As Graham wrote in the first edition of this book: "The investor cannot enter the arena of the stock market with any real hope of success unless he is armed with mental weapons that distinguish him in *kind*—not in a fancied superior *degree*—from the trading public."

described two types of learning environments. A "kind" setting provides prompt, accurate, unambiguous feedback on whether what you're doing works. A "wicked" environment offers feedback that is delayed, inaccurate, and ambiguous.[3]

The stock market is among the most wicked learning environments in the world, with murky feedback in constant flux. Let's say you're convinced a company is worth $14 to $16 a share. You buy the stock at 11:42 a.m. for $10. By 11:48 a.m., it's at $10.87: *The market already agrees with me!* An hour later, the stock has fallen to $9.94: *The market is wrong!* The next day, trading opens—and closes—at $10: *Well, at least I'm breaking even.* A week later, the stock is at $11.50: *Yes! It's up 15%!* The week after that, it sinks to $9, then to $8.50, then to $8: *No! I've lost 20%!* Over the next month the stock sinks to $6.66, at which point you panic and sell before you lose even more than a third of your money.

Later that day, a competitor announces it's buying the company for $14 per share.

Were you right?

Were you wrong?

You won't be able to tell unless you documented your reasoning. That's the only way to get kind feedback out of a wicked learning environment. Before you buy, make a record of your rationale: What specific evidence do you understand about the company that other investors are overlooking, and why did they miss it? Why do you think the company is worth $14 to $16 a share? How long should it take to reach that price? How confident are you that you're correct—are you 90% certain? 80%? 50%? 100%?

Gut Check

One of the best ways to create a record of your rationale and structure your feedback is with a checklist.

By imposing a rule on yourself—*I will never buy a stock without first completing a checklist*—you can avoid the heartache that comes from selling in a panic after buying on an impulse. And you can help determine whether you were right for the right reasons, or whether you just got lucky.

A checklist can't work miracles: It won't, all by itself, enable you to

---

[3] Robin M. Hogarth, *Educating Intuition* (Chicago, 2001).

find the next Amazon or Apple. But it takes much of the wickedness out of the stock market's feedback. It compels you to be consistent and ensures that you don't underemphasize or overlook factors you intend to rely on. Above all, it enables you to learn what works, what doesn't, and how to improve your analyses.[4]

Every investor's checklist will be different: It should be based partly on what you've learned from your successes and mistakes, and not every company or industry can be analyzed the same way. At a minimum, though, your checklist must refocus your attention away from the *stock* and onto the *business*. It might include such elements as these:

- **Have I read at least the last three annual reports and the past year's quarterly reports?** A company's financial reports consist of three key components: the balance sheet, the income statement, and the cash-flow statement. Do I understand the balance sheet well enough to determine whether the company is dangerously in debt? Can I tell from the income statement whether costs are under control and profits are rising? What does the statement of cash flows indicate about how the company generates and consumes cash? Is the business consistently generating more cash over time from its operations? From the narrative portion of the company's reports, what can I learn about the company's biggest competitors? How dependent is it on a few sources of raw materials, sales in one geographical region, or a handful of large customers? Has it grown by acquiring other companies or by expanding internally? Does management allocate surplus capital wisely, or has the company repeatedly taken accounting write-offs to cover the costs of investments or acquisitions that went bad?[5]

---

[4] Atul Gawande, *The Checklist Manifesto* (Metropolitan, 2009). See also the checklist guidelines compiled by Phil Ordway of Anabatic Investment Partners at bit.ly/43ue88u; Meb Faber of Cambria Investment Management at bit.ly/3uvjg0x; and investor Brett Caughran at bit.ly/45DGZsD.

[5] By "annual report," I mean the company's full financial statement. In the U.S., it is called Form 10-K and is freely available from the Securities and Exchange Commission's EDGAR website at sec.gov/edgar. I do *not* mean the report mailed to shareholders, a promotional document on glossy paper featuring pretty pictures and propaganda.

- **Have I read the latest proxy statement?** Relative to other firms in the same industry, is this company's management compensated fairly? Are managers engaging in extensive "related party transactions" or receiving lavish perks that raise troubling conflicts of interest? Do the directors have significant stock holdings? Are top executives using their own cash to buy shares, or simply being granted a free ride with stock options? Is incentive compensation tied to sensible measures of long-term profitability and financial soundness, such as growth in return on equity or book value per share over multiyear horizons—or purely to the raw share price or to make-believe metrics like growth in "adjusted EBITDA"?[6]
- **Does the company have durable advantages?** As Warren Buffett has said, "The key to investing is . . . determining the competitive advantage of any given company and, above all, the durability of that advantage." How dominant are its brands, and why? Does it have patents or other intellectual property that insulate it from competition? Does it continuously undercut its rivals' prices, providing consumers with compelling value? Does the business generate "network effects," in which its products or services become more valuable as more people use them? If the company disappeared tomorrow, how hard would it be for customers to find a comparable provider?[7]
- **Are the managers operators or promoters?** Do the top executives say what they will do and do what they say? Do they underpromise and overdeliver? Do they readily admit mistakes? Do they consistently follow conservative accounting rules, or do they repeatedly change how the company reports its financial

---

[6] See the Commentary on Chapter 19.

[7] Carol Loomis, "Mr. Buffett on the Stock Market," bit.ly/3Dbxi8x. For a classic discussion on identifying businesses with durable advantages, see Philip A. Fisher, *Common Stocks and Uncommon Profits* (Wiley, 1996). On competitive "moats" and network effects, see Pat Dorsey, *The Little Book That Builds Wealth* (Wiley, 2009); Michael J. Mauboussin and Dan Callahan, "Market Share," bit.ly/44u1hVg and "The Economics of Customer Businesses," bit.ly/3XSyK98. For its moat to endure, a company should be able to set prices without arbitrary actions by government regulators.

results? Are they focused on the long-term value of the business or the short-term price of the stock?
- **Have I conducted a premortem?** Do I understand the business well enough to imagine the competitive weaknesses that could kill it? Pretend it's one year from now and the company just filed for bankruptcy protection. What went wrong: Did new management fail to turn the business around, did rising interest rates turn its debt into an unbearable burden, did consumers abandon a hot product on which the company was overdependent, did an acquisition turn into a debacle?
- **What is my edge?** What, exactly, do I understand about this company that most other investors are missing, and why?
- **What are the odds?** Based on my experience, how confident am I that I'm right? How long do I estimate the stock will take to reach my target?
- **If the stock market shut down for the next five years, would I be happy owning a piece of this company?** Write down three to five reasons—having nothing to do with the stock price—why this is a good business that should be even better five years from now.

Above all, live by this rule: *If I haven't followed all the steps in my checklist, I can't buy this investment.*[8]

If complying with all the steps in a checklist sounds like too much work, you should reconsider whether you're an enterprising investor after all. Unless you're ready and willing to commit many hours of time and effort to analyzing a company before you invest, you're a defensive investor. And there's nothing wrong with that.

---

[8] The only permissible exception to this rule would be if you make the purchase in your "mad-money" account (see Chapter 1 and its Commentary)—in which case you can't put more than a minuscule amount into it.

CHAPTER 12

Things to Consider About Per-Share Earnings

by Benjamin Graham

*T*his chapter will begin with two pieces of advice to the investor that cannot avoid being contradictory in their implications. The first is: **Don't take a single year's earnings seriously. The second is: If you do pay attention to short-term earnings, look out for booby traps in the per-share figures.** If our first warning were followed strictly the second would be unnecessary. But it is too much to expect that most shareholders can relate all their common-stock decisions to the long-term record and the long-term prospects. The quarterly figures, and especially the annual figures, receive major attention in financial circles, and this emphasis can hardly fail to have its impact on the investor's thinking. He may well need some education in this area, for it abounds in misleading possibilities.

As this chapter is being written the earnings report of Aluminum Company of America (ALCOA) for 1970 appears in the *Wall Street Journal*. The first figures shown are

	1970	1969
Share earnings[a]	$5.20	$5.58

The little [a] at the outset is explained in a footnote to refer to "primary earnings," before special charges. There is much more footnote material; in fact it occupies twice as much space as do the basic figures themselves.

For the December quarter alone, the "earnings per share" are given as $1.58 in 1970 against $1.56 in 1969.

The investor or speculator interested in ALCOA shares, reading those figures, might say to himself: "Not so bad. I knew that 1970 was a recession year in aluminum. But the fourth quarter shows a gain over 1969, with earnings at the rate of $6.32 per year. Let me see. The stock is selling at 62. Why, that's less than ten times earnings. That makes it look pretty cheap, compared with 16 times for International Nickel, etc., etc."

But if our investor-speculator friend had bothered to read all the material in the footnote, he would have found that instead of one figure of earnings per share for the year 1970 there were actually *four*, viz.:

	1970	1969
Primary earnings	$5.20	$5.58
Net income (after special charges)	4.32	5.58
Fully diluted, before special charges	5.01	5.35
Fully diluted, after special charges	4.19	5.35

For the fourth quarter alone only two figures are given:

Primary earnings	$1.58	$1.56
Net income (after special charges)	.70	1.56

What do all these additional earnings mean? Which earnings are true earnings for the year and the December quarter? If the latter should be taken at 70 cents—the net income after special charges—the annual rate would be $2.80 instead of $6.32, and the price 62 would be "22 times earnings," instead of the 10 times we started with.

Part of the question as to the "true earnings" of ALCOA can be answered quite easily. The reduction from $5.20 to $5.01, to allow for the effects of "dilution," is clearly called for. ALCOA has a large bond issue convertible into common stock; to calculate the "earning power" of the common, based on the 1970 results, it must be assumed that the conversion privilege will be exercised if it should prove profitable to the bondholders to do so. The amount involved in the ALCOA picture is relatively small, and hardly deserves detailed comment. But in other cases, making allowance for conversion rights—and the existence of stock-purchase warrants—can reduce the apparent earnings by half, or more. We shall present examples of a really significant dilution factor below (p. 405). (The financial services are not always consistent in their allowance for the dilution factor in their reporting and analyses.)*

Let us turn now to the matter of "special charges." This figure of $18,800,000, or 88 cents per share, deducted in the fourth quarter, is not unimportant. Is it to be ignored entirely, or fully recognized as an earnings reduction, or partly recognized and partly ignored? The alert investor might ask himself also how does it happen that there was a virtual epidemic of such special charge-offs appearing after the close of 1970, but not in previous years? Could there possibly have been some fine Italian hands[†] at work with the accounting—but always, of course, within the limits of the permissible? When we look closely we may find that such losses, charged off before they actually occur, can be charmed away, as it were, with no unhappy effect on either past or future "primary earnings." In some extreme cases they might be availed of to make subsequent earnings appear nearly twice as large as in reality—by a more or less prestidigitous treatment of the tax credit involved.

---

* "Dilution" is one of many words that describe stocks in the language of fluid dynamics. A stock with high trading volume is said to be "liquid." When a company goes public in an IPO, it "floats" its shares. A company that drastically diluted its shares (with large amounts of convertible debt or multiple offerings of common stock) was said to have "watered" its stock. This term may have originated with the market manipulator Daniel Drew (1797–1879), who began as a livestock trader. He would drive his cattle south toward Manhattan, force-feeding them salt. When they got to the Harlem River, they would guzzle huge volumes of water to slake their thirst. Drew would then bring them to market, where the water they had just drunk would increase their weight. That enabled him to get a much higher price, since cattle on the hoof is sold by the pound. Drew later watered the stock of the Erie Railroad by massively issuing new shares without warning.

† Graham is referring to the elegant calligraphy of medieval and Renaissance scribes in Italy. The phrase later became a synonym for "sleight of hand." Accountants, likewise, can transform simple financial facts into intricate and even incomprehensible patterns.

In dealing with ALCOA's special charges, the first thing to establish is how they arose. The footnotes are specific enough. The deductions came from four sources, viz.:

1. Management's estimate of the anticipated costs of closing down the manufactured products division.
2. Ditto for closing down ALCOA Castings Co.'s plants.
3. Ditto for losses in phasing out ALCOA Credit Co.
4. Also, estimated costs of $5.3 million associated with completion of the contract for a "curtain wall."

All of these items are related to future costs and losses. It is easy to say that they are not part of the "regular operating results" of 1970—but if so, where do they belong? Are they so "extraordinary and nonrecurring" as to belong nowhere? A widespread enterprise such as ALCOA, doing a $1.5 billion business annually, must have a lot of divisions, departments, affiliates, and the like. Would it not be normal rather than extraordinary for one or more to prove unprofitable, and to require closing down? Similarly for such things as a contract to build a wall. Suppose that any time a company had a loss on any part of its business it had the bright idea of charging it off as a "special item," and thus reporting its "primary earnings" per share so as to include only its profitable contracts and operations? Like King Edward VII's sundial that marked only the "sunny hours."*

The reader should note two ingenious aspects of the ALCOA procedure we have been discussing. The first is that by *anticipating future losses* the company escapes the necessity of allocating the

---

* The king probably took his inspiration from a once-famous essay by the English writer William Hazlitt, who mused about a sundial near Venice that bore the words *Horas non numero nisi serenas,* or "I count only the hours that are serene." Companies that chronically exclude bad news from their financial results on the pretext that negative events are "extraordinary" or "nonrecurring" are taking a page from Hazlitt, who urged his readers to "compose our lives of bright and gentle moments, turning always to the sunny side of things, and letting the rest slip from our imaginations, unheeded or forgotten!" (William Hazlitt, "On a Sun-Dial," ca. 1827.) Unfortunately, investors must always count the sunny and dark hours alike.

losses themselves to an identifiable year. They don't belong in 1970, because they were not actually taken in that year. And they won't be *shown* in the year when they are actually taken, because they have already been provided for. Neat work, but might it not be just a little misleading?

The ALCOA footnote says nothing about the future tax saving from these losses. (Most other statements of this sort state specifically that only the "after-tax effect" has been charged off.) If the ALCOA figure represents future losses before the related tax credit, then not only will future earnings be freed from the weight of these charges (as they are actually incurred), but they will be *increased* by a tax credit of some 50% thereof. It is difficult to believe that the accounts will be handled that way. But it is a fact that certain companies which have had large losses in the past have been able to report future earnings without charging the normal taxes against them, in that way making a very fine profits appearance indeed—based paradoxically enough on their past disgraces. (Tax credits resulting from *past years'* losses are now being shown separately as "special items," but they will enter into future statistics as part of the final "net-income" figure. However, a reserve now set up for *future* losses, if *net* of expected tax credit, should not create an addition of this sort to the net income of later years.)

The other ingenious feature is the use by ALCOA and many other companies of the 1970 year-end for making these special charge-offs. The stock market took what appeared to be a blood bath in the first half of 1970. Everyone expected relatively poor results for the year for most companies. Wall Street was now anticipating better results in 1971, 1972, etc. What a nice arrangement, then, to charge as much as possible to the bad year, which had already been written off mentally and had virtually receded into the past, leaving the way clear for nicely fattened figures in the next few years! Perhaps this is good accounting, good business policy, and good for management-shareholder relationships. But we have lingering doubts.

The combination of widely (or should it be wildly?) diversified operations with the impulse to clean house at the end of 1970 has produced some strange-looking footnotes to the annual reports. The reader may be amused by the following explanation given by a New York Stock Exchange company (which shall remain unnamed) of its "special items" aggregating $2,357,000, or about a third of the income before charge-offs: "Consists of provision for closing Spalding United Kingdom operations; provision for reorganizational expenses of a division; costs of selling a small baby-pants and bib manufacturing company, disposing of part interest in a Spanish car-leasing facility, and liquidation of a ski-boot operation."*

Years ago the strong companies used to set up "contingency reserves" out of the profits of *good years* to absorb some of the bad effects of depression years to come. The underlying idea was to equalize the reported earnings, more or less, and to improve the stability factor in the company's record. A worthy motive, it would seem; but the accountants quite rightly objected to the practice as misstating the true earnings. They insisted that each year's results be presented as they were, good or bad, and the shareholders and analysts be allowed to do the averaging or equalizing for themselves. We seem now to be witnessing the opposite phenomenon, with everyone charging off as much as possible against forgotten 1970, so as to start 1971 with a slate not only clean but specially prepared to show pleasing per-share figures in the coming years.

It is time to return to our first question. What then were the true earnings of ALCOA in 1970? The accurate answer would be: The $5.01 per share, after "dilution," *less* that part of the 82 cents of "special charges" that may properly be attributed to occurrences in 1970. But we do not know what that portion is, and *hence we cannot properly state the true earnings for the year.* The management and the auditors should have given us their best judgment on this point, but they did not do so. And furthermore, the management and the auditors should have provided for deduction of the balance of these charges from the *ordinary earnings* of a suitable number of future years—say, not more than five. This evidently they will not do either, since they have already conveniently disposed of the entire sum as a 1970 special charge.

The more seriously investors take the per-share earnings figures as published, the more necessary it is for them to be on their guard against accounting factors of one kind and another

---

* The company to which Graham refers so coyly appears to be American Machine & Foundry (or AMF Corp.), one of the most jumbled conglomerates of the late 1960s.

that may impair the true comparability of the numbers. We have mentioned three sorts of these factors: the use of *special charges*, which may never be reflected in the per-share earnings, the reduction in the normal *income-tax* deduction by reason of past losses, and the *dilution* factor implicit in the existence of substantial amounts of convertible securities or warrants.[1] A fourth item that has had a significant effect on reported earnings in the past is the method of treating depreciation—chiefly as between the "straight-line" and the "accelerated" schedules. We refrain from details here. But as an example current as we write, let us mention the 1970 report of Trane Co. This firm showed an increase of nearly 20% in per-share earnings over 1969—$3.29 versus $2.76—but half of this came from returning to the older straight-line depreciation rates, less burdensome on earnings than the accelerated method used the year before. (The company will continue to use the accelerated rate on its income-tax return, thus deferring income-tax payments on the difference.) Still another factor, important at times, is the choice between charging off research and development costs in the year they are incurred or amortizing them over a period of years. Finally, let us mention the choice between the FIFO (first-in-first-out) and LIFO (last-in-first-out) methods of valuing inventories.

An obvious remark here would be that investors should not pay any attention to these accounting variables if the amounts involved are relatively small. But Wall Street being as it is, even items quite minor in themselves can be taken seriously. Two days before the ALCOA report appeared in the *Wall Street Journal*, the paper had quite a discussion of the corresponding statement of Dow Chemical. It closed with the observation that "many analysts" had been troubled by the fact that Dow had included a 21-cent item in regular profits for 1969, instead of treating it as an item of "extraordinary income." Why the fuss? Because, evidently, evaluations of Dow Chemical involving many millions of dollars in the aggregate seemed to depend on exactly what was the percentage gain for 1969 over 1968—in this case either 9% or 4½%. This strikes us as rather absurd; it is very unlikely that small differences involved in one year's results could have any bearing on future average profits or growth, and on a conservative, realistic valuation of the enterprise.

By contrast, consider another statement also appearing in

January 1971. This concerned Northwest Industries Inc.'s report for 1970.* The company was planning to write off, as a special charge, not less than $264 million in one fell swoop. Of this, $200 million represents the loss to be taken on the proposed sale of the railroad subsidiary to its employees and the balance a write-down of a recent stock purchase. These sums would work out to a loss of about $35 per share of common before dilution offsets, or twice its then current market price. Here we have something really significant. If the transaction goes through, and if the tax laws are not changed, this loss provided for in 1970 will permit Northwest Industries to realize about $400 million of future profits (within five years) from its other diversified interests without paying income tax thereon.† What will then be the real earnings of that enterprise; should they be calculated with or without provision for the nearly 50% in income taxes which it will not actually have to pay? In our opinion, the proper mode of calculation would be first to consider the indicated earning power on the basis of full income-tax liability, and to derive some broad idea of the stock's value based on that estimate. To this should be added some bonus figure, representing the value per share of the important but temporary tax exemption the company will enjoy. (Allowance must be made, also, for a possible large-scale dilution in this case. Actually, the convertible preferred issues and warrants would more than double the outstanding common shares if the privileges are exercised.)

All this may be confusing and wearisome to our readers, but it

---

* Northwest Industries was the holding company for, among other businesses, the Chicago and Northwestern Railway Co. and Union Underwear (the maker of both BVD and Fruit of the Loom briefs). It was taken over in 1985 by overindebted financier William Farley, who ran the company into the ground. Fruit of the Loom was bought in a bankruptcy proceeding by Warren Buffett's Berkshire Hathaway Inc. in early 2002.

† Graham is referring to the provision of Federal tax law that allows corporations to "carry forward" their net operating losses. These losses can be carried forward, with some restrictions, thereby reducing the company's future tax liability (and thus raising its after-tax earnings). Therefore, investors should consider whether recent severe losses could actually *improve* the company's net earnings in the future.

belongs in our story. Corporate accounting is often tricky; security analysis can be complicated; stock valuations are really dependable only in exceptional cases. For most investors it would be probably best to assure themselves that they are getting good value for the prices they pay, and let it go at that.

Use of Average Earnings

In former times analysts and investors paid considerable attention to the average earnings over a fairly long period in the past—usually from seven to ten years. This "mean figure"* was useful for ironing out the frequent ups and downs of the business cycle, and it was thought to give a better idea of the company's earning power than the results of the latest year alone. One important advantage of such an averaging process is that it will solve the problem of what to do about nearly all the special charges and credits. They should be *included* in the average earnings. For certainly most of these losses and gains represent a part of the company's operating history. If we do this for ALCOA, the average earnings for 1961–1970 (ten years) would appear as $3.62 and for the seven years 1964–1970 as $4.62 per share. If such figures are used in conjunction with ratings for growth and stability of earnings during the same period, they could give a really informing picture of the company's past performance.

Calculation of the Past Growth Rate

It is of prime importance that the growth factor in a company's record be taken adequately into account. Where the growth has been large the recent earnings will be well above the seven- or ten-year average, and analysts may deem these long-term figures irrelevant. This need not be the case. The earnings can be given in terms *both* of the average and the latest figure. We suggest that the growth rate itself be calculated by comparing the *average* of the last three years with corresponding figures ten years earlier. (Where

---

* "Mean figure" refers to the average that Graham describes in the preceding sentence.

TABLE 12-1

	ALCOA	Sears Roebuck	DJIA
Average earnings 1968–1970	$4.95[a]	$2.87	$55.40
Average earnings 1958–1960	2.08	1.23	31.49
Growth	141.0%	134.0%	75.0%
Annual rate (compounded)	9.0%	8.7%	5.7%

[a] Three-fifths of special charges of 82 cents in 1970 deducted here.

there is a problem of "special charges or credits" it may be dealt with on some compromise basis.) Note the following calculation for the growth of ALCOA as against that of Sears Roebuck and the DJIA group as a whole.

Comment: These few figures could be made the subject of a long discussion. They probably show as well as any others, derived by elaborate mathematical treatment, the actual growth of earnings for the long period 1958–1970. But how relevant is this figure, generally considered central in common-stock valuations, to the case of ALCOA? Its past growth rate was excellent, actually a bit better than that of acclaimed Sears Roebuck and much higher than that of the DJIA composite. But the market price at the beginning of 1971 seemed to pay no attention to this fine performance. ALCOA sold at only 11½ times the recent three-year average, while Sears sold at 27 times and the DJIA itself at 15+ times. How did this come about? Evidently Wall Street has fairly pessimistic views about the future course of ALCOA's earnings, in contrast with its past record. Surprisingly enough, the high price for ALCOA was made as far back as 1959. In that year it sold at 116, or 45 times its earnings. (This compares with a 1959 adjusted high price of 25½ for Sears Roebuck, or 20 times its then earnings.) Even though ALCOA's profits did show excellent growth thereafter, it is evident that in this case the future possibilities were greatly overestimated in the market price. It closed 1970 at exactly half of the 1959 high, while Sears tripled in price and the DJIA moved up nearly 30%.

It should be pointed out that ALCOA's earnings on capital funds* had been only average or less, and this may be the decisive factor here. High multipliers have been *maintained* in the stock market only if the company has maintained better than average profitability.

Let us apply at this point to ALCOA the suggestion we made in the previous chapter for a "two-part appraisal process."† Such an approach might have produced a "past-performance value" for ALCOA of 10% of the DJIA, or $84 per share relative to the closing price of 840 for the DJIA in 1970. On this basis the shares would have appeared quite attractive at their price of 57¼.

To what extent should the senior analyst have marked down the "past-performance value" to allow for adverse developments that he saw in the future? Frankly, we have no idea. Assume he had reason to believe that the 1971 earnings would be as low as $2.50 per share—a large drop from the 1970 figure, as against an advance expected for the DJIA. Very likely the stock market would take this poor performance quite seriously, but would it really establish the once mighty Aluminum Company of America as a relatively *unprofitable* enterprise, to be valued at less than its tangible assets behind the shares?‡ (In 1971 the price declined from a high of 70 in May to a low of 36 in December, against a book value of 55.)

---

* Graham appears to be using "earnings on capital funds" in the traditional sense of return on book value—essentially, net income divided by the company's tangible net assets.

† See p. 288.

‡ Recent history—and a mountain of financial research—have shown that the market is unkindest to rapidly growing companies that suddenly report a fall in earnings. More moderate and stable growers tend to suffer somewhat milder stock declines if they report disappointing earnings. Great expectations lead to great disappointment if they are not met; a failure to meet moderate expectations leads to a much milder reaction. Thus, one of the biggest risks in owning growth stocks is not that their growth will stop, but merely that it will slow down. And in the long run, that is not merely a risk, but a virtual certainty.

ALCOA is surely a representative industrial company of huge size, but we think that its price-and-earnings history is more unusual, even contradictory, than that of most other large enterprises. Yet this instance supports, to some degree, the doubts we expressed in the last chapter as to the dependability of the appraisal procedure when applied to the typical industrial company.

Commentary on Chapter 12
by Jason Zweig

> It's not a paranoid delusion—the issuers of financial statements really **are** out to get you!
> —Martin S. Fridson[1]

When companies announce their earnings, one question matters above all: Do these reported numbers fairly represent the profitability of the underlying business?

If only the question were as easy to answer as it is to ask.

Mind the GAAP

Under generally accepted accounting principles, or GAAP, income and expenses are typically booked within the fiscal period in which they occur. That sounds sensible, but it can paint a misleading picture.

Imagine an industrial company that bought a manufacturer of chemicals last year. This year, environmental regulators fined the company $80 million to clean up pollution at the site of a factory that its newly acquired subsidiary shut down 17 years ago. It no longer even makes the chemical that contaminated the factory site.

Under GAAP rules, that fine for activities in years past is an expense that reduces net earnings this year. However, it is—or at least should be—a one-time or nonrecurring expense, rather than a perennial cost of doing business. Such a cost says little about the company's fundamental health this year and next to nothing about its ability to generate cash and profits in future years.

---

[1] Personal communication.

Likewise, let's say a company wins $1 billion in a patent-infringement lawsuit against its only major competitor. That will inflate GAAP income, but it's almost certainly a one-time event. You'd be foolish to count on its recurrence.

Because GAAP isn't perfect, companies increasingly rely on non-GAAP reporting in which they exclude various items from expenses or income. Companies report these alternative numbers in their earnings announcements, parts of their financial statements, and conference calls. Analysts and investors rely on them. Corporate executives' compensation often does, too.[2]

The shadow numbers have become at least as important as the real ones. "The entire system has been conditioned to accept these non-GAAP notions as legitimate measures," says Lauren Taylor Wolfe, managing partner of Impactive Capital, an investment firm in New York.

As the U.S. Securities and Exchange Commission has said, whether a non-GAAP adjustment to expenses or income is fair or misleading "depends on a company's individual facts and circumstances." The SEC says non-GAAP financial statements should treat items consistently over time; shouldn't subtract "normal, recurring, cash operating expenses"; and shouldn't include nonrecurring gains if nonrecurring charges are excluded in the same period.

In principle, non-GAAP numbers should remove any unusual or extraordinary costs or income, creating a clearer picture of how well the company is doing and how profitable it is likely to be in the future.

In practice, non-GAAP numbers have become the devil's workshop. No regulatory or accounting standards determine exactly what can be excluded, when, and why. Companies can change their non-GAAP metrics whenever they want, without warning or explanation. How much of which types of income or expenses should be adjusted? What constitutes a normal cost of doing business? What defines whether a source of income is unlikely to recur? How should a company decide—and communicate—whether its adjustments are fair, sensible, and consistent? All that is up to each company's executives; the judgments are theirs to make, and the story is theirs to tell.

---

[2] Outside the U.S., most companies use International Financial Reporting Standards (IFRS) instead of GAAP; they may also present alternative performance numbers that raise similar issues of fairness and comparability.

Welcome to Non-GAAP Land

Naturally, when companies become storytellers, many choose to tell fairy tales. These fantasies are set in a place I call Non-GAAP Land.

In this magical world, every frog is a prince, every beanstalk grows into the stratosphere, and the emperor always has clothes. In Non-GAAP Land, companies can make expenses vanish and ephemeral income appear as durable as marble:

- In 2011, Groupon, Inc., concocted a non-GAAP measure of profitability called ACSOI, or adjusted consolidated segment operating income. In the three years ended December 31, 2010, Groupon lost $423 million under GAAP rules. Using its ACSOI measure, however, the company "earned" $63 million. In Non-GAAP Land, Groupon—an online marketing company!—decided it was fair to exclude online marketing expenses from its measure of earnings. (The SEC later compelled Groupon to include them.)
- In 2018, WeWork Cos., the office-sharing start-up, created a measure of purported profitability called "community-adjusted EBITDA." That waved away the costs of sales, marketing, and administration. It also effectively treated upfront discounts from landlords as a perennial, rather than transitory, source of income. In the real world, under GAAP rules, the company lost $933 million the year before. In Non-GAAP Land, WeWork "earned" $233 million. (WeWork bungled its attempted stock offering in 2019; after finally going public in 2021, the company filed for bankruptcy protection in late 2023.)[3]
- Year after year, measures of non-GAAP income at such pharmaceutical giants as Bristol-Myers Squibb Co., Eli Lilly & Co., and Pfizer Inc. excluded a portion of research and development costs—even though researching and developing new drugs is the heart of their business. That added billions of dollars to their "earnings" in Non-GAAP Land. (In 2022, under pressure from regulators, the companies finally changed that practice.)[4]

---

[3] Eliot Brown and Maureen Farrell, *The Cult of We* (Crown, 2021), pp. 196–98, 321–22.

[4] Olga Usvyatsky, "In-Depth: How Pharma Firms Use Non-GAAP," bit.ly/47R3BYa.

Do You Believe in Magic?

Elsewhere in Non-GAAP Land, some airlines exclude a portion of the cost of renting airplanes; energy companies strip out some of the cost of exploring for oil and gas; software firms wipe away part of the cost of developing software.

Because you don't live in Non-GAAP Land, you're probably thinking: *I can't pretend that my expenses don't reduce my income. Why should a business get to do that?*

The answer: Professional investors go along with the charade. If no one powerful questions a business practice, more businesses will practice it. Once stocks go up because of apparent earnings growth, demanding actual earnings growth seems like nitpicking. And when a rising tide lifts all boats, no one wants to rock any boat.

Yet people know better.

A survey of 169 chief financial officers of public companies asked what made reported earnings "high quality." Fully 94% of the CFOs said earnings should reflect "consistent reporting choices over time"; more than two-thirds said earnings shouldn't include "one-time or special items."

In a separate survey, more than half of professional analysts and investors said many non-GAAP adjustments are sometimes or always inappropriate.

Yet many of these CFOs oversee the production of financial reports that present a fantasy—and many of these professional investors own the very companies whose accounting they consider inadequate.

The survey of CFOs found that 93% believe that companies misrepresenting earnings do so to support their stock price and to satisfy "outside pressure" for ever-higher reported profits. And 89% think companies misrepresenting earnings want to "influence"—i.e., to inflate—executive compensation.[5]

Research also indicates that companies that habitually exclude items from non-GAAP earnings tend to be younger and smaller; they have wide institutional ownership, high recent stock returns, and thus great expectations for more hot returns in the future.[6]

---

[5] Ilia Dichev et al., "The Misrepresentation of Earnings," bit.ly/3YNVA27, and "Earnings Quality: Evidence from the Field," bit.ly/3stivng.

[6] Patricia Dechow et al., "A Rating System to Evaluate Non-GAAP Exclusion Quality," bit.ly/3KSOfc6.

Companies tell fairy tales because their audience doesn't want the spell to be broken. When investors want to believe in magic, companies will make wishes seem to come true.

We Swear It Won't Happen Ever Again . . . Until Next Year

One way companies can polish their performance is to exclude restructuring charges from non-GAAP results. A business can incur such costs when it sells assets at a loss, shuts down a division, or lays off employees.

In the real world, those are expenses. In Non-GAAP Land, they can disappear.

In principle, a healthy company shouldn't be chronically dumping assets and jettisoning workers. Overpaying for acquisitions and overexpanding the workforce aren't part of the ordinary cost of doing business.

In practice, however, every company needs to change course occasionally, so restructuring charges do crop up every few years. Excluding them from your assessment of a company's profitability can make sense: A cost that occurs sporadically in the short term isn't likely to constrict profits in the long term.

But if restructuring charges recur often, then they start to resemble a regular feature of how the business operates—in which case, you would be naïve to overlook them.

Many companies, however, are telling investors to do just that.

According to Calcbench, a financial-data firm, 68 companies in the S&P 500 took restructuring charges *every year* from 2013 to 2022. Of those, 36 adjusted their numbers in 2022 by adding restructuring charges back into their reported measures of non-GAAP income.

These companies are effectively taunting investors with the attitude of Chico Marx in the classic movie *Duck Soup*: "Well, who are you gonna believe: me or your own eyes?"

Look with your own eyes at HP Inc.

Over the 10 years through 2023, HP took restructuring charges 10 times; it also took "acquisition and divestiture" charges in every one of those years (although only for $1 million in 2015). Those charges totaled nearly $5.1 billion—an eighth of HP's $42.7 billion in cumulative operating profits (by the conventional GAAP measure).

After HP cleansed those charges in its financial statements, the company reported a cumulative $49.5 billion in non-GAAP operating income.

HP says such charges cover "nonrecurring costs" that are "inconsistent in amount and frequency" and unrepresentative of expected future operating expenses. After recurring year after year after year, that's a bit like saying the lyrics of "Happy Birthday to You" aren't repetitive because not every person has the same name.

Stocking Up Earnings

Another item that bloats measures of "income" in Non-GAAP Land is stock-based compensation: the cost companies incur to pay employees and executives with shares or options. Especially among software and other technology companies, that's a huge—and regular—cost of doing business. At many, it's the dominant component of pay.

Over the 10 fiscal years ending in May 2023, Oracle Corp.'s cumulative non-GAAP operating income of $178.9 billion was more than one-third higher than the operating earnings it reported under GAAP rules. That's partly because the software giant paid $15.6 billion of stock-based compensation to its management

FIGURE 12-1: An Ordinary Recurrence?

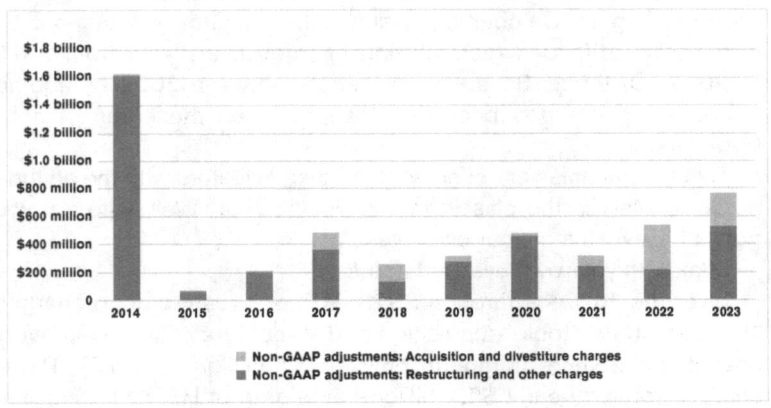

Source: HP earnings presentations, SEC.gov.

and employees—and added that expense back into its non-GAAP operating income.

Oracle concedes in its earnings reports that "stock-based compensation expenses will recur in future periods," but "we continue to evaluate our business performance excluding stock-based compensation expenses."

Over the same period, another software giant, Salesforce, Inc., reported $25.6 billion of cumulative operating income in its non-GAAP reports. Yet the company's cumulative operating income, as measured conventionally by GAAP, totaled just $3.1 billion.

How did Salesforce earn more than eight times as much in Non-GAAP Land than it did in the real world? By taking the $14.1 billion it had paid employees and management in stock-based compensation expense and declaring that it *wasn't* an expense.

Salesforce has explained that it adds stock-based compensation (and other expenses) into its non-GAAP calculations of income because such costs aren't incurred to "increase revenue in a particular period, but instead for the Company's long-term benefit over multiple periods."

Yet, over the same 10-year stretch, Microsoft Corp. paid out an enormous $48.1 billion in stock-based compensation. How much of that expense did Microsoft shovel into its non-GAAP income?

Zero.

By doing so, Microsoft recognized stock-based compensation as what it is: a normal, recurring cost of doing business that companies and investors shouldn't be adding back into a fairy-tale measure of income.

As Warren Buffett wrote in 2016:

> . . . it has become common for managers to tell their owners to ignore certain expense items that are all too real. "Stock-based compensation" is the most egregious example. The very name says it all: "compensation." If compensation isn't an expense, what is it? And, if real and recurring expenses don't belong in the calculation of earnings, where in the world do they belong?[7]

---

[7] Berkshire Hathaway 2015 annual report, bit.ly/3YQPgaj, p. 16.

TABLE 12-1: Stockpiling

Company	Year ended										
Salesforce, Inc.	1/31/14	1/31/15	1/31/16	1/31/17	1/31/18	1/31/19	1/31/20	1/31/21	1/31/22	1/31/23	Cumulative
GAAP operating income	(286)	(146)	115	64	454	535	297	455	548	1,030	3,066
Plus: adjustment for stock-based compensation expense	503	565	594	820	997	1,283	1,785	2,190	2,779	3,259	14,775
Plus: other adjustments (total)	147	155	121	225	287	447	792	1,121	1,624	2,779	7,698
Non-GAAP operating income	364	574	830	1110	1738	2,265	2,874	3,766	4,951	7,068	25,540
Oracle Corp.	5/31/14	5/31/15	5/31/16	5/31/17	5/31/18	5/31/19	5/31/20	5/31/21	5/31/22	5/31/23	Cumulative
GAAP operating income	14,759	13,871	12,604	12,710	13,264	13,535	13,896	15,213	10,926	13,093	133,871
Plus: adjustment for stock-based compensation expense	795	928	793	981	1,245	1,293	1,590	1,837	2,613	3,547	15,622
Plus: other adjustments (total)	2,524	2,567	2,379	2,305	2,599	2,536	1,892	1,948	6,054	4,262	29,066
Non-GAAP operating income	18,109	17,393	15,786	16,167	17,155	17,384	17,382	19,000	19,593	20,902	178,871
Microsoft Corp.	6/30/14	6/30/15	6/30/16	6/30/17	6/30/18	6/30/19	6/30/20	6/30/21	6/30/22	6/30/23	Cumulative
GAAP operating income	27,759	18,161	20,182	22,326	35,058	42,959	52,959	69,916	83,383	88,523	461,226
Plus: adjustment for stock-based compensation expense	–	–	–	7,013	–	–	–	–	–	1,171	26,075
Plus: other adjustments (total)	127	10,011	7,753	–	–	–	–	–	–	–	
Non-GAAP operating income	27,886	28,172	27,935	29,339	35,058	42,959	52,959	69,916	83,383	89,694	487,301

Notes: All numbers in $millions. Non-GAAP operating income totals may not exactly match sum of items above them because of rounding and other minor discrepancies.

Sources: Companies' annual earnings releases.

I once defined "income statement" as "the part of a company's financial statements in which it may exaggerate its income and understate its expenses."[8] The plague of non-GAAP adjustments has made that little joke deadly serious.

Some companies, to their credit, do use non-GAAP numbers to clarify rather than to camouflage or confuse. Far too many don't. One of the most important—and challenging—tasks for enterprising investors is figuring out whether the non-GAAP numbers paint a fair picture or a fantasy.[9]

---

[8] Jason Zweig, *The Devil's Financial Dictionary* (PublicAffairs, 2015), p. 114.
[9] For enterprising investors, an excellent forensic guide to the reliability of companies' financial statements is Howard M. Schilit et al., *Financial Shenanigans* (McGraw-Hill, 2018). See also Doron Nissim, "Earnings Quality, Fundamental Analysis and Valuation," bit.ly/3R2pkX8.

CHAPTER 13

A Comparison of Four Listed Companies
by Benjamin Graham

*I*n this chapter we should like to present a sample of security analysis in operation. We have selected, more or less at random, four companies which are found successively on the New York Stock Exchange list. These are ELTRA Corp. (a merger of Electric Autolite and Mergenthaler Linotype enterprises), Emerson Electric Co. (a manufacturer of electric and electronic products), Emery Air Freight (a domestic forwarder of air freight), and Emhart Corp. (originally a maker of bottling machinery only, but now also in builders' hardware).* There are some broad resemblances between the three manufacturing firms, but the differences will seem more significant. There should be sufficient variety in the financial and operating data to make the examination of interest.

In Table 13-1 we present a summary of what the four companies were selling for in the market at the end of 1970, and a few figures on their 1970 operations. We then detail certain key ratios, which relate on the one hand to *performance* and on the other to *price*. Comment is called for on how various aspects of the performance pattern agree with the relative price pattern. Finally, we shall pass the four companies in review, suggesting some comparisons and relationships and evaluating each in terms of the requirements of a conservative common-stock investor.

The most striking fact about the four companies is that the current price/earnings ratios vary much more widely than their operating performance or financial condition. Two of the enterprises—ELTRA

---

* Of Graham's four examples, only Emerson Electric still exists in the same form.

TABLE 13-1 A Comparison of Four Listed Companies

	ELTRA	Emerson Electric	Emery Air Freight	Emhart Corp.
A. Capitalization				
Price of common, Dec. 31, 1970	27	66	57¾	32¾
Number of shares of common	7,714,000	24,884,000[a]	3,807,000	4,932,000
Market value of common	$208,300,000	$1,640,000,000	$220,000,000	$160,000,000
Bonds and preferred stock	8,000,000	42,000,000		9,200,000
Total capitalization	216,300,000	1,682,000,000	220,000,000	169,200,000
B. Income Items				
Sales, 1970	$454,000,000	$657,000,000	$108,000,000	$227,000,000
Net income, 1970	20,773,000	54,600,000	5,679,000	13,551,000
Earned per share, 1970	$2.70	$2.30	$1.49	$2.75[b]
Earned per share, ave., 1968–1970	2.78	2.10	1.28	2.81
Earned per share, ave., 1963–1965	1.54	1.06	.54	2.46
Earned per share, ave., 1958–1960	.54	.57	.17	1.21
Current dividend	1.20	1.16	1.00	1.20
C. Balance-sheet Items, 1970				
Current assets	$205,000,000	$307,000,000	$20,400,000	$121,000,000
Current liabilities	71,000,000	72,000,000	11,800,000	34,800,000
Net assets for common stock	207,000,000	257,000,000	15,200,000	133,000,000
Book value per share	$27.05	$10.34	$3.96	$27.02

[a] Assuming conversion of preferred stock.
[b] After special charge of 13 cents per share.
[c] Year ended Sept. 1970.

TABLE 13-2 A Comparison of Four Listed Companies (*continued*)

	ELTRA	Emerson Electric	Emery Air Freight	Emhart Corp.
B. Ratios				
Price/earnings, 1970	10.0 ×	30.0 ×	38.5 ×	11.9 ×
Price/earnings, 1968–1970	9.7 ×	33.0 ×	45.0 ×	11.7 ×
Price/book value	1.00 ×	6.37 ×	14.3 ×	1.22 ×
Net/sales, 1970	4.6 %	8.5 %	5.4 %	5.7 %
Net per share/book value	10.0 %	22.2 %	34.5 %	10.2 %
Dividend yield	4.45 %	1.78 %	1.76 %	3.65 %
Current assets to current liabilities	2.9 ×	4.3 ×	1.7 ×	3.4 ×
Working capital/debt	Very large	5.6 ×	no debt	9.4 ×
Earnings growth per share:				
1968–1970 vs. 1963–1965	+ 81%	+ 87%	+ 135%	+14 %
1968–1970 vs. 1958–1970	+400%	+250%	Very large	+132%
C. Price Record				
1936–1968 Low	¾	1	⅛	3⅝
High	50¾	61½	66	58¼
1970 Low	18⅝	42⅛	41	23½
1971 High	29⅜	78¾	72	44⅜

and Emhart—were modestly priced at only 9.7 times and 12 times the average earnings for 1968–1970, as against a similar figure of 15.5 times for the DJIA. The other two—Emerson and Emery—showed very high multiples of 33 and 45 times such earnings. There is bound to be some explanation of a difference such as this, and it is found in the superior growth of the favored companies' profits in recent years, especially by the freight forwarder. (But the growth figures of the other two firms were not unsatisfactory.)

For more comprehensive treatment let us review briefly the chief elements of performance as they appear from our figures.

1. *Profitability.* (*a*) All the companies show satisfactory earnings on their book value, but the figures for Emerson and Emery are much higher than for the other two. A high rate of return on invested capital

often goes along with a high annual growth rate in earnings per share. All the companies except Emery showed better earnings on book value in 1969 than in 1961; but the Emery figure was exceptionally large in both years. (*b*) For manufacturing companies, the profit figure per dollar of sales is usually an indication of comparative strength or weakness. We use here the "ratio of operating income to sales," as given in Standard & Poor's *Listed Stock Reports*. Here again the results are satisfactory for all four companies, with an especially impressive showing by Emerson. The changes between 1961 and 1969 vary considerably among the companies.

2. *Stability.* This we measure by the maximum decline in per-share earnings in any one of the past ten years, as against the average of the three preceding years. No decline translates into 100% stability, and this was registered by the two popular concerns. But the shrinkages of ELTRA and Emhart were quite moderate in the "poor year" 1970, amounting to only 8% each by our measurement, against 7% for the DJIA.

3. *Growth.* The two low-multiplier companies show quite satisfactory growth rates, in both cases doing better than the Dow Jones group. The ELTRA figures are especially impressive when set against its low price/earnings ratio. The growth is of course more impressive for the high-multiplier pair.

4. *Financial Position.* The three manufacturing companies are in sound financial condition, having better than the standard ratio of $2 of current assets for $1 of current liabilities. Emery Air Freight has a lower ratio; but it falls in a different category, and with its fine record it would have no problem raising needed cash. All the companies have relatively low long-term debt. "Dilution" note: Emerson Electric had $163 million of market value of low-dividend convertible preferred shares outstanding at the end of 1970. In our analysis we have made allowance for the dilution factor in the usual way by treating the preferred as if converted into common. This decreased recent earnings by about 10 cents per share, or some 4%.

5. *Dividends.* What really counts is the history of continuance without interruption. The best record here is Emhart's, which has not suspended a payment since 1902. ELTRA's record is very good, Emerson's quite satisfactory, Emery Freight is a newcomer.

The variations in payout percentage do not seem especially significant. The current dividend yield is twice as high on the "cheap pair" as on the "dear pair," corresponding to the price/earnings ratios.

6. *Price History.* The reader should be impressed by the percentage advance shown in the price of all four of these issues, as measured from the lowest to the highest points during the past 34 years. (In all cases the low price has been adjusted for subsequent stock splits.) Note that for the DJIA the range from low to high was on the order of 11 to 1; for our companies the spread has varied from "only" 17 to 1 for Emhart to no less than 528 to 1 for Emery Air Freight.* These manifold price advances are characteristic of most of our older common-stock issues, and they proclaim the great opportunities of profit that have existed in the stock markets of the past. (But they may indicate also how overdone were the declines in the bear markets before 1950 when the low prices were registered.) Both ELTRA and Emhart sustained price shrinkages of more than 50% in the 1969–70 price break. Emerson and Emery had serious, but less distressing, declines; the former rebounded to a new all-time high before the end of 1970, the latter in early 1971.

General Observations on the Four Companies

Emerson Electric has an enormous total market value, dwarfing the other three companies combined.† It is one of our "good-will giants," to be commented on later. A financial analyst blessed (or handicapped) with a good memory will think of an analogy between Emerson Electric and Zenith Radio, and that would not be

---

* In each case, Graham is referring to Section C of Table 13-2 and dividing the high price during the 1936–1968 period by the low price. For example, Emery's high price of 66 divided by its low price of 1/8 equals 528, or a ratio of 528 to 1 between the high and low.

† At the end of 1970, Emerson's $1.6 billion in market value truly was "enormous," given average stock sizes at the time. In early 2024, Emerson's common stock had a total market value of approximately $54 billion.

reassuring. For Zenith had a brilliant growth record for many years; it too sold in the market for $1.7 billion (in 1966); but its profits fell from $43 million in 1968 to only half as much in 1970, and in that year's big selloff its price declined to 22½ against the previous top of 89. **High valuations entail high risks.**

Emery Air Freight must be the most promising of the four companies in terms of future growth, if the price/earnings ratio of nearly 40 times its highest reported earnings is to be even partially justified. The past growth, of course, has been most impressive. But these figures may not be so significant for the future if we consider that they started quite small, at only $570,000 of net earnings in 1958. **It often proves much more difficult to continue to grow at a high rate after volume and profits have already expanded to big totals.** The most surprising aspect of Emery's story is that its earnings and market price continued to grow apace in 1970, which was the worst year in the domestic air-passenger industry. This is a remarkable achievement indeed, but it raises the question whether future profits may not be vulnerable to adverse developments, through increased competition, pressure for new arrangements between forwarders and airlines, etc. An elaborate study might be needed before a sound judgment could be passed on these points, but the conservative investor cannot leave them out of his general reckoning.

Emhart and ELTRA. Emhart has done better in its business than in the stock market over the past 14 years. In 1958 it sold as high as 22 times the current earnings—about the same ratio as for the DJIA. Since then its profits tripled, as against a rise of less than 100% for the Dow, but its closing price in 1970 was only a third above the 1958 high, versus 43% for the Dow. The record of ELTRA is somewhat similar. It appears that neither of these companies possesses glamour, or "sex appeal," in the present market; but in all the statistical data they show up surprisingly well. Their future prospects? We have no sage remarks to make here, but this is what Standard & Poor's had to say about the four companies in 1971:

ELTRA—"Long-term Prospects: Certain operations are cyclical, but an established competitive position and diversification are offsetting factors."

Emerson Electric—"While adequately priced (at 71) on the current outlook, the shares have appeal for the long term.... A continued acquisition policy together with a strong position in industrial fields and an accelerated international program suggests further sales and earnings progress."

Emery Air Freight—"The shares appear amply priced (at 57) on current prospects, but are well worth holding for the long pull."

Emhart—"Although restricted this year by lower capital spending in the glass-container industry, earnings should be aided by an improved business environment in 1972. The shares are worth holding (at 34)."

Conclusions: Many financial analysts will find Emerson and Emery more interesting and appealing stocks than the other two—primarily, perhaps, because of their better "market action," and secondarily because of their faster recent growth in earnings. Under our principles of conservative investment the first is not a valid reason for selection—that is something for the speculators to play around with. The second has validity, but within limits. Can the past growth and the presumably good prospects of Emery Air Freight justify a price more than 60 times its recent earnings?[1] Our answer would be: Maybe for someone who has made an in-depth study of the possibilities of this company and come up with exceptionally firm and optimistic conclusions. But *not* for the careful investor who wants to be reasonably sure in advance that he is not committing the typical Wall Street error of overenthusiasm for good performance in earnings and in the stock market.* The same cautionary statements seem called for in the case of Emerson Electric, with a special reference to the market's current valuation of over a billion dollars for the intangible, or earning-power, factor here. We should add that the "electronics industry," once a fair-haired child of the stock market, has in general fallen on disastrous days. Emerson is an outstanding exception, but it will have to continue to be such an exception for a great many years in the future before the 1970 closing price will have been fully justified by its subsequent performance.

By contrast, both ELTRA at 27 and Emhart at 33 have the

---

* Graham was right. Of the "Nifty Fifty" stocks that were most fashionable and highly valued in 1972, Emery fared among the worst.

earmarks of companies with sufficient value behind their price to constitute reasonably protected investments. Here the investor can, if he wishes, consider himself basically a part owner of these businesses, at a cost corresponding to what the balance sheet shows to be the money invested therein.* The rate of earnings on invested capital has long been satisfactory; the stability of profits also; the past growth rate surprisingly so. The two companies will meet our seven *statistical* requirements for inclusion in a defensive investor's portfolio. These will be developed in the next chapter, but we summarize them as follows:

1. Adequate size.
2. A sufficiently strong financial condition.
3. Continued dividends for at least the past 20 years.
4. No earnings deficit in the past ten years.
5. Ten-year growth of at least one-third in per-share earnings.
6. Price of stock no more than 1½ times net asset value.
7. Price no more than 15 times average earnings of the past three years.

We make no predictions about the future earnings performance of ELTRA or Emhart. In the investor's diversified list of common stocks there are bound to be some that prove disappointing, and this may be the case for one or both of this pair. But the diversified list itself, based on the above principles of selection, plus whatever other sensible criteria the investor may wish to apply, should perform well enough across the years. At least, long experience tells us so.

A final observation: An experienced security analyst, even if he accepted our general reasoning on these four companies, would have hesitated to recommend that a holder of Emerson or Emery *exchange* his shares for ELTRA or Emhart at the end of 1970—unless the holder understood clearly the philosophy behind the recommendation. There was no reason to expect that in any short

---

* Graham's point is that, based on their prices at the time, an investor could buy shares in these two companies for little more than their book value, as shown in the third line of Section B in Table 13-2.

period of time the low-multiplier duo would outperform the high-multipliers. The latter were well thought of in the market and thus had a considerable degree of momentum behind them, which might continue for an indefinite period. The sound basis for preferring eltra and Emhart to Emerson and Emery would be the client's considered conclusion that he preferred value-type investments to glamour-type investments. Thus, **to a substantial extent, common-stock investment policy must depend on the attitude of the individual investor**. This approach is treated at greater length in our next chapter.

Commentary on Chapter 13
by Jason Zweig

> As a scientist I believe in proof without certainty, while other people tend to believe in certainty without proof.
> —Ashley Montagu[1]

In Chapter 13, Graham reminds you to shift your focus from the superficial to the fundamental. As an intelligent investor, you must look past the price of the stock to the performance of the business it represents. Graham maps out six dimensions on which you can measure performance—profitability, stability, growth, financial position, dividends, and price history. Only the last has anything to do with the stock directly; all the others require you to learn about the business.

Four Paths

Of the four companies Graham compared in this chapter, only Emerson Electric still exists independently. Let's see what we can learn from looking at Emerson and three other contemporary companies whose names begin with the letter E: Energizer Holdings Inc., Eastman Kodak Co., and Exact Sciences Corp.

Emerson is a manufacturing and engineering giant with more than $15 billion in annual revenue and a stock-market value that exceeded $54 billion in early 2024. It produces essential tools and technologies: valves, electric motors, temperature sensors, seismic analysis, laser-based welding equipment, process-control

---

[1] *Current Anthropology*, vol. 36, no. 5 (1995), p. 836.

software, heavy-duty vacuums, and many other devices and services. Like many conglomerates, Emerson frequently buys other companies and often sells some, too; it is continually remaking and redesigning itself. Emerson has been in the S&P 500 index since 1965.

Energizer is headquartered only 20 miles away from Emerson near St. Louis, Missouri, and its ticker symbol, ENR, is almost an exact match for Emerson's (EMR). But the two companies are far from twins. Energizer's primary business is manufacturing batteries under the Energizer, Eveready, and Rayovac brands; it also makes waxes, fragrances, and fuel additives for cars and trucks. The battery business has been losing power for years as smartphones have superseded cameras, clocks, calculators, flashlights, radios, videogame consoles, and audio and video recorders. As of 2024, Energizer was focused on trying to return to stable profitability, largely by cutting costs.

Eastman Kodak was the colossus of the photo industry for more than a century. Then it faded like a snapshot left out in the sun. After inventing digital photography in 1975, Kodak took nearly two decades to market its own electronic cameras to consumers. Making most of its money selling photographic film, the company was reluctant to advance a product that didn't use any. Rivals raced past Kodak; later, smartphones turned traditional cameras into dinosaurs and film into a fossil. Between 1993 and 2022, Kodak's annual revenues shrank by 93%; in 2012, the company filed for bankruptcy protection, then staggered on. By early 2020, Kodak's accountants were warning that it might not survive.

Exact Sciences, which develops cancer-screening tests, first sold stock to the public in early 2001. In its early years, it spent massively on research and development, as well as on sales and marketing. In its first eight years as a public company, Exact Sciences generated only $21 million in sales but $149 million in cumulative net losses. By the end of 2008 its stock-market value had dwindled below $20 million. Not until 2014 did the U.S. Food and Drug Administration finally approve Exact Sciences' Cologuard screening test for colorectal cancer. At that point, the business exploded, with annual revenues soaring from less than $2 million in 2014 to $454 million in 2018. The company also produces tests that can detect breast cancer, prostate cancer, and the Covid-19 virus.

Six Dimensions

Now let's briefly analyze each company along Graham's six dimensions.

1. *Profitability*

Although Emerson was profitable every year between 1993 and 2022, its growth was somewhat spasmodic. Earnings per share from continuing operations expanded by only 8% cumulatively over the five fiscal years ended in 2023 and barely surpassed their level in 2015. Return on equity was 13.8% in 2022, down from an average of more than 26% over the previous five years, partly because the sale of discontinued operations swelled Emerson's equity in 2023.

Energizer's profits have been erratic; the company earned $201 million in 2017, only to lose $231 million in 2022. In 2023, it earned a $141 million net profit. Worse, the company issued new stock along the way; its earnings had to be parceled out across a roughly 20% greater number of shares. Energizer's return on equity was wildly volatile, swinging from more than 700% in 2017 to negative 95% in 2022 to positive 82% in 2023, according to FactSet.

Eastman Kodak lost $3.3 billion over the past two decades and was profitable in only eight of those years. In 2022 it squeaked out a profit, earning a razor-thin return on equity of 1.4%; in the first nine months of 2023, Eastman Kodak earned $70 million, up from $19 million in the first three quarters of 2022.

Like many fast-growing technology companies, Exact Sciences sacrificed near-term earnings to pursue long-term growth and profitability. By 2023, its annual revenues had boomed to $2.5 billion, up more than 1,000-fold in a decade. Over that period, Exact Sciences' cumulative losses exceeded $3.1 billion—a sum that will seem like a pittance if (but only if) the company's growth continues.

2. *Stability*

Graham defines "stability" as no decline in earnings (measured against the average of the prior three years) in any of the past 10 years. None of our four companies passed that test, with Kodak and Exact Sciences faring the worst.

3. *Growth*

Here, Graham wants us to compare the rates at which companies' earnings per share grew over multiyear periods. That way, we account for expansion and contraction in the global economy; we also minimize the effects of short bursts of outperformance (or underperformance) that might be the result of luck or unrepeatable causes.

We'll use two five-year periods: 2014–18, and 2019–23. The first consisted almost entirely of an economic boom; the second includes both the pandemic-induced near-depression of 2020–21 and the rapid recovery afterward.

Emerson's earnings per share from continuing operations grew by a sluggish average of 2% annually from 2014 through 2018, then finished 2023 at $3.72, no higher than the $3.74 figure in 2019.

From 2015, its first year of independence from its former parent company, through 2018, Energizer's earnings grew from a loss of six cents per share to a $1.52 gain; then, between 2019 through 2023, they wobbled from a 58-cent gain to a $3.37 loss to a $1.94 gain.

Eastman Kodak's losses per share moderated from a ghastly $2.95 per share in 2014 to a grim 84 cents in 2018; it lost $2.74 and $9.77 per share in 2019 and 2020, then was thinly profitable from 2021 on, with a modest gain projected for 2023.

At Exact Sciences, from 2014 through 2018, losses widened at an average annual rate of almost 3%. They peaked, so far anyway, at more than $820 million in 2020. By late 2023, it looked as if the company might be able to report its first annual profit before much longer.

4. *Financial position*

Emerson has total assets of nearly $43 billion and book value of nearly $21 billion, although much of that is attributable to intangible assets such as goodwill (the excess above net worth that Emerson paid for many of its acquisitions). Its total debt of $16 billion looks manageable.

Energizer's $3.3 billion in long-term debt is substantial, especially on its small base of $211 million in shareholders' equity and $223 million in cash. The company did pay down well over $200 million in debt during 2023.

Eastman Kodak was able to increase its cash on hand by $29 million in the first nine months of 2023, although it was still carrying more than $450 million in long-term debt.

Exact Sciences has more than $700 million in cash. It has more than $2.3 billion in convertible notes, which are likely to be turned into new shares of common stock eventually; that will diffuse future earnings over a larger number of shares, leaving less for each stockholder. The company otherwise has little debt.

5. *Dividends*

Emerson has increased its dividend every year since 1956. Energizer raised its dividend from 25 cents in 2015 to $1.20 in 2019 and has sustained it since. Kodak hasn't paid a dividend since 2003; Exact Sciences has never paid one.

6. *Price history*

After a long period of outperformance, Emerson has strained to keep up. Over the decade ending in 2023, it underperformed the S&P 500 index by 5.7 percentage points annually.

Energizer has gained an average of 2% annually since it became an independent company in 2015, falling far behind the market.

Eastman Kodak's returns were punctuated by two absurdities. In early 2018, the stock more than doubled in a day when Kodak announced it would launch its own cryptocurrency—a venture it soon abandoned. In 2020, Kodak's shares shot from $2 to as high as $60 in three days when word leaked that the U.S. government might loan the company $765 million to develop a pharmaceutical division—money that never materialized. Over the decade ending in 2023, Kodak's shares fell more than 88%.

Exact Sciences' stock returned an average of more than 20% annually over the 10 years ending in 2023. It did so in stupendous swoops of interim gains and losses. From 2017 through early September 2019, the stock rose 817%. It then proceeded to fall 55% by March 2020. Next, it gained 180% in less than a year after celebrity stock-picker Cathie Wood amassed more than 5 million shares for her ARK funds. Then, in 2021 and 2022, Exact Sciences lost more than 80% in an 18-month stretch before partially recovering. In 2023 it soared 49%.

E-volution

Companies are artificial organizations of physical assets, but they resemble natural living organisms. They are born, they grow fast, their expansion slows, they become heavy, they grow old, and often they die.

Newly sprouted plants and newborn animals can grow extraordinarily fast—if they evade the ever-present risks of dying from disease, perishing in extreme weather, or being eaten by predators. Some

TABLE 13-1: E-valuation

	Emerson Electric	Energizer Holdings	Eastman Kodak	Exact Sciences
Capitalization				
Price of common stock, Dec. 31, 2023, $ per share	97.33	31.68	3.90	73.98
Total return, 2023, %	3.8	-2.2	27.9	49.4
Market value of common stock, Dec. 31, 2023, $ millions	55,954	2,360	315	13,996
Income items				
Revenue growth, latest 5 fiscal years, cumulative %	-17.4	18.7	-8.0	185.0
Earnings per share (EPS), latest 12 months, $	3.72	1.94	0.63	-1.58
EPS, average of latest 5 fiscal years, $	3.98	-0.35	-2.29	-2.97
Balance-sheet items (Sept. 30, 2023)				
Cash & short-term investments, $ millions	8,051	223	255	734
Total liabilities / total assets, %	37.8	95.3	50.5	51.4
Book value per share, $	36.17	2.95	12.06	17.26
Valuation, latest fiscal year end				
Price/earnings	26.0	16.5	6.7	NM
Price/book value	2.7	10.9	0.3	4.0

Price/sales (total revenue)	3.7	0.8	0.3	5.2
Return on common equity, %	13.8	82.3	6.2	-9.1
Return on invested capital, %	9.0	3.8	5.0	-5.1
Dividend yield, %	2.2	3.7	0	0
Working capital/total liabilities	0.54	0.19	0.37	0.20
Price history ($ per share)				
10-year high and low	105.70—38.08	65.06—25.14	37.20—1.55	155.01—4.94
2023 high and low	100.12—77.68	37.55—28.80	6.17—3.11	99.04—47.19

Notes: Prices and ratios as of August 2023. Figures according to GAAP.
Source: FactSet.

creatures, like sharks, tortoises, and bristlecone pines, can live for centuries or even millennia.

Emerson, founded in 1890, is reshaping itself in hopes of a burst of rejuvenating growth. Energizer, whose heritage also dates back to the 1890s, may have to reconcile itself to stagnation. Eastman Kodak, incorporated in 1892, is struggling to survive without any significant remnants of its original business. Exact Sciences barely outlasted childhood; after only seven years, its stock was nearly delisted from trading in 2009. Early in 2024 its stock had a market capitalization of $12 billion.

Recently, the stocks of all four companies have shot up, at least temporarily. If you focused only on the momentum of the share price, you could easily have gotten carried away extrapolating a trend of growth that often turned out to be an illusion.

When you instead evaluate a company along Graham's six dimensions, you reorient your focus from the stock price to the underlying business—and can better assess which period of the corporate lifecycle it is likely to be in. You can never be certain of any company's future, but methodically disengaging your attention from the stock price is the best way to assess whether the next phase of a business is distinction or extinction.

CHAPTER 14

Stock Selection for the Defensive Investor
by Benjamin Graham

*I*t is time to turn to some broader applications of the techniques of security analysis. Since we have already described in general terms the investment policies recommended for our two categories of investors,* it would be logical for us now to indicate how security analysis comes into play in order to implement these policies. The defensive investor who follows our suggestions will purchase only high-grade bonds plus a diversified list of leading common stocks. He is to make sure that the price at which he bought the latter is not unduly high as judged by applicable standards.

In setting up this diversified list he has a choice of two approaches, the DJIA-type of portfolio and the quantitatively-tested portfolio. In the first he acquires a true cross-section sample of the leading issues, which will include both some favored growth companies, whose shares sell at especially high multipliers, and also less popular and less expensive enterprises. This could be done, most simply perhaps, by buying the same amounts of all thirty of the issues in the Dow-Jones Industrial Average (DJIA). Ten shares of each, at the 900 level for the average, would cost an aggregate of about $16,000.[1] On the basis of the past record he might expect approximately the same future results by buying shares of several representative investment funds.†

---

* Graham describes his recommended investment policies in Chapters 4 through 7.
† As we have discussed in the Commentaries on Chapters 4 and 9, today's defensive investor can achieve this goal simply by buying a low-cost index fund, ideally one that tracks the return of the total U.S. stock market.

333

His second choice would be to apply a set of standards to each purchase, to make sure that he obtains (1) a minimum of *quality* in the past performance and current financial position of the company, and also (2) a minimum of *quantity* in terms of earnings and assets per dollar of price. At the close of the previous chapter we listed seven such quality and quantity criteria suggested for the selection of specific common stocks. Let us describe them in order.

1. Adequate Size of the Enterprise

All our minimum figures must be arbitrary and especially in the matter of size required. Our idea is to exclude small companies which may be subject to more than average vicissitudes especially in the industrial field. (There are often good possibilities in such enterprises but we do not consider them suited to the needs of the defensive investor.) Let us use round amounts: not less than $100 million of annual sales for an industrial company and, not less than $50 million of total assets for a public utility.

2. A Sufficiently Strong Financial Condition

For industrial companies current assets should be at least twice current liabilities—a so-called two-to-one current ratio. Also, long-term debt should not exceed the net current assets (or "working capital"). For public utilities the debt should not exceed twice the stock equity (at book value).

3. Earnings Stability

Some earnings for the common stock in each of the past ten years.

4. Dividend Record

Uninterrupted payments for at least the past 20 years.

5. Earnings Growth

A minimum increase of at least one-third in per-share earnings in the past ten years using three-year averages at the beginning and end.

6. Moderate Price/Earnings Ratio

Current price should not be more than 15 times average earnings of the past three years.

7. Moderate Ratio of Price to Assets

Current price should not be more than 1½ times the book value last reported. However, a multiplier of earnings below 15 could justify a correspondingly higher multiplier of assets. As a rule of thumb we suggest that the *product* of the multiplier times the ratio of price to book value should not exceed 22.5. (This figure corresponds to 15 times earnings and 1½ times book value. It would admit an issue selling at only 9 times earnings and 2.5 times asset value, etc.)

GENERAL COMMENTS: These requirements are set up especially for the needs and the temperament of defensive investors. They will eliminate the great majority of common stocks as candidates for the portfolio, and in two opposite ways. On the one hand they will exclude companies that are (1) too small, (2) in relatively weak financial condition, (3) with a deficit stigma in their ten-year record, and (4) not having a long history of continuous dividends. Of these tests the most severe under recent financial conditions are those of financial strength. A considerable number of our large and formerly strongly entrenched enterprises have weakened their current ratio or overexpanded their debt, or both, in recent years.

Our last two criteria are exclusive in the opposite direction, by demanding more earnings and more assets per dollar of price than the popular issues will supply. This is by no means the standard viewpoint of financial analysts; in fact most will insist that even conservative investors should be prepared to pay generous prices for stocks of the choice companies. We have expounded our contrary view above; it rests largely on the absence of an adequate *factor of safety* when too large a portion of the price must depend on ever-increasing earnings in the future. The reader will have to decide this important question for himself—after weighing the arguments on both sides.

We have nonetheless opted for the inclusion of a modest

requirement of growth over the past decade. Without it the typical company would show retrogression, at least in terms of profit per dollar of invested capital. There is no reason for the defensive investor to include such companies—though if the price is low enough they could qualify as bargain opportunities.

The suggested *maximum* figure of 15 times earnings might well result in a typical portfolio with an *average* multiplier of, say, 12 to 13 times. Note that in February 1972 American Tel. & Tel. sold at 11 times its three-year (and current) earnings, and Standard Oil of California at less than 10 times latest earnings. Our basic recommendation is that the stock portfolio, when acquired, should have an overall earnings/price ratio—the reverse of the P/E ratio—at least as high as the current high-grade bond rate. This would mean a P/E ratio no higher than 13.3 against an AA bond yield of 7.5%.*

Application of Our Criteria to the DJIA at the End of 1970

All of our suggested criteria were satisfied by the DJIA issues at the end of 1970, but two of them just barely. Here is a survey based on the closing price of 1970 and the relevant figures. (The basic data for each company are shown in Tables 14-1 and 14-2.)

1. Size is more than ample for each company.
2. Financial condition is adequate in the *aggregate*, but not for every company.[2]
3. Some dividend has been paid by every company since at least 1940. Five of the dividend records go back to the last century.

---

* In early 2024, the yield on highly rated corporate bonds was around 4.9%, suggesting—by Graham's formula—that a stock portfolio should have an earnings-to-price ratio at least that high. Taking the inverse of that number (by dividing 4.9 into 100), we can derive a "suggested maximum" P/E ratio of 20.4. At the beginning of this paragraph Graham recommends that the "average" stock be priced about 20% below the "maximum" ratio. That suggests Graham would consider stocks selling at roughly 16 times their three-year average earnings to be potentially attractive given recent interest rates and market conditions.

TABLE 14-1 Basic Data on 30 Stocks in the Dow Jones Industrial Average at September 30, 1971

	Price Sept. 30, 1971	"Earnings Per Share"[a] Sept. 30, 1971	Ave. 1968–1970	Ave. 1958–1960	Div. Since	Net Asset Value	Current Div.
Allied Chemical	32½	1.40	1.82	2.14	1887	26.02	1.20
Aluminum Co. of Am.	45½	4.25	5.18	2.08	1939	55.01	1.80
Amer. Brands	43½	4.32	3.69	2.24	1905	13.46	2.10
Amer. Can	33¼	2.68	3.76	2.42	1923	40.01	2.20
Amer. Tel. & Tel.	43	4.03	3.91	2.52	1881	45.47	2.60
Anaconda	15	2.06	3.90	2.17	1936	54.28	none
Bethlehem Steel	25½	2.64	3.05	2.62	1939	44.62	1.20
Chrysler	28½	1.05	2.72	(0.13)	1926	42.40	0.60
DuPont	154	6.31	7.32	8.09	1904	55.22	5.00
Eastman Kodak	87	2.45	2.44	0.72	1902	13.70	1.32
General Electric	61¼	2.63	1.78	1.37	1899	14.92	1.40
General Foods	34	2.34	2.23	1.13	1922	14.13	1.40
General Motors	83	3.33	4.69	2.94	1915	33.39	3.40
Goodyear	33½	2.11	2.01	1.04	1937	18.49	0.85
Inter. Harvester	28½	1.16	2.30	1.87	1910	42.06	1.40
Inter. Nickel	31	2.27	2.10	0.94	1934	14.53	1.00
Inter. Paper	33	1.46	2.22	1.76	1946	23.68	1.50
Johns-Manville	39	2.02	2.33	1.62	1935	24.51	1.20
Owens-Illinois	52	3.89	3.69	2.24	1907	43.75	1.35
Procter & Gamble	71	2.91	2.33	1.02	1891	15.41	1.50
Sears Roebuck	68½	3.19	2.87	1.17	1935	23.97	1.55
Std. Oil of Calif.	56	5.78	5.35	3.17	1912	54.79	2.80
Std. Oil of N.J.	72	6.51	5.88	2.90	1882	48.95	3.90
Swift & Co.	42	2.56	1.66	1.33	1934	26.74	0.70
Texaco	32	3.24	2.96	1.34	1903	23.06	1.60
Union Carbide	43½	2.59	2.76	2.52	1918	29.64	2.00
United Aircraft	30½	3.13	4.35	2.79	1936	47.00	1.80
U. S. Steel	29½	3.53	3.81	4.85	1940	65.54	1.60
Westinghouse	96½	3.26	3.44	2.26	1935	33.67	1.80
Woolworth	49	2.47	2.38	1.35	1912	25.47	1.20

[a] Adjusted for stock dividends and stock splits.
[b] Typically for the 12 months ended June 30, 1971.

TABLE 14-2 Significant Ratios of DJIA Stocks at September 30, 1971

	Price to Earnings		Current Div. Yield	Earnings Growth 1968–1970 vs. 1958–1960	CA/CL[a]	NCA/ Debt[b]	Price/ Net Asset Value
	Sept. 1971	1968–1970					
Allied Chemical	18.3 ×	18.0 ×	3.7%	(–15.0%)	2.1 ×	74%	125%
Aluminum Co. of Am.	10.7	8.8	4.0	149.0%	2.7	51	84
Amer. Brands	10.1	11.8	5.1	64.7	2.1	138	282
Amer. Can	12.4	8.9	6.6	52.5	2.1	91	83
Amer. Tel. & Tel.	10.8	11.0	6.0	55.2	1.1	—[c]	94
Anaconda	5.7	3.9	—	80.0	2.9	80	28
Bethlehem Steel	12.4	8.1	4.7	16.4	1.7	68	58
Chrysler	27.0	10.5	2.1	—[d]	1.4	78	67
DuPont	24.5	21.0	3.2	(–9.0)	3.6	609	280
Eastman Kodak	35.5	35.6	1.5	238.9	2.4	1764	635
General Electric	23.4	34.4	2.3	29.9	1.3	89	410
General Foods	14.5	15.2	4.1	97.3	1.6	254	240
General Motors	24.4	17.6	4.1	59.5	1.9	1071	247
Goodyear	15.8	16.7	2.5	93.3	2.1	129	80
Inter. Harvester	24.5	12.4	4.9	23.0	2.2	191	66
Inter. Nickel	13.6	16.2	3.2	123.4	2.5	131	213

Inter. Paper	22.5	14.0	4.6	26.1	2.2	62	139
Johns-Manville	19.3	16.8	3.0	43.8	2.6	—	158
Owens-Illinois	13.2	14.0	2.6	64.7	1.6	51	118
Procter & Gamble	24.2	31.6	2.1	128.4	2.4	400	460
Sears Roebuck	21.4	23.8	1.7	145.3	1.6	322	285
Std. Oil of Calif.	9.7	10.5	5.0	68.8	1.5	79	102
Std. Oil of N.J.	11.0	12.2	5.4	102.8	1.5	94	115
Swift & Co.	16.4	25.5	1.7	24.8	2.4	138	158
Texaco	9.9	10.8	5.0	120.9	1.7	128	138
Union Carbide	16.6	15.8	4.6	9.5	2.2	86	146
United Aircraft	9.7	7.0	5.9	55.9	1.5	155	65
U. S. Steel	8.3	6.7	5.4	(−21.5)	1.7	51	63
Westinghouse El.	29.5	28.0	1.9	52.2	1.8	145	2.86
Woolworth	19.7	20.5	2.4	76.3	1.8	185	1.90

[a] Figures taken for fiscal 1970 year-end co. results.
[b] Figures taken from *Moody's Industrial Manual* (1971).
[c] Debit balance for NCA. (NCA = net current assets.)
[d] Reported deficit for 1958–1960.

4. The aggregate earnings have been quite stable in the past decade. None of the companies reported a deficit during the prosperous period 1961–69, but Chrysler showed a small deficit in 1970.
5. The total growth—comparing three-year averages a decade apart—was 77%, or about 6% per year. But five of the firms did not grow by one-third.
6. The ratio of year-end price to three-year average earnings was 839 to $55.5 or 15 to 1—right at our suggested upper limit.
7. The ratio of price to net asset value was 839 to 562—also just within our suggested limit of 1½ to 1.

If, however, we wish to apply the same seven criteria to each individual company, we would find that only five of them would meet *all* our requirements. These would be: American Can, American Tel. & Tel., Anaconda, Swift, and Woolworth. The totals for these five appear in Table 14-3. Naturally they make a much better statistical showing than the DJIA as a whole, except in the past growth rate.[3]

Our application of specific criteria to this select group of industrial stocks indicates that the number meeting every one of our tests will be a relatively small percentage of *all* listed industrial issues. We hazard the guess that about 100 issues of this sort could have been found in the Standard & Poor's *Stock Guide* at the end of 1970, just about enough to provide the investor with a satisfactory range of personal choice.

The Public-Utility "Solution"

If we turn now to the field of public-utility stocks we find a much more comfortable and inviting situation for the investor. Here the vast majority of issues appear to be cut out, by their performance record and their price ratios, in accordance with the defensive investor's needs as we judge them. We exclude one criterion from our tests of public-utility stocks—namely, the ratio of current assets to current liabilities. The working-capital factor takes care of itself in this industry as part of the continuous financing of its growth by sales of bonds and shares. We do require an adequate proportion of stock capital to debt.[4]

TABLE 14-3 DJIA Issues Meeting Certain Investment Criteria at the End of 1970

	American Can	American Tel. & Tel.	Anaconda	Swift	Woolworth	Average, 5 Companies
Price Dec. 31, 1970	39¾	48⅛	21	30⅜	36½	
Price/earnings, 1970	11.0 ×	12.3 ×	6.7 ×	13.5 ×	14.4 ×	11.6 ×
Price/earnings, 3 years	10.5 ×	12.5 ×	5.4 ×	18.1 ×[b]	15.1 ×	12.3 ×
Price/book value	99%	108%	38%	113%	148%	112%
Current assets/current liabilities	2.2 ×	n.a.	2.9 ×	2.3 ×	1.8 ×[c]	2.3 ×
Net current assets/debt	110%	n.a.	120%	141%	190%	140%
Stability index[a]	85	100	72	77	99	86
Growth[a]	55%	53%	78%	25%	73%	57%

[a] See definition on p. 319.
[b] In view of Swift's good showing in the poor year 1970, we waive the 1968–1970 deficiency here.
[c] The small deficiency here below 2 to 1 was offset by margin for additional debt financing.
n.a. = not applicable. American Tel. & Tel.'s debt was less than its stock equity.

In Table 14-4 we present a résumé of the 15 issues in the Dow Jones public-utility average. For comparison, Table 14-5 gives a similar picture of a random selection of fifteen other utilities taken from the New York Stock Exchange list.

As 1972 began the defensive investor could have had quite a wide choice of utility common stocks, each of which would have met our requirements for both performance and price. These companies offered him everything he had a right to demand from simply chosen common-stock investments. In comparison with prominent industrial companies as represented by the DJIA, they offered almost as good a record of past growth, plus smaller fluctuations in the annual figures—both at a lower price in relation to earnings and assets. The dividend return was significantly higher. The position of the utilities as regulated monopolies is assuredly more of an advantage than a disadvantage for the conservative investor. Under law they are entitled to charge rates sufficiently remunerative to attract the capital they need for their continuous expansion, and this implies adequate offsets to inflated costs. While the process of regulation has often been cumbersome and perhaps dilatory, it has not prevented the utilities from earning a fair return on their rising invested capital over many decades.

For the defensive investor the central appeal of the public-utility stocks at this time should be their availability at a moderate price in relation to book value. This means that he can ignore stockmarket considerations, if he wishes, and consider himself primarily as a part owner of well-established and well-earning businesses. **The market quotations are always there for him to take advantage of when times are propitious—either for purchases at unusually attractive low levels, or for sales when their prices seem definitely too high.**

The market record of the public-utility indexes—condensed in Table 14-6, along with those of other groups—indicates that there have been ample possibilities of profit in these investments in the past. While the rise has not been as great as in the industrial index, the individual utilities have shown more price stability in most periods than have other groups. It is striking to observe in this table that the relative price/earnings ratios of the industrials and the utilities have changed places during the past two decades.

TABLE 14-4 Data on the Fifteen Stocks in the Dow Jones Utility Average at September 30, 1971

	Price Sept. 30, 1971	Earned[a]	Dividend	Book Value	Price/ Earnings	Price/ Book Value	Div. Yield	Earns. Per Share 1970 vs. 1960
Am. Elec. Power	26	2.40	1.70	18.86	11×	138%	6.5%	+87%
Cleveland El. Ill.	34¾	3.10	2.24	22.94	11	150	6.4	86
Columbia Gas System	33	2.95	1.76	25.58	11	129	5.3	85
Commonwealth Edison	35½	3.05	2.20	27.28	12	130	6.2	56
Consolidated Edison	24½	2.40	1.80	30.63	10	80	7.4	19
Consd. Nat. Gas	27¾	3.00	1.88	32.11	9	86	6.8	53
Detroit Edison	19¼	1.80	1.40	22.66	11	84	7.3	40
Houston Ltg. & Power	42¾	2.88	1.32	19.02	15	222	3.1	135
Niagara-Mohawk Pwr.	15½	1.45	1.10	16.46	11	93	7.2	32
Pacific Gas & Electric	29	2.65	1.64	25.45	11	114	5.6	79
Panhandle E. Pipe L.	32½	2.90	1.80	19.95	11	166	5.5	79
Peoples Gas Co.	31½	2.70	2.08	30.28	8	104	6.6	23
Philadelphia El.	20½	2.00	1.64	19.74	10	103	8.0	29
Public Svs. El. & Gas	25½	2.80	1.64	21.81	9	116	6.4	80
Sou. Calif. Edison	29¼	2.80	1.50	27.28	10	107	5.1	85
Average	28½	2.66	1.71	23.83	10.7×	121%	6.2%	+65%

[a] Estimated for year 1971.

TABLE 14-5 Data on a Second List of Public-Utility Stocks at September 30, 1971

	Price Sept. 30, 1971	Earned	Dividend	Book Value	Price/ Earnings	Price/ Book Value	Div. Yield	Earns. Per Share 1970 vs. 1960
Alabama Gas	15½	1.50	1.10	17.80	10×	87%	7.1%	+34%
Allegheny Power	22½	2.15	1.32	16.88	10	134	6.0	71
Am. Tel. & Tel.	43	4.05	2.60	45.47	11	95	6.0	47
Am. Water Works	14	1.46	.60	16.80	10	84	4.3	187
Atlantic City Elec.	20½	1.85	1.36	14.81	11	138	6.6	74
Baltimore Gas & Elec.	30¾	2.85	1.82	23.03	11	132	6.0	86
Brooklyn Union Gas	23½	2.00	1.12	20.91	12	112	7.3	29
Carolina Pwr. & Lt.	22½	1.65	1.46	20.49	14	110	6.5	39
Cen. Hudson G. & E.	22¼	2.00	1.48	20.29	11	110	6.5	13
Cen. Ill. Lt.	25¼	2.50	1.56	22.16	10	114	6.5	55
Cen. Maine Pwr.	17¾	1.48	1.20	16.35	12	113	6.8	62
Cincinnati Gas & Elec.	23¾	2.20	1.56	16.13	11	145	6.7	102
Consumers Power	29½	2.80	2.00	32.59	11	90	6.8	89
Dayton Pwr. & Lt.	23	2.25	1.66	16.79	10	137	7.2	94
Delmarva Pwr. & Lt.	16½	1.55	1.12	14.04	11	117	6.7	78
Average	23½	2.15	1.50	21.00	11×	112%	6.5%	+71%

TABLE 14-6 Development of Prices and Price/Earnings Ratios for Various Standard & Poor's Averages, 1948–1970.

	Industrials		Railroads		Utilities	
Year	Price[a]	P/E Ratio	Price[a]	P/E Ratio	Price[a]	P/E Ratio
1948	15.34	6.56	15.27	4.55	16.77	10.03
1953	24.84	9.56	22.60	5.42	24.03	14.00
1958	58.65	19.88	34.23	12.45	43.13	18.59
1963	79.25	18.18	40.65	12.78	66.42	20.44
1968	113.02	17.80	54.15	14.21	69.69	15.87
1970	100.00	17.84	34.40	12.83	61.75	13.16

[a] Prices are at the close of the year.

These reversals will have more meaning for the active than for the passive investor. But they suggest that even defensive portfolios should be changed from time to time, especially if the securities purchased have an apparently excessive advance and can be replaced by issues much more reasonably priced. Alas! there will be capital-gains taxes to pay—which for the typical investor seems to be about the same as the Devil to pay. Our old ally, experience, tells us here that it is better to sell and pay the tax than not sell and repent.

Investing in Stocks of Financial Enterprises

A considerable variety of concerns may be ranged under the rubric of "financial companies." These would include banks, insurance companies, savings and loan associations, credit and small-loan companies, mortgage companies, and "investment companies" (e.g., mutual funds). It is characteristic of all these enterprises that they have a relatively small part of their assets in the form of material things—such as fixed assets and merchandise inventories—but on the other hand most categories have short-term obligations well in excess of their stock capital. The question of financial soundness is, therefore, more relevant here than in the case of the typical manufacturing or commercial enterprise. This, in turn, has given rise to various forms of regulation and supervision, with the design and general result of assuring against unsound financial practices.

Broadly speaking, the shares of financial concerns have produced investment results similar to those of other types of common shares. Table 14-7 shows price changes between 1948 and 1970 in six groups represented in the Standard & Poor's stock-price indexes. The average for 1941–1943 is taken as 10, the base level. The year-end 1970 figures ranged between 44.3 for the 9 New York banks and 218 for the 11 life-insurance stocks. During the sub-intervals there was considerable variation in the respective price movements. For example, the New York City bank stocks did quite well between 1958 and 1968; conversely the spectacular life-insurance group actually lost ground between 1963 and 1968. These cross-movements are found in many, perhaps most, of the numerous industry groups in the Standard & Poor's indexes.

We have no very helpful remarks to offer in this broad area of investment—other than to counsel that the same arithmetical standards for price in relation to earnings and book value be applied to the choice of companies in these groups as we have suggested for industrial and public-utility investments.

Railroad Issues

The railroad story is a far different one from that of the utilities. The carriers have suffered severely from a combination of severe competition and strict regulation. (Their labor-cost problem has of course been difficult as well, but that has not been confined to railroads.) Automobiles, buses, and airlines have drawn off most of their passenger business and left the rest highly unprofitable; the trucks have taken a good deal of their freight traffic. More than half of the railroad mileage of the country has been in bankruptcy (or "trusteeship") at various times during the past 50 years.

But this half-century has not been all downhill for the carriers. There have been prosperous periods for the industry, especially the war years. Some of the lines have managed to maintain their earning power and their dividends despite the general difficulties.

The Standard & Poor's index advanced sevenfold from the

TABLE 14-7 **Relative Price Movements of Stocks of Various Types of Financial Companies Between 1948 and 1970**

	1948	1953	1958	1963	1968	1970
Life insurance	17.1	59.5	156.6	318.1	282.2	218.0
Property and liability insurance	13.7	23.9	41.0	64.7	99.2	84.3
New York City banks	11.2	15.0	24.3	36.8	49.6	44.3
Banks outside New York City	16.9	33.3	48.7	75.9	96.9	83.3
Finance companies	15.6	27.1	55.4	64.3	92.8	78.3
Small-loan companies	18.4	36.4	68.5	118.2	142.8	126.8
Standard & Poor's composite	13.2	24.8	55.2	75.0	103.9	92.2

[a] Year-end figures from Standard & Poor's stock-price indexes. Average of 1941–1943 = 10.

low of 1942 to the high of 1968, not much below the percentage gain in the public-utility index. The bankruptcy of the Penn Central Transportation Co., our most important railroad, in 1970 shocked the financial world. Only a year and two years previously the stock sold at close to the highest price level in its long history, and it had paid continuous dividends for more than 120 years! (On p. 423 below we present a brief analysis of this railroad to illustrate how a competent student could have detected the developing weaknesses in the company's picture and counseled against ownership of its securities.) The market level of railroad shares as a whole was seriously affected by this financial disaster.

It is usually unsound to make blanket recommendations of whole classes of securities, and there are equal objections to broad condemnations. The record of railroad share prices in Table 14-6 shows that the group as a whole has often offered chances for a large profit. (But in our view the great advances were in themselves largely unwarranted.) Let us confine our suggestion to this: There is no compelling reason for the investor to own railroad shares; before he buys any he should make sure that he is getting so much value for his money that it would be unreasonable to look for something else instead.*

Selectivity for the Defensive Investor

Every investor would like his list to be better or more promising than the average. Hence the reader will ask whether, if he gets himself a competent adviser or security analyst, he should not be able to count on being supplied with an investment package of really superior merits. "After all," he may say, "the rules you have outlined are pretty simple and easygoing. A highly trained analyst ought to be able to use all his skill and techniques to improve substantially on something as obvious as the Dow Jones list. If not, what good are all his statistics, calculations, and pontifical judgments?"

Suppose, as a practical test, we had asked a hundred security analysts to choose the "best" five stocks in the Dow Jones Average, to be bought at the end of 1970. Few would have come up with identical choices and many of the lists would have differed completely from each other.

This is not so surprising as it may at first appear. The underlying reason is that **the current price of each prominent stock pretty well reflects the salient factors in its financial record plus the general opinion as to its future prospects. Hence the view of any analyst that one stock is a better buy than the rest must arise to a great extent from his personal partialities and expectations, or from the placing of his emphasis on one set of factors rather than on another in his work of evaluation. If all analysts were agreed that one particular stock was better than all the rest, that**

---

* Only a few major rail stocks remain, including CSX, Norfolk Southern, and Union Pacific. The advice in this section is at least as relevant to airline stocks today—with their frequent massive losses and a half-century of almost incessantly poor results—as it was to railroads in Graham's day.

issue would quickly advance to a price which would offset all of its previous advantages.*

Our statement that the current price reflects both known facts and future expectations was intended to emphasize the double basis for market valuations. Correspondingly with these two kinds of value elements are two basically different approaches to security analysis. To be sure, **every competent analyst looks forward to the future rather than backward to the past, and he realizes that his work will prove good or bad depending on what *will* happen and not on what *has* happened. Nevertheless, the future itself can be approached in two different ways, which may be called the way of *prediction* (or projection) and the way of *protection*.†**

Those who emphasize prediction will endeavor to anticipate fairly accurately just what the company will accomplish in future years—in particular whether earnings will show pronounced and persistent growth. These conclusions may be based on a very careful study of such factors as supply and demand in the industry—or volume, price, and costs—or else

---

* Graham is summarizing the "efficient markets hypothesis," or EMH, an academic theory claiming that the price of each stock incorporates all publicly available information about the company. With millions of investors scouring the market every day, it is unlikely that severe mispricings can persist for long. An old joke has two finance professors walking along the sidewalk; when one spots a $20 bill and bends over to pick it up, the other grabs his arm and says, "Don't bother. If it was really a $20 bill, someone would have taken it already." While the market is not perfectly efficient, it is pretty close most of the time—so the intelligent investor will stoop to pick up the stock market's $20 bills only after researching them thoroughly and minimizing the costs of trading and taxes.

† This is one of Graham's central points. All investors labor under a cruel irony: We invest *in* the present, but we invest *for* the future. And, unfortunately, the future is almost entirely uncertain. Therefore, investing on the basis of *projection* is a fool's errand; even the forecasts of the so-called experts are less reliable than the flip of a coin. For most people, investing on the basis of *protection*—from overpaying for a stock and from overconfidence in the quality of their own judgment—is the best solution. See Chapter 20 and its Commentary.

they may be derived from a rather naïve projection of the line of past growth into the future. If these authorities are convinced that the fairly long-term prospects are unusually favorable, they will almost always recommend the stock for purchase without paying too much regard to the level at which it is selling. Such, for example, was the general attitude with respect to the air-transport stocks—an attitude that persisted for many years despite the distressingly bad results often shown after 1946. In the Introduction we have commented on the disparity between the strong price action and the relatively disappointing earnings record of this industry.

By contrast, **those who emphasize protection are always especially concerned with the price of the issue at the time of study. Their main effort is to assure themselves of a substantial margin of indicated present value above the market price—which margin could absorb unfavorable developments in the future. Generally speaking, therefore, it is not so necessary for them to be enthusiastic over the company's long-run prospects as it is to be reasonably confident that the enterprise will get along.**

The first, or predictive, approach could also be called the qualitative approach, since it emphasizes prospects, management, and other nonmeasurable, albeit highly important, factors that go under the heading of quality. The second, or protective, approach may be called the quantitative or statistical approach, since it emphasizes the measurable relationships between selling price and earnings, assets, dividends, and so forth. Incidentally, the quantitative method is really an extension—into the field of common stocks—of the viewpoint that security analysis has found to be sound in the selection of bonds and preferred stocks for investment.

In our own attitude and professional work we were always committed to the quantitative approach. From the first we wanted to make sure that we were getting ample value for our money in concrete, demonstrable terms. We were not willing to accept the prospects and promises of the future as compensation for a lack of sufficient value in hand. This has by no means been the standard viewpoint among investment authorities; in fact, the majority would probably subscribe to the view that prospects, quality of management, other intangibles, and "the human factor" far outweigh the indications supplied by any study of the past record, the balance sheet, and all the other cold figures.

Thus this matter of choosing the "best" stocks is at bottom a highly controversial one. Our advice to the defensive investor is that he let it alone. Let him emphasize diversification more than individual selection. Incidentally, the universally accepted idea of diversification is, in part at least, the negation of the ambitious pretensions of selectivity. If one *could* select the best stocks unerringly, one would only lose by diversifying. Yet within the limits of the four most general rules of common-stock selection suggested for the defensive investor (on pp. 114–115) there is room for a rather considerable freedom of preference. At the worst the indulgence of such preferences should do no harm; beyond that, it may add something worthwhile to the results. With the increasing impact of technological developments on long-term corporate results, the investor cannot leave them out of his calculations. Here, as elsewhere, he must seek a mean between neglect and overemphasis.

Commentary on Chapter 14

by Jason Zweig

> The temptation to "do something" is one of the worst temptations that investors face. There is always some bluebird on the horizon.
>
> —John C. Bogle

In Chapter 14, Graham punts.

Although he gives some general guidelines on how defensive investors can pick stocks, his heart isn't in it. Graham lists seven criteria that stocks should meet. By the end of the chapter, however, he advises defensive investors not to bother:

> ... this matter of choosing the "best" stocks is at bottom a highly controversial one. Our advice to the defensive investor is that he let it alone. Let him emphasize diversification more than individual selection.

So, if you meet Graham's definition of a defensive investor—if you're unwilling or unable to sink plenty of time and effort into building a portfolio—he doesn't think you have to pick stocks at all.

That doesn't absolve you of all responsibilities, though. While you don't have to learn how to pick stocks, you do have to learn how to stick to a plan.

Combating Your Inner Con Artist

We've already talked, in Chapters 5 and 8 and the accompanying Commentaries, about how the brokerage business and social contagion can conspire to turn you into a speculator.

But the ultimate challenge for any defensive investor is to defend against the con artist inside you. Ensuring that you don't fool yourself is the hardest struggle of all.

As a defensive investor, you can con yourself in two basic ways:

- by thinking you know less than you do;
- by thinking you know more than you do.

If you're *underconfident* about your knowledge and abilities, you'll be afraid to invest at all in what feel like markets where only experts can succeed.

If you're *overconfident*, you'll regard yourself as one of those experts and be much too certain that you know what the future holds.

You can overcome underconfidence by following Graham's guidelines for defensive investors and putting your behavior on autopilot with index funds, dollar-cost averaging, and rebalancing.[1]

Conquering overconfidence, however, is a greater challenge. Get a few big wins in the market—even if they came from sheer dumb luck—and overconfidence will undermine your ability to behave like a defensive investor.

Being content with being defensive is almost a violation of human nature. We tend to think we have more control than we do over a world that's often ruled by randomness. We believe that we understood the past better than we did and that we will foresee the future more accurately than we can.

Decades ago, two psychologists asked drivers in the Seattle area to rate their skills behind the wheel. They surveyed two groups: some with clean records, and some who had just had an accident. Here's a sample of the results:

All told, these drivers had totaled 28 of their own cars and six other vehicles; three of their passengers had been killed, and many of the drivers themselves suffered concussions and broken bones, with at least one being paralyzed. One driver who said he didn't know how well he was driving, the researchers found, had been "engaged in a drag race contest at the time of the accident."[2]

---

[1] See the Commentaries on Chapters 9, 5, and 4, respectively.
[2] Caroline E. Preston and Stanley Harris, "Psychology of Drivers in Traffic Accidents," bit.ly/3EziGAx.

How many said they were bad drivers?
Zero.

Psychologists sometimes call such inflated self-assessments *positive illusions*, but how positive they are depends on the setting. If you're going out on a date or applying for a job, overestimating your odds of success can give you the courage to take a risk that could change your life. If you're driving or flying, overestimating your skills can ruin or end your life. And if you're investing, overconfidence can wreck your financial life.

TABLE 14-1: Driving Lessons

Among 50 drivers who had recently been in severe auto accidents, how many . . .

denied responsibility	30
admitted partial responsibility	5
admitted full responsibility	15
had no auto insurance	10
had previously been cited for speeding or similar violations	29
admitted drinking alcohol before the accident	21
had previously been cited for negligent, reckless, or drunk driving	11
admitted failing driving tests at least once	11
had driver's license revoked at least once	6
were charged after the accident with negligent driving	15
were charged after the accident with reckless driving	3
were charged after the accident with other offenses	4
said their driving at the time was "normal," "usual," "good," "100%," or "extra good"	32
said they were driving less well than usual	16
didn't know how well they were driving	2
answered the survey while hospitalized with injuries from the accident	50
described themselves as "poor" or "very poor" drivers	0

Source: Caroline E. Preston and Stanley Harris, "Psychology of Drivers in Traffic Accidents" (1965).

Overconfidence is the clash between our beliefs and reality. It takes three main forms: *overestimation*, thinking our performance is better than it is; *overplacement*, exaggerating our performance relative to other people's; and *overprecision*, being sure we know the exact answer even though reality is so often random and murky.[3]

A related phenomenon is *unrealistic optimism*, or believing that good things are more likely to happen to ourselves than to others. In perhaps the ultimate expression of unrealistic optimism, one survey of 2,000 American adults found that 54% believe they will go to heaven after they die, but only 2% expect to go to hell.[4]

I'm the Greatest

When almost all assets go up, as they did in 2021, the impression that you've become a brilliant investor can be almost irresistible. No wonder such catchphrases as "wen moon" (when will the price soar to the moon?) and "WAGMI" (we're all gonna make it) went viral.

The more and the faster your holdings go up, the higher your self-esteem will, too. Soon, your inner con artist is whispering in your inner ear: *Look how good you are at this! Why are you wasting your time slogging away at work when you could be making a killing by trading stocks and options and crypto?*

I'm in Control

Another form of self-deception is feeling as if you're in control even when you have no influence over the situation.

Neuroscientists have found that the feeling of being in control (even if you're not) activates the medial prefrontal cortex, a region of the brain that helps inhibit stress and negative emotions. Fooling yourself into thinking you're in charge can fend off the anxiety you would otherwise feel in the face of uncertainty.[5]

---

[3] For an excellent overview of overconfidence, see Don A. Moore, *Perfectly Confident* (HarperCollins, 2020).

[4] Cultural Research Center, "American Worldview Inventory 2020," bit.ly/44rulrE.

[5] Lauren A. Leotti et al., "Born to Choose: The Origins and Value of the Need for Control," bit.ly/48clrnA.

If you're gambling, you might blow on dice for good luck, shake them longer until they "feel" right, or throw them harder when you need a high number. Pushing the elevator button over and over won't make it arrive any faster, but somehow it *seems* to. State lotteries took off in the U.S. only after the advent of scratch-off numbers gave players the sensation that they were creating their own tickets.

Decades ago, psychologist Ellen Langer identified the factors that fuel the illusion of control: choice, familiarity, personal involvement, and competition. Knowing your goal and succeeding at it are also important.[6]

Those factors make the financial markets the ideal material out of which your inner con artist can conjure illusions of control: You choose what, when, and how much to invest; the markets feel as familiar as today's headlines; you can watch (and trade) your portfolio nonstop; you compete against hundreds of millions of people; your goal is to make money; and you *will* make money some of the time, even if you have no clue what you're doing, just by luck alone.

In an environment over which you have little to no control, it's hard *not* to overestimate how much control you do have.

Just look at professional traders. In a study at investment banks in London, 107 traders played a computer simulation in which they were told they "may" be able to make a financial index go up or down by pressing buttons on their keyboard. In fact, the buttons had no effect on the prices of the index. After four rounds of the game, the traders were asked how much control they'd had.

Many thought they'd exerted at least some influence over the market index. And it turned out that those who were more prone to that illusion had poorer analytical ability, contributed less to their bank's profits, earned lower total annual compensation, and weren't as good at managing risk.[7]

When self-enhancement crosses the line into self-deception, you are likely to resist taking advice from others—and to treat the inevitable losses not as warnings that you're out of your depth but only as signals

---

[6] Ellen J. Langer, "The Illusion of Control," bit.ly/46OLptO; Suzanne C. Thompson, "Illusions of Control: How We Overestimate Our Personal Influence," bit.ly/3Qsnmyr.

[7] Mark Fenton-O'Creevy et al., "Trading on Illusions: Unrealistic Perceptions of Control and Trading Performance," bit.ly/46aUFv8.

that your success is bound to resume. Believing you have more control than you do is a sure way to end up earning lower returns than you should.

I Knew It All Along

Look at this detail from a photo I took of a FedEx envelope:

FIGURE 14-1

Source: Jason Zweig

Many people know there's something embedded in the logo besides the letters *F, e, d, E,* and *x*. But not everybody does. Either you spot it instantly, or you can't find it at all.

Look again. Do you see anything?

If not, turn the page and look at Figure 14-2, which is simply an enlarged detail of the same photo.

Now try something else. Look at the full FedEx logo again and try to unsee that arrow between the *E* and the *x*. Try as hard as you can to reconstruct your state of visual ignorance before you knew the arrow was there.

Can you see only the letters, without the arrow?

In much the same way, once we know what *has* happened in the financial markets, it becomes all but impossible to recall that we didn't know what would happen.

And fooling yourself into thinking you knew what *would* happen can delude you into thinking you know what *will* happen.

Psychologists call this "hindsight bias." It takes results that seemed improbable or impossible before they happened and transforms them into inevitabilities—because we now know they did happen. As the Nobel laureate Daniel Kahneman liked to say, hindsight bias "makes surprises vanish."

FIGURE 14-2

Source: Jason Zweig

After markets go up sharply, you will recall expecting them to rise more than you did at the time. If they go down steeply, you will remember being more bearish than you were. Hindsight isn't 20/20; it's close to legally blind.[8]

The effect is so powerful that investors who had no idea what would unfold over the coming year will look back, 12 months later, and recall that they expected the market to perform almost exactly as it did. It's yet another way your inner con artist will try to coax you into abandoning your resolve to be a defensive investor: *You knew all along what the market was about to do! That means you know what it's going to do next. Act on it before it's too late!*

Hindsight bias mixes with selective memory to create an intoxicating brew of self-delusion. Look back at your investing decisions and you're

---

[8] Baruch Fischhoff and Ruth Beyth, "I Knew It Would Happen: Remembered Probabilities of Once-Future Things," bit.ly/45PPH7u; Neal J. Roese and

likely to "remember" having even more gains and fewer losses than you did. Your inner con artist tricks you into thinking not only that you foresaw what was coming, but that the decisions you based on that forecast were better than they were.[9]

Handcuffing Your Inner Con Artist

You aren't an intelligent investor because your holdings have just gone up a lot.

You're an intelligent investor because you know your limitations.

And you're a *defensive* investor because you've already decided you aren't willing or able to commit the time and effort that are the prerequisites for success as an *enterprising* investor.

Overconfidence feasts on generalities. It's easy to believe you're a better investor than you are if you take your cues from whether your portfolio's market value has gone up. On the other hand, specific questions are the kryptonite of overconfidence. When your inner con artist starts telling you how brilliant an investor you are, force yourself to answer concrete inquiries like these:

- How much is my portfolio up *relative to the market*?
- What exactly do I know about this asset that most other people don't?
- How did I learn it? Why haven't they learned it?
- Can I give three detailed reasons why this asset is still undervalued?

Relying on specific questions will get you closer to what psychologist Don Moore calls "evidence-based confidence": a sense of your abilities grounded not in wishful thinking but in objective measures of reality.

Your answers could demonstrate that you do have a significant edge over other investors, in which case you should redefine yourself

---

Kathleen D. Vohs, "Hindsight Bias," bit.ly/3PCeGFB; Jason Zweig, *Your Money and Your Brain* (Simon & Schuster, 2007).

[9] Jason Zweig, "The Panic of 2020? Oh, I Made a Ton of Money—and So Did You," bit.ly/3RnXWTM, "Mirror, Mirror on the Wall, Who Knew That Stocks Would Fall?," bit.ly/45NHbWz, "Busting Your Hindsight Bias," bit.ly/3r3aJ3u; Katrin Gödker et al, "Investor Memory," bit.ly/3EDKDXS.

as an enterprising investor. More likely, though, by the time you finish answering the third question you should have silenced that little devil on your shoulder. Flick him off, recommit to following Graham's guidelines, and get back to living your life.

The Hindsight Bias-Buster

Nearly all investors, individuals and professionals alike, go through life blind to their hindsight bias. You can open your eyes to confront yours, though. Simply track your forecasts! What I call the Hindsight Bias-Buster takes only a few minutes a year.

Each January, make two copies of the following blank form and fill one out. Then, after December 31, as soon as the full year's results are available, try to recall your original forecasts as accurately as you can. *Without looking at your completed form*, write your recollections down on the remaining blank form. Then compare your original predictions against the page where you reconstructed them from memory.

You will almost certainly find that your recollection of what you expected has been skewed by what happened.

On December 31, what do you think will be . . .

. . . the closing value of the Dow Jones Industrial Average?

_____

. . . the total return of the S&P 500 for the calendar year?

_____ %

. . . the yield on the 10-year Treasury note?

____ %

. . . the official inflation rate (latest 12-month change in Consumer Price Index)?

____ %

. . . the price of bitcoin?

$_____

> ... *the price of gold?*
>
> $_____ per oz.
>
> ... *the price of crude oil?*
>
> $____ per barrel
>
> ... *the best-performing major financial asset?*
>
> _____
>
> Conducting this exercise a few years in a row just might cure you of the delusion that you know how to predict markets—and the itch to act on those predictions. (If you work with financial advisers, have them do it, too.)

CHAPTER 15

Stock Selection for the Enterprising Investor
by Benjamin Graham

In the previous chapter we have dealt with common-stock selection in terms of broad groups of eligible securities, from which the defensive investor is free to make up any list that he or his adviser prefers, provided adequate diversification is achieved. Our emphasis in selection has been chiefly on exclusions—advising on the one hand against all issues of recognizably poor quality, and on the other against the highest-quality issues if their price is so high as to involve a considerable speculative risk. In this chapter, addressed to the enterprising investor, we must consider the possibilities and the means of making *individual* selections which are likely to prove more profitable than an across-the-board average.

What are the prospects of doing this successfully? We would be less than frank, as the euphemism goes, if we did not at the outset express some grave reservations on this score. At first blush the case for successful selection appears self-evident. To get average results—e.g., equivalent to the performance of the DJIA—should require no special ability of any kind. All that is needed is a portfolio identical with, or similar to, those thirty prominent issues. Surely, then, by the exercise of even a moderate degree of skill—derived from study, experience, and native ability—it should be possible to obtain substantially better results than the DJIA.

Yet there is considerable and impressive evidence to the effect that this is very hard to do, even though the qualifications of those trying it are of the highest. The evidence lies in the record of the numerous investment companies, or "funds," which have been in operation for many years. Most of these funds are large enough to command the services of the best financial or security analysts in the field, together with all the other constituents of an adequate research department. Their expenses of operation, when spread over their ample capital, average about one-half of 1% a year thereon, or less. These costs are not negligible in themselves; but when they are compared with the approximately 15% annual overall return on common stocks generally in the decade 1951–1960, and even the 6% return in 1961–1970, they do not bulk large. A small amount of superior selective ability should easily have overcome that expense handicap and brought in a superior net result for the fund shareholders.

Taken as a whole, however, the all-common-stock funds failed over a long span of years to earn quite as good a return as was shown on Standard & Poor's 500-stock averages or the market as a whole. This conclusion has been substantiated by several comprehensive studies. To quote the latest one before us, covering the period 1960–1968:*

> It appears from these results that random portfolios of New York Stock Exchange stocks with equal investment in each stock performed on the average better over the period than did mutual funds in the same risk class. The differences were fairly substantial for the low- and medium-risk portfolios (3.7% and 2.5% respectively per annum), but quite small for the high-risk portfolios (0.2% per annum).[1]

As we pointed out in Chapter 9, these comparative figures in no way invalidate the usefulness of the investment funds as a financial institution. For they do make available to all members of the investing public the possibility of obtaining approximately average results on their common-stock commitments. For a variety of reasons, most members of the public who put their money in common stocks of their own choice fail to do nearly as well. But to the objective observer the failure of the funds to better the performance of a broad average is a pretty conclusive indication that such an achievement, instead of being easy, is in fact extremely difficult.

---

* Dozens of rigorous academic studies in later decades came to the same general conclusion: that mutual funds, on average, underperform the market by a margin roughly equal to their operating expenses and trading costs.

Why should this be so? We can think of two different explanations, each of which may be partially applicable. The first is the possibility that the stock market does in fact reflect in the current prices not only all the important facts about the companies' past and current performance, but also whatever expectations can be reasonably formed as to their future. If this is so, then the diverse market movements which subsequently take place—and these are often extreme—must be the result of new developments and probabilities that could not be reliably foreseen. This would make the price movements essentially fortuitous and random. To the extent that the foregoing is true, the work of the security analyst—however intelligent and thorough—must be largely ineffective, because in essence he is trying to predict the unpredictable.

The very multiplication of the number of security analysts may have played an important part in bringing about this result. With hundreds, even thousands, of experts studying the value factors behind an important common stock, it would be natural to expect that its current price would reflect pretty well the consensus of informed opinion on its value. Those who would prefer it to other issues would do so for reasons of personal partiality or optimism that could just as well be wrong as right.

We have often thought of the analogy between the work of the host of security analysts on Wall Street and the performance of master bridge players at a duplicate-bridge tournament. The former try to pick the stocks "most likely to succeed"; the latter to get top score for each hand played. Only a limited few can accomplish either aim. To the extent that all the bridge players have about the same level of expertness, the winners are likely to be determined by "breaks" of various sorts rather than superior skill. On Wall Street the leveling process is helped along by the freemasonry that exists in the profession, under which ideas and discoveries are quite freely shared at the numerous get-togethers of various sorts. **It is almost as if, at the analogous bridge tournament, the various experts were looking over each other's shoulders and arguing out each hand as it was played.**

The second possibility is of a quite different sort. **Perhaps many of the security analysts are handicapped by a flaw in** their basic approach to the problem of stock selection. They seek the industries with the best prospects of growth, and the companies in these industries with the best management and other advantages. The implication is that they will buy into such industries and such companies at any price, however high, and they will avoid less promising industries and companies no matter how low the price of their shares. This would be the only correct procedure if the earnings of the good companies were sure to grow at a rapid rate indefinitely in the future, for then in theory their value would be infinite. And if the less promising companies were headed for extinction, with no salvage, the analysts would be right to consider them unattractive at any price.

The truth about our corporate ventures is quite otherwise. Extremely few companies have been able to show a high rate of uninterrupted growth for long periods of time. Remarkably few, also, of the larger companies suffer ultimate extinction. For most, their history is one of vicissitudes, of ups and downs, of change in their relative standing. In some the variations "from rags to riches and back" have been repeated on almost a cyclical basis—the phrase used to be a standard one applied to the steel industry—for others spectacular changes have been identified with deterioration or improvement of management.

How does the foregoing inquiry apply to the enterprising investor who would like to make individual selections that will yield superior results? It suggests first of all that he is taking on a difficult and perhaps impracticable assignment. Readers of this book, however intelligent and knowing, could scarcely expect to do a better job of portfolio selection than the top analysts of the country. But if it is true that a fairly large segment of the stock market is often discriminated against or entirely neglected in the standard analytical selections, then the intelligent investor may be in a position to profit from the resultant undervaluations.

But to do so he must follow specific methods that are not generally accepted on Wall Street, since those that are so accepted do not seem to produce the results everyone would like to achieve. It would be rather strange if—with all the brains at work professionally in the stock market—there could be approaches which are both sound and relatively unpopular. Yet our own career and reputation have been based on this unlikely fact.*

A Summary of the Graham-Newman Methods

To give concreteness to the last statement, it should be worthwhile to give a brief account of the types of operations we engaged in during the thirty-year life of Graham-Newman Corporation, between 1926 and 1956.† These were classified in our records as follows:

Arbitrages: The purchase of a security and the simultaneous sale of one or more other securities into which it was to be exchanged under a plan of reorganization, merger, or the like.

Liquidations: Purchase of shares which were to receive one or more cash payments in liquidation of the company's assets.

Operations of these two classes were selected on the twin basis of (a) a calculated annual return of 20% or more, and (b) our judgment that the chance of a successful outcome was at least four out of five.

Related Hedges: The purchase of convertible bonds or convertible preferred shares, and the simultaneous sale of the common stock into which they were exchangeable. The position was established at close to a parity basis—i.e., at a small maximum loss if the senior issue had actually to be converted and the operation closed out

---

* In this section, as he did also on pp. 348–349, Graham is summarizing the Efficient Market Hypothesis. Recent appearances to the contrary, the problem with the stock market today is not that so many financial analysts are idiots, but rather that so many of them are so smart. As more and more smart people search the market for bargains, that very act of searching makes those bargains rarer—and, in a cruel paradox, makes the analysts look as if they lack the intelligence to justify the search. The advent of artificial-intelligence tools such as ChatGPT, by making analysis even more efficient, is likely to make the market harder to beat, not easier.

† Graham launched Graham-Newman Corp. in January 1936 and dissolved it when he retired from active money management in 1956; it was the successor to a partnership called the Benjamin Graham Joint Account, which he ran from January 1926 through December 1935.

in that way. But a profit would be made if the common stock fell considerably more than the senior issue, and the position closed out in the market.

Net-Current-Asset (or "Bargain") Issues: The idea here was to acquire as many issues as possible at a cost for each of less than their book value in terms of net-current-assets alone—i.e., giving no value to the plant account and other assets. Our purchases were made typically at two-thirds or less of such stripped-down asset value. In most years we carried a wide diversification here—at least 100 different issues.

We should add that from time to time we had some large-scale acquisitions of the control type, but these are not relevant to the present discussion.

We kept close track of the results shown by each class of operation. In consequence of these follow-ups we discontinued two broader fields, which were found not to have shown satisfactory overall results. The first was the purchase of apparently attractive issues—based on our general analysis—which were not obtainable at less than their working-capital value alone. The second were "unrelated" hedging operations, in which the purchased security was not exchangeable for the common shares sold. (Such operations correspond roughly to those recently embarked on by the new group of "hedge funds" in the investment-company field.* In both cases a study of the results realized by us over a period of ten years or more led us to conclude that the profits were not sufficiently dependable—and the operations not sufficiently "headache proof"—to justify our continuing them.

Hence from 1939 on our operations were limited to "self-liquidating" situations, related hedges, working-capital bargains, and a few control operations. Each of these classes gave us quite consistently satisfactory results from then on, with the special feature that the related hedges turned in good profits in the bear markets when our "undervalued issues" were not doing so well.

We hesitate to prescribe our own diet for any large number

---

* An "unrelated" hedge involves buying a stock or bond issued by one company and short-selling (or betting on a decline in) a security issued by a different company. A "related" hedge involves buying and selling different

of intelligent investors. Obviously, the professional techniques we have followed are not suitable for the defensive investor, who by definition is an amateur. As for the aggressive investor, perhaps only a small minority of them would have the type of temperament needed to limit themselves so severely to only a relatively small part of the world of securities. Most active-minded practitioners would prefer to venture into wider channels. Their natural hunting grounds would be the entire field of securities that they felt (a) were certainly not overvalued by conservative measures, and (b) appeared decidedly more attractive—because of their prospects or past record, or both—than the average common stock. In such choices they would do well to apply various tests of quality and price-reasonableness along the lines we have proposed for the defensive investor. But they should be less inflexible, permitting a considerable plus in one factor to offset a small black mark in another. For example, he might not rule out a company which had shown a deficit in a year such as 1970, if large average earnings and other important attributes made the stock look cheap. The enterprising investor may confine his choice to industries and companies about which he holds an optimistic view, but we counsel strongly against paying a high price for a stock (in relation to earnings and assets) because of such enthusiasm. If he followed our philosophy in this field he would more likely be the buyer of important cyclical enterprises—such as steel shares perhaps—when the current situation is unfavorable, the near-term prospects are poor, and the low price fully reflects the current pessimism.*

---

stocks or bonds issued by the same company. The "new group" of hedge funds described by Graham were widely available around 1968, but later regulation by the U.S. Securities and Exchange Commission restricted access to hedge funds for the general public.

* Today, an enterprising investor following Graham's train of thought might be searching for opportunities among (for example) small stocks, real-estate companies, electric utilities, European stocks, and perhaps Chinese-listed firms. History has shown that yesterday's losers are often tomorrow's winners.

Secondary Companies

Next in order for examination and possible selection would come secondary companies that are making a good showing, have a satisfactory past record, but appear to hold no charm for the public. These would be enterprises on the order of ELTRA and Emhart at their 1970 closing prices. (See Chapter 13 above.) There are various ways of going about locating such companies. We should like to try a novel approach here and give a reasonably detailed exposition of one such exercise in stock selection. Ours is a double purpose. Many of our readers may find a substantial practical value in the method we shall follow, or it may suggest comparable methods to try out. Beyond that what we shall do may help them to come to grips with the real world of common stocks, and introduce them to one of the most fascinating and valuable little volumes in existence. It is Standard & Poor's *Stock Guide*, published monthly, and made available to the general public under annual subscription. In addition many brokerage firms distribute the *Guide* to their clients (on request).*

The great bulk of the *Guide* is given over to about 230 pages of condensed statistical information on the stocks of more than 4,500 companies. These include all the issues listed on the various exchanges, say 3,000, plus some 1,500 unlisted issues. Most of the items needed for a first and even a second look at a given company appear in this compendium. (From our viewpoint the important missing datum is the net-asset-value, or book value, per share, which can be found in the larger Standard & Poor's volumes and elsewhere.)

The investor who likes to play around with corporate figures will find himself in clover with the *Stock Guide*. He can open to any page and see before his eyes a condensed panorama of the splendors and miseries of the stock market, with all-time high and low prices going as far back as 1936, when available. He will find companies that have multiplied their price 2,000 times from the minuscule low to the majestic high. (For prestigious IBM the

---

* The S&P Stock Guide is no longer distributed—but basic, free data on stocks is widely available online and on brokerage apps.

growth was "only" 333 times in that period.) He will find (not so exceptionally) a company whose shares advanced from ⅜ to 68, and then fell back to 3.² In the dividend record column he will find one that goes back to 1791—paid by Industrial National Bank of Rhode Island (which recently saw fit to change its ancient corporate name).* If he looks at the *Guide* for the year-end 1969 he will read that Penn Central Co. (as successor to Pennsylvania Railroad) has been paying dividends steadily since 1848; alas!, it was doomed to bankruptcy a few months later. He will find a company selling at only 2 times its last reported earnings, and another selling at 99 times such earnings.³ In most cases he will find it difficult to tell the line of business from the corporate name; for one U.S. Steel there will be three called such things as ITI Corp. (bakery stuff) or Santa Fe Industries (mainly the large railroad). He can feast on an extraordinary variety of price histories, dividend and earnings histories, financial positions, capitalization setups, and what not. Backward-leaning conservatism, run-of-the-mine featureless companies, the most peculiar combinations of "principal business," all kinds of Wall Street gadgets and widgets—they are all there, waiting to be browsed over, or studied with a serious objective.

The *Guides* give in separate columns the current dividend yields and price/earnings ratios, based on latest 12-month figures, wherever applicable. It is this last item that puts us on the track of our exercise in common-stock selection.

A Winnowing of the Stock Guide

Suppose we look for a simple *prima facie* indication that a stock is cheap. The first such clue that comes to mind is a low price in relation to recent earnings. Let's make a preliminary list of stocks that sold at a multiple of nine or less at the end of 1970. That datum is conveniently provided in the last column of the even-numbered pages. For an illustrative sample we shall take the first 20 such low-multiplier stocks; they begin with the sixth issue listed, Aberdeen Mfg. Co., which closed the year at 10¼, or 9 times its reported

---

* After many mergers, Industrial National Bank of Rhode Island ended up being absorbed into Bank of America Corp.

earnings of $1.25 per share for the 12 months ended September 1970. The twentieth such issue is American Maize Products, which closed at 9½, also with a multiplier of 9.

The group may have seemed mediocre, with 10 issues selling below $10 per share. (This fact is not truly important; it would probably—not necessarily—warn defensive investors against such a list, but the inference for enterprising investors might be favorable on balance.)* Before making a further scrutiny let us calculate some numbers. Our list represents about one in ten of the first 200 issues looked at. On that basis the *Guide* should yield, say, 450 issues selling at multipliers under 10. This would make a goodly number of candidates for further selectivity.

So let us apply to our list some additional criteria, rather similar to those we suggested for the defensive investor, but not so severe. We suggest the following:

1. Financial condition: *(a)* Current assets at least 1½ times current liabilities, and *(b)* debt not more than 110% of net current assets (for industrial companies).
2. Earnings stability: No deficit in the last five years covered in the *Stock Guide*.
3. Dividend record: Some current dividend.
4. Earnings growth: Last year's earnings more than those of 1966.
5. Price: Less than 120% net tangible assets.

The earnings figures in the *Guide* were generally for those ending September 30, 1970, and thus do not include what may be a bad quarter at the end of that year. But an intelligent investor

---

* For today's investor, the cutoff is more likely to be around $1 per share—the level below which many stocks are "delisted," or declared ineligible for trading on major exchanges. Just monitoring the stock prices of these companies can take a considerable amount of effort, making them impractical for defensive investors. The costs of trading low-priced stocks can be very high. Finally, companies with very low stock prices have a distressing tendency to go out of business. However, a diversified portfolio of dozens of these distressed companies may still appeal to some enterprising investors today.

can't ask for the moon—at least not to start with. Note also that we set no lower limit on the size of the enterprise. Small companies may afford enough safety if bought carefully and on a group basis.

When we have applied the five additional criteria our list of 20 candidates is reduced to only five. Let us continue our search until the first 450 issues in the *Guide* have yielded us a little "portfolio" of 15 stocks meeting our six requirements. (They are set forth in Table 15–1, together with some relevant data.) The group, of course, is presented for illustration only, and would not necessarily have been chosen by our inquiring investor.

The fact is that the user of our method would have had a much wider choice. If our winnowing approach had been applied to all 4,500 companies in the *Stock Guide*, and if the ratio for the first tenth had held good throughout, we would end up with about 150 companies meeting all six of our criteria of selection. The enterprising investor would then be able to follow his judgment—or his partialities and prejudices—in making a third selection of, say, one out of five in this ample list.

The *Stock Guide* material includes "Earnings and Dividend Rankings," which are based on stability and growth of these factors for the past eight years. (Thus *price* attractiveness does not enter here.) We include the S & P rankings in our Table 15-1. Ten of the 15 issues are ranked B+ (= average) and one (American Maize) is given the "high" rating of A. If our enterprising investor wanted to add a seventh mechanical criterion to his choice, by considering only issues ranked by Standard & Poor's as average or better in quality, he might still have about 100 such issues to choose from. One might say that a group of issues, of at least average quality, meeting criteria of financial condition as well, purchasable at a low multiplier of current earnings and below asset value, should offer good promise of satisfactory investment results.

Single Criteria for Choosing Common Stocks

An inquiring reader might well ask whether the choice of a better than average portfolio could be made a simpler affair than we have just outlined. Could a single plausible criterion be used to good advantage—such as a low price/earnings ratio, or a high

TABLE 15-1 A Sample Portfolio of Low-Multiplier Industrial Stocks

(The First Fifteen Issues in the *Stock Guide* at December 31, 1971, Meeting Six Requirements)

	Price Dec. 1970	Earned Per Share Last 12 Months	Book Value	S & P Ranking	Price Feb. 1972
Aberdeen Mfg.	10¼	$1.25	$9.33	B	13¾
Alba-Waldensian	6⅜	.68	9.06	B+	6⅜
Albert's Inc.	8½	1.00	8.48	n.r.[a]	14
Allied Mills	24½	2.68	24.38	B+	18¼
Am. Maize Prod.	9¼	1.03	10.68	A	16½
Am. Rubber & Plastics	13¾	1.58	15.06	B	15
Am. Smelt. & Ref.	27½	3.69	25.30	B+	23¼
Anaconda	21	4.19	54.28	B+	19
Anderson Clayton	37¾	4.52	65.74	B+	52½
Archer-Daniels-Mid.	32½	3.51	31.35	B+	32½
Bagdad Copper	22	2.69	18.54	n.r.[a]	32
D. H. Baldwin	28	3.21	28.60	B+	50
Big Bear Stores	18½	2.71	20.57	B+	39½
Binks Mfg.	15¼	1.83	14.41	B+	21½
Bluefield Supply	22¼	2.59	28.66	n.r.[a]	39½[b]

[a] n.r. = not ranked.
[b] Adjusted for stock split.

dividend return, or a large asset value? The two methods of this sort that we have found to give quite consistently good results in the longer past have been (a) the purchase of low-multiplier stocks of important companies (such as the DJIA list), and (b) the choice of a diversified group of stocks selling under their net-current-asset value (or working-capital value). We have already pointed out that the low-multiplier criterion applied to the DJIA at the end of 1968 worked out badly when the results are measured to mid-1971. The record of common-stock purchases made at a price below their working-capital value has no such bad mark against it; the drawback here has been the drying up of such opportunities during most of the past decade.

What about other bases of choice? In writing this book we have made a series of "experiments," each based on a single, fairly obvious criterion. The data used would be readily found in the Standard & Poor's *Stock Guide*. In all cases a 30-stock portfolio was assumed to have been acquired at the 1968 closing prices and then revalued at June 30, 1971. The separate criteria applied were the following, as applied to otherwise random choices: (1) A low multiplier of recent earnings (not confined to DJIA issues). (2) A high dividend return. (3) A very long dividend record. (4) A very large enterprise, as measured by number of outstanding shares. (5) A strong financial position. (6) A low price in dollars per share. (7) A low price in relation to the previous high price. (8) A high quality-ranking by Standard & Poor's.

It will be noted that the *Stock Guide* has at least one column relating to each of the above criteria. This indicates the publisher's belief that each is of importance in analyzing and choosing common stocks. (As we pointed out above, we should like to see another figure added: the net-asset-value per share.)

The most important fact that emerges from our various tests relates to the performance of stocks bought at random. We have tested this performance for three 30-stock portfolios, each made up of issues found on the first line of the December 31, 1968, *Stock Guide* and also found in the issue for August 31, 1971. Between these two dates the S & P composite was practically unchanged, and the DJIA lost about 5%. But our 90 randomly chosen issues declined an average of 22%, not counting 19 issues that were dropped from the *Guide* and probably showed larger losses. These comparative results undoubtedly reflect the tendency of smaller issues of inferior quality to be relatively overvalued in bull markets, and not only to suffer more serious declines than the stronger issues in the ensuing price collapse, but also to delay their full recovery—in many cases indefinitely. The moral for the intelligent investor is, of course, to avoid second-quality issues in making up a portfolio, unless—for the enterprising investor—they are demonstrable bargains.

Other results gleaned from our portfolio studies may be summarized as follows:

Only three of the groups studied showed up better than the

S & P composite (and hence better than the DJIA), viz: (1) Industrials with the highest quality ranking (A+). These advanced 9½% in the period against a decline of 2.4% for the S & P industrials, and 5.6% for the DJIA. (However, the ten public-utility issues rated A+ declined 18% against a decline of 14% for the 55-stock S & P public-utility index.) It is worth remarking that the S & P rankings showed up very well in this single test. In every case a portfolio based on a higher ranking did better than a lower-ranking portfolio. (2) Companies with more than 50 million shares outstanding showed no change on the whole, as against a small decline for the indexes. (3) Strangely enough, stocks selling at a high price per share (over 100) showed a slight (1%) composite advance.

Among our various tests we made one based on book value, a figure not given in the *Stock Guide*. Here we found—contrary to our investment philosophy—that companies that combined major size with a large good-will component in their market price did very well as a whole in the 2½-year holding period. (By "good-will component" we mean the part of the price that exceeds the book value.)* Our list of "good-will giants" was made up of 30 issues, each of which had a good-will component of over a billion dollars, representing more than half of its market price. The total market value of these good-will items at the end of 1968 was more than $120 billions! Despite these optimistic market valuations the group as a whole showed a price advance per share of 15% between December 1968 and August 1971, and acquitted itself best among the 20-odd lists studied.

A fact like this must not be ignored in a work on investment policies. **It is clear that, at the least, a considerable *momentum* is attached to those companies that combine the virtues of great size, an excellent past record of earnings, the public's expectation of continued earnings growth in the future, and strong market action over many past years. Even if the price may appear excessive by our quantitative standards the underlying market momentum**

---

* In Graham's terms, a large amount of goodwill can result from two causes: a corporation can acquire other companies for substantially more than the value of their assets, or its own stock can trade for substantially more than its book value.

may well carry such issues along more or less indefinitely. (Naturally this assumption does not apply to every individual issue in the category. For example, the indisputable good-will leader, IBM, moved down from 315 to 304 in the 30-month period.) It is difficult to judge to what extent the superior market action shown is due to "true" or objective investment merits and to what extent to long-established popularity. No doubt both factors are important here. Clearly, both the long-term and the recent market action of the good-will giants would recommend them for a diversified portfolio of common stocks. Our own preference, however, remains for other types that show a combination of favorable investment factors, including asset values of at least two-thirds the market price.

The tests using other criteria indicate in general that random lists based on a single favorable factor did better than random lists chosen for the opposite factor—e.g., low-multiplier issues had a smaller decline in this period than high-multiplier issues, and long-term dividend payers lost less than those that were not paying dividends at the end of 1968. To that extent the results support our recommendation that the issues selected meet a combination of quantitative or tangible criteria.

Finally we should comment on the much poorer showing made by our lists as a whole as compared with the price record of the S & P composite. The latter is weighted by the size of each enterprise, whereas our tests are based on taking one share of each company. Evidently the larger emphasis given to giant enterprises by the S & P method made a significant difference in the results, and points up once again their greater price stability as compared with "run-of-the-mine" companies.

Bargain Issues, or Net-Current-Asset Stocks

In the tests discussed above we did not include the results of buying 30 issues at a price less than their net-current-asset value. The reason was that only a handful, at most, of such issues would have been found in the *Stock Guide* at the end of 1968. But the picture changed in the 1970 decline, and at the low prices of that year a goodly number of common stocks could have been bought at below their working-capital value. It always seemed, and still seems, ridiculously simple to say that if one can acquire a diversified group of common stocks at a price less than the applicable net current assets alone—after deducting all prior claims, and counting as *zero* the fixed and other assets—the results should be quite satisfactory. They were so, in our experience, for more than 30 years—say, between 1923 and 1957—excluding a time of real trial in 1930–1932.

Has this approach any relevance at the beginning of 1971? Our answer would be a qualified "yes." A quick runover of the *Stock Guide* would have uncovered some 50 or more issues that appeared to be obtainable at or below net-current-asset value. As might be expected a good many of these had been doing badly in the difficult year 1970. If we eliminated those which had reported net losses in the last 12-month period we would be still left with enough issues to make up a diversified list.

We have included in Table 15-2 some data on five issues that sold at less than their working-capital value* at their *low* prices of 1970. These give some food for reflection on the nature of stock-price fluctuations. How does it come about that well-established companies, whose brands are household names all over the country, could be valued at such low figures—at the same time when other

TABLE 15-2 Stocks of Prominent Companies Selling at or Below Net-Current-Asset Value in 1970

Company	1970 Price	Net-Current-Asset Value Per Share	Book Value Per Share	Earned Per Share, 1970	Current Dividend	High Price Before 1970
Cone Mills	13	$18	$39.3	$1.51	$1.00	41½
Jantzen Inc.	11⅛	12	16.3	1.27	.60	37
National Presto	21½	27	31.7	6.15	1.00	45
Parker Pen	9¼	9½	16.6	1.62	.60	31¼
West Point Pepperell	16¼	20½	39.4	1.82	1.50	64

---

* Technically, the working-capital value of a stock is the current assets per share, minus the current liabilities per share, divided by the number of shares outstanding. Here, however, Graham means "*net* working-capital value," or the per-share value of current assets minus *total* liabilities.

concerns (with better earnings growth of course) were selling for billions of dollars in excess of what their balance sheets showed? To quote the "old days" once more, the idea of good will as an element of intangible value was usually associated with a "trade name." Names such as Lady Pepperell in sheets, Jantzen in swim suits, and Parker in pens would be considered assets of great value indeed. But now, if the "market doesn't like a company," not only renowned trade names but land, buildings, machinery, and what you will, can all count for nothing in its scales. **Pascal said that "the heart has its reasons that the reason doesn't understand."*** For "heart" read "Wall Street."

There is another contrast that comes to mind. **When the going is good and new issues are readily salable, stock offerings of no quality at all make their appearance. They quickly find buyers; their prices are often bid up enthusiastically right after issuance to levels in relation to assets and earnings that would put IBM, Xerox, and Polaroid to shame. Wall Street takes this madness in its stride, with no overt efforts by anyone to call a halt before the inevitable collapse in prices.** (The SEC can't do much more than insist on disclosure of information, about which the speculative public couldn't care less, or announce investigations and usually mild punitive actions of various sorts after the letter of the law has been clearly broken.) When many of these minuscule but grossly inflated enterprises disappear from view, or nearly so, it is all taken philosophically enough as "part of the game." Everybody swears off such inexcusable extravagances—until next time.

Thanks for the lecture, says the gentle reader. But what about your "bargain issues"? Can one really make money in them without taking a serious risk? Yes indeed, *if* you can find enough of them to make a diversified group, and *if* you don't lose patience if they fail to advance soon after you buy them. Sometimes the patience needed may appear quite considerable. In our previous edition we hazarded a single example (p. 188) which was current as we wrote.

---

* *Le coeur a ses raisons que la raison ne connaît point.* This poetic passage is one of the concluding arguments in the great French theologian's discussion of what has come to be known as "Pascal's wager" (see the Commentary on Chapter 20).

It was Burton-Dixie Corp., with stock selling at 20, against net-current-asset value of 30, and book value of about 50. A profit on that purchase would not have been immediate. But in August 1967 all the shareholders were offered 53¾ for their shares, probably at just about book value. A patient holder, who had bought the shares in March 1964 at 20, would have had a profit of 165% in 3½ years—a noncompounded annual return of 47%. Most of the bargain issues in our experience have not taken that long to show good profits—nor have they shown so high a rate. For a somewhat similar situation, current as we write, see our discussion of National Presto Industries below, p. 461.

Special Situations or "Workouts"

Let us touch briefly on this area, since it is theoretically includable in the program of operations of an enterprising investor. It was commented upon above. Here we shall supply some examples of the genre, and some further remarks on what it appears to offer an open-minded and alert investor.

Three such situations, among others, were current early in 1971, and they may be summarized as follows:

SITUATION 1. Acquisition of Kayser-Roth by Borden's. In January 1971 Borden Inc. announced a plan to acquire control of Kayser-Roth ("diversified apparel") by giving 1⅓ shares of its own stock in exchange for one share of Kayser-Roth. On the following day, in active trading, Borden closed at 26 and Kayser-Roth at 28. If an "operator" had bought 300 shares of Kayser-Roth and sold 400 Borden at these prices and if the deal were later consummated on the announced terms, he would have had a profit of some 24% on the cost of his shares, less commissions and some other items. Assuming the deal had gone through in six months, his final profit might have been at about a 40% per annum rate.

SITUATION 2. In November 1970 National Biscuit Co. offered to buy control of Aurora Plastics Co. at $11 in cash. The stock was selling at about 8½; it closed the month at 9 and continued to sell there at year-end. Here the gross profit indicated was originally about 25%, subject to the risks of nonconsummation and to the time element.

SITUATION 3. Universal-Marion Co., which had ceased its business operations, asked its shareholders to ratify dissolution of the concern. The treasurer indicated that the common stock had a book value of about $28½ per share, a substantial part of which was in liquid form. The stock closed 1970 at 21½, indicating a possible gross profit here, if book value was realized in liquidation, of more than 30%.

If operations of this kind, conducted on a diversified basis for spreading the risk, could be counted to yield annual profits of, say, 20% or better, they would undoubtedly be more than merely worthwhile. Since this is not a book on "special situations," we are not going into the details of the business—for it really is a business. Let us point out two contradictory developments there in recent years. On the one hand the number of deals to choose from has increased enormously, as compared with, say, ten years ago. This is a consequence of what might be called a mania of corporations to diversify their activities through various types of acquisitions, etc. In 1970 the number of "merger announcements" aggregated some 5,000, down from over 6,000 in 1969. The total money values involved in these deals amounted to many, many billions. Perhaps only a small fraction of the 5,000 announcements could have presented a clear-cut opportunity for purchase of shares by a special-situations man, but this fraction was still large enough to keep him busy studying, picking, and choosing.

The other side of the picture is that an increasing proportion of the mergers announced failed to be consummated. In such cases, of course, the aimed-for profit is not realized, and is likely to be replaced by a more or less serious loss. Reasons for nonsuccess are numerous, including antitrust intervention, shareholder opposition, change in "market conditions," unfavorable indications from further study, inability to agree on details, and others. The trick here, of course, is to have the judgment, buttressed by experience, to pick the deals most likely to succeed and also those which are likely to occasion the smallest loss if they fail.

Further Comment on the Examples Above

KAYSER-ROTH. The directors of this company had already rejected (in January 1971) the Borden proposal when this chapter was written. If the operation had been "undone" immediately the overall loss, including commissions, would have been about 12% of the cost of the Kayser-Roth shares.

AURORA PLASTICS. Because of the bad showing of this company in 1970 the takeover terms were renegotiated and the price reduced to 10½. The shares were paid for at the end of May. The annual rate of return realized here was about 25%.

UNIVERSAL-MARION. This company promptly made an initial distribution in cash and stock worth about $7 per share, reducing the investment to say 14½. However the market price fell as low as 13 subsequently, casting doubt on the ultimate outcome of the liquidation.

Assuming that the three examples given are fairly representative of "workout or arbitrage" opportunities as a whole in 1971, it is clear that they are not attractive if entered into upon a random basis. This has become more than ever a field for professionals, with the requisite experience and judgment.

There is an interesting sidelight on our Kayser-Roth example. Late in 1971 the price fell below 20 while Borden was selling at 25, equivalent to 33 for Kayser-Roth under the terms of the exchange offer. It would appear that either the directors had made a great mistake in turning down that opportunity or the shares of Kayser-Roth were now badly undervalued in the market. Something for a security analyst to look into.

Commentary on Chapter 15
by Jason Zweig

> The sense of danger must not disappear:
> The way is certainly both short and steep,
> However gradual it looks from here;
> Look if you like, but you will have to leap.
>
> —W. H. Auden[1]

If you're an enterprising investor trying to find mispriced stocks that can earn superior returns, you're taking on a challenge few people ever succeed at. Consistently beating the market by picking individual stocks is extraordinarily difficult.

That's why you should put your analytical energies into making only a few decisions. Most stocks won't usually be mispriced enough to justify the effort of researching how mispriced they are.

SOYA Investing

According to Warren Buffett, investors would be better off if all the trades of their lifetime had to fit on one punch card with 20 punches on it. Every investment decision they make would use up one of the punches. "They aren't going to get 20 great ideas in their lifetime," Buffett has said. "They're going to get five, or three, or seven, and you can get rich off five, or three, or seven. But what you can't get rich doing is trying to get one every day."

Buffett's longtime business partner, Charlie Munger, described the same idea more bluntly. Most of the time, Munger said, you should "sit

---

[1] W. H. Auden, "Leap Before You Look" (1940).

on your ass" waiting for one of the rare occasions when Mr. Market goes crazy. (For politeness, I'll abbreviate Munger's idea as "SOYA.") Although you shouldn't be trading while you wait, you should be learning: continually studying industries, reading annual reports, and compiling a watchlist of a few stocks you'd like to own if their prices plunge.[2] Sooner or later—perhaps years or even decades later—they will. Then, and only then, should you buy—and buy aggressively.

In the meantime, keep most of your money in a stock index fund; that way, while you wait for a specific opportunity, you'll participate all along in the general growth of the market.

To be a SOYA investor is thus the opposite of the common misconception of what an enterprising investor does: Instead of trading frequently, you almost never do.

By minimizing your activity, you maximize your probability of making money.

First, Look in the Mirror

As Max Heine, the late manager of the Mutual Shares stock fund, liked to say, "There are many roads to Jerusalem." You can be an enterprising investor by seeking:

- today's cheapest, "deep value" stocks, bargains even by Graham's standards;
- great companies at good prices, thanks to bad news;
- tomorrow's superstocks, companies that seldom trade cheaply but have the potential for high long-term growth.[3]

Which you choose depends on your temperament. *How enterprising you are* matters less than *how you are enterprising*. Do you enjoy hunting for bargains in thrift shops and working the system to maximize reward points on your credit cards? Then deep value may suit your

---

[2] On watchlists, see the Commentary on Chapter 7.

[3] Enterprising individual investors can also consider areas shunned by institutions, such as spinoffs, in which companies offer publicly traded shares in a subsidiary for the first time, and "orphans," or stocks that are removed from a market index.

spirit. Are you the kind of person who shuns the crowd and distrusts popular opinion? Then you may do well digging into companies battered by bad news. Do you like making bold bets in the pursuit of potentially big gains? Then superstocks may be a good fit for you.

No matter which enterprising approach you try, you must live by Graham's commandments to be disciplined and different.

The Bargain Basement

If you want deep value, you could buy a so-called "factor" or "smart-beta" fund that holds dozens or hundreds of stocks that clear a set of statistical hurdles of cheapness, such as low ratios of price to sales, earnings, and book value.

But the whole point of being an enterprising investor is that you're willing and able to commit time and effort in the attempt to outperform—rather than delegating the work to strangers. Buying a value fund makes sense for a defensive investor but is likely to leave an enterprising investor antsy and unsatisfied.

Graham's measure of deepest value was whether a stock is priced under the net current asset value of the underlying business. That means the shares trade below what the company's cash, accounts receivable, inventories, and other readily salable assets are worth, minus all liabilities.

As of late 2023, 80 out of roughly 3,100 regularly traded U.S. stocks—about 2.5% of the total—were priced at less than net current asset value, according to AJO Vista, an investment firm in Philadelphia.

Most were tiny start-up biotechnology or pharmaceutical firms that traded in low volume; the typical institutional investor won't touch them. An enterprising individual, however, could build a portfolio of all 80; if one of the companies discovers a major new drug, or some get bought by larger firms, the portfolio might do well even if most of the companies fade or go under.[4]

---

[4] This approach is extremely risky and would be a rare exception to our rule (see the Commentaries on Chapters 4 and 20) that once you diversify widely by putting most of your money in a total stock-market index fund, you can then focus the remainder of your assets on a handful of companies. Biotech stocks are so volatile that owning only a handful of them is a bad idea. Before

You could also focus on "microcaps," companies whose shares have a total market value of less than $100 million. Here, too, most institutions can't compete.

Otherwise, in the U.S. and many developed markets, deep-value stocks are remarkably scarce—at least until the next bear market finally creates a new crop of them.

When Opportunity Knocks, It Sounds Like Danger

Stocks are most likely to be severely mispriced when a company has an alarming setback—the failure of a product, a strategic stumble, turnover of top executives—or when the economy is in chaos, as in 2008–09 or 2020.

Such overreactions often create undervaluation. Paradoxically, when perceived risk goes up, actual risk often goes down. The perception of higher risk creates lower prices; lower prices create the potential for superior future returns.

Above all, shocks to a business or to the whole stock market create value by distracting attention from the most important question: Is this company likely to be able to produce consistently greater quantities of cash in the years to come?

Consider W. W. Grainger, Inc., a wholesale distributor of maintenance and repair equipment. In April 2017, under fierce competition from Amazon.com, Grainger suddenly announced it would slash its prices "across the board." Because of the price cuts, warned Grainger, its earnings in 2017 would likely be 9% to 12% lower than previously forecast.

That set Mr. Market's hair on fire.

Grainger's stock plunged 11% that day and kept dropping for months. In July, the company announced that its second-quarter profits were down 43% from a year earlier. Between its peak in February 2017 and when it finally hit bottom that August, nearly 40% of Grainger's stock-market value had been vaporized.

What about the business? Had that lost over a third of its value?

Grainger's customers didn't flee en masse. Nor did they continue

---

considering even this diversified approach, see Verdad Capital, "The Biotech Boneyard," bit.ly/48TDksc.

Screenwriting

Using the free stock screeners at websites and apps such as Koyfin, FinViz, Finchat.io, Finbox, TIKR, or Yahoo Finance, you can set filters to identify groups of companies that meet various criteria.[1]

In Graham's spirit, you could screen for low debt and low price/earnings (P/E) and price/book (P/B) ratios, as well as high dividend yields. If you're looking for superstocks (see p. 389), you could set filters to identify firms with rising net operating cash flow, return on assets, and return on invested capital. (Remember to average the results over three to five years.)[2]

You'll probably feel pretty clever the first time you run a stock screen and come up with companies you've never heard of that look like incredible bargains. But it's highly unlikely you've turned up a motherlode of great companies undiscovered by any of the professional investors, backed by supercomputers, artificial intelligence, and multimillion-dollar research budgets, who scour the markets all day long.

That's why you shouldn't think of the result of your stock screen as a buy list; it's a watchlist of companies you can study and monitor as a SOYA investor, waiting for them to become cheap.

---

[1] Stock screeners are also available for relatively low subscription fees at AAII.com, Morningstar.com, and YCharts.com. Most major brokerage firms offer stock screeners on their websites or apps. Also, tools that apply artificial intelligence to investment analysis are rapidly proliferating but uneven in quality. Before signing up to use any screener, be sure you're comfortable the tool isn't designed to goad you into frequent trading.

[2] The more criteria you screen for, the higher the odds that the resulting list will end up too arbitrary and brittle to be useful. If you use, say, 13 different criteria and the screen turns out not to work, good luck figuring out which of the 13 you should adjust or eliminate. Simple prediction models tend to work better than complex ones (Robyn M. Dawes, "The Robust Beauty of Improper Linear Models in Decision Making," bit.ly/3PQp5xy). Less is more!

flocking to Amazon; instead, they bought even more from Grainger, which was renowned for expert service and reliable delivery. Stocking more in its centralized warehouses to supply the rush of online buyers, Grainger didn't need to expand its number of local branches, helping to keep its profits high.

In 2018, Grainger's sales rose 8% over 2017; net income climbed 33%; its net operating cash flow held steady. All along, the company stayed profitable. (See Table 15-1.)

Over the five years after Mr. Market's overreaction to Grainger's price cuts, the stock gained an annual average of 22.2%, outperforming the S&P 500 by 6.8 percentage points annually.

By 2023, it seemed fair to ask whether Grainger was, if anything, too profitable. It was earning such high returns that a skeptic might wonder whether the company was treating its shareholders unfairly by not returning more of its excess capital to them.[5]

Overreaction

An enterprising investor is free to try taking the other side of the trade when Mr. Market overreacts to what's going on at a company or in the world.

Look at what happened to Fair Isaac Corp. during the global financial crisis of 2008–09. Fair Isaac's software provides the FICO credit scores that rate consumers seeking to borrow money or buy a house.

From their zenith in November 2006 to their low in March 2009, Fair Isaac's shares fell 76%. After that, the stock was valued at only one times sales, slightly over one times book value, four times cash flow, and nine times earnings—down, on each of those measures, by about two-thirds since 2006.

Was the business battered as badly?

Between its peak quarter ended December 31, 2006, and the depths of the credit crunch in the quarter ended March 31, 2009, Fair Isaac's sales shrank by 23%, and its net income shriveled by 43%. Yet, over that period, its return on invested capital and return on assets fell only about 25% apiece, while its return on equity barely dropped at all as Fair Isaac aggressively repurchased shares.

---

[5] See the Commentary on Chapter 19.

TABLE 15-1: Game Changer for Grainger

W. W. Grainger, Inc., years ending Dec. 31

	2012	2013	2014	2015	2016	2017	2018	2019	2020	2021	2022
Sales ($millions)	8,950.0	9,437.8	9,965.0	9,973.4	10,137.2	10,424.9	11,221.0	11,486.0	11,797.0	13,022.0	15,228.0
Net income ($millions)	677.5	785.4	792.2	761.4	600.5	581.0	776.0	849.0	695.0	1,043.0	1,547.0
Earnings per share ($)	9.52	11.13	11.45	11.58	9.87	10.02	13.73	15.46	12.94	19.98	30.27
Net margin (%)	7.6	8.3	7.9	7.6	5.9	5.6	6.9	7.4	5.9	8.0	10.2
Return on assets (%)	13.9	15.3	15.0	13.7	10.4	10.1	13.3	14.3	11.3	16.2	21.8
Return on equity (%)	24.0	25.0	24.5	27.8	29.5	33.3	43.0	45.0	37.7	56.3	71.7
Return on invested capital (%)	21.5	21.9	21.7	20.9	16.5	15.3	19.5	21.4	16.7	23.3	32.2
Dividends per share ($)	3.06	3.59	4.17	4.59	4.83	5.06	5.36	5.68	5.94	6.39	6.78
Payout ratio (%)	32.1	32.3	36.4	39.6	48.9	50.5	39.0	36.7	45.9	32.0	22.4

Source: FactSet.

Meanwhile, net cash flow from operations *rose* more than 10%.

Over the decade after it hit bottom in March 2009, Fair Isaac's stock gained more than 2,400%, growing at an average of 38.2% annually—crushing the S&P 500 by an average of 20.6 percentage points per year.

Another example:

In February and March 2020, during the worst of the panic over the Covid pandemic, NVR, Inc's stock dropped 45.1%—much worse than the S&P 500.

NVR is one of the largest homebuilders in the U.S. If Covid lasted for years or killed tens of millions of Americans, as seemed possible in the pandemic's early days, demand for homes would collapse.

But if Covid did last for years and kill tens of millions, you would have much bigger problems than losing whatever money you might have put into NVR's stock.

NVR had long been exceptionally profitable, with a return on invested capital that ran far above average in 15 of the preceding 20 years—slipping only during the housing slump that followed the 2008–09 financial crisis.

For the full year 2020, NVR's sales and net income rose slightly, and its net operating income went up 7% to what then was an all-time high.

From the market's low in 2020 through the end of 2023, NVR's stock gained 222%, far outpacing the 127% gain of the S&P 500.

What Makes Superstocks Super

Many people believe the highest-performing stocks come almost entirely from the technology industry. A look at the top 30 superstocks of the past 30 years—each with cumulative total returns of well over 10,000%—shows that isn't true.

Silicon and cell phones are on the list, but so are swimming pools, used cars, tobacco, and equipment for cops.

A warning: Profitability at many of the firms in Table 15.2 already seems to be fading. You can't get future winners by just blindly picking past winners.

One reason these stocks earned such high returns over the past 30 years is that they caught Wall Street by surprise. Most analysts and professional investors want what they call "consistent" earnings growth: profits that rise smoothly and steadily over time. The real

TABLE 15-2: Superstocks

Company	Cumulative total return, 1/1/1994–12/31/2023	Business
Monster Beverage Corp.	210,588%	energy drinks
Amazon.com	155,073%	online retailing & computing
NVIDIA Corp.	131,500%	computer hardware & software
Apple Inc.	89,085%	smartphones & computers
NVR Inc.	71,699%	homebuilding
Pool Corp.	57,572%	swimming pool supplies & equipment
HEICO Corp.	55,427%	aviation & electronics
Axon Enterprise Inc.	45,155%	police equipment
Ross Stores Inc.	44,932%	retail clothing stores
Netflix Inc.	40,594%	entertainment
Cognizant Technology Solutions Corp.	39,511%	technology services
Cooper Companies Inc.	37,529%	contact lenses & medical devices
Fair Isaac Corp.	36,728%	financial software & credit scoring
Balchem Corp.	35,382%	human nutrition, animal feed & industrial chemicals
Middleby Corp.	34,609%	food service & equipment

Company	Return	Industry
Copart Inc.	32,064%	online vehicle auctions
ResMed Inc.	30,161%	medical devices
Biogen Inc.	29,200%	biotechnology
Gilead Sciences Inc.	28,973%	biotechnology
Vector Group Ltd.	27,056%	cigarettes & real estate
O'Reilly Automotive Inc.	26,109%	auto parts
Old Dominion Freight Line Inc.	24,072%	trucking
Microsoft Corp.	23,924%	software
Watsco Inc.	23,419%	air-conditioning
Adobe Inc.	22,458%	software
Coherent Corp.	22,187%	lasers & electronics
Badger Meter Inc.	21,945%	water meters & equipment
AAON Inc.	21,154%	air-conditioning
National Beverage Corp.	20,955%	sparkling water & other beverages
Intuit Inc.	19,581%	software

Source: Center for Research in Security Prices.

world is so messy and unpredictable that no company can increase its profits every single quarter—and no one can reliably forecast corporate earnings to the penny. Nevertheless, Wall Street loves companies that repeatedly "meet expectations."

Especially in their earlier years, superstocks wreak havoc with expectations. They don't grow like automatons. They grow fast—but in fits and starts and huge swings.

If you're trying to identify the next superstock, you should look for a mix of qualitative and quantitative advantages.

Superstocks:

- have managers who focus five to 10 years into the future rather than on the next three months, so they don't bother producing smooth quarterly earnings growth or guiding analysts' expectations;
- have "moats" that defend them against competitors: processes, products, services, networks, or technologies so hard to surpass that customers become steadfastly loyal;[6]
- generate growing amounts of cash, even if their net income doesn't consistently rise (one reason Graham suggests averaging profits over three to five years);
- usually aren't commodity producers like mining or energy companies and seldom are found among cyclical industries such as airlines, chemicals, and hotels;
- grow not by acquisition but by inquisition, constantly interrogating their products, services, and technologies to find new ways of extracting revenue from existing lines of business.

> Over its first 18 quarters as a publicly traded company, Amazon lost $2.9 billion as founder Jeff Bezos made, in his own words, "bold rather than timid investment decisions . . . [for] long-term market leadership considerations rather than short-term profitability considerations or short-term Wall Street reactions."

---

[6] For more on moats, see the Commentary on Chapter 11.

> Balchem Corp., a superstock whose cumulative gain of 35,382% over 30 years vastly outperformed even Microsoft, develops techniques to coat nutrients and minerals. Decades ago, one of its engineers observed that its nutritional salts might prevent clay from absorbing too much water. Years went by before fracking for oil and gas turned that old technology into a new market for Balchem, producing tens of millions of dollars in additional revenue.[1]
>
> ---
>
> [1] Jason Zweig, "The Best Stock of the Last 30 Years? You've Never Heard of It," bit.ly/3PorE8C, and "How You Can Get Big Gains That Wall Street Can't," bit.ly/3ZtVKw0. For more on identifying companies with sustainably high growth, see Bruce Greenwald et al., *Value Investing: From Graham to Buffett and Beyond* (Wiley, 2021), Chapters 6–8.

The Intangibles

The economist John Burr Williams wrote in 1938, "a stock is worth *only what you can get out of it*"—the value, today, of all the net cash it can be expected to generate in the future.[7] That's why Warren Buffett has long emphasized that "growth is *always* a component in the calculation of value."

In Graham's day, industries such as railroads, automobiles, chemicals, and steel dominated. Value came largely from the *tangible* or physical assets on a company's balance sheet: its real estate, factories, and manufacturing and other equipment.

Nowadays, software, health care, financial, and consumer industries dominate. Value often comes largely from *intangible* assets that may be treated as expenses on a company's income statement: software development, employee training, advertising and marketing, patents, licenses, trademarks, and other forms of intellectual property.

Apple's logo, look, software, and brand name aren't physical

---

[7] John Burr Williams, The Theory of Investment Value (North-Holland, 1938), p. 57.

objects, but they are immensely valuable. So are Coca-Cola's iconic image, Amazon's logistical system for filling and delivering orders, and Google's algorithms for searching, organizing, and displaying information—all the result of pouring billions of dollars into advertising, human capital, and research and development.

The rise of intangibles is a reminder of what's always been true: Value is only an estimate—or, if your analysis is intellectually honest, a *range* of estimates. The future is uncertain, the distant future is more uncertain, and determining what the most important parts of a company are worth is an imprecise science.

Return on Invested Capital

If you think of a company as a living organism, return on invested capital is a vital diagnostic tool for measuring how cash flows through its circulatory system. Averaged over several years, is income growing? Are cash flows being diverted to areas that aren't essential for the survival and growth of the organism? Is the company not generating enough profit in the first place? Is the business hemorrhaging cash?

You can calculate ROIC several ways, but in its simplest form it is:

> net operating income after tax, divided by the book value of invested capital (equity plus debt, minus excess cash).

Not all companies choose to report ROIC in their financial disclosures, but various versions of the measure are available from third-party data providers. The long-term typical return on invested capital, across most industries in the U.S., is roughly 9%.

A high or steadily rising ROIC suggests not only that a business is becoming more profitable but also that its managers are good at identifying lucrative opportunities and allocating capital to them. Adjusting ROIC for intangibles is a key step that requires detailed analysis.[8]

Look at one of the superstocks of the past 30 years, Pool Corp.:

---

[8] For guidance on how to calculate and adjust return on invested capital, see Michael J. Mauboussin and Dan Callahan, "Return on Invested Capital," bit.ly/3L8ccMJ, "ROIC and the Investment Process," bit.ly/45cvLus, and

FIGURE 15-1: High Returns from a Low-Brow Business

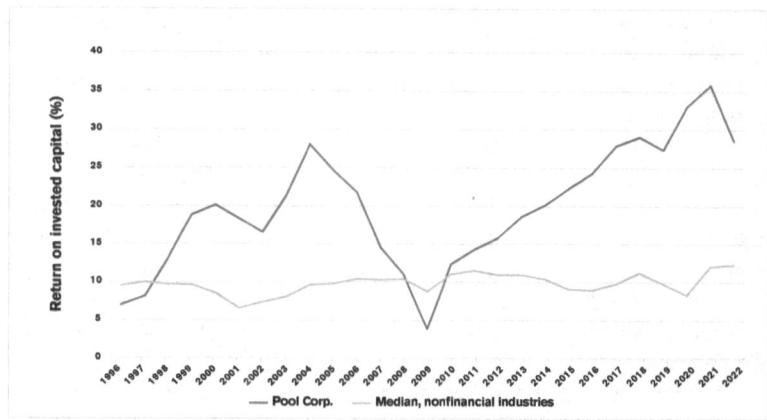

Sources: FactSet, Morgan Stanley.
Note: Not adjusted for intangibles.

Despite its unglamorous business of distributing swimming-pool supplies, this company generated returns on invested capital—except in 2009, during the global financial crisis—that would be the envy of more-prestigious industries such as software or online retailing. And especially in the earlier years, ROIC rose faster than the valuation of Pool's shares; in the late 1990s, its stock sold for well below the market's average price/earnings ratio. Pool then was small, followed by few analysts, and sparsely owned by institutional investors. (By the end of the period, its growth had become so impressive that Pool was arguably *overvalued*.)

If there's an opportunity for enterprising individuals to identify superstocks before Wall Street catches on, it's probably at companies that resemble Pool.

"ROIC and Intangible Assets," bit.ly/3GGRRvh; Kai Wu, "Intangible Value: A Sixth Factor," bit.ly/48g91f0. ROIC may well be the single best way to measure the quality of a business *and* its managers; see "The Siberian Solution" in Pulak Prasad, *What I Learned About Investing from Darwin* (Columbia Business School, 2023).

Cool Your Jets

Don't fool yourself, though. The odds are extremely low that you will be able to dentify tomorrow's superstocks today—*and* that you will be able to hold on long enough, despite shocking interim declines, for them to become super.

Of the 28,114 U.S. stocks whose returns can be tracked between 1926 and 2022, more than 16,000—nearly 59%—lost money for investors over their full histories. Only 966 stocks—3.4% of the total—accounted for the cumulative net gain of the entire U.S. stock market. And just under one-third of all the wealth created for investors over that nearly century-long period came from only 25 stocks—less than 0.09% of all the companies. Other stock markets worldwide show similar results.[9]

In fact, over all 10-year periods from 1926 through 2022, the typical stock underperformed the total market by a cumulative 27.1 percentage points, or an average of more than two percentage points annually. That 2% lag means investors in individual stocks typically sacrifice about one-fifth of the average long-term rate of return on stocks by choosing not to keep all their money in the entire market.

Over 20-year periods, the chance that an investment in any given stock will be worth less than half as much as it would have been in the market portfolio is nearly one-in-three. Only 0.55% of stocks turn out to be huge winners that beat the market by 1,000% or more over the long run.[10]

Trying to find the next superstock is like buying a lottery ticket that offers a remote shot at a giant jackpot years or decades into the future—but that also requires you to analyze the risks intensively before you buy it and for as long as you own it.

---

[9] "Cumulative net gain" and "wealth created" are measured relative to the return on U.S. Treasury bills; see Hendrik Bessembinder, "Shareholder Wealth Enhancement, 1926 to 2022," bit.ly/44yB08i, and Hendrik Bessembinder et al., "Long-Term Shareholder Returns: Evidence from 64,000 Global Stocks," bit.ly/3ROcJXz.

[10] Antti Petajsto, "Underperformance of Concentrated Stock Positions," bit.ly/48BFpd2. Results are for the median regularly traded stock relative to the CRSP market-capitalization-weighted portfolio of U.S. stocks.

The Upside of Enterprise

Against such long and discouraging odds, does it make any sense to try picking individual stocks yourself?

It can.

Although you aren't likely to succeed at picking individual stocks that will outperform, it isn't impossible. You might be skillful. Or you might just be lucky.[11]

Nor is outperformance even necessary for success.

So long as you follow Graham's procedural guidelines and Munger's SOYA principle, you will earn decent returns on the rest of your portfolio while you wait for enterprising opportunities—and, if you do find some, while you wait to see if they outperform.

Being an enterprising investor can also deliver psychological rewards even if it doesn't deliver conventional outperformance.

If you play recreational chess or soccer or basketball, it would be foolish to quit just because you'll never be as good as Magnus Carlsen or Kylian Mbappé or LeBron James. In much the same way, being an enterprising investor can be fun, improve your skills, and enable you to spend time with people you like—even if you're never able to beat the market.

What's more, the discipline of studying stocks from the ground up will sharpen your analytical tools, encourage you to think independently, cultivate your ability to defer gratification, and deepen your insights into what separates good businesses—and good ideas—from bad.

Those habits can pay enormous dividends your whole life long, even if none of the stocks you pick ever turn out to be super.

---

[11] As Graham writes in the Postscript, "one lucky break, or one supremely shrewd decision—can we tell them apart?—may count for more than a lifetime of . . . efforts" (p. 531). In the accompanying endnote he confesses that the greatest investment of his career might have been attributable to "dumb luck."

CHAPTER 16

Convertible Issues and Warrants
by Benjamin Graham

Convertible bonds and preferred stocks have been taking on a predominant importance in recent years in the field of senior financing. As a parallel development, stock-option warrants—which are long-term rights to buy common shares at stipulated prices—have become more and more numerous. More than half the preferred issues now quoted in the Standard & Poor's *Stock Guide* have conversion privileges, and this has been true also of a major part of the corporate *bond* financing in 1968–1970. There are at least 60 different series of stock-option warrants dealt in on the American Stock Exchange. In 1970, for the first time in its history, the New York Stock Exchange listed an issue of long-term warrants, giving rights to buy 31,400,000 American Tel. & Tel. shares at $52 each. With "Mother Bell" now leading that procession, it is bound to be augmented by many new fabricators of warrants. (As we shall point out later, they are a fabrication in more than one sense.)*

In the overall picture the convertible issues rank as much more important than the warrants, and we shall discuss them first. There are two main aspects to be considered from the standpoint of the investor. First, how do they rank as investment opportunities and risks? Second, how does their existence affect the value of the related common-stock issues?

Convertible issues are claimed to be especially advantageous to both the investor and the issuing corporation. The investor receives the superior protection of a bond or preferred stock, plus

---

* Graham detested warrants, as he makes clear on p. 407.

the opportunity to participate in any substantial rise in the value of the common stock. The issuer is able to raise capital at a moderate interest or preferred dividend cost, and if the expected prosperity materializes the issuer will get rid of the senior obligation by having it exchanged into common stock. Thus both sides to the bargain will fare unusually well.

Obviously the foregoing paragraph must overstate the case somewhere, for **you cannot by a mere ingenious device make a bargain much better for both sides.** In exchange for the conversion privilege the investor usually gives up something important in quality or yield, or both.[1] Conversely, if the company gets its money at lower cost because of the conversion feature, it is surrendering in return part of the common shareholders' claim to future enhancement. On this subject there are a number of tricky arguments to be advanced both pro and con. The safest conclusion that can be reached is that convertible issues are like any other *form* of security, in that their form itself guarantees neither attractiveness nor unattractiveness. That question will depend on all the facts surrounding the individual issue.*

We do know, however, that the group of convertible issues floated during the latter part of a bull market are bound to yield unsatisfactory results as a whole. (It is at such optimistic periods, unfortunately, that most of the convertible financing has been done in the past.) The poor consequences must be inevitable, from the timing itself, since a wide decline in the stock market must invariably make the conversion privilege much less attractive—and often, also, call into question the underlying safety of the issue itself. As a group illustration we shall retain the example used in our first edition of the relative price behavior of convertible and straight (nonconvertible) preferreds offered in 1946, the closing year of the bull market preceding the extraordinary one that began in 1949.

A comparable presentation is difficult to make for the years

---

* Graham is pointing out that, despite the promotional rhetoric that investors usually hear, convertible bonds do not automatically offer "the best of both worlds." Higher yield and lower risk do *not* go hand in hand. What Wall Street gives with one hand, it usually takes away with the other. An investment may offer the best of one world, or the worst of another; but the best of both worlds seldom becomes available in a single package.

TABLE 16-1 Price Record of New Preferred-Stock Issues Offered in 1946

Price Change from Issue Price to Low up to July 1947	"Straight" Issues	Convertible and Participating Issues
	(number of issues)	
No decline	7	0
Declined 0–10%	16	2
10–20%	11	6
20–40%	3	22
40% or more	0	12
	37	42
Average decline	About 9%	About 30%

1967–1970, because there were virtually no new offerings of nonconvertibles in those years. But it is easy to demonstrate that the average price decline of convertible preferred stocks from December 1967 to December 1970 was greater than that for common stocks as a whole (which lost only 5%). Also the convertibles seem to have done quite a bit worse than the older straight preferred shares during the period December 1968 to December 1970, as is shown by the sample of 20 issues of each kind in Table 16-2. These comparisons would demonstrate that convertible securities as a whole have relatively poor quality as senior issues and also are tied to common stocks that do worse than the general market except during a speculative upsurge. These observations do not apply to all convertible issues, of course. In 1968 and 1969 particularly, a fair number of strong companies used convertible issues to combat the inordinately high interest rates for even first-quality bonds. But it is noteworthy that in our 20-stock sample of convertible preferreds only one showed an advance and 14 suffered bad declines.*

---

* Recent structural changes in the convertible market have negated some of these criticisms. Between 1973 and 2020, convertible bonds slightly outperformed the S&P 500, with lower volatility. However, low-cost funds specializing in convertibles didn't exist for most of that period.

TABLE 16-2 Price Record of Preferred Stocks, Common Stocks, and Warrants, December 1970 versus December 1968
(Based on Random Samples of 20 Issues Each)

	Straight Preferred Stocks Rated A or Better	Rated Below A	Convertible Preferred Stocks	Listed Common Stocks	Listed Warrants
Advances	2	0	1	2	1
Declines:					
0–10%	3	3	3	4	0
10–20%	14	10	2	1	0
20–40%	1	5	5	6	1
40% or more	0	0	9	7	18
Average declines	10%	17%	29%	33%	65%

(Standard & Poor's composite index of 500 common stocks declined 11.3%.)

The conclusion to be drawn from these figures is not that convertible issues are in themselves less desirable than nonconvertible or "straight" securities. Other things being equal, the opposite is true. But we clearly see that other things are *not* equal in practice and that the addition of the conversion privilege often—perhaps generally—betrays an absence of genuine investment quality for the issue.

It is true, of course, that a convertible preferred is safer than the common stock of the same company—that is to say, it carries smaller risk of eventual loss of principal. Consequently those who buy new convertibles instead of the corresponding common stock are logical to that extent. But in most cases the common would not have been an intelligent purchase to begin with, at the ruling price, and the substitution of the convertible preferred did not improve the picture sufficiently. Furthermore, a good deal of the buying of convertibles was done by investors who had no special interest or confidence in the common stock—that is, they would never have thought of buying the common at the time—but who were tempted by what seemed an ideal combination of a prior claim plus a conversion privilege close to the current market. In a number of instances this combination has worked out well, but the statistics seem to show that it is more likely to prove a pitfall.

In connection with the ownership of convertibles there is a special problem which most investors fail to realize. Even when a profit appears it brings a dilemma with it. Should the holder sell on a small rise; should he hold for a much bigger advance; if the issue is called—as often happens when the common has gone up considerably—should he sell out then or convert into and retain the common stock?*

Let us talk in concrete terms. You buy a 6% bond at 100, convertible into stock at 25—that is, at the rate of 40 shares for each $1,000 bond. The stock goes to 30, which makes the bond worth at least 120, and so it sells at 125. You either sell or hold. If you hold, hoping for a higher price, you are pretty much in the position of a common shareholder, since if the stock goes down your bond will go down too. A conservative person is likely to say that beyond 125 his position has become too speculative, and therefore he sells and makes a gratifying 25% profit.

So far, so good. But pursue the matter a bit. In many cases where the holder sells at 125 the common stock continues to advance, carrying the convertible with it, and the investor experiences that peculiar pain that comes to the man who has sold out much too soon. The next time, he decides to hold for 150 or 200. The issue goes up to 140 and he does not sell. Then the market breaks and his bond slides down to 80. Again he has done the wrong thing.

Aside from the mental anguish involved in making these bad guesses—and they seem to be almost inevitable—there is a real arithmetical drawback to operations in convertible issues. It may be assumed that a stern and uniform policy of selling at 25% or 30% profit will work out best as applied to many holdings. This would then mark the upper limit of profit and would be realized only on the issues that worked out well. But, if—as appears to be true—these issues often lack adequate underlying security and tend to be floated and purchased in the latter stages of a bull market, then a goodly proportion of them will fail to rise to 125 but will not fail to

---

* A bond is "called" when the issuing corporation forcibly pays it off ahead of the stated maturity date, or final due date for the bond to be paid off.

collapse when the market turns downward. Thus the spectacular opportunities in convertibles prove to be illusory in practice, and the overall experience is marked by fully as many substantial losses—at least of a temporary kind—as there are gains of similar magnitude.

Because of the extraordinary length of the 1950–1968 bull market, convertible issues as a whole gave a good account of themselves for some 18 years. But this meant only that the great majority of common stocks enjoyed large advances, in which most convertible issues were able to share. The soundness of investment in convertible issues can only be tested by their performance in a declining stock market—and this has always proved disappointing as a whole.

In our first edition (1949) we gave an illustration of this special problem of "what to do" with a convertible when it goes up. We believe it still merits inclusion here. Like several of our references it is based on our own investment operations. We were members of a "select group," mainly of investment funds, who participated in a private offering of convertible $4\frac{1}{2}\%$ debentures of Eversharp Co. at par, convertible into common stock at $40 per share. The stock advanced rapidly to $65\frac{1}{2}$, and then (after a three-for-two split) to the equivalent of 88. The latter price made the convertible debentures worth no less than 220. During this period the two issues were called at a small premium; hence they were practically all converted into common stock, which was retained by a number of the original investment-fund buyers of the debentures. The price promptly began a severe decline, and in March 1948 the stock sold as low as $7\frac{3}{8}$. This represented a value of only 27 for the debenture issues, or a loss of 75% of the original price instead of a profit of over 100%.

The real point of this story is that some of the original purchasers converted their bonds into the stock and held the stock through its great decline. In so doing they ran counter to an old maxim of Wall Street, which runs: "Never convert a convertible bond." Why this advice? Because once you convert you have lost your strategic combination of prior claimant to interest plus a chance for an attractive profit. You have probably turned from investor into speculator, and quite often at an unpropitious time (because the stock has already had a large advance). If "Never convert a convertible" is a good rule, how came it that these experienced fund managers exchanged their Eversharp bonds for stock, to their subsequent embarrassing loss? The answer, no doubt, is that they let themselves be carried away by enthusiasm for the company's prospects as well as by the "favorable market action" of the shares. **Wall Street has a few prudent principles; the trouble is that they are always forgotten when they are most needed.** Hence that other famous dictum of the old-timers: "Do as I say, not as I do."

Our general attitude toward new convertible issues is thus a mistrustful one. We mean here, as in other similar observations, that the investor should look more than twice before he buys them. After such hostile scrutiny he may find some exceptional offerings that are too good to refuse. The ideal combination, of course, is a strongly secured convertible, exchangeable for a common stock which itself is attractive, and at a price only slightly higher than the current market. Every now and then a new offering appears that meets these requirements. By the nature of the securities markets, however, you are more likely to find such an opportunity in some older issue which has developed into a favorable position rather than in a new flotation. (If a new issue is a really strong one, it is not likely to have a good conversion privilege.)

The fine balance between what is given and what is withheld in a standard-type convertible issue is well illustrated by the extensive use of this type of security in the financing of American Telephone & Telegraph Company. Between 1913 and 1957 the company sold at least nine separate issues of convertible bonds, most of them through subscription rights to shareholders. The convertible bonds had the important advantage to the company of bringing in a much wider class of buyers than would have been available for a stock offering, since the bonds were popular with many financial institutions which possess huge resources but some of which were not permitted to buy stocks. The interest return on the bonds has generally been less than half the corresponding dividend yield on the stock—a factor that was calculated to offset the prior claim of the bondholders. Since the company maintained its $9 dividend rate for 40 years (from 1919 to the stock split in 1959) the result was the eventual conversion of virtually all the convertible issues into common stock. Thus the buyers of these convertibles have fared well through the years—but not quite so well as if they had bought the capital stock in the first place. This example establishes the soundness of American Telephone & Telegraph, but not the intrinsic attractiveness of convertible bonds. To prove them sound in practice we should need to have a number of instances in which the convertible worked out well even though the common stock proved disappointing. Such instances are not easy to find.

Effect of Convertible Issues on the Status of the Common Stock

In a large number of cases convertibles have been issued in connection with mergers or new acquisitions. Perhaps the most striking example of this financial operation was the issuance by the NVF Corp. of nearly $100,000,000 of its 5% convertible bonds (plus warrants) in exchange for most of the common stock of Sharon Steel Co. This extraordinary deal is discussed below (p. 427). Typically the transaction results in a pro forma increase in the reported earnings per share of common stock; the shares advance in response to their larger earnings, so-called, but also because the management has given evidence of its energy, enterprise, and ability to make more money for the shareholders. But there are two offsetting factors, one of which is practically ignored and the other entirely so in optimistic markets. The first is the actual dilution of the current and future earnings on the common stock that flows arithmetically from the new conversion rights. This dilution can be quantified by taking the recent earnings, or assuming some other figures, and calculating the adjusted earnings per share if all the convertible shares or bonds were actually converted. In the majority of companies the resulting reduction in per-share figures is not significant. But there are numerous exceptions to this statement, and there is danger that they will grow at an uncomfortable rate. The fast-expanding "conglomerates" have been the chief practitioners of convertible legerdemain. In Table 16-3 we list seven companies with large amounts of stock issuable on conversions or against warrants.*

---

* In recent years, convertible bonds have been heavily issued by companies in the financial, health-care, and technology industries.

TABLE 16-3 Companies with Large Amounts of Convertible Issues and Warrants at the End of 1969 (Shares in Thousands)

	Common Stock Outstanding	Additional Common Stock Issuable			Total Additional Common Stock
		On Conversion of			
		Bonds	Preferred Stock	Against Warrants	
Avco Corp.	11,470	1,750	10.436	3,085	15,271
Gulf & Western Inc.	14,964	9,671	5,632	6,951	22,260
International Tel. & Tel.	67,393	190	48,115		48,305
Ling-Temco-Vought	4,410[a]	1,180	685	7,564	9,429
National General	4,910	4,530		12,170	16,700
Northwest Industries[b]	7,433		11,467	1,513	12,980
Rapid American	3,591	426	1,503	8,000	9,929

[a] Includes "special stock."
[b] At end of 1970.

Indicated Switches from Common into Preferred Stocks

For decades before, say, 1956, common stocks yielded more than the preferred stocks of the same companies; this was particularly true if the preferred stock had a conversion privilege close to the market. The reverse is generally true at present. As a result there are a considerable number of convertible preferred stocks which are clearly more attractive than the related common shares. Owners of the common have nothing to lose and important advantages to gain by switching from their junior shares into the senior issue.

EXAMPLE: A typical example was presented by Studebaker-Worthington Corp. at the close of 1970. The common sold at 57, while the $5 convertible preferred finished at 87½. Each preferred share is exchangeable for 1½ shares of common, then worth 85½. This would indicate a small money difference against the buyer of the preferred. But dividends are being paid on the common at the annual rate of $1.20 (or $1.80 for the 1½ shares), against the $5 obtainable on one share of preferred. Thus the original adverse difference in price would probably be made up in less than a year, after which the preferred would probably return an appreciably higher dividend yield than the common for some time to come. But most important, of course, would be the senior position that the common shareholder would gain from the switch. At the *low* prices of 1968 and again in 1970 the preferred sold 15 points higher than 1½ shares of common. Its conversion privilege guarantees that it could never sell lower than the common package.[2]

Stock-Option Warrants

Let us mince no words at the outset. **We consider the recent development of stock-option warrants as a near fraud, an existing menace, and a potential disaster. They have created huge aggregate dollar "values" out of thin air. They have no excuse for existence except to the extent that they mislead speculators and investors.** They should be prohibited by law, or at least strictly limited to a minor part of the total capitalization of a company.*

For an analogy in general history and in literature we refer the reader to the section of *Faust* (part 2), in which Goethe describes the invention of paper money. As an ominous precedent in Wall Street history, we may mention the warrants of American & Foreign Power Co., which in 1929 had a quoted market value of over a billion dollars, although they appeared only in a footnote to the company's balance sheet. By 1932 this billion dollars had shrunk to $8 million, and in 1952 the warrants were wiped out in the company's recapitalization—even though it had remained solvent.

Originally, stock-option warrants were attached now and then to bond issues, and were usually equivalent to a partial conversion privilege. They were unimportant in amount, and hence did no harm. Their use expanded in the late 1920s, along with many other financial abuses, but they dropped from sight for long years

---

* Warrants were an extremely widespread technique of corporate finance in the nineteenth century and were fairly common even in Graham's day. They have since diminished in importance and popularity, despite a brief, ignominious comeback among SPACs in the early 2020s.

thereafter. They were bound to turn up again, like the bad pennies they are, and since 1967 they have become familiar "instruments of finance." In fact a standard procedure has developed for raising the capital for new real-estate ventures, affiliates of large banks, by selling units of an equal number of common shares and warrants to buy additional common shares at the same price. *Example:* In 1971 CleveTrust Realty Investors sold 2,500,000 of these combinations of common stock (or "shares of beneficial interest") and warrants, for $20 per unit.

Let us consider for a moment what is really involved in this financial setup. Ordinarily, a common-stock issue has the first right to buy additional common shares when the company's directors find it desirable to raise capital in this manner. This so-called "preemptive right" is one of the elements of value entering into the ownership of common stock—along with the right to receive dividends, to participate in the company's growth, and to vote for directors. When separate warrants are issued for the right to subscribe additional capital, that action takes away part of the value inherent in an ordinary common share and transfers it to a separate certificate. An analogous thing could be done by issuing separate certificates for the right to receive dividends (for a limited or unlimited period), or the right to share in the proceeds of sale or liquidation of the enterprise, or the right to vote the shares. Why then are these subscription warrants created as part of the original capital structure? Simply because people are inexpert in financial matters. **They don't realize that the common stock is worth less with warrants outstanding than otherwise.** Hence the package of stock and warrants usually commands a better price in the market than would the stock alone. Note that in the usual company reports the per-share earnings are (or have been) computed without proper allowance for the effect of outstanding warrants. The result is, of course, to overstate the true relationship between the earnings and the market value of the company's capitalization.*

The simplest and probably the best method of allowing for the

---

* If anyone ever offers to sell you "units" in any company, you can be quite certain that warrants are involved and that it's a bad deal.

existence of warrants is to add the equivalent of their market value to the common-share capitalization, thus increasing the "true" market price per share. Where large amounts of warrants have been issued in connection with the sale of senior securities, it is customary to make the adjustment by assuming that the proceeds of the stock payment are used to retire the related bonds or preferred shares. This method does not allow adequately for the usual "premium value" of a warrant above exercisable value. In Table 16-4 we compare the effect of the two methods of calculation in the case of National General Corp. for the year 1970.

Does the company itself derive an advantage from the creation of these warrants, in the sense that they assure it in some way of receiving additional capital when it needs some? Not at all. Ordinarily there is no way in which the company can require the warrant-holders to exercise their rights, and thus provide new capital to the company, prior to the expiration date of the warrants. In the meantime, if the company wants to raise additional common-stock funds it must offer the shares to its shareholders in the usual way—which means somewhat under the ruling market price. The warrants are no help in such an operation; they merely complicate the situation by frequently requiring a downward revision in their own subscription price. Once more we assert that large issues of stock-option warrants serve no purpose, except to fabricate imaginary market values.

The paper money that Goethe was familiar with, when he wrote his *Faust*, were the notorious French assignats that had been greeted as a marvelous invention, and were destined ultimately to lose all of their value—as did the billion dollars' worth of American & Foreign Power warrants.* Some of the poet's remarks apply equally

---

* The "notorious French assignats" were issued during the Revolution of 1789. They were originally debts of the Revolutionary government, purportedly secured by the value of the real estate that the radicals had seized from the Catholic church and the nobility. But the Revolutionaries were bad financial managers. In 1790, the interest rate on assignats was cut; soon they stopped paying interest entirely and were reclassified as paper money. But the government refused to redeem them for gold or silver

TABLE 16-4 Calculation of "True Market Price" and Adjusted Price/Earnings Ratio of a Common Stock with Large Amounts of Warrants Outstanding

(Example: National General Corp. in June 1971)

1. Calculation of "True Market Price."

Market value of 3 issues of warrants, June 30, 1971	$94,000,000
Value of warrants per share of common stock	$18.80
Price of common stock alone	24.50
Corrected price of common, adjusted for warrants	43.30

2. Calculation of P/E Ratio to Allow for Warrant Dilution

	Before Warrant Dilution	After Warrant Dilution Company's Calculation	After Warrant Dilution Our Calculation
(1970 earnings) A. Before Special Items.			
Earned per share	$ 2.33	$ 1.60	$ 2.33
Price of common	24.50	24.50	43.30 (adj.)
P/E ratio	10.5×	15.3×	18.5×
B. After Special Items.			
Earned per share	$ .90	$ 1.33	$ .90
Price of common	24.50	24.50	43.30 (adj.)
P/E ratio	27.2×	18.4×	48.1×

Note that, after special charges, the effect of the company's calculation is to increase the earnings per share and reduce the P/E ratio. This is manifestly absurd. By our suggested method the effect of the dilution is to increase the P/E ratio substantially, as it should be.

well to one invention or another—such as the following (in Bayard Taylor's translation):

> FAUST: Imagination in its highest flight
>   Exerts itself but cannot grasp it quite.

---

and issued massive amounts of new assignats. They were officially declared worthless in 1797.

MEPHISTOPHELES (the inventor): If one needs coin the brokers ready stand.
THE FOOL (finally): The magic paper . . . !

Practical Postscript

The crime of the warrants is in "having been born."* Once born they function as other security forms, and offer chances of profit as well as of loss. Nearly all the newer warrants run for a limited time—generally between five and ten years. The older warrants were often perpetual, and they were likely to have fascinating price histories over the years.

EXAMPLE: The record books will show that Tri-Continental Corp. warrants, which date from 1929, sold at a negligible 1/32 of a dollar each in the depth of the depression. From that lowly estate their price rose to a magnificent 75¾ in 1969, an astronomical advance of some 242,000%. (The warrants then sold considerably higher than the shares themselves; this is the kind of thing that occurs on Wall Street through technical developments, such as stock splits.) A recent example is supplied by Ling-Temco-Vought warrants, which in the first half of 1971 advanced from 2½ to 12½—and then fell back to 4.

No doubt shrewd operations can be carried on in warrants from time to time, but this is too technical a matter for discussion here. We might say that warrants tend to sell relatively higher than the corresponding market components related to the conversion privilege of bonds or preferred stocks. To that extent there is a valid argument for selling bonds with warrants attached rather than creating an equivalent dilution factor by a convertible issue. If the warrant total is relatively small there is no point in taking its theoretical aspect too seriously; if the warrant issue is large relative to the outstanding stock, that would probably indicate that the

---

* Graham, an enthusiastic reader of Spanish literature, is paraphrasing a line from the play *Life Is a Dream* by Pedro Calderon de la Barca (1600–1681): "The greatest crime of man is having been born."

company has a top-heavy senior capitalization. It should be selling additional common stock instead. Thus the main objective of our attack on warrants as a financial mechanism is not to condemn their use in connection with moderate-size bond issues, but to argue against the wanton creation of huge "paper-money" monstrosities of this genre.

Commentary on Chapter 16
by Jason Zweig

> I put two children through Harvard by trading options.
> Unfortunately, they were my broker's children.
> —old Wall Street joke[1]

Today, most convertible bonds in the U.S. trade privately: Only institutional investors are permitted to buy them when first issued, and only the wealthiest individuals might be able to buy them later. Even then, most brokers are reluctant to offer convertibles to individual investors for fear of regulatory and legal liability. (Mutual funds and ETFs specializing in convertibles are widely available, however.)[2]

For all the criticism about convertible securities and warrants that Graham includes in Chapter 16, it never would have occurred to him to warn investors to be cautious about stock options—which weren't even traded in standardized form on a national exchange until 1973. Today, millions of people trade them. Many barely understand options; some use them wisely; others abuse them recklessly.

Why You Pay the Premium

An option—from the Latin *optio*, "choice"—gives you the right to buy or sell an asset, usually a stock or market index, at a specified price on a fixed date. An option to buy is known as a call; an option to sell is a put.

---
[1] As told by Michael LeBoeuf, 2001.
[2] Tracy V. Maitland et al., *Convertible Securities* (McGraw Hill, 2022) is a comprehensive handbook for anyone interested in learning more about convertible bonds.

(A convertible bond is a kind of corporate debt featuring a call option on the company's common stock.)

Options are a form of insurance; that's one reason the price you pay for them is called a "premium." You can insure against the risk of losses, the risk of missing out on gains, or the risk of specific upward or downward fluctuations within a predetermined price range.

Options reshape risks and returns. Buy call options on a hot stock, and you will make much more, percentage-wise, than you would on the stock itself if it goes up a lot in a hurry—but the value of your options can go to zero if the stock goes down, doesn't go up enough, or doesn't go up soon enough. Sell call options on a stock you already own, and you reduce the risk of loss from a fall in its price—but, if the stock ends up rising sharply instead, you'll miss out on most of its future gains. Likewise, put options, and combinations of puts and calls, reshape the risk and reward of an underlying stock or other asset.

Because they expire and their price depends on the fluctuations of another asset, options are seldom a "set-it-and-forget-it" investment. Options trading is for enterprising investors only.

"You have to be involved in really deep risk analysis to use options successfully as an alternative to owning a stock or for targeting income or for reshaping returns," says Joanne Hill, chief adviser of research at Vest Financial, an investment-advisory firm in McLean, Virginia. "It's rare to find individuals who have the time and expertise to devote to an options strategy or an options speculation on their own."

It's common to find people who *think* they do, though.

Why Your Brokerage App Keeps Nagging You to Trade Options

You can trade options directly or buy funds that use them to manage risk or generate income. The first thing to understand about trading options directly is that Wall Street has a gigantic incentive to get you to do it.

Not long ago, brokers could earn 5% or more when you bought a mutual fund and 1% or more when you bought (or sold) a stock. After fierce competition from index funds, ETFs, and lightning-fast technology, those high commissions have withered away.

On options, however, brokerage firms still make a killing. Market makers, the firms that facilitate trades, pay brokers much bigger kickbacks for the right to handle orders on options than on stocks. And, unlike stocks, options expire—usually in a few months at most. That means you have to trade repeatedly to maintain the same position, generating more money for your broker every time.

As Figure 16.1 shows, in the first six months of 2023, Robinhood took in $260 million in revenue on its customers' trades in options. That was five times more than on stock transactions, even though customers traded stocks two and a half times more often.

No wonder brokerage firms are constantly badgering customers to try trading options. It's *their* best option for making a lot of money off you.

Gambling Without Knowing the Rules

Fortunately for the brokerage industry, many people don't know much about options trading—and don't even know they don't.

A survey of more than 2,800 U.S. investors in late 2021 found that almost one in seven had traded options. Among them, 62% incorrectly answered what should have been an embarrassingly easy question:

The option described here gives you the right to pay $50 for a stock

FIGURE 16-1: Where the Fees Are

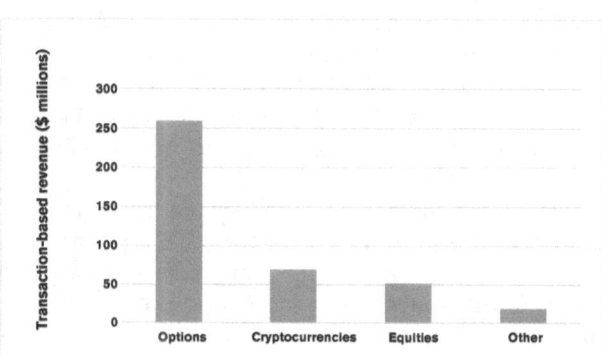

Source: Robinhood.
Note: Data for first half of 2023.

FIGURE 16-2: Failure Is an Option

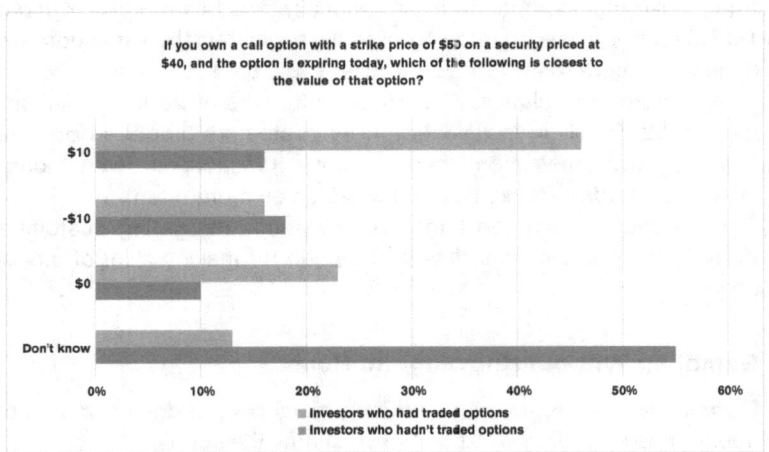

Source: FINRA Foundation.

that's trading at $40. Because it makes no sense to pay $50 today for something you can get for $40, no one will buy this option from you, so it will expire worthless. Its value is $0.

Yet nearly half of all the survey respondents who had traded options thought this one is worth $10. They were three times more likely to pick that wrong answer than people who had never traded options. They were also much less likely to admit they didn't know.

Trading options when you can't answer a question this easy is like expecting to win at poker if you think "four of a kind" means any hand with a 4 card in it. You aren't just gambling. You're gambling without even knowing the rules.

These risky behaviors have been exacerbated by the surging popularity of zero-days-to-expiration or "0DTE" options, which expire the same day you trade, giving them maximum volatility. Betting your money on whether a stock or index will go up or down by the end of the day is as close to unadulterated risk as you can get in the financial markets. If you turn out to be right, you'll make many times your money by the end of the same day. If you're wrong, you can lose all your money just as fast. It's thrilling—if you happen to win—but you might as well be betting on where the next raindrop will land on a windshield.

Fast Trades, Fast Losses

"The market, like the Lord, helps those who help themselves," Warren Buffett has written. "But, unlike the Lord, the market does not forgive those who know not what they do."

A study of more than 26,000 individuals who traded options at a Dutch online brokerage found that, after accounting for the costs of trading, their returns were worse than those of customers at the same firm who only traded stocks—by 2.75 percentage points *per month*.

Researchers recently estimated that individuals lost a total of $2.1 billion trading options in the U.S. between November 2019 and June 2021. Along the way, they incurred $7.3 billion in brokerage costs—a massively wasteful transfer of wealth from Main Street to Wall Street.

Between 2010 and 2021, retail traders placing option bets around companies' earnings announcements lost an average of 5% to 9%, or approximately $3 billion, a recent study found.[3]

None of this means trading options never makes sense. It does mean you should trade them only when they can accomplish specific goals that other assets can't. Options are taxed differently, carry steeper brokerage costs, and require more vigilant monitoring than other investments, so they need to clear a higher hurdle.

Uncovering Covered Calls

Conservative options strategies, when combined with a stock you own, can reduce risk, generate income, or both. When you sell call options on a stock you already own, you transform its uncertain returns in the future into certain income in the present. The premiums you earn upfront help cushion against any short-term decline in price. In exchange,

---

[3] Rob Bauer et al., "Option Trading and Individual Investor Performance," bit.ly/3ZITgdp; Svetlana Bryzgalova et al., "Retail Trading in Options and the Rise of the Big Three Wholesalers," bit.ly/46yemh2; Tim de Silva et al., "Losing Is Optional," bit.ly/3FqiPX7.

you give up the right to participate in the stock's future gains beyond a certain level.

Selling, or "writing," covered calls will work best on a stock or index that generates a moderate return. If the shares fall sharply, the income from selling the call options won't make up for all the loss. If the shares end up rising steeply, the buyer of the call could take the stock away from you cheaply at the strike price; you then will miss out on the potential for any future gains unless you buy the options back at a loss. Since the main reason most investors own stocks is to capture future growth, missing out on it is a major drawback.

If the stock fluctuates in a narrow band, though, selling covered calls will generate consistent income while reducing the risk of holding the stock alone. You can choose a strike price consistent with your target price for the stock; the higher the strike price at which the stock is covered, the lower your upfront premium income, but the greater your potential for gain.

After stocks and bonds alike took a beating in 2022, covered-call funds took off. JPMorgan Equity Premium Income ETF gathered a staggering $26 billion in new money from investors from the beginning of 2022 through the end of 2023; its sibling, JPMorgan Nasdaq Equity Premium Income ETF, took in $8 billion.

Such funds, and covered-call writing in general, have usually delivered as promised: You get much of the gains from stocks, with less of the losses and more income along the way. So-called "buffered" funds, using other options strategies, combine exposure to a stock index with put and call options, sacrificing the potential for big gains in exchange for reducing the risk of big declines. They also eliminate the need for investors to trade the options themselves.

However, other ways of reducing the risk of stocks are cheaper and simpler.

Interest rates have jumped since 2021, enabling you to earn 5% or more on money-market mutual funds, short-term U.S. Treasury bills, and certificates of deposit. That means a 20% allocation to cash adds one percentage point to the return of an all-stock portfolio. No method of generating income is safer or simpler than holding more cash alongside your stocks.

Alternatively, you could extract more income from your stock portfolio by selling a small portion every month. In the U.S., the proceeds would be taxable at the maximum capital-gains rate of about 20% (or, if you sell some positions at a loss, would even reduce your tax bill). Income from selling covered calls is typically taxed at a much higher rate.

When to Opt for Options

Here are some hypothetical scenarios in which options can make good sense.

- You want to set aside roughly $100,000 to $160,000 to make a down payment on a house 15 months in the future. You own 200 shares of Eli Lilly and Co. At one point in late 2023, the stock traded at about $600 per share—worth a total of slightly more than $120,000. You could sell calls on 200 shares, exercisable 15 months in the future at a strike price of $800, for $7,000. At the same time, you could buy puts on 200 shares, exercisable at the same time at a strike price of $500, for $7,000. You won't be able to sell for more than $800 a share, but you've ensured—at no net cost to you—that you won't have to sell for less than $500. You've locked in a final pre-tax value of between $100,000 and $160,000 no matter what the stock does.
- Your aunt has just died; in her will, she left you shares in an S&P 500 index fund worth $100,000. You will receive the shares in six months and would like to donate them to your favorite charity. To ensure that the amount of your gift totals no less than $100,000, you can buy puts on the S&P 500. You'll pay an option premium of a few thousand dollars, which you'll lose if the market goes up. In exchange, you have the certainty of knowing that the value of your donation six months from now can't fall below $100,000.
- If you want to speculate in your mad-money account (see the Commentary on Chapter 1), buying a call option on a stock you want to own could be worthwhile. Because the premium for options on 100 shares costs much less than buying the 100 shares outright, you could earn a greater percentage gain while committing less capital. However, this strategy incurs high brokerage costs and requires frequent trading and keen monitoring. You risk losing 100% of your option premium if the stock goes down instead of up—or if it doesn't go up *enough*. Even worse, you risk losing your identity as an investor if the adrenaline rush of options trading turns you into a speculator.

CHAPTER 17

Four Extremely Instructive Case Histories
by Benjamin Graham

The word "extremely" in the title is a kind of pun, because the histories represent extremes of various sorts that were manifest on Wall Street in recent years. They hold instruction, and grave warnings, for everyone who has a serious connection with the world of stocks and bonds—not only for ordinary investors and speculators but for professionals, security analysts, fund managers, trust-account administrators, and even for bankers who lend money to corporations. The four companies to be reviewed, and the different extremes that they illustrate, are:

Penn Central (Railroad) Co. An extreme example of the neglect of the most elementary warning signals of financial weakness, by all those who had bonds or shares of this system under their supervision. A crazily high market price for the stock of a tottering giant.

Ling-Temco-Vought Inc. An extreme example of quick and unsound "empire building," with ultimate collapse practically guaranteed; but helped by indiscriminate bank lending.

NVF Corp. An extreme example of one corporate acquisition, in which a small company absorbed another seven times its size, incurring a huge debt and employing some startling accounting devices.

AAA Enterprises. An extreme example of public stock-financing of a small company; its value based on the magic word "franchising," and little else, sponsored by important stock-exchange houses. Bankruptcy followed within two years of the stock sale and the doubling of the initial inflated price in the heedless stock market.

The Penn Central Case

This is the country's largest railroad in assets and gross revenues. Its bankruptcy in 1970 shocked the financial world. It has defaulted on most of its bond issues, and has been in danger of abandoning its operations entirely. Its security issues fell drastically in price, the common stock collapsing from a high level of 86½ as recently as 1968 to a low of 5½ in 1970. (There seems little doubt that these shares will be wiped out in reorganization.)*

Our basic point is that the application of the simplest rules of security analysis and the simplest standards of sound investment would have revealed the fundamental weakness of the Penn Central system long before its bankruptcy—certainly in 1968, when the shares were selling at their post-1929 record, and when most of its bond issues could have been exchanged at even prices for well-secured public-utility obligations with the same coupon rates. The following comments are in order:

1. In the S & P *Bond Guide* the interest charges of the system are shown to have been earned 1.91 times in 1967 and 1.98 times in 1968. The minimum coverage prescribed for railroad bonds in our textbook *Security Analysis* is 5 times before income taxes and 2.9 times after income taxes at regular rates. As far as we know the validity of these standards has never been questioned by any investment authority. On the basis of our requirements for earnings *after taxes*, the Penn Central fell short of the requirements for safety. But our after-tax requirement is based on a before-tax ratio of *five* times, with regular income tax deducted after the bond interest. In the case of Penn Central, it had been paying *no income taxes to speak of* for the past 11 years! Hence the coverage of its interest charges before taxes was less than two times—a totally inadequate figure against our conservative requirement of 5 times.

---

* How "shocked" was the financial world by the Penn Central's bankruptcy, which was filed over the weekend of June 20–21, 1970? The closing trade in Penn Central's stock on Friday, June 19, was $11.25 per share—hardly a going-out-of-business price. In more recent times, stocks like Enron, WorldCom, and Bed Bath & Beyond have also sold at relatively high prices shortly before filing for bankruptcy protection.

2. The fact that the company paid no income taxes over so long a period should have raised serious questions about the *validity* of its reported earnings.

3. The bonds of the Penn Central system could have been exchanged in 1968 and 1969, at no sacrifice of price or income, for far better secured issues. For example, in 1969, Pennsylvania RR 4½s, due 1994 (part of Penn Central) had a range of 61 to 74½, while Pennsylvania Electric Co. 4⅜s, due 1994, had a range of 64¼ to 72¼. The public utility had earned its interest 4.20 times before taxes in 1968 against only 1.98 times for the Penn Central system; during 1969 the latter's comparative showing grew steadily worse. An exchange of this sort was clearly called for, and it would have been a lifesaver for a Penn Central bondholder. (At the end of 1970 the railroad 4¼s were in default, and selling at only 18½, while the utility's 4⅜s closed at 66½.)

4. Penn Central reported earnings of $3.80 per share in 1968; its high price of 86½ in that year was 24 times such earnings. But any analyst worth his salt would have wondered how "real" were earnings of this sort reported without the necessity of paying any income taxes thereon.

5. For 1966 the newly merged company* had reported "earnings" of $6.80 a share—in reflection of which the common stock later rose to its peak of 86½. This was a valuation of over $2 billion for the equity. How many of these buyers knew at the time that the so lovely earnings were *before* a special charge of $275 million or $12 per share to be taken in 1971 for "costs and losses" incurred on the merger? O wondrous fairyland of Wall Street where a company can announce "profits" of $6.80 per share in one place and special "costs and losses" of $12 in another, and shareholders and speculators rub their hands with glee!†

6. A railroad analyst would have long since known that the

---

* Penn Central was the product of the merger, announced in 1966, of the Pennsylvania Railroad and the New York Central Railroad.

† This kind of accounting legerdemain, in which profits are reported as if "unusual" or "extraordinary" or "nonrecurring" charges do not matter, anticipates the recent reliance on non-GAAP financial statements (see the Commentary on Chapter 12).

operating picture of the Penn Central was very bad in comparison with the more profitable roads. For example, its transportation ratio was 47.5% in 1968 against 35.2% for its neighbor, Norfolk & Western.*

7. Along the way there were some strange transactions with peculiar accounting results.[1] Details are too complicated to go into here.

CONCLUSION: Whether better management could have saved the Penn Central bankruptcy may be arguable. But there is no doubt whatever that no bonds and no shares of the Penn Central system should have remained after 1968 at the latest in any securities account watched over by competent security analysts, fund managers, trust officers, or investment counsel. *Moral:* **Security analysts should do their elementary jobs before they study stock-market movements, gaze into crystal balls, make elaborate mathematical calculations, or go on all-expense-paid field trips.**†

Ling-Temco-Vought Inc.

This is a story of head-over-heels expansion and head-over-heels debt, ending up in terrific losses and a host of financial problems. **As usually happens in such cases, a fair-haired boy, or "young genius," was chiefly responsible for both the creation of the great empire and its ignominious downfall; but there is plenty of blame to be accorded others as well.**‡

---

* A railroad's "transportation ratio" (now more commonly called its operating ratio) measures the expenses of running its trains divided by the railroad's total revenues. The higher the ratio, the less efficient the railroad. Today even a ratio of 60% would be considered excellent.

† Today, Penn Central is a faded memory. In 1976, it was absorbed into Consolidated Rail Corp. (Conrail), a federally-funded holding company that bailed out several failed railroads. Conrail sold shares to the public in 1987 and, in 1997, was taken over jointly by CSX Corp. and Norfolk Southern Corp.

‡ Ling-Temco-Vought Inc. was founded in 1955 by James Joseph Ling, an electrical contractor who sold his first $1 million worth of shares to the public by becoming his own investment banker, hawking prospectuses from a booth set up at the Texas State Fair. His success at that led him to

The rise and fall of Ling-Temco-Vought can be summarized by setting forth condensed income accounts and balance-sheet items for five years between 1958 and 1970. This is done in Table 17-1. The first column shows the company's modest beginnings in 1958, when its sales were only $7 million. The next gives figures for 1960; the enterprise had grown twentyfold in only two years, but it was still comparatively small. Then came the heyday years to 1967 and 1968, in which sales again grew twentyfold to $2.8 billion with the debt figure expanding from $44 million to an awesome $1,653 million. In 1969 came new acquisitions, a further huge increase in debt (to a total of $1,865 million!), and the beginning of serious trouble. A large loss, after extraordinary items, was reported for the year; the stock price declined from its 1967 high of 169½ to a low of 24; the young genius was superseded as the head of the company. The 1970 results were even more dreadful. The enterprise reported a final net loss of close to $70 million; the stock fell away to a low price of 7⅛, and its largest bond issue was quoted at one time at a pitiable 15 cents on the dollar. The company's expansion policy was sharply reversed, various of its important interests were placed on the market, and some headway was made in reducing its mountainous obligations.

The figures in our table speak so eloquently that few comments are called for. But here are some:

1. The company's expansion period was not without an interruption. In 1961 it showed a small operating deficit, but—

---

acquire dozens of different companies, almost always using LTV's stock to pay for them. The more companies LTV acquired, the higher its stock went; the higher its stock went, the more companies it could afford to acquire. By 1969, LTV was the 14th biggest firm on the *Fortune* 500 list of major U.S. corporations. And then, as Graham shows, the whole house of cards came crashing down. (LTV Corp., then exclusively a steelmaker, ended up seeking bankruptcy protection in late 2000.) Companies that grow primarily through acquisitions are called "serial acquirers"—and the similarity to the term "serial killers" is no accident. As the case of LTV demonstrates, serial acquirers nearly always leave financial death and destruction in their wake. Investors who understood this lesson of Graham's would have avoided such later fiascos as Conseco, Tyco, WorldCom, and Valeant.

TABLE 17-1 Ling-Temco-Vought Inc., 1958–1970
(In Millions of Dollars Except Earned Per Share)

	1958	1960	1967	1969	1970
A. Operating Results					
Sales	$ 6.9	$143.0	$1,833.0	$3,750.0	$374.0
Net before taxes and interest	0.552	7.287	95.6	124.4	88.0
Interest charges	.1 (est.)	1.5 (est.)	17.7	122.6	128.3
(Times earned)	(5.5 ×)	(4.8 ×)	(54 ×)	(1.02 ×)	(0.68 ×)
Income taxes	0.225	2.686	35.6	cr. 15.2	4.9
Special items				dr. 40.6	dr. 18.8
Net after special items	0.227	3.051	34.0	dr. 38.3	dr. 69.6
Balance for common stock	0.202	3.051	30.7	dr. 40.8	dr. 71.3
Earned per share of common	0.17	0.83	5.56	def. 10.59	def. 17.18
B. Financial Position					
Total assets	6.4	94.5	845.0	2,944.0	2,582.0
Debt payable within 1 year	1.5	29.3	165.0	389.3	301.3
Long-term debt	.5	14.6	202.6	1,500.8	1,394.6
Shareholders' equity	2.7	28.5	245.0†	def. 12.0*	def. 69.0*
Ratios					
Current assets/current liabilities	1.27 ×	1.45 ×	1.80 ×	1.52 ×	1.45 ×
Equity/long-term debt	5.4 ×	2.0 ×	1.2 ×	0.17 ×	0.13 ×
Market-price range		28–20	169½–109	97¾–24⅜	29½–7⅞

* Excluding debt-discount as an asset and deducting preferred stock at redemption value.
† As published. *cr.*: credit. *dr.*: debit. *def.*: deficit.

adopting a practice that was to be seen later in so many reports for 1970—evidently decided to throw all possible charges and reserves into the one bad year.* These amounted to a round $13 million, which was more than the combined net profits of the preceding three years. It was now ready to show "record earnings" in 1962, etc.

2. At the end of 1966 the net tangible assets are given as $7.66 per share of common (adjusted for a 3-for-2 split). Thus the market price in 1967 reached 22 times (!) its reported asset value at the time. At the end of 1968 the balance sheet showed $286 million available for 3,800,000 shares of common and Class AA stock, or about $77 per share. But if we deduct the preferred stock at full value and exclude the good-will items and the huge bond-discount "asset,"† there would remain $13 million for the common—a mere $3 per share. This tangible equity was wiped out by the losses of the following years.

3. Toward the end of 1967 two of our best-regarded banking firms offered 600,000 shares of Ling-Temco-Vought stock at $111 per share. It had been as high as 169½. In less than three years the price fell to 7⅛.

4. At the end of 1967 the bank loans had reached $161 million, and a year later they stood at $414 million—which should have been a frightening figure. In addition, the long-term debt amounted to $1,237 million. By 1969 combined debt reached a total of $1,869

---

* The sordid tradition of hiding a company's true earnings picture under the cloak of restructuring charges is still with us. Piling up every possible charge in one year is sometimes called "big bath" or "kitchen sink" accounting. This bookkeeping gimmick enables companies to make an easy show of apparent growth in the following year—but investors should not mistake that for real business health.

† The "bond-discount asset" appears to mean that LTV had purchased some bonds below their par value and was treating that discount as an asset, on the grounds that the bonds could eventually be sold at par. Graham scoffs at this, since there is rarely any way to know what a bond's market price will be on a given date in the future. If the bonds could be sold only at values *below* par, this "asset" could in fact be a liability.

million. This may have been the largest combined debt figure of any industrial company anywhere and at any time, with the single exception of the impregnable Standard Oil of N.J.

5. The losses in 1969 and 1970 far exceeded the total profits since the formation of the company.

MORAL: The primary question raised in our mind by the Ling-Temco-Vought story is how the commercial bankers could have been persuaded to lend the company such huge amounts of money during its expansion period. In 1966 and earlier the company's coverage of interest charges did not meet conservative standards, and the same was true of the ratio of current assets to current liabilities and of stock equity to total debt. But in the next two years the banks advanced the enterprise nearly $400 million additional for further "diversification." This was not good business for them, and it was worse in its implications for the company's shareholders. If the Ling-Temco-Vought case will serve to keep commercial banks from aiding and abetting unsound expansions of this type in the future, some good may come of it at last.*

The NVF Takeover of Sharon Steel (A Collector's Item)

At the end of 1968 NVF Company was a company with $4.6 million of long-term debt, $17.4 million of stock capital, $31 million of sales, and $502,000 of net income (before a special credit of $374,000). Its business was described as "vulcanized fiber and plastics." The management decided to take over the Sharon Steel Corp., which had $43 million of long-term debt, $101 million of stock capital, $219 million of sales, and $2,929,000 of net earnings. The company it wished to acquire was thus seven times the size of NVF. In early 1969 it made an offer for all the shares of Sharon. The

---

* Graham would have been disappointed, though surely not surprised, to see that commercial banks have chronically kept supporting "unsound expansions." Enron, WorldCom, and Silicon Valley Bank, three of the biggest collapses in corporate history, were aided and abetted by billions of dollars in bank loans.

terms per share were $70 face amount of NVF junior 5% bonds, due 1994, plus warrants to buy 1½ shares of NVF stock at $22 per share of NVF. The management of Sharon strenuously resisted this takeover attempt, but in vain. NVF acquired 88% of the Sharon stock under the offer, issuing therefore $102 million of its 5% bonds and warrants for 2,197,000 of its shares. Had the offer been 100% operative the consolidated enterprise would, for the year 1968, have had $163 million in debt, only $2.2 million in tangible stock capital, $250 million of sales. The net-earnings question would have been a bit complicated, but the company subsequently stated them as a net loss of 50 cents per share of NVF stocks, before an extraordinary credit, and net earnings of 3 cents per share after such credit.*

FIRST COMMENT: Among all the takeovers effected in the year 1969 this was no doubt the most extreme in its financial disproportions. The acquiring company had assumed responsibility for a new and top-heavy debt obligation, and it had changed its calculated 1968 earnings from a profit to a loss into the bargain. A measure of the impairment of the company's financial position by this step is found in the fact that the new 5% bonds did not sell higher than 42 cents on the dollar during the year of issuance. This would have indicated grave doubt of the safety of the bonds and of the company's future; however, the management actually exploited the bond price in a way to save the company annual income taxes of about $1,000,000 as will be shown.

The 1968 report, published after the Sharon takeover, contained a condensed picture of its results, carried back to the year-end. This contained two most unusual items:

1. There is listed as an asset $58,600,000 of "deferred debt expense." This sum is greater than the entire "stockholders' equity," placed at $40,200,000.

---

* In June 1972 (just after Graham finished this chapter), a Federal judge found that NVF's chairman, Victor Posner, had improperly diverted the pension assets of Sharon Steel "to assist affiliated companies in their takeovers of other corporations." Sharon Steel, which Graham had singled out with his cold and skeptical eye, became known among Wall Street wags as "Share and Steal."

2. However, not included in the shareholders' equity is an item of $20,700,000 designated as "excess of equity over cost of investment in Sharon."

SECOND COMMENT: If we eliminate the debt expense as an asset, which it hardly seems to be, and include the other item in the shareholders' equity (where it would normally belong), then we have a more realistic statement of tangible equity for NVF stock, viz., $2,200,000. Thus the first effect of the deal was to reduce NVF's "real equity" from $17,400,000 to $2,200,000 or from $23.71 per share to about $3 per share, on 731,000 shares. In addition the NVF shareholders had given to others the right to buy 3½ times as many additional shares at six points below the market price at the close of 1968. The initial market value of the warrants was then about $12 each, or a total of some $30 million for those involved in the purchase offer. Actually, the market value of the warrants well exceeded the total market value of the outstanding NVF stock—another evidence of the tail-wagging-the-dog nature of the transaction.

The Accounting Gimmicks

When we pass from this pro forma balance sheet to the next year's report we find several strange-appearing entries. In addition to the basic interest expense (a hefty $7,500,000), there is deducted $1,795,000 for "amortization of deferred debt expense." But this last is nearly offset on the next line by a very unusual income item indeed: "amortization of equity over cost of investment in subsidiary: Cr. $1,650,000." In one of the footnotes we find an entry, not appearing in any other report that we know of: Part of the stock capital is there designated as "fair market value of warrants issued in connection with acquisition, etc., $22,129,000."

What on earth do all these entries mean? None of them is even referred to in the descriptive text of the 1969 report. The trained security analyst has to figure out these mysteries by himself, almost in detective fashion. He finds that the underlying idea is to derive a tax advantage from the low initial price of the 5% debentures. For readers who may be interested in this ingenious arrangement we set forth our solution in Appendix 6 (see p. 576 of the 2003 edition).

Other Unusual Items

1. Right after the close of 1969 the company bought in no less than 650,000 warrants at a price of $9.38 each. This was extraordinary when we consider that (*a*) NVF itself had only $700,000 in cash at the year-end, and had $4,400,000 of debt due in 1970 (evidently the $6 million paid for the warrants had to be borrowed); (*b*) it was buying in this warrant "paper money" at a time when its 5% bonds were selling at less than 40 cents on the dollar—ordinarily a warning that financial difficulties lay ahead.

2. As a partial offset to this, the company had retired $5,100,000 of its bonds along with 253,000 warrants in exchange for a like amount of common stock. This was possible because, by the vagaries of the securities markets, people were selling the 5% bonds at less than 40 while the common sold at an average price of 13½, paying no dividend.

3. The company had plans in operation not only for selling stock to its employees, but also for selling them a larger number of *warrants* to buy the stock. Like the stock purchases the warrants were to be paid for 5% down and the rest over many years in the future. This is the only such employee-purchase plan for *warrants* that we know of. Will someone soon invent and sell on installments a right to buy a right to buy a share, and so on?

4. In the year 1969 the newly controlled Sharon Steel Co. changed its method of arriving at its pension costs, and also adopted lower depreciation rates. These accounting changes added about $1 per share to the reported earnings of NVF before dilution.

5. At the end of 1970 Standard & Poor's *Stock Guide* reported that NVF shares were selling at a price/earnings ratio of only 2, the lowest figure for all the 4,500-odd issues in the booklet. As the old Wall Street saying went, this was "important if true." The ratio was based on the year's closing price of 8¾ and the computed "earnings" of $5.38 per share for the 12 months ended September 1970. (Using

these figures the shares were selling at only 1.6 times earnings.) But this ratio did not allow for the large dilution factor,* nor for the adverse results actually realized in the last quarter of 1970. When the full year's figures finally appeared, they showed only $2.03 per share earned for the stock, before allowing for dilution, and $1.80 per share on a diluted basis. Note also that the aggregate market price of the stock and warrants on that date was about $14 million against a bonded debt of $135 million—a skimpy equity position indeed.

AAA Enterprises

History

About 15 years ago a college student named Williams began selling mobile homes (then called "trailers").† In 1965 he incorporated his business. In that year he sold $5,800,000 of mobile homes and earned $61,000 before corporate tax. By 1968 he had joined the "franchising" movement and was selling others the right to sell mobile homes under his business name. He also conceived the bright idea of going into the business of preparing income-tax returns, using his mobile homes as offices. He formed a subsidiary company called Mr. Tax of America, and of course

---

* The "large dilution factor" would be triggered when NVF employees exercised their warrants to buy common stock. The company would then have to issue more shares, and its net earnings would be divided across a much greater number of shares outstanding.

† Jackie G. Williams founded AAA Enterprises in 1958. On its first day of trading, the stock soared 56% to close at $20.25. Williams later announced that AAA would come up with a new franchising concept every month (if people would step into a mobile home to get their income taxes done by "Mr. Tax of America," just imagine what else they might do inside a trailer!). But AAA ran out of time and money before Williams ran out of ideas. The history of AAA Enterprises is reminiscent of the saga of a later company with charismatic management and scanty assets: ZZZZ Best achieved a stock-market value of roughly $200 million in the late 1980s, even though its purported industrial vacuum-cleaning business was little more than a

started to sell franchises to others to use the idea and the name. He multiplied the number of corporate shares to 2,710,000 and was ready for a stock offering. He found that one of our largest stock-exchange houses, along with others, was willing to handle the deal. In March 1969 they offered the public 500,000 shares of AAA Enterprises at $13 per share. Of these, 300,000 were sold for Mr. Williams's personal account and 200,000 were sold for the company account, adding $2,400,000 to its resources. The price of the stock promptly doubled to 28, or a value of $84 million for the equity, against a book value of, say, $4,200,000 and maximum reported earnings of $690,000. The stock was thus selling at a tidy 115 times its current (and largest) earnings per share. No doubt Mr. Williams had selected the name AAA Enterprises so that it might be among the first in the phone books and the yellow pages. A collateral result was that his company was destined to appear as the first name in Standard & Poor's *Stock Guide*. Like Abou Ben Adhem's, it led all the rest.* This gives a special reason to select it as a harrowing example of 1969 new financing and "hot issues."

COMMENT: This was not a bad deal for Mr. Williams. The 300,000 shares he sold had a book value in December of 1968 of $180,000 and he netted therefor 20 times as much, or a cool $3,600,000. The underwriters and distributors split $500,000 between them, less expenses.

1. This did not seem so brilliant a deal for the clients of the selling houses. They were asked to pay about ten times the book value of the stock, after the bootstrap operation of increasing their equity

---

telephone and a rented office run by a teenager named Barry Minkow. ZZZZ Best went bust and Minkow went to jail. Even as you read this, another similar company is being formed, and a new generation of "investors" will be taken for a ride. No one who has read Graham, however, should climb on board.

* In "Abou Ben Adhem," by the British Romantic poet Leigh Hunt (1784–1859), a righteous Muslim sees an angel writing in a golden book "the names of those who love the Lord." The angel returns the next night to show Abou the book, in which "Ben Adhem's name led all the rest."

per share from 59 cents to $1.35 with their own money.* Before the best year 1968, the company's maximum earnings had been a ridiculous 7 cents per share. There were ambitious plans for the future, of course—but the public was being asked to pay heavily in advance for the hoped-for realization of these plans.

2. Nonetheless, the price of the stock doubled soon after original issuance, and any one of the brokerage-house clients could have gotten out at a handsome profit. Did this fact alter the flotation, or did the advance possibility that it might happen exonerate the original distributors of the issue from responsibility for this public offering and its later sequel? Not an easy question to answer, but it deserves careful consideration by Wall Street and the government regulatory agencies.[†]

Subsequent History

With its enlarged capital AAA Enterprises went into two additional businesses. In 1969 it opened a chain of retail carpet stores, and it acquired a plant that manufactured mobile homes. The results reported for the first nine months were not exactly brilliant, but they were a little better than the year before—22 cents a share against 14 cents. What happened in the next months was literally incredible. The company lost $4,365,000, or $1.49 per share. This consumed all its capital before the financing, plus the entire $2,400,000 received on the sale of stock plus two-thirds of the amount reported as earned in the first nine months of 1969. There was left a pathetic $242,000, or 8 cents per share, of capital for the

---

* By purchasing more common stock at a premium to its book value, the investing public increased the value of AAA's equity per share. But investors were only pulling themselves up by their own bootstraps, since most of the rise in shareholders' equity came from the public's willingness to overpay for the stock.

† Graham's point is that investment banks are not entitled to take credit for the gains a hot stock may produce right after its initial public offering unless they are also willing to take the blame for the stock's performance in the longer term. Many internet IPOs rose 1,000% or more in 1999 and early 2000; most of them lost more than 95% in the subsequent three years.

public shareholders who had paid $13 for the new offering only seven months before. Nonetheless the shares closed the year 1969 at 8⅛ bid, or a "valuation" of more than $25 million for the company.

FURTHER COMMENT: 1. It is too much to believe that the company had actually earned $686,000 from January to September 1969 and then lost $4,365,000 in the next three months. There was something sadly, badly, and accusingly wrong about the September 30 report.

2. The year's closing price of 8⅛ bid was even more of a demonstration of the complete heedlessness of stock-market prices than were the original offering price of 13 or the subsequent "hot-issue" advance to a high bid of 28. These latter quotations at least were based on enthusiasm and hope—out of all proportion to reality and common sense, but at least comprehensible. The year-end valuation of $25 million was given to a company that had lost all but a minuscule remnant of its capital, for which a completely insolvent condition was imminent, and for which the words "enthusiasm" or "hope" would be only bitter sarcasms. (It is true the year-end figures had not been published by December 31, but it is the business of Wall Street houses associated with a company to have monthly operating statements and a fairly exact idea of how things are going.)

Final Chapter

For the first half of 1970 the company reported a further loss of $1 million. It now had a good-sized capital deficit. It was kept out of bankruptcy by loans made by Mr. Williams, up to a total of $2,500,000. No further statements seem to have been issued, until in January 1971 AAA Enterprises finally filed a petition in bankruptcy. The quotation for the stock at month-end was still 50 cents a share bid, or $1,500,000 for the entire issue, which evidently had no more than wallpaper value. End of our story.

MORAL AND QUESTIONS: **The speculative public is incorrigible. In financial terms it cannot count beyond 3. It will buy anything, at any price, if there seems to be some "action" in progress. It will fall for any company identified with "franchising," computers, electronics, science, technology, or what have you, when the particular fashion is raging.** Our readers, sensible investors all, are of course above such foolishness. But questions remain: Should not responsible investment houses be honor-bound to refrain from identifying themselves with such enterprises, nine out of ten of which may be foredoomed to ultimate failure? (This was actually the situation when the author entered Wall Street in 1914. By comparison it would seem that the ethical standards of the "Street" have fallen rather than advanced in the ensuing 57 years, despite all the reforms and all the controls.) Could and should the SEC be given other powers to protect the public, beyond the present ones which are limited to requiring the printing of all important relevant facts in the offering prospectus? Should some kind of box score for public offerings of various types be compiled and published in conspicuous fashion? Should every prospectus, and perhaps every confirmation of sale under an original offering, carry some kind of formal warranty that the offering price for the issue is not substantially out of line with the ruling prices for issues of the same general type already established in the market? As we write this edition a movement toward reform of Wall Street abuses is under way. **It will be difficult to impose worthwhile changes in the field of new offerings, because the abuses are so largely the result of the public's own heedlessness and greed.** But the matter deserves long and careful consideration.*

---

* Just as the Surgeon General's warning on the side of a cigarette pack does not stop everyone from lighting up, no regulatory reform will ever prevent investors from overdosing on their own greed. (Not even Communism can outlaw market bubbles; the Chinese stock market shot up 101.7% in the first half of 1999, then crashed.) Nor can investment banks ever be entirely cleansed of their own compulsion to sell any stock at any price the market will bear. The circle can only be broken one investor, and one financial adviser, at a time. Mastering Graham's principles (see especially Chapters 1, 8, and 20) is the best way to start.

Commentary on Chapter 17
by Jason Zweig

> An unflinching determination to take the whole evidence into account is the only method of preservation against the fluctuating extremes of fashionable opinion. This advice seems so easy, and is in fact so difficult to follow.
> —Alfred North Whitehead[1]

In Graham's spirit, let's consider four companies that "represent extremes of various sorts that were manifest on Wall Street in recent years." Like Graham's original examples, these also "hold instruction, and grave warnings, for everyone who has a serious connection" with investing.

The four companies, and the extremes they exemplify, are:

Nikola Corp., an overhyped firm in an overhyped industry. As the stock roared higher, speculators ignored the red flags fluttering around the company. Nikola's main product, an electric truck, turned out to be fake; its founder was convicted of fraud.

Peloton Interactive Inc., a home-exercise stock in a short-term boom that traders extrapolated to the moon. In the 2020 pandemic, it felt as if no one would ever leave home or go to a gym again. When life normalized—as it normally does!—Peloton petered out.

Virgin Galactic Holdings Inc., a special-purpose acquisition company promoted by Chamath Palihapitiya, a ubiquitous pied piper for the meme-stock mania. He and other insiders reaped hundreds of millions of dollars. Outsiders lost more than 80% of their money.

---

[1] Alfred North Whitehead, *Science and the Modern World* (Free Press, 1967), p. 187.

Albemarle Corp., an old-time specialty-chemicals producer that got swept up in a new speculation. It became a hot potato tossed around by traders trying to grab any stock that might benefit from surging demand for a trendy technology. Then it went cold.

No Truck with That

Nikola purported to be on the verge of producing electric trucks that could haul freight using hydrogen fuel cells. It went public on June 4, 2020, when millions of people locked down in quarantine from Covid were trading as if their underpants were on fire. The stock shot up 136% in three days. At their peak of $79.73, the market capitalization of Nikola's shares surpassed $30 billion, briefly making the company more valuable than Ford Motor Co. or Fiat Chrysler Automobiles (now Stellantis N.V.), two of the largest carmakers in the world. Yet Nikola had no revenues, was bleeding tens of millions of dollars in losses, and had not sold—or even developed—a single vehicle.

Only three months later, investment firm Hindenburg Research published a devastating online report alleging more than a decade of lies and business failures by Nikola's founder, Trevor Milton. It demonstrated that a video of Nikola's truck driving down a highway at high speed was, in fact, a film of the truck coasting down a hill powered only by gravity. The vehicle couldn't propel itself, and Nikola had very little of its own battery or hydrogen technology, Hindenburg alleged.

Nikola's stock fell 24% in two days, sinking below $35. Soon the U.S. Securities and Exchange Commission and the Department of Justice were investigating. The *Wall Street Journal* reported that Nikola, which claimed to be developing its own batteries, had long been secretly planning to obtain them from an outside supplier.

Even so, Nikola remained among the most popular stocks on Robinhood, where more than 200,000 traders had owned it at one point. Egged on by Milton's aggressive tweets, individual speculators helped prop up the stock price, which remained above $20 for months and even recovered to $34.50 in November 2020.

From 2020 through 2022, Nikola lost $1.5 billion on a mere $51 million in sales.

In October 2022, Trevor Milton was convicted of securities fraud and wire fraud. He was sentenced to four years in federal prison.[1]

By year-end 2023, Nikola's stock had sunk below 90 cents, down 98% from its first day of trading.[2]

Late-Cycle Investing

For its initial public offering in September 2019, Peloton Interactive, Inc., the high-tech bike and exercise company, declared in its prospectus that it could land 45 million U.S. households as "members" or paying customers. That would be one out of every three households in the country.

A few months later, that audacious goal seemed plausible to many speculators. Millions of people who were hooked on exercise were going stir crazy from quarantine during the 2020 pandemic—and they

FIGURE 17-1: Stalled Out

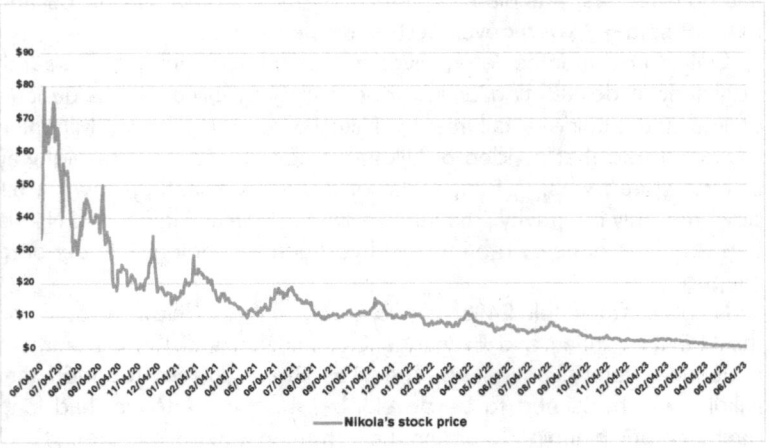

Source: FactSet.

---

[1] Milton, sentenced in December 2023, is appealing his conviction.

[2] The definitive account of Nikola is the six-part *Wall Street Journal* podcast *Bad Bets* by Ben Foldy at on.wsj.com/3VycmT1. See also Hindenburg Research, bit.ly/3Mb091p, and Robintrack, bit.ly/46K2VDm.

were awash in cash from government stimulus checks. Spending $2,495 for an exercise bike you could use in the safety of your own home—and connect to live-streaming video classes—didn't feel like an extravagance.

By July 2020, Peloton had a backlog of orders for more than 100,000 bikes. Its stock-market value hit $38 billion, roughly as large as eBay Inc., the giant online retailer, even though eBay's sales over the previous 12 months were approximately six times greater.

For the full year 2020, Peloton's stock rose 434%.

Peloton and the speculators who rode its stock insisted that even after the pandemic ended, people would still prefer to exercise at home. "When you say 'normalize coming out of Covid,' we don't see that," cofounder John Foley proclaimed during an earnings call in September 2020. But by mid-2021, the economy was reopening, and consumers were getting out—and going back to the gym. Once they were no longer locked down, people no longer wanted to sweat at home alone on a stationary bicycle.

Wall Street has a saying, "The trend is your friend." But it isn't your friend when it comes to an end.

Peloton lost a combined $3.9 billion in 2021 and 2022. By 2023, the company had only 6.5 million members—far below its original target of 45 million.

After its huge gain in 2020, the stock lost 76% in 2021, another 78% in 2022, and 23% in 2023.

Had you invested $10,000 in Peloton at the beginning of 2020, by the end of 2023 you would have had less than $2,150 left.

As of late 2023, used Peloton bikes were offered for sale on eBay for as little as $300.[3]

Unlike a Virgin

Virgin Galactic Holdings, Inc., originally known by the grandiloquent name of Social Capital Hedosophia Holdings Corp., is a space-travel company that launched its initial public offering of stock in October 2019 at an opening price of $12.34 per share.

---

[3] Peloton IPO prospectus, bit.ly/3FrLZFs; Sharon Terlep, "Inside a Year at Peloton: From Pandemic Winner to HBO Punchline," bit.ly/497qCXO.

FIGURE 17-2: Downshifting

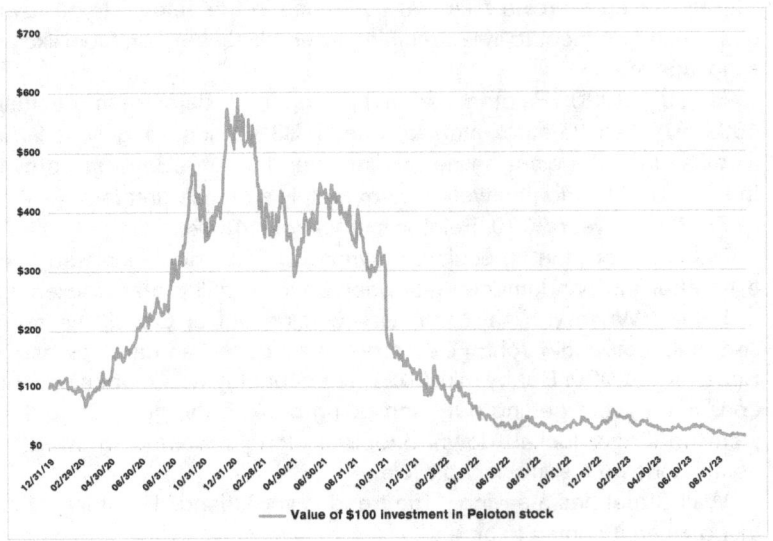

Source: FactSet.

Virgin Galactic's IPO came through a deal with a special purpose acquisition company, led by "SPAC King" Chamath Palihapitiya. The billionaire and former Facebook executive regularly whipped his more than 1 million Twitter followers into a buying frenzy with populist rants, boasts about the potential of his companies, and chest-thumping posts about his own trading.

Riled up by a charismatic "influencer," speculators blindly chased Virgin Galactic's stock and blithely ignored the fundamentals of its underlying business. The stock often traded 10 million shares per day, sometimes more than 50 million.

The shares skyrocketed, more than tripling to $59 by February 2021. That gave the company a total market value of approximately $14 billion.

What did buyers get for that price?

Imagine Mr. Market saying, "Wanna buy my business? It racked up $117 million in expenses in 2020, sold only $238,000 worth of our

products and services, and ended up losing $273 million. It's yours for $14 billion."
Would you take him up on that deal?
With social media at its most toxic, that's exactly what happened.
How did it work out?
After its shares hit the stratosphere in early 2021, Virgin Galactic's business generated $1.25 billion in losses by late 2023. Near its low in October 2023, its stock-market value had sunk to roughly $550 million—down 96% from its peak.

Palihapitiya, who goaded so many individuals into buying Virgin Galactic stock, had long since dumped it. He reaped at least $166 million in profit by selling most of his shares—which he'd bought at bargain prices as an insider—when the stock was near its zenith.[4]

FIGURE 17-3: Space Case

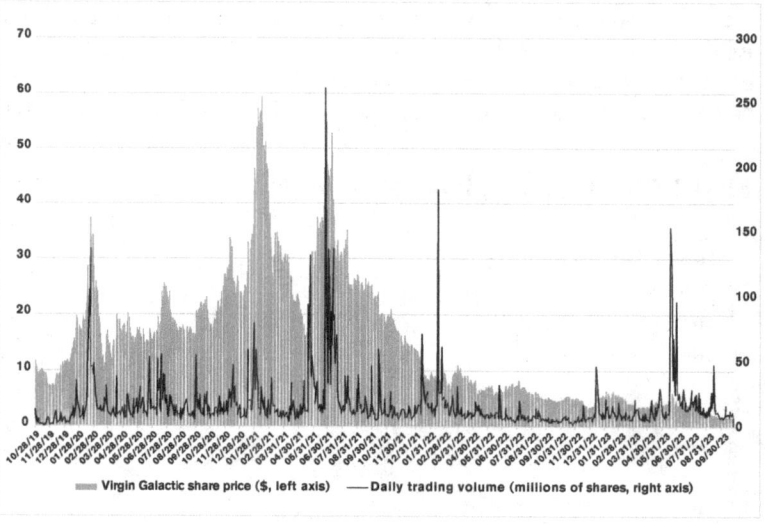

Virgin Galactic share price ($, left axis) ——Daily trading volume (millions of shares, right axis)

Source: FactSet.

---

[4] Peter Rudegeair and Maureen Farrell, "When SPAC-Man Chamath Palihapitiya Speaks, Reddit and Wall Street Listen," bit.ly/3QFwbWh; Tom McGinty et al., "Company Insiders Made Billions Before SPAC Bust," bit.ly/3rXfSdy.

Hot, Then Not

Albemarle Corp.'s history dates back to a paper company founded in 1887. It later morphed into a producer of lithium, bromine, and other chemicals.

Albemarle wasn't a fast grower; its sales were no higher in early 2020 than they had been in 2011. As recently as 2017, lithium accounted for only a third of net sales.

Then the growing market for electric-vehicle batteries sparked demand for lithium, and expectations of future growth exploded. In 2019, Albemarle's sales of lithium grew nearly 11%; in 2020, the stock shot up 102%. In 2021, its lithium sales rose 19%, and the shares jumped another 58%.

By the end of 2021, Albemarle's stock was trading at more than eight times sales and 218 times earnings—far and away the most expensive in the company's history.

As a glut of lithium poured out of mines, the price for the metal crumpled by more than half between October 2022 and late 2023. Albemarle's stock fell 7% in 2022 and a grim 33% in 2023. If you'd bought Albemarle at the beginning of 2019 as the lithium hype was heating up, by the end of 2023 you would have earned slightly less

FIGURE 17-4: To the Moon—and Back

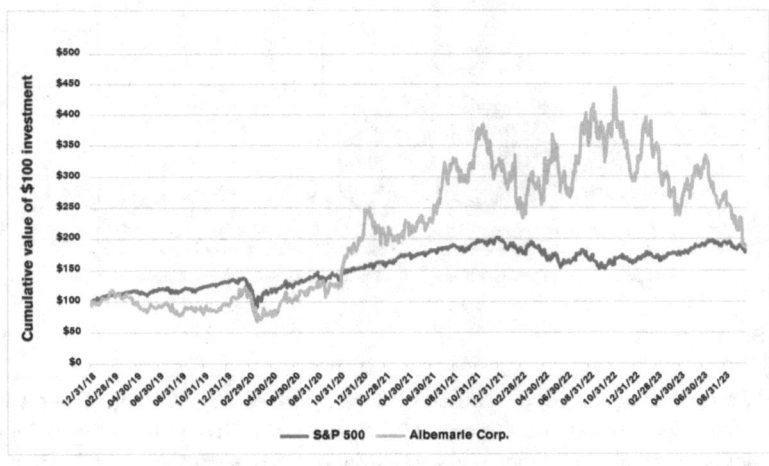

Source: FactSet.

than if you'd invested in an index fund—despite Albemarle's huge gains in 2020 and 2021.

In late 2023, the stock was trading at less than three times sales and under seven times earnings—close to the cheapest in Albemarle's history.

The more expensive Albemarle became, the more Mr. Market adored it. Then he got burned—and the cheaper it got, the more he hated it.

Riding the Tiger

As Graham says, "the speculative public is incorrigible." In August 2023, a Vietnamese electric-vehicle maker, VinFast Auto Ltd., sold shares to the public. It was as if no one had learned anything. In yet another IPO frenzy, Vinfast's stock went up more than eight-fold to $93 per share in less than two weeks, briefly hitting a total market capitalization of $190 billion. That was twice the market value of Ford Motor Co. and General Motors Co. *combined*, even though Vinfast had sold only 740 vehicles in the U.S. and was losing about $7 million a day.

Over the next two months the stock fell more than 90%.

For as long as companies and markets have existed, speculators have gone to extremes—buying when they know nothing about a stock except that other people are buying it, ignoring the most obvious warning signs, extrapolating short-term trends into eternity, paying almost infinite prices for slices of pie in the sky. Human nature doesn't change, and some people will chase dreams of greed until the end of time.

Should you join them?

Someone who bought Nikola, Peloton, Virgin Galactic, or Albemarle at the beginning of their run-ups and sold at the absolute peak could have made a lot of money. But that's like climbing onto the back of a wild tiger, hanging on until it's sprinting 40 miles per hour, and hopping off without getting mauled.

Somewhere on earth, someone might be able to do that.

But the hordes of speculators who thought they could were kidding themselves—and so are you if you think you can get rich by riding hot stocks and cashing out before it's too late.

CHAPTER 18

A Comparison of Eight Pairs of Companies
by Benjamin Graham

*I*n this chapter we shall attempt a novel form of exposition. By selecting eight pairs of companies which appear next to each other, or nearly so, on the stock-exchange list we hope to bring home in a concrete and vivid manner some of the many varieties of character, financial structure, policies, performance, and vicissitudes of corporate enterprises, and of the investment and speculative attitudes found on the financial scene in recent years. In each comparison we shall comment only on those aspects that have a special meaning and import.

Pair I: Real Estate Investment Trust (stores, offices, factories, etc.) and Realty Equities Corp. of New York (real estate investment; general construction)

In this first comparison we depart from the alphabetical order used for the other pairs. It has a special significance for us, since it seems to encapsulate, on the one hand, all that has been reasonable, stable, and generally good in the traditional methods of handling other people's money, in contrast—in the other company—with the reckless expansion, the financial legerdemain, and the roller-coaster changes so often found in present-day corporate operations. The two enterprises have similar names, and for many years they appeared side by side on the American Stock Exchange list. Their stock-ticker symbols—REI and REC—could easily have been confused. But one of them is a staid New England trust, administered by three trustees, with operations dating back nearly a century, and

A Comparison of Eight Pairs of Companies

with dividends paid continuously since 1889. It has kept throughout to the same type of prudent investments, limiting its expansion to a moderate rate and its debt to an easily manageable figure.*

The other is a typical New York-based sudden-growth venture, which in eight years blew up its assets from $6.2 million to $154 million, and its debts in the same proportion; which moved out from ordinary real-estate operations to a miscellany of ventures, including two racetracks, 74 movie theaters, three literary agencies, a public-relations firm, hotels, supermarkets, and a 26% interest in a large cosmetics firm (which went bankrupt in 1970).† This conglomeration of business ventures was matched by a corresponding variety of corporate devices, including the following:

1. A preferred stock entitled to $7 annual dividends, but with a par value of only $1, and carried as a liability at $1 per share.
2. A stated common-stock value of $2,500,000 ($1 per share), more than offset by a deduction of $5,500,000 as the cost of 209,000 shares of reacquired stock.
3. Three series of stock-option warrants, giving rights to buy a total of 1,578,000 shares.
4. At least six different kinds of debt obligations, in the form of mortgages, debentures, publicly held notes, notes payable to banks, "notes, loans, and contracts payable," and loans payable to the Small Business Administration, adding up to over $100 million in March 1969. In addition it had the usual taxes and accounts payable.

Let us present first a few figures of the two enterprises as they appeared in 1960 (Table 18-1A). Here we find the Trust shares selling in the market for nine times the aggregate value of Equities stock. The Trust enterprise had a smaller relative debt and a better ratio of

---

* Here Graham is describing Real Estate Investment Trust, which was acquired by San Francisco Real Estate Investors in 1983 for $50 a share. The next paragraph describes Realty Equities Corp. of New York.

† The actor Paul Newman was briefly a major shareholder in Realty Equities Corp. of New York after it bought his movie-production company, Kayos, Inc., in 1969.

TABLE 18-1A Pair 1. Real Estate Investment Trust vs. Realty Equities Corp. in 1960

	Real Estate Investment Trust	Realty Equities Corp. of New York
Gross revenues	$ 3,585,000	$1,484,000
Net income	485,000	150,000
Earned per share	.66	.47
Dividend per share	none	.10
Book value per share	$20.	$4.
Price range	20–12	5⅜–4¾
Total assets	$22,700,000	$6,200,000
Total liabilities	7,400,000	5,000,000
Book value of common	15,300,000	1,200,000
Average market value of common	12,200,000	1,360,000

net to gross, but the price of the common was higher in relation to per-share earnings.

In Table 18-1B we present the situation about eight years later. The Trust had "kept the noiseless tenor of its way," increasing both its revenues and its per-share earnings by about three-quarters.* But Realty Equities had been metamorphosed into something monstrous and vulnerable.

How did Wall Street react to these diverse developments? By paying as little attention as possible to the Trust and a lot to Realty Equities. In 1968 the latter shot up from 10 to 37¾ and the listed warrants from 6 to 36½, on combined sales of 2,420,000 shares. While this was happening the Trust shares advanced sedately from 20 to 30¼ on modest volume. The March 1969 balance sheet of Equities was to show an asset value of only $3.41 per share, less than a tenth of its high price that year. The book value of the Trust shares was $20.85.

---

* Graham, an avid reader of poetry, is quoting Thomas Gray's "Elegy Written in a Country Churchyard."

TABLE 18-1B Pair 1.

	Real Estate Investment Trust	Realty Equities Corp. of New York
Price, December 31, 1968	26½	32½
Number of shares of common	1,423,000	2,311,000 (March '69)
Market value of common	$37,800,000	$75,000,000
Estimated market value of warrants	—	30,000,000[a]
Estimated market value of common and warrants	—	105,000,000
Debt	9,600,000	100,800,000
Preferred stock	—	2,900,000
Total capitalization	$47,400,000	$208,700,000
Market value per share of common, adjusted for warrants	—	45 (est.)
Book value per share	$20.85 (Nov.)	$3.41
	November 1968	March 1969
Revenues	$6,281,000	$39,706,000
Net for interest	2,696,000	11,182,000
Interest charges	590,000	6,684,000
Income tax	58,000[b]	2,401,000
Preferred dividend		174,000
Net for common	2,048,000	1,943,000
Special items	245,000 cr.	1,896,000 dr.
Final net for common	2,293,000	47,000
Earned per share before special items	$1.28	$1.00
Earned per share after special items	1.45	.20
Dividend on common	1.20	.30
Interest charges earned	4.6 ×	1.8 ×

[a] There were warrants to buy 1,600,000 or more shares at various prices. A listed issue sold at 30½ per warrant.

[b] As a realty trust, this enterprise was not subjected to Federal income tax in 1968.

The next year it became clear that all was not well in the Equities picture, and the price fell to 9½. When the report for March 1970 appeared the shareholders must have felt shell-shocked as they read that the enterprise had sustained a net loss of $13,200,000, or $5.17 per share—virtually wiping out their former slim equity. (This disastrous figure included a reserve of $8,800,000 for future losses on investments.) Nonetheless the directors had bravely (?) declared an extra dividend of 5 cents right after the close of the fiscal year. But more trouble was in sight. The company's auditors refused to certify the financial statements for 1969–70, and the shares were suspended from trading on the American Stock Exchange. In the over-the-counter market the bid price dropped below $2 per share.*

Real Estate Investment Trust shares had typical price fluctuations after 1969. The low in 1970 was 16½, with a recovery to 26⅝ in early 1971. The latest reported earnings were $1.50 per share, and the stock was selling moderately above its 1970 book value of $21.60. The issue may have been somewhat overpriced at its record high in 1968, but the shareholders have been honestly and well served by their trustees. The Realty Equities story is a different and a sorry one.

Pair 2: Air Products and Chemicals (industrial and medical gases, etc.) and Air Reduction Co. (industrial gases and equipment; chemicals)

Even more than our first pair, these two resemble each other in both name and line of business. The comparison they invite is thus of the conventional type in security analysis, while most of our other pairs are more heteroclite in nature.† "Products" is a

---

* Realty Equities was delisted from the American Stock Exchange in September 1973. In 1974, the U.S. Securities and Exchange Commission sued Realty Equities' accountants for fraud. Realty Equities' founder, Morris Karp, later pleaded guilty to one count of grand larceny. In 1974–1975, the overindebtedness that Graham criticizes led to a financial crisis among large banks, including Chase Manhattan, that had lent heavily to the most aggressive realty trusts.
† "Heteroclite" is a technical term from classical Greek that Graham uses to mean abnormal or unusual.

newer company than "Reduction," and in 1969 had less than half the other's volume.* Nonetheless its equity issues sold for 25% more in the aggregate than Air Reduction's stock. As Table 18-2 shows, the reason can be found both in Air Reduction's greater profitability and in its stronger growth record. We find here the typical consequences of a better showing of "quality." Air Products sold at 16½ times its latest earnings against only 9.1 times for Air Reduction. Also Air Products sold well above its asset backing, while Air Reduction could be bought at only 75% of its book value.† Air Reduction paid a more liberal dividend; but this may be deemed to reflect the greater desirability for Air Products to retain its earnings. Also, Air Reduction had a more comfortable working-capital position. (On this point we may remark that a profitable company can always put its current position in shape by some form of permanent financing. But by our standards Air Products was somewhat overbonded.)

If the analyst were called on to choose between the two companies he would have no difficulty in concluding that the prospects of Air Products looked more promising than those of Air Reduction. But did this make Air Products more attractive at its considerably higher relative price? We doubt whether this question can be answered in a definitive fashion. **In general Wall Street sets "quality" above "quantity" in its thinking,** and probably the majority of security analysts would opt for the "better" but dearer Air Products as against the "poorer" but cheaper Air Reduction. Whether this preference is to prove right or wrong is more likely to depend on the unpredictable future than on any demonstrable investment principle. In this instance, Air Reduction appears to belong to the group of important companies in the low-multiplier class. If, as the studies referred to above‡

---

* By "volume," Graham is referring to sales or revenues—the total dollar amount of each company's business.

† "Asset backing" and book value are synonyms. In Table 18-2, the relationship of price to asset or book value can be seen by dividing the first line ("Price, December 31, 1969") by "Book value per share."

‡ Graham is citing his research on value stocks, which he discusses in Chapter 15 (see pp. 366–368).

would seem to indicate, that group *as a whole* is likely to give a better account of itself than the high-multiplier stocks, then Air Reduction should logically be given the preference—but only as part of a diversified operation. (Also, a thorough-going study of the individual companies could lead the analyst to the opposite conclusion; but that would have to be for reasons beyond those already reflected in the past showing.)

TABLE 18-2 Pair 2.

	Air Products & Chemicals	Air Reduction
Price, December 31, 1969	39½	16⅜
Number of shares of common	5,832,000[a]	11,279,000
Market value of common	$231,000,000	$185,000,000
Debt	113,000,000	179,000,000
Total capitalization at market	344,000,000	364,000,000
Book value per share	$22.89	$21.91
Sales	$221,500,000	$487,600,000
Net income	13,639,000	20,326,000
Earned per share, 1969	$2.40	$1.80
Earned per share, 1964	1.51	1.51
Earned per share, 1959	.52	1.95
Current dividend rate	.20	.80
Dividend since	1954	1917
Ratios:		
Price/earnings	16.5 ×	9.1 ×
Price/book value	165.0%	75.0%
Dividend yield	0.5%	4.9%
Net/sales	6.2%	4.25%
Earnings/book value	11.0%	8.2%
Current assets/liabilities	1.53 ×	3.77 ×
Working capital/debt	.32 ×	.85 ×
Growth in per-share earnings		
1969 versus 1964	+59%	+19%
1969 versus 1959	+362%	decrease

[a] Assuming conversion of preferred stock.

SEQUEL: Air Products stood up better than Air Reduction in the 1970 break, with a decline of 16% against 24%. However, Reduction made a better comeback in early 1971, rising to 50% above its 1969 close, against 30% for Products. In this case the low-multiplier issue scored the advantage—for the time being, at least.*

Pair 3: American Home Products Co. (drugs, cosmetics, household products, candy) and American Hospital Supply Co. (distributor and manufacturer of hospital supplies and equipment)

These were two "billion-dollar good-will" companies at the end of 1969, representing different segments of the rapidly growing and immensely profitable "health industry." We shall refer to them as Home and Hospital, respectively. Selected data on both are presented in Table 18-3. They had the following favorable points in common: excellent growth, with no setbacks since 1958 (i.e., 100% earnings stability); and strong financial condition. The growth rate of Hospital up to the end of 1969 was considerably higher than Home's. On the other hand, Home enjoyed substantially better profitability on both sales and capital.† (In fact, the relatively low rate of Hospital's earnings on its capital in 1969—only 9.7%—raises the intriguing question whether the business then was in fact a highly profitable one, despite its remarkable past growth rate in sales and earnings.)

When comparative price is taken into account, Home offered much more for the money in terms of current (or past) earnings and dividends. The very low book value of Home illustrates a basic ambiguity or contradiction in common-stock analysis. On the one hand, it means that the company is earning a high return on

---

* Air Products and Chemicals, Inc., still exists as a publicly-traded stock and is included in the Standard & Poor's 500-stock index. Air Reduction Co. became a wholly-owned subsidiary of British Oxygen, now part of Linde PLC, in 1978.

† You can determine profitability by referring to the "Ratios" section of Table 18-3. "Net/sales" measures return on sales; "Earnings/book value" is one way to measure return on capital.

TABLE 18-3 Pair 3.

	American Home Products	American Hospital Supply
Price, December 31, 1969	72	45⅛
Number of shares of common	52,300,000	33,600,000
Market value of common	$3,800,000,000	$1,516,000,000
Debt	11,000,000	18,000,000
Total capitalization at market	3,811,000,000	1,534,000,000
Book value per share	$5.73	$7.84
Sales	$1,193,000,000	$446,000,000
Net income	123,300,000	25,000,000
Earned per share, 1969	$2.32	$.77
Earned per share, 1964	1.37	.31
Earned per share, 1959	.92	.15
Current dividend rate	1.40	.24
Dividends since	1919	1947
Ratios:		
Price/earnings	31.0 ×	58.5 ×
Price/book value	1250.0%	575.0%
Dividend yield	1.9%	0.55%
Net/sales	10.7%	5.6%
Earnings/book value	41.0%	9.5%
Current assets/liabilities	2.6 ×	4.5 ×
Growth in per-share earnings		
1969 versus 1964	+75%	+142%
1969 versus 1959	+161%	+405%

its capital—which in general is a sign of strength and prosperity. On the other, it means that the investor at the current price would be especially vulnerable to any important adverse change in the company's earnings situation. Since Hospital was selling at over four times its book value in 1969, this cautionary remark must be applied to both companies.

CONCLUSIONS: Our clear-cut view would be that both companies were too "rich" at their current prices to be considered by the investor who decides to follow our ideas of conservative selection. This does not mean that the companies were lacking in promise. The trouble is, rather, that **their price contained too much "promise" and not enough actual performance.** For the two enterprises combined, the 1969 price reflected almost $5 billion of good-will valuation. How many years of excellent future earnings would it take to "realize" that good-will factor in the form of dividends or tangible assets?

SHORT-TERM SEQUEL: At the end of 1969 the market evidently thought more highly of the earnings prospects of Hospital than of Home, since it gave the former almost twice the multiplier of the latter. As it happened the favored issue showed a microscopic *decline* in earnings in 1970, while Home turned in a respectable 8% gain. The market price of Hospital reacted significantly to this one-year disappointment. It sold at 32 in February 1971—a loss of about 30% from its 1969 close—while Home was quoted slightly above its corresponding level.*

Pair 4: H & R Block, Inc. (income-tax service) and Blue Bell, Inc., (manufacturers of work clothes, uniforms, etc.)

These companies rub shoulders as relative newcomers to the New York Stock Exchange, where they represent two very different genres of success stories. Blue Bell came up the hard way in a highly competitive industry, in which eventually it became the largest factor. Its earnings have fluctuated somewhat with industry conditions, but their growth since 1965 has been impressive. The company's operations go back to 1916 and its continuous dividend record to 1923. At the end of 1969 the stock market showed no enthusiasm for the issue, giving it a price/earnings ratio of only 11, against about 17 for the S & P composite index.

By contrast, the rise of H & R Block has been meteoric. Its first published figures date only to 1961, in which year it earned $83,000 on revenues of $610,000. But eight years later, on our comparison date, its revenues had soared to $53.6 million and its net to $6.3 million. At that time the stock market's attitude toward

---

* American Home Products Co. was later absorbed into Pfizer Inc. American Hospital Supply Co. was acquired by Baxter Healthcare Corp. in 1985.

this fine performer appeared nothing less than ecstatic. The price of 55 at the close of 1969 was more than 100 times the last reported 12-months' earnings—which of course were the largest to date. The aggregate market value of $300 million for the stock issue was nearly 30 times the tangible assets behind the shares.* This was almost unheard of in the annals of serious stock-market valuations. (At that time IBM was selling at about 9 times and Xerox at 11 times book value.)

Our Table 18-4 sets forth in dollar figures and in ratios the extraordinary discrepancy in the comparative valuations of Block and Blue Bell. True, Block showed twice the profitability of Blue Bell per dollar of capital, and its percentage growth in earnings over the past five years (from practically nothing) was much higher. But as a stock enterprise Blue Bell was selling for less than one-third the total value of Block, although Blue Bell was doing four times as much business, earning 2½ times as much for its stock, had 5½ times as much in tangible investment, and gave nine times the dividend yield on the price.

INDICATED CONCLUSIONS: An experienced analyst would have conceded great momentum to Block, implying excellent prospects for future growth. He might have had some qualms about the dangers of serious competition in the income-tax-service field, lured by the handsome return on capital realized by Block.[1] But mindful of the continued success of such outstanding companies as Avon Products in highly competitive areas, he would have hesitated to predict a speedy flattening out of the Block growth curve. His chief concern would be simply whether the $300 million valuation for the company had not already fully valued and perhaps overvalued all that one could reasonably expect from this excellent business. By contrast the analyst should have had little difficulty in recommending Blue Bell as a fine company, quite conservatively priced.

SEQUEL TO MARCH 1971. The 1970 near-panic lopped one-quarter

---

* "Nearly 30 times" is reflected in the entry of 2920% under "Price/book value" in the Ratios section of Table 18-4. H & R Block remains a publicly-traded company, while Blue Bell was taken private in 1984 at $47.50 per share.

TABLE 18-4 Pair 4.

	H & R Block	Blue Bell
Price, December 31, 1969	55	49¾
Number of shares of common	5,426,000	1,802,000[a]
Market value of common	$298,000,000	$89,500,000
Debt	—	17,500,000
Total capitalization at market	298,000,000	107,000,000
Book value per share	$1.89	$34.54
Sales	$53,600,000	$202,700,000
Net income	6,380,000	7,920,000
Earned per share, 1969	$.51 (October)	$4.47
Earned per share, 1964	.07	2.64
Earned per share, 1959	—	1.80
Current dividend rate	.24	1.80
Dividends since	1962	1923
Ratios:		
Price/earnings	108.0 ×	11.2 ×
Price/book value	2920 %	142 %
Dividend yield	0.4 %	3.6 %
Net/sales	11.9 %	3.9 %
Earnings/book value	27 %	12.8 %
Current assets/liabilities	3.2 ×	2.4 ×
Working capital/debt	no debt	3.75 ×
Growth in per-share earnings		
1969 versus 1964	+630%	+68%
1969 versus 1959	—	+148%

[a] Assuming conversion of preferred stock.

off the price of Blue Bell and about one-third from that of Block. Both then joined in the extraordinary recovery of the general market. The price of Block rose to 75 in February 1971, but Blue Bell advanced considerably more—to the equivalent of 109 (after a three-for-two split). Clearly Blue Bell proved a better buy than Block as of the end of 1969. But the fact that Block was able to advance some 35% from that apparently inflated value indicates **how wary analysts and** investors must be to sell good companies short—either by word or deed—no matter how high the quotation may seem.*

Pair 5: International Flavors & Fragrances (flavors, etc., for other businesses) and International Harvester Co. (truck manufacturer, farm machinery, construction machinery)

This comparison should carry more than one surprise. Everyone knows of International Harvester, one of the 30 giants in the Dow Jones Industrial Average.† How many of our readers have even heard of International Flavors & Fragrances, next-door neighbor to Harvester on the New York Stock Exchange list? Yet, *mirabile dictu,* IFF was actually selling at the end of 1969 for a higher aggregate market value than Harvester—$747 million versus $710 million. This is more amazing when one reflects that Harvester had 17 times the stock capital of Flavors and 27 times the annual sales. In fact, only three years before, the *net earnings* of Harvester had been larger than the 1969 *sales* of Flavors! How did these extraordinary disparities develop? The answer lies in the two magic words: profitability and growth. Flavors made a remarkable showing in both categories, while Harvester left everything to be desired.

The story is told in Table 18-5. Here we find Flavors with a sensational profit of 14.3% of sales (before income tax the figure was 23%), compared with a mere 2.6% for Harvester. Similarly, Flavors had earned 19.7% on its stock capital against an inadequate

---

* Graham is alerting readers to a form of the "gambler's fallacy," in which investors believe that an overvalued stock must drop in price purely because it is overvalued. Just as a coin does not become more likely to turn up heads after landing on tails for nine times in a row, so an overvalued stock (or stock market!) can stay overvalued for a surprisingly long time. That makes short-selling, or betting that stocks will drop, too risky for mere mortals.

† International Harvester was the heir to McCormick Harvesting Machine Co., the manufacturer of the McCormick reaper that helped make the midwestern states the "breadbasket of the world." But International Harvester fell on hard times in the 1970s and, in 1985, sold its farm-equipment business to Tenneco. International Flavors & Fragrances is a member of the S&P 500.

TABLE 18-5 Pair 5.

	International Flavors & Fragrances	International Harvester
Price, December 31, 1969	65½	24¾
Number of shares of common	11,400,000	27,329,000
Market value of common	$747,000,000	$710,000,000
Debt	4,000,000	313,000,000
Total capitalization at market	751,000,000	1,023,000,000
Book value per share	$6.29	$41.70
Sales	$94,200,000	$2,652,000,000
Net income	13,540,000	63,800,000
Earned per share, 1969	$1.19	$2.30
Earned per share, 1964	.62	3.39
Earned per share, 1959	.28	2.83
Current dividend rate	.50	1.80
Dividends since	1956	1910
Ratios:		
Price/earnings	55.0 ×	10.7 ×
Price/book value	1050.0%	59.0%
Dividend yield	0.9%	7.3%
Net/sales	14.3%	2.6%
Earnings/book value	19.7%	5.5%
Current assets/liabilities	3.7 ×	2.0 ×
Working capital/debt	large	1.7 ×
Interest earned	—	(before tax) 3.9 ×
Growth in per-share earnings		
1969 versus 1964	+93%	+9%
1969 versus 1959	+326%	+39%

5.5% earned by Harvester. In five years the net earnings of Flavors had nearly doubled, while those of Harvester practically stood still. Between 1969 and 1959 the comparison makes similar reading. These differences in performance produced a typical stock-market divergence in valuation. Flavors sold in 1969 at 55 times its last reported earnings, and Harvester at only 10.7 times. Correspondingly, Flavors was valued at 10.4 times its book value, while Harvester was selling at a 41% *discount* from its net worth.

COMMENT AND CONCLUSIONS: The first thing to remark is that the market success of Flavors was based entirely on the development of its central business, and involved none of the corporate wheeling and dealing, acquisition programs, top-heavy capitalization structures, and other familiar Wall Street practices of recent years. The company has stuck to its extremely profitable knitting, and that is virtually its whole story. The record of Harvester raises an entirely different set of questions, but these too have nothing to do with "high finance." Why have so many great companies become relatively unprofitable even during many years of general prosperity? What is the advantage of doing more than $2½ billion of business if the enterprise cannot earn enough to justify the shareholders' investment? It is not for us to prescribe the solution of this problem. But we insist that not only management but the rank and file of shareholders should be conscious that the problem exists and that it calls for the best brains and the best efforts possible to deal with it.* From the standpoint of common-stock selection, neither issue would have met our standards of sound, reasonably attractive, and moderately priced investment. Flavors was a typical brilliantly successful but lavishly valued company; Harvester's showing was too mediocre to make it really attractive even at its discount price. (Undoubtedly there were better values available in the reasonably priced class.)

SEQUEL TO 1971: The low price of Harvester at the end of 1969 protected it from a large further decline in the bad break of 1970. It lost only 10% more. Flavors proved more vulnerable and declined to 45, a loss of 30%. In the subsequent recovery both advanced, well above their 1969 close, but Harvester soon fell back to the 25 level.

---

* For more of Graham's thoughts on shareholder activism, see Chapter 19 and its Commentary. In criticizing Harvester for its refusal to maximize shareholder value, Graham uncannily anticipated the behavior of the company's future management. In 2001, a majority of shareholders voted to remove Navistar's restrictions against outside takeover bids—but the board of directors simply refused to implement the shareholders' wishes. It's remarkable that an antidemocratic tendency in the culture of some companies can endure for decades.

Pair 6: McGraw Edison (public utility and equipment; housewares) McGraw-Hill, Inc. (books, films, instruction systems; magazine and newspaper publishers; information services)

This pair with so similar names—which at times we shall call Edison and Hill—are two large and successful enterprises in vastly different fields. We have chosen December 31, 1968, as the date of our comparison, developed in Table 18-6. The issues were selling at about the same price, but because of Hill's larger capitalization it was valued at about twice the total figure of the other. This difference should appear somewhat surprising, since Edison had about 50% higher sales and one-quarter larger net earnings. As a result, we find that the key ratio—the multiplier of earnings—was more than twice as great for Hill as for Edison. This phenomenon seems explicable chiefly by the persistence of a strong enthusiasm and partiality exhibited by the market toward shares of book-publishing companies, several of which had been introduced to public trading in the later 1960s.*

Actually, by the end of 1968 it was evident that this enthusiasm had been overdone. The Hill shares had sold at 56 in 1967, more than 40 times the just-reported record earnings for 1966. But a small decline had appeared in 1967 and a further decline in 1968. Thus the current high multiplier of 35 was being applied to a company that had already shown two years of receding profits. Nonetheless the stock was still valued at more than eight times its tangible asset backing, indicating a good-will component of not far from a billion dollars! Thus **the price seemed to illustrate—in Dr. Johnson's famous phrase—"The triumph of hope over experience."**

By contrast, McGraw Edison seemed quoted at a reasonable price in relation to the (high) general market level and to the company's overall performance and financial position.

SEQUEL TO EARLY 1971: The decline of McGraw-Hill's earnings continued through 1969 and 1970, dropping to $1.02 and then to $.82 per share. In the May 1970 debacle its price suffered a devastating break to 10—less than a fifth of the figure two years before. It had a good recovery thereafter, but the high of 24 in May 1971 was still

---

* McGraw-Hill and McGraw-Edison are no longer publicly traded.

TABLE 18-6 Pair 6.

	McGraw Edison	McGraw-Hill
Price, December 31, 1968	37⅝	39¾
Number of shares of common	13,717,000	24,200,000[a]
Market value of common	$527,000,000	$962,000,000
Debt	6,000,000	53,000,000
Total capitalization at market	533,000,000	1,015,000,000
Book value per share	$20.53	$5.00
Sales	$568,600,000	$398,300,000
Net income	33,400,000	26,200,000
Earned per share, 1968	$2.44	$1.13
Earned per share, 1963	1.20	.66
Earned per share, 1958	1.02	.46
Current dividend rate	1.40	.70
Dividends since	1934	1937
Ratios:		
Price/earnings	15.5 ×	35.0 ×
Price/book value	183.0%	795.0%
Dividend yield	3.7%	1.8%
Net/sales	5.8%	6.6%
Earnings/book value	11.8%	22.6%
Current assets/liabilities	3.95 ×	1.75 ×
Working capital/debt	large	1.75 ×
Growth in per-share earnings		
1968 versus 1963	+104%	+71%
1968 versus 1958	+139%	+146%

[a] Assuming conversion of preferred stock.

only 60% of the 1968 closing price. McGraw Edison gave a better account of itself—declining to 22 in 1970 and recovering fully to 41½ in May 1971.*

---

* In "the May 1970 debacle" that Graham refers to, the U.S. stock market lost 5.5%. From the end of March to the end of June 1970, the S&P 500 fell 19%, one of the worst three-month returns on record.

McGraw-Hill continues to be a strong and prosperous company. But its price history exemplifies—as do so many other cases—the speculative hazards in such stocks created by Wall Street through its undisciplined waves of optimism and pessimism.

Pair 7: National General Corp. (a large conglomerate) and National Presto Industries (diverse electric appliances, ordnance)

These two companies invite comparison chiefly because they are so different. Let us call them "General" and "Presto." We have selected the end of 1968 for our study, because the write-offs taken by General in 1969 made the figures for that year too ambiguous. The full flavor of General's far-flung activities could not be savored the year before, but it was already conglomerate enough for anyone's taste. The condensed description in the *Stock Guide* reads "Nation-wide theatre chain; motion picture and TV production, savings and loan assn., book publishing." To which could be added, then or later, "insurance, investment banking, records, music publishing, computerized services, real estate—and 35% of Performance Systems Inc. (name recently changed from Minnie Pearl's Chicken System Inc.)." Presto had also followed a diversification program, but in comparison with General it was modest indeed. Starting as the leading maker of pressure cookers, it had branched out into various other household and electric appliances. Quite differently, also, it took on a number of ordnance contracts for the U.S. government.

Our Table 18-7 summarizes the showing of the companies at the end of 1968. The capital structure of Presto was as simple as it could be—nothing but 1,478,000 shares of common stock, selling in the market for $58 million. Contrastingly, General had more than twice as many shares of common, plus an issue of convertible preferred, plus three issues of stock warrants calling for a huge amount of common, plus a towering convertible bond issue (just given in exchange for stock of an insurance company), plus a goodly sum of nonconvertible bonds. All this added up to a market capitalization of $534 million, not counting an impending issue of convertible bonds, and $750 million, including such issue. Despite National General's enormously greater capitalization, it had actually done

TABLE 18-7 Pair 7.

	National General	National Presto Industries
Price, December 31, 1968	44¼	38⅝
Number of shares of common	4,330,000[a]	1,478,000
Market value of common	$192,000,000	$58,000,000
Add market value of 3 issues of warrants	221,000,000	—
Total value of common and warrants	413,000,000	—
Senior issues	121,000,000	—
Total capitalization at market	534,000,000	58,000,000
Market price of common stock adjusted for warrants	98	—
Book value of common	$31.50	$26.30
Sales and revenues	$117,600,000	$152,200,000
Net income	6,121,000	8,206,000
Earned per share, 1968	$1.42 (December)	$5.61
Earned per share, 1963	.96 (September)	1.03
Earned per share, 1958	.48 (September)	.77
Current dividend rate	.20	.80
Dividends since	1964	1945
Ratios:		
Price/earnings	69.0 ×[b]	6.9 ×
Price/book value	310.0%	142.0%
Dividend yield	.5%	2.4%
Net/sales	5.5%	5.4%
Earnings/book value	4.5%	21.4%
Current assets/liabilities	1.63 ×	3.40 ×
Working capital/debt	.21 ×	no debt
Growth in per-share earnings		
1968 versus 1963	+48%	+450%
1968 versus 1960	+195%	+630%

[a] Assuming conversion of preferred stock.
[b] Adjusted for market price of warrants.

considerably less gross business than Presto in their fiscal years, and it had shown only 75% of Presto's net income.

The determination of the *true market value* of General's common-stock capitalization presents an interesting problem for security analysts and has important implications for anyone interested in the stock on any basis more serious than outright gambling. The relatively small $4½ convertible preferred can be readily taken care of by assuming its conversion into common, when the latter sells at a suitable market level. This we have done in Table 18-7. But the warrants require different treatment. In calculating the "full dilution" basis the company assumes exercise of all the warrants, and the application of the proceeds to the retirement of debt, plus use of the balance to buy in common at the market. These assumptions actually produced virtually no effect on the earnings per share in calendar 1968—which were reported as $1.51 both before and after allowance for dilution. We consider this treatment illogical and unrealistic. As we see it, the warrants represent a part of the "common-stock package" and their market value is part of the "effective market value" of the common-stock part of the capital. (See our discussion of this point on p. 408 above.) This simple technique of adding the market price of the warrants to that of the common has a radical effect on the showing of National General at the end of 1968, as appears from the calculation in Table 18-7. In fact the "true market price" of the common stock turns out to be more than twice the quoted figure. Hence the true multiplier of the 1968 earnings is more than doubled—to the inherently absurd figure of 69 times. The total market value of the "common-stock equivalents" then becomes $413 million, which is over three times the tangible assets shown therefor.

These figures appear the more anomalous when comparison is made with those of Presto. One is moved to ask how could Presto possibly be valued at only 6.9 times its current earnings when the multiplier for General was nearly 10 times as great. All the ratios of Presto are quite satisfactory—the growth figure suspiciously so, in fact. By that we mean that the company was undoubtedly benefiting considerably from its war work, and the shareholders should be prepared for some falling off in profits under peacetime conditions. But, on balance, Presto met all the requirements of a sound and reasonably priced investment, while General had all the earmarks of a typical "conglomerate" of the late 1960s vintage, full of corporate gadgets and grandiose gestures, but lacking in substantial values behind the market quotations.

SEQUEL: General continued its diversification policy in 1969, with some increase in its debt. But it took a whopping write-off of millions, chiefly in the value of its investment in the Minnie Pearl Chicken deal. The final figures showed a loss of $72 million before tax credit and $46.4 million after tax credit. The price of the shares fell to 16½ in 1969 and as low as 9 in 1970 (only 15% of its 1968 high of 60). Earnings for 1970 were reported as $2.33 per share diluted, and the price recovered to 28½ in 1971. National Presto increased its per-share earnings somewhat in both 1969 and 1970, marking 10 years of uninterrupted growth of profits. Nonetheless its price declined to 21½ in the 1970 debacle. This was an interesting figure, since it was less than four times the last reported earnings, and less than the net current assets available for the stock at the time. Late in 1971 we find the price of National Presto 60% higher, at 34, but the ratios are still startling. The enlarged working capital is still about equal to the current price, which in turn is only 5½ times the last reported earnings. If the investor could now find ten such issues, for diversification, he could be confident of satisfactory results.*

Pair 8: Whiting Corp. (materials-handling equipment) and Willcox & Gibbs (small conglomerate)

This pair are close but not touching neighbors on the American Stock Exchange list. The comparison—set forth in Table 18-8A—makes one wonder if Wall Street is a rational institution. The company with smaller sales and earnings, and with half the tangible assets for the common, sold at about four times the aggregate value of the other. The higher-valued company was about to report a large

---

* National Presto remains a publicly-traded company. National General was acquired in 1974 by another controversial conglomerate, American Financial Group, which at various times has had interests in cable television, banking, real estate, mutual funds, insurance, and bananas.

loss after special charges; it had not paid a dividend in thirteen years. The other had a long record of satisfactory earnings, had paid continuous dividends since 1936, and was currently returning one of the highest dividend yields in the entire common-stock list. To indicate more vividly the disparity in the performance of the two

Table 18-8A Pair 8.

	Whiting	Willcox & Gibbs
Price, December 31, 1969	17¾	15½
Number of shares of common	570,000	2,381,000
Market value of common	$10,200,000	$36,900,000
Debt	1,000,000	5,900,000
Preferred stock	—	1,800,000
Total capitalization at market	$11,200,000	$44,600,000
Book value per share	$25.39	$3.29
Sales	$42,200,000	$29,000,000
	(October)	(December)
Net income before special item	1,091,000	347,000
Net income after special item	1,091,000	def. 1,639,000
Earned per share, 1969	$1.91 (October)	$.08[a]
Earned per share, 1964	1.90 (April)	.13
Earned per share, 1959	.42 (April)	.13
Current dividend rate	1.50	—
Dividends since	1954	(none since 1957)
Ratios:		
Price/earnings	9.3 ×	very large
Price/book value	70.0%	470.0%
Dividend yield	8.4%	—
Net/sales	3.2%	0.1%[a]
Earnings/book value	7.5%	2.4%[a]
Current assets/liabilities	3.0 ×	1.55 ×
Working capital/debt	9.0 ×	3.6 ×
Growth in per-share earnings		
1969 versus 1964	even	decrease
1969 versus 1959	+354%	decrease

[a] Before special charge. *def.*: deficit.

TABLE 18-8B Ten-Year Price and Earnings Record of Whiting and Willcox & Gibbs

	Whiting Corp.		Willcox & Gibbs	
Year	Earned Per Share[a]	Price Range	Earned Per Share	Price Range
1970	$1.81	22½–16¼	$.34	18½–4½
1969	2.63	37–17¾	.05	20⅝–8¾
1968	3.63	43⅛–28¼	.35	20⅛–8⅓
1967	3.01	36½–25	.47	11–4¾
1966	2.49	30¼–19¼	.41	8–3¾
1965	1.90	20–18	.32	10⅜–6⅛
1964	1.53	14–8	.20	9½–4½
1963	.88	15–9	.13	14–4¾
1962	.46	10–6½	.04	19¾–8¼
1961	.42	12½–7¾	.03	19½–10½

[a] Year ended following April 30.

companies we append, in Table 18-8B, the earnings and price record for 1961–1970.

The history of the two companies throws an interesting light on the development of medium-sized businesses in this country, in contrast with much larger-sized companies that have mainly appeared in these pages. Whiting was incorporated in 1896, and thus goes back at least 75 years. It seems to have kept pretty faithfully to its materials-handling business and has done quite well with it over the decades. Willcox & Gibbs goes back even farther—to 1866—and was long known in its industry as a prominent maker of industrial sewing machines. During the past decade it adopted a policy of diversification in what seems a rather outlandish form. For on the one hand it has an extraordinarily large number of subsidiary companies (at least 24), making an astonishing variety of products, but on the other hand the entire conglomeration adds up to mighty small potatoes by usual Wall Street standards.

The earnings developments in Whiting are rather characteristic of our business concerns. The figures show steady and rather spectacular growth from 41 cents a share in 1960 to $3.63 in 1968. But they carried no assurance that such growth must continue indefinitely. The subsequent decline to only $1.77 for the 12 months ended January 1971 may have reflected nothing more than the slowing down of the general economy. But the stock price reacted in severe fashion, falling about 60% from its 1968 high (43½) to the close of 1969. Our analysis would indicate that the shares represented a sound and attractive secondary-issue investment—suitable for the enterprising investor as part of a group of such commitments.

SEQUEL: Willcox & Gibbs showed a small operating loss for 1970. Its price declined drastically to a low of 4½, recovering in typical fashion to 9½ in February 1971. It would be hard to justify that price statistically. Whiting had a relatively small decline, to 16¾ in 1970. (At that price it was selling at just about the current assets alone available for the shares.) Its earnings held at $1.85 per share to July 1971. In early 1971 the price advanced to 24½, which seemed reasonable enough but no longer a "bargain" by our standards.*

General Observations

The issues used in these comparisons were selected with some malice aforethought, and thus they cannot be said to present a random cross-section of the common-stock list. Also they are limited to the industrial section, and the important areas of public utilities, transportation companies, and financial enterprises do not appear. But they vary sufficiently in size, lines of business, and qualitative and quantitative aspects to convey a fair idea of the choices confronting an investor in common stocks.

The relationship between price and indicated value has also differed greatly from one case to another. For the most part the companies with better growth records and higher profitability have sold at higher multipliers of current earnings—which is logical enough in general. Whether the specific differentials in price/

---

* Whiting Corp. and Willcox & Gibbs are no longer publicly traded.

TABLE 18-9 Some Price Fluctuations of Sixteen Common Stocks (Adjusted for Stock Splits Through 1970)

	Price Range 1936–1970	Decline 1961 to 1962	Decline 1968–69 to 1970
Air Products & Chemicals	1⅜–49	43¼–21⅝	49–31⅜
Air Reduction	9⅜–45¾	22½–12	37–16
American Home Products	⅞–72	44¾–22	72–51⅛
American Hospital Supply	¾–47½	11⅝–5¾	47½–26¾[a]
H & R Block	¼–68½	–	68½–37⅛[a]
Blue Bell	8¾–55	25–16	44¾–26½
International Flavors & Fragrances	4¾–67½	8–4½	66⅜–44⅞
International Harvester	6¼–53	28¾–19¼	38¾–22
McGraw Edison	1¼–46¼	24⅜–14[b]	44¾–21⅝
McGraw-Hill	⅛–56½	21½–9⅛	54⅝–10¼
National General	3⅝–60½	14⅞–4¾[b]	60½–9
National Presto Industries	½–45	20⅝–8¼	45–21½
Real Estate Investment Trust	10½–30¼	25⅛–15¼	30¼–16⅜
Realty Equities of N.Y.	3¾–47¾	6⅞–4½	37¾–2
Whiting	2⅞–43⅜	12½–6½	43⅜–16¾
Willcox & Gibbs	4–20⅝	19½–8¼	20⅜–4½

[a] High and low both in 1970.
[b] 1959 to 1960.

earnings ratios are "justified" by the facts—or will be vindicated by future developments—cannot be answered with confidence. On the other hand we do have quite a few instances here in which a worthwhile judgment can be reached. These include virtually all the cases where there has been great market activity in companies of questionable underlying soundness. Such stocks not only were speculative—which means inherently risky—but a good deal of the time they were and are obviously overvalued.

Other issues appeared to be worth more than their price, being affected by the opposite sort of market attitude—which we might call "underspeculation"—or by undue pessimism because of a shrinkage in earnings.

In Table 18-9 we provide some data on the price fluctuations of the issues covered in this chapter. Most of them had large declines between 1961 and 1962, as well as from 1969 to 1970. Clearly the investor must be prepared for this type of adverse market movement in future stock markets. In Table 18-10 we show year-to-year fluctuations of McGraw-Hill common stock for the period 1958–1970. It will be noted that in each of the last 13 years the price either advanced or declined over a range of at least three to two from one year to the next. (In the case of National General fluctuations of at least this amplitude both upward and downward were shown in each two-year period.)

In studying the stock list for the material in this chapter, we were impressed once again by the wide difference between the usual

TABLE 18-10. Large Year-to-Year Fluctuations of McGraw-Hill, 1958–1971[a]

From	To	Advances	Declines
1958	1959	39–72	
1959	1960	54–109¾	
1960	1961	21¾–43⅛	
1961	1962	18¼–32¼	43⅛–18¼
1963	1964	23⅜–38⅞	
1964	1965	28⅜–61	
1965	1966	37½–79½	
1966	1967	54½–112	
1967	1968		56¼–37½
1968	1969		54⅝–24
1969	1970		39½–10
1970	1971	10–24⅛	

[a] Prices not adjusted for stock-splits.

objectives of security analysis and those we deem dependable and rewarding. Most security analysts try to select the issues that will give the best account of themselves in the future, in terms chiefly of market action but considering also the development of earnings. We are frankly skeptical as to whether this can be done with satisfactory results. Our preference for the analyst's work would be rather that he should seek the exceptional or minority cases in which he can form a reasonably confident judgment that the price is well below value. He should be able to do this work with sufficient expertness to produce satisfactory average results over the years.

Commentary on Chapter 18
by Jason Zweig

> There can be few fields of human endeavor in which history counts for so little as in the world of finance. Past experience, to the extent that it is part of memory at all, is dismissed as the primitive refuge of those who do not have the insight to appreciate the incredible wonders of the present.
> —John Kenneth Galbraith[1]

In Chapter 18, Graham compares and contrasts eight pairs of companies with similar names or ticker symbols.

His main lesson?

There's no such thing as a good or bad stock. There are only good or bad stock *prices*. The higher a company's stock price goes, the more people will want to buy it; the cheaper a stock gets, the less anyone will want to own it. The same stock at different times can be either cheap or expensive.

Let's zero in on eight comparisons from recent markets and see what Graham might have thought about them.

Pair 1: AMC Entertainment Holdings Inc. (movie theaters) and AMETEK, Inc. (electronics and electrical devices)

In 2021–22, AMC personified a "meme stock": a movie-theater chain with pallid prospects for growth, dangerous amounts of debt—and swarms of speculators bidding it up, motivated by conspiracy

---

[1] John Kenneth Galbraith, *A Short History of Financial Euphoria* (Penguin, 1994), p. 13.

theories and willfully blind to the ailing health of the underlying business.

"This isn't a trade about fundamentals. It's just not," one AMC fan said in July 2021. He argued that the "apes," as the online speculators called themselves to flaunt their scorn for traditional analysis, would use their collective buying power to drive up the share price—and the upside was almost unlimited.

The apes swore they would HODL, or hold on for dear life, until the MOASS, the mother of all short squeezes. In the MOASS, hedge funds and other professional investors betting against AMC would be forced to buy, the stock would soar to $100,000 or more, and the apes would be rich.

And in less than five months in early 2021, the apes pushed AMC's stock price up an astounding 3,050%.

AMETEK, which supplies equipment to aerospace, defense, automation, and medical customers, had no army of apes to boost its shares. Over the same period, AME rose 14%, piddling by comparison.

Yet AMC was at death's door in 2021, whereas AME was a reasonably profitable business.

Since 2017, AMC's sales had shrunk by half, it had earned only one paltry annual profit, its debt had doubled, and it was hemorrhaging cash.

At AME, sales and earnings had grown steadily, debt was moderate, and cash was plentiful.

The MOASS never came to pass. AMC's shares lost 76% in 2022 and another 83% for the full year 2023. A few folks who bought AMC at the bottom and sold at the top made a killing. Countless others bought at the top and got killed.

> **The point:** In the short run, fundamentals often don't matter. In the long run, they always do.[2]

---

[2] Alexander Gladstone and Erich Schwartzel, "Inside AMC's Crazy, Bonkers, Upside-Down Year of Apes, Memes and Shorts," bit.ly/40jSILe; Caitlin McCabe and Alexander Osipovich, "GameStop Investors Still Await Riches from Epic Short Squeeze," bit.ly/40mH0PT.

TABLE 18-1: AMC vs. AME

AMC

	12/31/17	12/31/18	12 months ended 12/31/19	12/31/20	12/31/21	12/31/22	9 months ended 9/30/23
Change in stock price (%)	-55.1	-18.7	-41.0	-70.7	1,183.0	-75.6	-77.8
Sales ($ millions)	5,079	5,461	5,471	1,242	2,528	3,911	3,708
Net income ($ millions)	-487	110	-149	-4,589	-1,269	-974	-215
Net profit margin (%)	-9.6	2.0	-2.7	-369.4	-50.2	-24.9	-5.8
Return on invested capital (%)	-7.3	1.6	-1.7	-48.8	-15.7	-12.9	-7.4
Earnings per share ($)	-33.53	3.62	-12.67	-345.46	-23.46	-8.20	-1.43
Book value per share ($)	146.03	119.18	103.16	-113.48	-30.72	-18.65	-10.78
Assets	9,806	9,496	13,676	10,276	10,822	9,136	8,793
Working capital	-537	-547	-1,260	-1,092	82	-811	-571
Long-term debt	4,799	5,201	9,737	10,737	10,116	9,427	8,778
Total debt as a percentage of capital	69.8	79.1	89.5	134.1	120.0	135.5	129.8
Free cash flow	-68	-53	61	-1,229	-707	-831	-295

AME

	12/31/17	12/31/18	12 months ended 12/31/19	12/31/20	12/31/21	12/31/22	9 months ended 9/30/23
Change in stock price (%)	49.1	-6.6	47.3	21.3	21.6	-5.0	6.3
Sales ($ millions)	4,300	4,846	5,159	4,540	5,547	6,151	4,866
Net income ($ millions)	681	778	861	872	990	1,160	970
Net profit margin (%)	15.8	16.1	16.7	19.2	17.9	18.9	19.9
Return on invested capital (%)	12.2	12.5	12.3	11.0	11.3	12.2	13.0
Earnings per share ($)	2.94	3.34	3.75	3.77	4.25	5.01	4.19
Book value per share ($)	17.42	18.68	22.33	25.81	29.66	32.50	36.15
Assets	7,796	8,662	9,845	10,358	11,898	12,431	13,093
Working capital	796	577	600	1,447	565	964	1,445
Long-term debt	1,866	2,274	2,414	2,410	2,358	2,288	1,856
Total debt as a percentage of capital	35.1	38.3	36.6	30.3	28.4	25.5	21.8
Free cash flow	758	843	1,012	1,207	1,050	1,010	1,445

Notes: Shares outstanding, fully diluted; working capital equals current assets minus current liabilities; free cash flow equals flow from operations minus fixed capital expenditures. Figures in shaded cells are for the 12 months ended 9/30/23.

Sources: The companies, FactSet.

Pair 2: Arcimoto Inc. (electric vehicles) and Arconic Corp. (aluminum)

In 2020, shares of Arcimoto, the minuscule manufacturer of a three-wheeled electric motorcycle called the Fun Utility Vehicle ("FUV®"), rose more than 720%. Its CEO appeared on countless podcasts and online videos, often gleefully whizzing around in an FUV, urging traders to snap up the stock.

Once traders labeled it "the next Tesla," Arcimoto's stock got an electrifying jolt.

Arcimoto's business, however, was a mess.

It delivered only 97 retail vehicles to customers in 2020. That year, the business generated a negligible $2 million in sales, but $18 million in net losses.

Arcimoto claimed to have "thousands of pre-orders." But it managed to deliver only 192 retail vehicles in 2021 and 228 in 2022.

The company lost a combined $144 million from 2021 through 2023. The stock fell 41% in 2021, 98% in 2022 and another 74% in 2023.

Arconic was volatile, too, for different reasons.

In February 2019, its corporate parent announced that Arconic Corp., which manufactures aluminum products, would be spun off as a separate company. A year later, the global economy locked down to combat the Covid pandemic. Arconic's new stock began trading on April Fool's Day 2020.

With manufacturing stalled and supply chains choked around the world, industrial demand for aluminum was imploding. In Arconic's first three months as a standalone company, its sales would plummet 38% from the same period one year earlier, and it swung from a $5 million profit to a $92 million loss.

The stock fell 54% on April 1. The next day, it sank another 11%.

Just as the people buying Arcimoto overextrapolated its promise, the people dumping Arconic overextrapolated its problems.

The company refinanced its debt, conserved cash, and cut hundreds of millions of dollars in costs. As quarantines lifted and demand for aluminum recovered, Arconic's sales rebounded and its operating income shot up. By June 2021, Arconic's shares hit $38, up more than 500% from their low the year before.

In August 2023, Arconic was acquired for $30 per share by a group led by Apollo Global Management.

> ➻ **The point:** In the long run, high returns don't come from great expectations. Often, they come from the reversal of *gloomy* expectations.

Pair 3: Bed Bath & Beyond (housewares) and Best Buy (home electronics)

The testosterone-poisoned atmosphere of 2021's meme-stock mania took time to clear. For at least two more years, hordes of individual traders periodically sent stocks skyrocketing in bursts of coordinating buying, regardless of whether the underlying businesses were worth anything. Seeking to punish professional investors for betting against companies, these traders kept hoping to create "short squeezes" that would force the pros to buy and send a stock soaring even higher.

As a business, Bed Bath & Beyond was beyond repair. In its fiscal year ended February 2021, sales totaled $9.2 billion—down 17%

FIGURE 18-1: Taking a Bath ... and Beyond

Source: FactSet.

from the year before and below the company's total nine years earlier. Bed Bath had lost $900 million in the prior three years, and its total liabilities had nearly tripled in 10 years. With a weak online presence, the company's business was crushed when Covid shuttered its stores.

Worse, since 2012, Bed Bath had spent an astounding $8.3 billion buying back its stock at prices often exceeding $40 per share. By late 2022 the stock had sunk below $4.

Bed Bath had fired its CEO, its chief financial officer had committed suicide, and the company had burned through roughly $1 billion of cash in 12 months. Its financial statements warned that BBBY might not survive.

In response, speculators bought the stock en masse.

"I think that Bed Bath & Beyond, even in bankruptcy, is one of the best deals in the stock market," one said in May 2023. "You can call me a conspiracy theorist."

Again and again from 2021 until Bed Bath's shares finally stopped trading in September 2023, traders piled into the stock based on one confabulation after another: *Let's get revenge on those hedge funds! Entrepreneur Ryan Cohen will rescue the company! Bankruptcy won't make the shares worthless!*

But the hedge funds had the last laugh after Bed Bath filed for bankruptcy protection in April 2023. Cohen sold his entire stake after only a few months. All the shares were extinguished, worthless, in September 2023.

At the same time, another retailer, Best Buy (ticker symbol: BBY), kept plodding along. Its online sales held up, and its customers went on a spending binge as the economy reopened after the pandemic faded. Best Buy's sales, net income, and earnings per share hit record highs in the year ending in January 2022.

Later in 2022 and in 2023, Best Buy's business slumped as inflation and higher interest rates hit home. After rising 66% in 2019 and moderately positive gains in 2020 and 2021, Best Buy's stock dropped 21% in 2022 and another 2% in 2023.

But BBY's investors fared far better than BBBY's, because they weren't chasing recent hot returns, pursuing a fantasy of punishing other people, or pretending that bankruptcy would shower them with wealth.

➻ **The point:** You can *feel* that a stock is going to make you rich even in bankruptcy, but your feelings can't change the facts. Furthermore, you aren't one penny poorer if someone else is making more money than you, and it isn't the job of the stock market to equalize everyone's wealth. Hedge-fund managers can become billionaires, but they aren't taking that money from you *unless you choose to be on the other side of the trade from them.*

Pair 4: H&R Block (tax preparation) and Block, Inc. (online payments)

Between early 1973, when Graham wrote his last version of this chapter, and early 2013, H&R Block's stock rose a remarkable 625-fold—quintupling in value four times, a feat achieved over the long run by fewer than 2.5% of all U.S. companies.[3] Most of that came in the earlier years, however. Between early 2013 and the end of 2023, H&R Block gained an average of 8.7% annually, well behind the 13% average annual return of the S&P 500.

Competition from online tax-preparation tools and the Internal Revenue Service's Free File, which enables people to do their own tax returns, helped slow H&R Block's growth from a torrent to a trickle. About 48% of U.S. taxpayers filed their own returns in 2022 and 2023, up from roughly 34% in 2012–13. Some used H&R Block's own online tools to do that, but many others used competing services.

Partly as a result, between its fiscal years 2018 and 2023, H&R Block's revenue grew only from $3.2 billion to $3.5 billion, and its net income shrank from $625 million to $560 million.

As the growth of the business slowed, the stock—valued richly at more than 20 times earnings a decade earlier—traded in late 2023 for only nine times H&R Block's earnings over the previous 12 months. That was much cheaper than the overall market's valuation of 21 times earnings.

Block, Inc., formerly Square, Inc., enables small businesses—even

---

[3] Hendrik Bessembinder, "Long-Run Stock Market Returns: Probabilities of Big Gains and Post-Event Returns," bit.ly/3QKh11N.

vendors at farmers' markets—to use a smartphone or tablet to take credit-card payments. That's the kind of electronic magic that dazzles Wall Street. In 2021, Square changed its name to Block, partly to evoke the blockchain technology that facilitates cryptocurrencies.

The company initially sold stock to the public in November 2015 at $9 per share. Less than three years later, the stock hit $99. In 2020 alone, the shares gained 248%.

By late 2020, Block, Inc.'s shares were trading at more than 550 times earnings, according to FactSet.

Why? Unlike H&R Block, Block, Inc. was booming. It grew from $1.2 billion in sales and a net loss of $212 million in 2015 to $9.5 billion in sales and a net profit of $213 million in 2020.

But no company can keep growing like that for long. In 2022, Block, Inc.'s revenue flatlined, and it lost $541 million. The stock fell 26% in 2021, 61% in 2022, and by the following October had lost nearly 38% in 2023. Then it made an astonishing comeback in the final two months, closing up 23% for the full year as bitcoin soared.

Meanwhile, although H&R Block is far from its former glory, it bounced back, returning 49% in 2021, 55% in 2022, and 37% in 2023.

FIGURE 18-2: Chopping Block

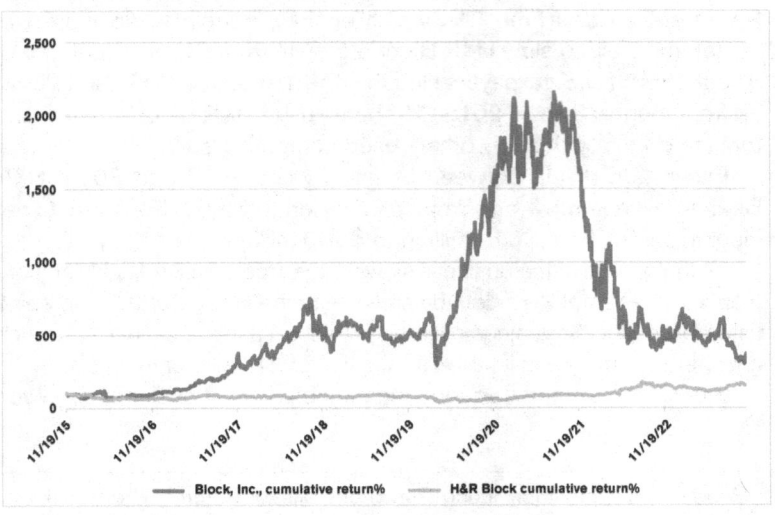

Source: FactSet.

By the end of 2023, you would have made more than three times as much on Block, Inc., as on H&R Block, but you would have had to survive a wild ride that included a death-defying 86% drop.

➻ **The point:** It doesn't matter how fast a company grows if you pay too much for the stock or can't bear to hang on.

Pair 5: Microsoft Corp. (computer software) and MicroStrategy Inc. (bitcoin)

Although both are ostensibly in the software business, Microsoft *is*, while MicroStrategy functions mainly as a corporate receptacle for one of the world's largest holdings of bitcoin.

From 2012 through 2019, MicroStrategy's revenues declined 19%; its existing data-analytics software business was profitable but stagnant. In 2020, as bitcoin's price was exploding, CEO Michael Saylor began putting MicroStrategy's ample cash reserves in bitcoin.

Trend-chasing traders not only binged on bitcoin; they snapped up MicroStrategy, too. That year, MicroStrategy's shares leaped 172%.

However, under an accounting rule disclosed in MicroStrategy's financial statements, the company had to review the market value of its bitcoin each quarter and write it down—taking a bite out of profits—if it fell below the purchase price. When the value of bitcoin rose, MicroStrategy could record a gain only if it sold the asset, not if it kept holding it.[4]

Because MicroStrategy bought bitcoin at fluctuating prices in a frenzied market, it booked "digital asset impairment losses" of $71 million in 2020, $831 million in 2021, and $1.3 billion in 2022.

That's one reason the stock's performance diverged sharply from bitcoin's:

---

[4] This accounting asymmetry was eliminated by regulators in 2023.

TABLE 18-2: Coin vs. Stock

	2020	2021	2022	2023
Bitcoin return (%)	303.9	59.9	-64.3	156.9
MicroStrategy stock return (%)	172.4	40.1	-74.0	346.2

Sources: Dow Jones Market Data, FactSet.

As of late 2023, MicroStrategy's $2.5 billion position in bitcoin made up more than three-quarters of its $3.4 billion in total assets. It was more a hedge fund than a computer software company—but a fund whose returns often sheared away from bitcoin's.

In just the first 15 trading days of 2024, MicroStrategy's stock fell 29% as U.S. regulators finally approved ETFs that may hold bitcoin directly—creating new competition for MicroStrategy as a way to own the digital currency.

Microsoft Corp. is at the other extreme: It minds its own business. Microsoft has made big acquisitions, paying $26 billion for careers website LinkedIn and $69 billion for videogame producer Activision Blizzard, along with a more than $10 billion investment in artificial-intelligence group OpenAI. But it remains focused on its primary strengths in software.

Its conservative accounting and vast reserves of more than $144 billion in cash make Microsoft the most stable among gigantic technology firms. Yet its stock has been nimble, outperforming the S&P 500 in most recent years. Microsoft seems—so far, at least—to be defying the sclerosis that strikes nearly all technology firms as they age.

> ➥ **The point:** If you want to invest in a company, buy the stock. If you want to own bitcoin, buy the digital currency itself, not a company that holds it.

Pair 6: NVIDIA Corp. (artificial-intelligence computer chips) and Novo Nordisk ADR (pharmaceuticals)

Even the biggest stocks can be inflamed with speculative fever if they're associated with a trendy new technology.

By late 2020, NVIDIA Corp., which makes chips for computer graphics, gaming, and other advanced uses, was valued at more than $330 billion. Novo Nordisk was Denmark's biggest company and one of the world's largest drug manufacturers.

Two technological breakthroughs soon set off buying panics.

Artificial intelligence, or AI, captured the popular imagination when ChatGPT was released in November 2022. NVIDIA is the dominant producer of the chips needed to power AI software.

And Novo Nordisk's weight-loss drugs, Wegovy and Ozempic, went viral after users started posting about them in 2021 on Facebook and TikTok—and after influential people like Elon Musk said on social media that the drugs had helped them slim down.

In May 2023, NVIDIA—whose stock was already up 109% since the beginning of the year—forecast that its quarterly sales would hit $11 billion, 64% higher than a year earlier and far above the $7.2 billion that Wall Street had expected.

Analysts following NVIDIA were as giddy as teenagers at a Taylor Swift concert. "It looks like the new gold rush is upon us," one research note read. "The magnitude of upside is stunning," said another. NVIDIA's market value quickly surpassed $1 trillion.

Then, in August 2023, NVIDIA stunned Wall Street again, reporting sales and earnings far above analysts' forecasts. Its revenue doubled over the prior year—a remarkable rate of growth for so gigantic a company. The stock surged again, up more than 230% since January 1. At its peak, NVIDIA traded at more than 250 times its earnings over the prior 12 months.

In November 2023, NVIDIA surpassed analysts' expectations yet again—but this time the stock tailed down, probably because its "upside surprise" wasn't big enough.

With Novo, too, Wall Street's hype machine had been hitting on all cylinders: Analysts predicted that consumers with newly controllable appetites would buy much less junk food, thinner passengers could save the typical airline $80 million in annual fuel costs, and demand for clothing fabric could decline by as much as 20% if fewer people needed extra-large sizes.

By August 2023 Novo traded at 50 times its earnings in the prior 12 months—almost triple what investors were willing to pay for the average pharmaceutical stock.

Can these leviathans keep growing larger? For that to happen, the future markets for their products don't only need to be bigger. They need to be even bigger than most people expect.

> **The point:** Great companies can be great stocks, too—but not at any price. Your returns always equal future reality minus present expectations—and the higher today's expectations go, the lower the odds that the future can live up to them.

Pair 7: Tesla Inc. (electric vehicles) and Tetra Tech, Inc. (environmental consulting)

Tesla first sold shares to the public in 2010. In mid-2012, Tesla began delivering its Model S, a luxury electric vehicle. As CEO Elon Musk, a master marketer with boundless energy, flogged the cars, reviewers raved about them, customers snapped them up, and the stock raced ahead.

As early as 2013 and 2014, analysts were warning that the rise in Tesla's stock was unjustified and unsustainable. So far, at least, Tesla has made skeptics seem like fools.

By December 2020, when Tesla was added to the S&P 500 index, its shares were trading at more than 1,100 times its earnings over the previous 12 months—over 35 times more expensive than the S&P 500 itself. From the beginning of 2011 through the end of 2021, a period when the S&P 500 rose 360%, Tesla's shares gained an astonishing 18,400%.

Tesla's stock finally crashed in 2022, falling 65%. But it promptly accelerated again, gaining 94% in 2023.

By late 2023, Tesla's stock-market value exceeded $750 billion, more than most of the world's major automakers—Ferrari, Ford, General Motors, Honda, Nissan, Renault, Stellantis, Toyota, and Volkswagen—*combined*. Then, in the first five months of 2024, Tesla's stock fell 28%.

Tetra Tech also benefited from the green-energy boom, but its

TABLE 18-3: Is the Sky the Limit?

	2023	2022	2021	2020	2019	2018	2017	2016	2015	2014	2013	2012
Revenue, fiscal years ($millions)												
Tesla	96,773.0	81,462.0	53,823.0	31,536.0	24,578.0	21,461.3	11,758.8	7,000.1	4,046.0	3,198.4	2,013.5	413.3
Tetra Tech	4,522.6	3,504.0	3,213.5	2,994.9	3,107.3	2,964.1	2,753.4	2,583.5	2,299.3	2,483.8	2,613.8	2,711.1
Net income, fiscal years ($millions)												
Tesla	14,997.0	12,556.0	5,524.0	690.0	-862.0	-976.1	-1,961.4	-674.9	-888.7	-294.0	-74.0	-396.2
Tetra Tech	273.4	263.1	232.8	173.9	158.7	136.9	117.9	83.8	39.1	108.3	-2.1	104.4
Earnings per share, fiscal years ($)												
Tesla	4.30	3.62	4.90	0.64	-4.92	-5.72	-0.79	-0.31	-0.46	-0.16	-0.04	-0.25
Tetra Tech	5.10	4.86	4.26	3.16	2.84	2.42	2.04	1.42	0.64	1.66	-0.03	1.63
Price / earnings ratio, fiscal year end												
Tesla	57.7	34.0	216.0	1,107.5	NM	NM	NM	NM	NM	NM	NM	NM
Tetra Tech	29.8	26.5	35.7	28.9	29.9	28.2	22.8	25.0	38.9	15.2	NM	16.1
Annual stock total return, calendar years (%)												
Tesla	101.7	-65.0	49.8	743.4	25.7	6.9	45.7	-11.0	7.9	47.9	344.1	18.5
Tetra Tech	15.7	-14.5	46.7	34.4	66.4	7.5	11.6	67.7	-1.4	-3.8	5.7	22.5

Notes: Fiscal years end Dec. 31 for Tesla and the last day of September or the first day of October for Tetra Tech.
Sources: FactSet, SEC.gov, tesla.com.

growth was tepid alongside Tesla's. Its earnings per share roughly tripled between 2012 and 2022, and investors bid up the stock. But consulting and engineering services are complicated to explain; contracts can take years to pay off; and Tetra Tech lacks a glamorous consumer product like electric cars and a charismatic, ubiquitous CEO like Elon Musk. Tetra Tech's stock had high returns—perhaps even higher than justified by the growth of the business—but it didn't thrill investors the way Tesla did.

➤➤ **The point:** No matter how overvalued a stock seems, it can keep going up much longer than even its harshest critics can imagine.

Pair 8: Valeant Pharmaceuticals International Inc. (prescription drugs) and Valmont Industries, Inc. (industrial equipment)

In 2015, Valeant looked like one of the stock market's greatest success stories. Since 2010, it had vacuumed up more than a dozen other drug manufacturers. As soon as it acquired these companies, Valeant promptly jacked up prices, sometimes raising the cost to consumers by at least 500% overnight.

Valeant was not a healthy company, however. It binged on borrowed money, racking up $31 billion in debt to make those acquisitions. In its earnings announcements, Valeant boasted about its booming "cash earnings," an unorthodox measure of profits that excluded almost all the company's major expenses. By the yardsticks of conventional accounting, Valeant lost money or barely broke even almost every quarter.[5]

Wall Street looked the other way. Valeant's stock rose nearly 1,900% from 2010 through August 2015.

Then short-sellers and journalists reported that Valeant had been using coercive sales at an affiliated firm to inflate its revenue. Congress held hearings on whether Valeant had been price-gouging patients.

---

[5] For other abuses of non-GAAP accounting, see the Commentary on Chapter 12.

By the end of 2017, shares in Valeant (now known as Bausch Health Companies) had fallen 97% from their peak.

In 2020, Valeant paid $45 million to settle civil charges of accounting fraud from the Securities and Exchange Commission.

As Valeant was watering down its assets with billions of dollars in debt and bogus accounting, Valmont Industries was watering wheatfields. Valmont makes metal coatings, utility poles and towers, and irrigation equipment.

Valmont's profits are moderate and sporadic; net earnings tripled from 2010 to 2013, then fell 38% over the next three years. In 2022 Valmont's net earnings were 10% lower than they had been in 2013.

From early 2010 through the end of 2023, Valmont's stock gained an average of 9.6% annually, well behind the 12.9% annualized return of the S&P 500. Still, that was much better than the 3.5% average annual loss of Valeant (now Bausch).

➽ **The point:** When a company grows only by buying other companies, it often doesn't end well—and you need to dissect the financial statements with the scalpel of a skeptic.

What have we learned?

Graham was fond of the French saying *Plus ça change, plus c'est la même chose* (The more things change, the more they stay the same). The excesses he highlighted decades ago differ only in name from the excesses of 1999–2000, the mid-2010s, and 2020–21.

No matter where or when you're reading this, another mania, more accounting chicanery, the latest outbreak of mass delusion, or a wild extrapolation of eternal growth is bound to burst out sooner or later. Understanding that we've been here before will help you avoid going there yourself.

CHAPTER 19

*Shareholders and Managements:
Dividend Policy*

by Benjamin Graham

*E*ver since 1934 we have argued in our writings for a more intelligent and energetic attitude by shareholders toward their managements. We have asked them to take a generous attitude toward those who are demonstrably doing a good job. We have asked them also to demand clear and satisfying explanations when the results appear to be worse than they should be, and to support movements to improve or remove clearly unproductive managements. Shareholders are justified in raising questions as to the competence of the management when the results (1) are unsatisfactory in themselves, (2) are poorer than those obtained by other companies that appear similarly situated, and (3) have resulted in an unsatisfactory market price of long duration.

In the last 36 years practically nothing has actually been accomplished through intelligent action by the great body of shareholders. A sensible crusader—if there are any such—would take this as a sign that he has been wasting his time, and that he had better give up the fight. As it happens our cause has not been lost; it has been rescued by an extraneous development—known as take-overs, or take-over bids. We said in Chapter 8 that **poor managements produce poor market prices.** The low market prices, in turn, attract the attention of companies interested in diversifying their operations—and these are now legion. Innumerable such acquisitions have been accomplished by agreement with the existing managements, or else by accumulation of shares in the market and by offers made over the head of those in control. The price bid has usually been within the range of the value of the enterprise under reasonably competent management. Hence, in many cases, the inert public shareholder has been bailed out by the actions of "outsiders"—who at times may be enterprising individuals or groups acting on their own.

It can be stated as a rule with very few exceptions that poor managements are not changed by action of the "public stockholders," but only by the assertion of control by an individual or compact group. This is happening often enough these days to put the management, including the board of directors, of a typical publicly controlled company on notice that if its operating results and the resulting market price are highly unsatisfactory, it may become the target of a successful take-over move. As a consequence, boards of directors have probably become more alive than previously to their fundamental duty to see that their company has a satisfactory top management. Many more changes of presidents have been seen in recent years than formerly.

Not all companies in the unsatisfactory class have benefited from such developments. Also, the change has often occurred after a long period of bad results without remedial action, and has depended on enough disappointed shareholders selling out at low prices to permit the energetic outsiders to acquire a controlling position in the shares. But the idea that public shareholders could really help themselves by supporting moves for improving management and management policies has proved too quixotic to warrant further space in this book. Those individual shareholders who have enough gumption to make their presence felt at annual meetings—generally a completely futile performance—will not need our counsel on what points to raise with the managements. For others the advice would probably be wasted. Nevertheless, let us close this section with the plea that shareholders consider with an open mind and with careful attention any proxy material sent them by fellow-shareholders who want to remedy an obviously unsatisfactory management situation in the company.

Shareholders and Dividend Policy

In the past the dividend policy was a fairly frequent subject of argument between public, or "minority," shareholders and managements. In general these shareholders wanted more liberal dividends, while the managements preferred to keep the earnings in the business "to strengthen the company." They asked the shareholders to sacrifice their present interests for the good of the enterprise and for their own future long-term benefit. But in recent years the attitude of investors toward dividends has been undergoing a gradual but significant change. The basic argument now for paying small rather than liberal dividends is not that the company "needs" the money, but rather that it can use it to the shareholders' direct and immediate advantage by retaining the funds for profitable expansion. Years ago it was typically the weak company that was more or less forced to hold on to its profits, instead of paying out the usual 60% to 75% of them in dividends. The effect was almost always adverse to the market price of the shares. Nowadays it is quite likely to be a strong and growing enterprise that deliberately keeps down its dividend payments, with the approval of investors and speculators alike.*

There was always a strong theoretical case for reinvesting profits in the business where such retention could be counted on to produce a goodly increase in earnings. But there were several strong counter-arguments, such as: The profits "belong" to the shareholders, and they are entitled to have them paid out within the limits of prudent management; many of the shareholders need their dividend income to live on; the earnings they receive in dividends are "real money," while those retained in the company may or may not show up later as tangible values for the shareholders. These counter-arguments were so compelling, in fact, that the stock market showed a persistent bias in favor of the liberal dividend payers as against the companies that paid no dividends or relatively small ones.[1]

In the last 20 years the "profitable reinvestment" theory has been gaining ground. The better the past record of growth, the readier investors and speculators have become to accept a low-pay-out

---

* The irony that Graham describes here grew even stronger in the 1990s, when it seemed the stronger the company was, the less likely it was to pay a dividend—or for its shareholders to want one. The "payout ratio" (the percentage of net income companies paid out as dividends) dropped from "60% to 75%" in Graham's day to roughly 35% to 40% in recent years.

policy. So much is this true that in many cases of growth favorites the dividend rate—or even the absence of any dividend—has seemed to have virtually no effect on the market price.*

A striking example of this development is found in the history of Texas Instruments, Incorporated. The price of its common stock rose from 5 in 1953 to 256 in 1960, while earnings were advancing from 43 cents to $3.91 per share and while no dividend of any kind was paid. (In 1962 cash dividends were initiated, but by that year the earnings had fallen to $2.14 and the price had shown a spectacular drop to a low of 49.)

Another extreme illustration is provided by Superior Oil. In 1948 the company reported earnings of $35.26 per share, paid $3 in dividends, and sold as high as 235. In 1953 the dividend was reduced to $1, but the high price was 660. In 1957 it *paid no dividend at all,* and sold at 2,000! This unusual issue later declined to 795 in 1962, when it earned $49.50 and paid $7.50.†

Investment sentiment is far from crystallized in this matter of dividend policy of growth companies. The conflicting views are well illustrated by the cases of two of our very largest corporations—American Telephone & Telegraph and International Business Machines. American Tel. & Tel. came to be regarded as an issue with good growth possibilities, as shown by the fact that in 1961 it sold at 25 times that year's earnings. Nevertheless, the company's cash dividend policy has remained an investment and speculative consideration of first importance, its quotation making an active response to even *rumors* of an impending increase in the dividend rate. On the other hand, comparatively little attention appears to

---

* In the late 1990s, technology companies were particularly strong advocates of the view that all of their earnings should be "plowed back into the business," where they could earn higher returns than outside shareholders could get elsewhere. Incredibly, investors seldom questioned the truth of this patronizing Daddy-Knows-Best principle—or recognized that a company's cash belongs to the shareholders, not its managers.

† Superior Oil's stock price peaked at $2,165 per share in 1959, when it paid a $4 dividend. For many years, Superior was the highest-priced stock listed on the New York Stock Exchange. Superior, controlled by the Keck family of Houston, was acquired by Mobil Corp. in 1984.

have been paid to the *cash* dividend on IBM, which in 1960 yielded only 0.5% at the high price of the year and 1.5% at the close of 1970. (But in both cases stock splits have operated as a potent stock-market influence.)

The market's appraisal of cash-dividend policy appears to be developing in the following direction: Where prime emphasis is not placed on growth the stock is rated as an "income issue," and the dividend rate retains its long-held importance as the prime determinant of market price. At the other extreme, stocks clearly recognized to be in the rapid-growth category are valued primarily in terms of the expected growth rate over, say, the next decade, and the cash-dividend rate is more or less left out of the reckoning.

While the above statement may properly describe present tendencies, it is by no means a clear-cut guide to the situation in all common stocks, and perhaps not in the majority of them. For one thing, many companies occupy an intermediate position between growth and nongrowth enterprises. It is hard to say how much importance should be ascribed to the growth factor in such cases, and the market's view thereof may change radically from year to year. Secondly, there seems to be something paradoxical about requiring the companies showing slower growth to be more liberal with their cash dividends. For these are generally the less prosperous concerns, and in the past the more prosperous the company the greater was the expectation of both liberal and increasing payments.

It is our belief that shareholders should demand of their managements either a normal payout of earnings—on the order, say, of two-thirds—or else a clear-cut demonstration that the reinvested profits have produced a satisfactory increase in per-share earnings. Such a demonstration could ordinarily be made in the case of a recognized growth company. But in many other cases a low payout is clearly the cause of an average market price that is below fair value, and here the shareholders have every right to inquire and probably to complain.

A niggardly policy has often been imposed on a company because its financial position is relatively weak, and it has needed all or most of its earnings (plus depreciation charges) to pay debts and bolster its working-capital position. When this is so there is not much the shareholders can say about it—except perhaps to criticize the management for permitting the company to fall into such an unsatisfactory financial position. However, **dividends are sometimes held down by relatively unprosperous companies for the declared purpose of expanding the business. We feel that such a policy is illogical on its face, and should require both a complete explanation and a convincing defense before the shareholders should accept it.** In terms of the past record there is no reason a priori to believe that the owners will benefit from expansion moves undertaken with their money by a business showing mediocre results and continuing its old management.

Stock Dividends and Stock Splits

It is important that investors understand the essential difference between a stock dividend (properly so-called) and a stock split. The latter represents a restatement of the common-stock structure—in a typical case by issuing two or three shares for one. The new shares are not related to specific earnings reinvested in a specific past period. Its purpose is to establish a lower market price for the single shares, presumably because such lower price range would be more acceptable to old and new shareholders. A stock split may be carried out by what technically may be called a stock dividend, which involves a transfer of sums from earned surplus to capital account; or else by a change in par value, which does not affect the surplus account.*

What we should call a *proper stock dividend* is one that is paid to shareholders to give them a tangible evidence or representation of *specific* earnings which have been reinvested in the business for their account over some relatively short period in the recent past—say, not more than the two preceding years. It is now approved practice to value such a stock dividend at the approximate value at the time of declaration, and to transfer an amount equal to such value from earned surplus to capital accounts. Thus the amount

---

* Today, virtually all stock splits are carried out by a change in value. In a two-for-one split, one share becomes two, each trading at half the former price of the original single share; in a three-for-one split, one share becomes three, each trading at a third of the former price; and so on. Only in very rare cases is a sum transferred "from earned surplus to capital account," as in Graham's day.

of a typical stock dividend is relatively small—in most cases not more than 5%. In essence a stock dividend of this sort has the same overall effect as the payment of an equivalent amount of cash out of earnings when accompanied by the sale of additional shares of like total value to the shareholders. However, a straight stock dividend has an important tax advantage over the otherwise equivalent combination of cash dividends with stock subscription rights, which is the almost standard practice for public-utility companies.

The New York Stock Exchange has set the figure of 25% as a practical dividing line between stock splits and stock dividends. Those of 25% or more need not be accompanied by the transfer of their market value from earned surplus to capital, and so forth. Some companies, especially banks, still follow the old practice of declaring any kind of stock dividend they please—e.g., one of 10%, not related to recent earnings—and these instances maintain an undesirable confusion in the financial world.

We have long been a strong advocate of a systematic and clearly enunciated policy with respect to the payment of cash and stock dividends. Under such a policy, stock dividends are paid periodically to capitalize all or a stated portion of the earnings reinvested in the business. Such a policy—covering 100% of the reinvested earnings—has been followed by Purex, Government Employees Insurance, and perhaps a few others.*

Stock dividends of all types seem to be disapproved of by most academic writers on the subject. They insist that they are nothing but pieces of paper, that they give the shareholders nothing they did not have before, and that they entail needless expense and inconvenience.† On our side we consider this a completely

---

* This policy, already unusual in Graham's day, is extremely rare today. In 1936 and again in 1950, roughly half of all stocks on the NYSE paid a so-called special dividend. By 1970, however, that percentage had declined to less than 10% and, by the 1990s, was well under 5%.
† The academic criticism of dividends was led by Merton Miller and Franco Modigliani, whose influential article "Dividend Policy, Growth, and the Valuation of Shares" (1961) helped win them Nobel Prizes in Economics. Miller and Modigliani argued that dividends were irrelevant, since investors shouldn't care whether their return comes through dividends and a rising

doctrinaire view, which fails to take into account the practical and psychological realities of investment. True, a periodic stock dividend—say of 5%—changes only the "form" of the owners' investment. He has 105 shares in place of 100; but without the stock dividend the original 100 shares would have represented the same ownership interest now embodied in his 105 shares. Nonetheless, the change of form is actually one of real importance and value to him. If he wishes to cash in his share of the reinvested profits he can do so by selling the new certificate sent him, instead of having to break up his original certificate. He can count on receiving the same cash-dividend rate on 105 shares as formerly on his 100 shares; a 5% rise in the cash-dividend rate without the stock dividend would not be nearly as probable.*

The advantages of a periodic stock-dividend policy are most evident when it is compared with the usual practice of the public-utility companies of paying liberal cash dividends and then taking back a good part of this money from the shareholders by selling them additional stock (through subscription rights).† As we mentioned above, the shareholders would find themselves in exactly the same position if they received stock dividends in lieu of the popular combination of cash dividends followed by stock subscriptions—except that they would save the income tax otherwise paid on the cash dividends. Those who need or wish the maximum annual cash income, with no additional stock, can get this result by selling their

---

stock price, or through a rising stock price alone, so long as the total return is the same.

* Today's investors can safely skip over this passage. Shareholders no longer need to worry about "having to break up" a stock certificate, since virtually all shares now exist in electronic rather than paper form.

† Subscription rights, often simply known as "rights," are used less frequently than in Graham's day. They confer upon an existing shareholder the right to buy new shares, sometimes at a discount to market price. A shareholder who does not participate will end up owning proportionately less of the company. Thus, as is the case with so many other things that go by the name of "rights," some coercion is often involved. Rights are most common today among closed-end funds and insurance or other holding companies.

stock dividends, in the same way as they sell their subscription rights under present practice.

The aggregate amount of income tax that could be saved by substituting stock dividends for the present stock-dividends-plus-subscription-rights combination is enormous. We urge that this change be made by the public utilities, despite its adverse effect on the U.S. Treasury, because we are convinced that it is completely inequitable to impose a second (personal) income tax on earnings which are not really received by the shareholders, since the companies take the same money back through sales of stock.

Efficient corporations continuously modernize their facilities, their products, their bookkeeping, their management-training programs, their employee relations. It is high time they thought about modernizing their major financial practices, not the least important of which is their dividend policy.

Commentary on Chapter 19

by Jason Zweig

> Whoever can be trusted with very little can also be trusted with much, and whoever is dishonest with very little will also be dishonest with much. So if you have not been trustworthy in handling worldly wealth, who will trust you with true riches?
>
> —Luke 16: 10–11

Over the lifetime of this book, Graham changed no chapter more than this.

It was originally part of a section titled "The Investor as Business Owner," nearly 34 pages long. In it, Graham urged intelligent investors to become intelligent owners: vigilant and outspoken in ensuring that companies are well-managed, executives fairly paid, and the interests of outside investors safeguarded.

In principle, Graham wrote, "the stockholders as a class are king . . . they can hire and fire managements and bend them completely to their will."

In practice, however,

> . . . the shareholders are a complete washout. . . . They vote in sheeplike fashion for whatever the management recommends and no matter how poor the management's record. . . . The only way to inspire the average American shareholder to take any independently intelligent action would be by exploding a firecracker under him.

By his last revision in 1971–72, Graham had shrunk the discussion to a few pages focused almost entirely on dividends. The effort to incite investors to take action must have exhausted him.

Insiders versus Outsiders

The tension between managers and owners is as old as capitalism. Left unchecked, many CEOs would binge on buying other companies, pour money into failing businesses, hoard more capital than they need, and pay themselves stupendous bonuses for tepid performance.

In fact, many do.

Centuries ago, investors expected dividends to be set at high rates of 6% to 10%, partly as a check on management's power. By transferring cash to outside shareholders, high dividends prevented managers from pilfering or frittering it all away.

Buybacks, in which companies use excess cash to repurchase some of their shares, appear to have originated for the same reason.

Today's critics, who contend that buybacks line the pockets of management and fat-cat investors, should ponder what can happen when companies *don't* repurchase stock.

In the 1970s, bursting with windfall profits from soaring oil prices, Exxon started manufacturing typewriters—right before personal computers wiped that business out. Mobil Oil bought Montgomery Ward department stores—just as Walmart was about to crush traditional retailers.

The oil giants wasted billions of dollars on businesses they had no business getting into. They and their investors would have been much better off if the companies had used that excess cash to buy back shares instead.

As one of Wall Street's first "activist" investors, Graham pioneered the fight against overpaid, underachieving corporate managers. He understood that cash is at the heart of the conflict between managers and investors:

> [M]anagement . . . almost always wants as much capital from the owners as it can possibly get, in order to minimize its own financial problems. Thus the typical management will operate with more capital than necessary, if the stockholders permit it—which they often do.[1]

---

[1] Benjamin Graham, *The Intelligent Investor* (Harper & Row, 1949), p. 233.

The better companies get at producing what their customers want to buy, the more the profits pile up. Superior businesses eventually accumulate more cash than they know what to do with.

On the other hand, businesses that are struggling will cling to cash for dear life. "The more dubious the company's prospects . . . the more anxious management is to retain all the cash it can in the business," Graham wrote. "But the stockholders would be well advised to take out all the capital *that can be safely spared*, because these funds are much more valuable to them if in their own pockets, or invested elsewhere."[2]

Buyback Baloney

The most important task of a CEO is to allocate capital to its most productive use. That could mean making capital expenditures, such as maintaining and upgrading factories or replacing an aging fleet of trucks or airplanes. It could mean pouring surplus cash into research and development to create better software, develop promising drugs, or come up with innovative goods or services. It could mean buying another company to acquire its products, technology, or marketing prowess. It could mean hiring more workers or paying more to the existing staff.[3]

Once those essential needs of the business are met, what should managers do with excess cash?

Unless the business can use it productively, management should give the cash back to the owners—either through dividends or buybacks.

The two choices are fundamentally similar.

With a dividend, you decide whether to keep the payment in cash or reinvest it in more shares of the company.

With a buyback, you choose whether to accept the company's offer to buy your shares. If you do, you end up with cash. If you don't, you end up owning a slightly larger stake in a company that now has fewer shares.

---

[2] Benjamin Graham and David Dodd, *Security Analysis* (McGraw-Hill, 1951 edition), p. 600; italics in original.

[3] Michael J. Mauboussin and Dan Callahan, "Capital Allocation," bit.ly /3MQIBbj.

FIGURE 19-1: The Buyback Boom

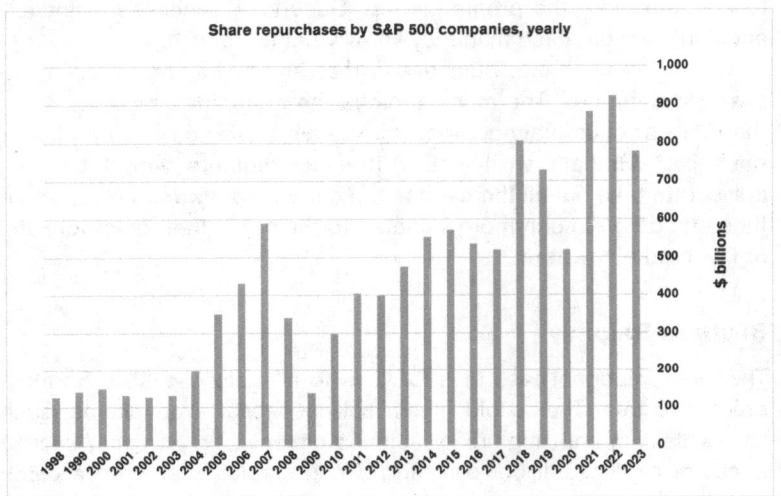

Source: S&P Dow Jones Indices.

In either case, the company has less capital, its owners have more, and some of its return has shifted from the uncertain future to the present, where it is certain.

Buybacks have incited furious debate. From 2014 through 2023, U.S. companies repurchased a staggering $6.8 trillion of their own shares:

In theory, companies should buy back their stock only when it's cheap. In practice, they almost always think it is. In the spring of 2020, with Covid raging and the stock market crashing, 83% of chief financial officers thought their stock was undervalued. However, more than 80% of CFOs also thought their stock was undervalued in the first quarter of 2000, during one of the wildest market manias in history! Always trusting their subjective opinions would be a dumb idea.[4]

Lehman Brothers Holdings Inc. spent more than $4 billion

---

[4] John R. Graham, "Presidential Address: Corporate Finance and Reality," bit.ly/46IcNfG. To be fair, executives may think their stock is undervalued without necessarily buying it back.

repurchasing its shares in 2007 and 2008. In September 2008, Lehman went bust from reckless bets on complex risks—precipitating the worst global financial crisis since the Great Depression.

Citigroup Inc. bought back over $20 billion in its shares from 2004 through 2008, then needed a $45 billion bailout from the U.S. government to survive the financial crisis.

As we saw in the Commentary on Chapter 18, Bed Bath & Beyond spent billions buying back its stock, only to end up filing for bankruptcy protection. Years earlier, so did Sears, another failed retailer.

Your instinct might be to say: *Imagine how much better those companies would have done if they hadn't wasted all that money buying back their stock!*

Your better judgment should tell you: *Imagine how much more damage those companies could have done with billions of extra dollars to spend on their managers' whims!*

If the companies hadn't repurchased all that stock, wouldn't they have been wallowing in so much cash that the temptation to overpay their CEOs would have been even greater?

Despite what the critics say, the evidence that CEOs get giant boosts in pay from buybacks is unpersuasive; nor do the stocks of companies doing repurchases get big pops in price.

The argument that CEOs are starving capital expenditures and research and development to fund buybacks is also hollow; those commitments have risen to record highs despite the surge in share repurchases.[5]

The Bottom Line on Buybacks

The bottom line is that buybacks are neither good nor evil.

They're simply a tool.

Just as you can use a hammer either to build a house or knock it down, buybacks can be either constructive or destructive. They are an effective tool to distribute surplus cash when a company has no better use for it—but a damaging tool when the company repurchases shares with reckless disregard for warning signs about its own future.

---

[5] Jason Zweig, "Stock Buybacks Aren't Bad. They Aren't Good, Either," bit .ly/3sAl2N1.

Blindly opposing all buybacks makes no sense. Nor does blindly applauding them. As an intelligent investor, you must assess any company's buyback based on the circumstances: How cheap is the stock? How bright are the prospects for growth? Is the company borrowing money to finance the buyback? Are the repurchases simply counteracting the issuance of new shares to pay incentive compensation to management? Would the company and its owners be better off if it spent the money for other purposes?

When, in August 2023, NVIDIA announced that it would repurchase up to $25 billion of stock, many shareowners cheered. Instead, they should have worried about the wisdom of a big buyback near the highest valuations in NVIDIA's history.[6]

Pay for "Performance"

With musicians and athletes earning tens of millions of dollars a year and often becoming billionaires, you shouldn't automatically criticize CEOs earning similar sums.

However, you always should be skeptical.

Consider Warner Bros. Discovery, Inc. (WBD).

After several acquisitions orchestrated by its CEO, David Zaslav, WBD consists of CNN, DC Comics, Discovery Channel, Food Network, HBO, the Warner Bros. movie and television studios, and other entertainment assets.

The company went public, as Discovery Communications, Inc., in late 2008. In the first five years after that IPO, the stock was on fire, gaining an average of 46% annually while the S&P 500 averaged 18%. After that blazing start, the board of directors awarded Zaslav $156 million in total compensation in 2014—the year Discovery began a decline that, so far, has lasted a decade.

In the 2010s and early 2020s, online and mobile streaming wreaked havoc on traditional networks and studios.

---

[6] Cliff Asness et al., "Buyback Derangement Syndrome," bit.ly/40Izgbe; Alex Edmans, "The Case for Share Buybacks," bit.ly/3sGqZbk; Joachim Klement, "About Those Share Buybacks," bit.ly/3umPn2I; Michael J. Mauboussin and Dan Callahan, "Thoughts on Dividends and Buybacks," bit.ly/3G6Plho; Patrick O'Shaughnessy, "High-Conviction Buybacks," bit.ly/40Mil7y.

Despite its hot start, from its IPO to the end of 2023 WBD's stock returned an annual average of 2%, trailing the U.S. stock market by an abysmal 8.6 percentage points annually. A $10,000 investment in WBD would have crept up to just over $13,400 over that period; the same amount in the S&P 500 burgeoned to nearly $42,500.

Although Warner Bros. Discovery's revenues rose more than 10-fold over that period, its net income jolted up and down; in 2022, WBD lost $7.4 billion. By late 2023 it was carrying $45 billion of debt.

WBD's shares performed slightly better than rivals Paramount Global and Lions Gate Entertainment, but significantly worse than Comcast Corp. or Walt Disney Co., two other media giants.

Nevertheless, from 2009 through the end of 2022, Zaslav, the CEO of WBD, earned $956 million in total potential compensation—and took home more than $750 million.[7]

TABLE 19-1: That's Showbusiness

Year	Total return, Warner Bros. Discovery stock (%)	S&P 500 total return (%)	WBD total market capitalization ($ millions)	Total compensation for Warner Bros. Discovery CEO ($)
2009	116.6	26.5	13,065	11,655,850
2010	36.0	15.1	17,764	42,589,296
2011	1.8	2.1	16,511	52,404,119
2012	54.9	16.0	25,094	49,932,867
2013	42.4	32.4	34,920	33,349,798
2014	-25.4	13.7	16,567	156,077,912
2015	-22.6	1.4	12,166	32,377,346
2016	2.7	12.0	11,457	37,192,354

---

[7] Much of his potential total hasn't been paid out in cash, but resides in stock options whose ultimate value is contingent on whether WBD's stock can hit ambitious targets before the end of 2027.

TABLE 19-1: That's Showbusiness

Year	Total return, Warner Bros. Discovery stock (%)	S&P 500 total return (%)	WBD total market capitalization ($ millions)	Total compensation for Warner Bros. Discovery CEO ($)
2017	-18.4	21.8	8,639	42,247,984
2018	10.5	-4.4	13,112	129,499,005
2019	32.3	31.5	17,352	45,843,912
2020	-8.1	18.4	14,804	37,710,462
2021	-21.8	28.7	12,005	246,573,481
2022	-59.7	-18.1	23,036	39,288,458
Cumulative compensation for Warner Bros. Discovery CEO ($)				956,742,844
Annualized total return (%)	1.9	13.1		

Sources: WBD proxy statements, FactSet.

WBD's 2023 proxy statement said that paying top management with stock helps "align our executives' interests with those of our stockholders" and that Zaslav's "exceptional performance" as CEO included "over-delivery of the strategic objectives established for him." (After the stock fell nearly 60% in 2022, the board decided not to award him "any additional or above-target bonus.")

Much of Zaslav's cumulative compensation was based on an inventive measure of profits called Adjusted OIBDA. The company adds the *expense* of stock-based compensation back into that measure of its *income*—so the more WBD pays its top executives in stock, the higher adjusted OIBDA goes. And an increase in adjusted OIBDA is one of the things the CEO gets rewarded for.

As we saw in the Commentary on Chapter 12, this sort of arrangement is far from unusual, and its daffy logic has become so common that Wall Street treats it as normal—even though, as David Zion of Zion Research Group says, "it's flat-out wrong."

If what seems like excessive pay for unimpressive performance bothers you—as it should!—then exercise your rights. When you receive the annual proxy statement, don't merely vote against an unfair compensation plan. Vote against the reelection of every single director. They approved the plan. The least you can do is voice your disapproval of them.

You can also attend the company's annual meeting and speak out. In the U.S., you can check how your mutual funds and ETFs voted on pay packages by searching their Form N-PX filings at the SEC's EDGAR database (sec.gov/edgar/searchedgar/n-px). And you can try seeking out and banding together with like-minded investors using apps and online tools such as Civex, iconikapp.com, and Troop.[8]

Once you buy a stock, you must seek to be not only an intelligent investor, but also an intelligent owner. That means you have a responsibility to assert your rights.

Rewarding the Right Things

To reduce the risk of overpaying for underperformance, how *should* a company incentivize its management?

At Costco Wholesale Corp., executives' bonuses depend primarily on hitting targets for growth in sales and pre-tax income—two standard measures that are difficult to manipulate.

---

[8] Be selective; some apps come and go quickly. And you should associate with other investors who are serious and analytical, not with speculators who whip each other into a frenzy. The "apes" who bought AMC stock in 2021 egged each other on in adoration of the company's management, ignoring the fact that the executives had dumped nearly all their own shares before issuing new stock that radically reduced the apes' ownership. To be an intelligent owner, you must first think for yourself before you join a group.

Markel Corp., an insurance company, bases incentive compensation on the growth in per-share book value and the total return of the stock over five years.

At ExxonMobil Corp., most incentive pay for top executives is in special shares with restricted ownership rights; 50% vest after five years, the other half after 10 years. That rewards focusing on long-term goals.

Investors should expect pay for performance to be based on simple, clear measurements of the health and growth of the business—not on accounting chicanery. Multiyear results should weigh much more heavily than the short term. And performance hurdles shouldn't get easier to clear from year to year.

Decades ago, Graham advocated measuring the success of corporate managers with these criteria: return on invested capital, net profit margin, and the rate of growth in sales and net income. Each should be compared to that of other companies in the same industry. I'm not aware of any company that bases its incentive compensation on such sensible standards, but boards of directors should consider following Graham's advice.[1]

---

[1] Benjamin Graham and David Dodd, *Security Analysis* (McGraw-Hill, 1951), pp. 581–83. Measuring performance against other companies in the same industry is vital, since corporate results are often driven more by luck than by management's strategies. When interest rates fall, for example, most homebuilders will thrive even if their CEOs are barely competent. Only those executives whose firms did significantly better than the industry average over multiyear periods should be rewarded with big incentive pay.

CHAPTER 20

"Margin of Safety" as the Central Concept of Investment
by Benjamin Graham

*I*n the old legend the wise men finally boiled down the history of mortal affairs into the single phrase, "This too will pass."* Confronted with a like challenge to distill the secret of sound investment into three words, we venture the motto, MARGIN OF SAFETY. This is the thread that runs through all the preceding discussion of investment policy—often explicitly, sometimes in a less direct fashion. Let us try now, briefly, to trace that idea in a connected argument.

All experienced investors recognize that the margin-of-safety concept is essential to the choice of sound bonds and preferred stocks. For example, a railroad should have earned its total fixed charges better than five times (before income tax), taking a period of years, for its bonds to qualify as investment-grade issues. This *past* ability to earn in excess of interest requirements constitutes the margin of safety that is counted on to protect the investor against loss or discomfiture in the event of some *future* decline in net income. (The margin above charges may be stated in other ways—for example, in the percentage

---

* "It is said an Eastern monarch once charged his wise men to invent a sentence, to be ever in view, and which should be true and appropriate in all times and situations. They presented him the words: '*And this, too, shall pass away.*' How much it expresses! How chastening in the hour of pride!—how consoling in the depths of affliction! 'And this, too, shall pass away.' And yet let us hope it is not *quite* true."—Abraham Lincoln, Address to the Wisconsin State Agricultural Society, September 30, 1859, bit.ly/3OOT60g.

by which revenues or profits may decline before the balance after interest disappears—but the underlying idea remains the same.)

The bond investor does not expect future average earnings to work out the same as in the past; if he were sure of that, the margin demanded might be small. Nor does he rely to any controlling extent on his judgment as to whether future earnings will be materially better or poorer than in the past, if he did that, he would have to measure his margin in terms of a carefully *projected* income account, instead of emphasizing the margin shown in the past record. Here the function of the margin of safety is, in essence, that of rendering unnecessary an accurate estimate of the future. If the margin is a large one, then it is enough to assume that future earnings will not fall far below those of the past in order for an investor to feel sufficiently protected against the vicissitudes of time.

The margin of safety for bonds may be calculated, alternatively, by comparing the total value of the enterprise with the amount of debt. (A similar calculation may be made for a preferred-stock issue.) If the business owes $10 million and is fairly worth $30 million, there is room for a shrinkage of two-thirds in value—at least theoretically—before the bondholders will suffer loss. The amount of this extra value, or "cushion," above the debt may be approximated by using the average market price of the junior stock issues over a period of years. Since average stock prices are generally related to average earning power, the margin of "enterprise value" over debt and the margin of earnings over charges will in most cases yield similar results.

So much for the margin-of-safety concept as applied to "fixed-value investments." Can it be carried over into the field of common stocks? Yes, but with some necessary modifications.

There are instances where a common stock may be considered sound because it enjoys a margin of safety as large as that of a good bond. This will occur, for example, when a company has outstanding only common stock that under depression conditions is selling for less than the amount of bonds that could safely be issued against its property and earning power.* That was the position of a host

---

* "Earning power" is Graham's term for a company's potential profits or, as he puts it, the amount that a firm "might be expected to earn year after year if the business conditions prevailing during the period were to continue

of strongly financed industrial companies at the low price levels of 1932–33. In such instances the investor can obtain the margin of safety associated with a bond, *plus* all the chances of larger income and principal appreciation inherent in a common stock. (The only thing he lacks is the legal power to insist on dividend payments "or else"—but this is a small drawback as compared with his advantages.) Common stocks bought under such circumstances will supply an ideal, though infrequent, combination of safety and profit opportunity. As a quite recent example of this condition, let us mention once more National Presto Industries stock, which sold for a total enterprise value of $43 million in 1972. With its $16 million of recent earnings before taxes the company could easily have supported this amount of bonds.

In the ordinary common stock, bought for investment under normal conditions, the margin of safety lies in an expected earning power considerably above the going rate for bonds. In former editions we elucidated this point with the following figures:

> Assume in a typical case that the earning power is 9% on the price and that the bond rate is 4%; then the stockbuyer will have an average annual margin of 5% accruing in his favor. Some of the excess is paid to him in the dividend rate; even though spent by him, it enters into his overall investment result. The undistributed balance is reinvested in the business for his account. In many cases such reinvested earnings fail to add commensurately to the earning power and value of his stock. (That is why the market has a stubborn habit of valuing earnings disbursed in dividends more generously than the portion retained in the business.) But, if the picture is viewed as a whole, there is a reasonably close connection between the growth of corporate surpluses through reinvested earnings and the growth of corporate values.
>
> Over a ten-year period the typical excess of stock earning power over bond interest may aggregate 50% of the price paid.

---

unchanged" (*Security Analysis*, 1934 ed., p. 354). Graham intended the term to cover periods of five years or more.

This figure is sufficient to provide a very real margin of safety—which, under favorable conditions, will prevent or minimize a loss. If such a margin is present in each of a diversified list of twenty or more stocks, the probability of a favorable result under "fairly normal conditions" becomes very large. That is why **the policy of investing in representative common stocks does not require high qualities of insight and foresight to work out successfully. If the purchases are made at the average level of the market over a span of years, the prices paid should carry with them assurance of an adequate margin of safety. The danger to investors lies in concentrating their purchases in the upper levels of the market, or in buying nonrepresentative common stocks that carry more than average risk of diminished earning power.**

As we see it, the whole problem of common-stock investment under 1972 conditions lies in the fact that "in a typical case" the earning power is now much less than 9% on the price paid.* Let us assume that by concentrating somewhat on the low-multiplier issues among the large companies a defensive investor may now acquire equities at 12 times recent earnings—i.e., with an earnings return of 8.33% on cost. He may obtain a dividend yield of about 4%, and he will have 4.33% of his cost reinvested in the business for his account. On this basis, the excess of stock earning power over bond interest over a ten-year basis would still be too small to constitute an adequate margin of safety. For that reason we feel that there are real risks now even in a diversified list of sound common

---

* Graham elegantly summarized the discussion that follows in a lecture he gave in 1972: "The margin of safety is the difference between the percentage rate of the earnings on the stock at the price you pay for it and the rate of interest on bonds, and that margin of safety is the difference which would absorb unsatisfactory developments. At the time the 1965 edition of *The Intelligent Investor* was written the typical stock was selling at 11 times earnings, giving about 9% return as against 4% on bonds. In that case you had a margin of safety of over 100 per cent. Now [in 1972] there is no difference between the earnings rate on stocks and the interest rate on stocks, and I say there is no margin of safety . . . you have a negative margin of safety on stocks . . ."

stocks. The risks may be fully offset by the profit possibilities of the list; and indeed the investor may have no choice but to incur them—for otherwise he may run an even greater risk of holding only fixed claims payable in steadily depreciating dollars. Nonetheless the investor would do well to recognize, and to accept as philosophically as he can, that the old package of *good profit possibilities combined with small ultimate risk* is no longer available to him.*

However, the risk of paying too high a price for good-quality stocks—while a real one—is not the chief hazard confronting the average buyer of securities. Observation over many years has taught us that the chief losses to investors come from the purchase of *low-quality* securities at times of favorable business conditions. The purchasers view the current good earnings as equivalent to "earning power" and assume that prosperity is synonymous with safety. It is in those years that bonds and preferred stocks of inferior grade can be sold to the public at a price around par, because they carry a little higher income return or a deceptively attractive conversion privilege. It is then, also, that common stocks of obscure companies can be floated at prices far above the tangible investment, on the strength of two or three years of excellent growth.

These securities do not offer an adequate margin of safety in any admissible sense of the term. Coverage of interest charges and preferred dividends must be tested over a number of years, including preferably a period of subnormal business such as in 1970–71. The same is ordinarily true of common-stock earnings if they are to qualify as indicators of earning power. Thus it follows that **most of the fair-weather investments, acquired at fair-weather prices, are destined to suffer disturbing price declines when the horizon clouds over—and often sooner than that. Nor can the investor count with confidence on an eventual recovery—although this does come about in some proportion of the cases—for he has never had a real safety margin to tide him through adversity.**

The philosophy of investment in growth stocks parallels in part

---

* This paragraph—which Graham probabaly wrote in early 1972—is an approximation of market conditions in the early 2020s.

and in part contravenes the margin-of-safety principle. The growth-stock buyer relies on an expected earning power that is greater than the average shown in the past. Thus he may be said to substitute these expected earnings for the past record in calculating his margin of safety. In investment theory there is no reason why carefully estimated future earnings should be a less reliable guide than the bare record of the past; in fact, security analysis is coming more and more to prefer a competently executed evaluation of the future. Thus the growth-stock approach may supply as dependable a margin of safety as is found in the ordinary investment—provided the calculation of the future is conservatively made, and provided it shows a satisfactory margin in relation to the price paid.

The danger in a growth-stock program lies precisely here. For such favored issues the market has a tendency to set prices that will not be adequately protected by a conservative projection of future earnings. (It is a basic rule of prudent investment that all estimates, when they differ from past performance, must err at least slightly on the side of understatement.) The margin of safety is always dependent on the price paid. It will be large at one price, small at some higher price, nonexistent at some still higher price. If, as we suggest, the average market level of most growth stocks is too high to provide an adequate margin of safety for the buyer, then a simple technique of diversified buying in this field may not work out satisfactorily. A special degree of foresight and judgment will be needed, in order that wise individual selections may overcome the hazards inherent in the customary market level of such issues as a whole.

The margin-of-safety idea becomes much more evident when we apply it to the field of undervalued or bargain securities. We have here, by definition, a favorable difference between price on the one hand and indicated or appraised value on the other. That difference is the safety margin. It is available for absorbing the effect of miscalculations or worse than average luck. The buyer of bargain issues places particular emphasis on the ability of the investment to withstand adverse developments. For in most such cases he has no real enthusiasm about the company's prospects. True, if the prospects are definitely bad the investor will prefer to avoid the security no matter how low the price. But the field of undervalued issues is drawn from the many concerns—perhaps a majority of the total—for which the future appears neither distinctly promising nor distinctly unpromising. If these are bought on a bargain basis, even a moderate decline in the earning power need not prevent the investment from showing satisfactory results. The margin of safety will then have served its proper purpose.

Theory of Diversification

There is a close logical connection between the concept of a safety margin and the principle of diversification. One is correlative with the other. **Even with a margin in the investor's favor, an individual security may work out badly. For the margin guarantees only that he has a better chance for profit than for loss—not that loss is impossible. But as the number of such commitments is increased the more certain does it become that the aggregate of the profits will exceed the aggregate of the losses.** That is the simple basis of the insurance-underwriting business.

Diversification is an established tenet of conservative investment. By accepting it so universally, investors are really demonstrating their acceptance of the margin-of-safety principle, to which diversification is the companion. This point may be made more colorful by a reference to the arithmetic of roulette. If a man bets $1 on a single number, he is paid $35 profit when he wins—but the chances are 37 to 1 that he will lose. He has a "negative margin of safety." In his case diversification is foolish. The more numbers he bets on, the smaller his chance of ending with a profit. If he regularly bets $1 on every number (including 0 and 00), he is certain to lose $2 on each turn of the wheel. But suppose the winner received $39 profit instead of $35. Then he would have a small but important margin of safety. Therefore, the more numbers he wagers on, the better his chance of gain. And he could be certain of winning $2 on every spin by simply betting $1 each on all the numbers. (Incidentally, the two examples given actually describe the respective positions of the player and proprietor of a wheel with 0 and 00.)*

---

* In "American" roulette, most wheels include 0 and 00 along with numbers 1 through 36, for a total of 38 slots. The casino offers a maximum payout of 35 to 1. What if you bet $1 on every number? Since only one slot can

A Criterion of Investment versus Speculation

Since there is no single definition of investment in general acceptance, authorities have the right to define it pretty much as they please. Many of them deny that there is any useful or dependable difference between the concepts of investment and of speculation. We think this skepticism is unnecessary and harmful. It is injurious because it lends encouragement to the innate leaning of many people toward the excitement and hazards of stock-market speculation. We suggest that the margin-of-safety concept may be used to advantage as the touchstone to distinguish an investment operation from a speculative one.

Probably most speculators believe they have the odds in their favor when they take their chances, and therefore they may lay claim to a safety margin in their proceedings. Each one has the feeling that the time is propitious for his purchase, or that his skill is superior to the crowd's, or that his adviser or system is trustworthy. But such claims are unconvincing. They rest on subjective judgment, unsupported by any body of favorable evidence or any conclusive line of reasoning. We greatly doubt whether the man who stakes money on his view that the market is heading up or down can ever be said to be protected by a margin of safety in any useful sense of the phrase.

By contrast, the investor's concept of the margin of safety—as developed earlier in this chapter—rests upon simple and definite arithmetical reasoning from statistical data. We believe, also, that it is well supported by practical investment experience. There is no guarantee that this fundamental quantitative approach will continue to show favorable results under the unknown conditions of the future. But, equally, there is no valid reason for pessimism on this score.

---

be the one into which the ball drops, you would win $35 on that slot, but lose $1 on each of your other 37 slots, for a net loss of $2. That $2 difference (or a 5.26% spread on your total $38 bet) is the casino's "house advantage," ensuring that, *on average*, roulette players will always lose more than they win. Just as it is in the roulette player's interest to bet as seldom as possible, it is in the casino's interest to keep the roulette wheel spinning.

Thus, in sum, we say that **to have a true investment there must be present a true margin of safety. And a true margin of safety is one that can be demonstrated by figures, by persuasive reasoning, and by reference to a body of actual experience.**

Extension of the Concept of Investment

To complete our discussion of the margin-of-safety principle we must now make a further distinction between conventional and unconventional investments. Conventional investments are appropriate for the typical portfolio. Under this heading have always come United States government issues and high-grade, dividend-paying common stocks. We have added state and municipal bonds for those who will benefit sufficiently by their tax-exempt features. Also included are first-quality corporate bonds when, as now, they can be bought to yield sufficiently more than United States savings bonds.

Unconventional investments are those that are suitable only for the enterprising investor. They cover a wide range. The broadest category is that of undervalued common stocks of secondary companies, which we recommend for purchase when they can be bought at two-thirds or less of their indicated value. Besides these, there is often a wide choice of medium-grade corporate bonds and preferred stocks when they are selling at such depressed prices as to be obtainable also at a considerable discount from their apparent value. In these cases the average investor would be inclined to call the securities speculative, because in his mind their lack of a first-quality rating is synonymous with a lack of investment merit.

It is our argument that **a sufficiently low price can turn a security of mediocre quality into a sound investment opportunity—provided that the buyer is informed and experienced and that he practices adequate diversification. For, if the price is low enough to create a substantial margin of safety, the security thereby meets our criterion of investment.** Our favorite supporting illustration is taken from the field of real-estate bonds. In the 1920s, billions of dollars' worth of these issues were sold at par and widely recommended as sound investments. A large proportion had so little margin of value over debt as to be in fact highly speculative in character. In the depression of the 1930s an enormous quantity of these bonds defaulted their interest, and their price collapsed—in some cases below 10 cents on the dollar. At that stage the same advisers who had recommended them at par as safe investments were rejecting them as paper of the most speculative and unattractive type. But as a matter of fact the price depreciation of about 90% made many of these securities exceedingly attractive and reasonably safe—for the true values behind them were four or five times the market quotation.*

The fact that the purchase of these bonds actually resulted in what is generally called "a large speculative profit" did not prevent them from having true investment qualities at their low prices. The "speculative" profit was the purchaser's reward for having made an unusually shrewd investment. They could properly be called *investment* opportunities, since a careful analysis would have shown that the excess of value over price provided a large margin of safety. **Thus the very class of "fair-weather investments" which we stated above is a chief source of serious loss to naïve security buyers is likely to afford many sound profit opportunities to the sophisticated operator who may buy them later at pretty much his own price.**†

The whole field of "special situations" would come under our definition of investment operations, because the purchase is always predicated on a thoroughgoing analysis that promises a larger realization than the price paid. Again there are risk factors in each individual case, but these are allowed for in the calculations and absorbed in the overall results of a diversified operation.

To carry this discussion to a logical extreme, we might suggest that a defensible investment operation could be set up

---

* Graham is saying that there is no such thing as a good or bad stock; there are only cheap stocks and expensive stocks. Even the best company becomes a "sell" when its stock price goes too high, while the worst company is worth buying if its stock goes low enough.

† The very people who considered technology and telecommunications stocks a "sure thing" in late 1999 and early 2000, when they were hellishly overpriced, shunned them as "too risky" in 2002—even though, in Graham's exact words from an earlier period, "the price depreciation

by buying such intangible values as are represented by a group of "common-stock option warrants" selling at historically low prices. (This example is intended as somewhat of a shocker.)* The entire value of these warrants rests on the possibility that the related stocks may some day advance above the option price. At the moment they have no exercisable value. Yet, since all investment rests on reasonable future expectations, it is proper to view these warrants in terms of the mathematical chances that some future bull market will create a large increase in their indicated value and in their price. Such a study might well yield the conclusion that there is much more to be gained in such an operation than to be lost and that the chances of an ultimate profit are much better than those of an ultimate loss. If that is so, there is a safety margin present even in this unprepossessing security form. A sufficiently enterprising investor could then include an option-warrant operation in his miscellany of unconventional investments.[1]

To Sum Up

Investment is most intelligent when it is most *businesslike*. It is amazing to see how many capable businessmen try to operate in Wall Street with complete disregard of all the sound principles through which they have gained success in their own undertakings. Yet every corporate security may best be viewed, in the first instance, as an ownership interest in, or a claim against, a specific business enterprise. And if a person sets out to make profits from security purchases and sales, he is embarking on a

---

of about 90% made many of these securities exceedingly attractive and reasonably safe." Similarly, Wall Street's analysts have always tended to call a stock a "strong buy" when its price is high, and to label it a "sell" after its price has fallen—the exact opposite of what Graham (and simple common sense) would dictate. As he does throughout the book, Graham is distinguishing speculation—or buying on the hope that a stock's price will keep going up—from investing, or buying on the basis of what the underlying business is worth.

* See Graham's criticisms of warrants in Chapter 16.

business venture of his own, which must be run in accordance with accepted business principles if it is to have a chance of success.

The first and most obvious of these principles is, "Know what you are doing—know your business." For the investor this means: Do not try to make "business profits" out of securities—that is, returns in excess of normal interest and dividend income—unless you know as much about security values as you would need to know about the value of merchandise that you proposed to manufacture or deal in.

A second business principle: "Do not let anyone else run your business, unless (1) you can supervise his performance with adequate care and comprehension or (2) you have unusually strong reasons for placing implicit confidence in his integrity and ability." For the investor this rule should determine the conditions under which he will permit someone else to decide what is done with his money.

A third business principle: "Do not enter upon an operation—that is, manufacturing or trading in an item—unless a reliable calculation shows that it has a fair chance to yield a reasonable profit. In particular, keep away from ventures in which you have little to gain and much to lose." For the enterprising investor this means that his operations for profit should be based not on optimism but on arithmetic. For every investor it means that when he limits his return to a small figure—as formerly, at least, in a conventional bond or preferred stock—he must demand convincing evidence that he is not risking a substantial part of his principal.

A fourth business rule is more positive: "Have the courage of your knowledge and experience. If you have formed a conclusion from the facts and if you know your judgment is sound, act on it—even though others may hesitate or differ." (You are neither right nor wrong because the crowd disagrees with you. You are right because your data and reasoning are right.) Similarly, in the world of securities, courage becomes the supreme virtue *after* adequate knowledge and a tested judgment are at hand.

Fortunately for the typical investor, it is by no means necessary for his success that he bring these qualities to bear upon his program—*provided* he limits his ambition to his capacity and confines his activities within the safe and narrow path of standard, defensive investment. **To achieve *satisfactory* investment results is easier than most people realize; to achieve *superior* results is harder than it looks.**

Commentary on Chapter 20
by Jason Zweig

> There are old pilots, and there are bold pilots. But there are no old, bold pilots.
>
> —traditional saying among flight instructors[1]

Having a margin of safety is what distinguishes an intelligent investor from the crowd.

Most large passenger jets have two engines, but can safely fly for extended periods if one fails. Engineers design the structural components of skyscrapers to withstand more weight than they are ever likely to experience. A bridge required to bear a load of 40 tons is built to hold 70 or 80 tons.

Precaution is prepackaged into aircraft, buildings, and bridges. As a result, air travel is remarkably safe, tall buildings almost never collapse, and major bridges can carry millions of vehicles. We take their margin of safety for granted.

---

[1] bit.ly/413BsdL.

"Always Dependent on the Price Paid"

When you invest, the simplest measure of the margin of safety is the value of the business (V) minus the price of the stock (P):

$$MoS = V - P$$

When the value of the business exceeds the price of the stock, the margin of safety is positive. When the price of the stock is higher than the value of the business, the margin of safety is negative.[2]

"The margin of safety is always dependent on the price paid," says Graham. "It will be large at one price, small at some higher price, nonexistent at some still higher price."

For a vivid example of how current price affects future returns, let's look at what would have happened, years ago, if you had bought Amazon.com either when the margin of safety was deeply negative or when it was less extreme.

Imagine you invested in Amazon on December 10, 1999, when the stock hit what then was its all-time high. Branching out from its original specialty of selling books, the ambitious young company was losing millions of dollars a day. Yet, after rising nearly 970% in 1998, the stock was up another 99% so far in 1999. Because it had no earnings, you couldn't use a price/earnings ratio to estimate how expensive Amazon was. But the stock was selling for more than 15 times the company's sales over the prior year—a ratio 10 times higher than that of Walmart, the world's largest retailer. For Amazon, "the calculation of the future," as Graham put it, was *not* being "conservatively made."

Had you bought Amazon then, convinced that it would become one of the greatest growth companies in history, you would have been absolutely right. But because it had no margin of safety, you would

---

[2] Graham formally defines the margin of safety as the earnings yield (or reciprocal of the price/earnings ratio) minus the interest rate on investment-grade bonds. The lower a stock's P/E ratio, the higher the earnings yield and the greater the likelihood that the resulting number will exceed the bond yield. The lower interest rates go, the less it takes for an earnings yield to exceed the bond yield. Conversely, higher P/E ratios and interest rates shrink the margin of safety.

have had to wait 10 years—*and survive a 94% loss along the way!*—to make even a modest profit at the very end:

FIGURE 20-1: Ten Long Years

Source: FactSet.

Now imagine you waited to buy Amazon until September 28, 2001, when it hit rock bottom after internet stocks crashed. The company's losses had narrowed, and its sales over the previous four quarters had nearly doubled from their level in December 1999. But the stock had been trashed: Now you could buy Amazon for a price/sales ratio of only 0.74, or less than half that of Walmart, even though Amazon was growing far faster. The internet retailer's margin of safety was much less negative than before.

Your investment would have boomed more than 35-fold over the following 10 years:

FIGURE 20-2: Ten Better Years

Value of $100 Investment in Amazon.com Stock (2001–2011)

Source: FactSet.

These examples are hypothetical; you would have needed unbelievable luck to buy on the exact date when the stock was either at its absolute peak or at its lowest point.

But these rules are perfectly realistic:

- Buying when a stock is expensive reduces your margin of safety.
- Buying whenever it's extraordinarily expensive reduces your margin of safety to zero.
- And buying whenever it's cheap increases your margin of safety.

What You Get

Viewed this way, *the margin of safety is itself a source of return.* Buy a business when the stock is cheap, and that positive margin of safety will raise your return. Buy the same business when the stock is expensive, and that negative margin of safety will reduce your return. If an excessively high stock price makes the margin of safety extremely negative, you can lose money even if the business thrives for years to come.

That's what Graham meant when he said, according to Warren Buffett, "Price is what you pay; value is what you get."

The higher the expectations for a stock and the further into the future its eventual profits may materialize, the wider the margin of safety you should seek—because even the slightest interim decline in growth can crush the stock.

Think of it this way: Invest $100 at a 25% average annual growth rate, and it will be worth $80,779 thirty years from now. Invest $100 at a 20% average annual growth rate, and it will be worth "only" $23,738 in three decades. Investors will pay a lot more for an expected long-term growth rate of 25% than for 20%—even though either would be a spectacular, and extraordinarily rare, result. (See Figure 20-3.)

Spreading Your Bets Over Time and Space

Today's investors have an advantage they didn't in Graham's day: They can diversify easily, cheaply, and widely.

You can diversify over *time* by

- investing steadily for years and decades—eliminating the risk that you will buy (or sell) too much at an inopportune moment.[3]

You can diversify across *space* in index funds that

- hold hundreds, even thousands, of stocks, mitigating the risk that your estimate of the margin of safety for one or more of your holdings might be wrong;
- hold unfamiliar stocks along with household names, exposing you to the serendipity of great returns that can come like happy surprises from unexpected sources;

---

[3] See the discussion of dollar-cost averaging in Chapter 5 and its Commentary.

FIGURE 20-3: Great Expectations

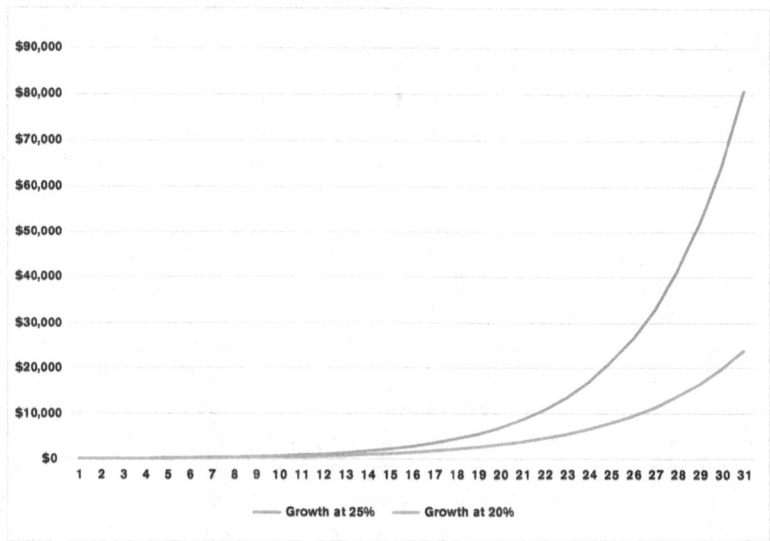

Source: Author's calculations.

- hold stocks from around the world, reducing the risk of being overconcentrated in your home country's stocks.

And keeping some of your money in cash, bonds, and other assets lowers the risk that poor performance in stocks alone will harm your results.

As your individual decisions become a small part of a broad portfolio over time, diversification drapes a margin of safety around them. A mistake can't destroy you: Even if you lose 100% on an investment that amounts to (say) 5% of your total portfolio, you still have 95% of your money left, and it's spread widely across the world's markets. On the other hand, the potential upside of any given holding is unbounded: If a stock or fund that's only 5% of your portfolio goes up 1,000% and *the rest of your holdings go nowhere*, you will still gain 50%.

Often, only a few stocks account for much of the value of an index fund, as with Reliance Industries and Infosys in India and Tencent Holdings and Alibaba Group in China. Even in the U.S., nearly all the returns of funds that follow major indexes like the S&P 500 have been driven in recent years by only a handful of stocks, including Amazon, Apple, Microsoft, and NVIDIA. If almost all of an index's performance comes from very few of its stocks, that dilutes the diversification benefit.

However, the other holdings in an index fund should provide at least some ability to zig when the biggest positions zag, and the U.S. market has thrived even though it has often been even more concentrated in the largest stocks in the past.[4]

The most important thing to understand about diversification is that you're doing it wrong if all your assets rise together when markets go up. Then they will surely all fall together when markets go down. A portfolio consisting entirely of winners in good times is also likely to consist entirely of losers in bad times. And the whole purpose of diversification is to reduce risk. So, if you don't own any losers during up markets, you won't own any winners during down markets.

This, in turn, means that a well-diversified portfolio should always be at least partly disappointing, although the disappointments should come from different investments at different times. Even if you had been able to invest in a hypothetical portfolio constructed with perfect hindsight to hold the exact combination of assets that performed best over the long term, you still would have lost money over many short-term periods. As analyst and investor Brian Portnoy likes to say, "Diversification means always having to say you're sorry."[5]

Diversification will not feel good *all* the time, but it will feel good over time. This margin of safety isn't free. The price you pay is short-term psychological pain; the benefit you get is long-term financial gain.

---

[4] Jason Zweig, "What Amazon's Rise to No. 1 Says About the Stock Market," bit.ly/3R2v3ea.

[5] Brian Portnoy, bit.ly/4aUtwyz; Nick Maggiulli, "The Downsides of Diversification," bit.ly/47G1gz4; Wesley Gray, "Even God Would Get Fired as an Active Investor," bit.ly/3qoTLfz.

Superforecasting

To be an intelligent investor, you need not only an external margin of safety to protect yourself from Mr. Market's misbehavior but also an internal margin of safety to protect yourself from *yourself*.

One of the blessings of today's investment world is also a curse: Information is freely, instantaneously, boundlessly available. That's great, since it puts you in a position closer to the biggest investors in the world. It's also terrible, since new information adds much more to your conviction than to your knowledge; any fresh trivia echoing what you already believe will deepen your certainty that your views are correct.

The more information you encounter confirming your views, the less you will feel the need to seek out *disconfirming* information. The abundance of "proof" will discourage you from looking for dissenting views, even though it should be obvious that they must be abundant, too.

The best way to build a margin of safety around your own judgments is to convert your forecasts from guesstimates to a formal process.

Anyone can—and all enterprising investors should—sign up online to participate in the Good Judgment Open. This forecasting competition also features a training program that can uproot many of the common errors that threaten to strangle good decision-making. (Go to GJOpen.com/training to register and view the training materials; it's free.)

The Good Judgment project trains people to think of their own opinions "as hypotheses to be tested, not treasures to be guarded," says Philip Tetlock, a psychologist at the University of Pennsylvania and coleader of the program.

Because most people are "too quick to make up their minds and too slow to change them," he says, the project is designed to force forecasters to be "ruthlessly honest about why they think what they do." That can turn you into what Tetlock calls a superforecaster—if you are willing to invest the necessary time and energy into the effort.

> **Start by auditing your sources of information.** Make sure you're taking in all kinds of evidence—not only supportive and positive, but also skeptical and negative, what Tetlock calls "a balanced cognitive diet."
>
> **Then establish a reference class.** Instead of thinking of this company (or any asset) as a unique case, classify it as a member of a category: all the companies in the same industry, all that depend

on this type of strategy, all those at a similar phase of development, all that have recently replaced their CEO, or whatever constitutes a fair group for comparison.

Next, determine the base rate—the average historical experience for the reference class, using the longest-term data available. Consider an example from daily life. You *could* estimate the likelihood that a newlywed couple will divorce by observing how happy they seem, but you *should* estimate it by realizing that (in the U.S.) the divorce rate in the first decade of marriage is approximately 40%. Then adjust that base rate up or down by what you know about this couple.

Likewise, if you're thinking of investing in an initial public offering, you *could* simply extrapolate the company's past growth rate into the indefinite future. Instead, you *should* determine the average return of all IPOs, readily available at bit.ly/417ESfh. That long-term base rate is at least 1.5 percentage points lower than the return of the overall stock market. Then adjust that up or down based on the specific characteristics of this particular business.

Use your checklist (see the Commentary on Chapter 11) to ensure you base your forecasts on consistent criteria. Be specific and probabilistic: "I'm 80% certain that this company's earnings will double in the next five years." Record your reasoning: Will that growth come from new products, international sales, price increases, or elsewhere? This way, you'll later be able to tell not only whether you were right but whether you were right for the right reasons.

Now consider the opposite. What information would you need in order to prove that your prediction *won't* come true? Seek it out, soak it up, and evaluate whether it justifies changing your forecast.

Next, update and revise your views as new information becomes available. Because you're focused on the long-term future, all your estimates are rough, so your forecasts must stay flexible.

A forecast isn't an *event*; it's a continuous *process* that consists of what Tetlock calls trying, failing, analyzing, adjusting, and trying again.

As Amazon.com founder Jeff Bezos has said, "People who are right a lot change their mind a lot."[6]

Follow the principle that the great investor Charlie Munger called "over, under, kapow." Munger liked to say that in artillery training, military recruits would bracket a target by overshooting it, undershooting it, and then hitting it with a *kapow!* Munger followed the same practice in estimating values, deliberately oversizing, undersizing, and then *kapow!* Being open to new information is the key component of being able to hit the target.

Repeatedly practicing these superforecasting procedures until they become routine is a way of "mentally rewiring yourself," says Tetlock. With enough disciplined repetition, overriding your intuitive, emotional responses and replacing them with deliberative decisions will come to feel natural.[7]

When to Cut Loose

The ultimate way to create a margin of safety is by selling: If you were wrong, selling out keeps you from being wiped out. However, only a fine line separates counting your blessings from kicking yourself. The stock or asset you sell could go to zero, in which case you got out just in time—or it could go up and keep going, in which case you'll miss out on potentially gigantic gains.

Here are a few ways to determine whether selling makes sense.

> **Review.** Whenever a stock, fund, or other asset drops a fixed amount below what you paid, automatically revisit your original reasons for buying to see whether they still hold. Many brokerage firms allow you to set such price alerts in advance. Pinning these thresholds at intervals you consider significant—25%, 33%, and 50%, for example—will compel you to think before you sell.
>
> **Reappraise.** If you liked this asset at a higher price, shouldn't you like it more now that the price has fallen? All else being

---

[6] bit.ly/4bol7mx.
[7] Philip E. Tetlock and Dan Gardner, *Superforecasting: The Art and Science of Prediction* (Crown, 2015); Jason Zweig, "The Trick to Making Better Forecasts," bit.ly/3GrKgAv; and "Five Ways to See the Financial Future," bit.ly/3uKtrhK.

equal, a lower price means a wider margin of safety—unless the value of the business has also dropped. That requires a separate appraisal—centered on the business and its operations, not on the stock market and its madness. Ask yourself: What has changed about the fundamentals of this business that could justify this decline in the stock price? Base that judgment on facts about the company, not opinions in the market. If the facts have changed, then you should sell.

Reprice. Look up what you originally paid. Divide it by 10 and ask whether, if you had paid that much lower price, you would be willing to hold on. If the answer is no, you definitely should sell.

Reflect. Getting angry at everyone who disagrees with you is a sure sign that your investment thesis might be wrong. Deep understanding is calmly confident, never touchy and defensive. If you find yourself mocking or sniping at critics, catch yourself and ask: What am I angry about? Could I be angry not because they're wrong, but because I am? Force yourself to go back and redo your analysis.

Reframe. Finally, selling at a loss is hard because it compels you to face up, and fess up, to making a mistake. Frame it instead as an opportunity: In the U.S., you can deduct up to $3,000 of your losses from your taxable income annually. You can also use a sale to improve your diversification. Imagine that you decide that your analysis of a particular stock was wrong. Sell it, then invest the proceeds in a widely diversified holding like a total stock-market index fund. By spreading a little more of your money across all stocks, you incrementally increase your margin of safety.

Safe at Last

Many people who call themselves investors, whether they are sheer speculators or honestly trying to invest intelligently, never factor in a margin of safety. Intelligent investors always do. That's because success doesn't depend only on making money. It depends also on avoiding loss. If you build in a margin of safety, your portfolio will prosper from your good decisions without being destroyed by your bad ones.

Having a margin of safety is the natural and inevitable result of following the rules, policies, and procedures we've outlined in this book. Maintaining a margin of safety means you've successfully laid the foundations, brick by brick, for being an intelligent investor.

For the rest of your investing lifetime, with Graham as your guide, not even Mr. Market will be able to knock that fortress off its foundations.

Pascal's Wager

The French mathematician and theologian Blaise Pascal (1623–1662) argued that it isn't possible, with logic alone, to prove—or disprove—that God exists. How, then, should you decide whether to believe? Framing the question as a wager, Pascal asked what the gambler stands to win or lose. "Let us weigh up the gain and the loss involved in [betting] that God exists," he wrote. ". . . If you win you win everything, if you lose you lose nothing."

As the investing writer Peter L. Bernstein explained Pascal's Wager in 2003:

> Suppose you act as though God is and [you] lead a life of virtue and abstinence, when in fact there is no god. You will have passed up some goodies in life, but there will be rewards. Now suppose you act as though God is not and spend a life of sin, selfishness, and lust when in fact God is. You may have had fun and thrills during the relatively brief duration of your lifetime, but when the day of judgment rolls around you are in big trouble.

Framing decisions in the light of Pascal's Wager helps you focus not only on how much you stand to gain from being right, but on how much you stand to lose if you turn out to be wrong.

Consequences are at least as important as probabilities. You will survive your gains, but you might not be able to survive your losses.

Building a margin of safety into all your investing decisions is the best insurance against the consequences of being wrong.

Postscript
by Benjamin Graham

We know very well two partners who spent a good part of their lives handling their own and other people's funds on Wall Street. Some hard experience taught them it was better to be safe and careful rather than to try to make all the money in the world. They established a rather unique approach to security operations, which combined good profit possibilities with sound values. They avoided anything that appeared overpriced and were rather too quick to dispose of issues that had advanced to levels they deemed no longer attractive. Their portfolio was always well diversified, with more than a hundred different issues represented. In this way they did quite well through many years of ups and downs in the general market; they averaged about 20% per annum on the several millions of capital they had accepted for management, and their clients were well pleased with the results.*

In the year in which the first edition of this book appeared an opportunity was offered to the partners' fund to purchase a half-interest in a growing enterprise. For some reason the industry did not have Wall Street appeal at the time and the deal had been turned down by quite a few important houses. But the pair was impressed by the company's possibilities; what was decisive for them was that the price was moderate in relation to current earnings and asset value. The partners went ahead with the acquisition, amounting

---

* The two partners Graham coyly refers to are Jerome Newman and Benjamin Graham himself.

in dollars to about one-fifth of their fund. They became closely identified with the new business interest, which prospered.*

In fact it did so well that the price of its shares advanced to two hundred times or more the price paid for the half-interest. The advance far outstripped the actual growth in profits, and almost from the start the quotation appeared much too high in terms of the partners' own investment standards. But since they regarded the company as a sort of "family business," they continued to maintain a substantial ownership of the shares despite the spectacular price rise. A large number of participants in their funds did the same, and they became millionaires through their holding in this one enterprise, plus later-organized affiliates.†

Ironically enough, **the aggregate of profits accruing from this single investment decision far exceeded the sum of all the others realized through 20 years of wide-ranging operations in the partners' specialized fields, involving much investigation, endless pondering, and countless individual decisions.**

Are there morals to this story of value to the intelligent investor? An obvious one is that **there are several different ways to make and keep money in Wall Street.** Another, not so obvious, is that **one lucky break, or one supremely shrewd decision—can we tell**

---

* Graham is describing the Government Employees Insurance Co., or GEICO, in which he and Newman purchased a 50% interest in 1948, right around the time he finished writing *The Intelligent Investor*. The $712,500 that Graham and Newman put into GEICO was roughly 25% of their fund's assets at the time. Graham was a member of GEICO's board of directors for many years. In a nice twist of fate, Graham's greatest student, Warren Buffett, made an immense bet of his own on GEICO in 1976, by which time the big insurer had slid to the brink of bankruptcy. It turned out to be one of Buffett's best investments as well.

† Because of a legal technicality, Graham and Newman were directed by the U.S. Securities & Exchange Commission to "spin off," or distribute, Graham-Newman Corp.'s GEICO stake to the fund's shareholders. An investor who owned 100 shares of Graham-Newman at the beginning of 1948 (worth $11,413) and who then held on to the GEICO distribution would have had $1.66 million by 1972. GEICO's "later-organized affiliates" included Government Employees Financial Corp. and Criterion Insurance Co.

them apart?—may count for more than a lifetime of journeyman efforts.[1] But behind the luck, or the crucial decision, there must usually exist a background of preparation and disciplined capacity. One needs to be sufficiently established and recognized so that these opportunities will knock at his particular door. One must have the means, the judgment, and the courage to take advantage of them.

Of course, we cannot promise a like spectacular experience to all intelligent investors who remain both prudent and alert through the years. We are not going to end with J. J. Raskob's slogan that we made fun of at the beginning: "Everybody can be rich." But interesting possibilities abound on the financial scene, and the intelligent and enterprising investor should be able to find both enjoyment and profit in this three-ring circus. Excitement is guaranteed.

Commentary on the Postscript
by Jason Zweig

> Human Felicity is produc'd not so much by great Pieces of good Fortune that seldom happen, as by little Advantages that occur every day.
>
> —Benjamin Franklin[1]

In the end, the advice in this book isn't only about what kind of investor you want to become.

It's also about what kind of person you want to become.

Do you want investing to be primarily an endeavor or entertainment?

Do you want to treat low costs, instantaneous trading, and limitless information as *obligations* to be constantly acted on, or as *options* to be invoked as rarely as possible?

Do you want to chase every hunch and gut feeling? Or do you want to follow policies, procedures, and rules that will give you growing mastery with the passage of time?

Do you want to live in blind self-delusion, or do you want to use investing as a means of becoming more honest about your strengths and weaknesses?

Do you want to spend the rest of your life trading like a maniac? Or do you want to treat investing as a way to achieve serenity?

Do you want your decisions and emotions to be held hostage by millions of strangers? Do you want Mr. Market to tell you what to think? Or do you want to think for yourself?

These choices are yours, not other people's, to make. And you know by now which path Graham and I want you to take.

---

[1] *The Autobiography of Benjamin Franklin* (Yale, 1964), p. 207.

Appendixes

1. The Superinvestors of Graham-and-Doddsville

by Warren E. Buffett

EDITOR'S NOTE: *This article is an edited transcript of a talk given at Columbia University in 1984 commemorating the fiftieth anniversary of* Security Analysis, *written by Benjamin Graham and David L. Dodd. This specialized volume first introduced the ideas later popularized in* The Intelligent Investor. *Buffett's essay offers a fascinating study of how Graham's disciples have used Graham's value investing approach to realize phenomenal success in the stock market.*

Is the Graham and Dodd "look for values with a significant margin of safety relative to prices" approach to security analysis out of date? Many of the professors who write textbooks today say yes. They argue that the stock market is efficient; that is, that stock prices reflect everything that is known about a company's prospects and about the state of the economy. There are no undervalued stocks, these theorists argue, because there are smart security analysts who utilize all available information to ensure unfailingly appropriate prices. Investors who seem to beat the market year after year are just lucky. "If prices fully reflect available information, this sort of investment adeptness is ruled out," writes one of today's textbook authors.

Well, maybe. But I want to present to you a group of investors who have, year in and year out, beaten the Standard & Poor's 500 stock index. The hypothesis that they do this by pure chance is at least worth examining. Crucial to this examination is the fact that these winners were all well known to me and pre-identified as superior investors, the most recent identification occurring over fifteen years ago. Absent this condition—that is, if I had just recently searched among thousands of records to select a few names for you this morning—I would advise you to stop reading right here. I should add that all these records have been audited. And I should further add that I have known many of those who have invested with these managers, and the checks received by those participants over the years have matched the stated records.

Before we begin this examination, I would like you to imagine a national coin-flipping contest. Let's assume we get 225 million Americans up tomorrow morning and we ask them all to wager a dollar. They go out in the morning at sunrise, and they all call the flip of a coin. If they call correctly, they win a dollar from those who called wrong. Each day the losers drop out, and on the subsequent day the stakes build as all previous winnings are put on the line. After ten flips on ten mornings, there will be approximately 220,000 people in the United States who have correctly called ten flips in a row. They each will have won a little over $1,000.

Now this group will probably start getting a little puffed up about this, human nature being what it is. They may try to be modest, but at cocktail parties they will occasionally admit to attractive members of the opposite sex what their technique is, and what marvelous insights they bring to the field of flipping.

Assuming that the winners are getting the appropriate rewards from the losers, in another ten days we will have 215 people who have successfully called their coin flips 20 times in a row and who, by this exercise, each have turned one dollar into a little over $1 million. $225 million would have been lost, $225 million would have been won.

By then, this group will really lose their heads. They will probably write books on "How I Turned a Dollar into a Million in Twenty Days Working Thirty Seconds a Morning." Worse yet, they'll probably start jetting around the country attending seminars on efficient coin-flipping and tackling skeptical professors with, "If it can't be done, why are there 215 of us?"

But then some business school professor will probably be rude enough to bring up the fact that if 225 million orangutans had engaged in a similar exercise, the results would be much the same—215 egotistical orangutans with 20 straight winning flips.

I would argue, however, that there *are* some important differences in the examples I am going to present. For one thing, if (a) you had taken 225 million orangutans distributed roughly as the U.S. population is; if (b) 215 winners were left after 20 days; and if (c) you found that 40 came from a particular zoo in Omaha, you would be pretty sure you were on to something. So you would probably go out and ask the zookeeper about what he's feeding them, whether they had special exercises, what books they read, and who knows what else. That is, if you found any really extraordinary concentrations of success, you might want to see if you could identify concentrations of unusual characteristics that might be causal factors.

Scientific inquiry naturally follows such a pattern. If you were trying to analyze possible causes of a rare type of cancer—with, say, 1,500 cases a year in the United States—and you found that 400 of them occurred in some little mining town in Montana, you would get very interested in the water there, or the occupation of those afflicted, or other variables. You know that it's not random chance that 400 come from a small area. You would not necessarily know the causal factors, but you would know where to search.

I submit to you that there are ways of defining an origin other than geography. In addition to geographical origins, there can be what I call an *intellectual* origin. I think you will find that a disproportionate number of successful coin-flippers in the investment world came from a very small intellectual village that could be called Graham-and-Doddsville. A concentration of winners that simply cannot be explained by chance can be traced to this particular intellectual village.

Conditions could exist that would make even that concentration unimportant. Perhaps 100 people were simply imitating the coin-flipping call of some terribly persuasive personality. When he called heads, 100 followers automatically called that coin the same way. If the leader was part of the 215 left at the end, the fact that 100 came from the same intellectual origin would mean nothing. You would simply be identifying one case as a hundred cases. Similarly, let's assume that you lived in a strongly patriarchal society and every family in the United States conveniently consisted of ten members. Further assume that the patriarchal culture was so strong that, when the 225 million people went out the first day, every member of the family identified with the father's call. Now, at the end of the 20-day period, you would have 215 winners, and you would find that they came from only 21.5 families. Some naïve types might say that this indicates an enormous hereditary factor as an explanation of successful coin-flipping. But, of course, it would have no significance at all because it would simply mean that you didn't have 215 individual winners, but rather 21.5 randomly distributed families who were winners.

In this group of successful investors that I want to consider, there has been a common intellectual patriarch, Ben Graham. But the children who left the house of this intellectual patriarch have called their "flips" in very different ways. They have gone to different places and bought and sold different stocks and companies, yet they have had a combined record that simply can't be explained by random chance. It certainly cannot be explained by the fact that they are all calling flips identically because a leader is signaling the calls to make. The patriarch has merely set forth the intellectual theory for making coin-calling decisions, but each student has decided on his own manner of applying the theory.

The common intellectual theme of the investors from Graham-and-Doddsville is this: they search for discrepancies between the *value* of a business and the *price* of small pieces of that business in the market. Essentially, they exploit those discrepancies without the efficient market theorist's concern as to whether the stocks are bought on Monday or Thursday, or whether it is January or July, etc. Incidentally, when businessmen buy businesses—which is just what our Graham & Dodd investors are doing through the medium of marketable stocks—I doubt that many are cranking into their purchase decision the day of the week or the month in which the transaction is going to occur. If it doesn't make any difference whether all of a business is being bought on a Monday or a Friday, I am baffled why academicians invest extensive time and effort to see whether it makes a difference when buying small pieces of those same businesses. Our Graham & Dodd investors, needless to say, do not discuss beta, the capital asset pricing model, or covariance in returns among securities. These are not subjects of any interest to them. In fact, most of them would have difficulty defining those terms. The investors simply focus on two variables: price and value.

I always find it extraordinary that so many studies are made of price and volume behavior, the stuff of chartists. Can you imagine buying an entire business simply because the price of the business had been marked *up* substantially last week and the week before? Of course, the reason a lot of studies are made of these price and volume variables is that now, in the age of computers, there are almost endless data available about them. It isn't necessarily because such studies have any utility; it's simply that the data are there and academicians have worked hard to learn the mathematical skills needed to manipulate them. Once these skills are acquired, it seems sinful not to use them, even if the usage has no utility or negative utility. As a friend said, to a man with a hammer, everything looks like a nail.

I think the group that we have identified by a common intellectual home is worthy of study. Incidentally, despite all the academic studies of the influence of such variables as price, volume, seasonality, capitalization size, etc., upon stock performance, no interest has been evidenced in studying the methods of this unusual concentration of value-oriented winners.

I begin this study of results by going back to a group of four of us who worked at Graham-Newman Corporation from 1954 through 1956. There were only four—I have not selected these names from among thousands. I offered to go to work at Graham-Newman for nothing after I took Ben Graham's class, but he turned me down as overvalued. He took this value stuff very seriously! After much pestering he finally hired me. There were three partners and four of us at the "peasant" level. All four left between 1955 and 1957 when the firm was wound up, and it's possible to trace the record of three.

The first example (see Table 1, pages 549–550) is that of Walter Schloss. Walter never went to college, but took a course from Ben Graham at night at the New York Institute of Finance. Walter left Graham-Newman in 1955 and achieved the record shown here over 28 years.

Here is what "Adam Smith"—after I told him about Walter—wrote about him in *Supermoney* (1972):

He has no connections or access to useful information. Practically no one in Wall Street knows him and he is not fed any ideas. He looks up the numbers in the manuals and sends for the annual reports, and that's about it.

In introducing me to [Schloss] Warren had also, to my mind, described himself. "He never forgets that he is handling other people's money and this reinforces his normal strong aversion to loss." He has total integrity and a realistic picture of himself. Money is real to him and stocks are real—and from this flows an attraction to the "margin of safety" principle.

Walter has diversified enormously, owning well over 100 stocks currently. He knows how to identify securities that sell at considerably less than their value to a private owner. *And that's all he does.* He doesn't worry about whether it's January, he doesn't worry about whether it's Monday, he doesn't worry about whether it's an election year. He simply says, if a business is worth a dollar and I can buy it for 40 cents, something good may happen to me. And he does it over and over and over again. He owns many more stocks than I do—and is far less interested in the underlying nature of the business: I don't seem to have very much influence on Walter. That's one of his strengths; no one has much influence on him.

The second case is Tom Knapp, who also worked at Graham-Newman with me. Tom was a chemistry major at Princeton before the war; when he came back from the war, he was a beach bum. And then one day he read that Dave Dodd was giving a night course in investments at Columbia. Tom took it on a noncredit basis, and he got so interested in the subject from taking that course that he came up and enrolled at Columbia Business School, where he got the MBA degree. He took Dodd's course again, and took Ben Graham's course. Incidentally, 35 years later I called Tom to ascertain some of the facts involved here and I found him on the beach again. The only difference is that now he owns the beach!

In 1968 Tom Knapp and Ed Anderson, also a Graham disciple, along with one or two other fellows of similar persuasion, formed Tweedy, Browne Partners, and their investment results appear in Table 2. Tweedy, Browne built that record with very wide diversification. They occasionally bought control of businesses, but the record of the passive investments is equal to the record of the control investments.

Table 3 describes the third member of the group who formed Buffett Partnership in 1957. The best thing he did was to quit in 1969. Since then, in a sense, Berkshire Hathaway has been a continuation of the partnership in some respects. There is no single index I can give you that I would feel would be a fair test of investment management at Berkshire. But I think that any way you figure it, it has been satisfactory.

Table 4 shows the record of the Sequoia Fund, which is managed by a man whom I met in 1951 in Ben Graham's class, Bill Ruane. After getting out of Harvard Business School, he went to Wall Street. Then he realized that he needed to get a real business education so he came up to take Ben's course at Columbia, where we met in early 1951. Bill's record from 1951 to 1970, working with relatively small sums, was far better than average. When I wound up Buffett Partnership I asked Bill if he would set up a fund to handle all our partners, so he set up the Sequoia Fund. He set it up at a terrible time, just when I was quitting. He went right into the two-tier market and all the difficulties that made for comparative performance for value-oriented investors. I am happy to say that my partners, to an amazing degree, not only stayed with him but added money, with the happy result shown.

There's no hindsight involved here. Bill was the only person I recommended to my partners, and I said at the time that if he achieved a four-point-per-annum advantage over the Standard & Poor's, that would be solid performance. Bill has achieved well over that, working with progressively larger sums of money. That makes things much more difficult. Size is the anchor of performance. There is no question about it. It doesn't mean you can't do better than average when you get larger, but the margin shrinks. And if you ever get so you're managing two trillion dollars, and that happens to be the amount of the total equity evaluation in the economy, don't think that you'll do better than average!

I should add that in the records we've looked at so far, throughout this whole period there was practically no duplication in these portfolios. These are men who select securities based on discrepancies between price and value, but they make their selections very differently. Walter's largest holdings have been such stalwarts as Hudson Pulp & Paper and Jeddo Highland Coal and New York Trap Rock Company and all those other names that come instantly to mind to even a casual reader of the business pages. Tweedy Browne's selections have sunk even well below that level in terms of name recognition. On the other hand, Bill has worked with big companies. The overlap among these portfolios has been very, very low. These records do not reflect one guy calling the flip and fifty people yelling out the same thing after him.

Table 5 is the record of a friend of mine who is a Harvard Law graduate, who set up a major law firm. I ran into him in about 1960 and told him that law was fine as a hobby but he could do better. He set up a partnership quite the opposite of Walter's. His portfolio was concentrated in very few securities and therefore his record was much more volatile but it was based on the same discount-from-value approach. He was willing to accept greater peaks and valleys of performance, and he happens to be a fellow whose whole psyche goes toward concentration, with the results shown. Incidentally, this record belongs to Charlie Munger, my partner for a long time in the operation of Berkshire Hathaway. When he ran his partnership, however, his portfolio holdings were almost completely different from mine and the other fellows mentioned earlier.

Table 6 is the record of a fellow who was a pal of Charlie Munger's—another non–business school type—who was a math major at USC. He went to work for IBM after graduation and was an IBM salesman for a while. After I got to Charlie, Charlie got to him. This happens to be the record of Rick Guerin. Rick, from 1965 to 1983, against a compounded gain of 316 percent for the S&P, came off with 22,200 percent, which, probably because he lacks a business school education, he regards as statistically significant.

One sidelight here: it is extraordinary to me that the idea of buying dollar bills for 40 cents takes immediately with people or it doesn't take at all. It's like an inoculation. If it doesn't grab a person right away, I find that you can talk to him for years and show him records, and it doesn't make any difference. They just don't seem able to grasp the concept, simple as it is. A fellow like Rick Guerin, who had no formal education in business, understands immediately the value approach to investing and he's applying it five minutes later. I've never seen anyone who became a gradual convert over a ten-year period to this approach. It doesn't seem to be a matter of IQ or academic training. It's instant recognition, or it is nothing.

Table 7 is the record of Stan Perlmeter. Stan was a liberal arts major at the University of Michigan who was a partner in the advertising agency of Bozell & Jacobs. We happened to be in the same building in Omaha. In 1965 he figured out I had a better business than he did, so he left advertising. Again, it took five minutes for Stan to embrace the value approach.

Perlmeter does not own what Walter Schloss owns. He does not own what Bill Ruane owns. These are records made *independently*. But every time Perlmeter buys a stock it's because he's getting more for his money than he's paying. That's the only thing he's thinking about. He's not looking at quarterly earnings projections, he's not looking at next year's earnings, he's not thinking about what day of the week it is, he doesn't care what investment research from any place says, he's not interested in price momentum, volume, or anything. He's simply asking: What is the business worth?

Table 8 and Table 9 are the records of two pension funds I've been involved in. They are not selected from dozens of pension funds with which I have had involvement; they are the only two I have influenced. In both cases I have steered them toward value-oriented managers. Very, very few pension funds are managed from a value standpoint. Table 8 is the Washington Post Company's Pension Fund. It was with a large bank some years ago, and I suggested that they would do well to select managers who had a value orientation.

As you can see, overall they have been in the top percentile ever since they made the change. The Post told the managers to keep at least 25 percent of these funds in bonds, which would not have been necessarily the choice of these managers. So I've included the bond performance simply to illustrate that this group has no particular expertise about bonds. They wouldn't have said they did. Even with this drag of 25 percent of their fund in an area that was not their game, they were in the top percentile of fund management. The Washington Post experience does not cover a terribly long period but it does represent many investment decisions by three managers who were not identified retroactively.

Table 9 is the record of the FMC Corporation fund. I don't manage a dime of it myself but I did, in 1974, influence their decision to select value-oriented managers. Prior to that time they had selected managers much the same way as most larger companies. They now rank number one in the Becker survey of pension funds for their size over the period of time subsequent to this "conversion" to the value approach. Last year they had eight equity managers of any duration beyond a year. Seven of them had a cumulative record better than the S&P. All eight had a better record last year than the S&P. The net difference now between a median performance and the actual performance of the FMC fund over this period is $243 million. FMC attributes this to the mindset given to them about the selection of managers. Those managers are not the managers I would necessarily select but they have the common denominator of selecting securities based on value.

So these are nine records of "coin-flippers" from Graham-and-Doddsville. I haven't selected them with hindsight from among thousands. It's not like I am reciting to you the names of a bunch of lottery winners—people I had never heard of before they won the lottery. I selected these men years ago based upon their framework for investment decision-making. I knew what they had been taught and additionally I had some personal knowledge of their intellect, character, and temperament. It's very important to understand that this group has assumed far less risk than average; note their record in years when the general market was weak. While they differ greatly in style, these investors are, mentally, always *buying the business, not buying the stock.* A few of them sometimes buy whole businesses. Far more often they simply buy small pieces of businesses. Their attitude, whether buying all or a tiny piece of a business, is the same. Some of them hold portfolios with dozens of stocks; others concentrate on a handful. But all exploit the difference between the market price of a business and its intrinsic value.

I'm convinced that there is much inefficiency in the market. These Graham-and-Doddsville investors have successfully exploited gaps between price and value. When the price of a stock can be influenced by a "herd" on Wall Street with prices set at the margin by the most emotional person, or the greediest person, or the most depressed person, it is hard to argue that the market always prices rationally. In fact, market prices are frequently nonsensical.

I would like to say one important thing about risk and reward. Sometimes risk and reward are correlated in a positive fashion. If someone were to say to me, "I have here a six-shooter and I have slipped one cartridge into it. Why don't you just spin it and pull it once? If you survive, I will give you $1 million." I would decline—perhaps stating that $1 million is not enough. Then he might offer me $5 million to pull the trigger twice—now that would be a positive correlation between risk and reward!

The exact opposite is true with value investing. If you buy a dollar bill for 60 cents, it's riskier than if you buy a dollar bill for 40 cents, but the expectation of reward is greater in the latter case. The greater the potential for reward in the value portfolio, the less risk there is.

One quick example: The Washington Post Company in 1973 was selling for $80 million in the market. At the time, that day, you could have sold the assets to any one of ten buyers for not less than $400 million, probably appreciably more. The company owned the *Post*, *Newsweek*, plus several television stations in major markets. Those same properties are worth $2 billion now, so the person who would have paid $400 million would not have been crazy.

Now, if the stock had declined even further to a price that made the valuation $40 million instead of $80 million, its beta would have been greater. And to people who think beta measures risk, the cheaper price would have made it look riskier. This is truly Alice in Wonderland. I have never been able to figure out why it's riskier to buy $400 million worth of properties for $40 million than $80 million. And, as a matter of fact, if you buy a group of such securities and you know anything at all about business valuation, there is essentially no risk in buying $400 million for $80 million, particularly if you do it by buying ten $40 million piles for $8 million each. Since you don't have your hands on the $400 million, you want to be sure you are in with honest and reasonably competent people, but that's not a difficult job.

You also have to have the knowledge to enable you to make a very general estimate about the value of the underlying businesses. But you do not cut it close. That is what Ben Graham meant by having a margin of safety. You don't try and buy businesses worth $83 million for $80 million. You leave yourself an enormous margin. When you build a bridge, you insist it can carry 30,000 pounds, but you only drive 10,000-pound trucks across it. And that same principle works in investing.

In conclusion, some of the more commercially minded among you may wonder why I am writing this article. Adding many converts to the value approach will perforce narrow the spreads between price and value. I can only tell you that the secret has been out for 50 years, ever since Ben Graham and Dave Dodd wrote *Security Analysis*, yet I have seen no trend toward value investing in the 35 years that I've practiced it. There seems to be some perverse human characteristic that likes to make easy things difficult. The academic world, if anything, has actually backed away from the teaching of value investing over the last 30 years. It's likely to continue that way. Ships will sail around the world but the Flat Earth Society will flourish. There will continue to be wide discrepancies between price and value in the marketplace, and those who read their Graham & Dodd will continue to prosper.

Tables 1–9 follow:

TABLE 1 Walter J. Schloss

Year	S&P Overall Gain, Including Dividends (%)	WJS Ltd Partners Overall Gain per year (%)	WJS Partnership Overall Gain per year (%)		
1956	7.5	5.1	6.8	Standard & Poor's 28¼ year compounded gain	887.2%
1957	−10.5	−4.7	−4.7		
1958	42.1	42.1	54.6	WJS Limited Partners 28¼ year compounded gain	6,678.8%
1959	12.7	17.5	23.3		
1960	−1.6	7.0	9.3	WJS Partnership 28¼ year compounded gain	23,104.7%
1961	26.4	21.6	28.8		
1962	−10.2	8.3	11.1	Standard & Poor's 28¼ year annual compounded rate	8.4%
1963	23.3	15.1	20.1		
1964	16.5	17.1	22.8	WJS Limited Partners 28¼ year annual compounded rate	16.1%
1965	13.1	26.8	35.7		
1966	−10.4	0.5	0.7	WJS Partnership 28¼ year annual compounded rate	21.3%
1967	26.8	25.8	34.4		
1968	10.6	26.6	35.5		

During the history of the Partnership it has owned over 800 issues and, at most times, has had at least 100 positions. Present assets under management approximate $45 million. The difference between returns of the partnership and returns of the limited partners is due to allocations to the general partner for management.

TABLE 1 Walter J. Schloss (*continued*)

Year	S&P Overall Gain, Including Dividends (%)	WJS Ltd Partners Overall Gain per year (%)	WJS Partnership Overall Gain per year (%)
1969	−7.5	−9.0	−9.0
1970	2.4	−8.2	−8.2
1971	14.9	25.5	28.3
1972	19.8	11.6	15.5
1973	−14.8	−8.0	−8.0
1974	−26.6	−6.2	−6.2
1975	36.9	42.7	52.2
1976	22.4	29.4	39.2
1977	−8.6	25.8	34.4
1978	7.0	36.6	48.8
1979	17.6	29.8	39.7
1980	32.1	23.3	31.1
1981	6.7	18.4	24.5
1982	20.2	24.1	32.1
1983	22.8	38.4	51.2
1984 1st Qtr.	2.3	0.8	1.1

TABLE 2 Tweedy, Browne Inc.

Period Ended (September 30)	Dow Jones* (%)	S & P 500* (%)	TBK Overall (%)	TBK Limited Partners (%)
1968 (9 mos.)	6.0	8.8	27.6	22.0
1969	−9.5	−6.2	12.7	10.0
1970	−2.5	−6.1	−1.3	−1.9
1971	20.7	20.4	20.9	16.1
1972	11.0	15.5	14.6	11.8
1973	2.9	1.0	8.3	7.5
1974	−31.8	−38.1	1.5	1.5
1975	36.9	37.8	28.8	22.0
1976	29.6	30.1	40.2	32.8
1977	−9.9	−4.0	23.4	18.7
1978	8.3	11.9	41.0	32.1
1979	7.9	12.7	25.5	20.5
1980	13.0	21.1	21.4	17.3
1981	−3.3	2.7	14.4	11.6
1982	12.5	10.1	10.2	8.2
1983	44.5	44.3	35.0	28.2

Total Return				
15¾ years	191.8%	238.5%	1,661.2%	936.4%
Standard & Poor's 15¾ year annual compounded rate				7.0%
TBK Limited Partners 15¾ year annual compounded rate				16.0%
TBK Overall 15¾ year annual compounded rate				20.0%

* Includes dividends paid for both Standard & Poor's 500 Composite Index and Dow Jones Industrial Average.

TABLE 3 Buffett Partnership, Ltd.

Year	Overall Results From Dow (%)	Partnership Results (%)	Limited Partners' Results (%)
1957	−8.4	10.4	9.3
1958	38.5	40.9	32.2
1959	20.0	25.9	20.9
1960	−6.2	22.8	18.6
1961	22.4	45.9	35.9
1962	−7.6	13.9	11.9
1963	20.6	38.7	30.5
1964	18.7	27.8	22.3
1965	14.2	47.2	36.9
1966	−15.6	20.4	16.8
1967	19.0	35.9	28.4
1968	7.7	58.8	45.6
1969	−11.6	6.8	6.6

On a cumulative or compounded basis, the results are:

Year	Overall Results From Dow (%)	Partnership Results (%)	Limited Partners' Results (%)
1957	−8.4	10.4	9.3
1957–58	26.9	55.6	44.5
1957–59	52.3	95.9	74.7
1957–60	42.9	140.6	107.2
1957–61	74.9	251.0	181.6
1957–62	61.6	299.8	215.1
1957–63	94.9	454.5	311.2
1957–64	131.3	608.7	402.9
1957–65	164.1	943.2	588.5
1957–66	122.9	1156.0	704.2
1957–67	165.3	1606.9	932.6
1957–68	185.7	2610.6	1403.5
1957–69	152.6	2794.9	1502.7
Annual Compounded Rate	7.4	29.5	23.8

TABLE 4 Sequoia Fund, Inc.

Year	Annual Percentage Change**	
	Sequoia Fund (%)	S&P 500 Index* (%)
1970 (from July 15)	12.1	20.6
1971	13.5	14.3
1972	3.7	18.9
1973	−24.0	−14.8
1974	−15.7	−26.4
1975	60.5	37.2
1976	72.3	23.6
1977	19.9	−7.4
1978	23.9	6.4
1979	12.1	18.2
1980	12.6	32.3
1981	21.5	−5.0
1982	31.2	21.4
1983	27.3	22.4
1984 (first quarter)	−1.6	−2.4
Entire Period	775.3%	270.0%
Compound Annual Return	17.2%	10.0%
Plus 1% Management Fee	1.0%	
Gross Investment Return	18.2%	10.0%

* Includes dividends (and capital gains distributions in the case of Sequoia Fund) treated as though reinvested.
** These figures differ slightly from the S&P figures in Table 1 because of a difference in calculation of reinvested dividends.

TABLE 5 Charles Munger

Year (%)	Mass. Inv. Trust (%)	Investors Stock (%)	Lehman (%)	Tri-Cont. (%)	Dow (%)	Overall Partnership (%)	Limited Partners
Yearly Results							
1962	−9.8	−13.4	−14.4	−12.2	−7.6	30.1	20.1
1963	20.0	16.5	23.8	20.3	20.6	71.7	47.8
1964	15.9	14.3	13.6	13.3	18.7	49.7	33.1
1965	10.2	9.8	19.0	10.7	14.2	8.4	6.0
1966	−7.7	−9.9	−2.6	−6.9	−15.7	12.4	8.3
1967	20.0	22.8	28.0	25.4	19.0	56.2	37.5
1968	10.3	8.1	6.7	6.8	7.7	40.4	27.0
1969	−4.8	−7.9	−1.9	0.1	−11.6	28.3	21.3
1970	0.6	−4.1	−7.2	−1.0	8.7	−0.1	−0.1
1971	9.0	16.8	26.6	22.4	9.8	25.4	20.6
1972	11.0	15.2	23.7	21.4	18.2	8.3	7.3
1973	−12.5	−17.6	−14.3	−21.3	−23.1	−31.9	−31.9
1974	−25.5	−25.6	−30.3	−27.6	−13.1	−31.5	−31.5
1975	32.9	33.3	30.8	35.4	44.4	73.2	73.2

Compound Results

1962	−9.8	−13.4	−14.4	−12.2	−7.6	20.1
1962–3	8.2	0.9	6.0	5.6	11.5	77.5
1962–4	25.4	15.3	20.4	19.6	32.4	136.3
1962–5	38.2	26.6	43.3	32.4	51.2	150.5
1962–6	27.5	14.1	39.5	23.2	27.5	171.3
1962–7	53.0	40.1	78.5	54.5	51.8	273.0
1962–8	68.8	51.4	90.5	65.0	63.5	373.7
1962–9	60.7	39.4	86.9	65.2	44.5	474.6
1962–70	61.7	33.7	73.4	63.5	57.1	474.0
1962–71	76.3	56.2	119.5	100.1	72.5	592.2
1962–72	95.7	79.9	171.5	142.9	103.9	642.7
1962–73	71.2	48.2	132.7	91.2	77.2	405.8
1962–74	27.5	40.3	62.2	38.4	36.3	246.5
1962–75	69.4	47.0	112.2	87.4	96.8	500.1
Average Annual Compounded Rate	3.8	2.8	5.5	4.6	5.0	13.7

TABLE 6 Pacific Partners, Ltd.

Partnership Year	S & P 500 Index (%)	Limited Partnership Results (%)	Overall Results (%)
1965	12.4	21.2	32.0
1966	−10.1	24.5	36.7
1967	23.9	120.1	180.1
1968	11.0	114.6	171.9
1969	−8.4	64.7	97.1
1970	3.9	−7.2	−7.2
1971	14.6	10.9	16.4
1972	18.9	12.8	17.1
1973	−14.8	−42.1	−42.1
1974	−26.4	−34.4	−34.4
1975	37.2	23.4	31.2
1976	23.6	127.8	127.8
1977	−7.4	20.3	27.1
1978	6.4	28.4	37.9
1979	18.2	36.1	48.2
1980	32.3	18.1	24.1
1981	−5.0	6.0	8.0
1982	21.4	24.0	32.0
1983	22.4	18.6	24.8

Standard & Poor's 19 year compounded gain	316.4%
Limited Partners 19 year compounded gain	5,530.2%
Overall Partnership 19 year compounded gain	22,200.0%
Standard & Poor's 19 year annual compounded rate	7.8%
Limited Partners 19 year annual compounded rate	23.6%
Overall Partnership 19 year annual compounded rate	32.9%

TABLE 7 Perlmeter Investments

Year	PIL Overall (%)	Limited Partner (%)		
8/1–12/31/65	40.6	32.5	Total Partnership Percentage Gain 8/1/65 through 10/31/83	4277.2%
1966	6.4	5.1	Limited Partners Percentage Gain 8/1/65 through 10/31/83	2309.5%
1967	73.5	58.8	Annual Compound Rate of Gain Overall Partnership	23.0%
1968	65.0	52.0	Annual Compound Rate of Gain Limited Partners	19.0%
1969	−13.8	−13.8	Dow Jones Industrial Average 7/31/65 (Approximate)	882
1970	−6.0	−6.0	Dow Jones Industrial Average 10/31/83 (Approximate)	1225
1971	55.7	49.3	Approximate Compound Rate of Gain of DJI including dividends	7%
1972	23.6	18.9		
1973	−28.1	−28.1		
1974	−12.0	−12.0		
1975	38.5	38.5		
1/1–10/31/76	38.2	34.5		
11/1/76–10/31/77	30.3	25.5		
11/1/77–10/31/78	31.8	26.6		
11/1/78–10/31/79	34.7	28.9		
11/1/79–10/31/80	41.8	34.7		
11/1/80–10/31/81	4.0	3.3		
11/1/81–10/31/82	29.8	25.4		
11/1/82–10/31/83	22.2	18.4		

TABLE 8 The Washington Post Company, Master Trust, December 31, 1983

Ended*	Current Quarter		Year Ended		2 Years Ended*		3 Years Ended*		5 Years Ended	
	% Ret.	Rank	% Ret.	Rank	% Ret.	Rank	% Ret.	Rank	% Ret	Rank
All Investments										
Manager A	4.1	2	22.5	10	20.6	40	18.0	10	20.2	3
Manager B	3.2	4	34.1	1	33.0	1	28.2	1	22.6	1
Manager C	5.4	1	22.2	11	28.4	3	24.5	1	—	—
Master Trust (All Managers)	3.9	1	28.1	1	28.2	1	24.3	1	21.8	1
Common Stock										
Manager A	5.2	1	32.1	9	26.1	27	21.2	11	26.5	7
Manager B	3.6	5	52.9	1	46.2	1	37.8	1	29.3	3
Manager C	6.2	1	29.3	14	30.8	10	29.3	3	—	—
Master Trust (All Managers)	4.7	1	41.2	1	37.0	1	30.4	1	27.6	1
Bonds										
Manager A	2.7	8	17.0	1	26.6	1	19.0	1	12.2	2
Manager B	1.6	46	7.6	48	18.3	53	12.7	84	7.4	86
Manager C	3.2	4	10.4	9	24.0	3	18.9	1	—	—
Master Trust (All Managers)	2.2	11	9.7	14	21.1	14	15.2	24	9.3	30
Bonds & Cash Equivalents										
Manager A	2.5	15	12.0	5	16.1	64	15.5	21	12.9	9
Manager B	2.1	28	9.2	29	17.1	47	14.7	41	10.8	44
Manager C	3.1	6	10.2	17	22.0	2	21.6	1	—	—
Master Trust (All Managers)	2.4	14	10.2	17	17.8	20	16.2	2	12.5	9

* Annualized
Rank indicates the fund's performance against the A.C. Becker universe.
Rank is stated as a percentile: 1 = best performance, 100 = worst.

TABLE 9 FMC Corporation Pension Fund, Annual Rate of Return (Percent)

Period ending	1 Year	2 Years	3 Years	4 Years	5 Years	6 Years	7 Years	8 Years	9 Years
FMC (Bonds and Equities Combined)									
1983	23.0								*17.1
1982	22.8	13.6	16.0	16.6	15.5	12.3	13.9	16.3	
1981	5.4	13.0	15.3	13.8	10.5	12.6	15.4		
1980	21.0	19.7	16.8	11.7	14.0	17.3			
1979	18.4	14.7	8.7	12.3	16.5				
1978	11.2	4.2	10.4	16.1					
1977	−2.3	9.8	17.8						
1976	23.8	29.3							
1975	35.0							* 18.5 from equities only	
Becker large plan median									
1983	15.6								12.6
1982	21.4	11.2	13.9	13.9	12.5	9.7	10.9	12.3	
1981	1.2	10.8	11.9	10.3	7.7	8.9	10.9		
1980	20.9	NA	NA	NA	10.8	NA			
1979	13.7	NA	NA	NA	11.1				
1978	6.5	NA	NA	NA					
1977	−3.3	NA	NA						
1976	17.0	NA							
1975	24.1								

TABLE 9 FMC Corporation Pension Fund, Annual Rate of Return (Percent) *(continued)*

Period ending	1 Year	2 Years	3 Years	4 Years	5 Years	6 Years	7 Years	8 Years	9 Years
S&P 500									
1983	22.8								15.6
1982	21.5	7.3	15.1	16.0	14.0	10.2	12.0	14.9	
1981	-5.0	12.0	14.2	12.2	8.1	10.5	14.0		
1980	32.5	25.3	18.7	11.7	14.0	17.5			
1979	18.6	12.4	5.5	9.8	14.8				
1978	6.6	-0.8	6.8	13.7					
1977	7.7	6.9	16.1						
1976	23.7	30.3							
1975	37.2								

2. The New Speculation in Common Stocks[1]

What I shall have to say will reflect the spending of many years in Wall Street, with their attendant varieties of experience. This has included the recurrent advent of new conditions, or a new atmosphere, which challenge the value of experience itself. It is true that one of the elements that distinguish economics, finance, and security analysis from other practical disciplines is the uncertain validity of past phenomena as a guide to the present and future. Yet we have no right to reject the lessons of the past until we have at least studied and understood them. My address today is an effort toward such understanding in a limited field—in particular, an endeavor to point out some contrasting relationships between the present and the past in our underlying attitudes toward investment and speculation in common stocks.

Let me start with a summary of my thesis. In the past the speculative elements of a common stock resided almost exclusively in the company itself; they were due to uncertainties, or fluctuating elements, or downright weaknesses in the industry, or the corporation's individual setup. These elements of speculation still exist, of course; but it may be said that they have been sensibly diminished by a number of long-term developments to which I shall refer. But in revenge a new and major element of speculation has been introduced into the common-stock arena from *outside* the companies. It comes from the attitude and viewpoint of the stock-buying public and their advisers—chiefly us security analysts. This attitude may be described in a phrase: primary emphasis upon future expectations.

Nothing will appear more logical and natural to this audience than the idea that a common stock should be valued and priced primarily on the basis of the company's expected future performance. Yet this simple-appearing concept carries with it a number of paradoxes and pitfalls. For one thing, it obliterates a good part of the older, well-established distinctions between investment and speculation. The dictionary says that "speculate" comes from the Latin "specula," a lookout. Thus it was the speculator who looked out and saw future developments coming before other people did. But today, if the investor is shrewd or well advised, he too must have his lookout on the future, or rather he mounts into a common lookout where he rubs elbows with the speculator.

Secondly, we find that, for the most part, companies with the best investment characteristics—i.e., the best credit rating—are the ones which are likely to attract the largest speculative interest in their common stocks, since everyone assumes they are guaranteed a brilliant future. Thirdly, the concept of future prospects, and particularly of continued growth in the future, invites the application of formulas out of higher mathematics to establish the present value of the favored issues. But the combination of precise formulas with highly imprecise assumptions can be used to establish, or rather to justify, practically any value one wishes, however high, for a really outstanding issue. But, paradoxically, that very fact on close examination will be seen to imply that no one value, or reasonably narrow range of values, can be counted on to establish and maintain itself for a given growth company; hence at times the market may conceivably value the growth component at a strikingly *low* figure.

Returning to my distinction between the older and newer speculative elements in common stock, we might characterize them by two outlandish but convenient words, viz.: endogenous and exogenous. Let me illustrate briefly the old-time speculative common stock, as distinguished from an investment stock, by some data relating to American Can and Pennsylvania Railroad in 1911–1913. (These appear in Benjamin Graham and David L. Dodd, *Security Analysis*, McGraw-Hill, 1940, pp. 2–3.)

In those three years the price range of "Pennsy" moved only between 53 and 65, or between 12.2 and 15 times its average earnings for the period. It showed steady profits, was paying a reliable $3 dividend, and investors were sure that it was backed by well over its par of $50 in tangible assets. By contrast, the price of American Can ranged between 9 and 47; its earnings between 7 cents and $8.86; the ratio of price to the three-year average earnings moved between 1.9 times and 10 times; it paid no dividend at all; and sophisticated investors were well aware that the $100 par value of the common represented nothing but undisclosed "water," since the preferred issue exceeded the tangible assets available for it. Thus American Can common was a representative speculative issue, because American Can Company was then a speculatively capitalized enterprise in a fluctuating and uncertain industry. Actually, American Can had a far more brilliant long-term future than Pennsylvania Railroad; but not only was this fact not suspected by investors or speculators in those days, but even if it had been it would probably have been put aside by the investors as basically irrelevant to investment policies and programs in the years 1911–1913.

Now, to expose you to the development through time of the importance of long-term prospects for investments. I should like to use as my example our most spectacular giant industrial enterprise—none other than International Business Machines, which last year entered the small group of companies with $1 billion of sales. May I introduce one or two autobiographical notes here, in order to inject a little of the personal touch into what otherwise would be an excursion into cold figures? In 1912 I had left college for a term to take charge of a research project for U.S. Express Company. We set out to find the effect on revenues of a proposed revolutionary new system of computing express rates. For this purpose we used the so-called Hollerith machines, leased out by the then Computing-Tabulating-Recording Company. They comprised card punches, card sorters, and tabulators—tools almost unknown to businessmen, then, and having their chief application in the Census Bureau. I entered Wall Street in 1914, and the next year the bonds and common stock of C.-T.-R. Company were listed on the New York Stock Exchange. Well, I had a kind of sentimental interest in that enterprise, and besides I considered myself a sort of technological expert on their products, being one of the few financial people who had seen and used them. So early in 1916 I went to the head of my firm, known as Mr. A. N., and pointed out to him that C.-T.-R. stock was selling in the middle 40s (for 105,000 shares); that it had earned $6.50 in 1915; that its book value—including, to be sure, some nonsegregated intangibles—was $130; that it had started a $3 dividend; and that I thought rather highly of the company's products and prospects. Mr. A. N. looked at me pityingly. "Ben," said he, "do not mention that company to me again. I would not touch it with a ten-foot pole. [His favorite expression.] Its 6 per cent bonds are selling in the low 80s and they are no good. So how can the stock be any good? Everybody knows there is nothing behind it but water." (Glossary: In those days that was the ultimate of condemnation. It meant that the asset account of the balance sheet was fictitious. Many industrial companies—notably U.S. Steel—

despite their $100 par, represented nothing but water, concealed in a written-up plant account. Since they had "nothing" to back them but earning power and future prospects, no self-respecting investor would give them a second thought.)

I returned to my statistician's cubbyhole, a chastened young man. Mr. A. N. was not only experienced and successful, but extremely shrewd as well. So much was I impressed by his sweeping condemnation of Computing-Tabulating-Recording that I never bought a share of it in my life, not even after its name was changed to International Business Machines in 1926.

Now let us take a look at the same company with its new name in 1926, a year of pretty high stock markets. At that time it first revealed the good-will item in its balance sheet, in the rather large sum of $13.6 million. A. N. had been right. Practically every dollar of the so-called equity behind the common in 1915 had been nothing but water. However, since that time the company had made an impressive record under the direction of T. L. Watson, Sr. Its net had risen from $691,000 to $3.7 million—over fivefold—a greater percentage gain than it was to make in any subsequent eleven-year period. It had built up a nice tangible equity for the common, and had split it 3.6 for one. It had established a $3 dividend rate for the new stock, while earnings were $6.39 thereon. You might have expected the 1926 stock market to have been pretty enthusiastic about a company with such a growth history and so strong a trade position. Let us see. The price range for that year was 31 low, 59 high. At the average of 45 it was selling at the same 7-times multiplier of earnings and the same 6.7 per cent dividend yield as it had done in 1915. At its low of 31 it was not far in excess of its tangible book value, and in that respect was far more conservatively priced than eleven years earlier.

These data illustrate, as well as any can, the persistence of the old-time investment viewpoint until the culminating years of the bull market of the 1920s. What has happened since then can be summarized by using ten-year intervals in the history of IBM. In 1936 net expanded to twice the 1926 figures, and the average multiplier rose from 7 to $17\frac{1}{2}$. From 1936 to 1946 the gain was $2\frac{1}{2}$ times, but the average multiplier in 1946 remained at $17\frac{1}{2}$. Then the pace accelerated. The 1956 net was nearly 4 times that of 1946, and the average multiplier rose to $32\frac{1}{2}$. Last year, with a further gain in net, the multiplier rose again to an average of 42, if we do not count the unconsolidated equity in the foreign subsidiary.

When we examine these recent price figures with care we see some interesting analogies and contrasts with those of forty years earlier. The one-time scandalous water, so prevalent in the balance sheets of industrial companies, has all been squeezed out—first by disclosure and then by writeoffs. But a different kind of water has been put back into the valuation by the stock market—by investors and speculators themselves. When IBM now sells at 7 times its book value, instead of 7 times earnings, the effect is practically the same as if it had no book value at all. Or the small book-value portion can be considered as a sort of minor preferred-stock component of the price, the rest representing exactly the same sort of commitment as the old-time speculator made when he bought Woolworth or U.S. Steel common entirely for their earning power and future prospects.

It is worth remarking, in passing, that in the thirty years which saw IBM transformed from a 7-times earnings to a 40-times earnings enterprise, many of what I have called the endogenous speculative aspects of our large industrial companies have tended to disappear, or at least to diminish greatly. Their financial positions are firm, their capital structures conservative: they are managed far more expertly, and even more honestly, than before. Furthermore, the requirements of complete disclosure have removed one of the important speculative elements of years ago—that derived from ignorance and mystery.

Another personal digression here. In my early years in the Street one of the favorite mystery stocks was Consolidated Gas of New York, now Consolidated Edison. It owned as a subsidiary the profitable New York Edison Company, but it reported only dividends received from this source, not its full earnings. The unreported Edison earnings supplied the mystery and the "hidden value." To my surprise I discovered that these hush-hush figures were actually on file each year with the Public Service Commission of the state. It was a simple matter to consult the records and to present the true earnings of Consolidated Gas in a magazine article. (Incidentally, the addition to profits was not spectacular.) One of my older friends said to me then: "Ben, you may think you are a great guy to supply those missing figures, but Wall Street is going to thank you for nothing. Consolidated Gas with the mystery is both more interesting and more valuable than ex-mystery. You youngsters who want to stick your noses into everything are going to ruin Wall Street."

It is true that the three M's which then supplied so much fuel to the speculative fires have now all but disappeared. These were Mystery, Manipulation, and (thin) Margins. But we security analysts have ourselves been creating valuation approaches which are so speculative in themselves as to pretty well take the place of those older speculative factors. Do we not have our own "3M's" now—none other than Minnesota Mining and Manufacturing Company—and does not this common stock illustrate perfectly the new speculation as contrasted with the old? Consider a few figures. When M. M. & M. common sold at 101 last year the market was valuing it at 44 times 1956 earnings, which happened to show no increase to speak of in 1957. The enterprise itself was valued at $1.7 billion, of which $200 million was covered by net assets, and a cool $1½ billion represented the market's appraisal of "good will." We do not know the process of calculation by which that valuation of good will was arrived at; we do know that a few months later the market revised this appraisal downward by some $450 million, or about 30 per cent. Obviously it is impossible to calculate accurately the intangible component of a splendid company such as this. It follows as a kind of mathematical law that the more important the good will or future earning-power factor the more uncertain becomes the true value of the enterprise, and therefore the more speculative inherently the common stock.

It may be well to recognize a vital difference that has developed in the valuation of these intangible factors, when we compare earlier times with today. A generation or more ago it was the standard rule, recognized both in average stock prices and in formal or legal valuations, that intangibles were to be appraised on a more conservative basis than tangibles. A good industrial company might be required to earn between 6 per cent and 8 per cent on its tangible assets, represented typically by bonds and preferred stock; but its excess earnings, or the intangible assets they gave rise to, would be valued on, say, a 15 per cent basis. (You will find approximately these ratios in the initial offering of Woolworth preferred and common stock in 1911, and in numerous others.) But what has happened since the 1920s? Essentially the exact reverse of these relationships may now be seen. A company must now typically earn about 10 per cent on its common equity to have it sell in the average market at full book value. But its excess earnings, above 10 per cent on capital, are usually valued more liberally, or at a higher multiplier, than the base earnings required to support the book value in the market. Thus a company earning 15 per cent on the equity may well sell at 13½ times earnings, or twice its net assets. This would mean that the first 10 per cent earned on capital is valued at only 10 times, but the next 5 per cent—what used to be called the "excess"—is actually valued at 20 times.

Now there is a logical reason for this reversal in valuation procedure, which is related to the newer emphasis on growth expectations. Companies that earn a high return on capital are given these liberal appraisals not only because of the good profitability itself, and the relative stability associated with it, but perhaps even more cogently because high earnings on capital generally go hand in hand with a good growth record and prospects. Thus what is really paid for nowadays in the case of highly profitable companies is not the good will in the old and restricted sense of an established name and a profitable business, but rather their assumed superior expectations of increased profits in the future.

This brings me to one or two additional mathematical aspects of the new attitude toward common-stock valuations, which I shall touch on merely in the form of brief suggestions. If, as many tests show, the earnings multiplier tends to increase with profitability—i.e., as the rate of return on book value increases—then the arithmetical consequence of this feature is that value tends to increase directly as the square of the earnings, but *inversely* the book value. Thus in an important and very real sense tangible assets have become a drag on average market value rather than a source thereof. Take a far from extreme illustration. If Company A earns $4 a share on a $20 book value, and Company B also $4 a share on $100 book value, Company A is almost certain to sell at a higher multiplier, and hence at higher price than Company B—say $60 for Company A shares and $35 for Company B shares. Thus it would not be inexact to declare that the $80 per share of greater assets for Company B are responsible for the $25 per share lower market price, since the earnings per share are assumed to be equal.

But more important than the foregoing is the general relationship between mathematics and the new approach to stock values. Given the three ingredients of (a) optimistic assumptions as to the rate of earnings growth, (b) a sufficiently long projection of this growth into the future, and (c) the miraculous workings of compound interest—lo! the security analyst is supplied with a new kind of philosopher's stone which can produce or justify any desired valuation for a really "good stock." I have commented in a recent article in the *Analysts' Journal* on the vogue of higher mathematics in bull markets, and quoted David Durand's exposition of the striking analogy between value calculations of growth stocks and the famous Petersburg Paradox, which has challenged and confused mathematicians for more than two hundred years. The point I want to make here is that there is a special paradox in the relationship between mathematics and investment attitudes on common stocks, which is this: Mathematics is ordinarily considered as producing precise and dependable results; but in the stock market the more elaborate and abstruse the mathematics the more uncertain and speculative are the conclusions we draw therefrom. In forty-four years of Wall Street experience and study I have never seen dependable calculations made about common-stock values, or related investment policies, that went beyond simple arithmetic or the most elementary algebra. Whenever calculus is brought in, or higher algebra, you could take it as a warning signal that the operator was trying to substitute theory for experience, and usually also to give to speculation the deceptive guise of investment.

The older ideas of common-stock investment may seem quite naïve to the sophisticated security analyst of today. The great emphasis was always on what we now call the defensive aspects of the company or issue—mainly the assurance that it would continue its dividend unreduced in bad times. Thus the strong railroads, which constituted the standard investment commons of fifty years ago, were actually regarded in very much the same way as the public-utility commons in recent years. If the past record indicated stability, the chief requirement was met; not too much effort was made to anticipate adverse changes of an underlying character in the future. But, conversely, especially favorable future prospects were regarded by shrewd investors as something to look for but not to pay for.

In effect this meant that the investor did not have to pay anything substantial for superior long-term prospects. He got these, virtually without extra cost, as a reward for his own superior intelligence and judgment in picking the best rather than the merely good companies. For common stocks with the same financial strength, past earnings record, and dividend stability all sold at about the same dividend yield.

This was indeed a shortsighted point of view, but it had the great advantage of making common-stock investment in the old days not only simple but also basically sound and highly profitable. Let me return for the last time to a personal note. Somewhere around 1920 our firm distributed a series of little pamphlets entitled *Lessons for Investors*. Of course it took a brash analyst in his middle twenties like myself to hit on so smug and presumptuous a title. But in one of the papers I made the casual statement that "if a common stock is a good investment it is also a good speculation." For, reasoned I, if a common stock was so sound that it carried very little risk of loss it must ordinarily be so good as to possess excellent chances for future gains. Now this was a perfectly true and even valuable discovery, but it was true only because nobody paid any attention to it. Some years later, when the public woke up to the historical merits of common stocks as long-term investments, they soon ceased to have any such merit, because the public's enthusiasm created price levels which deprived them of their built-in margin of safety, and thus drove them out of the investment class. Then, of course, the pendulum swung to the other extreme, and we soon saw one of the most respected authorities declaring (in 1931) that no common stock could *ever* be an investment.

When we view this long-range experience in perspective we find another set of paradoxes in the investor's changing attitude toward capital gains as contrasted with income. It seems a truism to say that the old-time common-stock investor was not much interested in capital gains. He bought almost entirely for safety and income, and let the speculator concern himself with price appreciation. Today we are likely to say that the more experienced and shrewd the investor, the less attention he pays to dividend returns, and the more heavily his interest centers on long-term appreciation. Yet one might argue, perversely, that precisely because the old-time investor did not concentrate on future capital appreciation he was virtually guaranteeing to himself that he would have it, at least in the field of industrial stocks. And, conversely, today's investor is so concerned with anticipating the future that he is already paying handsomely for it in advance. Thus what he has projected with so much study and care may actually happen and still not bring him any profit. If it should fail to materialize to the degree expected he may in fact be faced with a serious temporary and perhaps even permanent loss.

What *lessons*—again using the pretentious title of my 1920 pamphlet—can the analyst of 1958 learn from this linking of past with current attitudes? Not much of value, one is inclined to say. We can look back nostalgically to the good old days when we paid only for the present and could get the future for nothing—an "all this and Heaven too" combination. Shaking our heads sadly we mutter, "Those days are gone forever." Have not investors and security analysts eaten of the tree of knowledge of good and evil prospects? By so doing have they not permanently expelled themselves from that Eden where promising common stocks at reasonable prices could be plucked off the bushes? Are we doomed always to run the risk either of paying unreasonably high prices for good quality and prospects, or of getting poor quality and prospects when we pay what seems a reasonable price?

It certainly looks that way. Yet one cannot be sure even of that pessimistic dilemma. Recently, I did a little research in the long-term history of that towering enterprise, General Electric—stimulated by the arresting chart of fifty-nine years of earnings and dividends appearing in their recently published 1957 Report. These figures are not without their surprises for the knowledgeable analyst. For one thing they show that prior to 1947 the growth of G. E. was fairly modest and quite irregular. The 1946 earnings, per share adjusted, were only 30 per cent higher than in 1902—52 cents versus 40 cents—and in no year of this period were the 1902 earnings as much as doubled. Yet the price-earnings ratio rose from 9 times in 1910 and 1916 to 29 times in 1936 and again in 1946. One might say, of course, that the 1946 multiplier at least showed the well-known prescience of shrewd investors. We analysts were able to foresee then the really brilliant period of growth that was looming ahead in the next decade. Maybe so. But some of you remember that the next year, 1947, which established an impressive new high for G.E.'s per-share earnings, was marked also by an extraordinary fall in the price-earnings ratio. At its low of 32 (before the 3-for-1 split) G.E. actually sold again at only 9 times its current earnings and its average price for the year was only about 10 times earnings. Our crystal ball certainly clouded over in the short space of twelve months.

This striking reversal took place only eleven years ago. It casts some little doubt in my mind as to the complete dependability of the popular belief among analysts that prominent and promising companies will now always sell at high price-earnings ratios—that this is a fundamental fact of life for investors and they may as well accept and like it. I have no desire at all to be dogmatic on this point. All I can say is that it is not settled in my mind, and each of you must seek to settle it for yourself.

But in my concluding remarks I can say something definite about the structure of the market for various types of common stocks, in terms of their investment and speculative characteristics. In the old days the investment character of a common stock was more or less the same as, or proportionate with, that of the enterprise itself, as measured quite well by its credit rating. The lower the yield on its bonds or preferred, the more likely was the common to meet all the criteria for a satisfactory investment, and the smaller the element of speculation involved in its purchase. This relationship, between the speculative ranking of the common and the investment rating of the company, could be graphically expressed pretty much as a straight line descending from left to right. But nowadays I would describe the graph as U-shaped. At the left, where the company itself is speculative and its credit low, the common stock is of course highly speculative, just as it has always been in the past. At the right extremity, however, where the company has the highest credit rating because both its past record and future prospects are most impressive, we find that the stock market tends more or less continuously to introduce a highly speculative element into the common shares through the simple means of a price so high as to carry a fair degree of risk.

At this point I cannot forbear introducing a surprisingly relevant, if quite exaggerated, quotation on the subject which I found recently in one of Shakespeare's sonnets. It reads:

> Have I not seen dwellers on form and favor
> Lose all and more by paying too much rent?

Returning to my imaginary graph, it would be the center area where the speculative element in common-stock purchases would tend to reach its minimum. In this area we could find many well-established and strong companies, with a record of past growth corresponding to that of the national economy and with future prospects apparently of the same character. Such common stocks could be bought at most times, except in the upper ranges of a bull market, at moderate prices in relation to their indicated intrinsic values. As a matter of fact, because of the present tendency of investors and speculators alike to concentrate on more glamorous issues, I should hazard the statement that these middle-ground stocks tend to sell on the whole rather below their independently determinable values. They thus have a margin-of-safety factor supplied by the same market preferences and prejudices which tend to destroy the margin of safety in the more promising issues. Furthermore, in this wide array of companies there is plenty of room for penetrating analysis of the past record and for discriminating choice in the area of future prospects, to which can be added the higher assurance of safety conferred by diversification.

When Phaëthon insisted on driving the chariot of the Sun, his father, the experienced operator, gave the neophyte some advice which the latter failed to follow—to his cost. Ovid summed up Phoebus Apollo's counsel in three words:

> *Medius tutissimus ibis*
> You will go safest in the middle course

I think this principle holds good for investors and their security analyst advisers.

3. Technological Companies as Investments

In the Standard & Poor's services in mid-1971 there were listed about 200 companies with names beginning with Compu-, Data, Electro-, Scien-, Techno-. About half of these belonged to some part of the computer industry. All of them were traded in the market or had made applications to sell stock to the public.

A total of 46 such companies appeared in the S & P *Stock Guide* for September 1971. Of these, 26 were reporting deficits, only six were earning over $1 per share, and only five were paying dividends.

In the December 1968 *Stock Guide* there had appeared 45 companies with similar technological names. Tracing the sequel of this list, as shown in the September 1971 *Guide*, we find the following developments:

Total Companies	Price Advanced	Price Declined Less Than Half	Price Declined More Than Half	Dropped from Stock Guide
45	2	8	23	12

COMMENT: It is virtually certain that the many technological companies not included in the *Guide* in 1968 had a poorer subsequent record than those that were included; also that the 12 companies dropped from the list did worse than those that were retained. The harrowing results shown by these samples are no doubt reasonably indicative of the quality and price history of the entire group of "technology" issues. The phenomenal success of IBM and a few other companies was bound to produce a spate of public offerings of new issues in their fields, for which large losses were virtually guaranteed.

Notes

Introduction: What This Book Expects to Accomplish

1. "Letter stock" is stock not registered for sale with the Securities and Exchange Commission (SEC), and for which the buyer supplies a letter stating the purchase was for investment.
2. The foregoing are Moody's figures for AAA bonds and industrial stocks.

Chapter 1. Investment versus Speculation: Results to Be Expected by the Intelligent Investor

1. Benjamin Graham, David L. Dodd, Sidney Cottle, and Charles Tatham, McGraw-Hill, 4th. ed., 1962. A fascimile copy of the 1934 edition of *Security Analysis* was reissued in 1996 (McGraw-Hill).
2. This is quoted from *Investment and Speculation,* by Lawrence Chamberlain, published in 1931.
3. In a survey made by the Federal Reserve Board.
4. 1965 edition, p. 8.
5. We assume here a top tax bracket for the typical investor of 40% applicable to dividends and 20% applicable to capital gains.

Chapter 2. The Investor and Inflation

1. This was written before President Nixon's price-and-wage "freeze" in August 1971, followed by his "Phase 2" system of controls. These important developments would appear to confirm the views expressed above.
2. The rate earned on the Standard & Poor's index of 425 industrial stocks was about $11\frac{1}{2}$% on asset value—due in part to the inclusion of the large and highly profitable IBM, which is not one of the DJIA 30 issues.

3. A chart issued by American Telephone & Telegraph in 1971 indicates that the rates charged for residential telephone services were somewhat less in 1970 than in 1960.
4. Reported in the *Wall Street Journal*, October 1970.

Chapter 3. A Century of Stock-Market History: The Level of Stock Prices in Early 1972

1. Both Standard & Poor's and Dow Jones have separate averages for public utilities and transportation (chiefly railroad) companies. Since 1965 the New York Stock Exchange has computed an index representing the movement of all its listed common shares.
2. Made by the Center for Research in Security Prices of the University of Chicago, under a grant from the Charles E. Merrill Foundation.
3. This was first written in early 1971 with the DJIA at 940. The contrary view held generally on Wall Street was exemplified in a detailed study which reached a median valuation of 1520 for the DJIA in 1975. This would correspond to a discounted value of, say, 1200 in mid-1971. In March 1972 the DJIA was again at 940 after an intervening decline to 798. Again, Graham was right. The "detailed study" he mentions was too optimistic by an entire decade: The Dow Jones Industrial Average did not close above 1520 until December 13, 1985!

Chapter 4. General Portfolio Policy: The Defensive Investor

1. A higher tax-free yield, with sufficient safety, can be obtained from certain *Industrial Revenue Bonds*, a relative newcomer among financial inventions. They would be of interest particularly to the enterprising investor.

Chapter 5. The Defensive Investor and Common Stocks

1. *Practical Formulas for Successful Investing*, Wilfred Funk, Inc., 1953.
2. In current mathematical approaches to investment decisions, it has become standard practice to define "risk" in terms of average price variations or "volatility." See, for example, *An Introduction to Risk and Return*, by Richard A. Brealey, The M.I.T. Press, 1969. We find this use of the word "risk" more harmful than useful for sound investment decisions—because it places too much emphasis on market fluctuations.
3. All 30 companies in the DJIA met this standard in 1971.

Chapter 6. Portfolio Policy for the Enterprising Investor: Negative Approach

1. In 1970 the Milwaukee road reported a large deficit. It suspended interest payments on its income bonds, and the price of the 5% issue fell to 10.
2. For example: Cities Service $6 first preferred, not paying dividends, sold at as low as 15 in 1937 and at 27 in 1943, when the accumulations had reached $60 per share. In 1947 it was retired by exchange for $196.50 of 3% debentures for each share, and it sold as high as 186.
3. An elaborate statistical study carried on under the direction of the National Bureau of Economic Research indicates that such has actually been the case. Graham is referring to W. Braddock Hickman, *Corporate Bond Quality and Investor Experience* (Princeton University Press, 1958). Hickman's book later inspired Michael Milken of Drexel Burnham Lambert to offer massive high-yield financing to companies with less than sterling credit ratings, helping to ignite the leveraged-buyout and hostile takeover craze of the late 1980s.
4. A representative sample of 41 such issues taken from Standard & Poor's *Stock Guide* shows that five lost 90% or more of their high price, 30 lost more than half, and the entire group about two-thirds. The many not listed in the *Stock Guide* undoubtedly had a larger shrinkage on the whole.

Chapter 7. Portfolio Policy for the Enterprising Investor: The Positive Side

1. See, for example, Lucile Tomlinson, *Practical Formulas for Successful Investing;* and Sidney Cottle and W. T. Whitman, *Investment Timing: The Formula Approach*, both published in 1953.
2. A company with an ordinary record cannot, without confusing the term, be called a growth company or a "growth stock" merely because its proponent expects it to do better than the average in the future. It is just a "promising company." Graham is making a subtle but important point: If the definition of a growth stock is a company that will thrive in the future, then that's not a definition at all, but wishful thinking. It's like calling a sports team "the champions" before the season is over. This wishful thinking persists today; among mutual funds, "growth" portfolios describe their holdings as companies with "above-average growth potential" or

"favorable prospects for earnings growth." A better definition might be companies whose net earnings per share have increased by an annual average of at least 15% for at least five years running. (Meeting this definition in the past does not ensure that a company will meet it in the future.)
3. See Table 7-1.
4. Here are two age-old Wall Street proverbs that counsel such sales: "No tree grows to Heaven" and "A bull may make money, a bear may make money, but a hog never makes money."
5. Two studies are available. The first, made by H. G. Schneider, one of our students, covers the years 1917–1950 and was published in June 1951 in the *Journal of Finance*. The second was made by Drexel Firestone, members of the New York Stock Exchange, and covers the years 1933–1969. The data are given here by their kind permission.
6. See pp. 379–381, for three examples of special situations existing in 1971.

Chapter 8. The Investor and Market Fluctuations

1. Except, perhaps, in dollar-cost averaging plans begun at a reasonable price level.
2. But according to Robert M. Ross, authority on the Dow theory, the last two buy signals, shown in December 1966 and December 1970, were well below the preceding selling points.
3. The top three ratings for bonds and preferred stocks are Aaa, Aa, and A, used by Moody's, and AAA, AA, A by Standard & Poor's. There are others, going down to D.
4. This idea has already had some adoptions in Europe—e.g., by the state-owned Italian electric-energy concern on its "guaranteed floating rate loan notes," due 1980. In June 1971 it advertised in New York that the annual rate of interest paid thereon for the next six months would be $8\frac{1}{8}$%.

One such flexible arrangement was incorporated in The Toronto-Dominion Bank's "7%–8% debentures," due 1991, offered in June 1971. The bonds pay 7% to July 1976 and 8% thereafter, but the holder has the option to receive his principal in July 1976.

Chapter 9. Investing in Investment Funds

1. The sales charge is universally stated as a percentage of the selling price, which includes the charge, making it appear lower than if applied to net asset value. We consider this a sales gimmick unworthy of this respectable industry.
2. *The Money Managers*, by G. E. Kaplan and C. Welles, (Random House, 1969).
3. See definition of "letter stock" on p. 573.
4. Title of a book first published in 1852. The volume described the "South Sea Bubble," the tulip mania, and other speculative binges of the past. It was reprinted by Bernard M. Baruch, perhaps the only continuously successful speculator of recent times, in 1932. *Comment:* That was locking the stable door after the horse was stolen. Charles Mackay's *Extraordinary Popular Delusions and the Madness of Crowds* (Metro Books, 2002) was first published in 1841. Neither a light read nor always strictly accurate, it is an extensive look at how large numbers of people often believe very silly things—for instance, that iron can be transmuted into gold, that demons most often show up on Friday evenings, and that it is possible to get rich quick in the stock market. For a more factual account, consult Edward Chancellor's *Devil Take the Hindmost* (Farrar, Straus & Giroux, 1999); for a lighter take, try Robert Menschel's *Markets, Mobs, and Mayhem: A Modern Look at the Madness of Crowds* (Wiley 2002).

Chapter 10. The Investor and His Advisers

1. The examinations are given by the Institute of Chartered Financial Analysts, which is an arm of the Financial Analysts Federation. The latter now embraces constituent societies with over 50,000 members.
2. The NYSE had imposed some drastic rules of valuation (known as "haircuts") designed to minimize this danger, but apparently they did not help sufficiently.
3. New offerings may now be sold only by means of a prospectus prepared under the rules of the Securities and Exchange Commission. This document must disclose all the pertinent facts about the issue and issuer, and it is fully adequate to inform the *prudent investor* as to the exact nature of the security offered him. But the very copiousness of

the data required usually makes the prospectus of prohibitive length. It is generally agreed that only a small percentage of *individuals* buying new issues read the prospectus with thoroughness. Thus they are still acting mainly not on their own judgment but on that of the house selling them the security or on the recommendation of the individual salesman or account executive.

Chapter 11. Security Analysis for the Lay Investor: General Approach

1. Our textbook, *Security Analysis* by Benjamin Graham, David L. Dodd, Sidney Cottle, and Charles Tatham (McGraw-Hill, 4th ed., 1962), retains the title originally chosen in 1934, but it covers much of the scope of financial analysis.
2. With Charles McGolrick, Harper & Row, 1964, reissued by HarperBusiness, 1998.
3. These figures are from Salomon Bros., a large New York bond house.
4. At least not by the great body of security analysts and investors. Exceptional analysts, who can tell in advance what companies are likely to deserve intensive study and have the facilities and capability to make it, may have continued success with this work. For details of such an approach see Philip Fisher, *Common Stocks and Uncommon Profits,* Harper & Row, 1960.
5. On p. 283 we set forth a formula relating multipliers to the rate of expected growth.
6. Part of the fireworks in the price of Chrysler was undoubtedly inspired by two two-for-one stock splits taking place in the single year 1963—an unprecedented phenomenon for a major company. In the early 1980s, under Lee Iacocca, Chrysler did a three-peat, coming back from the brink of bankruptcy to become one of the best-performing stocks in America. However, identifying managers who can lead great corporate comebacks is not as easy as it seems. When Al Dunlap took over Sunbeam Corp. in 1996 after restructuring Scott Paper Co. (and driving its stock price up 225% in 18 months), Wall Street hailed him as little short of the Second Coming. Dunlap turned out to be a sham who used improper accounting and false financial statements to mislead Sunbeam's investors—including the revered money managers Michael Price and Michael Steinhardt, who had hired him. For a keen dissection of Dunlap's career, see John A. Byrne, *Chainsaw* (HarperCollins, 1999).

7. Note that we do not suggest that this formula gives the "true value" of a growth stock, but only that it approximates the results of the more elaborate calculations in vogue.

Chapter 12. Things to Consider About Per-Share Earnings

1. Our recommended method of dealing with the warrant dilution is discussed below. We prefer to consider the market value of the warrants as an addition to the current market price of the common stock as a whole.

Chapter 13. A Comparison of Four Listed Companies

1. In March 1972, Emery sold at 64 times its 1971 earnings!

Chapter 14. Stock Selection for the Defensive Investor

1. Because of numerous stock splits, etc., through the years, the actual average price of the DJIA list was about $53 per share in early 1972.
2. In 1960 only two of the 29 industrial companies failed to show current assets equal to twice current liabilities, and only two failed to have net current assets exceeding their debt. By December 1970 the number in each category had grown from two to twelve.
3. But note that their combined market action from December 1970 to early 1972 was poorer than that of the DJIA. This demonstrates once again that no system or formula will guarantee superior market results. Our requirements "guarantee" only that the portfolio-buyer is getting his money's worth.
4. As a consequence we must exclude the majority of gas pipeline stocks, since these enterprises are heavily bonded. The justification for this setup is the underlying structure of purchase contracts which "guarantee" bond payments; but the considerations here may be too complicated for the needs of a defensive investor.

Chapter 15. Stock Selection for the Enterprising Investor

1. *Mutual Funds and Other Institutional Investors: A New Perspective,* I. Friend, M. Blume, and J. Crockett, McGraw-Hill, 1970. We should add that the 1966–1970 results of many of the funds we studied

were somewhat better than those of the Standard & Poor's 500-stock composite and considerably better than those of the DJIA.
2. Personal note: Many years before the stock-market pyrotechnics in that particular company the author was its "financial vice-president" at the princely salary of $3,000 per annum. It was then really in the fireworks business. In early 1929, Graham became a financial vice president of Unexcelled Manufacturing Co., the nation's largest producer of fireworks. Unexcelled later became a diversified chemical company and no longer exists in independent form.
3. The *Guide* does not show multipliers above 99. Most such would be mathematical oddities, caused by earnings just above the zero point.

Chapter 16. Convertible Issues and Warrants

1. This point is well illustrated by an offering of two issues of Ford Motor Finance Co. made simultaneously in November 1971. One was a 20-year nonconvertible bond, yielding 7½%. The other was a 25-year bond, subordinated to the first in order of claim and yielding only 4½%; but it was made convertible into Ford Motor stock, against its then price of 68½. To obtain the conversion privilege the buyer gave up 40% of income and accepted a junior-creditor position.
2. Note that in late 1971 Studebaker-Worthington common sold as low as 38 while the $5 preferred sold at or about 77. The spread had thus grown from 2 to 20 points during the year, illustrating once more the desirability of such switches and also the tendency of the stock market to neglect arithmetic. (Incidentally the small premium of the preferred over the common in December 1970 had already been made up by its higher dividend.)

Chapter 17. Four Extremely Instructive Case Histories

1. See, for example, the article "Six Flags at Half Mast," by Dr. A. J. Briloff, in *Barron's*, January 11, 1971.

Chapter 18. A Comparison of Eight Pairs of Companies

1. The reader will recall from p. 431 above that AAA Enterprises tried to enter this business, but quickly failed. Here Graham is making a

profound and paradoxical observation: The more money a company makes, the more likely it is to face new competition, since its high returns signal so clearly that easy money is to be had. The new competition, in turn, will lead to lower prices and smaller profits. This crucial point was overlooked by overenthusiastic internet stock buyers, who believed that early winners would sustain their advantage indefinitely.

Chapter 19. Shareholders and Managements: Dividend Policy

1. Analytical studies have shown that in the typical case a dollar paid out in dividends had as much as four times the positive effect on market price as had a dollar of undistributed earnings. This point was well illustrated by the public-utility group for a number of years before 1950. The low-payout issues sold at low multipliers of earnings, and proved to be especially attractive buys because their dividends were later advanced. Since 1950 payout rates have been much more uniform for the industry.

Chapter 20. "Margin of Safety" as the Central Concept of Investment

1. This argument is supported by Paul Hallingby, Jr., "Speculative Opportunities in Stock-Purchase Warrants," *Analysts' Journal*, third quarter 1947.

Postscript

1. Veracity requires the admission that the deal almost fell through because the partners wanted assurance that the purchase price would be 100% covered by asset value. A future $300 million or more in market gain turned on, say, $50,000 of accounting items. By dumb luck they got what they insisted on.

Appendixes

1. Address of Benjamin Graham before the annual Convention of the National Federation of Financial Analysts Societies, May 1958.

Acknowledgments from Jason Zweig

I thank David Reilly, Charles Forelle, Marie Beaudette, Liz Harris, and Emma Tucker of the *Wall Street Journal* for so graciously giving me the time away to work on this book.

I'm grateful to Hollis Heimbouch, Kirby Sandmeyer, and the entire staff at HarperCollins for their meticulous and brilliant work in bringing this new edition to life.

In rough alphabetical order, these people generously provided analysis, criticism, data, feedback, or perspective: Amy Arnott and Jeff Ptak, Morningstar; Ted Aronson, Jesse Barnes, and John Jacques, AJO Vista; William Bernstein, Efficient Frontier Advisors; Hank Bessembinder, Arizona State University; Laurence Black, the Index Standard; Warren Buffett; Deborah Fuhr, ETFGI; Pranav Ghai, Calcbench; Roy Haya, Fort Point Capital Partners; Joanne Hill, Cboe Vest; Matt Hougan, Bitwise Asset Management; Elisabeth Kashner, FactSet; Paul Marsh, London Business School; Michael Mauboussin, Counterpoint Global; Don Moore, University of California, Berkeley; Nina Munk, for delivering me into serendipity's path; Jeremy Perler and Yoni Engelhart, Schilit Forensics; Antti Petajisto, Brooklyn Investment Group; Alex Poukchanski and Diane Roman, Center for Research in Security Prices; Robert Shiller, Yale University; Howard Silverblatt, S&P Dow Jones Indices; Todd Sohn, Strategas Securities; Jocelyn Wilk, Rare Book & Manuscript Library, Columbia University; Lauren Taylor Wolfe, Impactive Capital; Jun Wu, Wharton Research Data Service.

Above all, I thank my wife: She did everything but this so I could do nothing but this.

Index

Note: Page numbers in *italics* indicate figures and tables.

A. & P. *see* Great Atlantic & Pacific Tea Co.
AAA Enterprises, 144–145, 420, 431–435, 433n
AAII, 386
AAON Inc., *391*
Aberdeen Mfg. Co., 370–371, *373*
account executives. *see* "customers' brokers"
accounting practices. *see also specific company*
  "big bath"/"kitchen sink," 426n
  case histories about, 420, 422, 422n, 423
  and dividends, 491–492, 491n
  and GAAP rules, 307–315, 484n5
  and market fluctuations, 199n
  and per-share earnings, 295–306, 297n
  railroads, 170
  and stock splits, 491–492, 491n
acquisitions. *see* mergers and acquisitions; takeovers; *specific company*
active investor. *see* aggressive investors
Activision Blizzard, 480
Adobe Inc., *391*
advice. *see also* type of source
  for aggressive investors, 247, 259
  basic thesis about, 247
  for defensive investors, 117–118, 132–133, 247–248, 259
  and for defensive investors, 348–349
  fees/commissions for, 247, 250–251, 254, 258, 260–265, 266n3
  Graham's views about, 246–259
  and interviewing potential advisers, 265–268
  and investments vs. speculation, 19, 26–28
  knowing what you need, 264–265
  and role of adviser, 246
  sources of, 246–259
  and speculation, 559
  and trust and verification of advisers, 264, 266n2
  Zweig's comments about, 260–268
Aetna Maintenance Co., 144–145
Affiliated Fund, *224*
aggressive investors
  characteristics of, 6, 134, 158, 161n, 176
  definition of, 134n
  "dont's" for, 134–145, 146–156
  "do's" for, 157–179, 180–184
  expectations for, 27–33, 259
  and investments vs. speculation, 17–33
  and mixing aggressive and defensive, 176–177, 178–179
  and overconfidence, 359–360
  portfolio for, 104, 134–145, 146–156, 157–179, 180–184

585

aggressive investors (*cont.*)
  and preferred stocks, 99, 134,
    135–138, 135n, 139–141, 142–
    143, 167–168, 174, 176–178, 366
  psychology of, 367–368
  recommended fields for, 164–176
  return for, 27–33, 90
  and risk, 104–105
  rules for, 176–179
  security analysis for, 362–381
  stock selection for, 362–381,
    382–397
AI. *see* artificial intelligence (AI)
airlines, 6, 6n, 7, 30, 309, 347–348,
    349–350
Air Products & Chemicals Inc.,
    448–451, *450*, 451n, *468*
Air Reduction Co., 448–451, *450*,
    451n, *468*
AJO Vista, 384
Alabama Gas Co., 344
Alba-Waldensian, 373
Albemarle Corp., 437, 442–443, *442*
Albert's Inc., 373
ALCOA. *see* Aluminum Company of
    America (ALCOA)
Allegheny Power Co., 344
Allied Chemical Co., 278, *281*, 337,
    338
Allied Mills, 373
alternative assets, 106, 147–149
Aluminum Company of America
    (ALCOA), 278, 295–306, 337,
    338
Amazon.com, 20n, *390*, 392, 394,
    519–522, *520*, *521*, 524, 527
AMC Entertainment Holdings Inc.,
    41, *42*, 128, 216, 471–472, *473*,
    503n19
American & Foreign Power Co., 407,
    409
American Brands Co., 337, *338*
American Can Co., 278, 337, *338*,
    340, *341*, 559–561
American Electric Power Co., 343
American Financial Group, 464n

American Gas & Electric Co., 97–98
American Home Products Co.,
    451–453, *452*, 453n, *468*
American Hospital Supply Co.,
    451–453, *452*, 453n, *468*
American International Group, 183
American Machine & Foundry, 300n
American Maize Products, 371–372,
    373
American Rubber & Plastics Co., 373
American Smelting & Refining Co.,
    373
American Stock Exchange, 197, 398,
    444, 448, 448n
American Telephone & Telegraph,
    67, 136, 174, 196–197, *278*, *285*,
    336, *337*, *338*, 340, *341*, 344, 398,
    404, 489
American Tobacco Co., *278*
American Water Works, 344
AMETEK, Inc., 471–472, *473*
AMF Corp., 300n
Anaconda, 169, *278*, 337, *338*, 340,
    341, 373
analysts. *see* financial analysts
Anderson, Ed, 540
Anderson Clayton Co., 373
anger, 217
annual earnings multipliers, *285*
annual meetings, 487
annual reports, 292, 292n5
annuities, 146n2, 264–265
anxiety, 217
Apple Inc., *390*, 393–394, 524
appreciation, 23–25, *52*, 136
apps, trading
  embedded costs in, 127n7
  and finding investing community,
    503, 503n19
  as a gamblified investing tool,
    125–126
  and investing myopia, 153
  negative-sum game, 126–127
  and stock screeners, 386
arbitrages, 31, 32n, 174–175, 176,
    366, 380–381

Archer-Daniels-Midland, 373
Arcimoto Inc., 474–475
Arconic Corp., 474–475
Aristotle, 76
ARK Innovation, 244–245, *245*
artificial intelligence (AI), 261, 481
artwork, 55
"as if" statements. *see* pro forma statements
asset allocation. *see also* diversification
   50-50 plan of, 5, 91–93, 158–159
   and aggressive investors, 134, 158–159
   and defensive investors, 20–28, 90–93
   and history and forecasting of stock market, 75
   and inflation, 47–48
   and institutional investors, 190
   and investments vs. speculation, 10
   and market fluctuations, 190, 193
   tactical, 190
asset backing. *see* book value
assets. *see also* asset allocation; *specific company*
   alternative, 106, 147–149
   average annual, 60n4
   financial capital, 59
   human capital, 59
   inflation and, 59–60
   and per-share earnings, 302n, 305n
   physical capital, 59
   and security analysis, 270, 273–274
   and stock selection for aggressive investors, 367, 369, 371–372, 374, 375–376, 377n, *377*, 378
   and stock selection for defensive investors, 323–324, 334, 335, 340–342, *341*, 345, 350–351
assets under management (AUM), 261–262

Association for Investment Management and Research, 269n
AT&T Corp. *see* American Telephone & Telegraph
Atchison, Topeka & Santa Fe, 136, 202–203, *205*
Atlantic City Electric Co., 344
AUM. *see* assets under management (AUM)
Aurora Plastics Co., 379, 380–381
Avco Corp., *406*
Avon Products, 454
Axon Enterprise Inc., *390*

Babson's Financial Service, 247–248
Badger Meter Inc., *391*
Bagdad Copper, 373
balanced funds, 230
balance sheets, 196–197, 273–274, 302n, *317*, 322–323, 350–351, 378. *see also specific company*
balance-sheet value. *see* book value
Balchem Corp., *390*, 393
Baldwin (D.H.), 373
Baltimore Gas & Electric Co., 344
Bankers Trust, 227n
bank-loan funds, 106
Bankman-Fried, Sam, 149
Bank of America Corp., 370n
Bank of Southwark, 141n
bankruptcy. *see also specific company*
   and aggressive investors, 144–145, 174–176, 370
   of brokerage houses, 254–255
   case histories about, 420–435, 421n
   and defensive investors, 100–101, 347–348
   and history and forecasting of stock market, 70
   and investment funds, 227
   and market fluctuations, 3–4, 4n
   and price, 421n
   of railroads, 3–4, 4n, 347–348, 370, 421n
   and security analysis, 275–276

banks. *see also* type of bank or specific bank
  and advice, 256–258, 259
  and bond valuation, 206
  as corporate lenders, 420
  and delivery and receipt of securities, 256–257, 256n
  and dividends, 491–492
  investing in, 345–346
  and investment funds, 227
  and new offerings, 257
  and real estate ventures, 408
  and stock selection for defensive investors, 347
  trust departments of, 4, 27–28, 225, 227, 247–248
bargains
  and aggressive investors, 134–135, 157, 158, 167–174, 176, 177–179, 366n, 367, 374, 376–379
  and bonds, 167–168, 174
  and common stock, 167–174, 177–178
  and defensive investors, 90, 97, 336
  definition of, 167–168, 177–178
  and investments vs. speculation, 32–33
  and margin of safety, 510–511
  and market fluctuations, 198, 202–203
  and preferred stocks, 167–168, 174
  in secondary companies, 171–174, 173n, 177–179
  and value, 177–178
Bausch & Lomb Co., 234
Bausch Health Companies, 485
Baxter Healthcare Corp., 453n
bear markets
  and aggressive investors, 140n, 367–368
  and defensive investors, 90
  and history and forecasting of stock market, 65–72, 74, 80–81, 206
  and market fluctuations, 189–190, 190n, 206
"beating the market/average," 9–10, 76, 120–121, 159–160, 159n, 230–231, 362–363, 535–536
Bed Bath & Beyond Inc., 41, 42, 128, 475–477, 475, 499
Belgian Congo bonds, 138–139
Benjamin Graham Joint Account, 366n
Berkshire Hathaway, 215, 302n, 541, 542
Bernstein, Peter L., 529
Bernstein, William, 2n, 84, 110
Best Buy, 475–477, 475
Bethlehem Steel, 278, 337, 338
Bezos, Jeff, 392, 527
Bieber, Justin, 154
Big Ben Stores, 373
Binks Manufacturing Co., 373
Biogen Inc., 391
biotechnology stocks, 384
bitcoin, 63–64, 479–480
Blackberry Ltd, 42
blank-check companies, 155
Block, Inc., 477–479, 478
Bloomberg U.S. Aggregate Bond Index, 238
Blue Bell, Inc., 453–456, 454n, 455, 468
Bluefield Supply Co., 373
BOC Group, 451n
Bogle, John, 238
bond funds, 230, 272n
Bond Guide (Standard & Poor's), 421
bonds. *see also* bond funds; convertible issues; *specific company or type of bond*
  and advice, 248, 250, 257, 259
  and aggressive investors, 134–136, 135n, 136n, 139–141, 157, 167–168, 174, 174–178
  and asset allocation, 10, 20–28, 90–93
  and bargains, 167–168, 174

calls on, 98–99, 139–140
common stocks compared with, 5n, 17–28, 56, 190
and convertible issues and warrants, 206–207, 400, *406*, 407, 409, 411–412
coupons for, 99, 99n, 135, 135n, 136, 139–140
"coverage" for, *284*
defaults on, 89–90, 174, 275–276, 421, 514
and defensive investors, 20–28, 90–101, 106, 113n, 114, 114n, 119, 121–122, 176–177, 333, 336, 350–351
discount, 136n
distressed, 158n
and diversification, 272n
earnings on, 272–276
and Graham's business principles, 515–516
and history and forecasting of stock market, 70, 75, 76, 77, 78, 84–85
I bonds, 61
inflation and, 5, 24–25, 47, 48, 50–51, 56
inflation-linked, 61–62
interest on, 2, 3, 5, 20–28, 70, 76, 77, 78, 90, 94–95, 96, 99, 99n, 114, 121–122, 135n, 203–208, 507–509, 508n
and investment funds, 230, 234–235
and investments vs. speculation, 17–21
long- and short-term, 92–93, 106, 185
and margin of safety, 505–506, 507, 508–509, 508n, 512–513
and market fluctuations, 185, 189–190, 203–208
and new offerings, 8, 139–141
price of, 21–23, 136, 136n, 203–208
ratings for, 96, 206, 207, 272n, 336n
and risk, 272–276
and role of investment bankers, 256
safety of, 272–276
second-grade, 135–138, 139–140
and security analysis, 270, 272–276, 282–283, 286n
selling at par, 137–138
and size of enterprise, 273–274
taxes and, 20–24, 92–93, 94, 95, 96, 97, 97n, 100, 157, 512–513
types of, 92–99
yield on, 5, 8–9, 25–26, 78, 90, 92, 93, 94, 96, 97–98, 99, 114, 114n, 135, 138–139, 189–190, 203–208, 399, 568–569
books, 55
book value. *see also specific company*
and aggressive investors, *278*, 366, 369–370, 374, 375n, 379
and defensive investors, 334, 335, *337, 338–339*, 340, *341*, 342
and market fluctuations, 194–197, 194n, 199n
and per-share earnings, 305–306, 305n, 565
and return on capital, 451n
Borden Inc., 379, 380–381
Bored Ape Yacht Club NFT, 154
Branson, Richard, 154
bridge players analogy, 364–365
Bristol-Myers Squibb Co., 309
brokerage firms. *see also* online trading; *specific firm*
and advice, 117–118, 246, 250–253, 251n, 254–255, 259, 260–264
commissions, 85, 85n5
discount, 251n
fees/commissions of, 117–118, 127n7, 153, 414–417, *415*
financial troubles of, 4, 4n, 254–255
full-service, 251n
margin accounts with, 20n
online, 39
and options trading, 414–417

brokerage firms (*cont.*)
  and portfolio policy for defensive investors, 117–118, 120–121
  and stock screeners, 386
  volume of trades in, 254–255
  websites, 182–183
brokerage transactions, delivery of, 255–256, 256n
Brooklyn Union Gas Co., 344
Brooks, John, 254n
Brown, Eliot, 149n5
buffered funds, 418
Buffett, Warren E. *see also* Berkshire Hathaway
  on difference between price and value, 522
  and diversification, 279n
  on durable advantages, 293
  and GEICO, 531n
  on intelligent investing, 14
  on investing for the long run, 87
  on the market, 417
  on per-share earnings, 313
  on price, 538–539
  on risk, 544–545
  preface by, xiii–xiv
  and SOYA investing, 382–383
  "Superinvestors of Graham-and-Doddsville" talk by, 535–558
  on valuing stocks, 64, 535
Buffett Partnership, Ltd., 541, *550*
bull markets
  and bargains, 171, 173–174, 177–178
  characteristics of, 140–141, 189–190
  and common stock, 565–566
  and convertible issues and warrants, 399–400, 403
  and dealings with brokeragefirms, 139–140, 254–255
  death/end of, 142–143, 206
  and defensive investors, 104
  history and forecasting of, 65–73, 74, 76, 78, 206

  length of, 190n
  and market fluctuations, 54–55, 171, 189–190, 190n, 193, 206
  and new offerings, 140–141, 140n, 142–145
  and performance funds, 226–227
  and portfolio policy for aggressive investors, 140–141, 140n, 142–145, 171, 173–174, 177–178
Bureau of Labor Statistics, 86n1
Burlington Northern Railroad, 348n
Burton-Dixie Corp., 379
Bush, George W., 495
business
  buying the, 544
  knowing your, 515–516
  "businessman's investment," 136–137
business principles, Graham's, 515–516
buybacks of shares, 497–500, *498*
buy-low-sell-high approach, 189–190
buzzwords, investing, 173n

Calcbench, 311
Callahan, Dan, 293n7, 394n7
calls and call options, 98–99, 139–140, 400n, 401–402, 402n, 413–414, 417–419
CAPE ratio, 81–83, *81*
capital, 52–53, 59, 303, 305n, 399, 408. *see also* capital gains; capitalization; return on invested capital (ROIC); *specific company*
capital gains, 75, 221, 345, 567–568
capitalization, 123, 123n, 229–230, 276–277, 279–283, *317*, 370, 407, 408, 409
Career Academy, *234*
Carolina Power & Light Co., *344*
case histories
  Graham's comparison of eight pairs of companies, 444–470

Graham's discussion of four "extremely instructive," 420–435
Zweig's comparison of eight pairs of companies, 471–485
Zweig's discussion of four "extremely instructive," 436–443
cash/"cash equivalents," 22–24, 106
Caughran, Brett, 292n4
Central Hudson Gas and Electric Co., 344
Central Illinois Light Co., 344
Central Maine Power Co., 344
certificates, stock, 194, 194n, 493, 493n
certificates of deposit, 97–98
Certified Financial Planner (CFP), 263
Certified Public Accountant (CPA), 263
charitable institutions, 47, 47n
Chartered Financial Analyst (CFA), 253, 253n, 263
Chase Manhattan Bank, 448n
checklists, 291–294
chemical companies, 279–280, 280n, 281
Chicago, Milwaukee, St. Paul and Pacific Bonds, 136
Chicago and Northwestern Railway Co., 302n
China, stock market in, 435n
Chrysler Corp., 166, *167*, 168, 169, *278*, 280, *337*, *338*, 340
Cincinnati Gas & Electric Co., 344
Citigroup Inc, 499
Civex, 503
Cleveland Electric Co., 343
CleveTrust Realty Investors, 408
closed-end funds, 141n, 221, 230, 231–235, 493n
Clover Health Investments Corp., 42
coal, 64
Coca-Cola, 394

Cognizant Technology Solutions Corp., *390*
Cohen, Ryan, 476
Coherent Corp., *391*
Coinbase Global Inc., 42
coin flipping, 536, 537, 538
coins, buying and selling, 55
Columbia Gas System, 343
commercial banks, 97–98, 225, 246, 258, 427, 427n
commodities, inflation and, 64
common stock. *see also specific topic*
  and advice, 257, 259
  for aggressive investors, 135, 137, 139–140, 157–179, 362–381
  and asset allocation, 10, 90–93, 158–159
  bonds compared with, 5n, 17–28, 56, 190
  characteristics of, 158
  for defensive investors, 20–28, 90–101, 113–123, 124–133, 176–177, 323–324, 333, 334–351
  dividends on, 20–21, 100, 114–115, 274n, 282–283, 319–320, 565–566, 567, 568
  earnings on, 115, 276–289, 564–565
  expected growth (1963 and 1969) of, *285*
  general long-term prospects for, 279–280
  general observations on, 321–322
  as growth stock, 116–117, 159–160, 283–287, 510
  and history and forecasting of stock market, 70, 73, 74, 75, 76, 78
  inflation and, 47–56
  investment merits of, 113–115
  investment rules for, 176–179
  and investments vs. speculation, 17–21
  investor's personal situation and, 119–121
  as "junior stock issues," 274n

common stock (*cont.*)
  and margin of safety, 506–511, 567, 570
  and market fluctuations, 185, 186, 189–190, 191–193, 195–197, 197, 199–200, 201
  performance of, 222–223
  portfolio changes in, 117–118
  price decline in, 3
  price record of, 400
  public attitude toward, 18–19, 18n
  return on, 114, 363
  and risk, 19–20, 121–122, 380
  security analysis of, 270, 273–274, 276–289, 316–324
  selection of, 114–115, 135, 137, 139–140, 157, 159, 160, 161–162, 167–168, 170, 176–179, 333, 334–351
  valuation of, 276–279, 565–566
  Value Line Forecast (1967-1969) about, 278
Commonwealth Edison Co., 343
companies. *see also* case histories; corporations; secondary companies; *specific company*
  annual reports, 292, 292n5
  change in character of, 199–200
  comparison of eight pairs of, 444–470, 471–485
  comparison of four listed, 316–324, 436–443
  and GAAP rules, 307–315
  general observations about, 467–470
  investors' relationship with, 162, 164n, 199–200
  "large, prominent conservatively financed," 122–123
  with large amounts of convertible issues (1969), 406
  second-line, 192–193, 192n
  unpopular large, 164–168, 169
compensation, stock-based, 312–315, 314
computer industry, 6–7, 29, 173–174, 173n, 434–435

Cone Mills, 377
Conseco, 424n
conglomerates, 3, 405
Consolidated Edison, 343, 562–564
Consolidated Gas of New York, 562–564
Consolidated Natural Gas Co., 343
Consolidated Rail Corp. (Conrail), 423n
Consolidation Coal, 280
Consumers Power Co., 344
Consumers' Research Council of America, 263
control, illusion of, 355–357
convertible issues. *see also* warrants; *specific company*
  and aggressive investors, 135, 366
  and defensive investors, 91, 98, 100–101
  Graham's discussion about, 398–407
  and market fluctuations, 206–207
  and per-share earnings, 300–301, 302–303, 405, 408, *410*
  Zweig's comments about, 413–414
Cooper Companies Inc., 390
Copart Inc., 391
corporate bonds
  and aggressive investors, 135n
  and convertible issues and warrants, 398
  and defensive investors, 93, 96, 336n
  and dividends, 22–23
  and inflation, 50
  and investment funds, 234–235
  and margin of safety, 512–513
  and market fluctuations, 199–200, 203–208
  return on, 399n
  and security analysis, 272, 272n
corporations. *see also* companies; corporate bonds; *specific corporation*
  annual reports, 292, 292n5
  debt of, 53–54, 135

and fluctuations in bond prices, 207–208
and GAAP rules, 307–315
governance of, 202–204, 203n
investor's relationship with, 162, 164n, 199–200
"large, prominent, conservatively financed," 122–123, 191–192
misleading reporting by, 229–230
taxes on, 100, 177–178
unpopular large, 164–168, 169
Costco Wholesale Corp., 503
costs. *see* expenses/costs; fees/commissions
coupons, 99, 99n, 135, 135n, 136, 139–140
courage, investor virtue of, 16
Covid pandemic, 38–39, 106, 218, 389, 436, 437, 438–439, 476, 498
Cowles Commission, 65, *66*
crash, stock market
of 1929, 188, 229–230
of 1987, 141n
of 2000, 141n, 280n, 435n
of 2007–09, 87
of 2020, 498
and the human brain, 218–219
credit companies, investing in, 345–346
credit ratings, 135, 161–162, 568–569
Criterion Insurance Co., 531n
crowd contagion, 128–132
cryptocurrencies, 39, 40, 63–64, 148–149
CSX Corp., 348n, 423n
C.-T.-R. Co., 560–562
The Cult of We (Brown & Farrell), 149n5
curiosity, investor virtue of, 14–15
Curry, Stephen, 154
"customers' brokers," 250–251, 252–253, 259

"Daddy-Knows-Best," 489n
Davis, Christopher, 183
Davis Advisors, 183

Dawkins, Richard, 41
Dayton Power & Light Co., 344
debt. *see also* bonds; *specific company or type of bond*
and aggressive investors, 371
corporate, 53–54, 135
and defensive investors, 334, 335, *338–339*, 341
and dividends, 490–491
of emerging markets, 106
limit on, of U.S. government, 95, 97
margin debt, 151
and margin of safety, 506
of public utilities, 334
and selection of stock, 334, 335, *338–339*, *341*, 371
decumulation, 80–81
Deere & Co., 174
defaults
and bargains, 174
on bonds, 89–90, 174, 275–276, 421, 514
and portfolio policy for aggressive investors, 138–139, 158n, 174
defensive investors
characteristics of, 5–6
definition of, 20–21
vs. enterprising investors, 104–105
exclusions for, 176–178
expectations for, 20–28
and inflation, 47–56
and the inner con artist, 352–361
and investments vs. speculation, 17–28
and margin of safety, 508–509, 516–517
and market fluctuations, 195–197
and mixing aggressive and defensive, 176–177, 178–179
portfolio for, 90–101, 103–106, 109–111, *112*, 113–123, 124–133
return for, 20–28, 24n, 25–26, 176–177
and risk tolerance, 102–105
rules for, 176–178

defensive investors (cont.)
  and security analysis, 282–283, 333–351
  selectivity for, 348–351
  stock selection for, 333–351, 371n
deflation, 51
delisted stocks, 371n
Delmarva Power & Electric Co., 344
Deltona Co., 234
denominator blindness, 262n1
Department of Justice, 437
depreciation, 300–301, 490–491
Depression (1930s), 72, 137–138, 152, 171, 199–200, 411–412, 514
Detroit Edison Co., 343
diamonds, 55
dilution. see also specific company
  and convertible issues and warrants, 405, 410, 411–412
  and per-share earnings, 296–299, 297n, 300–301, 302–303
directors, 408, 487
discipline, investor virtue of, 15
Discord, 128
discount brokerage firms, 251n
Discovery Communications, Inc., 500–501
diversification
  and aggressive investors, 366, 372–376, 377, 378–379
  and alternative assets, 55–56
  and defensive investors, 114–115, 333, 350–351
  and delisted stocks, 371n
  and ETFs, 241–242
  and Graham's disciples, 540
  importance of, 530
  and margin of safety, 508–509, 510, 511, 512n, 514, 514–515, 522–524, 523
  and market fluctuations, 212
  and security analysis, 272n, 277, 279, 279n
dividends. see also yield; specific company or type of security
  academic criticism of, 492–493, 492n
  and advice, 247
  and bargains, 167–168, 170, 173–174
  and comparison of four listed companies, 319–320, 329
  cumulative or noncumulative, 100
  and earnings, 492–493
  and expectations for defensive investors, 20–26, 24n
  fixed, 100
  Graham's comments about, 487–494
  and growth, 488–489, 490–491
  and history and forecasting of stock market, 65, 67, 69, 71, 72, 76, 77, 78
  inflation and, 48, 50, 52, 54–55
  and investor-management relations, 487–494, 489n
  and margin of safety, 507, 508–509, 515–516
  and market fluctuations, 188, 189–190, 198, 201, 203
  overview about, 487–494
  and "payout ratio," 283n, 488n
  and performance (1871-1970), 71
  and portfolio policy for aggressive investors, 135n, 137–138, 167–168, 170, 173–174
  and portfolio policy for defensive investors, 92, 99, 100, 100n, 114–115, 116–117, 118–119, 121–122
  and price, 488–489, 492n
  proper stock, 491–492
  record of paying, 114–115
  reinvestment of, 487–491
  of secondary companies, 173–174
  and security analysis, 272, 274n, 276–277, 282–283, 286–287, 286n
  special, 492n
  and speculation, 487, 488–489, 565–566, 567, 568

Index 595

and stock selection for aggressive
  investors, 370, 371–372, 374,
  375–376
and stock selection for defensive
  investors, 322–323, 334, 335,
  336, *337*, *338–339*, 340–342,
  347–348, 350–351
stock split and, 491–494, 491n
taxes on, 20–24, 100, 283n,
  493–494
Dixon, Richard, 47n
Dodd, David, 540. *see also* Security
  Analysis (Graham and Dodd)
Dogecoin, 40
"Dogs of the Dow," 165, 165n
dollar-cost averaging, 2, 26–28, 75,
  118–119, 119n, 132–133, 190,
  522n3
Dorsey, Pat, 293n7
dot.com stocks, 173n
Dow Chemical Co., 301
Dow Jones Industrial Average
  (DJIA). *see also specific company*
  aggressive investors and, 137, 160,
    161, 164–165, 165–166, 165n,
    172, 362, 372–376
  and bargains, 172
  "best" stocks in, 348–349
  and comparison of four listed
    companies, 318, *318*, 321–322
  defensive investors and, 92,
    114–115, 118–119, 333, 336–340,
    340–342, 348–349
  and dividend return on common
    stocks, 20–21
  in early 1970s, 4, 72–79
  and expectations for investors,
    21–27, 26n, 32, 33
  growth of, 284–286
  and growth stocks, 160
  and history and forecasting of
    stock market, *66*, 67, 70–73, 74,
    75, 76, 78, 79, 1069
  inflation and, 50, 51–55, 56
  and investment funds, 225,
    226–227, 235n

and market fluctuations, 188–189,
  190n, 191–193, 196–197, 197,
  198, 204
and per-share earnings, 303–306
and Raskob's prescription, 2
rise of (1915-1970), 50
and security analysis, 278,
  279–280, *281*, 282–283, *285*,
  287–288
and selection of stocks, 333,
  336–342, 348–349, 362, 372–376
and unpopular large companies,
  164–166, 165n
yield of stocks (2003) on, 5n
"Dow Theory," 3, 32, 188–189,
  191–192
DraftKings Inc., 42
Drew, Daniel, 297n
Drexel Burnham Lambert, 165n, 427n
Drexel Firestone Co., 165, 165n
Dreyfus Fund, *224*
drug industry, 29
dual-purpose funds, 221–222, 221n
Du Pont, Glore, Forgan & Co., 254n
Du Pont Co., *278*, *281*, *337*, *338*
durable advantages, 293
Durand, David, 195n, 565–566

"earning power," 52–53, 506, 506n,
  507–509, 510, 511, 563–564
earnings. *see also* "earning power";
  per-share earnings; price/
  earnings ratio; *specific company
  or type of security*
  average, 303–306
  and bargains, 167–170, 174
  on capital funds, 303, 305n
  debt and profits on capital (1950-
    1969), 53
  and dividends, 492–493
  and expectations for investors,
    24n, 25–26, 32
  hiding true, 426n
  and history and forecasting of
    stock market, 65, 69, 71, 72, 76,
    77, 78

earnings (*cont.*)
  inflation and, *49*, 51–55
  and margin of safety, 506, 508n, 509–510
  and market fluctuations, 196–197, 198
  and performance (1871-1970), *71*
  and per-share earnings, 300–301
  and portfolio policy for aggressive investors, 135, 136, 137, 140–141, 161–162, 164–165, 166, 167–170, 173–174, *174*
  and portfolio policy for defensive investors, 115, 115n, 116–117
  real, 422
  and security analysis, 270, 272, 276–277, 279–280, *281*, 282–284, *284*, *285*, 286–287
  and speculation, 564–565
  and stock selection for aggressive investors, 367–368, 370, 371–372, 374, 375–376, 378
  and stock selection for defensive investors, 322–323, 334, 335, *338–339*, 340–342, 349–351
  and superstocks, 389–396
earnings-covered test, 272–276
Eastman Kodak Co., *278*, 325–332, *330–331*, *337*, *338*
eBay Inc., 439
Edison Electric Light Co., 20n
Edward VII (king of Great Britain), 298, 298n
"efficient markets hypothesis" (EMH), 348–349, 349n, 365–366, 366n
Electric Autolite Co., 316
electronics industry, 29, 173–174, 173n, 322–323, 434–435
Eli Lilly & Co., 309
ELTRA Corp., 316–324
Emerson, Ralph Waldo, 380–381
Emerson Electric Co., 316–324, 320n, 325–332, 330n, *330–331*
Emery Air Freight, 316–324, 322n
Emhart Corp., 316–324, 369

Eminem, 154
employee-purchase plans, 429–430, 431n
employees, compensation for, 312–315, *314*. *see also* managers/management
endowment funds, 150–151, 190, 215, 227, 227n
Energizer Holdings Inc., 325–332, *330–331*
Ennis, Richard, 150
Enron Corp., 421n, 427n
enterprising investors. *see also* aggressive investors
  stock selection for, 382–397
EPS. *see* per-share earnings
Erb, Claude B., 60n4
Erie Railroad, 297n
ESG funds, 242–244
ETFGI, 241
ethics, 250–251, 251n, 257, 269
eToro, 125
Eversharp Co., 403
evidence-based confidence, 359–360
Exact Sciences Corp., 325–332, *330–331*
exchange-traded funds (ETFs), 236, 238n2, 239–242
expenses/costs. *see also* fees/commissions
  of doing business, 302n
  and GAAP rules, 307–315
  of mutual funds, 362–363
  and per-share earnings, 302n
  of research, 362–363
  and stock selection for aggressive investors, 362–363
  of trading, 349n, 371n
ExxonMobil Corp., 496, 504

Faber, Meb, 292n4
Facebook, 131, 162n
factor funds, 384–385
Fair Isaac Corp., 387, 389, *390*
"fair-weather investments," 514
Farley, William, 302n

Farrell, Maureen, 149n5
Faust (Goethe), 409–411
Fedders Co., 234
Federal Reserve Board, 2n, 18n, 50, 121–122
feedback, 290-291
fees/commissions. *see also* expenses/costs
    for advice, 247, 250–251, 254, 258, 260–265, 266n3
    for aggressive investors, 146–150, 146n2, 147
    of brokerage firms, 117–118, 127n7, 153
    of investment funds, 221, 221n, 231n, 237, 238n2
    and IPOs, 140n
    and market fluctuations, 196–197
    and options trading, 414–417, 415
    and portfolio changes, 117–118
    and trading apps, 127n7
Fidelity Funds, 224
Fidelity Magellan Fund, 241
fiduciaries, 264
50-50 plan, 5, 91–93, 158–159
financial analysts. *see also* securities analysis
    and advice, 250–251, 251n, 252–253, 259
    collective intelligence of, 366n
    consensus opinion of, 363–364
    as creating valuation, 563–564, 565–566
    flaw in approach to selection by, 364–365
    functions of, 250–251, 252n, 253, 363–364
    and investments vs. speculation, 26–28
    and margin of safety, 510
    and market fluctuations, 187, 202–203
    requirements for, 252–253
    role of, 250–251, 269–270
    and speculation, 559, 563–564, 565–566, 570
    and stock selection for aggressive investors, 362, 363–364
    and stock selection for defensive investors, 348–349
financial capital, 59
financial condition. *see also specific company*
    and common stock, 282–283
    and dividends, 490–491
    and stock selection for aggressive investors, 370, 371–372, 374
    and stock selection for defensive investors, 322–323, 334, 335, 336
financial crisis (2008–09), 100n, 106, 236
financial institutions/industry, 139–140, 257, 345–346, 405n. *see also* type of institution or specific institution
financial markets, history and forecasting of, 1–2, 10, 23n, 54, 54n, 65–79. *see also* stock market
financial planners, 258n
financial position, and comparison of four listed companies, 319, 328–329
financial reports. *see* financial statements; *specific report*
financial service organizations/industry, 248–250
financial statements, 229–230, 429–430. *see also* per-share earnings; security analysis; type of report
Finbox, 386
Finchat.io, 386
FinViz, 386
Fisher, Lawrence, 67n
Fisher, Philip A., 293n7
fixed-value investments, 505–506. *see also* type of investment
Florida real estate, collapse of, 144–145
fluctuations, market
    and aggressive investors, 32
    and asset allocation, 193

fluctuations, market (cont.)
  in bond prices, 203–208
  book value and, 194–197, 194n, 199n
  and the human brain, 217–219
  and buy-low-sell-high approach, 189–190
  and defensive investors, 186
  example of, 196–201, 229n
  and forecasting, 186–189, 187n, 202–203, 206
  and formula investment plans, 191–192, 191n
  as guide to investment decisions, 186–189
  history of (1871-1972), 4, 65–72
  and investors, 185–219
  of investor's portfolio, 191–193
  managers and, 202–204
  Morgan's comments about, 54, 54n
  and Mr. Market parable, 200–201, 209–219
  timing and pricing of, 186–189, 202–203
  and valuation, 185, 186, 191–193, 207
FMC Corp., 543–544, *557–558*
Foley, John, 439
footnotes to financial statements, 300, 429–430
forced sale of stock, 199–200
Ford Motor Co., 443
forecasting
  and advice, 248–250
  and aggressive investors, 363–364
  and defensive investors, 349–350, 349n
  foreign stocks/bonds, 135, 138–139, 176–178, 233–234
  and history of stock market, 72–79
  of inflation, 48, 50, 54, 54n
  and investments vs. speculation, 23n
  and market fluctuations, 186–189, 187n, 202–203, 206

and Raskob's prescription, 2
reliability of, 10
and security analysis, 270, 271n, 276–279, 280n, 286–288
and selection of stock, 349–350, 349n, 363–364
and speculation, 568
the unpredictable, 363–364
formula investing/trading, 26–28, 91–93, 188–189. *see also specific formula*
formula plans/planners, 191–192, 191n
formula timing, 158–159
Fortune 500 list, 424n
Four Seasons Nursing, 234
"franchise" companies, 173–174, 173n, 420, 431–435
fraud, 229–230, 407, 427n, 448n
French assignats, 409, 409n
Friend-Blume-Crockett study, 363
friends or relatives, advice from, 258
Fruit of the Loom, 302n
FTX, 148–149
FuelCell Energy Inc., 42
Fundamental Investments Co., 224
fund industry. *see* investment funds

GAAP. *see* generally accepted accounting principles (GAAP)
Galton, Francis, 129
"gambler's fallacy," 456n
gambling, 18n, 19–20, 37, 195n, 356, 463, 511, 512n
  gamblified investing tools, 125–127
  and options trading, 416–417
GameStop Corp., 41, 42, 128, 216–217
Gawande, Atul, 292n4
GEICO. *see* Government Employees Insurance Co.
General American Investors, 234–235
General Electric Co., 54–55, 161–162, *278, 285, 337, 338*

General Foods Corp., *278, 337, 338*
generally accepted accounting principles (GAAP), 307–315, 484n5
General Motors Corp., *2,* 168, *278, 281, 285, 337, 338,* 443
Gilead Sciences Inc., *391*
Goethe, Johann Wolfgang von, 409–411
gold, buying, 55, 55n, 60–61, 60n3
Goodbody & Co., 254n
Good Judgment Open, 525–527
goodwill, 374, 375–376, 375n, 378, 424–426, 451, 563–564
Goodyear Tire Co., *278, 337, 338*
Google, 217, 394
Gordon, Myron, 84
Gordon equation, 24n, 84
Government Employees Financial Corp., 531n
Government Employees Insurance Co. (GEICO), 221n, 492–493, 531n
Graham, Benjamin
 Buffett's tribute to, xiv–xv
 business principles of, 515–516
 definition of investment of, 18, 34, 34n2
 disciples of, 535–558
 forecasts of, 23–24, 24n
 misjudgments of, 48–50, 50n
 photo, *xvi*
 Zweig's comments about, xviii–xxi
Graham-Newman Corp., 221n, 366–368, 366n, 531n, 539
Graham-Newman methods, summary of, 366–368
Grainger (W.W.), 385, 387, *388*
Great Atlantic & Pacific Tea Co., 196–201, 199n
greed, 193, 434–435, 435n
Groupon, Inc., 309
growth. *see also specific company*
 average, 303–306
 calculation of past rate of, 303–306
 and common stock, 408

and comparison of four listed companies, 319, 327–328
definition of, 159
and dividends, 488–489, 490–491
and growth stocks, 221–222
and history and forecasting of stock market, 73
and margin of safety, 508–509, 510
and market fluctuations, 9, 195n
mutual funds for, 160n, 161n, *161,* 221n
and per-share earnings, 303–306, 305n
and portfolio policy for aggressive investors, 158, 159–160, 160n, 180–184
and portfolio policy for defensive investors, 114–115, 116–117, 123
and risk, 161–162
and security analysis, 270, 271, 271n, 282–287
slow down in, 305n
speculative, 564–566
and stock selection for aggressive investors, 364–365, 370, 371–372, 375–376, 378
and stock selection for defensive investors, 323–324, 333, 334, 335–336, *338–339,* 340–342, *341,* 349–350
and types of investors, 6–8
Guerin, Rick, 542
Gulf & Western Inc., *406*

H&R Block, Inc., 453–456, *455, 468,* 477–479, *478*
Harrison, Arthur, 86n1
Hart, Kevin, 154
Harvey, Campbell R., 60n4
Hayden, Stone & Co., 254n
Hazlitt, William, 298n
hedge funds, 14n3, 106, 147–149, 152
hedging
 and aggressive investors, 366
 and expectations for investors, 25n, 31, 32n

hedging (*cont.*)
  and inflation, 55–56
  and investment funds, 221n, 230–231
  "related" and "unrelated," 366–368, 367n
HEICO Corp., *390*
Heine, Max, 383
herding, 544
high-yield bonds. *see* junk bonds
Hill, Joanne, 414
Hindenburg Research, 437
hindsight bias, 357–359, 360–361
Hogarth, Robin, 290–291
Horizon Corp., *234*
hostile takeovers, 32n, 427n
Housing and Urban Development (HUD), U.S. Department of, 97n
Houston Light & Power Co., *343*
"How much?" question, 8–9
HP Inc., 311–312, *312*
Hudson Pulp & Paper, 541
human capital, 59
"human factor" in selection, 350–351
humility, investor virtue of, 15, 151

IBM. *see* International Business Machines (IBM)
I bonds, 61
iconikapp.com, 503
Impactive Capital, 308
income, 137, 248, 307–315, 508–509, 567–568. *see also specific company*
income bonds, 100–101, 137
income tax. *see* taxes
independence, investor virtue of, 15, 151
index funds. *see also* exchange-traded funds (ETFs)
  and defensive investors, 109, 333n
  and margin of safety, 524
  and security analysis, 279n
  of total U.S. stock market, 333n
  types of, 238–241, *240*
industrial bonds, 157, 273–274, 275–276, *284*

Industrial National Bank of Rhode Island, 370, 370n
industrial stocks, *345*, 372–376
industry. *see also* type of security
  analysis of, 276–288
  and defensive investors, 21–22, 24–25, 24n, 25n, 114–115, 349n
  and history and forecasting of stock market, 48, 50, 54, 54n
inflation, 3, 22–23, 47–56, 282–283
  and money illusion, 57–58
  predicting growth of, 6–8, 6n
  and price, *49*
  and protection against, 21–22, 55–56
  and Raskob's prescription, 2n
  and returns/yield, 50, 54, 56
  and risk, 47n, 55, 56
  and survivorship bias, 86
  and taxes, 50
influencers, 153–155, 440
Infosys, 524
initial public offerings (IPOs), 139–141, 140n, 143n, 146n2, 147, 154, 258n, 297n, 432–433, 433n. *see also specific company*
institutional investors, 115, 190, 210–214, *211*, 212n2, *213*, 253n, 413
insurance companies, 177–178, 206, 207–208, 493n, 511
intangible assets, 393–394
intelligent investors
  as businesslike, 515–516
  and margin of safety, 518–529
  virtues of, 14–16
interest. *see also specific company or type of security*
  and aggressive investors, 135, 135n, 136, 137, 140–141, 161–162, 174
  and bargains, 174
  compound, 565–566
  and defensive investors, 90, 94–95, 96, 98, 99, 99n, 100–101, 114, 121–122, 349n

Index 601

and expectations for investors, 20–28, 32
fixed, 207
and history and forecasting of stock market, 70, 76, 77, 78
inflation and, 54, 55
and margin of safety, 508–509, 508n
and security analysis, 272, *284*, 286–287, 286n
and taxes, 100–101
International Business Machines (IBM), 6, 7, 73, 116–117, 161–162, 195, *234*, *285*, 369, 376, 378, 454, 489, 560–563, 571
International Financial Reporting Standards (IFRS), 308n2
International Flavors & Fragrances, 456–458, 456n, *457*, 468
International Harvester Co., *278*, *285*, *337*, *338*, 456–458, 456n, *457*, 458n, 468
International Nickel, *278*, 296, *337*, *338*
International Paper Co., *278*, *337*, *339*
International Telephone & Telegraph, *406*
internet companies, 258n, 433n, 435n
Intuit Inc., *391*
inverse funds, 241
investment banks/bankers
and advice, 246, 256–258
and aggressive investors, 140–142, 143n, 173n
IPOs, 433n, 434–435
and reform of Wall Street, 434–435, 435n
role of, 256–258
Investment Company of America, *224*
investment counseling firms, 19, 26–28, 247–249, 258
investment funds. *see also* closed-end funds; mutual funds; ETFs
advice about, 223, 225

and aggressive investors, 161, 362–364
aim/purpose of, 221–223
and balanced fund investments, 234–235
bank-operated, 4, 227
closed end vs. open end, 231–235
and common stock, 222–223, 225, 229–230, 234–235
and defensive investors, 27–28, 230, 345–346
dividends on, 221, 231–232
and earnings, 221, 225–226
expenses/costs of, 221, 221n, 231n
Graham's comments about, 220–235
and growth stocks, 7, 221–222
and "hot" stocks, 6–7n
influences on, 130n11
and interest, 221
managers of, 4, 222–226
method of sale of, 221
number of, 230
overvalued, speculative investments of, 4–5
performance of, 222–226, 230–231
questions about, 221–222
registration of, 230
regulation of, 230–231
return on, 234–235
and risk, 225–227, 230–231
selection of, 345–346, 362–364
taxes on, 234–235
type/classification of, 221–222, 230
Zweig's comments about, 236–245
investment operations, 34–35
investment policy statement (IPS), 107–108
investments. *see also specific topic*
conventional and nonconventional, 512–513
definition of, 512
expectations for, 20–33
"fair-weather," 514

investments (*cont.*)
  Graham's comments about, 17–33, 513–517
  Graham's definition of, 18, 34, 34n2
  importance of long-term, 560–562
  of large sums of money, 541
  major change since 1964 in, 20–23
  margin of safety as central concept, 505–517
  opportunities for, 514, 530–532
  speculation vs., 10, 17–33, 35–46, 512–513
  Zweig's comments about, 34–46
investors. *see also* type of investor
  active and passive, 109
  activism of, 458, 458n, 496
  and amusement investing, 37
  checklists for, 291–294
  controlling behavior of, 23n
  courage of, 516–517
  defensive, 89
  discipline of, 23n, 190n
  and dividends, 487–494
  emotions of, 8, 18, 190n, 217–218
  and endeavor investing, 37
  enterprising, 104–105
  expectations for, 20–33, 24n
  Graham's comments about, 486–494
  inexperienced, 127
  inflation and, 47–56
  ironical situation of, 349n
  managers/management, 486–494
  meaning of term, 17–21
  as mixed aggressive and defensive, 176–177, 178–179
  novice, 39–41
  online communities for, 131–132
  and other people's mistakes, 199–200
  and overconfidence, 352–361
  personal situation of, 119–121
  prediction behavior of, 23n
  psychology of, 8, 51, 109–110, 119, 192–193
  "reckless," 18
  relationship with company of, 162, 164n, 199–200
  self-defeating behavior of, 12–13
  self-knowledge of, 106
  speculators distinguished from, 1–2, 10, 17–33, 35–46, 201–203
  types of, 5–6
  and uncertainty, 88
  values of, 242–244
  willfully ignorant, 40–41
  Zweig's comments about, 495–504
Investors Stock Fund, 224
IPOs. *see* initial public offerings
IPS. *see* investment policy statement (IPS)
ITI Corp., 370

Jacob (Ryan) Internet Fund, 229n
Jantzen Inc., 377, 378
Jeddo Highland Coal, 541
Johns Manville Corp., *278*, *337*, *339*
JPMorgan Equity Premium Income ETF, 418
JPMorgan Nasdaq Equity Premium Income ETF, 418
junior stock issues. *see* common stock
junk bonds, 97, 97n, 427n

Kahneman, Daniel, 358
Kaplan, G.E., 229
Karp, Morris, 448n
Kashner, Elisabeth, 241–242
Kayos, Inc., 445n
Kayser-Roth Co., 379, 380–381
Keck family, 489n
Keynes, John Maynard, 134n
King Resources Co., 234
Kitces, Michael, 262
Knapp, Tom, 540
Koyfin, 386

Langer, Ellen, 356
lawsuits, 176, 176n
learning environments, 290–291

Lehman Brothers Holdings, 498–499
Lehman Corp., 234–235
Lessons for Investors (Graham), 567, 568
LetsMakeAPlan.org, 264
letter stocks, 3, 3n, 220–221, 220n, 229–230
leverage, 282–283
leveraged buyouts, 32n, 427n
leveraged funds, 241
liabilities, 334, 340–342, *341*, 371, 377n. *see also specific company*
life insurance, 90, 118–119, *347*
Ling-Temco-Vought Inc., 4n, *406*, 411–412, 420, 423–427, 423n
LinkedIn, 480
liquidations, 31, 366–367
liquidity, 199–200, 297n
lithium, 64
load funds, 221
loneliness, 218
Long-Term Capital Management L.P., 14
Loomis, Carol, 293n7
Lordstown Motors Corp., *42*
Lorie, James H., 67n
losses. *see also specific company*
  "carrying forward," 302n
  and Graham's definition of investment, 34n2
  and margin of safety, 508–509, 511
  and per-share earnings, 299, 300–301, 302n
  low-multiplier stocks, 372–376, 449, 508–509
LTV Corp., 424n
Lubin, Melanie Senter, 267n6
Lucent Technologies Inc., 183
luck, 356, 397n11, 532
Lynch, Peter, 241

Mackintosh, James, 243
"mad money" account, 20, 46, 294n8, 419

managers/management
  compensation for, 312–315, *314*, 503–504
  competence of, 280, 486
  and convertible issues and warrants, 405
  and dividends, 487–491
  Graham's comments about, 486–494
  of investment funds, 222–226, 237–238, 279n
  investor's relations with, 486–494
  and market fluctuations, 202–204
  and per-share earnings, 300–301
  poor, 487
  and security analysis, 280
  and stock selection for aggressive investors, 364–365
  Zweig's comments about, 495–504
Manhattan Fund, Inc., 226–229
margin accounts, 20, 20n, 47n, 189–190, 254–255
margin debt, 151
margin of safety, 10, *285*, 335, 505–529, 508n, 512n, 535, 545, 567, 570
Markel Corp., 504
Massachusetts Investment Trust, 224
Master Financial Planner (MFP), 263
mathematics, 565–566
Mattel Inc., *234*
Mauboussin, Michael J., 129n9, 293n7, 394n7, 497n3
Maxwell Motors Co., 280
Maxwell Tailwagger, 263
McCormick Harvesting Machine Co., 456n
McGraw Edison, 459–461, 459n, *460*, *468*
McGraw-Hill, Inc., 136, 459–461, 459n, *460*, *468*, *469*, *469*
McQuarrie, Edward, 86
meme stocks, 41, *42–44*, 128, 216, 471–472
Mergenthaler Linotype Enterprises, 316

mergers and acquisitions
    and aggressive investors, 174–175, 366–367, 375n, 379
    and case histories, 420, 422, 422n, 424, 424n
    and investments vs. speculation, 31, 32n
Merrill Lynch & Co., 254n, 400n
Meta Platforms, 162n
microcaps, 385
Microsoft Corp., 313, *314*, *391*, 393, 479–480, *480*, 524
MicroStrategy Inc., 43, 479–480, *480*
Middleby Corp., *390*
Miller, Merton, 492n
Milton, Trevor, 437–438
Minkow, Barry, 431n
Minnie Pearl's Chicken System Inc., 461, 464
moats, 392
Mobil Oil, 489n, 496
Modigliani, Franco, 492n
"money managers," 229, 230–231
monopolies, 340–342
Monster Beverage Corp., *390*
Montgomery Ward, 496
Moody's Investment Service, 96, 248–249
Moomoo, 39
Moore, Don, 359
Morgan, J.P., 54, 54n
Morgan Guaranty Bank, 227n
Morningstar, 386
mortgages, 174, 345–346
Mr. Market parable, 200–201, 209–219, 366n, 385, 387, 440–441, 525
Mr. Tax of America, 431, 431n
MSCI All-Country World Index, 109, 238
MSCI Global Pollution Prevention Index, 243
Munger, Charles T. ("Charlie"), 14, 215, 382–383, 397, 527, 542, 552–553

municipal bonds
    and aggressive investors, 135n, 157
    and defensive investors, 93, 96
    fluctuations in price of, 204, 206
    and speculation, 22–23, 512–513
Musk, Elon, 162n, 216, 481, 482, 484
mutual funds. *see also* investment funds; *specific fund*
    and aggressive investors, 141n, 160n, 161n, 363
    closed-end funds vs. open-end, 231–235
    closing of, 231n
    and corporate bonds, 272n
    and defensive investors, 26–27, 27n, 90, 97n, 345–346
    expenses/costs of, 362–363
    "focused" portfolios of, 279n
    and growth stocks, 160n, 161n, *161*
    managers of, 279n
    and market fluctuations, 6n, 7
    and new offerings, 141n
    performance of, 222–226, 236–238, *237*, 363, 376n
    and public attitude about stocks, 18n
    registration of, 230
    as "regulated investment company" (RIC), 221n
    return on, 279n
    and secondary companies, 173n
    and security analysis, 279n
    and speculation, 4–5
    and survivorship bias, 86n1
    taxes on, 221n
    type of, 221n, 230–231
Mutual Shares, 383
myopia, 153

name brands, 378
NAPFA.org, 264
NASDAQ, 87, 400n, 1359
National Beverage Corp., *391*
National Biscuit Co., 379

National Cash Register, 234
National General Corp., 4n, *406*, 409, 461–464, *462*, 464n, *468*, 469
National Investors Fund, 224
National Presto Industries, 169, *377*, *379*, 461–464, *462*, 464n, *468*, 507
National Student Marketing Corp., 227n, 234
Navistar, 456n, 458n
net asset value. *see* book value
net current assets. *see* working capital
Netflix Inc, *390*
New Community debentures, 96, 97, 157
New Haven Railroad, 275
New Housing Authority, 97, 97n, 157
Newman, Jerome, 530n, 531n
Newman, Paul, 445n
new offerings. *see also* initial public offerings
  and advice, 256–257
  and aggressive investors, 135, 139–145, 173–178, 378
  and case histories, 431–435
  of common stock, 140n, 141–145, 257
  and defensive investors, 176–177
  and investments vs. speculation, 26–27
  and market fluctuations, 189–190
  and per-share earnings, 297n
  and price, *400*
  and role of investment bankers, 256–257
  and valuation, 173–174
Newton, Isaac, 13–14
New York Central Railroad, 422n
New York Edison Co., 562–564
New York Stock Exchange (NYSE)
  advice from members of, 250, 252–253, 254–255, 258, 259
  bankruptcy of firms registered with, 254
  comparison of four companies listed on, 316–324
  and comparison of securities, 1
  and convertible issues and warrants, 407n
  "customers' brokers" as registered with, 252–253
  and dealings with brokerage firms, 138–140, 254–255
  and dividends, 491–492, 492n
  highest-price stock on, 489n
  and per-share earnings, 299–300
  and stock selection for aggressive investors, 198, 363
  and stock selection for defensive investors, 340–342
  and stock splits, 491–492
  turnover of stock on, 254–255
  and World War I, 10
New York Trap Rock Co., 541
NFTs. *see* non-fungible tokens (NFTs)
Niagara-Mohawk Power Co., 343
"Nifty Fifty" stocks, 322n
Nikola Corp., *43*, 436, 437–438, *438*
NIO Inc., *43*
Nixon, Richard M., 50n
no-load funds, 221, 221n, 232
nonconvertible bonds, 99–100, 135
non-fungible tokens (NFTs), 154–156
non-traded real estate, 106
Norfolk & Western, 423
Norfolk Southern Railroad, 348n, 423n
Northern Pacific Railway, 169, 204, *205*
Northwest Industries Inc., 302, 302n, *406*
Norway bonds, 138–139
Novo Nordisk ADR, 481–482
NVF Corp., 405, 420, 427–431, 427n, 431n
NVIDIA Corp., *390*, 481–482, 500, 524
NVR Inc., 389, *390*

oil companies, 279–280, 280n, *281*
Old Dominion Freight Line Inc.,
    391
online trading, 39, 131–132, 153
Ontario Securities Commission, 126
OpenAI, 480
open-end funds, 116–117, 231–235,
    231n. *see also* mutual funds
opportunities, recognizing, 530–532
options, stock, 3, 3n, 413–419. *see
    also* calls and call options;
    put options; warrants; *specific
    company*
Oracle Corp., 312–313, *314*
orders, execution of, 255–256
Ordway, Phil, 292n4
O'Reilly Automotive Inc., *391*
orphan stocks, 383n3
overconfidence, 353-355
overvaluation, 5, 173–174, 250, 395.
    see also specific company
    and aggressive investors, 164–165,
        173–174, 367–368
    "gambler's fallacy" about, 456n
Owens-Illinois Glass Co., *278, 337,
    339*
Ozempic, 481

Pacific Gas & Electric Co., *343*
Pacific Partners, Ltd., *554*
Palantir Technologies Inc., *43*
Palihapitiya, Chamath, 154, 436,
    440–441
Paltrow, Gwyneth, 154
Panhandle Eastern Pipe Line Co.,
    343
Parker Pen Co., *377, 378*
Pascal, Blaise, 378, 529
"Pascal's wager," 378n, 529
patience, investor virtue of, 16
Peloton Interactive Inc., *43*, 436,
    438–439
Penn Central Railroad, 4n, 95, 275,
    347–348, 370, 420, 421–423,
    421n, 422n, 423n, 559–561
Pennsylvania Electric Co., 422

pension funds, 150–151, 190, 427n,
    543–544. *see also specific company*
Peoples Gas Co., *343*
P/E ratio. *see* price/earnings ratio
performance. *see also* "beating
    the market/average"; *specific
    company or type of security*
    and aggressive investors, 173n,
        362–364, 374
    and defensive investors, 334,
        340–342
    and Graham's definition of
        investment, 34n2
    of growth stocks, 451n
    and market fluctuations, 199–200
    and per-share earnings, 305–306
    of secondary companies, 173n
    and security analysis, 280n, *281*,
        288–289
    of value stocks, 451n
    vogue of, 4
performance funds, 221–222, 222n,
    226–231
Performance Systems Inc., 461
Perlmeter (Stan) Investments, 543,
    555
periodicals, as source of advice,
    246–247
Perot, H. Ross, 254n
per-share earnings. *see also specific
    company*
    and common stock, 302–303
    and convertible issues and
        warrants, 300–301, 302–303, 405,
        408, *410*
    and defensive investors, 323–324,
        334, *337*
    and dividends, 490–491
    Graham's comments about,
        295–306
    Zweig's comments about,
        307–315
Petersburg Paradox, 565–566
Pfizer, Inc., 309, 453n
pharmaceutical stocks, 384
Philadelphia Electric Co., *343*

Index 607

physical capital, 59
PitchBook Data, 147
PlugPower Inc., *43*
Polaroid, *234*, 378
Pool Corp., *390*, 394–395
portfolio. *see also* asset allocation; selection, stock
   for aggressive investors, 104, 134–145, 146–156, 157–179, 180–184, 362–381
   basic characteristics of, 90
   changes to, 117–118
   and common stocks, 113–123, 124–133
   for defensive investors, 90–101, 103–106, 109–111, *112*, 113–123, 124–133, 323–324, 333–351
   Graham's concept of appropriate individual, 17–33
   inflation and, 47–56
   market fluctuations and, 191–193
   monitoring, 184
   negative approach to development of, 134–145, 146–156
   overview about, 1–11
   positive approach to development of, 157–179, 180–184
   rebalancing of, 193
Portnoy, Dave, 40
positive illusions, 354–355
Posner, Victor, 427n
precious metals, 55
predictions. *see* forecasting
"pre-emptive right," 408
preferred stock. *see also specific company*
   and aggressive investors, 99, 135–138, 135n, 139–141, 142–143, 167–168, 174, 176–178, 366–367
   and balanced funds, 234–235
   and bargains, 167–168, 174
   and convertible issues and warrants, 399–400, 400n, *406*, 409, 411–412

   and defensive investors, 90, 99–101, 121–122, 176–177, 350–351
   dividends on, 99–100, 100n, 135n, 274n, 399, 508–509
   and Graham's business principles, 515–516
   and inflation, 48
   and investment funds, 234–235
   and margin of safety, 505, 506, 508–509, 512–513
   and new offerings, 140–141, 142–143, 399–400
   and per-share earnings, 302–303
   price fluctuations in, 206–207
   price record of, 399–400
   ratings for, 206
   recommended "coverage" for, *284*
   and risk, 272–276
   and security analysis, 270, 272–276, 282–283
   as senior stock issues, 274n
   switches between common and, 405–407
   yield on, 568–569
price. *see also* appreciation; bargains; fluctuations, market; inflation; price/earnings ratio; *specific company*
   and advice, 250
   and bankruptcy, 421n
   Buffett's comments about, 538–539
   calculation of true market, *410*
   and comparison of four listed companies, 316–324, 320n, 323n, 329
   and convertible issues and warrants, 399–400, 409, *410*
   decline in common stock, 3
   of delisted stocks, 371n
   and dividends, 488–489, 492n
   and earnings, 116, 302n
   and expectations for investors, 22–23, 23n, 30, 31
   "gambler's fallacy" about, 456n

price (cont.)
  and history and forecasting of
    stock market, 65, 69, 70, 71, 73,
    74, 77, 78, 80–81, 320
  and investment funds, 231–232,
    232, 234–235
  and investor-management
    relations, 486, 487
  and margin of safety, 506, 508–509,
    508n, 510–511, 514–515, 514n,
    519–522
  and market fluctuations, 21–23,
    186–189, 203–208
  and mispricing of stock, 349n,
    383–387
  and new offerings, 140–141, 142–145
  and portfolio policy for aggressive
    investors, 4, 134–135, 136n,
    160, 161, 164–166, 172, 173–174,
    174–179
  and portfolio policy for defensive
    investors, 98, 113–117, 122,
    176–177
  and risk, 122
  and speculation, 568
  and stock selection for aggressive
    investors, 363–364, 367–368,
    370, 371–372, 374, 375–376, 377
  and stock selection for defensive
    investors, 323–324, 333, 334,
    335, 336, 336n, 337, 340,
    340–342, 341, 345, 348–350,
    349n, 350–351
  and timing, 186–189
  unpredictability of, 22–23, 23n
  and value, 10, 31, 122, 202–203,
    514–515, 539
  wholesale, 76, 77
price-and-wage freeze, 50n
price/earnings ratio. *see also specific
  company*
  and bargains, 169
  calculation of, 161n
  CAPE ratio, 81–83, *81*
  and convertible issues and
    warrants, *410*
  definition of, 70n
  and growth stocks, 161
  and history and forecasting of
    stock market, 70, 71, 76, 78
  and margin of safety, 519n2
  and market fluctuations, 189–190,
    196–197, 198
  and per-share earnings, 305–306
  and portfolio policy for aggressive
    investors, 161, 161n, 169
  and portfolio policy for defensive
    investors, 115, 116–117, 117n
  and security analysis, 279–280,
    281, 283–284, *285*
  and stock selection for aggressive
    investors, 367–368, 370, 371
  and stock selection for defensive
    investors, 323–324, 335, 336,
    336n, *338–339*, 340, *341*, 345
price-to-assets ratio, 335
primary stock issues, 123
private-credit funds, 147–149, 152
private equity and private-equity
  funds, 106, 147–149, 152, 172
Procter & Gamble, *278*, 337
profitability. *see also specific measure
  of profitability*
  and comparison of four listed
    companies, 318–319, 327
  determining, 451n
  and superstocks, 389–396
profitable reinvestment theory,
  487–493, 489n
pro forma ("as if") statements, 405,
  422n, 429
prospectus, 434–435
Public Service Commission, 563–564
Public Service Electric & Gas Co.,
  343
public utilities
  and aggressive investors, 176, 374
  and bonds, 275–276
  debt of, 334
  as defensive investment, 340–345
  and defensive investors, 122, 334,
    340–345, 347–348

dividends of, 491–492, 493–494
and inflation, 54
and investments vs. speculation, 25–26
and market fluctuations, 9, 196–197
regulation of, 275n
and security analysis, 273–274, 275–276, *284*
and selection of stock, 334, 340–345, 347–348, 374
and subscription rights, 493–494
Public Utility Holding Company Act (1935), 275n
Purex Co., 492–493
Putnam Growth Fund, *224*
put options, 413–414

quicken.com, 159n
"quotational" value/loss, 19
quotations, market, 73n, 194–196, 199–200, 201, 202–203

railroads. *see also specific railroad*
and aggressive investors, 137, 174–176
bankruptcy of, 3–4, 4n, 347–348, 370, 421, 421n
and bargains, 174
bonds of, 173–176, 273–274, 275–276, *284*, 421, 422, 505
and defensive investors, 100–101, 122, *345*, 347–348, 348n
and market fluctuations, 3–4, 4n, *347*
and security analysis, 273–274, 275–276, *284*
and speculation, 566–567
Randell, Cort, 227n
Rapid American, *406*
Raskob, John J., 1–2, 2n
rating, of bonds, 96, 206, 207, 272n, 336n
Rea, James, 182
Rea-Graham fund, 182

real estate, 55–56, 62, 106, 147–149, 199–200, 408, 409n, 513–514
Real Estate Investment Trust Company, 444–448, *446*, *449*, *468*
Realty Equities Corp. of New York, 444–448, 445n, *446*, 448n, *468*
rebalancing, 109–111, *112*, 193
Reddit, 128
reinvestment
and defensive investors, 114
and dividends, 487–491, 489n, 490–493
and margin of safety, 508–509
and portfolio for aggressive investors, 173–174
REITs. *see* Real Estate Investment Trusts
Reliance Industries, 524
research, 161n, 253n, 349n, 362–363
research and development (R&D), 300–301
ResMed Inc., *391*
restructuring charges, 311–312, 424–426, 426n
retail bonds, *284*
retirement plans. *see* pension plans; *specific plan*
return. *see also* dividends; interest; performance; return on invested capital (ROIC); yield; *specific company or type of security*
aggregate, 25–26
for aggressive investors, 27–33, 90, 136, 174–175, 363, 366–367, 379
average annual, 24n, 33, 113n
compound annualized, 60n4
for defensive investors, 20–28, 24n, 90, 92, 93, 97, 113n, 114, 121–122, 176–178
geometric mean, 60n4
and Graham's business principles, 515–516
Graham's comments about, 17–33
and Graham's definition of investment, 34n2

return (*cont.*)
  and history and forecasting of stock market, 67, 78, 81–84, 85
  and inflation, 50, 54
  and investment vs. speculation, 17, 18n
  and margin of safety, 521–522
  measures of, 451n
  and public attitude about stocks, 18n
  on Raskob's prescription, 2
  and risk, 90
  and security analysis, 279n
  Zweig's comments about, 35–46, 45n
return on invested capital (ROIC), 394–395, *395*
revenue bonds, 95
Riot Blockchain Inc., 43
risk. *see also specific company or type of security*
  and aggressive investors, 31, 134n, 135n, 136–137, 152, 156, 161–162, 161n, 164–168, 174–176, 180, 184, 363, 378–379
  Buffett's comments about, 544–545
  and call options, 417–419
  and defensive investors, 90, 97n, 102–105, 113, 114–115, 114n, 116–117, 121–122
  and enterprising investors, 384n4
  and Graham's business principles, 515–516
  and history and forecasting of stock market, 84–88
  and inflation, 47n, 55, 56
  and investment vs. speculation, 19–20, 20n
  and margin of safety, 508, 508–509, 514–515, 514n
  and market fluctuations, 185, 212–213, 214n6
  and options trading, 415–417
  and price, 122
  and return/reward, 90, 544–545
  and security analysis, 272–276
  and short selling, 456n
  and speculation, 567
  and value, 122
  Zweig's comments about, 533
Rivian Automotive Inc., *43*
Robinhood, 39, 125, 126, 127n7, 437
robo-advisors, 261
Rogozinski, Jaime, 40
Ross Stores Inc., *390*
Roth, Allan, 263
Rothschild family, 32, 32n
roulette, 511, 512n
Rouse Corp., *234*
Ruane, Bill, 541, 542, 543
"Rule of 72," 116n, 286n
"rule of opposites," 204, 204n

sadness, 218
"safety of principle," 17
safety tests, for bonds, 272–276
Salesforce, 313
San Francisco Real Estate Investors, 445n
Santa Fe Industries, 370
Santayana, Geoge, 1
savings accounts, 22–23, 55, 75, 98
savings and loan associations, 345–346
savings banks, 90, 98
savings bonds, 22–23, 61, 207
Saxon Industries, *234*
Schloss, Walter J., 539–540, 541–542, 543, *547–548*
screenwriting, 386
Scudder, Stevens & Clark, 248
Sears Roebuck Co., *278*, 304, *304*, *337*, *339*, 499
SEC. *see* Securities and Exchange Commission
secondary companies, 5, 123, 171–174, 173n, 176–179, 192–193, 192n, 282–283, 369–370, 512–513
securities, delivery and receipt of, 255–256, 256n

Securities & Exchange Commission (SEC)
and GAAP rules, 308
and GEICO, 531n
and hedge funds, 367n
investigations by, 437
and investment funds, 221n, 230
and IPOs, 434–435
and letter-stocks, 3n
and mutual funds, 116–117
and new issues, 378
and NVF-Sharon Steel case, 427n
and Realty Equities case, 448n
regulation of brokerage firms by, 229–230, 254
regulation of public utilities by, 275n
and security analysis, 275–276, 275n
website for, 292n5
Securities Investor Protection Corp. (SIPC), 256
security analysis. *see also* case histories; financial analysts; per-share earnings; selection, stock; type of security
and advice, 248–249
for aggressive investors, 362–381
and comparison of four listed companies, 316–324
and growth stocks, 283–287
and per-share earnings, 295–306
prediction/qualitative approach to, 349–351, 349n
protection/quantitative approach to, 349n, 350–351
and risk, 272–276
and speculation in common stocks, 568
techniques for, 270, 271, 271n
and two-part appraisal process, 305–306
and valuation, 270–271
Zweig's comments about, 290–294

Security Analysis (Graham and Dodd), 17, 272, 421, 535, 546, 559–560
security analyst. *see* financial analysts
security and analysis
and capitalization, 276–277
characteristics of, 271
and comparison of four listed companies, 316–324
concept of, 269–270
for defensive investors, 282–283, 333–351
and forecasting, 270, 271n, 276–279, 280n, 286–288
and growth stocks, 270, 271
Seidt, Andrea, 267n6
selection, stock. *see also* asset allocation
and adoption of schemes by large numbers of people, 191n
for aggressive investors, 29–30, 362–381
and bargain issues, 376–379
and "best" stocks in DJIA, 348–349
and bridge player analogy, 364–365
criteria for, 323–324, 334–351, 371–372
for defensive investors, 323–324, 333–361, 371n
for enterprising investors, 382–397
Graham-Newman methods for, 366–368
Graham's comments about, 335–336, 362–381
Graham's criteria for, 352, 353
"human factor" in, 350–351
for long- and short-term, 28–29, 30
and low-multiplier industrial stocks, 372–376
and market fluctuations, 196–197, 202–203
"pick the winners," 76

selection, stock (*cont.*)
  prediction/qualitative approach to, 349–350, 349n
  protection/quantitative approach to, 333–334, 349–351, 349n
  rules for common stock, 114–115, 117–118
  and secondary companies, 369–370
  single criteria for, 372–376
  and special situation, 379–381
  and stock-picking "systems," 40–41
  Zweig's comments about, 352–361
selling, and margin of safety, 527–528
Sequoia Fund, 541, *551*
share repurchases, *see* buybacks of shares
shareholders. *see* investors
Sharon Steel Co., 405, 427–431, 427n
Shiller, Robert, 82
shorting, 18–19, 29, 31, 31n, 367n, 456n
Siegel, Jeremy, 2n, 47n, 84–85
size of enterprise, 322–323, 334, 335, 336, 371–372, 374, 375–376
skepticism, investor virtue of, 15, 151
Small Business Administration, 445
smart-beta funds, 384–385
smartphones, 153
Smith, Adam, 539–540
Smith, Walter Buckingham, 86n1
Social Capital Hedosophia Holdings Corp., 439
social media, 128, 130–131, 216, 440–441
Southern California Edison, *343*
South Sea Co., 14
SOYA (sit on your ass) investing, 382–383, 397
SPACs. *see* special-purpose acquisition companies (SPACs)

Spalding United Kingdom, 300
special charges, 296, 297–299, 300–301, 304, *410*, 422. *see also specific company*
special-purpose acquisition companies (SPACs), 153–156, *155*
special situations. *see* "workouts"
speculation
  and advice, 248–249, 251–252, 256, 257, 559
  and aggressive investors, 141n, 143–144, 161–162, 166, 173, 176, 378
  and bargains, 173
  behavioral life cycle of the speculator, 36
  benefits of, 20n
  and case histories, 431–435
  and convertible issues and warrants, 400, 403
  and crowd contagion, 128–132
  and defensive investors, 90, 113, 115, 116–117, 119, 128–130
  and dividends, 487, 488–489
  expectations from, 22–33
  Graham's comments about, 17–33, 559–560
  and history and forecasting of stock market, 74, 81–84
  and inflation, 47
  and influencers, 440
  intelligent, 20
  investing distinguished from, 1–2, 10, 17–33, 35–46, 201–203, 512–513
  and investment funds, 4–5, 222–223, 225–227, 230–231
  and margin of safety, 512–514
  and market fluctuations, 4–5, 185, 186, 187–188, 189–190, 195
  and new offerings, 141n, 143–144, 378
  and problems of brokeragefirms, 255
  and Raskob's prescription, 2

and role of investment bankers, 256
and security analysis, 282–283
Zweig's comments about, 35, 37–38, 45–46
Spinoza, Baruch, 191–192
splits, stock, 489, 491–494, 491n
Square, Inc., 478
stability, 178–179, 319, 327, 334, 335, 371–372. *see also* volatility
stamps, rare, 55
Standard & Poor's. *see also* Stock Guide; *specific company*
500 index, 44
and advice, 248
and bargains, 170, 172–173
bond ratings by, 96, 421
and convertible issues and warrants, 398, 400n
and dividends, 283n
and expectations for investors, 26–27, 26n, 27n
and Graham's disciples, 535–536, 541, 542, 544
and history and forecasting of stock market, 65–72, 76, 77, 81–84
and inflation, 50
and investment funds, 223, 225, 226–227, 230–231, *232*, 235n, 238
listing of constituent companies in, 319
and market fluctuations, 189–190, *205*, 208
and May 1970 debacle, 460n
and mutual funds, *224*
and portfolio for aggressive investors, 160, *161*, 170, 172–173
and portfolio for defensive investors, 109, 113n
and price/earnings ratio, 70n, 81–83, *81* price record from, *401*
and "second-line companies," 192–193, 192n
and security analysis, 283n, 287–288

and stock selection for aggressive investors, 198, 363, 369–373, 374, 376
and stock selection for defensive investors, 340, *345*, 346, 347–348, *347*
and technology companies, 571
website for, 192n
Standard Oil of California, 169–170, *278*, *281*, 336, *337*, *339*
Standard Oil of New Jersey, *278*, *281*, *337*, *339*, 427
state bonds, 22–23, 96, 248, 512–513
steel industry, 168, 364–365, 369
stock. *see also* common stock; preferred stock; *specific stock or sector of stock*
"delisting of," 371n
good and bad, 514n
group approach to buying, 181–182
method of "selecting," 148
mistakes, 183–184
and portfolio for defensive investors, 109–111, *112*
public attitude about, 18–19, 18n
rebalancing, 109–111, *112*
turnover rate of, 254–255
watchlists, 182–183
"watered," 297n
stockbrokers. *see* brokerage firms
stock/equity ratio, 273–274
Stock Guide (Standard & Poor's), 144–145, 170, 340, 369–373, 369n, 374, *377*, 398, 430, 461, 571
stockholders. *see* investors
stock market. *see also* financial market
1972 level in, 72–79
in China, 435n
Covid pandemic gains, 39–40
and crowd contagion, 128–132
easy ways to make money in, 191n
as going wrong, 198–200

stock market (*cont.*)
  history and forecasting of, 1, 2, 10, 23n, 54, 54n, 65–79, 80–88
  market declines, 80–81
  meme stocks, 41, 42–44
  positive-sum game, 127
  structure of, 569–570
  as a wicked learning environment, 291
stocks
  inflation and, 62–63
  vs. socks analogy, 81
stock screeners, 386
Stocks for the Long Run (Siegel), 84–85
stress, 218
Studebaker-Worthington Corp., 406–407
subscription rights, 493–494, 493n
Sundial Growers Inc., 43
superforecasting, 525–527
Superior Oil, 489, 490–491
superstocks, 389–396
"sure things," 514n
survivorship bias, 85, 86, 151
Swensen, David, 149
Swift & Co., *278, 337, 339,* 340, *341*

takeovers, 427–431, 427n, 486–487. *see also specific company*
tangible-asset value. *see* book value
tastytrade, 125
taxes. *see also specific company*
  and aggressive investors, 135, 157
  on capital gains, 75, 345
  on corporations, 100, 177–178
  and defensive investors, 92–97, 97n, 100–101, 349n
  on dividends, 100, 283n, 491–492, 493–494
  and expectations for investors, 21–24, 25–26, 33
  and history and forecasting of stock market, 75
  and inflation, 50, 54
  and interest, 100–101
  and margin of safety, 512–513

  and market fluctuations, 203–208
  and per-share earnings, 299, 300–301, 302–303, 302n
  and security analysis, 273–274, 283n, *284*
"technical approaches," 2–3
technology stocks. *see also specific company*
  and aggressive investors, 29, 173n
  and convertible issues and warrants, 405n
  and dividends, 489n
  and history and forecasting of stock market, 87
  and margin of safety, 514n
  and security analysis, 280n, 287–288
  and superstocks, 389
telecommunications stocks, 280n, 435n, 514n
Teleprompter Corp., *234*
Telex Corp., *234*
Tencent Holdings, 524
Tenneco, 456n
Tesla Inc., 162n, 243, 482–484, *483*
Tetlock, Philip, 525, 526
Tetra Tech, Inc., 482–484, *483*
Texaco, *278, 281, 337, 339*
Texas Instruments, 489
Theranos Inc., 148–149
3M Co., 563–564
TIKR, 386
TikTok, 131, 481
timing, 158–159, 186–189, 202–203
TIPS. *see* Treasury Inflation-Protected Securities
Tobin, James, 215
Tomlinson, Lucile, 118–119
trade names. *see* brand names
trades
  costs of, 302n, 349n, 371n
  of delisted stocks, 371n
  gamblification of, 125–127
  long- and short-term, 126–127

Index

online, 39
volume of, 254–255
"trading in the market," 29
Tran, Danny, 41
Trane Co., 300–301
Treasury bonds, *see* U.S. Treasury bonds
Treasury Inflation-Protected Securities (TIPS), 25n, 61–62, 62n6, 207n
Tri-Continental Corp., 411–412
Troop, 503
trust, 223, 225
trust companies, 27–28, 258
trust funds, 4, 47, 90, 225–226, 233, 247–248
Tweedy Browne Partners, 540, 541–542, *549*
Twitter, 128, 131
two-part appraisal process, 288–289, 305–306
Tyco International Ltd., 424n

uncertainty, 88
unconscious bias, 217–218
undervaluation, 250, 498n4
  and aggressive investors, 31, 33, 168, 171, 173–174, 176, 367–368, 383–387
  and bargains, 168, 171, 173–174
  Buffett's comments about, 535
  and margin of safety, 510–511, 512–513
underwriting, 256–258, 432–433, 511. *see also specific company or underwriter*
Union Carbide Co., *278, 337, 339*
Union Pacific Railroad, 348n
Union Underwear, 302n
United Accumulative Fund, 224
United Aircraft Co., *278, 337, 339*
"units," 408n
Universal Marion Co., 379, 380–381
University of Michigan, 18n

unpopular large companies, 164–168, 169
unrealistic optimism, 355
U.S. bonds (other than savings), 22–23, 95–96, 97, 119
U.S. savings bonds, 93, 94–95, 96, 118–119, 120–122, 185, 206, 207, 234–235, 512–513
U.S. Steel Corp., *278, 337, 339*, 370
U.S. Treasury, 495
U.S. Treasury bonds, 61, 95, 106, 113n
U.S. Treasury certificates, 95–96

Valeant Pharmaceuticals International Inc., 484–485
Valmont Industries Inc., 484–485
Value Line (investment service), 276–277
value/valuation. *see also* earnings; fluctuations; market; overvaluation; price/earnings ratio; undervaluation; *specific company or type of security*
  and advice, 248, 250
  and aggressive investors, 31, 32, 137–138, 167–168, 177–179, 366n, 377n
  and bargains, 167–168, 177–179
  Buffett's comments about, 538–539
  business vs. stock market, 194–203
  and dealings with brokerage firms, 255
  and defensive investors, 20–26, 120–121, 122, 349–350
  dependability of, 302n, 305–306
  financial analysts as creating, 563–564
  and history and forecasting of stock market, 74, 81–84
  importance of, 531
  inflated, 255
  and inflation, 54
  and investment funds, 231–232, *232, 234*

value/valuation (*cont.*)
    and margin of safety, 512–515
    and options trading, 415–416, *416*
value/valuation (*cont.*)
    and per-share earnings, 302–303, 302n, 304
    and price, 10, 32n, 122, 202–203, 513–515, 539
    and problems of brokerage firms, 255
    "quotational," 19
    and risk, 122
    and security analysis, 270–271, 273–274, 276–279, 282–287
    and selection of stock, 349–350, 366n, 377n
    and speculation, 564–565
    and stock splits, 491n
    and two-part appraisal process, 288–289
Vanguard Group, 238
Vector Group Ltd., *391*
venture capital, 106
venture capital funds, 147–149
Veres, Robert, 262
Vest Financial, 414
VinFast Auto Ltd., 443
Virgin Galactic Holdings Inc., 41, *43*, 436, 439–441, *440*, *441*
virtues of intelligent investors, 14–16
volatility, 400n. *see also* stability
volume, trading, 297n

Wall Street, reform of, 434–435
WallStreetBets, 40, 216–217
Wall Street Journal, 29, 243, 295, 301, 437
Walmart, 496, 519, 520
Warner Bros. Discovery, Inc, 500–502, *501*, *502*
warrants, 3, 3n, 135, 296–297, 300–301, 302–303, 398–407, 398n, 400, 405–406, *406*, 407–409, 407n, 408n, 514–515. *see also specific company*

Washington Post Co., 543–544, 545, *556*
"watered" stock, 297n
Watsco Inc., *391*
Watson, T.L., Sr., 561–562
Webull, 125
Wegovy, 481
Welles, C., 229
Westinghouse Corp., *337*, *339*
Westinghouse Electric Co., *278*
West Point Pepperell, *377*, 378
WeWork, 148, 309
Whiting Corp., 464–467, *465*, *466*, 467n, *468*
Wiesenberger Financial Services, 160, *224*, *232*, 234
Willcox & Gibbs, 464–467, *465*, *466*, 467n, *468*
Williams, Jackie G., 431n, 434
Williams, John Burr, 393
Williams, Serena, 154
Wilshire indexes, 26–27n
wireless stocks, 173n
Wolfe, Lauren Taylor, 308
Wood, Cathie, 244
Woolworth Company (F.W.), *278*, *337*, 340, *341*, 564–565
working capital
    and aggressive investors, 167–168, 170, 170n, 171, 366–368, 371, 372–379, 377n
    and defensive investors, 334, 340–342
    and dividends, 490–491
    and security analysis, 270
"workouts," 157, 158, 174–176, 379–381, 514–515
WorldCom, 421n, 424n, 427n
Wyeth, 453n

X, *see* Twitter
Xerox Corp., 195, 283–286, 378, 454

Yahoo Finance, 386
Yale University, 149–150

YCharts, 386
yield. *see also* dividends; interest; performance; return; type of security
  and aggressive investors, 135–139, 380
  and convertible issues and warrants, 399, 399n, 405–406
  and defensive investors, 24–25, 90, 92–93, 94, 96, 97, 98–99, 114–115, 336
  fluctuations in, 189–190, 203–208
  and history and forecasting of stock market, 71, 77, 78
  and inflation, 56
  and speculation, 568–569
YouTube, 217

Zaslav, David, 500–502
Zeckhauser, Richard, 262n1
Zenith Radio, 320–321
Zion, David, 502
Zion Research Group, 502
Zoom Video Communications Inc., 44, 117n
Zuckerberg, Mark, 162n
Zuckerman, Gregory, 212n2
Zweig's comments. *see specific topic*
ZZZZ Best, 431n

www.ingramcontent.com/pod-product-compliance
Lightning Source LLC
LaVergne TN
LVHW031534060526
838200LV00056B/4487